Music in Evolution
and
Evolution in Music

Music in Evolution
and
Evolution in Music

Steven Bradley Jan

https://www.openbookpublishers.com

©2022 Steven Bradley Jan

ISBN Paperback: 9781800647350
ISBN Hardback: 9781800647367
ISBN Digital (PDF): 9781800647374
ISBN Digital ebook (EPUB): 9781800647381
ISBN Digital ebook (AZW3): 9781800647398
ISBN XML: 9781800647404
ISBN HTML: 9781800647411
DOI: 10.11647/OBP.0301
Cover image by Gareth Price, all rights reserved. Cover design by Anna Gatti.

To
Maureen Jan
and
Philip Partridge

for care, understanding and forbearance
on this journey.

Contents

List of Figures

List of Tables

Acknowledgements

Thanks are owed to several people who provided encouragement and assistance in the writing of this book.

First and foremost (and happily primary alphabetically), Nicholas Bannan, for the inspiration of his comprehensive knowledge of the evolutionary basis of musicality – and indeed of very many other aspects of music – his kind encouragement of this project from its inception, and his support of my work more generally for many years. His passionate belief in music education, and his conviction that a knowledge of the evolutionary history of our species can foster a more democratic and organic approach to music education (Bannan, 2019), represent a significant advance in music pedagogy. More broadly, his work has been instrumental in the increasing acknowledgement that music is at the heart of humans' evolutionary story and is therefore key to unlocking our potential, developmentally and creatively. On a practical level, Nicholas kindly read the whole manuscript and offered numerous insightful suggestions for improvement.

Susan Blackmore, for a useful discussion of memetic drive that helped me to improve and expand the treatment of this issue in §3.7.1.

Alan Harvey, who served as one of my publisher's reviewers, for his numerous insightful comments, incorporation of which has significantly improved the text, particularly in Chapter 2. During the review process, Patrick Savage kindly drew my attention to some recently published work relevant to that chapter.

Michal Hoftich, for kindly undertaking the production of the ebook.

Lesley Jeffries and Dan McIntyre, for their advice in writing the article (Jan, 2015b) that forms the basic framework, considerably expanded here, for much of the discussion of the relationship between music and language.

Moreover, their formidable knowledge of corpus linguistics, directly relevant to memetics, has inspired several ideas here.

Robin Laney, my Co-Editor at the *Journal of Creative Music Systems*,[1] for helping me to understand better many of the intricacies of music-AI and the algorithmic generation of music.

Daniel Leech-Wilkinson, for encouraging my continued application of evolutionary ideas to music with his warm review of *The memetics of music* (Leech-Wilkinson, 2009b).

Gareth Price, for designing the cover image.

Trevor Rawbone, for reading and commenting extensively on earlier drafts, for providing incisive critiques of my arguments, for making numerous suggestions for improvement (not all of which I have adopted), and for proof-reading the manuscript. The best PhD students are those who teach their supervisors more than they are taught, and Trevor (and Valerio Velardo, below) certainly comes into this category. Beyond this, I thank Trevor for useful discussions of schemata in music, and the extent to which they draw upon innate perceptual-cognitive factors. Trevor skilfully pulled me towards a "generative" position in a joint article we wrote (Rawbone & Jan, 2020), so he will perhaps be disappointed to see that I have reverted to type here in endorsing a more "associative-statistical" view, and thus a more full-blooded Darwinism, to understand cultural evolution, in schemata as in other types of musical patterning. Nevertheless, I did stick with his wise advice to change the title (or, rather, to make the planned subtitle the title): as well as being satisfyingly palindromic, *Music in Evolution and Evolution in Music* is a better reflection of the content of the book than was my original title.

Stephen Robertson, for generously sharing a LaTeX template developed for his own book (S. Robertson, 2020) for Open Book Publishers.

Alessandra Tosi, Luca Baffa, Rupert Gatti and Lucy Barnes at Open Book Publishers, for guiding me through the publication process so reassuringly.

---

[1] At https://www.jcms.org.uk/.

Valerio Velardo, for stimulating discussions of music-AI, and for practical help with LaTeX. Valerio's work at the cutting-edge of music-AI builds strongly upon an evolutionary understanding of music and shows, in the starkest way possible, how musicality and music are no longer the province of our own species, and that they are moving into the new realms opened up by advances in computer technology.

Bennett Zon, for organising the conference in Durham in 2007 – *Music and Evolutionary Thought* – that encouraged me to think beyond memetics to consider how evolution operated in the wider context of the human capacity for musicality. The unfortunate failure to materialise of a planned proceedings volume arising from this conference – my contribution was eventually published as Jan (2015a) – was, in part, a stimulus to write this book: like Beethoven's Diabelli Variations, I have attempted here, hopefully not as a result of a surfeit of arrogance, to contribute a complete opus rather than a single variation. I draw upon Bennett's own exemplary analysis of evolutionary metaphors in nineteenth-century musicology (Zon, 2016) in §4.3.

My colleagues in the Department of Music and Music Technology at the University of Huddersfield, for creating such a fertile and conducive research environment; and the staff of the Library, particularly Janet di Franco, Christopher Beevers and the inter-library loans team.

Of course, any errors and infelicities are entirely my own. In the light of ideas presented in Chapters 3 and 4, I hope that any such deficits are not seized upon by cultural evolution – often blind to matters of truth and falsity – and replicated.

Preface

> Is evolution a theory, a system or a hypothesis? It is much more: it is a general condition to which all theories, all hypotheses, all systems must bow and which they must satisfy henceforward if they are to be thinkable and true. Evolution is a light illuminating all facts, a curve that all lines must follow. (Teilhard de Chardin, 2008, p. 219)

This book is not a sequel to my *The memetics of music* (Jan, 2007); if anything, it is a prequel. I wrote *The memetics of music* because I was interested in understanding how Darwinism might operate *within* music, both as process and as product. That is, I tried to consider how a Darwinian perspective might help us to see musical works as the products of myriad replicating particles that can be understood in terms of Richard Dawkins' concept of the meme (Dawkins, 1989); and I tried to frame the various processes attendant upon the generation of music and its cultural-evolutionary change as being motivated by the variation, replication and selection of memes. In this sense, I attempted to develop a model of music that understood it as governed by mechanisms equivalent to those that also operate, on larger scales, in other realms, most notably biology.

In the present book, my field of reference is somewhat wider – indeed, the book covers some topics I deemed outside the scope of *The memetics of music* – although a return visit is made unapologetically to memetics, most significantly in Chapter 3, in order to continue to advocate its merits, to consider recent developments in the field, and to integrate it into the broader context of this study. In a nutshell, I try to consider here all the various ways in which music might relate to, or be amenable to understanding in terms of, Darwin's theory of evolution, in order to see the wider connections between the natural and the cultural. Broadly speaking, this includes seeing music and musicality (human and non-human) in the context of evolutionary theory – *music in evolution* – as a counterpoint to seeing (in the way that memetics

 https://doi.org/10.11647/OBP.0301.08

does) evolutionary theory operating in the context of music – *evolution in music*.

The "Universal Darwinism" hypothesised by Dawkins (1983b) and Plotkin (1995) – that is, the extension of Darwinism to realms beyond the biological (§1.5) – is fortified by incorporating music because the reach of Darwinism can, this book argues, readily be demonstrated in a central realm of human culture. Similarly, our understanding of music is deepened by incorporating evolutionary theory because many questions concerning music's nature can only be fully answered by considering how and why it arose in our species and why it is such a defining attribute of seemingly all human cultures. As the only truly "Universal Acid" (Dennett, 1995, p. 63), Darwinism has the disconcerting tendency to dissolve the boundaries between different phenomena and processes in the world, making music melt into the wider unity of a universe governed by the operation of evolutionary laws and processes.

It is tempting to use the term "evolutionary musicology" (Wallin et al., 2000) to encompass these concerns, provided the second word is not understood too restrictively, and provided that the balance of power between the scientific and the artistic dimensions implicit in the term – C. P. Snow's "two cultures" (1964) – is broadly equitable. Nevertheless, the way this discipline developed in its initial phase has indeed often privileged the biological dimension over the socio-cultural, to the detriment of a fuller understanding of both.[2] By taking the synergistic perspective inherent in evolutionary musicology seriously, both domains may be enriched. Indeed, impelled by Wallin (1991) and significantly consolidated by Wallin et al. (2000), a number of recent books have appeared that to some extent balance the scientific and the artistic, including Patel (2008), Fitch (2010), Changizi (2011), Bannan (2012), Schulkin (2013), Honing (2018b) and Spitzer (2021), not to mention several dozen articles. This book attempts to continue this tradition, perhaps ranging more widely than some of its predecessors by covering certain less well explored areas where music and evolution intersect.

---

[2] Apropos Snow's scientific-artistic dualism, it should be stressed that the socio-cultural dimension is not wholly analogous to the artistic, for it is itself amenable to understanding using the scientific method.

Building on ideas proposed by Darwin and others over a century ago, one factor in the growth of evolutionary musicology over the last twenty years has been its insistence that only an interdisciplinary perspective can unpick the complex relationships between music and human nature. Thus, it brings together a range of interlocking disciplines – evolutionary biology, genetics, neuroscience, psychology, archaeomusicology, memetics, zoomusicology and computational creativity – that, in conjunction, afford compelling evidence that music is not a frivolous diversion but something central to our nature and our existence. Indeed, one of the hard claims of evolutionary musicology, and one that I hope comes across strongly in this book, is that antecedents of what we now term "music" helped to drive the evolution of primate vocalisations in ways that underpinned the development of human sociality, language and complex thought: music shaped our societies (and thus our history), it nourished our languages and, most importantly, it structured our minds. Thus, music may be, as Cross (1999) asserts, "the most important thing we ever did": we have survived and prospered on earth in large part because of the phenomenon of musicality.

From the foregoing it will be clear that the methodology of the book is broadly synoptic, taxonomic, integrative and comparative. This arguably represents the best approach for organising an account of the contributions to the evolutionary understanding of musicality and music afforded by the disciplines listed above, but also for highlighting their overlaps, common concerns and synergies. This is particularly important given that, in many cases, two or more disciplines may often consider the same issue from different standpoints, doing so by means of different vocabularies and methodologies. A synoptic approach also helps to highlight directions for future research, particularly interdisciplinary work. I try to be as scrupulous as possible in referencing the different disciplinary ingredients before mixing them together synergystically, not least in order to allow the reader to follow them up systematically. At times, however, the tone becomes more speculative and, because it is in the nature of many of the ideas considered here that concrete evidence is difficult to find, it follows that such speculations must remain open to future research to verify, or falsify, them. While the book is designed to be accessible to an intelligent general reader, its main constituencies are musicians interested in how scientific ideas can illuminate our understanding of music; and, perhaps to a lesser extent, scientists interested in how music can exemplify, and help expand, their theories.

Structurally, the book reviews a sequence of interconnected topics in an ordering that is a mixture of the chronological and the conceptual. Chapter 1 outlines the key tenets of evolutionary theory needed to contextualise the rest of the book, focusing particularly on the extensions of Darwin's theory to other domains that have proved fruitful in recent decades, and on which understanding of the ideas presented in subsequent chapters depends. Chapter 2 considers the evolution of human musicality, attempting to understand the role music played in shaping our morphological and cognitive development. Chapter 3 turns to cultural evolution, considering the mechanisms by which the same basic human design plan can have given rise to the rich diversity and complexity of human musics and how cultural evolution and biological evolution interact. Chapter 4 serves in part as a corollary to Chapter 3 in taking a memetic view, not in relation to music itself, but in regard to the discourses surrounding it. Again, a coevolutionary perspective attempts to relate cultural evolution within music to cultural evolution in music-scholarly discourse. Chapter 5 moves the focus partly away from human music, attempting to understand certain animal vocalisations as proto-musical and proto-linguistic, and conceiving them as supporting evidence for the account of human musical/linguistic development offered in Chapter 2. Chapter 6, like Chapter 5, also turns away from human music to consider that generated by computers, this body of AI-generated music posing profound challenges to our understandings of musicality and music. Chapter 7 turns to the thorny question of consciousness, in an attempt to connect it to aspects of the foregoing discussion of music. This is not in order to offer any novel solutions to what is arguably the most intractable of all intellectual problems (spoiler alert: I do not solve the "hard problem" of consciousness). Rather, it attempts to relate the mechanism for the operation of consciousness hypothesised in certain theories (most notably that of Dennett) to the wider perspective on music developed here, in order to reinforce the book's overarching narrative of the power of Universal Darwinism.

Having previewed these chapters, it is important to stress that each one of them could have been expanded into a book-length study in its own right – indeed, some other studies, including those cited in the paragraph above discussing evolutionary musicology, attempt this, wholly or in part – such is the breadth and depth of the topics covered and the vitality of the research associated with them. From this, it follows that the book – like most others tackling such weighty subjects – is necessarily constrained, and thus several interesting topics have not found their way into it, or have had their discussion curtailed. Examples of the former include formal mathematical models of replicator transmission and the learned song of animals other than the bird and cetacean species considered in Chapter 5; examples of the latter include the narrative of human evolution sketched in Chapter 2, the overviews of music-scholarly literature offered in Chapter 4, and the discussion of consciousness in Chapter 7, to name only a handful.

As will be evident from the foregoing, one important theme running, in various ways, throughout the book, is the relationship between music and language. As a "book within a book", it is dealt with in each of Chapters 2–7 from various perspectives. Whenever it is discussed, I aim to make the point that the sound patterns of music and those of language are not so dissimilar as to warrant entirely separate consideration; and that the way they are implemented in the brain helps us, in conjunction with other evidence, to reconstruct their evolutionary history and to understand how patterning in both domains acquires syntactic structure and semantic content. In short, because the sounds of music and those of language are in many ways similar phonologically and so tightly connected physiologically and neurobiologically, it is highly likely that they are closely related evolutionarily, even though their subsequent bifurcation – in relation to their common "musilinguistic" ancestor (§2.7.2) – has to some extent obscured their commonalities.

Most of the music examples in this book are drawn from works of the European common-practice period. With this focus inevitably comes a concentration on male-composed musics. This is not in any way to imply that the ideas presented here relate only to this repertoire, or to this sex. Rather, this is simply the music with which I (and, I imagine, many of my readers) will be most familiar. Were I a proper ethnomusicologist, I would have drawn from a range of non-European musics, so there is nothing here that is intrinsically Eurocentric. Indeed, the ideas expressed in this book would be very much diminished if they were only applicable to a narrow historical and geographical sample of music rather than, as is maintained here, the broad sweep of human cultures. I therefore attempt to stress throughout the universality of the processes underpinning human musicality and music, even though their products are richly diverse.

Steven Jan
Didsbury, Manchester, 27th November 2022.

Credits

I am grateful to the following publishers for their permission to reproduce certain images. Unless listed below, the figures in this book have been created by the author and are under license CC BY-NC-ND. Those figures preceded by an asterisk below have been re-drawn and modified by the author, and are also under license CC BY-NC-ND.

Chapter 1

Springer Nature, for permission to reproduce the image in *Figure 1.2.

Chapter 2

Proceedings of the National Academy of Sciences of the United States of America, for permission to reproduce the image in Figure 2.1.

MIT Press, for permission to reproduce the image in *Figure 2.2.

Chapter 3

Sage Publishing, for permission to reproduce the images in Figure 3.9 and Figure 3.11.

Craig Stuart Sapp, for permission to reproduce the images in Figure 3.12.

Cambridge University Press, for permission to reproduce the image in *Figure 3.16.

Chapter 4

The University of Chicago Press, for permission to reproduce the image in *Figure 4.1.

MIT Press, for permission to reproduce the image in Figure 4.5.

Princeton University Press, for permission to reproduce the image in *Figure 4.9.

Chapter 5

Henrike Hultsch, for permission to reproduce the image in Figure 5.1.

Elsevier, for permission to reproduce the image in Figure 5.4.

Elsevier, for permission to reproduce the image in Figure 5.5.

Chapter 6

Valerio Velardo, for permission to reproduce the images in *Figure 6.11 and *Figure 6.12.

Chapter 7

Taylor and Francis and the Institute of Materials, Minerals and Mining, for permission to reproduce the image in *Figure 7.1.

Note on Symbols

The analytical overlay-symbology for identifying musemes in those figures that contain musical score-extracts is that employed in Jan (2007, pp. 49–51, Fig. 3.1). Pitch designations in the text use Helmholtz notation, where the pitches two octaves below, one octave below and one octave above "middle" C ($= c^1$) are, respectively, C, c and c^2. Non-register-specific pitches are referred to using capital letters ("C").

Chord symbols in the text are generally given in "upper-case" Roman numerals (e.g., I, II, VI, etc.), except where a distinction is necessary between chord-forms in the major and those in the minor modes (e.g., I *versus* i, vi *versus* VI, etc.). Alternative forms of triads on the same root are indicated by a vertical line (e.g., I|i (the tonic chords in the major or the minor), etc.). Diminished and augmented triads are, where necessary, identified by post-pended symbols (e.g., vii$_\circ$ (a diminished triad on the seventh scale degree in the major), III$_+$ (an augmented triad on the third scale degree in the (harmonic) minor), etc.). No attempt is made to specify the nature (major, minor, etc.) of a seventh used in connection with a Roman numeral (e.g., I7 (a major seventh over a tonic-major chord), vii7 (a minor seventh over a leading-note diminished chord in the major), etc.). Chord symbols separated by a forward-slash usually indicate "secondary-dominant" relationships (e.g., V/V (the dominant ($= \mathrm{II}_{3\sharp}^7$) of the dominant), etc.). As in the previous example, figured-bass symbols are occasionally used to clarify chord content and inversion (e.g., I$_4^6$ (a tonic chord in second inversion), V$_5^6$ (a dominant seventh chord in first inversion), etc.). Scale degrees are indicated using careted Arabic numerals (e.g., $\hat{5}$, $\hat{3}$–$\hat{2}$–$\hat{1}$, etc.).

While the book is intended to be read in sequence, cross-references (indicated by "§") connect sections where the same or a related topic is covered, allowing the reader to follow a particular thematic "thread" through the book.

1. Introduction:
Music and Darwinism

… a beautifully simple and easily understood idea … evolution by
natural selection …. is one of the most powerful ideas in all areas of
science, and is the only theory that can seriously claim to unify biology. It
can give meaning to facts from the invisible world in a drop of rain water,
or from the many colored delights of a botanic garden, to thundering
herds of big game.… As Theodosius Dobzhansky, one of the twentieth
century's most eminent evolutionary biologists, remarked in an often
quoted but scarcely exaggerated phrase, 'nothing in biology makes sense
except in the light of evolution'. (Ridley, 2004, p. 4; see also Dobzhansky,
1973)

1.1 Prologue: What Can Evolution Tell Us about Music, and What Can Music Tell Us about Evolution?

Two questions motivate this book. The first is: "what can evolution tell us
about music?" The second is its inversion: "what can music tell us about evolution?" The following subsections expand upon these questions, allowing
us to understand the implications of the book's title, *Music in evolution and
evolution in music*, and to see the two phenomena – one a universal process,
the other an ostensibly human-specific art-form – as intimately connected
and reciprocally illuminating. In pursuing answers to these questions, the
book will attempt, in Ridley's phrase, to "give meaning to facts" about music
using the unifying power of the theory of evolution (2004, p. 4).

  https://doi.org/10.11647/OBP.0301.01

1.1.1 What Can Evolution Tell Us about Music?

I begin with the proviso that, when discussing "evolution" in this book, I am, unless otherwise stated, referring to *Darwin's theory of evolution by natural selection*. This will be defined more formally in §1.5.1. As will be discussed in §1.8, other theories of evolution have been developed, but these will not figure extensively here. At first thought, evolution might seem to bear little relation to most people's experience and understanding of music. To the teenager absorbed in the sounds emanating from her headphones, the child haltingly learning his first notes on the clarinet, or the retired person guiltily dividing her attention between the Beethoven symphony playing in the concert hall and the text message from her granddaughter, evolution – insofar as these individuals may apprehend the details of the theory – is probably something they see as quite separate from their varied experiences of music. These cultural stereotypes aside, however, I contend that evolution can shed a powerful light on music and, as explained in §1.2, it is the aim of this book to show how and why this is the case. The illumination of music by evolutionary theory works in two main ways.

Firstly, evolutionary theory can help us to understand how we came, as a species, to be so musical. No other organism on earth is so adept at manipulating sounds in such dazzlingly complex ways and so relentless in making them bear such an intense weight of emotion and meaning – to borrow Meyer's (1956) phrase – as *Homo sapiens*. While there are certainly species who are talented sound-makers/vocalisers (§5.4.1, §5.4.2), their apparent lack of a (human-like) consciousness (insofar as we can know this) precludes their "music" – if this is how one chooses to perceive and conceive it – from having the intentionality and the personal and group significance of human music. By regarding musicality — the morphology and propensity to make sounds that can be regarded by others as music/musical — as a biological attribute, it is possible to trace its development in the human lineage, a development that involved both physical and mental changes. These changes include modifications to the body that enabled (vocal) sound production; and developments of the brain that enabled perception and cognition of such sounds as constituting what we came to regard (whatever conceptual vocabulary we used) as music.

Of course, seeing musicality in this way involves regarding it as an *adaptation* – as something that made some contribution, alone or in conjunction with other competences, to the survival of individuals, groups and, ultimately, *Homo sapiens* as a species (§2.5). Some adaptationist accounts see musicality as fostering the group coordination (physical and in terms of common purpose) necessary for overcoming intra-group rivalries and extra-group threats. Others see music as a sexually selected factor in female mate-choice, being used for extravagant male displays of health, intelligence and rhythmic co-ordination. Others see it in terms of the communicative rituals that enable mothers and their infants to bond. Still others – and these explanations are not mutually exclusive – consider it in conjunction with language, arguing that not much separated early "music" and early "language" (§2.7). As organised, "communicative" vocalisations produced by the same sound-producing organs and controlled by many similar brain regions (§2.7.7), music and language are increasingly seen as two sides of the same evolutionary coin and so cannot be understood in isolation: music is broadly communicative, certainly of affect; and language has many musical features, certainly in terms of prosody and rhythm. All of these adaptationist accounts have merit, and will be discussed and evaluated in Chapter 2.

Secondly, evolutionary theory can help us to understand how musics themselves came to be as they are – to understand why there are so many different musical cultures in the world, and how they have reached their present states. Extensively documented by ethnomusicology and historical musicology, different musical forms, genres and styles have come and gone over the course of recorded history and even though the post-Renaissance western developmental model of constant striving for progress is far from universal or normative, it is reasonable to infer (even in conservative traditions) that gradual, continual change is the norm in most if not all musical cultures. It is important to understand that such change is not the result of biological evolution, because the period of known human musics – roughly that of the last two millennia – is far too short for significant music-affecting biological-evolutionary change to have occurred in our species. As Harari argues,

> [t]he large societies found in some other species, such as ants and bees, are stable and resilient because most of the information needed to sustain

them is encoded in the genome. A female honeybee larva can, for example, grow up to be either a queen or a worker, depending on what food
it is fed. Its DNA programmes the necessary behaviours for whatever
role it will fulfil in life. Hives can be very complex social structures, containing many different kinds of workers, such as harvesters, nurses and
cleaners. But so far researchers have failed to locate lawyer bees. Bees
don't need lawyers because there is no danger that they might forget
or violate the hive constitution. The queen does not cheat the cleaner
bees of their food, and they never go on strike demanding higher wages.
(Harari, 2014, pp. 119–120)

Harari's point is that several animal societies are entirely and self-sufficiently
regulated by their genes: the structure of apian social relations could change
at some point in the future – perhaps moving from a monarchical system
to a Roman-Republic-style two-consul-bee system – but only as a result of
biological evolution in response to some selection pressure.[3] Humans, by
contrast, create "imagined orders" (Harari, 2014, pp. 113–118) – virtual models of the world, descriptive and prescriptive, that often bear little connection
to the biological imperatives of our DNA. Most such imagined orders define
socio-political, economic or religious structures, such as the Roman Republic, communism or Christianity. For Harari, the growth of state-supported
market capitalism went hand in hand with the growth of individualism
(sometimes discussed under the rubric of "bourgeois subjectivity" (Pippin,
2005, p. 12; see also McClary, 1994)); but this was not an easy alliance, for

[t]he deal between states, markets and individuals is an uneasy one.... it
breaches countless generations of human social arrangements. Millions
of years of evolution have designed us to live and think as community
members. Within a mere two centuries we have become alienated individuals. Nothing testifies better to the awesome power of culture [to
overcome/circumvent biological evolution]. (Harari, 2014, p. 360)

Another imagined order, perhaps more properly a durable sub-order common to numerous imagined orders, is a musical culture – the idea of a valued
(canonic, perhaps) body of sound-manipulation practices and their resultant
sound-objects. As will be clear from Harari's account, the key feature of

---

[3] See Grimaldi and Engel (2005, p. 408) for a discussion of the "haplodiploid" genetic basis
of such "social" insects as bees, wasps and ants (all of the order *Hymenoptera*). A move to a
two-consul system would require a significant change in bees' genetic code.

this and other imagined orders is that it is a *cultural* rather than a *biological* (genetic) fact. As such, it is highly mutable, changing at rates many times faster than the "parent" genetic evolution and often doing so in ways that do not align with the "interests" – the survival imperatives – of the genes.

To understand this dichotomy – and to support the claim above that "evolutionary theory can help us to understand how musics themselves came to be as they are" – we need to invoke the concept of the *replicator*. A fundamental concept in evolutionary theory, a replicator, as its name implies, is a small particle with the remarkable property of being able to cause copies of itself to be made. From such seemingly unpromising beginnings, "systems of great complexity" can arise (Dawkins, 1989, p. 322). In biology, genes are the fundamental replicator, and they have given rise to the dizzying variety and richness of the natural world. To account for musical culture we require not one *replicator system* (genes, plus their replication-fostering adjuncts), but two. As Chapter 3 argues, that second replicator system might be understood in terms of the *meme* concept developed by Dawkins (1989). This argues that there exist replicated particles in culture, memes, that function as the equivalent of the gene. Without this second, cultural, replicator system, it is virtually impossible to explain the rich imagined order of human musics.

1.1.2 What Can Music Tell Us about Evolution?

Having outlined briefly how music might be illuminated by an evolutionary perspective on its production, structure and reception, it would appear that evolutionary theory can, conversely, draw fruitfully on and be evidenced by what is known of musicality and music. This is because the origin of this most singular of human competences, in both its biological and cultural dimensions, poses significant challenges to scientific understanding. Specifically, the evolution of the substrates for musicality and music – morphological, neurobiological and psychological – was associated with significant changes in the design of our species, modifications that the chimpanzee line, our closest evolutionary relative, did not undergo. Whether one takes musicality and music (and, indeed, the related capacity for language) as the *cause* or the *effect* of these adaptive changes (§2.1) – and the reality may not have been either/or – attempting to reconstruct and explain their markers in the human fossil record and in the behaviour of ourselves and our closest evolutionary relatives offers a reasonably coherent body of evidence upon which evolutionary theory can develop and test its wider claims. More dramatically, this central attribute of humanity throws down a gauntlet to evolutionary theory.

Indeed, for Cross (1999), music may be "the most important thing we ever did". He believes that, far from being cost-heavy and benefit-light – a "pleasure technology" amounting to mere "auditory cheesecake", in Pinker's dismissive view (1997, pp. 528, 534) (§2.2, §2.5) – music was key to our endurance on and domination of this planet: it shaped our species physically, cognitively and socially in ways that maximised our survival chances. He argues that

> 'music' as an identifiable human pursuit, emerges from its developmental precursors as a distinct and socially-conditioned activity in the particular processes of human evolution that gave rise to *Homo sapiens* .... Music is integrally bound up with those processes, and can be considered to have been either evolutionarily adaptive or what Stephen Jay Gould would term 'exaptive'. In other words, music propels the development, and propelled the evolution, of mind by enabling consequence-free representational redescription[4] across domains; music also facilitates the development, and facilitated the evolution, of social behaviours by enabling risk-free action and risky interaction. At the very least it may have contributed to the emergence of one of our most distinguishing features, our cognitive flexibility; at most, it may have been the single most important factor enabling the capacities of representational redescription to evolve. (Cross, 1999, pp. 33–34)

Returning to the capacity of music to illuminate evolutionary theory, for those who advocate the extension of orthodox Darwinism to culture – the "neo-Darwinians" or "Universal Darwinians" (Dawkins, 1983b), most of whom would also advocate a memetic perspective – human music offers a rich resource for the study of cultural replicators and the evolutionary processes they impel. Although some biologists reject the claims of memetics, it offers evidence in support of Darwinism that is arguably more direct, more

---

[4] A term of Karmiloff-Smith's, this is the process whereby, during child development, and in knowledge building generally, implicit, domain-specific knowledge becomes explicit, domain-general (Cross, 1999, pp. 15–16; Karmiloff-Smith, 1992, pp. 15–16).

tractable, and more readily accessible than that available to biology. While the computer simulation of biological evolution can "accelerate" the process and make it more tangible – the same is true for simulations of language-cultural and music-cultural evolution (Chapter 6) – cultural evolution is already intrinsically many orders of magnitude faster than biological evolution. Thus, the processes and artefacts of musical culture (and those of other realms of culture) are sufficiently tangible, diverse and robust to motivate an evolutionary explanation and serve as evidence for multi-domain evolutionary hypotheses.

1.2 Aims, Claims, Objectives and Structure

Given the above points, necessarily expounded at some length, I am now in a position to outline more formally what this book is about and what it intends to cover. Stated systematically, its aims, claims, objectives and structure are as follows.

1.2.1 Aims

The principal aims of this book are as follows:

- To demonstrate the operation of the "evolutionary algorithm" in the origin and development of human musicality – that is, to situate *music in evolution* and so to understand it as a suite of competences humans acquired in response to various selection pressures that afforded us a survival advantage over our competitors.

- To demonstrate the operation of the evolutionary algorithm (or, as I generally term it, the "Variation-Replication-Selection" (VRS) algorithm, explained in §1.5.1) in the development of musical style and structure itself – that is, to show the workings of *evolution in music*.

- To show the integration and continuity of music in evolution with evolution in music, and thereby to argue for the broad validity of the evolutionary algorithm in shaping musicality and music within a broader biological-naturalistic context.

1.2.2 Claims

The principal claims of this book are as follows:

- That music was intrinsic to the evolution and survival of *Homo sapiens* in its shaping of our morphology and cognition, its fostering of the development of language (as the impeller of a "protomusic-protolanguage"), and its mediation of our social interactions; and that similar organised-sound-related processes, at a less advanced stage of development, are at work in other species.

- That music, as process and product, cannot be understood in isolation from the biological processes that shaped the musicality that engenders it and that shapes its development.

- That music as process and product *itself* internalises evolutionary mechanisms and so affords a microcosm of the algorithms that paved the way for its existence.

- That music has been understood by means of discourses that, as a subset of culture more generally, also manifest evolutionary change. This coevolution of music and discourse-about-music is a rich field for cultural-evolutionary analysis.

- That music is a particularly powerful manifestation of a kind of "Darwinism-as-consciousness", whereby the millisecond-level processes underpinning the awareness and decision-making intrinsic to human consciousness are mirrored, at a somewhat slower pace, in musical cultures.

1.2.3 Objectives

The principal objectives of this book (and the chapters in which they are primarily addressed) are as follows:

- To survey the principal ideas and concepts of evolutionary theory insofar as they relate to musicality and music (Chapter 1).

- To summarise what is known of the evolution of *Homo sapiens*, particularly those physical and psychological attributes related to the capacities for musicality and language (Chapter 2).

- To survey theories of cultural evolution and to argue that in its most radical form – the theory of memetics – it is a direct equivalent to Darwinism in biological evolution (Chapter 3).

- To give an account of the metaphorical uses of evolutionary theory in western music historiography and western music theory and analysis, and to argue that discourse on music is itself subject to the same cultural-evolutionary forces operating on the music that is the object of that discourse (Chapter 4).

- To assess the relationship between certain animal vocalisations and human music and language, and to consider the extent to which these might be regarded as musical and/or linguistic, and the extent to which they might be deemed creative (Chapter 5).

- To explore how musicality, music and the creativity normally associated with them have been rendered using evolutionary simulations in computers (Chapter 6).

- To consider the relationships between evolution and consciousness and to explore music's relationship to these interconnected processes (Chapter 7).

1.2.4 Structure

The structure of this book is as follows.

Chapter 1 attempts to define the nature and scope of the evolutionary algorithm, exploring the characteristics of the materials and mechanisms that fall under its ambit in biology and culture.

Chapter 2 explores the biological foundations for musicality and music in humans, tracing the evolution of our species from our hominin ancestors and attempting to locate the origins of musicality in this process.[5] In the first of six treatments of this issue in the book, it will be argued that it is impossible to consider the evolution of language separately from that of music, not least given the close analogies in brain substrates relating the two competences.

---

[5] I employ the term "homin*in*", in accordance with modern usage, to refer to modern humans and our immediate ancestors (i.e., the genera *Homo*, *Australopithecus*, *Paranthropus* and *Ardipithecus*). This is in contrast to the term "homin*id*", which refers more widely to modern great apes (i.e., humans, gorillas, chimpanzees and orangutans) and their immediate ancestors (Bannan, 2012, p. xii; but see Fitch, 2010, 235, note to Box 6.1).

Chapter 3 revisits memetics, and a number of antecedent models, in part to develop
it and integrate it into a wider evolutionary framework, and in part to set the
context for the metaphorical uses of evolutionary concepts in music-scholarly
discourses covered in Chapter 4. Exploring the extent to which memetics might
illuminate our understanding of musical performance affords an opportunity
to connect a number of different issues considered up to this point. Chapter 3
returns to the issue of the relationship between music and language, attempting
to understand the sound patterns of music ("musemes") in ways similar to
how the sound patterns of language ("lexemes") were understood in Chapter
2.[6]

Chapter 4 traces the application of evolutionary metaphors in scholarly discourses
on music, both historiographic and theoretical/analytical. Since their peak in
the nineteenth century, such metaphors have become less overt, partly as a
result of criticisms that the organicism from which they spring is reductive
and deterministic, but they still arguably govern much musical scholarship,
albeit implicitly. Their status as what might be termed "verbal-conceptual"
memeplexes (§3.8) is discussed and thus a multi-layered treatment of the issue
is offered: the consideration of evolutionary metaphors in scholarly discourse
is related to the memetic-evolutionary development of those discourses, which
itself occurs in coadaptation with meme (musical and non-musical) evolution.

Chapter 5 discusses musicality in animals, particularly certain species of primates,
birds and cetaceans, and the extent to which these organisms might be said
to have a musical culture and the creativity normally associated with it. An
application of memetic analysis to certain cases of animal culture indicates that
process operating in human musics also govern animal "musics". The chapter
concludes with a discussion of the extent to which the vocalisations of certain
animals are musical and/or linguistic, and to what extent they betray evidence
of consciousness.

Chapter 6 considers, after an examination of the computer simulation of language
evolution, a number of computer systems developed to generate music via the
simulation of evolutionary processes (and other approaches), and examines

---

[6] I use these terms in a slightly different sense in this book to their conventional usage,
employing the suffix "-eme" to denote derivation from "meme", a unit of cultural replication.
Thus, "museme" refers to a unit of music-cultural replication, and is a contraction of "musical
meme" (and not, in Tagg's sense, and after Seeger, "a complete, independent unit of music-
logical form or mood" (in Tagg, 1999, p. 31)); and "lexeme" refers to a unit of linguistic-cultural
replication (and not (just) "a unit of lexical meaning, which exists regardless of any inflectional
endings it may have or the number of words it may contain" (Crystal, 2019, p. 128)).

whether creativity is an attribute of any of them. It is argued that various technologies are on the threshold of this property, and consequently that distinctions between human and machine creativity, as evolutionary phenomena, are becoming increasingly blurred.

Chapter 7 concludes this study with a broadly philosophical review and extension of the subjects considered. It principally explores the relationships between evolution and consciousness and examines the extent to which musical processes and products might be seen as manifestations of consciousness in a sense rather wider than that which is normally accepted.

From this overview, it will be clear that the book moves broadly along a dual nature (biology)-to-nurture (culture) and human-to-post-human trajectory: it starts with a discussion of the biological basis of human musicality (Chapter 2); moves through an extension of Darwinism to culture, both via memetics (Chapter 3) and via metaphor (Chapter 4); and it concludes with a consideration of animal-musical (Chapter 5) and incipient "post-human" cultures, as implemented in computer systems (Chapter 6) and in the internet (Chapter 7).

This first chapter begins by exploring the distinction between music and musicality (§1.3), before considering the academic disciplines, and their associated terminology, relevant to the book's concerns (§1.4). It then assesses the scope of the evolutionary algorithm and how it operates across a number of different substrates (§1.5). The next section considers the elements key to all evolutionary systems, attempting to discern commonalities across a number of different realms within which evolution operates (§1.6). Classification is an important concern of evolutionary theory and this is considered in order to set up later cross-comparisons between biological and cultural taxonomies (§1.7). The final part of the chapter looks at the tensions between Lamarckian and Darwinian accounts of evolution, again to enable later cross-comparisons with analogous phenomena in music (§1.8).

1.3 Music and Musicality in Evolutionary Thought

Despite what was said in §1.1, it might be thought that the paradigms currently in use for understanding music are adequate. Certainly in the field of musicology – or "music scholarship" as Joseph Kerman enjoined us to call it (Kerman, 1994a, pp. 7–8) – there are well developed models for considering music in its social and historical contexts and for understanding its structure, both generally (via music theory) and specifically (via music analysis). In addition to the growing status of ethnomusicology, and its recontextual-isation of European musics as just as "ethnic" as any other, recent decades have seen an expansion in the range of musics admitted to the scholarly canon (Randel, 1992) and a concomitant broadening of the methodologies deployed to understand them.

Ethnomusicology, as part of the recontextualisation mentioned above, poses a challenge to other types of music scholarship, in that its scope, chronolo-gical and geographical, is radically more expansive. It also sees music as part of culture in a way that only became fashionable for western "art" music with the inception of the "New Musicology" of the 1980s (L. Kramer, 2010), and that, in our increasingly fragmented post-postmodern culture, may yet become unfashionable (J. D. Kramer, 2016) (see also §4.6). Moreover, and in conjunction with its sister discipline anthropology, ethnomusicology at-tempts to see music in the broader context of human biological attributes. Thus, it is not enslaved to the work-centric, aestheticised view of music that began to arise in the mid-eighteenth century and that, fuelled by Romanti-cism, privileges the creative artist and his – and it usually is "his" – intellectual offspring (Goehr, 1992). While attenuated, this way of seeing music – as text, not act (Taruskin, 1995) – persists, and it is perhaps a consequence, in part, of western capitalism and its fixation on the possession of, and commerce in, objects.

What ethnomusicology opens up to us is not only the broad vista of *music/mu-sics* in (global, human) culture, but also – to add the complementary term to one of the principal dualisms that inform this book – of *musicality/musicalities* in the context of evolution. That is, it allows us to make a distinction between music as *product* – as something we make and do as part of our daily lives – and music as *competence* – as a set of skills necessary for making and doing music that are underpinned by various physical attributes and neurological substrates and that have evolved in our species over millennia. As Honing argues, "[p]otential candidates for the basic components of musicality that have been proposed in the recent literature are relative pitch (e.g., contour and interval analysis …), regularity and beat perception …, tonal encoding of pitch …, and metrical encoding of rhythm …. Some of these musical traits may be common to humans and other species, and other might be uniquely human …" (2018a, pp. 6, 8).

In this sense musicality and music are broadly analogous to what Chomsky terms "I-language" – "internal language", which is a biologically evolved function of human brains – and "E-language" – "external language", which is a culturally evolved function of human communities (Chomsky, 1986, pp. 20, 22; Fitch, 2010, p. 32). Thus, and while not completely separable, I-language inheres in "some element of the mind of the person who knows the language" (Chomsky, 1986, p. 22), whereas E-language encompasses "actual or potential speech events" (1986, p. 20). The equivalents to these are what might be termed "I-music" – musicality as capacity – and "E-music" – music as process and product. There are, however, two caveats to this mapping. Firstly, whereas I-language is primarily neural/cognitive, with some derivative neural/motor elements (for vocal production), I-music involves greater motor functionality (for rhythmicity) than its linguistic counterpart. Secondly, it is important to note that Chomsky would not advocate the "gradualist" approach to the evolution of language (and music) advocated here: indeed, he adopts an explicitly "saltationist" account (§1.7.3), speaking of the origin of (I-)language occurring via a "great leap forward" (2006, pp. 176, 184; see also Chomsky, 2009, p. 34).

As argued in §1.7.3, however, the distinction between gradualism and saltationism is perhaps not as clear-cut as it might seem, resting in part on the granularity with which evolutionary processes are conceived and measured and in part on the mechanisms driving them (what are termed there *single-step* and *cumulative* selection). In this sense, the "Cognitive Revolution" discussed in §2.5.5 – a driver of Chomsky's "great leap forward" – represents the product of accelerated cumulative-selection gradualism, not of single-step-selection saltationism. Rejecting such ontogenetic (organism/I-level) and phylogenetic (species/E-level) saltationism in favour of gradualism, one might speak, apropos E-music, of "musogeny" – cultural-historical musical change – as the musical analogue to the "glossogeny" – cultural-historical linguistic change – of E-language (Fitch, 2010, pp. 33–34).

As will be explored in detail in this book, the fact that all human cultures possess what might (in the most catholic sense) be called music and/or musicality; the manifestation of musicality in even very young infants of our species; the likelihood that musicality appears to have been present from the earliest days of our species; the fact that music making is a profound force for social communication and cohesion; and the fact that brain circuits for musical competences are "cross/inter-wired" with circuits for many other competences (perhaps most importantly language), makes music a central part of what it is to be human. That many of the points I have just listed appear to have been strongly shaped by evolution – they are not present, or are present to a much lesser extent, in other species, even those with which we share a close common ancestor – ties music firmly into an *adaptationist* view (§2.5), in opposition to one that sees it merely as a source of (Pinkerian) sensory pleasure.

An adaptationist perspective regards musicality as having subserved one or more functions that have contributed to our survival. As suggested in §1.1.1, and as will be explored in more detail in §2.5, the three most fundamental of these appear to be group sociality, sexual selection, and infant nurturing; a higher-level, emergent, benefit appears to be pre/protolinguistic communication (§2.7). Adaptationism implies a Darwinian process by which those individuals who possessed genes for what we would now regard as musical competences had a higher differential "fitness" – however defined; see Dawkins (1983a, Ch. 10) – than those without. Over time, such genes inevitably spread in the gene-pool and musicality became established as one of the things that made us human and that helped us to face the challenges of our early existence.

The other term of the dualism, music, also needs to figure in any adaptationist account. Key to the argument here is that it is insufficient only to consider the evolution of musicality, important though this is; one must also consider the intra-musical Darwinian processes that have shaped music over time in human cultures. This is because, even in the most conservative, traditional musical societies, change in what might be termed musical style has been extensively documented over time. Much of the research agenda of western historical musicology, like those of other humanistic disciplines, is predicated upon the idea of constant change and development in the materials of music and their use in constantly changing genres, forms and styles. Faced with such indisputable change, one needs a mechanism to account for it, and Darwinism appears the prime candidate. Just as Darwinism is the only mechanism capable of explaining the evolution of human beings and their (musical) competences from precursor species, I contend that Darwinism, as incorporated into a number of cultural replication theories of which memetics is the most promising, is the only mechanism capable of explaining the evolution of music itself. In this sense I advocate a *coevolutionary* account of the evolution of musicality and music that, as noted, attempts to integrate understanding of *music in evolution* with understanding of *evolution in music*. As Brown, Merker and Wallin express it,

> [t]he term 'music evolution' ... refers both to biological evolution of a capacity and to cultural evolution of that capacity's output. In other words, the term refers both to the biological emergence of music through evolution of the capacity to make it (an evolutionary psychological consideration [in addition to other disciplines]) as well as to the historical changes in musical systems and styles that occur over time and place (a comparative musicological consideration [in addition to other disciplines]). (Wallin et al., 2000, p. 18)

There are five scientific alternatives to adopting a Darwinian explanation for musicality and/or music: leaving aside the non-scientific "explanation" of creationism, Mayr identifies six theories of biological evolution (1982, pp. 360–361), that, in Dawkins' formulation, are: (i) "built-in capacity for, or drive toward, increasing perfection" (1983b, p. 406); (ii) "use and disuse plus inheritance of acquired characters" (Lamarckism; considered later in terms of its applicability to biological (§1.8) and cultural (§3.4.3) evolution) (1983b, pp. 406–409); (iii) "direct induction by the environment" (1983b, pp. 409–411); (iv) "saltationism" (1983b, 412—418); (v) "random evolution" (1983b, pp. 419–420); and (vi) "direction (order) imposed on random variation by natural selection" (1983b, p. 420). All but one of these – Darwinian natural selection – are elegantly refuted by Dawkins (1983a, pp. 406–420);

and these refutations chime with the broad consensus of opinion of modern evolutionary biology, which is squarely Darwinian.

A creationist account of musicality would simply see musicality as a gift from God, one, like sight, hearing or any other human attribute, bestowed fully formed and without antecedents. Similarly, many accounts of music are also "creationist", albeit in a more implicit and metaphorical sense. That is, the act of producing music is often framed, certainly in originality-dominated western culture, as singular and unmediated, the sovereign will of the composer imposing order on musical material in a way that seems to call out "let there be sound!" and that results in the miracle of musical genesis. If one takes a creationist account of musicality or of music, one is unlikely to find anything in this book with which one might agree, and it would perhaps be better to stop here and turn to a different book. Actually – like Dawkins' "[n]o, on second thoughts I don't give up" (Dawkins, 2006, p. xvi) – I should not be so defeatist and should urge sceptical readers to press on and give my arguments a chance.

In both domains there is an obligation to explain the varied recurrence of features from earlier forms, one that is arguably met neither by biological nor by cultural creationism. Just as (biological) creationists struggle to explain the similarities between fossils and presently living creatures, or morphological parallels between humans and other life forms, "musical creationists" – that is, those who do not see one piece of music as connected, in an intertextual web, to others – must account for similarities between patterns in music from widely separated time-periods. In both these domains it is important to distinguish between fortuitous similarities – analogies or, more technically, *homoplasies* – and similarities resulting from evolutionary transmission from a common ancestor – or *homologies* (Dennett, 1995, p. 357), discussed in §1.7.2. To give two biological examples, octopus and human eyes are very similar in their morphology, but are actually homoplasious, not homologous: they evolved independently from each other, converging on a similar design. Paradoxically, arms and wings are, in some respects, quite different, but are in fact homologous: they evolved from structures in a common ancestor.[7]

---

[7] I am grateful to Alan Marsden (personal communication) for this point.

To give a musical example, Figure 1.1 shows a clear "morphological" similarity between the passages in Figure 1.1a and Figure 1.1b, one perhaps also resonating in Figure 1.1c (but see also Ringer (1961), and note 195 on page 336).

This resemblance is unlikely to be the result of coincidence: while these patterns are clearly two different entities, certain features render the likelihood of their being coincidentally alike improbable. Both use a I–V … V–I harmonic structure associated with a $\hat{1}$–$\hat{7}$ … $\hat{2}$–$\hat{1}$ melodic pattern (the latter circled in Figure 1.1), forming an *Aprile* schema, in Gjerdingen's terms (2007a, pp. 122–123). While this schema is, almost by definition, common in the music of this period, further similarities – recurrence of scale-degree sequences additional to those constituting the *Aprile* – suggest the relationship between the two passages goes beyond one of generic schema-deployment (i.e., a many-to-one connection between several schema-exemplars and Mozart's and Beethoven's passages), and thus implies a more focused route of transmission (i.e., a one-to-one connection from Wranitzky's passage to Mozart's and, perhaps, from Mozart's to Beethoven's). Further contextual connections suggest Mozart may indeed have directly adapted his phrase from Wranitzky,[8] and Beethoven would certainly have known Mozart's Singspiel, and perhaps Wranitzky's. Thus, the pattern-replication suggests a homological rather than a homoplasious relationship, and so the connection between Figure 1.1a and Figure 1.1b is in principle as much Darwinian as is the relationship between an arm and a wing.[9] This issue is taken up more fully in §3.6.5.

As this book will attempt to argue, the evolutionary theory that many believe offers the best explanation for the origin and development of human musicality also offers the best explanation of the origin and development of human music itself. In short, while it is useful to speak of the dualism of nature

---

[8] Bauman notes that "[t]he popular enthusiasm generated by *Oberon* at Vienna provided an important impulse for the creation of a generation of popular spectacles trading in magic and the exotic. *Die Zauberflöte* in particular shares many features with *Oberon*, musical as well as textual", and was performed at the same theatre as *Oberon*, the Theater auf der Wieden (2001).

[9] As multiparametric entities, it is possible that certain features of a schema (such as the metrical and phrasal elements) are more likely to be homoplasious, whereas others (such as the harmonic and voice-leading patterns) are more likely to be homologous (adapting an idea of Trevor Rawbone, personal communication).

(a) Wranitzky: *Oberon, König der Elfen* (1789), no. 17, "Sie lebt, sie ist's" bb. 42–54.

(b) Mozart: *Die Zauberflöte* K. 620 (1791), no. 21, "Was hör' ich? Paminens Stimme?", bb. 249–253.

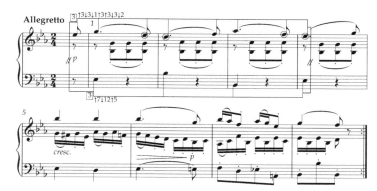

(c) Beethoven: *Die Geschöpfe des Prometheus* op. 43 (1801), no. 16, bb. 1–8.

Figure 1.1: "Morphological" Similarity Between Three Musical Patterns.

and/*versus* nurture, when it comes to the relationship between musicality and music, the nurtural is itself natural.

1.4 Disciplines and Interdisciplines

As a truly multi/interdisciplinary enquiry, the subject(s) of this book – music in evolution and evolution in music – encompass a number of ostensibly separate scientific and humanistic disciplines, or at least these disciplines have pursued separate lines of development until relatively recently; and the book's concerns have previously been partly addressed (although without the overarching synthesis attempted here) under a variety of terminological rubrics. These are outlined below.

1.4.1 Disciplines

The book's contributory disciplines are as shown in Table 1.1; the second column is arranged as *definition of the discipline's scope*/application to evolutionary-music/language questions. Section references here and in §1.4.2 refer to those parts of the book wherein issues cognate with that discipline are treated.

Biology	*The study of living organisms, incorporating evolutionary biology, human evolution* (§2.3), *genetics and taxonomy* (§1.7) / the origin and adaptive benefits of the physical and mental substrates for human musicality, language and related competences (§2.5).
Anthropology	*The study of human beings* / musicality as a characteristic of *Homo sapiens* and the similarities and differences between musical cultures; the universal attributes, if any, of human musical cultures (§3.6).
Sociology	*The study of humans in society* / the nature and functions of musics in human societies and their relationships with social structures (§2.3).
Neuroscience	*The study of brain structure and function* / the structural and functional localisation of music and language in the brain and its relationship to evolutionary changes (§2.7.7); the neuronal encoding and implementation of music and language (§3.8.3).
Linguistics	*The study of the structure and functions of language* / structural and functional analogies / homologies between music and language (§2.7, §3.8, §4.5, §5.6, §6.3 and §7.4); studies of language origin and linguistic "speciation" (§1.7.3).
Psychology	*The study of the human mind* / perception and cognition of music and language; human creativity; consciousness as it applies to musicality (§3.5.2, §7.3).[10]
Ethology	*The study of animal behaviour* / vocalisations in certain species of primates, birds and cetaceans and their potential musical / linguistic function(s) (§5.4); animal creativity (§5.5.3).
Memetics	*The study of cultural replicators* / the factors affecting the genesis and replication of the particles constituting music and language; the population dynamics of musical and linguistic replicators *vis-à-vis* that of their associated biological replicators (§3.4, §3.7).
Musicology	*The study of music as an art and a science* / contribution to evolutionary models of music historiography and of music theory and analysis (§4.3, §4.4).

---

[10] Sometimes neuroscience and psychology are treated together under the rubric of cognitive science, singular or plural.

Ethnomusicology	*The study of music in its socio-cultural contexts*/comparative studies of musical style and structure and its relationship to other "performative" social rituals.[11]
Computer Science	*The study of the theory and practice of computation*/techniques for agent-based simulation of music/linguistic cultural-evolutionary processes (§6.5, §6.3); issues of artificial intelligence (AI) related to musicality; emergent machine creativity (§6.6).
Philosophy	*The study of general problems of being, knowledge and reason*/ the meaning of music and language and their connection to other domains of experience and knowledge (§7.1); the evolutionary basis of knowledge (Evolutionary Epistemology, §3.3.2).

Table 1.1: Disciplines.

1.4.2 Interdisciplines

Many commentators – to be referred to *passim* – have attempted to synthesise two or more of the above disciplines in the pursuit of deeper understanding of music in evolution and/or evolution in music. These hybrid/inter/trans disciplines, which this book seeks further to reconcile and integrate, have a number of different terms, as indicated in Table 1.2.

Evolutionary Psychology	A field consolidated by Leda Cosmides and John Tooby, this concerns the adaptive shaping of perception and cognition, including responses to music and language, by evolution (Barkow et al., 1992; Tooby & Cosmides, 2005).

---

[11] It is not always straightforward to determine whether something is a discipline in its own right or a sub-discipline of a higher-level field of enquiry. With ethnomusicology, geographical-institutional structures (certainly in the North-American academy), a certain tension between it and "traditional" (ethnomusicologists would say "Eurocentric") musicology, and its close links with anthropology and sociology, perhaps warrant its presentation and treatment as a discipline increasingly separate from (non-ethno) musicology. See N. Cook (1998, pp. 86, 99).

Sociobiology	Established by Edward O. Wilson, this encompasses the study of social behaviours (including their cultural processes and products) in terms of biologically/evolutionarily determined constraints (E. O. Wilson, 2000).
Biomusicology	A term coined by Nils Wallin (Wallin, 1991), this is "the analysis of music origins and its application to the study of human origins" (Brown et al., 2000, p. 5). It encompasses three subcategories: (i) *Evolutionary Musicology*, concerned with "the evolutionary origins of music, both in terms of a comparative approach to vocal communication in animals and in terms of an evolutionary psychological approach to the emergence of music in the hominid line" (2000, p. 5); (ii) *Neuromusicology*, examining "the nature and evolution of the neural and cognitive mechanisms involved in musical production and perception . . . " (2000, p. 5); (iii) *Comparative Musicology*, dealing with "the diverse functional roles and uses of music in all human cultures . . . " (2000, p. 5) (see also Table 1.1, "Ethnomusicology").
Sound Archaeology	The study of the sound-world, natural and fabricated, of hominins (Till, 2014; Till, 2019), incorporating music archaeology/archaeomusicology (the study of evidence for human music-making in the material record (Kunej & Turk, 2000; Dumbrill, 2005)), and archaeoacoustics (the study and reconstruction of the sound-worlds of ancient societies and cultures (Fazenda et al., 2017)).
Zoomusicology	The comparative study of animal behaviour, specifically their vocalisations, in terms of musical (and linguistic) characteristics (M. S. Keller, 2012) (Chapter 5).
Evolutionary Computer Music	The use of evolutionary algorithms to compose, perform and analyse music (Miranda & Biles, 2007). Incorporates Computer Simulation of Musical Creativity/Evolution (and related interdisciplinary rubrics): the use of evolutionary algorithms to emulate/replicate/simulate human-level music-creative processes in machines, including (by means of agent-based simulations) interaction between musicians (Fernández & Vico, 2013; Herremans et al., 2017) (Chapter 6).

Table 1.2: Interdisciplines.

As suggested in the Preface, the term "evolutionary musicology" has a certain appeal, but it is arguably excessively restricted to the biological origins of music: it is too strongly orientated towards evolutionary psychology and therefore does not sufficiently acknowledge the power of cultural-evolutionary forces working with (and against) biological imperatives (Chapter 3), or the nature (and cultural evolution) of evolutionary thought in discourses on music (Chapter 4), or attempts to transcend human (and animal) biology and culture in the generation of music (Chapter 6).

1.5 The Ambit of the Evolutionary Algorithm

As Dennett asserted in the phrase quoted in the Preface, the (Darwinian) evolutionary algorithm is the "Universal Acid" (1995, p. 63): it eats away at everything, and so nothing in the universe is impervious to it or resistant to its effects. After defining what exactly is meant by the concept, this section considers the different domains in which the evolutionary algorithm operates and argues – entirely in accordance with the implications of Dennett's phrase – that musicality and music have no claim to be resistant to the acid.

1.5.1 What Is Evolution?

At its most basic level, evolution is reducible to an algorithm. An algorithm is a mindless, "if-then" process that works on a given substrate to produce outcomes or outputs of a certain type. In Dennett's formulation,

> evolution occurs whenever the following conditions exist: (1) *variation*: there is a continuing abundance of different elements[;][12] (2) heredity or *replication*: the elements have the capacity to create copies or replicas of themselves[; and][13] (3) differential 'fitness' [leading to *selection*]: the number of copies of an element that are created in a given time varies, depending on interactions between the features of that element and features of the environment in which it persists. (Dennett, 1995, p. 343; emphases mine)

---

[12] *Mutation*, in both genes and memes, is a driver of variation.
[13] Replication is normally associated with *transmission* in biological evolution and generally engendered by it in cultural evolution.

Calvin expresses the same idea slightly differently, arguing that

> 1. There must be a reasonably complex pattern involved. 2. The pattern
> must be *copied* [*replicated*] somehow (indeed, that which is copied may
> serve to define the pattern). 3. *Variant* patterns must sometimes be
> produced by chance. 4. The pattern and its variant must compete with
> one another for occupation of a limited work space.... 5. The competition
> is biased by a multifaceted environment .... That's natural *selection*. 6.
> There is a skewed survival to reproductive maturity (environmental
> selection is mostly juvenile mortality) or a skewed distribution of those
> adults who successfully mate (sexual selection), so new variants always
> preferentially occur around the more successful of the current patterns.
> (Calvin, 1998, p. 21; emphases mine)

Both formalisations have in common the three interconnected principles of
variation (a fund of pattern forms consisting of a notional original[14] (antecedent) and one or more variants (consequents)); *replication* (copying, leading to the existence of multiple forms of the same variant); and some form
of *selection* (whereby attributes of the pattern, in conjunction with those of
its environment, lead to some variants being more extensively copied than
others). In summary, one might say that the evolutionary algorithm, in its
most abstract form, is reducible to "VRS" – i.e., the interconnected processes
of variation, replication and selection. Plotkin (1995, p. 84), after Lewontin
(1970), uses a different acronym to signify essentially the same process: the
"g-t-r heuristic" aligns g (generate) with V, t (test) with S and r (regenerate) with R (see also Dennett, 2017, pp. 43, 384). Framing this process as
a heuristic captures the essence of the VRS/g-t-r algorithm as an adaptive/
survival-related problem-solver – and thus as an accumulator of information and knowledge, broadly understood, in a domain. Any system that
instantiates this algorithm – in whatever substrate and at whatever structural-
hierarchic level – is, in Calvin's phrase, a "Darwin machine" (Calvin, 1987b;
Calvin, 1987a; Calvin, 1998, p. 6; Plotkin, 1995). That is, it is an engine driven
by the VRS algorithm that, within some substrate, produces some output –
usually a change of form or state – in response to some adaptive imperative.

---

[14] The concept of originality is problematic in this context because multiple "originals" may
be intractably interconnected with multiple variants in a nexus of evolutionary processes. More
fundamentally, and in a cascade of regress, a candidate original may itself be a variant of an
earlier form.

The implication of Dennett's Universal Acid is that the VRS algorithm is not confined to any particular domain or medium – it is "substrate-neutral" (1995, p. 82). On earth, we encounter it (albeit indirectly, and in virtual/ reconstructed form) via the biological evolution of our own species and of other living creatures. But there is no reason, in principle, why the algorithm needs gene-based VRS – it is not tied to it in any structural or functional manner. This means that any entity of which copies can be made, and that exists in an environment that provides some kind of raw material for that entity and its future copies, will be amenable to the VRS algorithm. It is this point that prompted Dawkins to claim that terrestrial/biological Darwinism is merely a subset of a much more far-reaching process: a Universal Darwinism whose reach, logic dictates, is limitless (Dawkins, 1983b; see also Plotkin, 1995, Ch. 3).

Having made the last point, it is nevertheless possible to identify certain specific domains in which the VRS algorithm operates, as discussed in the following subsections.

1.5.2 Physical Evolution

By this highly speculative concept – upon which none of the specific arguments concerning music and evolution hinges – is meant evolution in the laws of physics, and not evolution in the morphologies of living creatures. To assert that these laws are themselves subject to Universal Darwinism is to make a claim that is both bold and intrinsically difficult to verify. After all, we know (very imperfectly) only one universe; and its laws, insofar as we understand them, appear immutable. But some physicists argue that our universe is only one of many.[15] In "multiverse" theories, the big bang gave rise not to one but to a multiplicity of universes (Carr, 2007), each with a different system of physical laws and constituent particles. Other physicists argue that the existence of multiverses is a philosophical, not a scientific, problem, principally on account of the non-amenability of multiverse theories to verification (by means of deduction or induction) or, in Popper's (1959) concept, to falsification.

---

[15] There is clearly a semantic problem here, because it is illogical to speak of a number of "universes" within a "multiverse".

Another difficulty with multiverse theories, beyond the aforementioned problem of verification/falsification, is that they are difficult to reconcile with certain features of the VRS algorithm that occur in other substrates, specifically the distinction between replicators and vehicles (§1.6.1). Briefly stated, that which is copied often creates for itself a framework to expedite its replication – this being physical, sentient bodies, in our case.[16] All other replicator systems discussed in this book operate within the trinity of replicator, vehicle and environment. In multiverse theories the replicator is the system of physical laws, the environment is the body of matter upon which those laws operate, but there is no obvious vehicle. Nevertheless, some terrestrial replicators, notably certain viruses, are coterminous with their vehicles, so this is perhaps not a significant discrepancy. More fundamentally, a replicator is normally something that operates *within* an environment, and that is largely subject to its vicissitudes, not something that (as in multiverse theories) *controls* an environment. Again, there are exceptions: the biological notion of the *extended phenotype* (§1.5.3) encompasses cases where genes act to remodel their environment in order to optimise their own replication.

Another way of conceiving the issue of universe/multiverse-level Darwinism is to be found in Vanchurin's audacious claim that, "on the most fundamental level, the dynamics of the entire universe is described by a microscopic neural network that undergoes learning evolution" (2020, p. 2; see also Vazza & Feletti, 2020). By this, he is "not just saying that the artificial neural networks can be useful for analyzing physical systems … or for discovering physical laws …"; rather, he is claiming that "this is how the world around us actually works" (2020, p. 17). When Vanchurin says the universe "is a neural network" (2020, p. 1), there is nevertheless a level of generalisation in that, as in the operation of the brain and its electronic simulacra, there are nodes ($\equiv$ neurons) and connections between them, forming a matrix. This matrix is comprised, in Vanchurin's model of particles and energy that instantiate physical laws and principles. As will be discussed in §6.5.1.2 apropos neural networks designed to generate music, Vanchurin's universal neural network implements a Darwin machine. This "Vanchurin machine" is able to: (i) generate and sustain a number of alternative systems of physical organisation

---

[16] This is perhaps the key to the "meaning" of life: we exist, from an evolutionary perspective, merely to expedite the survival of our genes into the next generation. Beyond that, we are meaningless, evolutionarily speaking.

(variants), each represented by specific patterns of connection between the particle-energy neurons, with each configuration representing a replicator; (ii) select from this range of configurations according to some survival criterion (such as coherence and immutability); and (iii) differentially replicate the "winning" candidates, these collectively instantiating and engendering the laws of physics. This *problem-solving via solution-exploration* (§5.5.2) is the basis for Vanchurin's above-cited assertion that physical phenomena arise through a process of Darwinian "learning evolution" implemented in a neural network. Indeed, in a ringing endorsement of Universal Darwinism, he claims that

> if the entire universe is a neural network, then something like natural selection might be happening on all scales from cosmological ($> 10^{+15}m$) and biological ($10^{+2} - -10^{-6}m$) all the way to subatomic ($< 10^{-15}m$) scales. The main idea is that some local structures (or architectures) of neural networks are more stable against external perturbations (i.e., interactions with the rest of the network) than other local structures. As a result, the more stable structures are more likely to survive and the less stable structures are more likely to be exterminated. There is no reason to expect that this process might stop at a fixed time or might be confined to a fixed scale and, so, the evolution must continue indefinitely and on all scales. (Vanchurin, 2020, p. 18)

As with many models at the cutting edge of theoretical physics, Vanchurin's is, as he concedes, "very speculative" (2020, p. 19), and thus provisional. Moreover, for all the rigour and logic of the underlying mathematics, it is inherently difficult to falsify. Yet its appeal lies in the fact that it regards as *emergent phenomena* certain theories – such as quantum mechanics and general relativity – that other physicists hold to be *fundamental theories*; and it sees (albeit not in these terms) the VRS algorithm as driving this emergence (Vanchurin, 2020, p. 17). In this sense, his neural-network model confirms Darwinism as the Universal Acid: indeed, it is a "proposal for the theory of everything" (Vanchurin, 2020, p. 17).

1.5.3 Biological Evolution

The coming of the Age of Enlightenment imposed increasing pressure on the immutable, God-centred world that had been accepted as accurate for centuries. Indeed, from the 1500s onwards one can speak of a scientific revolution characterised by the "discovery of ignorance" – the rejection of religious texts as a source of truth and their replacement by the scientific method and its attendant cycle of *a posteriori* and *a priori* interaction (Harari, 2014, pp. 250–251). By the end of the eighteenth century, advances in natural sciences, including the exploration of the fossil record, had suggested the mutability of living things. For all the controversy attending its publication, Darwin's *On the origin of species* (Darwin, 2008; see also S. Jones, 1999) was increasingly accepted as a valid model of the way by which the living world had taken shape over time. All this marks what might be called the *first phase* of Darwinism – the application of evolutionary theory to the physical forms and adaptations of living things on earth.

A *second phase* of Darwinism is represented by the discovery that Darwinian principles are operative in processes *internal* to the functioning of living creatures, such as homeostasis (the maintenance of a "steady state") and the immune response. In the latter, and according to "clonal selection theory", an invading organism is confronted by specialist cells (lymphocytes) that present a range of variant strategies – specifically, forms of adhesion to an antigen, the external marker of the pathogen – to combat the invading agent. That which manifests an optimal fit to the antigen is selected to be further replicated (cloned) as an antibody, thus arriving at and mass-producing the most effective weapon in the battle against the infection (Plotkin, 1995, p. 72). As Plotkin argues,

> [t]here are no ifs and buts about how, in general terms, the immune system works. It is a 'Darwin machine' – an organ system whose trans-formation through successive adaptational states in time is explained by a Darwinian evolutionary process. The immune system does not work *like* an evolutionary process. Immune system function *is* an evolutionary process. (Plotkin, 1995, p. 72; emphases in the original)

A *third phase* of Darwinism incorporates extensions of Darwinian ideas to phenomena and processes external to the body. This is the notion, referred to in §1.5.2, of the extended phenotype (Dawkins, 1983a),[17] wherein genes are

---

[17] In brief, and in advance of the fuller discussion in §1.6.1, an organism's phenotype – its body and its instinctive behaviours – is the vehicle produced by its replicators.

understood to shape the world at increasingly distant remove by motivating their vehicles to adapt their environment in certain ways in order to enhance the genes' replicative advantage, thus forming a distributed Darwin machine. The classic example of this extension is the beaver's dam. Dam-building behaviour in beavers is seemingly entirely innate (genetically determined), not learned (culturally determined) (Wilsson, 1968). Thus, when a beaver builds a dam and the environment around the structure changes – the vicinity of the dam is flooded, and other organisms are forced to adapt their behaviours accordingly – that effect on the world is genetically motivated and selected for (Dawkins, 1983a, p. 59). Other extended-phenotypic phenomena include changes to host phenotypes motivated by parasite genes, which disadvantage the former's genes and advantage the latter's (Hughes, 2014).

1.5.4 Cultural Evolution

From the 1970s onwards, and building upon some much earlier foundations (§3.3), a number of biologists argued for the operation of evolution in and of culture (for overviews, see Lewens, 2015 and Savage, 2019), what might be regarded as a *fourth phase* of Darwinism. Their extension of evolutionary thinking to culture was largely intended to advance the cause of Darwinian ideas more generally, but it had the complementary effect of opening up a new paradigm for cultural studies that, today, has coalesced under the rubric of memetics (Chapter 3). Linking cultural evolution with biological evolution is the contention that Darwinian processes are implicated in the operation of the brain, the ultimate location and foundation of culture. In what might be regarded as a *fifth phase* of Darwinism, variation, replication and selection of patterns of neuronal interconnection are hypothesised by some neuroscientists to account for key aspects of perception and cognition (Edelman, 1987; Calvin, 1998), making the brain a Darwin machine (§3.8.3).

From this perspective it is difficult to separate cultural evolution from what is arguably the supreme manifestation of Darwinism, namely human consciousness (§7.3). Always "switched on" during our waking hours, consciousness performs a number of functions, one of which is the processing and exchange of the ideas that constitute culture. In this sense, culture is understood as a subset of consciousness, dependent upon it but not coterminous with it.

Regarding consciousness as arising from the neuronal Darwin machine of the fifth phase of Darwinism perhaps allows us to understand it as representing a *sixth phase* of Darwinism. Yet the evolutionary hierarchy does not stop here: there is arguably a *seventh phase* of Darwinism, represented by the evolution of information on the internet, this information functioning as a form of extended, distributed consciousness (§7.6).

Even those who accept its existence in principle might argue that cultural evolution is intrinsically less significant than biological evolution, because it is dependent upon structures (neurons) that are provided and controlled by biological evolution. But this criticism might also be levelled, in turn, against biological evolution, which is contingent upon the laws of chemistry to furnish the molecules – primarily amino acids and nucleotides – upon which it depends.[18] In turn, the structures of chemistry themselves depend upon the laws of physics, which regulate how atoms can combine to form molecules. In this sense there is an interdependent structural hierarchy – a *recursive ontology* – regulating the organisation of phenomena in the universe, which is the subject of the next section.

1.5.5 Evolution and Recursive Ontology

Velardo hypothesises a recursive ontology wherein all the realms considered in §§1.5.2–1.5.4 are unified into a single entity (or master-system), termed "being", which encompasses everything in the universe. Being is characterised by certain common laws that relate its four constituent "ontological (macro) categories", the latter termed the physical, the biological, the psychological and the socio-cultural (Velardo, 2016, p. 104, Fig. 3). The common laws are four in number: (i) the *Law of Building Blocks* (in brief, ontological categories are each constituted from a number of *systems* of varying degrees of complexity; a network of systems with comparable degrees of complexity constitutes a *level*); (ii) the *Law of Recursive Organisation* (systems and levels

---

[18] Amino acids are the building blocks of proteins, molecules essential for life whose assembly (or "translation") is coded for by genes. Nucleotides are the building blocks of the nucleic acids DNA and RNA, segments of DNA functioning as genes. The five nucleotide molecules – adenine, cytosine, guanine, thymine and (substituting for thymine in RNA) uracil – connect to form "base pairs" that link the two chains of the DNA double helix (Berg et al., 2019). Representing a mere four "letters" (A[denine], C[ytosine], G[uanine] and T[hymine]/U[racil]), nucleotides constitute the "alphabet" by means of which the information underpinning life on earth is transmitted.

build in bottom-up fashion, to create higher-order systems); (iii) the *Law of Emergence* (new properties arise at higher levels from the attributes of lower levels; these properties are neither completely chaotic nor completely deterministic, but are rather "on the edge of chaos", or "quasi-chaotic"); and (iv) the *Law of Isomorphism Between Levels* (despite their qualitative differences, all systems and levels may be described by the same unifying mathematical model) (2016, pp. 95–100).

Summarising the attributes of the four ontological categories, Velardo argues that

> The physical category embraces all physical systems. This ontological category [as with the others] is structured in hierarchical levels that show different amounts of complexity. Starting from scratch, elementary particles build up protons, electrons and neutrons. These new particles connected together generate atoms, which in turn create molecules. This process keeps going until it reaches a threshold which allows chemistry to turn into biology. Indeed, the physical category acts as the basis for the biological category. The biological category arises when *biological replicators* emerge. Replicators are anything in the universe of which copies are made .... DNA is the main replicator within the biological category. Replicators allow the evolutionary process to unfold because they mutate over time and are selected depending on their fitness. The biological category considers hierarchical constructs such as cells, organs[s] and animals. The psychological category arises when *mind* emerges. Mind is an emergent property that arises by the non-linear local interactions of a large number of neurons .... The psychological [category] considers constructs such as perception, memory, and different functional modules of mind ... that allow an individual to interact with its environment. The socio-cultural category arises when *cultural replicators* emerge. These are called *memes* ... and are pattern[s] of information that can spread within a society. Memes are also characterised by an evolutionary process. The socio-cultural domain considers constructs such as society and philosophy. It is worth remembering that the four ontological categories altogether represent the entirety of being. (Velardo, 2016, pp. 104–105; emphases in the original)

Velardo illustrates their relationship as shown in Figure 1.2 (after 2016, p. 104, Fig. 3).

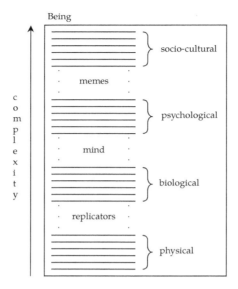

Figure 1.2: Recursive Ontology.

Whereas I frame cultural evolution as the successor to biological evolution, and therefore delineate three ontological categories – the physical, the biological and the (socio-)cultural – Velardo (2016) intercalates the psychological, giving his model four categories in total. For him, the psychological category – characterised by the operation of perception, memory and, by implication, consciousness (2016, p. 105) – is a distinct Darwinian system. While, as noted above, I certainly do not dispute the Darwinian nature of consciousness (§7.3), the differences between the psychological and the socio-cultural ontological categories seem less significant than those between the physical and the biological and between the biological and the psychological categories. These differences inhere in: (i) what I term, after the genome-phenotype distinction in biology, the memome-phemotype distinction in culture (§1.6.1) – i.e., the distinction between somatic/brain-resident replicators and their extrasomatic, physical products; (ii) the singular/plural distinction – the difference between one individual consciousness and a group of socially/culturally interacting minds; and (iii) the distinction (arising from (ii)) between the relatively fast processes of consciousness and the relatively slow processes of culture.

Moreover, the "threshold property" separating the biological from the psychological category is mind; and the threshold property separating the psychological from the socio-cultural category is the meme (Velardo, 2016, pp. 104–105). In some theories of consciousness, however, mind is held to be *constituted* by memes (§7.3.1). Thus, taken together, the similarities between the psychological and socio-cultural categories – between consciousness and culture – are arguably greater than their differences and, for the purposes of this book, do not materially affect any application of Darwinism to them. Indeed, Velardo's concept of the *domain* – "functionally coherent systems that can transcend the boundaries of ontological categories" (2016, p. 106, Tab. 1) – allows systems such as music and language to be understood in terms of processes distributed *across* the psychological and socio-cultural categories.

A four-category hierarchy might nevertheless emerge when one considers quasi-independent extensions of the socio-cultural category such as are found in the arguably nascent ontological category of the *digital* – the evolutionary domain of electron-based information-particles stored in computer systems and networks (§7.6). Thus, the psychological and the socio-cultural categories might, as inter-blending strata, be crowned by the digital, which is nevertheless partially dependent (at least at present) upon the socio-cultural. In this sense, and contrary to Velardo's assertion, the four ontological categories he identifies do not "altogether represent the entirety of being" (2016, p. 105).

1.6 Core Elements in Universal Darwinism

One of the challenges facing Universal Darwinism is that of determining which elements of biological evolution on earth are fundamental to the VRS algorithm – and which are therefore common to Darwinism in all the substrates in which it operates – and which elements are simply "local" peculiarities of gene-based evolution on our planet. It is in the nature of algorithms that they are formulated parsimoniously and so, in the case of the VRS algorithm, while it affords us a sense of how a Darwinian system operates in principle, the system's detailed functional implementation is necessarily not specified, lest the algorithm's wider applicability be curtailed by unnecessary substrate-specific constraints.

If a set of common elements beyond the minimal trinity of variation, replication and selection definitive of all systems held to implement the VRS algorithm can be found, then it would reinforce the case for a Universal Darwinism. I would contend that one can indeed see beyond the superficial dissimilarities motivated by the algorithm's operating in different substrates, and can arrive at a core of elements – second-order, ancillary properties – regularly manifested by all systems implementing the (first-order) evolutionary algorithm. These elements are simply consequences of the operation of the VRS algorithm itself, repeatedly found in a number of Darwinian systems on account of their utility and parsimony for the functioning of the algorithm. Put another way, a substrate capable of sustaining the VRS algorithm will not only "boot up" the algorithm itself, but will also tend to optimise its operation by drawing upon these ancillary elements. The following subsections outline them, with particular reference to the ways in which they impinge upon musicality and music.

1.6.1 Replicators and Vehicles

A minimal implementation of the VRS algorithm requires free-floating replicators in an environment containing the raw materials of which those replicators are constituted (Dawkins, 1989, pp. 14–15). It appears that for millions of years this worked perfectly well, certainly from the "perspective" of the replicators. Yet one can imagine that if a chance variant arose that used some environmental element not as a constituent of that which is replicated but to expedite the process of replication, then a distinction would arise between *that which is replicated* and *that which facilitates replication*. While this distinction might initially appear hard to resolve – after all, if some facilitatory element is consistently replicated along with the replicator itself, then the former arguably becomes a replicator (or at least a part of the replicator) in its own right – over time the distinction between a sacrosanct, protected replicator and the temporary vehicle that encompasses it grew ever clearer and wider. The replicator acquired a kind of immortality, because it existed in distributed form, scattered across numerous copies; while the vehicle, similar though it might be to other vehicles, was essentially transient and dispensable – it had no existence independent of the replicators that caused it to be fabricated.[19]

In Dawkins' formulation, the vehicle is presented as a passive intermediary between the replicator and the world – a puppet whose strings are pulled by a replicator lurking behind the scenes. In reality, the vehicle might assume a more active role, as is captured in Hull's (1988a) alternative notion of the "interactor". Interactors are "causal agents in their own right: [they] do things that are not reducible to the orders served up by the replicators riding about within them" (Plotkin, 1995, p. 97). References to vehicles in this book should be understood as encompassing the instrumentality ascribed to them by Hull. Sometimes a vehicle serving the interests of one replicator may subsequently provide the conditions for the origin of another replicator. The conduit connecting the lungs to the outside world primarily evolved in many species to facilitate oxygen ingress and carbon dioxide egress. In several species, including in hominins, it evolved various secondary sound-producing adaptations, whose initial selection pressure was the use of such vocalisations for the demarcation of territory and for other gene-advantageous forms of signalling (§5.1). While initially innate, such sound sequences in *Homo sapiens* were increasingly learned, being transmitted between conspecifics (members of the same species) by imitation. The resulting patterns eventually themselves became replicators in their own right – they constituted the memes of cultural evolution. To invoke what Plotkin terms the "replicator-interactor-lineage (RIL) formulation" (1995, p. 88), a lineage of interactors became a lineage of replicators.

The distinction between replicators and vehicles is usually discussed in biology in terms of the genome-phenotype distinction, already mentioned briefly in note 17 on page 28 and in §1.5.5. Table 1.3, after Ball (1984, p. 156, Fig. 2) and Jan (2007, p. 30, Tab. 2.1), extends the concept to encompass cultural replicators, positing the existence of various analogous categories.

---

[19] Two examples of this replicator immortality-vehicle mortality are given by Harari (2014). One is the modern industrialised farming of wheat. Wheat genes are among the most successful on the planet, owing to the sheer extent of wheat-vehicle cultivation; but wheat plants are destroyed after harvesting their seed (2014, p. 80). A sentient equivalent is cattle farming. Cow genes are similarly prolific, owing to the vast numbers of cows being bred; but the life of each individual cow-vehicle is usually short and often miserable (2014, p. 96, plate 15).

Gene	Genome	Phenotype	Somatic	Behaviour	Extrasomatic	Artefacts
A unit of biological replication. Manifesting itself as:	A constellation of nucleotides encoding a discrete, particulate unit of protein-generating information that is replicated (via its phenotype) in more than one body.	The somatic and extrasomatic products of a genome, by virtue of which genes are reconstituted in other bodies.	Feathers	Nest-building		Nests
Meme	**Memome**	**Phemotype**	**Somatic**	**Behaviour**	**Extrasomatic**	**Artefacts**
A unit of cultural replication. Manifesting itself as:	A constellation of discrete, particulate unit of cultural information that is replicated (via its phemotype) in more than one brain.	The somatic and extrasomatic products of a memome, by virtue of which memes are reconstituted in other brains.	Culturally determined modifications to the body.	Playing, singing, conducting.		Scores, configurations of sound waves, recordings.
Mnemon	**Mnemotype**	**Phmnemotype**	**Somatic**	**Behaviour**	**Extrasomatic**	**Artefacts**
An item of brain-stored memory (Lynch, 1998). Manifesting itself as:	A constellation of neurons encoding a discrete, particulate unit of information that is not (yet) replicated in another brain.	The somatic and extrasomatic products of a mnemotype, by virtue of which reconstitution of the mnemon in another brain (thereby creating a meme) may occur.	As phemotype.			

Table 1.3: Overview of Gene and Meme Forms.

Table 1.3 might be held to illustrate three underlying commonalities: (i) replicator systems are agnostic as to the substrate – DNA sequences, neuronal interconnections – implementing the replicator; (ii) there is a clear distinction between the replicator and its vehicular products; and (iii) the latter mediate the replication of the former, such that those replicators able to engender the most impactful vehicles have the greatest chances, in a statistical sense, of being replicated.

1.6.2 Replication Hierarchies and the Unit(s) of Selection

Velardo's recursive ontology (§1.5.5) divided reality, or being, into a hierarchy of four ontological *categories*: the physical, the biological, the psychological and the socio-cultural. Within each category a number of (also) hierarchic *levels* exist. Velardo defines a level as "the set of all the systems that share a similar amount of complexity and similar emergent properties" (2016, p. 111); and a *system*, after Backlund (2000), as "a set of interacting or interdependent components forming an integrated whole" (2016, p. 95). A replication hierarchy is a contiguous set of such intra-ontological-category levels manifesting increasing structural complexity as one proceeds up the ladder of the hierarchy. Given the existence of such hierarchies *within* and *across* ontological categories, the possibility exists of identifying structural similarities – systemic cross-mappings – *between* corresponding levels of two or more ontological categories.

On this second point, and reworking Figure 1.2 (partly by inversion), Table 1.4 (after Jan, 2013, p. 152, Fig. 1) proposes a replication hierarchy of eight levels spanning the physical and biological ontological categories, and it hypothesises the corresponding levels – by positing certain structural and functional analogies – in the psychological and socio-cultural categories.[20]

---

[20] It should be stressed that the nature-culture distinction represented by Table 1.4 – a form of the nature-nurture dichotomy – is somewhat artificial, in that, from the point of view of Universal Darwinism, culture is just as "natural" as nature.

[21] Meyer argues that rules "constitute the highest, most encompassing level of stylistic constraints". While "[d]ifferences in rules … distinguish large periods such as Medieval, Renaissance, and Baroque from one another", paradoxically a "commonality of rules … links Classic and Romantic musics together". For this reason, a dialect is equated here with a species, because, like Classical and Romantic musics, several distinct species may share the same underlying biochemical "rules" (1996, p. 17).

[22] An operon is a gene-complex: a group of genes that act in concert biochemically. In this sense, and as Table 1.4 indicates, it is analogous to a m(us)emeplex.

Level	Nature	Culture
	Genetic-"Cultural"	*Memetic-Cultural*
1	Physical Laws	Acoustical and Psychological Laws (Meyer, 1996, p. 13)
2	Biochemical Systems	Rules (Meyer, 1996, p. 17)[21]
3	Species	Dialect (Meyer, 1996, p. 23)
4	Sub-group of Organisms	Idiom (Meyer, 1996, p. 24)/ Genre/Formal-Structural Type
	Genetic-Structural	*Memetic-Structural*
5	Individual Organism	Intraopus Style (Meyer, 1996, p. 24) (Movement/Work/ Musemesatz)
6	Operon[22]	M(us)emeplex (schema (Gjerdingen, 1988, p. 6)/style structure (Narmour, 1990, p. 34))
7	Gene	M(us)eme (schema-feature (Gjerdingen, 1988, p. 6)/style shape (Narmour, 1990, p. 34))
8	Nucleotide	M(us)eme-element (single, discrete musical pitch plus duration)

Table 1.4: The Hierarchies of Nature and Culture.

In a similar vein, Sereno posits four analogies between biological and cultural (specifically linguistic) evolution (1991, p. 473, Fig. 1; see also Victorri, 2007): (i) species/language (1991, p. 471) (associated with historical linguistics and corresponding to level 3 (nature)–3 (culture) in Table 1.4); (ii) genes/culture (1991, p. 474) (associated with sociobiology and corresponding to levels 7–7); (iii) organism/concept (1991, p. 476) (associated with evolutionary epistemology (§3.3.2) and corresponding to levels 5–6/7); and (iv) cell/person (1991, p. 478) (associated with molecular biology and corresponding to levels ? (nature)–5 (nature)).

Sereno favours analogy (iv), arguing, in a nutshell, that a "symbolic-representational system" (Sereno, 1991, p. 484) – i.e., one encoding relationships between *symbols* and the *things they symbolise* – has arisen only twice on earth: in cellular protein synthesis and in human language (so the analogy is strictly cell/*cortex*, not cell/*person*); and that the mechanisms underpinning symbolisation in these two domains – that involve internal (intracellular/cortical) connections between internal representations of external *symbols* and internal representations of external *things* – are structurally very similar (1991, p. 488, Fig. 5; p. 489, Fig. 6). While his formulation fails to account for the operation of the VRS algorithm, which is most evident in analogy (ii), it may nevertheless be reconciled with the gene/meme-selectionist perspective adopted here by conflating the internal meme-representation (the memome) with what Sereno terms the "symbol representation" (1991, p. 489, Fig. 6). A model for implementing this representation in cortex is discussed in §3.8.3, and other implications of the cell/person analogy for the evolution of music and language, are considered in §3.8.7.

While Universal Darwinism and recursive ontology imply that replication will tend to give rise to structures at a number of different hierarchic levels – some of these constituting ever more complex vehicles arising in the service of their masters, the replicators (§1.6.1) – and while the phenomena at the eight levels shown in Table 1.4 are individually meaningful, the proposed cross-category mapping is, ultimately, hypothetical. That is, while it is based on arguably sensible analogies between the ways nature and culture are organised, these have no necessary validity. There is no fundamental reason, for instance, why a musical dialect should be equated to a species in biology, and there are many reasons why the mapping is problematic. For one thing, a species in biology is sustained by breeding within (but not without) itself; whereas there is no direct equivalent to this in culture: different musical dialects can readily "cross-fertilise" each other, as often happened when musicians travel widely or, more recently, as a result of the transmission of information via the internet.

Another potential criticism of the proposed mapping is that, while the distinction between them is not always clear, the biological levels in between the species and the level of biochemical systems – i.e., domain, kingdom, phylum, class, order, family and genus (§1.7) – are at least widely recognised in the history and literature of biology, whereas in culture there are no clear levels between rules and dialect, unless one invokes such concepts as national styles or such problematic notions as stylistic eras (Renaissance, Baroque, Classical, etc.). Thus, the gap between levels 2 and 3 of Table 1.4 is wider than might appear to be the case from the table's layout.

Nevertheless, the hypothesised mappings are suggestive and, particularly at the extremes of the continuum (arguably levels 1 and 2, and levels 6–8), they are telling in that they appear to accord with the "Humboldtian" nature of reality (Merker, 2002).[23] That is, they support a view of the way reality – Velardo's "being" – is assembled by particles (of whatever type) conglomerating to form higher-order particles that themselves assemble to form particles on the next higher level, and so on. While these levels are in some cases "analogue" – some slide imperceptibly into others – a "digital" order might nevertheless, as in Table 1.4, be read in them. These mappings are revisited in Chapter 3, apropos the issue of cultural taxonomies (§3.6), because Table 1.4's level three in nature, the species, is a fundamental taxonomic category in biology (§1.7), and it is fruitful to consider whether any equivalents to it in musical culture might meaningfully be subject to a taxonomic approach.

---

[23] Ideas stemming from Wilhelm von Humboldt, and indeed the notion of Recursive Ontology, suggest that the potentially infinite complexity of several systems – including music and language – arises from the recombination of a finite set of elements. This issue is discussed more fully in §5.6.

While the details of variation and replication are not unproblematic, it is selection that has perhaps proved to be the most controversial aspect of the VRS algorithm. In particular, it is not generally agreed by biologists upon what entities selection actually operates: what, in other words, are the meaningful "units" that might survive or perish? This question underpins one of the most fiercely contested debates in biology, the "unit(s) of selection controversy" (Lewontin, 1970). Some biologists maintain that selection operates at a collective level, the level of the species (species selectionism) or that of the group of organisms within a species (group selectionism). Others, including Darwin himself, argue that selection operates at the level of the individual (individual selectionism). A third group, including Dawkins, contend that selection operates at a level below that of the individual. Supporting this, he argues that biologists have confused two types of selection, *replicator selection* and *vehicle selection* (§1.6.1). In this dichotomy, "[r]eplicator selection is the process by which some replicators survive at the expense of other replicators. Vehicle selection is the process by which some vehicles are more successful than other vehicles in ensuring the survival of their replicators" (Dawkins, 1983a, p. 82). Thus, because selection devolves to the survival of replicators, not vehicles, then the units of selection are replicators, not vehicles (individually or in groups).

The replicator-selection/vehicle-selection dichotomy allows Dawkins to refine the concept of the gene. Extending Benzer's (1957) concepts of the "muton" ("the minimum unit of mutational change"), the "recon" ("the minimum unit of recombination"), and the "cistron" ("the unit responsible for synthesizing one polypeptide chain"), Dawkins proposes a fourth category, the "optimon", which he defines as "the unit of natural selection" (1983a, p. 81). This formulation represents a condensation of a longer definition, one that regards the gene as

> any portion of chromosomal material that potentially lasts for enough generations to serve as a unit of natural selection.... a genetic unit that is small enough to last for a large number of generations and to be distributed around in the form of many copies.... a unit which, to a high degree, *approaches* the ideal of indivisible particulateness. (Dawkins, 1989, pp. 28, 32, 33; emphasis in the original)

The level at which selection operates – and thus the unit of selection – is closely related to Dawkins' (1989) notion of "selfishness", arguably the most important, but perhaps the most misunderstood, concept in *The selfish gene*. If, on the basis of the foregoing, the gene is taken to be the unit of selection (the optimon), then it is by definition "the entity for whose benefit adaptations may be said to exist" (Dawkins, 1983a, p. 81). While somewhat downplaying the importance of replicator collaboration, adaptations (§2.5.1) might be understood as those changes to a vehicle driven by a replicator in response to some selection pressure, which serve to optimise the replicator's survival. Adaptations appear to suggest the presence of intentionality – usually ascribed to the work of a conscious designer (Dawkins, 2006) – in fashioning an effective vehicle; but they are simply the artefacts built by the "winners" of replicator competition. Those replicators that cause the most effective vehicles to be built will, self-evidently, augment their chances of replication, and thus will differentially increase their numerical representation in future generations. As Dawkins notes, "[t]his is not a theory; it is not even an observed fact: it is a tautology" (1989, p. 86).

This tautology means that, without agency or intentionality, the blind and mechanistic processes of the VRS algorithm afford the illusion of successful replicators selfishly pursuing their own interests, to the detriment of their rivals. Seen in these terms, selfishness is an intrinsic attribute of all replicators, be they genes in a human's cell nuclei or memes encoded in that human's brain. In the latter category, it is also an attribute of musemes (Chapter 3), such that individual musical patterns in a range of parameters may be said to pursue their self-interests above those of their rivals.

1.6.3 Replicator Attributes

Dawkins identifies three attributes that characterise all replicators: longevity, fecundity and copying-fidelity (1989, pp. 17–18). They relate to genes and memes in different ways but, in accordance with the precepts of Universal Darwinism, the characterising principles are common, irrespective of the substrate.

1.6.3.1 Longevity

This refers to the life-span of an individual copy of a replicator. A gene in the cells of a human body exists for as long as that body is alive; thereafter, it decomposes into its component molecules and atoms. Yet that same gene might exist as copies in countless other bodies, past and present. Given this distributed occurrence, the continuity of its future existence is highly likely and so it is, for all practical purposes, immortal. The same is true for other replicators: a meme we cannot get out of our heads might have similarly troubled a composer of the eighteenth century. It survived the death of its composer, it will survive our death, and likely that of its future hosts so, again, it is effectively immortal. Moreover, the memome-phemotype distinction (§1.6.1), given current technology, means that while a brain-stored version of a meme (a memome) faces numerous threats to its integrity, its phemotypic products, such as sounds or images on a DVD or on the internet, are highly durable.

1.6.3.2 Fecundity

The infectivity of a replicator contributes directly to its survival. If its innate attributes in some way positively motivate or facilitate its copying, then a replicator's fecundity will be high. In the case of genes, fecundity usually hinges upon the contribution of the gene to some survival advantage conferred upon the organism possessing it and manifested in the organism's phenotype.[24] In the case of memes, fecundity is usually contingent upon a meme's *perceptual-cognitive salience* – how distinctive or striking it is – and thus its capacity to stand out from surrounding cultural information. While not in conflict with the notion of the smallest unit of selection (§1.6.2), and with it gene/meme selfishness, such replication is collective, rather than individual: in biology, a gene cannot replicate in isolation; and the processes and products of culture

---

[24] While having no direct analogues in cultural evolution, it is important to acknowledge here the existence of genetic drift, whereby the frequency of an allele (an alternative gene-form; see §1.7.2) increases or decreases in a population as a result of random chance. While "[g]enetic drift, together with mutation and recombination, randomly produces the gametes that selection can act on" (Masel, 2011, p. 837), it was earlier understood as anti-Darwinian and anti-adaptationist. Indeed, "[m]ost evolutionists of the 1960s viewed genetic drift only as a random force of evolutionary change – a prime anomaly under adaptationist hardening ...". Yet "[Sewall Wright's] later interpretation of genetic drift invoked this concept primarily as an aid to an enlarged style of adaptationism, and not as a contrary force in evolutionary change (as he had originally argued)" (Gould, 2002, p. 555).

are multimemetic, not unimemetic. In this sense, intra-individual-replicator cooperation is a microcosm of intra-society-individual cooperation: such collaboration is a price often worth paying for the individual/selfish benefits it (statistically) confers.

1.6.3.3 Copying-Fidelity

A subtle balance obtains in the attribute of copying-fidelity. If all replicators possessed 100% copying-fidelity (i.e., if they had faultlessly accurate replication), then evolutionary systems would be static and no responses to external change would be possible. If all replicators had 0% copying-fidelity, then no replication would be possible and potentially evolutionary systems would be too chaotic for the VRS algorithm to be initiated. In biological evolution a limited degree of copying-*in*fidelity allows for intelligent systemic responses to environmental change (§7.3.2), such as rising or falling temperatures, or varying availability of food sources (these constituting what might be regarded as "hard" environmental factors). In cultural evolution the same attribute allows for similarly flexible responses to environmental change, the environment of a meme consisting of other memes in a given culture (what might be regarded as "soft" environmental factors, the latter analogous to the environment of a gene consisting also of other genes), together with the (hard-environmental) gene-determined perceptual-cognitive environment of the human mind.

1.7 Taxonomy

> Taxonomies are not neutral or arbitrary hat-racks for a set of unvarying concepts; they reflect (or even create) different theories about the structure of the world. As Michel Foucault has shown ..., when you know why people classify in a certain way, you understand how they think. (Gould & Vrba, 1982, p. 4)

Contrary to that normally thought of, taxonomy has been termed "the world's oldest profession" (Serrat, 2010, p. 1), because its concerns – the urge to sort and classify objects and phenomena in the world around us – appear universal in human cultures. This stems, perhaps, from the innate gestalt-psychological tendency to separate and group that which we perceive (Reybrouck, 1997; Guberman, 2017). I explore the issue in some detail here because much of what is said about taxonomy in biology is also applicable to culture, albeit with significantly more difficulty on account of the faster and more convoluted nature of cultural evolution.

Taxonomy is central in biology because an important foundation for the study of living organisms is understanding how they are related to each other and thus what similarities and dissimilarities exist between them. Indeed, one of the key stages in the progress of biology as a discipline was the development of a formalised system of taxonomy, and an associated ("binomial" – genus-species, "*Homo sapiens*") nomenclature, by Carl Linnaeus (1707–1778). Not only does the categorisation of organisms into (morphological) types allow the natural world to be studied in a systematic and structured way, it also affords evidence for lines of evolutionary development and relationship, an aspect central to some approaches to classification.[25]

The issue of taxonomy is relevant throughout this book because if we are positing a Universal-Darwinian relationship between nature and culture (§1.5), and if the study of the natural world is facilitated and illuminated by a taxonomic perspective, then the same may well be true of cultural phenomena. Of course, much work in musicology, both historical and theoretical-analytical, is broadly taxonomic in motivation, from the identification of "schools" and traditions of composition to the discussion of generic, formal and structural models and types (Caplin et al., 2009); but it is arguably possible to make deeper connections between natural and cultural categories. An overview of taxonomy is therefore given here not only in order to lay the foundations for the biomusical observations of Chapter 2 and Chapter 5, but also to provide the context for the application of taxonomy to music-cultural evolution in Chapter 3 (§3.6).

In biological taxonomy, organisms are associated on the basis of one or more criteria in order to form a group termed a *taxon*; and this collection is then situated at a specific structural-hierarchical level or *taxonomic rank*. The number of taxonomic ranks in a *taxonomic hierarchy* varies according to the

---

[25] The terms "classification", "systematics" and "taxonomy" are generally used interchangeably, the second and third being approaches to achieve the first. The second and third are sometimes used to mean slightly different things (Ridley, 2004, pp. 683, 689). For present purposes, however, the nuances are not significant.

Rank	Description	Animal Example	Plant Example
Domain	One of the three basic categories into which life on earth may be divided, namely *Archaea, Bacteria* (both unicellular prokaryotes) and *Eukaryota*.[26]		
Kingdom	Depending upon the system, a five- or six-part subdivision of the three Domains.	*Animalia*	*Plantae*
Phylum (in botany, Division)	A subdivision of the Kingdoms, with *Animalia* being divided into *c.* 35 phylla and *Plantae* into *c.* 14 divisions (A. G. Collins & Valentine, 2001, p. 432).	*Chordata*	*Tracheophyta*
Class	Intermediate between Phylum and Order.	*Mammalia*	*Pteropsida*
Order	Intermediate between Class and Family.	*Primates*	*Coniferales*
Family	Intermediate between Order and Genus.	*Hominidae*	*Pinaceae*
Genus	Intermediate between Family and Species and denoted by the first name in Linnaean binomial nomenclature.	*Homo*	*Pinus*
Species	The lowest category and denoted by the second name in binomial nomenclature.	[*Homo*] *sapiens*	[*Pinus*] *strobus*

Table 1.5: Taxonomic Ranks.

particular classification system utilised, and the concepts and terminology underpinning taxonomic ranks often have varied historical origins, but seven or eight divisions, or ranks, are common. These categories are often refined by associated subdivisions, indicated by such prefixes as *infra-* (below), *parv-* (small), *sub-* (under) and *super-* (above). The most commonly used taxonomic ranks are listed and exemplified in Table 1.5 (after Cain, 2020, Tab. 1). Common rank-associated suffixes are underlined in columns three and four.

For all the apparent clarity of these categories, their definition is often problematic, an issue perhaps most evident in the middle ranks (Class, Order and Family), and only partly addressed by their subdivision. This is because

---

[26] Prokaryotic organisms are single-celled and lack a distinct nucleus. Eukaryotic organisms are single-celled or multicellular and possess a distinct nucleus and other membrane-bound cell-structures (organelles) (Ridley, 2004, pp. 684, 687; Fitch, 2010, pp. 210–211).

a taxonomic hierarchy of ranks is an attempt to impose a synchronic, digital order on a process of diachronic, analogue change, the (fossil) records of which are, moreover, often incomplete. In particular, modern phylogenetic approaches (§1.7.1) – which represent evolution in terms of branching trees (Ridley, 2004, p. 479, Fig. 16.3) and which are informed by molecular evidence – give rise to a greater number of distinctions than can be accommodated by the standard (Linnean) ranks. Thus, "[w]e cannot naively say that each successive branching point (or node) in the phylogeny can have its own Linnean rank. There are just too many nodes" (Ridley, 2004, p. 483). What is true of nature is even more so of culture: unconstrained by the temporal-reproductive constraints of biology, cultural "speciation" involves an even greater proliferation of nodes.

1.7.1 A Metataxonomy of Taxonomy

There are several philosophically and methodologically distinct approaches to taxonomy, these being in part the result of the long development of the sub-discipline over time. An unfortunate consequence of its diverse, even fragmented, traditions is that, in Dawkins' view, taxonomy is "one of the most rancorously ill-tempered of biological fields. Stephen [Jay] Gould has well characterized it with the phrase 'names and nastiness'" (Dawkins, 2006, p. 391). It is important to understand the differences behind the distinct schools of taxonomy, and their motivations, in order to determine which, if any, aligns optimally with a Universal-Darwinian focus.

Much of the "nastiness" of which Gould speaks stems from disagreements over the extent to which taxonomy should be guided by the insights of evolutionary thought. Some approaches hold, even at the risk of circularity, that all taxonomic practice (that is, the categorisation of resemblances) should both draw upon and validate Darwinian evolutionary theory. Others believe that taxonomic practice should be conducted without such theoretical frameworks, lest evolutionary preconceptions bias outcomes – even though most advocates of this second approach would certainly not deny the existence and relevance of evolution itself (Dawkins, 2006, pp. 391–392). In this sense, the fundamental distinction in biological taxonomy is between essentially *static* (synchronic) and *dynamic* (diachronic) methods of classification: in a "metataxonomy" of taxonomic traditions, Ridley states that "two main methods are used to classify species into groups: the *phenetic* and the *phylogenetic* methods" (2004, p. 472; emphases in the original); and that while "[t]he phenetic and phylogenetic principles are the two fundamental types of biological classification, ... three schools of thought exist about how classification should be carried out" (2004, p. 474). This metataxonomy can be summarised as follows:

Phenetic methods avoid evolutionary preconceptions in examining relationships, using measurements of morphological similarity to determine groupings:

- The most rigorous advocates of phenetic principles constitute the school of *Numerical Taxonomy* (Sneath & Sokal, 1973), which uses detailed statistical analysis of measurements in order to create indices of morphological (as opposed to genetic-evolutionary) affinity and proximity in multidimensional space. Because morphological attributes can be captured via any number of measurements, and because the relative weightings ascribed to these measurements are ultimately subjective, Ridley argues that "[p]henetic classification ... is not objective. It can produce classifications, but classifications that lack a deep philosophical justification" (2004, p. 479).

Phylogenetic methods aim to arrange categories on the basis of evolutionary connections:

- The most systematic school within this method, the *cladists* (from the Greek *clade* (κλαδος), meaning branch), seeks to trace evolutionary development in terms of branching lineages – the chronological sequences in which organisms diverge and form discrete groups (i.e., species) – and to represent them using dendritic (tree-like) diagrams (Hennig, 1999) (§1.7.2).

A third school is:

- *Evolutionary Classification*, which synthesises the phenetic and the phylogenetic approaches, taking both the observed morphological resemblances of the former and the consideration of evolutionary descent of the latter into account.

Considering the history of these approaches, Ridley gives the heyday of evolutionary classification as the period *c*. 1930–*c*. 1980; that of numerical taxonomy the period *c*. 1960–*c*. 1970; and that of cladism, now pre-eminent, the period after *c*. 1960 (2004, p. 489).

1.7.2 Concepts of Cladism

While the methodology of pheneticists is in many ways both admirable and defensible, the rigorously evolutionary orientation of cladism – this unalloyed with the pheneticist elements of evolutionary classification – perhaps explains the method's aforementioned pre-eminence, and aligns most closely with the Universal-Darwinian focus of this book. In particular, if we accept Teilhard de Chardin's assertion (page xxv) that "[e]volution is a light which illuminates all facts, a trajectory which all lines of thought must follow", then we have to accept that all natural categories are products of Darwinian evolution and no categorisation makes sense – to echo Dobzhansky (1973) – except when it reflects this process.

The fundamental principles of cladism are: (i) that taxonomic groupings of species should reflect a hierarchical branching (Darwin, 2008, p. 90), with all branches deriving from a single common ancestor[27] represented by the trunk; (ii) that hierarchical relationships are strictly inclusive, not overlapping (i.e., higher branches are "perfectly nested" within their parent lower ones, as "rings within rings" (Dawkins, 2006, p. 367)), represented in a dendritic form called a *cladogram* (thus, a type of dendrogram); and (iii) that for any group of species there is *one and only one* evolutionarily correct branching hierarchy – itself part of "the one true tree of life" (Dawkins, 2006, Ch. 10). A species divides into two (perhaps because of some environmentally induced separation) and the "branch" of the parent species gives rise to two "sub-branches" representing the derived species. Because the new species share a common ancestor (the parent species/branch), they may be grouped together to form a clade. Note that cladograms align broadly with the taxonomic ranks shown in Table 1.5 (Ridley's point about there being "too many nodes" (page 47) notwithstanding) by *inversion*: the trunk of the cladogram maps

---

[27] Life on earth is thought to have arisen (successfully) only once, so all extant species ultimately share a single common ancestor (Dawkins, 2006, p. 366).

onto the top of the rankings (domain),[28] whereas the uppermost branches map onto the bottom of the rankings (species) – hence, in part, the biological concept of *descent* (Darwin, 2004).

Strict hierarchical inclusion (Dawkins' "perfect nesting") is related to the concept of *monophyly* in cladistic taxonomy. Two other situations obtain in regard to categorisation conducted in the light of hierarchical branching, namely *paraphyly* and *polyphyly*. These are defined below and represented in Figure 1.3 (after Ridley, 2004, p. 480, Fig. 16.4).

Related by Homology: "a character shared between two or more species that was present in their common ancestor" (Ridley, 2004, pp. 427, 480) – i.e., resemblances resulting from (direct) *evolution*.

> **Monophyly:** a monophyletic group is "[a] set of species containing a common ancestor and all its descendants" (Ridley, 2004, p. 686).
> "*Shared derived* homologies [– i.e., "homologies that evolved after the common ancestor, within the group of species under study" (Ridley, 2004, p. 431) –] are found in *all* the descendants of the common ancestor" (Ridley, 2004, p. 480; emphases mine).

> **Paraphyly:** a paraphyletic group is "[a] set of species containing an ancestral species together with some, but not all, of its descendants. The species included in the group are those that have continued to resemble the ancestor; the excluded species have evolved relatively rapidly and no longer resemble their ancestor" (Ridley, 2004, p. 687).
> "*Shared ancestral* homologies [– i.e., "characters ... present in the common ancestor of the group of species under study" (Ridley, 2004, p. 431) –] are found in *some but not all* of the descendants of the common ancestor" (Ridley, 2004, p. 480; emphases mine).

Related by Homoplasy: "a character shared between two or more species that was not present in their common ancestor" (Ridley, 2004, pp. 427–428, 480) – i.e., resemblances (analogies) most often resulting from *convergent evolution*, these arising "when the same selection pressure has operated in two lineages" (Ridley, 2004, p. 429).

---

[28] Strictly, it maps onto the superordinate category, life, a category that distinguishes this sequence of biological rankings from those of non-living things, such as cultural hierarchies (§1.6.2, §3.6).

Polyphyly: a polyphyletic group is "[t]he set of species descended from more than one common ancestor. The ultimate common ancestor of all the species in the group is not a member of the polyphyletic group" (Ridley, 2004, p. 687).

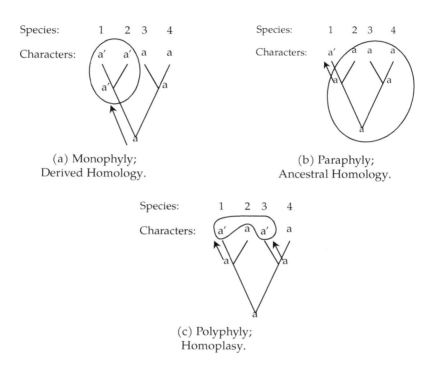

(a) Monophyly;
Derived Homology.

(b) Paraphyly;
Ancestral Homology.

(c) Polyphyly;
Homoplasy.

Figure 1.3: Monophyly, Paraphyly and Polyphyly.

The concepts of monophyly, paraphyly and polyphyly, and their associated character/resemblance-types, allow phenetic, cladistic and evolutionary classification systems (page 48) to be clearly differentiated:

- All three schools accept monophyletic groups; cladists alone reject paraphyletic groups; and pheneticists alone accept polyphyletic groups.

- Only pheneticists accept homoplasies.

- All three schools accept derived homologies; cladists alone reject ancestral homologies (after Ridley, 2004, p. 475, Tab. 16.1).

Thus, cladists arguably pursue the most rigorously evolutionary approach, insisting that the only meaningful groupings are monophyletic and are thus based exclusively on the derived homologies resulting from direct evolutionary descent.

A good example of the differences between monophyletic and paraphyletic groupings – and therefore between the approaches of cladists and pheneticists – is the class (Table 1.5) *Reptilia* (reptiles), a paraphyletic grouping. Lizards and crocodiles are sometimes grouped together in this class, but their common ancestor lived *before* the common ancestor of crocodiles and birds. In other words, birds and crocodiles are more closely related – they form a monophylum – than are crocodiles and lizards, even though (because of birds' much more rapid evolution compared to that of crocodiles) crocodiles resemble lizards more closely than they resemble birds, and thus have been linked, paraphyletically, with lizards. Because it is a paraphyletic, not monophyletic grouping, "[t]he class Reptilia, therefore, is disbanded in cladistic classification" (Ridley, 2004, p. 482).

One of the main factors in the growth of cladism is the rise of molecular biology, which, by tracing DNA and protein sequences, affords an additional category of evidence – in addition to morphological and embryological data – for the investigation of evolutionary relationships. On the basis that the smaller the differences between forms of a given molecule the closer the likely evolutionary connection, morphologically *similar* organisms with strong *divergences* between forms of a specific molecule might be homoplasious, whereas morphologically *dissimilar* organisms with strong *convergences* between forms of a specific molecule might be homologous. Nevertheless, the contrast between the near infinity of potential morphological states and the relatively limited number of "fixed states" of certain molecules such as nucleotides and amino acids (four and twenty types, respectively) means that some molecular evidence is less powerful for resolving the homology/homoplasy distinction than morphological evidence, because "it is fairly probable that the same informational state could independently evolve [homoplasy] in ... two species" (Ridley, 2004, pp. 437–438).

This issue is ameliorated by considering more complex molecules, such as cytochrome *c*, which has over one hundred amino acids and which exists in a number of variant forms that result from differences in amino acid type-position structure (Ridley, 2004, p. 438). Notwithstanding the potential effects of genetic "dark matter" – the *c.* 98% of DNA that regulates the *c.* 2% of protein-coding DNA (Ahmad et al., 2020; Flores-Ferrer et al., 2021) – and of epigenetic factors (§1.8), such molecular variants are the consequence of evolutionarily shaped gene *polymorphism*. Here, two or more *alleles* – alternative, rival forms, these competing to occupy the same *locus* (position) on a chromosome (Dawkins, 1983a, p. 283; Griffiths et al., 2015, p. 4) – give rise to different versions of a given protein and, potentially, to different phenotypic characteristics. As will be discussed in §3.5.2, the concept of an allele is relevant to cultural as well as to biological replicators.

1.7.3 Punctuationism *versus* Gradualism, The Unit(s) of Selection, and Taxonomy

In §1.6.2, it was noted that selection appears to operate most powerfully on the lowest level of a natural hierarchy – on the "selfish gene" as the fundamental unit of selection. While, as Table 1.4 shows, this is well below the level of the group, let alone that of the species, some would argue for a role for the species in selection, in particular those who advocate the evolutionary doctrine of *punctuated equilibrium* ("punk eek", in biologists' slang) (Eldredge & Gould, 1972, pp. 78–85; Prothero, 2007). This is the notion that species are stable for long periods of time – "stasis", driven by *stabilising selection* – and that evolutionary change is concentrated in speciation (species-forming) events, particularly in cases of *allopatric* speciation (Ridley, 2004, pp. 599–600, Fig. 21.5). The latter occurs where clear ecological/geographical separation of members of a species leads to evolutionary divergence (bifurcation) between the original species and the "outgroup"; by contrast, *sympatric* speciation relates to evolutionary divergence occurring within the same location; an intermediate type is *parapatric* speciation, where the divergent species lives adjacent to its antecedent (Ridley, 2004, pp. 382–383, Fig. 14.1). From the claims of punctuationism, it follows that the greater their discreteness and stability, the greater the opportunity for species to act as units of selection. Punctuated equilibrium is sometimes held to be opposed to *gradualism* (sometimes termed *phyletic gradualism*), which argues that evolution proceeds steadily and incrementally, and that species, far from being discrete and stable entities, are merely staging posts on a "smeary continuum" (Dawkins, 2006, p. 374; Hull, 1976), and so do not possess sufficient identity and stability to act as units of selection.[29]

At its heart, the debate between punctuated equilibrium and (phyletic) gradualism rests on two distinct senses in which the term gradualism may be (mis)understood (Ridley, 2004, 601, box 21.1). On the one hand, it may relate to the *rate* of evolution. Even extreme phyletic-gradualist neo-Darwinians, like Dawkins, acknowledge that the speed at which evolution proceeds is not constant, varying according to such factors as mutation rates and selection pressures. Adherents of punctuated equilibrium go further, however, in arguing for the existence of relatively long periods of stasis followed by relatively rapid change, the latter driven by allopatric speciation: for them, evolution proceeds not metronomically, and at andante, but in terms of short spurts of allegro embedded in long passages of adagio. In part, this is a matter of (time)scale, perspective and granularity: just as a seemingly unified image on a computer screen will reveal discrete pixels if viewed at close quarters, so gradualism in evolution will appear increasingly jumpy when one moves in from expansive to more constrained geological time-frames.

On the other hand, and perhaps more fundamentally, gradualism may relate to the *mechanism* of evolution. True mechanistic gradualism – advocated by *both* gradualists and adherents of punctuated equilibrium – rejects *single-step* selection in favour of *cumulative* selection. The former accomplishes a

---

[29] Dawkins considers the moral implications of gradualism, particularly the issue of where, if anywhere, rights start and finish for those creatures closest to humans (2006, p. 373).

large amount of evolutionary work in a single action (high-level digital); the latter covers the same distance by a multiplicity of small increments, each building upon the achievements of its direct predecessor (low-level digital, high-level analogue) (Dawkins, 2006, pp. 64–65, 70–71). It is in the nature of evolution that the greater the distance between two states, the lower the statistical probability of its occurring in one single "move". The saltation (large, single-step evolutionary leaps (Dawkins, 1983b, pp. 412–418)) required to give rise to new organisms of radically different character has very low statistical probability (Dawkins, 2006, pp. 332–333) because the resulting "hopeful monsters" (Goldschmidt, in Dennett, 1995, p. 288) are generally unviable. Renouncing saltation, Carl Linnaeus (1707–1778), an early advocate of cumulative (in opposition to single-step) selection, insisted in 1751 that *"Natura non facit saltus"* ("nature does not make leaps") (in Dennett, 1995, p. 288). Indeed, in Dawkins' view, the "blind watchmaker" of Darwinism (2006) proceeds exclusively via cumulative selection, this being the only means of building complexity, irrespective of gradualist-punctuationist debates on the (relative) speed of the process.[30]

The implications of this issue for taxonomy are that the neat branchings of cladograms tend to oversimplify evolution by representing a finite set of states. They show the beginnings and ends of evolutionary motions – these terms of course themselves loaded against a gradualist view – but not the continuum connecting them. Thus an inherent philosophical issue in taxonomy is that the very act of labelling an entity and assigning it to a position on a two-dimensional tree-diagram implies the (single-step) oversimplification, by time-slicing, of a complex (cumulative) process. In part this is a consequence of the numerous gaps in the fossil record, which render the (likely) "smeary continuum" invisible. Such gaps have indeed been used as evidence in the debate between gradualism and punctuated equilibrium, advocates of the latter arguing that discontinuities in fossil evidence indicate rapid evolution connecting otherwise static antecedent species to their

---

[30] As a final point in this line of discussion, it is nevertheless clear that the outcome of a single mutation may sometimes be disproportionately consequential. For instance, Harvey (2017, pp. 63, 67–74) discusses the effects of single base-pair changes in certain genes that may have had potentially significant evolutionary consequences for the augmentation of human cognitive capacity. One such is the Brain-derived neurotrophic factor (BDNF) gene (Harvey, 2017, p. 71), implicated in neural development, memory formation and brain plasticity, and subject to epigenetic mediation (§1.8; see also note 81 on page 138).

consequents. The (rate-of-evolution) gradualist alternative would maintain that a consequent (outgroup) species, gradualistically evolved, might have re-invaded the territory originally occupied by its antecedent, leaving discontinuity in the fossil record between the antecedent and consequent species, "because the interesting [gradual] evolution took place elsewhere" (Ridley, 2004, p. 599).

1.8 Lamarckism *versus* Darwinism in Biological Evolution

One of the greatest controversies in evolutionary theory was that between Lamarckism and Darwinism. At a time when the existence of evolution was increasingly recognised, Jean-Baptiste Lamarck (1744–1829) offered one of the earliest generally accepted theories to explain it (Lamarck, 2011). While his ideas were discredited in the late-nineteenth century, some have been re-examined in the light of modern genetics. The Lamarck-Darwin debate is significant not merely in terms of the historical development of evolutionary thought, but because if one is attempting to develop a Universal Darwinism that subsumes as many substrates as possible, including human musicality and music, then one needs to be clear on the contribution, if any, of "Universal Lamarckism" to Universal Darwinism.

Lamarck's account of evolution is multifaceted, but his most persistent idea was that of *the inheritance of acquired characteristics*. Put simply, if an organism developed a trait during the course of its lifetime – perhaps bigger muscles, as a result of sustained exertion; or longer arms, as a result of repeated stretching – then those attributes would, Lamarck suggested, be passed on to its offspring, conferring upon them, like the inheritance of wealth in human cultures, a survival advantage in life. One of his most celebrated examples was the case of the long front legs and neck of the giraffe, which he believed had evolved because successive generations of giraffes had struggled to reach the highest leaves of tall trees. Their exertions had, little by little, stretched their front legs and necks (*"ses jambes de devant sont devenues plus longues que celles de derrière, et que son col s'est tellement allongé"*) and these traits were passed to their offspring, who were able to pick up where their parents had left off (Lamarck, 2011, pp. 256–257). For such cases of inheritance of features augmented by use, there are also converse cases of those diminished by disuse.

In distinct contrast to this "soft inheritance", Darwinism's "hard inheritance" (E. Mayr, 1982, p. 687) holds that an organism's attributes (while to some extent environmentally malleable) are genetically coded for at conception, and this code cannot be "back-altered" by the environment. So central to modern Darwinism is this principle that Dawkins concedes that "I can think of few things that would more devastate my world view than a demonstrated need to return to the theory of evolution that is traditionally attributed to Lamarck" (1983a, pp. 164–165). Lacking understanding of genetics, Darwin was not able convincingly to rebut Lamarckism in his lifetime; indeed, in response to criticism of his ideas, he became progressively more Lamarckian in subsequent editions of *On the origin of species*: Darwin produced six in total, these appearing in 1859, 1860, 1861, 1866, 1869 and 1872 (Darwin, 2006; Darwin, 2012), each arguably slightly more Lamarckian than its predecessor.

Nevertheless, the integration, pioneered by Ronald Fisher (Fisher, 1930) in the 1930s, of Darwin's observations on morphological change with the foundational research of Gregor Mendel in genetics (Mendel, 1901) – the "Modern Synthesis" (Ridley, 2004, pp. 14–15) – made Lamarckism incompatible with the "Central Dogma" of modern genetics. This holds that there is – to use Weismann's distinction first articulated in 1885 – a "germ line" (the line of the genome, carried by sperms and eggs), and a "soma line" (the line of the phenotype, an expression of the genome in interaction with the environment); and that the former is connected to the latter by a strictly one-way arrow (E. Mayr, 1982, p. 700). In Crick's formulation, nucleic acids make proteins, not *vice-versa*: thus, "the amino acid sequence in a protein cannot be reverse-translated into DNA or RNA" (Jablonka & Lamb, 2014, p. 150). In terms of concepts discussed in §1.6.1, the germ line is that of the replicator whilst the soma line is that of the vehicle.[31]

---

[31] Some species, most notably certain plants, nevertheless have a capacity for somatic embryogenesis, where "a new generation may be formed from cells other than those in specialized reproductive organs" (Ridley, 2004, p. 296).

This, it might seem, makes the issue cut-and-dried; but some aspects of genetics, discussed from the time of the Modern Synthesis, appear to leave the Lamarckian door ajar, if only slightly. Through this door, *epigenetic inheritance* – inheritance "in addition to the gene" – might enter. This notion describes the "soft" transmission of information from one cell to another or from one organism to another, in ways that are separate from the "hard" transmission of the DNA (germ) line. As Jablonka and Lamb argue,

> [a]though their DNA sequences remain unchanged during development, [specialised soma] cells nevertheless acquire information that they can pass to their progeny. This information is transmitted through what are known as *epigenetic inheritance systems* (or EISs for short).... evolution is possible on the basis of heritable epigenetic variation, even when there is no genetic variation at all. (Jablonka & Lamb, 2014, pp. 111, 112; emphasis in the original)

Jablonka and Lamb (2014) identify four mechanisms for epigenetic inheritance, which they regard, like genetic inheritance, as a form of information transmission: (i) self-sustaining loops (where the activation of a specific gene in a parent cell is transmitted to daughter cells as a form of "cell memory" (2014, p. 117)); (ii) structural inheritance (where "three-dimensional templating" motivates the replication of some acquired cell structure (2014, p. 120)); (iii) chromatin marking (where certain molecules attached to DNA affect its *expression* (2014, p. 126)); and (iv) RNA interference (where certain small RNA molecules cause the "stable and cell heritable silencing of specific genes" (2014, p. 131)). Mechanisms (i), (iii) and (iv) mediate – by activation or silencing – the expression of genes, which devolves to the types of protein the DNA-segment codes for. The third of these mechanisms is of particular interest in the Lamarckism-Darwinism debate.

This third mechanism is driven by the process of *chromatin marking*. One way of understanding a chromosome is to regard it as consisting of two broad categories of molecules: the DNA (from which genes are built), and everything else. The "everything else" consists of molecules such as RNA, proteins, and various other chemicals. Together, DNA plus the "everything else" constitute *chromatin*, the material constituting chromosomes. One specific chromatin-marking EIS, *methylation*, involves the "labelling" of certain cytosine nucleotides in C-G pairs (see note 18 on page 30) with molecules from the non-DNA chromatin, specifically with a *methyl* group (CH_3). Methylation results from a variety of complex internal and external (environmental) causes, and is entirely natural: it is an important element of cell metabolism and development; and errors in methylation are believed to be a cause, or an effect, of the ageing process. Nevertheless, methylation affects certain components of DNA in ways that usually suppress their expression in cells. For present purposes, chromatin marking provides a mechanism whereby an acquired characteristic – the phenotypic consequences of gene suppression via environmentally induced methylation – is not only manifested in the individual acquiring that characteristic, but it is also potentially transmissible to that individual's descendants.

The latter property results from the fact that epigenetic transmission may occur not only via the soma line, but also, crucially, via the germ line. That is, not only are such (category (iii)) epigenetic changes transmissible to daughter cells, as a result of normal soma-cell division *within* an individual organism's tissues; but they are also able to be transmitted *from* an organism *to* its descendants. The mechanisms for this are imperfectly understood, but it appears that, in one process, chromosomes in gametes (sex cells, carrying the germ line) are marked – "imprinted" (Jablonka & Lamb, 2014, p. 137) – by differential patterns of methylation. Sometimes this differential is correlated with sex, which some believe affords an explanation for the fact that the offspring of a female horse (*Equus ferus caballus*) and a male donkey (*Equus africanus asinus*) (a mule) and the offspring of a male horse and a female donkey (a hinny), while genetically identical, are nevertheless phenotypically very different (Jablonka & Lamb, 2014, p. 136). It is thought that their male and female chromosomes are somehow "tagged" differently by methylation and that this leads to gross differences in gene expression in their offspring. Indeed, "[w]hen a chromosome passes from one sex to the other [such as a male-gamete chromosome ending up in a female offspring], the [methylation] marks that it originally carried are erased, and new sex-specific marks are established" (Jablonka & Lamb, 2014, p. 137; see also Wei et al., 2014). A related phenomenon is the commonly observed difference in the flower-shape of the Toadflax (*Linaria vulgaris*), where both normal and "peloric" ("monstrous", i.e., unusually spherical) flower-forms exist

(Jablonka & Lamb, 2014, pp. 138–139, Fig. 4.9). As in the equine examples, such stably transmitted variants, equivalents to which occur in other plant species, do not result from genetic differences: "[t]he morphological [phenotypic] change [is] due not to a [gene] mutation, but to an epimutation: the pattern of methylation of a particular gene in the normal and peloric plants [differs]" (Jablonka & Lamb, 2014, p. 139).

Both these examples seem dangerously close to suggesting that the epigenetic inheritance of acquired characteristics – a normal-flowered Toadflax plant can revert during the course of its life to a peloric form – is a seemingly Lamarckian process (Dawkins (1983a, p. 164) discusses a similar "Lamarckian scare"). In fact, there are two reasons to dismiss such illusory Lamarckism. First, even though epigenetic factors may mediate gene expression, genes are still the foundations on which the biological inheritance system is built. They remain the fundamental unit of selection – the optimon (§1.6.2) – because epigenetic markers, unlike DNA, cannot carry the vast quantity of information necessary to build the "survival machines" (vehicles) (Dawkins, 1989, p. 19) that ensure gene (replicator) transmission. Secondly, even though the gene-as-optimon is the fundamental unit of selection, it is gene *products* (in phenotypes) that are actually selected for or against. Because a Universal-Darwinian system is agnostic as to the means by which variation, replication and selection occur – it does not, strictly, require a distinction between replicators and vehicles – it follows that, while gene-based VRS is Darwinian, non-Gene based (or non-exclusively gene-based) VRS is not necessarily non-Darwinian.[32]

While the existence of epigenetic inheritance may certainly pose a challenge to the supremacy of the gene, it does not in the slightest undermine the (substrate-neutral) VRS algorithm itself. Epigenetics simply claims that, while the key elements of the VRS algorithm in terrestrial biology are implemented via gene-based processes, other mechanisms, such as methylation-induced phenotypic changes, should also be acknowledged as potential causes of variation. In this sense, epigenetic inheritance is as much Dar-

---

[32] This fact allows Jablonka and Lamb (2014, pp. 112–116) to imagine the fictional planet of Jaynus, where all life-forms are genetically identical, and where epigenetic factors alone drive the variation upon which Darwinian natural selection operates. This non-gene-based Darwinism gives rise to a plethora of diversely formed and beautifully adapted creatures.

winian (and is as much non-Lamarckian) as is genetic inheritance: both mechanisms spawn variation, this variation is able to be replicated, and the variants are selected from according to some adaptive constraints.

Lastly, a further issue in the Lamarckism-Darwinism debate relates to another means, broadly analogous to that underpinning epigenetics, whereby the expression of a gene is potentially mediated by acquired, non-genetic factors. The "Baldwin Effect" (first theorised by James Baldwin (1861–1934)) is distinct from epigenetic inheritance because the acquired characteristics it encompasses are *culturally*, not *biologically*, inherited, via some form of learning (Sznajder et al., 2012). As cognitive/psychological rather than morphological enhancements, they constitute a factor in Darwinian natural selection because they potentially advantage the genes of the organism that has learned the behaviour, provided the behaviour were in some way adaptive. If the learned behaviour were also transmissible – if it did not have to be learned afresh, but could be passed on from one individual to another by imitation – then it would represent an example of memetic inheritance and would therefore make this particular category of Baldwinism an example of gene-meme *coevolution* (§3.7), one with perhaps particular significance for the evolution of creativity (see also §5.5.2).

The distinction between genetic and epigenetic inheritance and their relationship to memetic transmission, is considered further in §3.4.3 and §4.4.1.1.

1.9 Summary of Chapter 1

Chapter 1 has argued that:

1. Evolutionary theory has the power to illuminate our understanding of musicality and music; conversely, light can be shed on evolutionary theory by the study of musicality and music.

2. The VRS algorithm operates not just in biological evolution on earth, but also in cultural evolution. Indeed, according to the precepts of Universal Darwinism, it operates in any substrate anywhere in the universe where the VRS algorithm is capable of being initiated and sustained. It is the driving force behind a recursive ontology connecting all phenomena in the universe.

3. In addition to the fundamental elements of the VRS algorithm, various other phenomena appear common to a number of evolutionary systems, such that they appear core to any definition of Universal Darwinism. These include a distinction between replicators and vehicles, a tendency for evolutionary systems to form multilevelled structural hierarchies, a focus upon the smallest unit(s) of selection, and the presence of the invariant replicator attributes of longevity, fecundity and copying-fidelity, irrespective of the substrate.

4. There are a number of distinct approaches to taxonomy, but that built upon charting evolutionary relationships, cladism, appears most powerful in biological and – as will be argued in Chapter 3 – cultural classification.

5. While the war between Lamarckism and Darwinism appears essentially won, and while Darwinism appears the clear victor over the core territory, skirmishes continue to occur at the periphery that indicate debate over the continuing relevance of a limited degree of Lamarckian transmission. Even epigenetic inheritance can be understood as conformant with Darwinism, not contradictory to it.

Chapter 2 will explore what is known of how humans came to be so musical, given that none of our primate cousins has anything approximating our level of facility and creativity with organised sounds. It will: consider what is and is not music; evaluate non-evolutionary and evolutionary explanations for musicality; trace our physical and social evolution from humans' earliest common ancestor with chimpanzees (delving briefly into sound archaeology as evidence for the sonic markers of this evolution); ask why music (initially vocal, but subsequently also instrumental) is so important to the history, and the survival, of our species; and examine the evolutionary relationships between music and language (both understood as forms of communicative vocalisation), this concluding with a consideration of the physical markers this evolution has left in the form of the various brain structures and systems responsible for processing music and language.

2. The Evolution of Human Musicality

Although all of the mechanisms involved in music perception and production may be grouped together, for convenience, as 'the music faculty'
or 'the capacity for music', it is important to remember that different
components of this capacity may have different evolutionary histories.
Thus, discussing 'Music' as an undifferentiated whole, or as a unitary
cognitive 'module', risks overlooking the fact that music integrates a
wide variety of domains (cognitive, emotional, perceptual, motor, ...),
may serve a variety of functions (mother-infant bonding, mate choice,
group cohesion ...) and may share key components with other systems
like language or speech. (Fitch, 2006, p. 174)

2.1 Introduction: What Is and What Is Not Music?

Of all creatures on earth, humans are the most musical. Of course this
statement is inherently solipsistic, since we as humans define what does and
does not constitute music and, in a related assessment, we ultimately judge
what is and is not (musically) creative (§5.5). As will be explored in Chapter
5, members of certain animal groups – most notably a number of bird and
cetacean species – are capable of producing structured sound sequences that
transcend their innate (genetic) capacities and that, to the human ear, have
many attributes of music. Indeed, as Jerison asserts,

> [t]here is no real question that we share with other mammals the basic
> bodily structures used to vocalize and generate musical sounds and
> thus share with other species many aspects of our capacity for musical
> expression. We are evidently unique, however, in the way we know (i.e.,
> 'cognize') and understand sounds as musical.... the biological basis of
> our musical experience is related to the biology of human intelligence;
> that is, to our capacity to know the external world. (Jerison, 2000, p. 178)

 https://doi.org/10.11647/OBP.0301.02

Thus, how non-human animals cognise their sound-producing activities, if they do so in any structured, "conscious" way at all, is likely to be very different from how humans conceive the sound sequences we regard as musical.[33] This is because human music is a mixture of the intentional (Dennett, 1989) and the aesthetic (Dahlhaus, 1982; Scruton, 1997). The highest and most abstract level of a hierarchy consisting of (at the bottom) the "physical stance" (where, for a relevant system, one must employ "knowledge of the laws of physics to predict the outcome for any input"), and (above that) the "design stance" (where one predicts that a system "will behave *as it is designed to behave* [including design by evolution] under various circumstances") (Dennett, 1989, pp. 16, 17; emphasis in the original), the (top-level) "intentional stance" requires that

> first you decide to treat the object whose behavior is to be predicted as a rational agent; then you figure out what beliefs that agent ought to have, given its place in the world and its purpose. Then you figure out what desires it ought to have, on the same considerations, and finally you predict that this rational agent will act to further its goals in the light of its beliefs. A little practical reasoning from the chosen set of beliefs and desires will in many – but not all – instances yield a decision about what the agent ought to do; that is what you predict the agent *will* do. (Dennett, 1989, p. 17; emphasis in the original; see also Dennett, 1988)

While the non-human animal groups referred to above might possess at least some degree of intentionality, it is doubtful they experience anything analogous to an aesthetic sense (unless the aesthetic is regarded as an extension of sexual-selective tendencies (§2.5.3)). Thus – to return to Jerison's distinction between the ability to produce sounds (the capacity for intentional sound-structuring; musicality); and the capacity to comprehend sounds in specific ways (the ability to deploy cognition in order to process them intellectually and aesthetically; as music) – it is clear that humans are superior to all other organisms on earth in terms of our ability to organise sounds in a multitude

---

[33] As a further complication, some objects or experiences regarded, or certainly presented, as music lack that which most humans would regard as an essential prerequisite, namely sound itself. John Cage's 4'33" is perhaps the obvious case in point, but more recent composers, including Peter Ablinger, have coded as musical things that cannot or do not produce any sound; or they have attempted to draw a distinction between (musical) sounds experienced in an aesthetic context and other sounds, even noises, experienced in different contexts (Ablinger, 2013; see also Velardo, 2014).

of inventive and expressive ways in order to define and transmit our emotions, thoughts, beliefs and cultures; and then to reflect coherently upon the products and consequences of this behaviour – even if some other species are closer to us in these regards than we might comfortably admit.

This chapter considers, insofar as currently available evidence permits, how and why the various human capacities that subserve musicality have arisen over the course of our evolutionary history. It takes musicality to be, certainly initially, *vocality*: while a good proportion of the world's musics involve instruments,[34] the first music, what we might regard as a form of singing, grew out of pre-musical and pre-linguistic utterances. Later, objects were co-opted to support dancing and to imitate vocal sounds. It is difficult to ascribe priority, but it appears likely that such early "instrumental" music included both percussion and wind instruments. On the former, it is evident that some of our primate cousins sometimes beat their own bodies and other objects percussively (§5.3.4), so it is reasonable to infer that early hominins did the same, perhaps as an accompaniment to vocalisation and to the movements and gestures of dancing (§5.1). On the latter, there is a growing body of evidence for the existence of various early bone and ivory flutes, even though there is ongoing debate as to the chronology of some of these candidate artefacts.[35]

---

[34] Indeed, by the beginning of the nineteenth century, Europe witnessed the "emancipation of instrumental music" from vocal models (Dahlhaus, 1982, p. 24).

[35] By convention, the *prehistory* within which the developments discussed in this chapter occurred is divided – necessarily imprecisely, and varying according to geography – into the *Stone Age* (units are MYBP (Million Years Before Present; the "present" taken as the year 1950)) (*c.* 3.300–0.008 [i.e., 3,300,000–8,000 years ago]), the *Bronze Age* (*c.* 0.008–0.003), and the *Iron Age* (*c.* 0.003–0.002). The Stone Age is itself divided into the *Palaeolithic* (*c.* 3.300–0.015), the *Mesolithic* (*c.* 0.015–0.012), the *Neolithic* (*c.* 0.012–0.010 years BP), and the *Chalcolithic* (*c.* 0.010–0.008). The Palaeolithic is itself divided into the *Lower Palaeolithic* (*c.* 3.300–0.300), the *Middle Palaeolithic* (*c.* 0.300–0.050), and the *Upper Palaeolithic* (*c.* 0.050–0.015) (Fitch, 2010, p. 209, Fig. 5.1; Fagan & Durrani, 2020; Wikipedia, 2020). The Palaeolithic is loosely contemporary with the Pleistocene (colloquially, the "Ice Age") (*c.* 2.600–0.0118), this being a geological, rather than a natural/cultural-historical, category. The coalescence of the substrates for human musicality is thought to have occurred in the Middle Palaeolithic, with the aforementioned "pre-musical and pre-linguistic utterances" appearing before *c.* 0.200. The "emergence of modern syntactic language and articulate speech, increased memory capacity, new patterns of technology and social organization, the evolution of a modern cortical interconnectional architecture, enhanced and more adaptable intercellular communication, and along with all of this, the origin of the modern human mind" (Harvey, 2017, p. 75) occurred before the transition from the Middle to the Upper Palaeolithic (*c.* 0.050), perhaps *c.* 0.070–0.060, and was broadly coincident with our species' founder population's move out of its birthplace, Africa (Bannan, 1999; Stringer, 2003; Harvey, 2017, p. 86; Harvey, 2018, p. 2). The earliest evidence for this "modern human mind"

The chapter continues by considering categories of explanation for musicality, comparing non-evolutionary with evolutionary varieties (§2.2). It moves on to survey, necessarily briefly, certain evolutionary developments in the lineages that led to modern humans and the varying potentially music/musicality-related morphological, behavioural and social changes that accompanied (or perhaps drove) those developments (§2.3). The following section assesses the material evidence, assembled by the interdiscipline of sound archaeology, for sound-making by our ancestors that might have been fostered by the hypothesised evolutionary changes underpinning musicality (§2.4). The next section considers, under the rubric of aptation – an expansion of the notion of adaptation to encompass later re-purposings of features evolved earlier for other purposes – to what extent musicality and music were advantageous to our species (§2.5). Then the issue of instrumental music is examined, relating the nature of early instruments to the previously corporeal basis of music-making (§2.6). Thereafter, the chapter turns to the important issue of music and its evolutionary relationships with language, arguing that it is meaningless to consider the evolution of one without also considering that of the other. Here the specific issue addressed is the hypothesised common origin of music and language, in the form of what some term "musilanguage" (Brown, 2000, p. 277) (§2.7).

2.2 Non-Evolutionary and Evolutionary Explanations for Musicality

While this book is self-evidently concerned with exploring evolutionary explanations for musicality and music, it is important to admit the possibility that they have no such basis – that they are the effects of non-evolutionary causes, or indeed that they are the effects of a mixture of non-evolutionary and evolutionary causes. Note that this distinction relates to the second and third of Tinbergen's (1963) four categories of explanation for biological questions. These "four whys", in Fitch's terms/sequence (Fitch, 2006, pp. 174–175; see also Fitch, 2010, pp. 68–70), are: (i) *mechanistic* ("causation" in Tinbergen (1963, p. 413)); (ii) *developmental* ("ontogeny" (1963, p. 423)); (iii) *phylogen-*

in the form of musical instruments – this more tangible than evidence for vocality – has been dated somewhat later, at *c.* 0.040 (§2.6). See Table 2.1.

etic ("evolution" (1963, p. 427)); and (iv) *adaptive* ("survival value" (1963, p. 417)). The first two constitute – in a reference to the Aristotelian underpinning of Tinbergen's framework (Dennett, 2017, p. 33) – what are sometimes termed "proximate" causes, and the second two "ultimate" causes (Hladký & Havlíček, 2013). Given Dobzhansky's injunction that "nothing in biology makes sense except in the light of evolution" (1973), the latter two – adaptation, driving phylogeny – must surely take precedence, notwithstanding Fitch's view that "all four types of question are equally valid and interesting" (2006, p. 175).

Foley (2012, pp. 49–50) offers a useful taxonomy of the issues involved in this distinction, identifying both non-evolutionary and evolutionary explanations for the origin of musicality (see also Honing, 2018a).

- Non-Evolutionary: Musicality has/had No Adaptive Benefit/Function

  1. Musicality *has* (and, by implication, *had*) no adaptive function, arising merely as a by-product of attributes evolved/adapted to serve other purposes (Pinker's "Auditory Cheesecake" hypothesis; §1.1.2, §2.5).

  2. Musicality *had* no adaptive function, but its substrates were subsequently *exapted* (redeployed for other purposes) (§2.5.1), which then conferred a selective advantage.

- Evolutionary: Musicality had/has Adaptive Benefit/Function

  1. Musicality arose as a result of *sexual selection*, serving to advertise genetic superiority to potential mates (§2.5.3).

  2. Musicality arose to foster *group cohesion*, its rhythmic aspects in particular serving to bind individuals into a collective enterprise (§2.5.2).

  3. Musicality arose as a content-focused, *information-signalling system*, eventually bifurcating into music and language (§2.7).[36]

A number of interconnecting cautions are necessary, however, these suggested by the quotation at the head of this chapter. *Firstly*, whatever its origins, musicality – what Fitch (2006, p. 174) terms "'the music faculty' or 'the

---

[36] While the first two items in this sub-list also refer to the communication of information, this third category refers to the communication of more specific propositions (Foley, 2012, p. 50).

capacity for music"' – is complex and multi-faceted.[37] It consists of a range
of interlocking competences that implicate hearing, perception, cognition,
memory (cognitive and embodied/muscular), vocal production, rhythmic-
muscular action, abstract social-relational proficiencies, affective states, and
others. In this sense, musicality is a "mosaic" (Foley, 2012), upon each tessera
of which Darwinian selection acted independently; and not a unified entity
upon which selection operated monolithically – it "is more a cognitive toolkit
than a single tool" (Savage et al., 2021, p. 3). Moreover, and *secondly*, one or
more of the brain or body structures that currently subserve musicality may
not originally have arisen to do so: something that subsequently became
pressed into the service of musicality may initially have been selected for
a different function (assuming we can ever securely know the functions
hypothesised and/or extant competences served in early human societies);
it may have been *exapted* for use in musicality (Gould & Vrba, 1982), rather
than *adapted* for it (§2.5.1). Underpinning these two points, and as a *third*,
the genetic variation upon which selection acts often affects a number of
biological systems and functions that are implicated in a range of attributes
and competences, many of which may not have related to musicality during
the period of selection. Thus, while musicality as we understand it draws
upon many substrates, it is only one of a multitude of interconnected human
abilities upon which selection operates (Bickerton, 2000, pp. 156–157, 160).

Of course much of the previous paragraph relies on our conception of musicality and, by extension, that of music. For the former, it is not entirely clear
what competences (exclusively) constitute musicality, because – for reasons
discussed in the previous paragraph – many that are pressed into its service
also do double-duty in other areas of our lives. For the latter, we need to be
careful not to universalise the western European model of musical culture
that, certainly in much scholarship on "art" music, sees it as channelled into
author-associated "works" (Goehr, 1992), which are the focus of econom-
ically mediated interactions between performers and listeners, and which
underpin a notion of canonicity (Bergeron & Bohlman, 1992). Instead, it
is necessary to attempt to understand what features, if any, are common to

---

[37] If musicality preceded linguisticality – as is argued in §2.7 – the same is true of what might
be termed "the language faculty" or "the capacity for language", as a set of competences derived
from and substantially overlapping with musicality, and to which many of the points in this
paragraph apply.

the musics of all human societies. The search for such "musical universals" is fraught with controversy (Nattiez, 1990, pp. 62–68), and is impeded by the fact that many musical cultures do not have a word equivalent to the "music" (or its counterparts) of Indo-European languages. This is partly because music and ritual are inseparable in surviving tribal cultures: for such cultures, to separate singing, instrumental sound-production, dancing, religious ritual and group bonding is meaningless, because all these constitute elements of a holistic, performative social activity. I return to the issue of musical universals in §2.5.5.

2.3 Hominin Evolution from *Australopithecus afarensis* to *Homo sapiens*

It is necessary briefly to summarise the biological-evolutionary changes that provided the foundation for human music-language cultural evolution. Table 2.1, after Foley (2012) and Smithsonian Institution (2019), outlines the principal members of the hominin lineage leading up to *Homo sapiens* (see also Sawyer et al., 2007).[38] Note that the overviews of pre-human species' characteristics in the "attributes" column are necessarily speculative, given that the fossil record permits only a limited reconstruction of their likely morphology and cognitive/socio-cultural development.

The salient developmental events linking the last common ancestor of *Homo sapiens* and *Pan troglodytes* (chimpanzee) to the first cognitively modern humans appear to have been as outlined in the following subsections. It is important to note that the concepts identified below do not characterise separate and distinct evolutionary stages, but overlapping segments on a continuum that is still imperfectly understood. Moreover, there is disagreement over the chronological priority and evolutionary significance of the phenomena discussed, particularly communal living (§2.3.2), infant altriciality (§2.3.4), and "vocal grooming" (§2.3.5), which are thought to have interacted in complex ways. The following discussion attempts to correlate

---

[38] Not all known/posited species are indicated in Table 2.1. Omitted, for instance, is *Homo antecessor* (Foley, 2012, p. 35, Fig. 2.1), which some regard as the last common ancestor of *Homo neanderthalensis* and *Homo sapiens* (Bermúdez-de-Castro et al., 2017, p. 27; see also Fitch, 2010, p. 234). Table 2.1 attributes this status to *Homo helmei* or to *Homo heidelbergensis*.

Era (Million Years BP)	Species	Extant (Million Years BP)	Attributes
Lower Palaeolithic (*c.* 3.300–*c.* 0.300)	*Australopithecus afarensis*	*c.* 3.900–*c.* 2.900	Partly or wholly bipedal. Antecedent (*Australopithecus anamensis*) and descendant (*Australopithecus africanus*) species known (Smithsonian Institution, 2019). Some similar species are assigned to the genus *Paranthropus* (Foley, 2012, p. 38).
	Homo habilis	*c.* 2.400–*c.* 1.400	Earliest extant member of the genus *Homo*, but ancestry (perhaps australopithecine or paranthropine) is unknown. Initially thought to be the first tool-making *Homo* species, but this practice is now thought to pre-date evidence for the earliest *Homo* (Smithsonian Institution, 2019).
	Homo rudolfensis	*c.* 1.900–*c.* 1.200	Few differences are evident between *Homo habilis*, *Homo rudolfensis* and australopithecines, and some advocate removal from *Homo* (Foley, 2012, p. 40).
	Homo erectus / Homo ergaster	*c.* 1.900–*c.* 0.400	Some regard *Homo erectus* as a variant form of *Homo ergaster*. Others see them as separate, with Klein regarding *Homo erectus* as a distinct Asian species, one perhaps aetiologically antecedent to *Homo ergaster*, which he terms "African *H. erectus*" (2009, p. 305; see also Foley, 2012, p. 35, Fig. 2.1; p. 38). A candidate ancestor of *Homo heidelbergensis* (Foley, 2012, p. 48, Fig. 2.4). Hypothesised to have been the first vocal-learning (§2.7.5) *Homo* (Mithen, 2006, p. 158; Merker, 2012, p. 233; see also point 9 of the list on page 139).
	Homo floresiensis	*c.* 0.190–*c.* 0.050	Localised to south-east Asia. Dwarf, compared with Eurasian species of *Homo*, perhaps on account of resource limitations (Smithsonian Institution, 2019).

(a) Australopithecines and Smaller-Brained Homo.

Era (Million Years BP)	Species	Extant (Million Years BP)	Attributes
Middle Palaeolithic (c. 0.300–c. 0.050)	*Homo heidelbergensis*	c. 0.700–c. 0.200	A candidate ancestor of *Homo neanderthalensis* and *Homo sapiens*, either directly or via *Homo helmei* (Foley, 2012, p. 46, Fig. 2.3). Perhaps the first *Homo* species to have used fire (Foley, 2012, p. 41).
	Homo helmei	c. 0.350–c. 0.250	A candidate ancestor of *Homo neanderthalensis* and *Homo sapiens*, seemingly larger-brained than its ancestors (Foley, 2012, pp. 41, 46, Fig. 2.3).
	Homo neanderthalensis	c. 0.400–c. 0.040	Localised and adapted to the colder climates of Eurasia. An approximate contemporary of *Homo sapiens* and seemingly sharing many aspects of the latter's morphology and behaviour, for a variety of posited genetic- and cultural-evolutionary reasons (Foley, 2012, pp. 45, 46, Fig. 2.3).
	Homo sapiens	c. 0.300–	A gap appears to have existed between the origin of *anatomically modern* (c. 0.200) and *cognitively modern* (after c. 0.100?) *Homo sapiens*, as judged by evidence of behaviour (Foley, 2012, p. 42). See note 35 on page 65.
Upper Palaeolithic (c. 0.050–c. 0.015)			

(b) Larger-Brained Homo.

Table 2.1: Hominin Species.

the hypothesised morphological and socio-cultural changes with potentially associated developments in the evolution of musicality.

2.3.1 Bipedalism

The evolution of bipedalism – consolidated in *Australopithecus afarensis c.* 2 MYA (million years ago) (Fitch, 2010, p. 259) – was associated with movement from a predominantly arboreal lifestyle to one of savannah (grassland-plain) dwelling (Mithen, 2006, pp. 144–145). The picture is complicated and, according to Mithen (2006, p. 144), occurred in two stages. In the first stage, hypothesised by Hunt (1994), bipedalism may have initially evolved to facilitate fruit-picking in species that otherwise moved predominantly using a combination of quadrupedal "knuckle-walking" and brachiation (swinging from branch to branch using the arms). Hunt (1994) observed that this type of object-grasping is a behaviour still manifested in modern-day chimpanzees, who sometimes stand on the ground using their feet in order to reach the fruit of small trees using their hands. Such "bipedal shuffling" avoids the energy expenditure of repeatedly raising and lowering the body, and it facilitates using the hands for grasping – both a tree's branches (for stabilisation) and the fruit itself (Mithen, 2006, p. 145).[39]

In the second stage, full bipedalism may have arisen as a response to the spread of savannah landscapes, these perhaps appearing as a consequence of global temperature rises thought to have occurred *c.* 2 MYA, which would have reduced forestation and fostered the spread of more drought-resistant plants such as grasses and low-growing, small-leaved shrubs (Mithen, 2006, p. 145).[40] In such environments, and lacking the cooling shade of densely clustered trees, bipedalism reduced heat stress by focusing sunlight primarily on the head and shoulders, rather than on the whole back (as occurs in knuckle-walking quadrupedal primates) – what Wheeler terms the "stand tall and stay cool" hypothesis (in Mithen, 2006, p. 145). For Fitch, the argument for "habitual bipedalism" in *Australopithecus afarensis*, one supported

---

[39] Bipedal shuffling in *Australopithecus*, while having a genetic underpinning, might also have been culturally transmitted between conspecifics, potentially leading to some Baldwinian enhancement of the behaviour's genetic basis (§1.8).

[40] A more recent theory argues that cosmic radiation from supernovae *c.* 2.6 MYA led to more frequent lightning and an increase in the number of wildfires, thereby reducing the density of forestation (Melott & Thomas, 2019).

by skeletal morphology, is "clinched" by some fossilised footprints found in Kenya, which appear to indicate tracks formed by two upright-walking individuals as long ago as 3.6 MYA (2010, pp. 259–260).

Beyond the perspectival shift – the move away from a "mostly two-dimensional world" (Bannan, 2019, p. 8), with all the cognitive expansion that implies – another consequence of the various anatomical and physiological changes bipedalism impels is of particular relevance to the evolution of musicality (and to that of the capacity for language). This is the lowering of the larynx (the vocal sound-producing organ) in the throat over the course of hominin evolution, which also occurs ontogenetically in our species (Clegg, 2012, pp. 64–65). The lowering of the larynx led to an increase in space in the pharynx (used in part by modern humans for vocal sound manipulation), and an associated augmentation of human vocal range and control (Clegg, 2012, pp. 58–59). This is nevertheless a particularly complex aspect of hominin phylogeny because, as always in evolution, there are a multitude of interacting adaptive factors at play, and it is not always clear which is a *cause* and which is an *effect*, in this case, of the ability to produce controlled vocalisations.

These factors include: (i) changes to the base of the cranium motivated by bipedalism,[41]; (ii) the mechanical (weight-balance) consequences of brain expansion, however driven (§3.7.1); (iii) jawbone and dentition changes resulting from savannah-dwelling[42] (Clegg, 2012, pp. 63–64); and (iv) the relationship between the lowered larynx and the potentially increased risk of choking owing to the greater chance of food ingress to the trachea via the lower human larynx compared with earlier, higher-larynx, hominins (a risk argued by Clegg to have been exaggerated by other commentators (2012, pp. 67–69)). As the only fossilising component of the vocal tract, the location of the hyoid bone – a marker of the position of the larynx – can be used to some extent to reconstruct the structure and evolution of the vocal tract and related cranial morphology in different hominin species (Clegg, 2012,

---

[41] The *foramen magnum*, the aperture through which the spinal cord passes, is located underneath the cranium in hominins, but to its rear in modern great apes and other quadrupedal mammals (Mithen, 2006, p. 122)

[42] This mode of life facilitates a move from a herbivorous-insectivorous to an omnivorous diet, because hominins could search (individually or collectively) for carcasses and/or (collectively) hunt animals more easily in deforested areas.

pp. 69–72), and thus to assess the degree to which a species is potentially "vocalisation-capable".

Having said all this – but having focused on the structural/mechanical aspects of vocal production as opposed to its neurological/cognitive substrates – one must consider the issue of virtuosic sound (re)production in certain birds (§5.4.1), perhaps most notably parrots. Birds have a completely different anatomy of sound production to primates – they have an organ called the syrinx instead of the primate larynx – but they far exceed our nearest evolutionary relatives in the range and dexterity of their vocalisations. This suggests that

> if the dearth of monkey talking and singing was merely a production limitation, we'd expect them to be able to learn to recognize music (and speech), perhaps to develop musical listening preferences, but researchers have found no evidence of this. There is a cognitive, not simply a motor limitation; they just don't get it. (Levitin, 2009, p. 293)

Whether parrots or other skilful vocalisers such as certain cetaceans (§5.4.2) "get it" or not is an open question; but they clearly have the cognitive resources to support memorisation and (re)production of fine vocal detail – the power of vocal learning (§2.7.5) – that non-human primates conspicuously lack. Thus – in an argument that cast doubts on the validity of studies of the evolution of the human vocal tract "for" language – "[i]t is not because the vocal tract of a chimpanzee has the wrong shape that it cannot do what parrots do ... but because chimpanzees lack the capacity for vocal learning [§2.7.5] that allows parrots to perform their imitative feats" (Merker, 2012, p. 232; see also Merker's point on fossil indicators of vocal biomechanics cited on page 130 below).

This complex body of evidence suggests that the evolution-driven alignment of morphological features in the hominin vocal tract that facilitated fine control of a range of vocalisations likely had a number of intersecting causes – it served a range of adaptive functions. Nevertheless, without the necessary associated cognitive infrastructure – either as cause or effect of the morphological features – then the type of vocalisations that we regard as musical and/or linguistic would not have evolved.

2.3.2 Communal Living

The relatively exposed environment of savannah dwelling is thought to have driven a greater tendency to communal living, for mutual protection and the maximisation of resources, leading to the appearance of "hunter-gatherer" societies. Rejecting the generally solitary, paired or small-group lifestyle of arboreal hominins,

> larger groups are likely to be more successful at repelling outside invaders. In a hunter-gatherer society, in which foodstuffs are often difficult to find and secure, the risks of any individual coming home empty-handed are diluted through the actions of many dozens or hundreds of hunter-gatherers; with cooperation, a given individual may come home empty-handed today, but full-armed tomorrow – in either case, the supplies are shared. (Levitin, 2009, p. 49)

For males, communal living was probably associated with greater cooperation in hunting, on account of the increasingly carnivorous diet implied by this lifestyle (see note 42 on page 73). The need to chase, kill and carry prey may also have driven an increase in body mass in males, although there is also a countervailing tendency towards similarity in body size between males (who generally hunted) and females (who generally gathered) (§2.3.3). For females, communal living implied increased cooperation in foraging for food and in infant-rearing, the latter including "grandmothering" – the co-opting of post-menopausal females for infant care in support of food-gathering mothers (Mithen, 2006, p. 186).[43] For both sexes, there were presumably strong selection pressures for the evolution of the cooperative behaviour that underpins communal living, in the ultimate service of individual selfish advantage.

The adaptive benefits of the melodic-rhythmic synchronisation believed to have been characteristic of rituals in such communally living societies are discussed more fully in §2.5.2.

---

[43] The co-option of grandmothers, and aunts, is not unique to hominins, being found in a number of other animal species (Nicholas Bannan, personal communication).

2.3.3 Sexual Non-Dimorphism

The broader context for this issue is that the dynamics of male-female inter-action in *Mammalia* are shaped by gamete size, whereby females generally produce a limited number of eggs and carry the developing offspring; and males generally produce an unlimited number of sperm. This "quality *versus* quantity" dichotomy of reproductive investment (see also note 47 on page 79) tends to create systems whereby females are strongly focused upon the survival of their offspring, to whom they devote considerable time and en-ergy; and males are strongly motivated to mate with as many females as possible. Nevertheless, this dichotomy is not wholly deterministic, and the evolution of the hominin line indicates that other factors can moderate its more extreme implications.

High levels of sexual dimorphism – in the sense of pronounced body-size difference between the sexes, as observed in *Australopithecus afarensis* (Mithen, 2006, p. 123)[44] – tend to correlate with *polygyny*. This is a system whereby "harems" of females are controlled by dominant males (Mithen, 2006, p. 134), who compete violently with each other for female attention, as in Gorillas, or for the unencumbered liberty to force themselves upon females.[45] This type of dimorphism, as well as others, may have arisen as a result of sexual selection (§2.5.3), "operating through male-male competition, female choice, or a combination of both" (Mithen, 2006, p. 182). Thus – and augmenting the effect of the gamete-size dichotomy – the larger the male is in relation to the female, the greater the violence involved in competition between males, and the larger the number of sexual partners potentially available to the dominant male(s).

Starting with *Homo erectus/Homo ergaster* at *c*. 1.8 MYBP, the modern human male : female body size ratio of *c*. 1.2 : 1 became established, perhaps because males had reached the sustainable limits of their size and/or perhaps because

---

[44] This phenomenon constitutes a continuum, ranging from extreme sexual dimorphism to its complete absence, i.e., sexual monomorphism.

[45] Pronounced sexual dimorphism is not invariably associated with the "harem" type of mating system: it can alternatively correlate with a promiscuous multi-male/multi-female dynamic, as is the case in chimpanzees (Alan Harvey, personal communication).

females had almost caught up with them.[46] This equalisation appears to have been related, in part, to dietary factors: Merker notes that "postcanine dental size and the masticatory apparatus were reduced as well ..., implying a diminished need for oral processing. To be compatible with an increase in stature [especially in females] and brain expansion relative to body size, this reduced need for oral processing indicates increased access to high quality nutrients", often high fat/high protein fish/shellfish (2012, pp. 233–234). Acquiring these foodstuffs in riverside, lakeside or coastal locations may have provided a selection pressure for the acquisition of swimming and diving, and may even have fostered a semi-aquatic lifestyle (Merker, 2012, 237, note 4).

The lower levels of sexual dimorphism in *Homo erectus/Homo ergaster* appear to have correlated with "colonial monogamy" (Merker, 2012, p. 235) – whereby communities of conspecifics live in reasonably stable pair-bonds and form members of extended family units. This structure may have arisen for two interconnected reasons. First, the "high quality nutrients" referred to above were "non-monopolizable" by dominant males (Merker, 2012, p. 234), meaning that subordinate males could avoid conflict with their more powerful rivals and concentrate instead upon "direct reproductive investment in a female and her offspring by provisioning them with high quality nutrients" (Merker, 2012, p. 234). Second, unable to dominate females physically – especially when the latter banded together for mutual protection – males needed to attract females and then provide food and care for them and their dependent children by means of the provisioning just referred to (Mithen, 2006, p. 187). While male-*versus*-male competition appears to have continued in these species after the reduction in sexual dimorphism, it was likely reorientated towards the domain of female choice.

Males in these species therefore needed to have used charm, not force, to advance their reproductive agenda, essentially by convincing females that they possessed good genes. Yet in this environment the attractiveness of a male to a female in many species is a result not only of: (i) an assessment of the male's genetic fitness (and thus his capacity to give a female gran-

---

[46] Bannan et al. (2023) consider the remaining *vocal* dimorphism, in the form of the disproportionately low male human voice and the associated phenomenon of octave equivalence, whereby adult male and female voices generally sing the "same" note an octave apart.

doffspring); but also of (ii) an assessment of the male's potential as a good parent (and thus of his capacity to help her care for her offspring to maturity). That these two roles may not necessarily be fulfilled by the *same* male is an explanation for deviations from monogamy in such pair-bonds (Fitch, 2010, pp. 245–247; see also page 400 below). Essentially, a female may mate with a short-term partner for his perceived good genes, but bond with a (different) long-term partner for his anticipated parental investment. Consequently, male commitment to the kind of extended involvement underpinning (ii) rests upon sufficient *paternal certainty*. In this environment, males evolved to provide for their offspring, but only when they could be reasonably certain – via various evolved counter-measures to female infidelity – that the infant they undertook to expend so much time and energy upon did indeed carry their own genes and not those of a rival (Fitch, 2010, p. 244).

As a further consequence of the reduction of sexual dimorphism, fitness-advertisement has significance for musicality because *much of this female-directed persuasion may have taken the form of vocalisation and dancing* (Mithen, 2006, p. 187). As manifestations of cognitive and physical capacity, and thus as useful markers of male genetic fitness, such performances may well have become currencies implicated in sexual selection (G. Miller, 2000, pp. 338–344) (§2.5.3), in addition to their fostering group cohesion (§2.3.2). To summarise a complex chain of interconnected causes and effects, one which attenuates the effects of gamete-size dichotomy, the available evidence suggests that: (i) the better the quality of nutritional resources became, the closer in size the female evolved in relation to the male; (ii) the more equal among themselves males became, partly on account of their becoming more adept at foraging, the more persuasive their courtship behaviour became; and (iii) the more durable pair-bonds became, the more cooperative – and perhaps the more musical – the relationships between the sexes became.

2.3.4 Infant Altriciality

Another consequence of bipedalism (§2.3.1) was that it tended to reduce infant birth-size in hominins, compared with non-bipedal primates, on account of the associated repositioning of the birth-canal. This resulted in increasing *altriciality* in hominin infants – i.e., the requirement for several years of nurture, on account of their helplessness, before they become in-dependent of their parents (Mithen, 2006, p. 185; see also Werneburg et al., 2016). The provisioning-sustained co-parenting discussed in §2.3.3 afforded an environment in which this nurture could be provided, allowing early weaning and replacement of breast milk with foraged high fat/high protein nutrients (Merker, 2012, p. 235).[47] As Dissanayake argues, "[t]he trend toward increasingly helpless infants surely created intense selective pressure for proximate physiological and cognitive mechanisms to ensure longer and better maternal care" (2000, p. 390).

Decreasing birth-size was associated with a countervailing tendency to *en-cephalisation*, i.e., towards increasing absolute and/or relative brain size (Dis-sanayake, 2000, p. 390). The *encephalisation quotient* (EQ) formalises relative brain size by calculating the ratio of body size : brain size for a group of species and then calculates the difference (or "residual") between this group and a target species. The EQ metric shows that "humans have high positive residuals or EQ values, no matter which group we use as the comparison set .... Our brains are roughly three times larger than predicted for an ape of our size" (Fitch, 2010, p. 281). Because decreasing (overall) birth-size is an imperfect attempt on the part of evolution to compensate for increasing head-size, it follows that encephalisation must have had adaptive benefits, to genes and/or to memes, which outweighed its birth-related risks to mother and infant. The evidence discussed in §2.7.5 and §3.7.1 suggests that those benefits accrued disproportionately to memes.

Extended parental care is thought to have included various proto/musiling-uistic vocalisations – gentle, reassuring singing – of the type discussed in §2.7. Such infant-directed *singing* and infant-directed *speech* – IDS[inging/peech], the latter sometimes called "motherese" and, despite its predominance in fe-males, "parentese" – was perhaps partly motivated by the inability of human infants, unlike those of other primates, to cling to their mothers until they are several years old. The consequence of the evolution of infant altriciality, an additional factor here is the gradual loss of fur in hominins. While modern great ape females often use their hands while their young infants cling to

---

[47] Merker argues that this lifestyle permitted the shortening of inter-birth intervals, allowing "*K*-selected" – quality-over-quantity reproduction; the converse, as in insects, is *r*-selection – apes to maximise their "reproductive output" (2012, p. 235).

their fur (Falk, 2004, p. 499), humans, while retaining some body hair, are, as Morris (1967) famously said, "the naked ape". Owing to these two factors, and to the additional complication of the predominantly vertically orientated back and belly of a bipedal species (Falk, 2004, p. 499), for a female hominin to undertake manual work, such as gathering food, it would have been necessary (in the absence of grandmothering (§2.3.2)) for her to place her infant on the ground. To provide comfort and reassurance to infants in such situations of separation, hominin vocalisations may have taken the place, at times, of an embrace (Patel, 2008, p. 370). This use of music as a proxy for physical contact is analogous to the vocal grooming hypothesis discussed below, whereby vocalisation uses the diffusion properties of sound (which, unlike those of light, are non-rectilinear) to compensate for the absence of direct physical proximity.

The adaptive benefits of IDS are discussed more fully in §2.5.4.

2.3.5 Vocal Grooming

Another significant driver of sociality, beyond the "strength-in-numbers" and rhythmic synchronisation arguments discussed in §2.3.2, is the vocal grooming hypothesised by Aiello and Dunbar (1993) and Dunbar (2017) to have underpinned social relationships in hominin societies. A common behaviour in primates is ritualised physical contact, in the form of reciprocal "stroking and patting" (Dunbar, 2017, p. 209), termed grooming. This appears to foster one-to-one networks of social relationships based on affection and trust, these dispositions arising in part from the release of endorphins triggered by this contact (Dunbar, 2017, p. 209).[48] As hominin social groups increased in size (§2.3.2), it became more difficult for such grooming-fostered networks to

---

[48] While several neurotransmitters are implicated in the response to music, and thus may be evolutionarily significant, Harvey, in contrast to Dunbar, foregrounds the role of oxytocin – an "ancient peptide" that is "highly conserved in evolution" – in "pair-bonding and maternal attachment, in moderating affiliative behaviors and conspecific social recognition, and in modulating the formation and maintenance of episodic memories, whether they be positive or negative" (2020, pp. 3, 5). Overlaps between the physiological and psychological effects of oxytocin and the psychological and social effects of music and dancing suggest causal linkages, such that "the unique prosocial, harmonizing activities of music and dance incorporated, perhaps even required, elements of [a] pre-existing oxytocinergic network" (2020, p. 5). Harvey's inclusion of pair-bonding and maternal attachment as behaviours "rewarded" by oxytocin suggests that the peptide's role in human evolution encompasses aptive dimensions in addition to social bonding, including those considered in §2.5.3 and §2.5.4. See also Savage et al. (2021, p. 10, Fig. 3; pp. 11–12) and note 60 on page 97.

be sustained, owing to the difficulty of individuals finding sufficient time to service a growing number of relationships in daylight hours, a period of the day that also had to be devoted to other survival-critical activities. Dunbar hypothesises that one-to-one physical grooming was gradually supplemented with, and eventually supplanted by, one-to-many vocal grooming (Fitch, 2010, pp. 417–420). In this way, musilinguistic vocalisations allowed one individual efficiently to interact with multiple others, maximising that individual's pay-off in the form of gene-advantageous reciprocal attention and affiliation.

The evolution of vocal grooming involved breaking a number of evolutionary "glass ceilings" (Dunbar, 2017, p. 209). In a first stage, and building on Provine (2001), Dunbar hypothesises that one-to-one grooming was expanded to encompass groups of around three individuals by the evolution of laughter in communities of *Homo ergaster* and *Homo erectus* (2017, p. 210). As with physical grooming, laughter – a form of "wordless, amusical chorusing" that is physiologically different in humans compared with great apes (Dunbar, 2017, p. 210)[49] – triggers the endorphin release necessary for social bonding, but has the efficiency advantage of engaging multiple conspecifics.[50]

In a second stage, the larger social groups typical of *Homo sapiens* rendered laughter alone inadequate to address the vocal grooming demands necessary to maintain the cohesion of social networks. Dunbar hypothesises that laughter was therefore supplemented by musilinguistic vocalisations – "singing, or musical chorusing" – that built upon and extended the "segmentation and breath control" underpinning laughter and that engaged a larger number of conspecifics (2017, p. 210). Such vocalisations also took advantage of various anatomical changes – again, as cause or effect – that arose in the modern human vocal tract. These include: (i) certain enhancements in nerve structure related to breath control and tongue movement; (ii) the repositioning of the hyoid bone, which lowered the larynx and poten-

---

[49] Great ape laughter is made up of patterns of exhalation-inhalation, whereas human laughter is purely exhalatory (Dunbar, 2017, p. 210). Perhaps this is one of the senses in which we should understand bb. 25–28 of the Queen of the Night's (second) aria (no. 14, "Der Hölle Rache") from Mozart's *Die Zauberflöte* K. 620 (1791).

[50] Note that laughter is not dependent upon language. While language is a medium and catalyst for the most sophisticated categories of humour, the earliest forms of laughter are likely to have been the result of the non-injurious pratfalls that befell hapless conspecifics (Dunbar, 2017, p. 210).

tially facilitated greater articulatory control (§2.3.1); and (iii) refinements in ear-canal structure to optimise it for the perception (and thus also production-enhancement) of vocalisations (Dunbar, 2017, p. 210). As perhaps the key factor underpinning the socialisation processes outlined in §2.3.2, "singing triggers the same endorphin mechanism as grooming and laughter, *and* at the same time increases the sense of belonging or social bonding" (Dunbar, 2017, p. 210; emphasis in the original).

In a third stage, Dunbar argues for the importance of fire – consolidated, it would appear, by *c.* 0.400 BP – in augmenting the power of singing-driven vocal grooming (2017, p. 211). Mithen suggests that the discovery of fire as a source of warmth led to the gradual reduction in hominin body hair density. This facilitated thermoregulation in hot climates (§2.3.1) and reduced the need for physical grooming to remove skin and hair parasites, thus allowing more time to focus on vocal grooming (2006, pp. 199–200). Fire, and the building of hearths to control it, also lengthens the usable day and divides it into the work-time of the daylight hours and the social-time of the evening. The latter period may have served as a congenial forum for communal vocalisation and therefore facilitated the evolution of language, because "if wordless chorusing began to be used to allow communal chorusing on a conversational or even camp-wide scale, it would have provided a natural template for the evolution of voiced speech, and hence language, by the very short additional step of mapping meaning onto sound" (Dunbar, 2017, p. 211). While Dunbar perhaps underestimates the enormous intellectual leap represented by his "very short additional step" – from the distorting perspective of our present position, it is tempting to see this likely chronologically extended and epistemologically cumulative process in terms of a single conceptual shift – this hypothesis of the attaching of meaning to components of segmented vocalisations appears evolutionarily convincing, partly owing to its parsimony. It is discussed further, with the necessary cautions, in §2.7.5 and §2.7.6.

Fire as a means of cooking food may have had further evolutionary consequences on hominin musicality related to changes in jaw morphology and associated dentition (§2.3.1). These may have arisen because the softening through cooking of previously unpalatable foods, primarily fibrous vegetable matter and tough meats (the latter made more accessible as a result of savannah-dwelling), perhaps increasingly favoured an omnivorous diet, rather than the herbivorous-insectivorous diet thought to have been consumed by the partly arboreal *Australopithecus afarensis* (Mithen, 2006, p. 123). Cooking thus made available a wider range of nutrients to hominins, allowing, some have argued, both the shrinkage of the gut and the allocation of greater resources to the brain (Wrangham, 2009; Patel, 2018, p. 114; see also Fernández-Armesto, 2001 for other potentially evolutionarily significant methods of food preparation that extend the diet without the use of heat). Jaw and dentition changes might also have had effects on sound-production, owing to their reconfiguration of the pharyngeal space. More radically – switching hypothesised cause and effect – the evolution of vocalisation might have itself driven changes to the structure of the jaw, owing to its adaptive benefits, which subsequently motivated certain dietary changes.

2.4 Sound Archaeology as Evidence for Hominin Musicality

Having outlined in the previous section the various evolutionary opportunities and motivations for musicality, it is reasonable to ask what evidence survives for its having existed in hominin communities. Sources of evidence include findings from the disciplines of *music archaeology* (a term that has largely superseded *archaeomusicology* (Hickmann, 1984)), and *archaeoacoustics* (Scarre & Lawson, 2006). The former, which focuses on the reconstruction and performance of very ancient instruments, has been developed since the 1980s; the latter, which attempts to analyse and reconstruct the likely sound environments of the ancient sites whose material environment is the province of music archaeology, is a more recent discipline (Till, 2014, pp. 292–294). Archaeoacoustics recognises that the concept of music is problematic when considering ancient cultures. As noted in §2.2, the modern western aestheticised notion of music does not align with the holistic use of vocalisation, dance and ritual observed in contemporary traditional cultures and which, by inference, may well have obtained in ancient human societies (Till, 2014, p. 293). Till advocates the use of the term *sound archaeology* for these research strands because it "includes research framed by [music archaeology and archaeoacoustics] as well as research excluded by them" (2014, p. 300).

The underlying rationale of sound archaeology is the notion that, initially, hominins selected their living and ritual spaces not only because they afforded protection from harmful aspects of the environment – both climatic and in terms of predators – but also because they were acoustically rich and/or unusual, maximising the sensory and aesthetic pleasure of music-making. Moreover, later built environments – for example, stone circles such as Stonehenge and other ritual auditoria, and Classical-era theatres – had a similar sensitivity to their acoustic properties. Growing human knowledge of acoustics (in an informal sense) led to the gradual supplanting of the *discovery* of sonically rich spaces by their active *construction* based on the intuitions of sonic-architectural principles (Till, 2019, p. 689; see also Till, 2017).

Sound archaeology attempts to reconstruct the sonic ecologies of ancient human societies using both analytical and synthetic methodologies. Analysis involves the exploration of sound-spaces by means of acoustic measurements of spatialisation and reverberation, allowing hypotheses to be developed on the kinds of vocalisations, instruments and musical behaviours the space might have supported or optimised – its affordances for musicality. These measurements are sometimes used to develop virtual models of acoustic spaces, which can then facilitate further simulation (Till et al., 2014a; Till et al., 2014b). Synthesis permits the testing of hypotheses on sonic ecologies by creating opportunities for present-day musicians to emulate possible styles and sonorities of ancient musics by techniques including vocalisation and performance on reconstructed instruments in original archaeological contexts, or to reconfigure recording-studio performances to sound as if there were performed in a specific ancient space (Potengowski & Wagner, 2017). The two dimensions may be combined to create a "multimedia time machine", as in the audiovisual *Soundgate* exhibit (and its associated app) that forms a component of the *European music archaeology project* (Various, 2015) touring exhibition *Archaeomusica: The sounds and music of ancient Europe* (De Angeli et al., 2018). The exhibition's bold aim is to transport present-day humans to the distant soundscapes of their ancestors by means of "phenomenological multi-sensory immersive experiences, which allow one to explore an archaeological site by virtual immersion within it" (Till, 2014, p. 294).

Studies of palaeolithic cave acoustics are most relevant to the concerns of this chapter, given that caves formed sites of both habitation and ritual for hominins: it is thought that the outermost parts of cave-complexes (near the entrance) were used for the former, whereas the innermost parts were used for the latter (Fazenda et al., 2017, p. 1339). Fazenda et al. (2017) explore Reznikoff's (2002) hypothesis that there is an association between cave "motifs" – the former's term for various intentionally made shapes and images carved or painted on cave walls, sometimes termed cave "paintings" or, perhaps anachronistically, cave "art" – and the acoustic properties of the adjacent spaces. This is potentially significant because "[t]he acoustic ecology of a space is part of what turns a space into a place" (Till, 2014, p. 295) – transforming an ostensibly neutral void into a meaningful environment in which, for instance, rituals might be performed. Indeed, Till notes that

> [t]he deeper parts of caves provided a very particular and powerful acoustic for humans in Palaeolithic times. In an animist cosmology, the lack of background and environmental noise differentiated caves from outdoor spaces. With no experience of stone buildings, these were alien natural spaces that featured variable reverberation, low frequency effects, and transformation of sounds made by human speech and movement. These were natural formations[;] humans entered into them, becoming enveloped by these other worlds' acoustics, going into an environment over which they had no control, leaving as a record of their presence visual motifs charged with spiritual meanings, and engaging with altered states and what they probably regarded as powerful supernatural forces. (Till, 2019, p. 689)

The hypothesised chronology of painting and musicality does not rule out such juxtapositions of visual imagery and music: Aubert et al. (2019) date a cave painting in Sulawesi, Indonesia at *c.* 0.044 MYBP; and Fitch (2006, p. 197) dates the earliest human music, perhaps conservatively, to *c.* 0.040 MYBP (§2.6). This is not to say that such images were necessarily functionally associated with music-making, but there is certainly the potential for some form of coexistence between the two. Indeed, any functional relationship – which the acoustic evidence discussed below to some extent supports – might suggest that Fitch (2006) is being too conservative in his dating, and that the earliest human music might potentially be nearer to *c*. 0.044 MYBP than to *c*. 0.040 MYBP. Because the rituals of hominins are likely to have involved rhythmically coordinated dance and vocalisation, any evidence that they were performed in sonically rich and/or unusual spaces, with or without an association with imagery, affords further support for the special importance of these musilinguistic practices.

To test Reznikoff's (2002) hypothesis that "the location for a rock painting was chosen to a large extent because of its sound value" (Fazenda et al., 2017, p. 1334), Fazenda et al. (2017) conducted a study of a number of palaeolithic caves in northern Spain that were decorated with painted motifs. They used twenty-three metrics designed to give a comprehensive account of the acoustic fingerprint of the caves, and concluded that "there is statistical, although weak, evidence, for an association between acoustic responses measured within these caves and the placement of motifs", specifically an "association between the position of motifs, particularly dots and lines, and places with low frequency resonances and moderate reverberation" (2017, p. 1347). This supports Till's observation, apropos the same caves, that "[s]ome lithophones, rocks that ring when struck, were already known in the caves, and one was marked with paint in prehistory" (2014, p. 299). The latter point suggests that the converse of Reznikoff's hypothesis – that the location for musical behaviours was chosen to a large extent because of its graphical-imagistic potential – was not the case.

In a later study, Till (2019) explores further the data from the Spanish caves in Fazenda et al. (2017) and compares them with data from other sites, namely Stonehenge and the Graeco-Roman theatre at Paphos on Cyprus, plus acoustic data from modern concert halls. The findings are, predictably, complex and nuanced, but they broadly align with those of Fazenda et al. (2017). One of the main conclusions – as the passage from Till (2019) quoted on page 85 suggests – is that many spaces in the caves have very resonant, reverberant acoustics, particularly favouring low-frequency sounds, as measured by the EDT (Early Decay Time) metric. The "strong low frequency support" (Till, 2019, p. 688) provided by such acoustics would have modulated the normal human voice, particularly the male voice, giving it a transformative, mystical intensity and power, thus intensifying the cathartic-spiritual dimension engendered by the caves' other-wordly environment. The affinity between such "amplified" sounds – Till describes them as "alive, or even larger than life" (2019, p. 690) – and deeply resonant natural sounds, such as thunder, perhaps further dissolved the imagined boundary between the natural and the supernatural and gave hominins access to the intense experiences afforded by contact with the sublime.

Till also argues that "speech is clear when judged using [the] ALcons [Articulation Loss of consonants metric] or [the] RASTI [Room Acoustic Speech Transmission Index metric], but at different octaves identified by [the] C (50) [speech clarity metric], clarity of speech can be either extremely high or low, indicating speech is understandable, but may be changed by support or transformation of one or other frequency range" (2019, p. 688). Of course such a statement is intrinsically problematic, because Till is using metrics designed for the analysis of speech sounds at a time when it is likely that only (or primarily) musilinguistic vocalisations were in the repertoire of hominins. One might nevertheless conclude that these data suggest that – in some caves, using certain metrics, and at certain frequency ranges[51] – the acoustics certainly afford sufficient clarity to support not only the perception of melodic contour but also that of consonants. Thus, they do not actively militate against the segmentation of musilanguage to form compositional language, in which the articulation of consonants is implicated – a process that, in any case, may have taken place primarily outside cave environments. Beyond issues of clarity, the favouring of low-frequency sounds might suggest that male, not female, vocalisations took precedence in cave-based rituals. Moreover, and aside from vocalisations in sacral contexts, the general modulation of the normal "outdoor" human voice by the acoustics of caves created opportunities for vocal play – the acoustic equivalent of exploring a hall of mirrors – that supported the kind of cognitive expansion via musical scaffolding hypothesised by Cross (2012) to have been central to our evolution, to be discussed in §2.5.4.

Of course, such studies as Fazenda et al. (2017) and Till (2019) are far from conclusive, offering only tantalising evidence for ritualistic music-dance

---

[51] In the La Garma cave, for instance, C50 clarity is good from 125Hz – within the range of a male voice – and above (Till, 2019, p. 685, Tab. 7).

behaviours in motif-adorned, resonant caves. But they certainly align with the hypothesised flowering of human cognitive-symbolic behaviour to be discussed below under the rubric of the "Cognitive Revolution" (§2.5.5). Even more conjecturally, there appears to be a degree of sensory-modality correlation between the "dots and lines" of some cave paintings identified by Fazenda et al. (2017, p. 1347) and their equivalents in music. Understood in terms of *image schemata* – metaphorical alignments between perceptions and conceptions of phenomena in two domains (§2.5.2) – "dots and lines" are arguably (and potentially retrospective) synchronic, visual equivalents of the diachronic, aural punctuations marked out in time by a regular rhythmic pulse and the rises and falls of musilinguistic vocalisations. If the suggestion made on page 86 concerning the potential precedence of music over images ("the converse of Reznikoff's hypothesis") is true, then "dots and lines" are consequent, not antecedent, to music.

2.5 The Aptive Benefits of Musicality

One issue that arises when considering music in the evolutionary context summarised in §2.3 is its often considerable biological costs. Singing and dancing in early hominin societies would have consumed a significant amount of time and energy, which might have been better spent on acquiring food or on resting. Assuming that such societies lived under constant pressure, often on the edge of survival, it is reasonable to assume that the suite of competences constituting musicality had either: (i) some *adaptive* aetiology – i.e., cost-exceeding benefits in enhancing survival that were *directly* selected for; or (ii) some *exaptive* aetiology – i.e., cost-exceeding benefits in enhancing survival that were *indirectly* selected for, being (possibly staggered) re-purposings of competences originally evolved for some other purpose; or (iii) some combination of adaptive and exaptive aetiologies.[52] An alternative view, Pinker's "auditory cheesecake" hypothesis (§1.1.2), is that: (iv) music arose merely for amusement and titillation, a situation that would only hold true in societies that lived with surpluses of resources, including

---

[52] It will be understood that, hitherto, I have used the term "adaptation" largely indiscriminately, potentially encompassing cases that are more likely to be exaptations than true adaptations. From the explanation of the distinction given in §2.5.1 onwards, I will, wherever possible, distinguish between the two cases.

time. Assuming that early hominins made music in varying conditions of adversity, it is reasonable to infer that musicality conferred some advantage upon them (and perhaps continues to do so today, even in affluent societies), and therefore an adaptive and/or exaptive explanation is the most likely.

What follows is a discussion of perhaps the three most significant ways in which musicality might have contributed to the survival of early hominins, this being undertaken with the proviso (given in §2.2) that many of the competences discussed would have had wider benefits, including those pertaining to the evolution of motor skills, of audition, of language (§2.7), and of other attributes. Naturally, it draws upon several of the themes outlined in §2.3, expanding upon the potentially *aptive* – this term is explained in the next section – role of music in the various developmental stages outlined there. It also accords with (but treats in a different order) the three "adaptationist explanations" for musicality – sexual selection, parent-infant bonding, and group cohesion – identified in (Honing, 2018a, p. 9). On the question of ordering, and as noted in §2.3, it is difficult to ascertain the detailed evolutionary chronology of these phenomena, which would almost certainly have interacted synergystically. The discussion concludes with a summary (§2.5.5) that nevertheless attempts to extrapolate an evolutionary trajectory for musicality from the aptation-based evidence currently available.

2.5.1 Aptation, Adaptation and Exaptation

In order to frame an evolutionary account of human musicality, G. Miller (2000) maintains that four questions need to be addressed.

> First, what is music *for*? Second, what adaptive *functions* are served by the specific behaviors of singing, chanting, humming, whistling, dancing, drumming, and instrument playing? Third, why did the fitness *benefits* of music making and music listening exceed the fitness *costs*? Fourth, consider music as a set of *signals* emitted to influence the *behavior* of other organisms …: who *generates* these signals, under what conditions, to what purpose? [W]ho *receives* these signals, with what sensitivity, resulting in what behavioral changes, benefiting whom? (G. Miller, 2000, p. 333; emphases mine)

One problem in addressing these questions is the fact that organisms live in an ever-changing physical and biological environment – one of often constant geological change and pressure from other (evolving) organisms – and so adaptation, driven by the VRS algorithm, is an attempt to track a constantly moving target, the ecological niche best suited to the survival of the organism in question. The considerable time-scales over which this process has occurred means that some adaptations are left behind when the evolutionary world moves on. Sometimes these "floating" adaptations are subsequently found useful by organisms: they serve to enhance their fitness, and so they are thereby propagated. Rejecting the earlier term *preadaptation* on the grounds that evolution does not have foresight (Fitch, 2010, pp. 63–64), Gould and Vrba (1982), in a classic formulation, argue that

> we may designate as an *adaptation* any feature that promotes fitness and was built by selection for its current role (criterion of *historical genesis*). The operation of an adaptation is its *function*.... We may also follow [G.C.] Williams in labelling the operation of a useful character not built by selection for its current role as an *effect*.... But what is the unselec- ted, but useful character itself to be called? .... We suggest that such characters, evolved for other usages (or for no function at all), and later 'coopted' for their current role, be called *exaptations*.... They are fit for their current role, hence *aptus*, but they were not designed for it, and are therefore not *ad aptus*, or pushed towards fitness. They owe their fitness to features present for other reasons, and are therefore *fit (ap- tus) by reason of (ex)* their form, or *ex aptus*. (Gould & Vrba, 1982, p. 6; emphases in the original)

They go on to assert that "[t]he general, static phenomenon of being fit should be called *aptation*, not *adaptation*. (The set of aptations existing at any one time consists of two partially overlapping subsets: the subset of *adaptations* and the subset of *exaptations*....)" (Gould & Vrba, 1982, p. 6; emphases mine). This formulation to some extent addresses the critique of adaptationism, in a famous paper, by Gould and Lewontin (1979). The latter argued that adaptationism had gone too far in biology, and that biologists were too keen to see every feature of an organism, in a "Panglossian" manner, as adaptive.[53] For Gould and Lewontin (1979), some features of organisms

---

[53] This term derives from the character of Doctor Pangloss in Voltaire's *Candide* of 1759, who – satirising Leibniz – uncritically exalts the optimism resulting from belief in a benevolent designer,

were not adaptations; rather, they were *spandrels*[54] – that is, by-products of the evolutionary process that, in themselves, served no adaptive purpose. Inverting the adaptive argument, Dennett argues that spandrels/pendentives might indeed have been adaptive, not exaptive, arising as surfaces upon which religious iconography – made up of "graphemes" or graphical memes (in written or artistic symbology) – could be displayed (1995, p. 274). This issue is, in part, an element of the critique of Darwinism advanced by Fodor and Piattelli-Palmarini (2011). If one accepts the position of Gould and Lewontin (1979), five possibilities present themselves: (i) a feature that was adapted retains its original utility; (ii) a feature that was adapted loses its original utility; (iii) a feature that was adapted loses its original utility and is subsequently exapted; (iv) a feature that was not adapted (a spandrel) is not subsequently exapted; (v) a feature that was not adapted (a spandrel) is subsequently exapted.

Given the distinction formalised in Gould and Vrba (1982), it seems clear that all four of the questions posed by G. Miller (2000) in the quotation on page 89 might have an adaptive and/or an exaptive answer. This is not to say that these answers are easy to arrive at: the difficulty in developing an aptationist account of music/ality lies, in part, in identifying the nature of the advantages that might arise from it, because (for reasons outlined in §2.1) musicality – specifically its physical, neurological and psychological substrates – presumably overlapped with other evolutionarily useful "-alities", and so finding unequivocal and specific examples of adaptations and exaptations relevant to musicality is not straightforward. For instance, sound production in hominins is closely integrated with respiration, just as rhythmic movement is a function of locomotion. In the first example, the adaptations subserving breathing (the lungs and associated blood supply and musculature) were subsequently exapted to serve vocalisation in a number of species, serving to drive the flow of air into sound-producing organs (the larynx, in tetrapods) in ways that were not, presumably, their original adaptive motivation. Moreover, these vocalisations, which initially

---

maintaining that "in this best of all possible worlds ..., all is for the best" (Voltaire, 1918, pp. 2, 3).

[54] In architecture, a spandrel is a broadly triangular feature resulting from the enclosure of an arch within a square frame, or from the intersection of the base of a dome and the square formed by its supporting walls or arches. Strictly, what Gould and Lewontin (1979) term a spandrel might more correctly be termed a *pendentive* (Dennett, 1995, pp. 271–272).

may have served a relatively limited range of functions in primates, were likely further exapted in human prehistory to subserve what we might regard as musicality. We might thus assume that the VRS algorithm found it similarly difficult, or unnecessary, to disentangle what was a coordinated suite of survival-enhancing attributes. As always, evolution builds upon what is at hand to secure immediate survival: it does not plan ahead in order to ensure its trajectory is parsimonious or elegant.

I return to the distinction between adaptation and exaptation in §3.4.2, in the context of music-cultural evolution.

2.5.2 Rhythm, Sociality and Embodiment

While clubs, festivals, gigs and karaoke are a significant exception, for many people today music is a solitary pursuit. The growth of sound-reproduction technology from the early-twentieth century onwards has had the effect of increasingly personalising the listening experience, first reducing it to a few people huddled round a phonograph or radio and then restricting it to the entirely headphone-enclosed world of the personal music player and, most recently, the smartphone. While one might agree with Rosen that "[w]e take a work of music specifically written for a public concert as the norm, and we do not realize to what extent it is actually an anomaly in the history of music" (Rosen, 2001, pp. 300–301), much secular (and probably even more sacred) music was intended to be played to at least a small group of people, the former category perhaps in an aristocratic salon or intimate domestic gathering. While art music in Europe from the sixteenth to the nineteenth centuries was rarely either solitary or mass-participatory, it was generally *social*.[55]

The same appears to have been true of music in its earliest forms in hominin societies. Evidence suggests that music-making – which, as will be argued in §2.7, was also vocalisation-making and eventually language-making – was communal and participatory. It was a group activity in which all members of a hominin community were involved and through which, by the

---

[55] The same is arguably true of literature: in the eighteenth and nineteenth centuries, poetry and novels were often read aloud, performatively, the silent reading taken as normative today being unusual.

act of participation, belonging and investment in the group were cemented (Merker, 2000a; Merker, 2000b). Such communal vocalisation is not restricted to hominins: many other animals, including members of certain non-human primate, cetacean, canine and avian species "repeat (or at least mimic or vocally match as closely as they can)" conspecifics' utterances (Richman, 2000, pp. 309–310), so it appears to be a reasonably common aptation. Richman stresses that

> [f]or these animals this [matching] also is part of a strong biological drive to remain attached and stay in *behavioral synchrony* with others. Joint production of utterances and vocal matching of melodic contours function as signals in a group context that all participants are in behavioral synchrony, that they are in solidarity with each other, and that they are attempting to resolve social and emotional conflicts. (Richman, 2000, p. 310; emphasis mine)

As in the species discussed by Richman, such synchrony is thought to have been characterised in hominins by coordinated *rhythmic* movement and, for our ancestors, by the musical – vocal and percussive – behaviours that both impel and arise from it.[56] Indeed, what sets humans apart from other behaviourally synchronising primates is the fact that, for us, the rhythmic coordination often occurs in the context of a *constant* pulse, or *tactus* (Temperley, 2001, p. 26). A tactus is, in hominins, afforded by bipedalism (§2.3.1), which represents an embodied binarism whereby left-right alternations of arms and legs arise naturally in locomotion. Changizi (2011, p. 129) speaks of the harnessing of bipedalism to new functions, including the subdivision by the arms of the tactus provided by the legs, turning pulse into rhythm, with all the opportunities for elaboration – for rhythmic stratification (Yeston, 1976) – that it affords (see also Bannan, 1999, p. 9).

A tactus therefore provides the framework upon which both variable durations and/or unequal attack points in percussion and vocalisation can be built. To the natural tactus generated by the movement of the limbs, it appears that evolution added the phenomenon of (rhythmic) *entrainment*, whereby

---

[56] Borderline Personality Disorder (BPD) in modern humans is characterised by impaired socialisation and problems with emotional regulation. It is also marked by an inability to synchronise musically with others (Foubert et al., 2017), thus speaking to the tight connection between these three domains in normal humans (see also the quotation from Levitin (2009) on page 98).

conspecifics synchronise their movements to each other and to a regular external rhythmic stimulus, or to a shared stable internal pulse, in dance (Merchant et al., 2018, p. 171). Significantly, the "innate neural mechanisms underlying rhythmic entrainment ... seem to have evolved convergently in humans and several vocal-learning lineages of birds and mammals, but not in nonhuman primates ..." (Savage et al., 2015, p. 8989), suggesting a connection, explored below and in §2.7.5, between rhythmic entrainment and vocal learning. Nevertheless, the "gradual audiomotor evolution hypothesis" of Merchant and Honing (2014) argues that the picture is more nuanced than Savage et al. (2015) implies.

Considering the "ecological meaning of pitch", Changizi links rhythmic entrainment to the phenomenon of aural discrimination (2011, p. 159, Fig. 28; p. 161; see also Bannan, 2019, p. 10). He argues that humans learned to interpret the Doppler Effect – the change in frequency or wavelength when a sound-source is moving relative to an observer – as a method for determining the speed and direction of movement of environmental objects. While ostensibly an adaptation selected for its predator-evasion potential, the visceral sensitivity to contour it motivated was perhaps exapted to support sonic templates – "signatures of the Doppler effect" (Changizi, 2011, p. 161), serving as musico-emotional shape-archetypes – that, arguably, still underpin extant human musics. They might be understood in terms of image schemata (§4.2, §4.5), which are "fundamental embodied cognitive structures generalized from recurring physical experiences, especially the experience of our own bodies.... [Such schemata] include up and down, centrality, linkage, causation, tension, pathways leading to a goal, and containment" (Snyder, 2000, pp. 108, 110; see also Arndt, 2011, 96–97, Figs. 2a–2c). Thus, one consequence of rhythmically regulated group vocalisation is its tendency to reify patterning. It forms a framework that fosters repetition, "formulaicness" and expectancy – three attributes contributing to the redundancy that permits learning and transmission of information (Richman, 2000, p. 304). The resultant formulae, on account of their oft-repeated status, likely served to encode patterns of expectation – if the beginning of a formula was heard, its continuation and conclusion could generally be predicted.

As evidence for rhythmic entrainment/synchrony in humans, Patel notes that

> [i]n every culture, there is some form of music with a regular beat, a periodic pulse that affords temporal coordination between performers and elicits a synchronized motor response from listeners .... Humans are able to extract periodicities from complex auditory stimuli, and can focus their expectancies on periodicities at different hierarchical levels in music .... These periodic expectancies are the basis of motor synchronization to the beat on the part of listeners, as shown by the fact that listeners typically tap or move slightly *ahead* of the actual beat, indicating that synchronization is based on structured temporal anticipation .... [However,] there is not a single report of [a non-human] animal being trained to tap, peck, or move in synchrony with an auditory beat. (Patel, 2008, pp. 402, 403, 409; emphasis in the original)

The neural substrates underpinning structured temporal anticipation, or "synchronisation-continuation" (Merchant et al., 2018, p. 172), are found in several brain regions, both subcortical and cortical. The former include the "cerebellum,[57] the basal ganglia (most often the putamen,[58] but also caudate nucleus and globus pallidus), and thalamus ...". The latter include the "supplementary motor area (SMA) and pre-SMA, premotor cortex (PMC), as well as auditory cortex" (Merchant et al., 2018, pp. 173–174) (see also note 84 on page 153). These various regions are connected in a "motor cortico-basal-ganglia-thalamo-cortical (mCBGT) circuit" (Merchant et al., 2018, p. 183). It appears that, by means of the mCBGT, "auditory and motor regions connect through oscillatory activity, particularly at delta [1–3 Hz] and beta [15–30 Hz] frequencies, with motor regions providing the [top-down] predictive timing needed for the [bottom-up] perception of, and entrainment to, musical rhythms" (Merchant et al., 2018, pp. 179, 182).

Moreover, there is evidence that "small ensembles of interconnected neurons" in the SMA are "tuned" to sequential organisation in a manner seemingly analogous to the "tonotopic" tuning of specific cells in the auditory cortex to

---

[57] The cerebellum appears to subserve "absolute" timing (i.e., note-duration-based (rhythmic) timing), rather than the "relative" timing underpinning the perception of the tactus and associated metrical hierarchies (Merchant et al., 2018, pp. 174–175).

[58] The basal ganglia are subcortical structures, situated at the base of the cerebrum, on top of the midbrain (mesencephalon) (Johns, 2014, p. 40).

specific frequencies (via topographically aligned connections with corresponding frequency-sensitive regions of the cochlea), and the "phototopic" or "retinotopic" sensitisation of specific cells in the visual cortex to specific elements of the visual field (via topographically aligned connections with corresponding orientation-sensitive regions of the retina), discussed in §3.8.3 (Merchant et al., 2018, pp. 187–188). This "temporal and sequential information is multiplexed in a cell population signal across the mCBGT that works as the notes of a musical score in order to define the duration of the produced interval and its position in the learned … sequence" (Merchant et al., 2018, p. 188).

While the mCBGT circuit is found in all primates, studies underpinning the gradual audiomotor evolution hypothesis (Merchant & Honing, 2014) suggest that "the complex entrainment abilities of humans seem to have evolved gradually across primates, with a duration [rhythm]-based timing mechanism present across the entire primate order …, and a beat [metre]-based mechanism that is most developed in humans …" (Merchant et al., 2018, p. 172).[59] Similarly, Patel notes that "the basal ganglia subserve interval timing and motor control functions across a wide range of species, including primates and rodents …" (2008, p. 410; see also Fitch, 2010, pp. 365–366, who notes their hypothesised implication in the comprehension of syntax), so it is natural to ask what is special about our own species that allows us to entrain rhythmically when members of these other species (as the last sentence of the quotation from Patel (2008) on page 95 indicates) cannot.

Patel's answer, the "vocal learning and rhythmic synchronization hypothesis" (2008, p. 411), asserts that vocal learning – the ability "to produce vocal signals based on auditory experience and sensory feedback" (Patel, 2008, p. 410) (§2.7.5) – bootstrapped the capacity of the basal ganglia by fostering the "online integration of the auditory and motor system" (Patel, 2008, p. 410; see also Patel, 2018, p. 120). This integration connects systems for sound and motion *production* (vocalisation and periodic beat-generation, respectively) with those for sound and motion *perception* (audition and proprioception,

---

[59] The "beat-based mechanism … shows some of the properties [of the fully developed human system] in monkeys [specifically macaques], and is present at an intermediate level in chimpanzees" (Merchant et al., 2018, p. 172), the latter evidenced by the swaying-motion entrainment discussed in §5.3.4.

respectively) in a synergistic feedback loop.[60] The capacity for vocal learning is very rare among animals, appearing to exist only in *Homo sapiens*, certain birds and certain cetaceans (Patel, 2008, p. 410), the latter two groups being the most "musical" after our own species.[61] This issue is taken up in §2.7.5 (apropos humans) and in §5.4 (apropos non-human animals).[62]

Morley also foregrounds the close coordination between vocal and motor centres in the brain (2012, 128-–130), emphasising the strongly embodied and enactive aspects of musical and linguistic perception and production (see also Leman, 2008; Shapiro, 2011; Cox, 2016). More broadly, and as suggested in §2.2, "the integral importance of bodily movement in musical behavior has been overlooked in the way we define music in Western culture. Typically, hearers are also participants. What is atypical is silent and motionless listening" (Dissanayake, 2000, p. 397). Thus, unlike the often passive nature of the listening culture of "classical music" – which is often as static as it is solitary – the dancing-vocalisation of early hominins was in all probability urgently and relentlessly physical. While aptive on account of its general group-bonding effects, the social synchrony engendered by rhythmic synchrony served a number of specific, interconnecting functions, including labour-enhancement (this surviving in modern-day work-songs), defensive alignment (persisting in modern-day marching music), and religious intensification. For these visceral reasons, music today continues to impel movement and synchronisation in its participants, as seen most strongly –

---

[60] As with the role of oxytocin discussed in note 48 on page 80, there is a likely neurochemical basis for rhythmic anticipation and entrainment, in the form of the "reward" circuits associated with the neurotransmitter dopamine. Harvey notes that "[t]he limbic system, which includes the hippocampus, parahippocampal gyrus, amygdala, and cingulate cortex, is involved in several functions including *learning, memory, motivation and emotional responsiveness*. Music can induce activity in all these regions, while music that is perceived as arousing and is appreciated also drives dopaminergic activity in nucleus accumbens in the ventral striatum, an *anticipatory and reward center*" (2020, p. 6; emphases mine). In short, there is an affective pay-off in entraining to a tactus, one in synergy with the warm prosociality motivated by the release of oxytocin when this entrainment is communal. See also Savage et al. (2021, p. 10, Fig. 3; p. 11).

[61] Counter-evidence to the vocal learning and rhythmic synchronization hypothesis – or certainly evidence counter to the last sentence of the previous paragraph – may be found in the case of the California sea lion (*Zalophus californianus*), which, while not considered a vocal learner, is nevertheless able to entrain to an external rhythmic stimulus (P. Cook et al., 2013).

[62] Additional evidence for this connection, in the form of a motor-vocal link between movement prediction and precise sound control, may be found in the capacity of birds (§5.4.1), dolphins and seals – all capable, to varying degrees, of vocal learning – to intercept moving objects and, as far as is known, the absence of this capacity in the non-vocal-learning apes (Nicholas Bannan, personal communication).

apropos the last of the aforementioned three purposes – in the quasi-religious, trance-inducing dance cultures of many contemporary popular musics (Till, 2010) and their homologues in extant indigenous hunter-gatherer societies. The *motion* motivated by music, individually and as part of a group, is also inherently *emotional*, for according to Levitin,

> [w]hat we call emotions are nothing more than complex neurochemical states in the brain that motivate us to act. Emotion and motivation are thus intrinsically linked to each other, and to our motor centers. But the system can work in the other direction, because most neural pathways are bi-directional. In addition to emotions causing us to move, movement can make us feel emotional. (Levitin, 2009, p. 54)

Augmenting the process by which we can sometimes help ourselves to feel more cheerful simply by smiling, the collective "e/motion" of rhythmically synchronised communal music-making serves powerfully to enhance emotion, binding a group together by means of an intense feeling of shared purpose. According to Tarr et al. (2014, p. 6), this results from the synergy between two interconnected mechanisms: "self-other merging" resulting from synchrony (an important component of the quasi-religious states referred to above); and the motivating release of endorphin (and, *pace* Harvey (2020), oxytocin and dopamine; note 48 on page 80, and note 60 on page 97, respectively) resulting from such synchronised physical-social activity.

It is clear that anything that binds individuals into a community – in this case emotionally intense musilinguistic and physically coordinated vocalisations – is likely to offer a survival advantage to the individual and thus be aptive. This is because cooperation – the one being protected by the many, in return for individual contribution to the collective – is often more successful than a solitary existence. Assuming the presence of a neural "system for processing and keeping track of social contracts" (Carruthers, 2002, p. 663) (§3.8.1), the dynamics of such groups tend to reward limited self-sacrifice/denial and to penalise individual acts of selfish transgression. This is not to argue for a group-selection (§1.6.2) hypothesis in such cases, although some do in this connection (Levitin, 2009, p. 45). Rather, it is to say that individual selfishness is often best served by the kinds of altruistic acts group living requires to function effectively (discussed in §3.7 under the rubric of "game theory"). Indeed, G. Miller (2000, p. 352) argues strongly against group selectionism as an force in the evolution of human musicality, advocating instead sexual selection – considered in the following section – as its principal driver (§2.5.3). Nevertheless, he argues that "if music did have individual-level benefits, such as courtship benefits under sexual selection, it may be possible for group selection to reinforce them with group benefits" (2000, p. 352).

2.5.3 Sexual Selection

The elaborate tail-feathers of the Indian peacock (*Pavo cristatus*) and of other peafowl species, which overwhelm those of the peahen in size and coloration, represent the *locus classicus* of sexual selection theory. This concerns

> the process by which individuals compete for access to mates and fertiliz-ation opportunities .... Darwin (1871 [(Darwin, 2004)]) developed the concept of sexual selection to explain the evolution of exaggerated and flamboyant characters such as calls, odors, ornaments, and conspicuous behaviors that are present in one sex only and cannot be easily explained as adaptations to the ecological conditions of a species. (Kuijper et al., 2012, p. 288)

The mechanisms underpinning sexual selection are especially complicated because, unlike natural selection, sexual selection requires the coevolution of two traits: the (usually male) *ornament* (i.e., the "calls, odors, ornaments, and conspicuous behaviors") and the (usually female) *preference for the ornament*. These traits exist in a state of "linkage disequilibrium" (LD), where there is "a nonrandom association of alleles at two or more loci" (Slatkin, 2008, p. 477). That is, in the case of sexual selection, the alleles for the ornament and those for the preference are associated in a population at a frequency that is higher than that which might be expected on the basis of purely random linkage. In one of the first systematic treatments of the subject, Fisher (1915) hypothesised that

> female preferences could evolve through a self-reinforcing runaway pro-cess. Fisher argued that, once a female preference for a certain ornament has gained a foothold in a population (for whatever reason), both the preference and the ornament are subject to positive selection, but for

different reasons. *For the ornament*, the argument is simple: Ornamented males will have a mating advantage if sufficiently many females mate preferentially with such males. *For the preference*, the argument is more sophisticated because selection on the preference is indirect. Because females with a strong preference tend to mate with males with a pronounced ornament, preference and ornament alleles often co-occur in the offspring of such matings, leading to a statistical association [i.e., a linkage disequilibrium] among these alleles. As a consequence, [direct] positive selection on the ornament will induce correlated [indirect] positive selection on the preference. Hence, preferences induce the evolution of ornaments and subsequently become selected owing to their association with the ornament. Fisher realized that this self-reinforcing process could explain the huge exaggeration of sexual ornaments observed in many organisms. Interestingly, Fisher's arguments apply to arbitrary ornaments. In other words, ornaments that evolved through the so-called Fisher process do not necessarily indicate any inherent quality of their bearers. (Kuijper et al., 2012, p. 290; emphases mine)

It took until the 1980s for Fisher's qualitative verbal articulation of the mechanisms underpinning sexual selection, initially not fully accepted, to be modelled quantitatively using computer simulations (Kuijper et al., 2012, p. 290). Four approaches have been developed to this end: (i) population genetics; (ii) quantitative genetics; (iii) invasion analysis; and (iv) individual-based simulations (summarised in Kuijper et al., 2012, pp. 290–291). The first "directly models the evolutionary dynamics in terms of changing genotype frequencies" (2012, p. 289). The second "describes evolution at the phenotypic level but still takes account of genetics . . . , thus yielding plausible assumptions on the transmission of phenotypic traits from parents to their offspring" (2012, p. 293). The third is focused on situations where populations are "repeatedly challenged by the invasion attempts of rare mutants. . . . evolution proceeds by a series of subsequent invasion and trait-substitution events" (2012, p. 294). The fourth "keeps track of a finite population of [virtual] individuals, each of which has a set of properties (e.g., genotypes, sex, degree of preference, degree of ornamentation)" (2012, p. 291).

Zahavi and Zahavi (1997) relate sexual selection to what they term the "handicap principle". Contradicting the assertion in the quotation on page 99 that "ornaments that evolved through the so-called Fisher process do not necessarily indicate any inherent quality of their bearers", this is the notion that by investing resources into such displays, an organism is indicating that it can cope with the "handicap" this investment entails, on account of the organism's having sufficient genetic wherewithal – in part the result of an unimpeded developmental trajectory (Merker, 2012, p. 226) – to shoulder the burden the handicap imposes. In Miller's formulation, "an indicator [i.e., an ornament] must have a higher relative cost to an unfit animal than it does to a highly fit animal", leading to the "apparent paradox that animals advertise their fitness with displays that, being most costly, most reduce their fitness" (2000, p. 339). The handicap principle relates to the wider issue of *signalling* (in its broadest sense) by organisms as a means of communicating with each other, and the associated tendency, in some situations, for organisms to use "dishonest" (false, deceptive) signals for their own evolutionary advantage (discussed in §3.7). A sexually selected ornament, like other types of handicap, represents an "honest" signal, on account of its genuine and unavoidable – nevertheless bearable – costliness to the organism that possesses it.

As outlined in the quotation on page 99, the Fisher process hypothesises that selection on the (male) ornament is *direct* whereas selection on the (female) preference is *indirect*. The benefits to a female may themselves be either direct or indirect. *Direct* benefits accrue to a female in the form of her own fecundity, because the genetic health conveyed by the honest signals of the handicapping ornament benefits her genes by helping to create strong offspring (Kuijper et al., 2012, p. 297). *Indirect* benefits accrue to a female in the form of the likelihood of her having grandchildren as a result of: *not only* (i) mating with a genetically robust male (the direct benefit); *but also* (ii) mating with a male whose genes are able to produce a successful female-wooing ornament in any male child. Indeed, in what is sometimes termed the "sexy sons" hypothesis (Blackmore, 1999, p. 79), "[t]he key benefit associated with the Fisher process is a greater number of grandoffspring: [a]ccording to this theory, choosy females will produce attractive [i.e., convincingly ornamented] sons, which in turn will have a higher mating rate" (Kuijper et al., 2012, p. 297), thus potentially advantaging the female's genes further into the future than would be the case for the direct benefits alone.

Turning specifically to vocalisations (as opposed to other sexually selected attributes), sexual selection was for Darwin the most powerful factor in the origin of music (Fitch, 2010, pp. 490–492). He believed music played a significant role in enhancing the appeal (usually) of males to females at a stage in human evolution where coaxing rather than coercion had become the default context (§2.3.3). In *The descent of man, and selection in relation to sex* (Darwin, 2004), he argued – in a passage that also indicates his views on the (music-before-words hypothesis) origins of language (§2.7) – that

> [a]s the males of several quadrumanous[63] animals have their vocal or-
> gans much more developed than in the females, and as a gibbon, one of
> the anthropomorphous apes, pours forth a whole octave of musical notes
> and may be said to sing, it appears probable that the progenitors of man,
> either the males or females or both sexes, before acquiring the power
> of expressing their mutual love in articulate language, endeavoured to
> charm each other with musical notes and rhythm. (Darwin, 2004, p. 639)

Assuming that the sexual selection hypothesis is correct in principle and practice, and also assuming that "the [male] progenitors of man" did use music to "charm" their (female) mates – a probability Darwin extrapolates on the basis of the behaviour of various extant species of non-human primates (§5.3) – the issue for present purposes is whether the genetic underpinnings for sexually selected vocalisations in our hominin ancestors passed into the human line and, if they did, whether they formed, if not the sole, at least one basis for the evolution of human musicality (and possibly for the evolution of language competences). In other words, can human music be regarded as having been founded, in whole or in part, upon the kind of innate (gene-driven) calling and "conspicuous behaviors" (to recall the quotation on page 99) made by certain male non-human primates and, indeed, by the males of other species with sexually divergent vocalisations? Note that sexual selection is not necessarily a prerequisite for human musicality, because non-differentiated vocalisations (i.e., ones very similar across both sexes) could alone have formed a substrate for musicality. In the case of sexual selection, the argument is that, like the peacock's feathers, male vocal displays "supercharged" (and unbalanced) an evolutionary process that may in all likelihood already have been under way.

---

[63] Having four feet, all specialised for use as hands owing to opposable digits.

G. Miller (2000) argues that sexual selection played a central role in the evolution of human musicality, ranking it above (but not necessarily to the exclusion of) the other candidate explanations considered in this section (see also G. Miller (2001)). In humans, "complex psychological adaptations", such as music, are particularly effective ornaments, given their dependence upon a brain that consumes a substantial part of our genetic, ontological and ongoing energy resources (G. Miller, 2000, pp. 339–340). Nevertheless, such ornaments may initially arise as a result of aesthetic preferences – "psychological foibles" – on the part of the animal, leading Miller to distinguish between fitness-revealing indicators/ornaments and aesthetic displays (2000, pp. 341–342). The two categories are difficult to separate, however, because a trait initially selected on the basis of a random aesthetic preference may, through the Fisher process, subsequently be co-opted as a reliable indicator of fitness.

Miller's early work on music as a sexually selected adaptation came with a plea for "much more detailed quantitative data about music production and reception" (2000, p. 353), which, as discussed below, has indeed appeared in recent years. Writing initially in the absence of such data, he offers certain pieces of circumstantial evidence that might support the hypothesis. Taking Jimi Hendrix as an exemplar, he discusses the seeming predominance of males over females in much of recent and contemporary musical culture, particularly in popular music; the common age-profile (often under thirty) of the most commercially successful male pop-music performers; the common sexual promiscuity of many such musicians; and the fast-living, early-dying lifestyle of the pop musician (2000, p. 331).[64] Miller's claims do not always align comfortably with the tenor of our age, which, often for legitimate political reasons, tends to try to balance arguments for (natural) differences in various capacities between the sexes with (nurtural) socio-economic and socio-cultural explanations. Whatever the causes of differences between the careers of male and female musicians, even some women commentators

---

[64] The "27 Club" refers to the not insubstantial group of pop musicians who died prematurely at the age of twenty-seven, whose number includes not only Hendrix but also Kurt Cobain, Jim Morrison and – unsupportive of the sexual selection hypothesis – Janis Joplin and Amy Winehouse (but see Wolkewitz et al. (2011)). As a counter to the "'pheromonal' power of a guitar case" (Harvey, 2017, p. 98), Fitch argues that "[a] woman choosing a one-night-fling with an itinerant musician today might have made quite different decisions knowing she might become pregnant with a bastard son in earlier times or other cultures" (2006, p. 201).

notice, and indeed celebrate, at least some differences in the manifestations of musicality in males and females, which are often held to extend to musico-stylistic distinctions (Rieger, 1992).

As mentioned, some recent studies have attempted to test empirically the sexual selection hypothesis for the origin of human musicality. In an over-view of what is still a relatively small body of research, Ravignani (2018) identifies four areas within which testing has been focused and, on the basis of extant literature, assesses to what extent these components of sexual se-lection theory might have received experimental support. These areas are: (i) genes coding for musical abilities (positive evidence for effects of natural and sexual selection exists); (ii) associations between musicality and traits relating to higher fitness (positive evidence for effects of natural and sexual selection exists); (iii) higher mating success in musically skilled individuals (negative evidence for both natural selection and sexual selection exists); and (iv) sexually dimorphic preferences (neutral evidence for natural selection and positive evidence for sexual selection exists) (2018, p. 717, Tab. 1).[65]

One of the most comprehensive studies to which Ravignani (2018) refers, Mosing et al. (2014), is based on a large sample of Swedish monozygotic (identical) twins, which afforded the opportunity to compare differences in musical aptitude and reproductive success in genetically identical pairs of individuals. The study's three main hypotheses (Mosing et al., 2014, p. 360), derived from the principles of sexual selection theory, and the associated findings in summary, were: (i) musical ability is correlated with mating success ("men with higher music achievement had more children; however, this association was not found for men with higher musical aptitude and there were no significant associations of the two musical ability measures with number of children in women" (2014, p. 363)); (ii) musical ability is associated in males with traits indicative of genetic fitness, such as physical agility and cognitive ability ("there were significant positive correlations of musical aptitude and music achievement with general intelligence as well

---

[65] This research tradition has its wilder fringes: after complaints about Guéguen et al. (2014) – the article's research methodology involved the soliciting of young women in the street by a confederate of the researchers carrying variously a guitar case, a sports bag, or nothing – the journal in which it was published, *Psychology of Music*, issued an "Expression of Concern". Find-ing this insufficient, some researchers organised a petition (at https://tinyurl.com/PoMletter) calling for the article's retraction.

as negative correlations [i.e., quicker reactions] with simple reaction time" (2014, p. 363)); and (iii) the correlation in (ii) is genetically based ("musical aptitude is moderately heritable" and "genetically correlated with IQ" (2014, pp. 363–364)).

The study's findings are more nuanced than the brief summary just given indicates but, as a final overview, Mosing et al. (2014) conclude that

> [t]he findings provided little support for a role of sexual selection in the evolution of music. Individuals with higher musical ability were generally not more sexually successful (at least not quantitatively), although *men scoring higher on the music achievement scale did have more offspring* [hypothesis (i) above]. Musical aptitude was correlated with other potential indicators of fitness, such as general intelligence, simple reaction time, and – for females – height. However, the genetic components of these associations were not significant with the exception of the genetic covariation between musical aptitude and general intelligence. (Mosing et al., 2014, p. 365; emphasis mine)

In a similar study, Madison et al. (2018), like Mosing et al. (2014), assess the correlations between the two variables of musical ability and reproductive success (which sexual selection theory maintains are *dependent* variables); but they also incorporate a cluster of other mate-value variables, related to the perceived attractiveness of potential mates, both physically and in terms of assessments of health, status and reliability. Essentially, respondents were asked how sexually attracted they were, and how emotionally committed they might be, to a series of candidate individuals represented by images of faces (of varying attractiveness), whilst hearing music (of varying quality) those mate-candidates were asserted to have produced. The study's three main hypotheses (Madison et al., 2018, p. 122),[66] derived from the principles of sexual selection theory, and the associated findings in summary, were: (i) males and females prefer mates with higher attractiveness and musical performance quality (MPQ) ("participants of both sexes assign both higher mate value and mate preferences as a function of greater attractiveness and performance skill" (2018, p. 125)); (ii) females are more sensitive to MPQ than are males ("this [is] the case for all mate preferences and all mate

---

[66] Unlike those of Mosing et al. (2014), the hypotheses of Madison et al. (2018) are orientated to the demand (female) rather than the supply (male) side of the sexual selection equation.

values except Parenting Skill" (2018, p. 125)); and (iii) for females, likely offspring-engendering relationships are more influenced by MPQ than non-offspring-engendering relationships ("the only significant effect of MPQ on any mate preference scale pertains to women's preference for a long-term relationship, which is that most likely to lead to children" (2018, p. 125)).

Charlton (2014) adopts a much more direct approach than Madison et al. (2018) and Mosing et al. (2014), attempting to correlate women's preference for complex music with their menstrual cycles. The aim is to determine whether a preference for complex music, as a putative sexually selected ornament, is related to women's assessment of a partner's genetic fitness and thus his direct contribution to an offspring (which sexual selection theory would predict), or to his long-term co-parenting value and thus his indirect contribution (see also note 68 on page 108). There are, however, two factors that militate to some extent against the efficacy of the study as a test of sexual selection theory: the non-vocal-performative design of the experiment (see the next paragraph), and the fact that the subjects could not (unlike in Madison et al. (2018)) actually see any males in conjunction with the musical extracts they heard. Nevertheless, Charlton concludes that "women have sexual preferences for composers of more complex music during peak conception times, but not outside this time. By contrast, a menstrual cycle shift in preferences was not seen when women were asked to choose which composer they would prefer as a long-term partner ..." (2014, p. 4). The first of these two outcomes was not observed in a visual-art control experiment, which Charlton suggests – but see Levitin (2008, pp. 254–255) for evidence to the contrary – rules out the involvement of sexual selection in any "general attraction towards creative skill" (2014, p. 4).[67]

---

[67] In a related study, G. Miller et al. (2007) demonstrated that the earnings from tips of lap dancers are highest when ovulating. This goes against the view that our species has lost the obvious oestrus ("heat") phase of the menstrual cycle found in other mammals, including non-human primates, because it appears clear that the male viewers were somehow able to detect the dancers' maximum period of fertility (ovulation) and calibrated their tips according to the dancers' perceived sexual potential (assuming that economic and sexual motives aligned). If males can indeed detect (consciously or not) females' period of peak fertility, and if females can indeed capitalise proceptively (consciously or not) on that capacity to detect, then it suggests that: (i) the male (ornament) element of the sexual selection hypothesis for music can be most efficiently targeted towards the most receptive females; and (ii) the female (preference) element can be most effectively directed to profiting (genetically) from the most interested and valuable males (even though lap dancers may normally target "men who are profligate, drunk, and gullible rather than those who are intelligent, handsome, and discerning" (G. Miller et al., 2007, p. 379)). See also point 14 of the list on page 148.

There seems currently to be no incontrovertible evidence proving the sexual selection hypothesis in relation to human musicality, although the findings of Madison et al. (2018), while hedged by more caveats than the above summary indicates, are somewhat more favourable than those of Mosing et al. (2014). That is not to say that such evidence is not there: it may simply be waiting to be discovered by an appropriate methodology. Yet there are inherent difficulties in designing experiments to test the hypothesis. Such studies necessarily use modern humans and the music of our own time in order to test a hypothesis relating to the very different environment of our prehistory (but see Apicella et al. (2007) for cognate evidence from present-day hunter-gatherers). Both the dynamics of contemporary human mating (not least the availability of birth control and assisted conception, together with online dating technologies), and the nature of present-day musical culture (often mixing vocal and instrumental sounds, or using purely instrumental, and often consumed via recordings), make robust tests difficult. At its heart, sexual selection relies strongly on a *live performative* element – incorporating not just music but also dancing (§2.5.2) – whereby males advertise their fitness to females using displays of musical and choreographic virtuosity, and this element has not yet figured in experiments. Moreover, for understandable reasons, studies have not yet attempted to measure the large-scale dynamics of the reproductive choices multiple females make over extended periods of time in the presence of multiple displays of live male vocalisation and dancing (§5.4.1.3 makes similar points about evidencing sexual selection experimentally in the case of bird-song). It is nevertheless telling that Mosing et al. (2014) find a correlation in men between musical achievement and reproductive success (hypothesis (i) of the list on page 104 and italicised in the following quotation). This relates to the distinction made in their study between musical *aptitude* and musical *achievement*: the first tests the kind of knowledge needed to pass the music theory and aural-discrimination tests favoured by examination boards and educational institutions; whereas the second reflects individuals' real-world artistic and financial success as musical performers (Mosing et al., 2014, p. 361). The latter is arguably a much better representation of the kind of musicality implicated in sexual selection than the former, and the fact that Mosing et al. (2014) are able to correlate it with reproductive success is, if not definitive, then certainly telling.[68]

If sexual selection – or even non-sex-differentiated, non-sexually-selected vocalisation – were a driver of human musicality, it alone clearly cannot account for the richness and diversity of human musics, historical and extant. At most, it can explain musical capacities and motivations (musicality), not the nature of their outcomes (music). A further "crane", as opposed to a "skyhook" (Dennett, 1995, pp. 73–75), was needed to build upon and augment the innate capacity, in order to connect primeval calls to sophisticated melodies. The strongest candidate for that crane is, perhaps unsurprisingly, cultural evolution, which, on this analysis, would have built upon the (perhaps sexually selected) genetic capacity for vocalisation, and far outstripped what was possible on the basis of an innate competence alone. The case for this having happened in human evolution is strengthened by its seeming occurrence in other non-human animal species, such as in certain birds and cetaceans (§5.4).

Going beyond the notion that cultural evolution built music on top of the genetically evolved substrate of musicality, it is tempting to ask if there might additionally have been the operation of something akin to sexual selection purely in the domain of culture. That is, could a culturally transmitted ornament – a particular complement of musemes and associated "choreoemes" (to assign a name to a unit of choreographic imitation) – have been associated with a culturally transmitted preference – a taste-related liking for the ornament represented by those musemes and choreoemes – such that they existed in a cultural linkage disequilibrium, i.e., in an alignment that is more consistent than would be expected on the basis of random association alone? The linkage disequilibrium might arise as a result of repeated exposure, such that the ornament and the preference become associated in a meme/musemeplex. This is essentially the process underpinning taste-formation (§6.6.2), which

---

[68] In all sexually reproducing species there is a tension between quantity and quality of mating. Prolific (multi-partner) mating does not necessarily result in greater genetic advantage (as measured by the number of viable offspring and grand-offspring) compared with that arising from enhanced parental care and investment. The sexual selection hypothesis is, however, compatible with both the "males compete/females choose" and the "bi-parental investment/ good dad" scenarios, with musical achievement perhaps relating more directly to the former and musical ability to the latter (Mosing et al., 2014, p. 364).

Rosen attempts to explain when he argues, apropos "difficult" (modernist) music, that

> [i]t is not at all natural to want to listen to classical music. Learning to appreciate it is like Pascal's wager: you pretend to be religious, and suddenly you have faith. You pretend to love Beethoven – or Stravinsky – because you think that will make you appear educated and cultured and intelligent, because that kind of music is prestigious in professional circles, and suddenly you really love it, you have become a fanatic, you go to concerts and buy records and experience true ecstasy when you hear a good performance .... (Rosen, 2001, pp. 317–318)

While this is ostensibly a process operating at the individual level, it is also necessarily socially contagious (in the same way that sexual selection is genetically "contagious"). This is because (to paraphrase Rosen) "think[ing] that [liking x] will make you appear [y]" – on the basis of having seen other admirable, y-characterised individuals who like x (the ornament) – is what motivates the exposure to, in this case, difficult music, which then establishes the linkage disequilibrium connecting the musemes of the ornament with the memes mediating the preference for them. Of course, this is not *sexual* selection, because it is not directly concerned with gene-reproductive dynamics (although preferences for certain types of music might form the ornament component of sexual selection, making males appear "cool" in the eyes of females); but it is nevertheless a functionally analogous cultural linkage disequilibrium between two traits, one of which is a given phenomenon and the other is a liking or preference for it.

Having discussed gene-based sexual selection, and having tentatively extended it to candidates for analogous cultural linkage disequilibria, are there any ways in which the two might interact, synergystically or antagonistically, to form four-way linkage disequilibria? The example of males appearing more attractive on the basis of musical preferences just given might, when understood in the light of the theory of "memetic drive" (§3.7.1), afford the basis of a hypothesis. Without pre-empting the full discussion of memetic drive in Chapter 3, suffice it to say that it holds that there is a similar correlation between an ornament and a preference for that ornament, except that in memetic drive, the ornament is the *capacity to imitate* and the preference is one for *mating with good imitators*. Moreover, the principle underpinning memetic drive is sex-neutral: those with the ornament and those with the preference can be either male or female (point 140 and point 141 of the list on page 255). If, however, there is a consistent sex-division between "ornamenter" and "preferrer", then classical sexual selection can work synergystically with memetic drive, to the advantage (at least initially) of the genes subserving the capacity for imitation, and to that of the memes that capitalise on that capacity (point 141 of the list on page 255).

2.5.4 Music and Infant-Caregiver Interaction

As indicated in §2.3.4, infant-directed vocalisation exists in two (overlapping) forms: ID singing and ID speech. These are types of rhythmically framed speech-song-gesture communication ubiquitous in human cultures (Morley, 2012, p. 126). Patel summarises the differences between ID singing and ID speech by arguing that the former has "slightly lower average pitch, more tightly controlled pitch variation (as expected, because singing involves moving between well-defined pitch levels), and slower tempo" than the latter (2008, p. 381). Despite these differences, there are many similarities, as might be expected when discussing musilinguistic vocalisations. Dissanayake conflates the two forms – as I will, here and in §2.7.4 – arguing that

> the solution to this problem [of infant altriciality] was accomplished by coevolution in infants and mothers of rhythmic, temporally patterned, jointly maintained communicative interactions that produced and sustained positive affect – psychobiological brain states of interest and joy – by displaying and imitating emotions and motivations of affiliation, and thereby sharing, communicating, and reinforcing them. (Dissanayake, 2000, p. 390)

Of course, this aligns closely with Levitin's principle of motion as a motivator of emotion (e/motion) articulated in the passage cited on page 98. While the motion of IDS is in part internal to the vocalisations – these being "rhythmic, temporally patterned" – it is also often associated with rocking actions on the part of the parent, even when the utterances are not directed towards an infant currently being held (Dissanayake, 2000, p. 397). As Harvey argues, such "maternal attachment" is rewarded by oxytocin (2020, p. 3; see also

2017, p. 140 and note 48 on page 80), another of the effects of which is stress-alleviation (Dissanayake, 2008, p. 181).

Dissanayake (2008) assigns a fundamental role to IDS in the evolution of music. Subject to the provisos given on the difficulty of reconstructing evolutionary chronologies, the ordering of this section, and that of §2.3, has placed consideration of IDS (§2.3.4, §2.5.4) after that of rhythmically mediated sociality (§2.3.2, §2.5.2). For Dissanayake, however, the communal took second place to the familial – the dyadic, as she terms it. Dissanayake maintains that

> the cognitive capacities and emotional sensitivities that are used in human music as it is and has been practiced in societies all over the world emerged, for good evolutionary reasons, from affinitive mechanisms in interactions that evolved gradually between ancestral mothers and infants as early as two million years ago, long before music as we think of it existed. We can call these capacities and sensitivities *proto*-musical and even find their antecedents in the ritualized behaviors of other animals. Unlike many other survival-related behaviors, they were performed *dyadically* – by two communicatively engaged people. They specifically used and built upon neural substrates and hormonal mechanisms [the latter including those discussed in note 48 on page 80 and note 60 on page 97] for social affiliation and coordination that already existed in primates and other mammals and became essential for the survival of helpless infants and for the reproductive success of mothers. In a later, *cultural*, development – ceremonial rituals – these same biological capacities and sensitivities became 'arts', including or especially music. (Dissanayake, 2008, p. 172; emphases in the original; see also Dissanayake, 2012)

Thus, for Dissanayake, rhythmically structured vocalisations initially appeared as an exclusively mother-infant form of communication and then spread more widely within hominin cultures to create the basis of musicality and, some would argue, of linguistic competence (the relationship between IDS and the (co)evolution of music and language is discussed further in §2.7.4). She therefore stresses the fundamental importance of IDS in our species' survival, and sees it as an antecedent of the "temporal arts", of which music is arguably primary (Dissanayake, 2000). As with other music-evolutionary sequences, it is difficult to see how this hypothesised dyadic-then-communal ordering might be verified; and it is possible that the two forms of "proto-music" – mother-infant and communal – might have originated very closely in time. This is because the capacities thought to have underpinned mother-infant vocalisation may not have been confined to females (clearly their motivations were strongest in mothers), and were therefore potentially available across social groups for purposes – such as social bonding, work-motivation and battle-preparation – other than the nurturing of infants.

This issue of the relative evolutionary priority of dyadic *versus* communal vocalisation is perhaps less relevant than the more fundamental point Dissanayake (2008) is making. This is that a number of proto-musical attributes of hominins – including auditory predispositions, vocal-production capacities and motor competences – shaped by selection for a variety of non-musical purposes, were drawn together by mother-infant bonding and communal-survival imperatives. Through ritualisation – which provides an opportunity for the ingress of cultural-evolutionary forces – they became the basis for the constellation of competences, some genetically controlled, some culturally driven, underpinning the "temporal art" we now term music. In Cross's term, musicality arose as an "emergent exaptation" (2012), in his view one that to some extent reconciles the dyadic-communal dichotomy by stressing the assimilation into adult settings of the social-cognitive benefits of infants' play. Taking communal music-making as a form of adult play – even if it has very serious functions – he suggests that

> in an increasingly altricial lineage, the need to accommodate to population structures with an increasing proportion of members with access to juvenile modes of cognition and behaviour … may have favoured the emergence of something like musicality as a means of assimilating the exploratory value of those juvenile modes of cognition into the adult behavioural repertoire …. Given that play is particularly a feature of the behaviour of juveniles in social mammals, and given that it is likely to have positive survival value for members of those species who engage in it, it is probable that group behaviours that enable yet regulate it so as to co-opt its utility into the adult repertoire are likely to have some adaptive – or exaptive – value …. (Cross, 2012, p. 273)

The continuing significance of play to adults indicates that neoteny (or paedomorphosis) – the aptation-related survival into adulthood of features from infants and juveniles in *K*-selected species (see note 47 on page 79) resulting from "the retardation of somatic development for selected organs and parts" (Gould, 1977, p. 9) – while primarily relating to morphological features,[69] also encompasses behaviour. Thus, "there is neoteny of the mind as much as of the body" (Bannan, 2019, p. 37). The neotenic persistence of play into adulthood found in our species engenders a behavioural plasticity (see note 81 on page 138) that supports creativity and socialisation, the latter arising in part from the turn-taking behaviours fostered by IDS (Bannan, 2019, p. 15).

The "emergent exaptation" view parallels Patel's hypothesis of music as "neither adaptation nor frill" (Patel, 2008, p. 400) – "frill" here being ana-logous to Pinker's "auditory cheesecake" hypothesis (§1.1.2). Seeing music in these terms is, for Patel, a "false dichotomy", for "music belongs in a different category", being (like fire) "something we invented that transforms human life" (2008, pp. 400, 401). He argues that "music was an invention because each of the components of musicality (the cognitive [and morpho-logical] foundations of musical behaviour) was cognitively linked to some nonmusical mental [and/or physical] ability" (Patel, 2018, p. 114). As a "transformative technology of the mind" (TTM), "once invented and exper-ienced, it becomes virtually impossible to give it up" (Patel, 2008, p. 401), partly on account of the neurotransmitter-system rewards music motivates (§2.3.5, §2.5.2) and partly because of the aptive benefits it affords.

In an "update" of his TTM theory, Patel acknowledges the importance of cultural evolution and gene-culture coevolution (GCC; §3.2, §3.7) in hu-man evolution, especially for the origin of pitch control in group singing, group auditory-motor synchrony (§2.5.2), and the augmentation of working memory (2018, pp. 119–122). He argues that "some components of music cognition might originate as secondary uses of other brain functions (i.e., as exaptations . . .), but then may become specialized through processes of GCC to support musical behavior" (Patel, 2018, pp. 116–117). Thus, an exaptation (the musical use of a function not originally evolved for that purpose) may become an adaptation (the further gene-survival-enhancing development of extant functions turned to musical use). Nevertheless, Patel arguably

---

[69] As an example, our nearest evolutionary relative, the chimpanzee, shows significant changes between infant and adult forms, including a degree of jawbone development not seen in humans (Bannan, 2019, p. 37).

shies away from the full implications of this extension of TTM theory in that, while endorsing GCC in principle – he acknowledges, for instance, the gene-beneficial effects of the discovery and propagation of fire-use (§2.3.5) – he does not adopt a thoroughgoing dual-replicator model. He does not, in other words, acknowledge the existence, and self-interests, of memes for fire-use or for other forms of culture, including music, and so does not admit of their survival benefits as a TTM accruing to anything other than genes. Unlike the theory of memetic drive (§3.7.1), Patel does not see musemes as benefiting from the invention of music, nor does he acknowledge their power to manipulate genes in order to serve their own selfish advantage.

2.5.5 Summary of the Aptive Benefits of Musicality

The foregoing discussion strongly suggests that human musicality is a constellation of competences that were drawn together because of their aptive synergy. Some of these are shared with other species, but none of these other species possesses them in the number, development and alignment that, in our species, gives rise to musicality. For example,

> neural mechanisms underlying rhythmic entrainment … seem to have evolved convergently in humans and several vocal-learning lineages of birds and mammals, but not in nonhuman primates …. However, communicative signaling using instruments (e.g., African great ape drumming) and semantically meaningful vocalizations (e.g., vervet monkey alarm calls) are found in nonhuman primates but are rare or absent in birds …. Thus, although multiple features of human music have parallels in other species, it is the *combination* of these features as a package that seems unique to humans. (Savage et al., 2015, p. 8989; emphasis mine)

From the evidence considered hitherto, it seems likely that musicality's and music's hypothesised role in social bonding, sexual selection and infant nurture was strongly aptive and thus played a key role in leveraging our survival. While their detailed evolutionary chronology is imperfectly understood, they are not in principle mutually exclusive, and so it is reasonable to assume that they interacted synergystically. Indeed, Savage et al. (2021, pp. 3–4, Fig. 1) integrate them as "complementary sub-components of a broader social bonding function" under the rubric of a "music and social bonding (MSB)

hypothesis" (see also Mehr et al. (2021), the peer commentaries responding to these two articles 2021, pp. 39–131, and the authors' responses 2021,
pp. 132–147). Speculating on the broad sequence of events that underpinned
the evolution of human musicality, one possible scenario is as follows.

1. A number of competences – auditory, cognitive, vocal-production, and motor – existed in the early hominin line as adaptations, some of these being
   homologous, others homoplasious with other mammals. These were probably
   "modular", being subserved by distinct brain sub-systems, but there was no
   discrete module "for" music or "for" language, then or now.

2. These competences for "musilinguisticality" were drawn together by various
   aptive forces, including social bonding, sexual selection and infant nurturing, which enhanced the interconnections between them by favouring those
   individuals with ever tighter neural connections between the individual sub-
   systems that subserved them. Bannan et al. (2023, p. 25) hypothesise a "time
   course" starting with "chorusing as a social bonding mechanism" (*c.* 0.500
   MYBP), followed by "maternal crooning" (*c.* 0.300), and continuing with
   "singing or voice-matching in mate choice and retention contexts" (*c.* 0.250?).

3. These biological-evolutionary developments created a platform of rhythmic-
   melodic potentialities upon which cultural-evolutionary processes could be
   initiated and sustained and so give rise to proto-music and proto-language,
   principally stereotypical musilinguistic vocalisations and coordinated rhythmic-
   motor patterns.

4. Gene-culture coevolution shaped the ongoing adaptation and exaptation of
   the biological competences underpinning musilinguisticality, expanding and
   refining certain capacities – such as memory for musilinguistic patterns and
   fine vocal-motor coordination – and thereby creating an increasingly fertile
   environment for continued cultural, and indeed biological, evolution in the
   interconnected domains of music and language.

As this summary suggests, the process was almost certainly long and convoluted; it involved many brain and body systems; it involved combining
and re-purposing systems that arose for different purposes; it involved both
biological and cultural evolution; and it saw the bifurcation of musilanguage
into melodic-rhythmic-expressive music and prosodic-syntactic-semantic
language. Its effect was to spark what is sometimes termed the "Cognitive

Revolution" – the appearance of Harvey's "modern human mind" (note 35 on page 65) – which was likely to have been in full swing by *c.* 0.070 MYBP. According to Harari,

> [t]he period from about 70,000 years ago to about 30,000 years ago witnessed the invention of boats, oil lamps, bows and arrows and needles (essential for sewing warm clothing). The first objects that can reliably be called art date from this era . . . , as does the first clear evidence for religion, commerce and social stratification. Most researchers believe that these unprecedented accomplishments were the product of a revolution in Sapiens' cognitive abilities.... The appearance of new ways of thinking and communicating ... constitutes the Cognitive Revolution. (Harari, 2014, p. 21)

Harari ascribes the causes of the Cognitive Revolution to "accidental genetic mutations [that] changed the inner wiring of the brains of Sapiens, enabling them to think in unprecedented ways and to communicate using an altogether new type of language" (2014, p. 21). From what has been said in §2.3 and in the foregoing subsections, it is not unreasonable to invert this sequence and to hypothesise that the "altogether new type of language" – musilinguistic vocalisations (point 2 of the list on page 115) – came first, creating a selective environment whereby those "accidental genetic mutations" that enhanced such musilinguistic capacities were then favoured by gene-culture coevolution (point 4).

Given the foregoing, it follows that, despite the enormous diversity of extant and historical human musics, and of the cultural frameworks that sustain them, there should be some underlying features – sometimes termed "universals of music" (§2.2) – that are common to all its manifestations and that, therefore, can be assumed to be the markers of biologically driven aptations, whatever cultural evolution subsequently goes on to build upon them. Savage et al. (2015) note that "[c]lassic typologies from anthropology and linguistics distinguish between *absolute* universals that occur without exception and *statistical* universals that occur with exceptions but significantly above chance"; and between "universal *features* that concern the presence or absence of particular individual features and universal *relationships* that concern the conditional associations between multiple features" (2015, p.

8987; emphases mine). Savage et al. (2015) undertook a study that tested the distribution of 32 candidate musical features in a database of 304 recordings representing a "diverse global music collection" that divides human music into nine geographical regions (2015, p. 8988). Their findings are represented in Figure 2.1 (2015, p. 8990, Fig. 3; see also Savage et al., 2021, p. 8, Tab. 1).

From the candidate thirty-two features, they identify eighteen statistical-universal features meeting the criteria of global predominance across all regions and majority prevalence within each region; but there are no absolute-universal features, according to their dataset and methodology (Savage et al., 2015, p. 8988). The eighteen statistical-universal features are categorised according to pitch (e.g., use of discrete pitches), rhythm (e.g., use of isochronous beat), form (e.g., use of short phrases), instrumentation (e.g., use of voice plus instruments), performance style (e.g., use of chest voice), and social context (e.g., group performance) (2015, pp. 8988–8989). Also represented in Figure 2.1, they identify ten features that constitute "a single interconnected [statistical-universal] network centered on group performance and dance" (shown enclosed by bold boxes and connected by bold black lines) (2015, p. 8989). They argue that

> [w]ithin this network of universal relationships, group performance (1), isochronous beat (2), motivic patterns (3), and few durational values (4) were also identified … as universal features, with phrase repetition (5) narrowly failing this designation. This suggests that simple, repetitive rhythms play a fundamental role in coordinating group performance in almost all of the world's music. The remaining five – percussion instruments (6; including both membranophones (7) and idiophones (8)), dance accompaniment (9), and syllabic singing (10; i.e., one or two syllables per note without melismatic embellishment) – were not necessarily common individually but tended to appear with these other features when they did appear. (Savage et al., 2015, p. 8989)

If one takes this constellation of features as "musical fossils" of our evolutionary past, then there are many resonances with the ideas outlined in this section. In particular, the constellation, in the opinion of Fitch, "includes all four 'core components of human musicality' – song, drumming, social synchronization, and dance" (in Savage et al., 2015, p. 8991). It aligns strongly with the arguments of §2.3.2 and §2.5.2: that one of the driving forces in

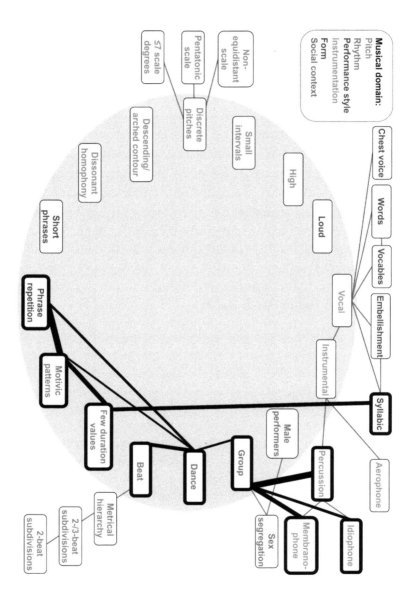

Figure 2.1: Statistical Universals in Music.

the coalescence of musicality was communal music-making based on: (i) rhythmic coordination of vocalisation (Savage et al. (2015, p. 8990) note that syllabic singing (feature 10 in the quotation above) optimises vocal co-ordination); and (ii) rhythmic coordination of bodily movements. They are (statistically) universal today, and are likely to have been so at the origin of our species. This is not to underestimate the importance of the forms of solo singing discussed in §2.5.3 and §2.5.4 – which might be understood in terms of Lomax's category of "individualized" singing ("characterized by embellished solo singing in free rhythm"), as opposed to his "groupy" singing ("characterized by syllabic communal singing and dancing to simple, regular rhythms") typical of the "single interconnected network" of Figure 2.1 (Savage et al., 2015, p. 8990).[70] As will be explored in §2.7, "individualized" singing, increasingly detached from its original reproductive imperatives, is believed to have played a key role in the evolution of language.

2.6 The Evolution of Instrumental Music

Hitherto little attention has been given in this chapter to instrumental music, partly because most evolutionary accounts of musicality focus primarily upon the hominin body and the capacities with which evolution is understood to have endowed it. As §2.5.5 indicates, early humans appear to have been able to move in synchrony with their conspecifics in coordinated rhythmic movement against a tactus; and they seem to have been able produce complex vocalisations, either in conjunction with movement or alone. As a result, a complex suite of music-related behaviours appears to have characterised early human social groups involving coordinated singing and dancing. These behaviours were variously adaptive or exaptive, or more likely a complex and ever-changing mixture of the two.

"In sharp contrast to song, which has evolved repeatedly [in humans, birds and whales, among other creatures], instrumental music is quite rare among vertebrates" (Fitch, 2006, p. 183). A fuller explanation of the evolution of musicality needs to account for the origin of instrumental music in humans – its manifestations in animals are considered briefly in §5.3.4 – which, in

---

[70] Lomax's "Cantometrics" project represents an early, arguably imperfect, attempt to classify song in cross-cultural terms (Lomax, 1976; Savage, 2018).

most extant human cultures, is tightly integrated with vocalisation and dancing. Perhaps the most parsimonious explanation for the origin of musical instruments is that they serve a *prosthetic* function: they extend the capacities of the body, magnifying its innate potential for musicality and augmenting the sonic reach and effects of music. In a manner that aligns with the aptive hypotheses discussed in §2.5, it seems the case that each of the two major components of human musicality – synchronised rhythmic movement and affective-communicative vocalisation – gave rise to instruments that supported and enhanced them. In the former category are various percussion instruments; in the latter are various wind instruments. The prosthetic nature of instruments also means that their repertoire is likely to have assimilated from the parent domain (gesture and vocality) figures appropriate to it. Thus, on the basis of usage in current instruments, it is likely that the earliest percussion instruments recreated the combination of unequal durations against a tactus (perhaps sometimes giving rise to syncopation); and the earliest wind instruments emulated the types of figures produced by the vocal tract. The converse process – whereby the voice (and potentially the moving body) borrows figures from the idioms of instrumental music – may also have occurred, and is discussed in §2.7.4.

While "[t]he oldest uncontested bone flutes are a pair, made from wing bones of a swan, from Geissenklösterle in Germany, dated to 36,800 ± 1,000 years ago" (i.e., *c.* 0.036 MYBP) (Fitch, 2006, pp. 196–197; see also Conard et al., 2009, p. 739, Tab. 1), other materials may also have been used for this purpose. These include reed and wood, which are considerably easier to work than bone but which, unlike bone, do not fossilise. These properties suggest the possibility that reed and wood flutes appeared before – and served as design templates for – bone versions. One of the earliest candidate bone flutes has been "unambiguously radiocarbon-dated to 43,100 ± 700 years of age" (i.e., *c.* 0.043 MYBP) and was found at a site in Divje Baba, Slovenia associated with the Mousterian tradition – of *c.* 0.160–0.040 MYBP, and cultivated by *Homo neanderthalensis* – of the Middle Palaeolithic period (see note 35 on page 65) (Fitch, 2006, p. 197). Despite the claims of Kunej and Turk (2000), there remains considerable disagreement as to whether this object is indeed a musical instrument or merely a piece of bone that was pierced by the teeth of another animal; of course, it could have been exapted as a flute as a result of having been "adapted" by animal teeth. If it were indeed a Neanderthal flute – it can certainly be used to produce musical sounds, but this cannot be taken as substantive evidence of its having being designed for this purpose – then "it would date the origins of instrumental music to the common ancestor of Neanderthals and anatomically modern *Homo sapiens* – often equated with *Homo heidelbergensis* or *H. antecessor* ... – and estimated to have split around 500,000 years ago ..." (i.e., *c.* 0.500 MYBP; see note 38 on page 69) (Fitch, 2006, p. 197).

Secure candidates for an "intentional" flute of an earlier date than the Geissenklösterle swan-bone pair are four examples worked from mammoth ivory found at Geissenklösterle, and at Hohle Fels and Vogelherd (also Germany) discussed in Conard et al. (2009). This material demands considerably more labour than reed, wood or bone to fashion it into a workable instrument: "[i]t requires forming the rough shape along the long axis of a naturally curved piece of mammoth ivory, splitting it open at the interface of the cementum and dentine or along one of the other bedding plains in the ivory, carefully hollowing out the halves, carving the holes and then rejoining the halves of the flute with air-tight seals along the seams that connected the halves of the flute" (Conard et al., 2009, p. 738). These constraints indicate that hollow pierced tubes made of ivory found in the material culture of hominins are, unlike those made of bone, unlikely to have been bitten by other animals and are thus intentionally shaped for sound-production. These four objects are thought to be associated with the early part of the Aurignacian tradition – of *c.* 0.043–0.026 MYBP, and cultivated by *Homo sapiens* – of the Upper Palaeolithic period. Thus, ignoring the Slovenian candidate – which "predates the onset of full spoken language posited by many scientists" (Fitch, 2006, p. 197) – and taking a more conservative assessment, one can assert that "instrumental music is at least 36,000 years old [on the basis of the (later Aurignacian) Geissenklösterle swan-bone flutes], but is almost certainly older, perhaps much older [on the basis of the (earlier Aurignacian) ivory flutes]. As a rough figure, we can thus take 40,000 years [0.040 MYBP] as the *minimum* age of human music" (Fitch, 2006, p. 197; emphasis in the original). Given the aforementioned prosthetic function of instrumental music, it is likely that what we would regard as musical melodic-rhythmic vocalisation may well have pre-dated this "minimum age" by many thousands of years.

2.7 The (Co)evolution of Music and Language I: Bifurcation from Musilanguage

> music and language should be seen as complex constellations of sub-
> processes, some of which are shared, and others not .... [From this, it
> follows that:] 1. As cognitive and neural systems, music and language
> are closely related. 2. Comparing music and language provides a power-
> ful way to study the mechanisms that the mind uses to make sense out
> of sound (Patel, 2008, p. 417)

Theorisation on the origin of language – the "hardest problem in science"
(Fitch, 2010, p. 15), or at least one of them – has been enriched in the last two
decades or so by considering the issue in conjunction with discussion of the
origin of music (Patel, 2008, Ch. 7).[71] This follows decades of separating their
treatment,[72] a strategy that often goes hand in hand with theorising language
as prior to music. Recent research has considered more systematically views
first expressed in the eighteenth and nineteenth centuries that saw the two
domains as intimately connected. Such integrated conceptions tend to view
music not as a successor to but rather as a precursor of language. While
Darwin's statement that "the progenitors of man probably uttered musical
tones before they had acquired the power of articulate speech; and that
consequently, when the voice is used under any strong emotion, it tends to
assume, through the principle of association, a musical character" (in Gamble,
2012, p. 83) is perhaps the most well known articulation of this viewpoint
(see also the quotation on page 102), the dependence of language upon
music was recognised not only by Otto Jespersen after Darwin's time but,
in the eighteenth century, by Jean-Jacques Rousseau (1712–1778) (Mithen,
2006, p. 2) and Johann Gottfried Herder (1744–1803) (Bohlman, 2002, p. 39),
and, in the nineteenth century, by the naturalist Alexander and the linguist
Wilhelm von Humboldt, both of whom corresponded with Darwin (Lansley,
2018; Lehmann, 2018).

---

[71] The most comprehensive and sophisticated treatment of the evolution of language to date
is given in Fitch (2010), upon which I draw in various places in this book. See also (Dennett,
2017, Ch. 12)

[72] This separation was encouraged by the prohibition by the Société de Linguistique de Paris
at its inception in 1866 of any discussion of the origins of language (Mithen, 2006, p. 1).

An increasing body of evidence suggests that music and language are, in many ways, different sides of the same coin (functionally, morpho-structurally and evolutionarily): both are communicative (in the broadest sense); both use organised sound in the form (initially) of melodic-rhythmic vocalisation; and both are deeply interconnected in the brain in ways that suggests an extended, shared evolutionary history (§2.7.7). As a result, this book will consider language as well as music and will attempt to present the evolution of human musicality as a shared journey with the evolution of human linguistic ability. Both substrates appear to have contributed, as facilitators of the development of symbolism, to the augmentation of mental capacity – the Cognitive Revolution – that has led to the dominance of our species on earth. In this sense, music and language have strong aptive benefits, although, as the foregoing has suggested, disambiguating the specific benefits of each domain – as with distinguishing musicality from other human competences – is difficult.

Paralleling the argument made here in connection with the evolution of music, Fitch stresses that the evolution of language built upon a broad collection of physical, neural and psychological competences, each of which may have had distinct evolutionary trajectories and may have evolved originally to subserve other functions (2010, p. 21). To his "faculty of language in a broad sense (FLB)" (Fitch, 2010, pp. 21–22, Fig. 1.1; p. 141, Tab. 3.1) – that is, the constellation of interconnecting competences underpinning language – one might add an intersecting "faculty of music in a broad sense" (FMB); and thus admit the possibility that a particular physical, neural or psychological attribute presently subserving musicality, or language competence, may have had a different adaptive purpose originally. In such cases, the attribute's musical or linguistic use constitutes an exaptation (§2.5.1). By contrast, the "faculty of language in a narrow sense" (FLN) – and the corresponding "faculty of music in a narrow sense" (FMN) – refer to "those mechanisms that are both unique to humans and special to language [or to music]" (Fitch, 2010, p. 22). There remains debate on which "sub-components" of the "multi-component" FLB model are constitutive of the FLN and on the extent to which elements of the super- and sub-sets are shared by non-human animals (Fitch, 2010, pp. 22–23), an issue that, on the basis of the foregoing, also applies to the FMB and the FMN.

The (co)evolution of music and language is a complex issue and, as noted, will be treated as a strand running through a number of related sections across the course of this book (§2.7, §3.8, §4.5, §5.6, §6.3 and §7.4).[73] To give a framework for the discussion to come, the following outlines the principal issues involved and indicates the section(s) where they are treated:

1. Vocalisations are common in many animal species and serve a number of functions. These include territorial demarcation, predator alerting, food-source advertising and mate-attraction (§5.3).

2. While most such vocalisations are innate, some are learned (often on the basis of an innate framework). The vocal learning underpinning the latter category has been hypothesised to be a fundamental driver of music and language origin, and of the brain expansion that supports it (§2.7.5).

3. Early hominin vocalisations appear to have existed in two main forms, both broadly "holistic" in nature:

   - Group vocalisation, involving rhythmically coordinated singing and dancing, which appears to have relied, in part, on the rhythmic tactus afforded by the bipedal orientation concomitant with a move from arboreal to savannah dwelling. Their main aptive function appears to have been the fostering of social cohesion (§2.5.2).

   - Individual vocalisations, which were more melodic than those in the previous sub-category. Their main aptive functions appear to have been mate-attraction (§2.5.3), mother-infant communication (§2.3.4), and/or vocal grooming (§2.3.5).

4. On account of likely short-term memory (STM) constraints, holistic vocalisations were subject to segmentation pressures that divided them into smaller units that were thus more memorable than their parent holistic utterances. By this point, cultural as well as biological evolution was operative, because the segmented patterns were themselves subject to the operation of the VRS algorithm (§2.7.6).

5. The association of segmented units with objects and events in the external world appears to have initiated a process of semanticisation and a concomitant "linguistification" of utterances. That which remained became music, retaining

---

[73] Some material in these sections is adapted from Jan (2016b).

its powerful expressive/emotional charge, but lacking the semantic specificity and high degree of syntactic regularity of language (§2.7.5).

6. The hypothesised evolutionary history of music and language has left its traces in the structure of the modern human brain. Centres for music and for the melodic aspects of language are broadly localised in the right hemisphere, whereas centres for the syntactic and semantic aspects of music and language are broadly localised in the left hemisphere. Rhythm appears evolutionarily separate and older, being localised in subcortical brain regions, including the basal ganglia (§2.5.2, §2.7.7).

7. The segmentation pressures referred to in point 4 appear also to have operated in a number of bird and cetacean species, suggesting that biologically evolved memory "bottlenecks" are an important factor – as replicator-makers and replicator-shapers – in the cultural evolution of several species (§5.4). Moreover, the early stages of a semanticisation process (point 5) are perhaps also observable today in certain non-human animal species, offering an opportunity tentatively to reconstruct the evolutionary history of human music and language (§5.6).

8. The processes hypothesised to have underpinned the evolution of music and language in organic forms have been simulated, and arguably verified, using computers, which have evolved rich musical and linguistic cultures with significant isomorphisms to those in human societies (§6.5, §6.3).

9. Language is deeply implicated in thought and consciousness, the latter understandable as a higher-level evolutionary system operating many orders of magnitude faster than biological or cultural evolution (§7.4).

To boil this summary down further, the argument of the music-language (co)evolution strand of this book is, in a nutshell, that while music and language had a common musilinguistic origin, they bifurcated into their present forms as a result of the tendency of musilanguage to undergo segmentation and for one of the derivative forms to acquire more concrete meaning than the other. This meaning-acquisition is part of the wider human development of symbolism/symbolisation, whereby a thing in one domain is understood, by virtue of association and/or of some isomorphism, to stand for a different thing in another domain.

2.7.1 Structural and Functional Commonalities between Language and Music

As primarily vocal utterances, music and language share many morpho-structural features: singing and speaking are generated by the same sound-producing organs; they consist of temporally structured sound-sequences; and they are communicative to varying degrees, information-transmission being primarily affective/emotional in music and primarily referential in speech. These similarities underpin the hypothesis that the two domains have followed a shared evolutionary history – that, in some ways, their development was intertwined. In order to identify structural and functional commonalities between music and language, Fitch (2006, p. 176) draws upon Hockett's (1960) classic enumeration of the "design features" of human language. These features are as follows (those *not* shared by (specifically vocal) music are shown in italics): (i) vocal auditory channel; (ii) broadcast transmission; (iii) rapid fading; (iv); interchangeability (that which can be understood can also be said); (v) total feedback (one can hear what one says or sings); (vi) specialisation (the vocal signal triggers a desired result); (vii) *semanticity* (sounds are associated with things); (viii) *arbitrariness*; (ix) *displacement* (referring to absent things); (x) *duality of patterning* (combination of finite set of meaningless elements to produce infinite set of meaningful elements); (xi) productivity (novelty and counterfactuality); (xii) discreteness (words and music are digital, whereas innate human calls (laughter, crying, screaming, etc.) are analogue); and (xiii) cultural transmission (Fitch, 2006, p. 177, Tab. 1). Hockett later added three more features: (xiv) prevarication (the ability to lie); (xv) reflexivity (using language to talk about language); and (xvi) learnability (the capacity for a speaker to learn more than one language) (Fitch, 2010, p. 19, Tab. 1.1; see also Fitch, 2010, p. 469, Tab. 14.1).

One of Hockett's motivations in formulating these design features was to identify aspects unique to human language, and thus not found in often ostensibly communicative animal vocalisations. Subsequent research has, however, indicated that several of the features Hockett believed to be unique to human language are also evident in certain non-human animal vocalisations (Fitch, 2006, p. 176) (§5.6). The present focus, however, is upon the relationships between human language and human music. To help elucidate these connections, Fitch (2006, p. 177, Tab. 1) maps Hockett's design features of language against human music, both vocal and instrumental. On the basis of the relatively small number of items italicised in the previous paragraph, Fitch concludes that "most of Hockett's design features of language are shared by music .... Furthermore, most of the nonshared features appear to derive from one core difference between music and language: referentiality or 'semanticity'. Language can be used to convey an unlimited set of discrete, propositional meanings, and music cannot" (2006, p. 176). Thus, aside from the issue of semanticity, Hockett's design feature (vii), there is a substantial "shared formal core of music and language" (Fitch, 2006, p. 173), which suggests a close evolutionary relationship.

Brown (2000) identifies five scenarios that might account for the origin of these design-feature similarities between music and language. One is that there is *parallelism* between them: an early form of music and an early form of language evolved separately, following distinct evolutionary tracks, and any present-day similarities between them are homoplasies (resemblances owing to parallel selection pressures), not homologies (derivation from a common ancestor) (§1.7.2). A second scenario is *binding*, whereby despite separate, parallel evolution, the two domains influenced each other at a relatively late stage of their development, this accounting for the similarities observable today. A third and fourth pair of scenarios concern *outgrowth* (side-branching) of one from the other: either the evolutionary outgrowth of music from an earlier form of communication that itself went on to develop into language; or the evolutionary outgrowth of language from an earlier form of communication that itself went on to develop into music. A fifth and final scenario describes a *common ancestor* – a *protolanguage* or, the term I prefer, *musilanguage* (Harvey, 2017, pp. 109–114) – for both music and language. This antecedent, hybrid utterance – which many believe *was much closer to song than to speech* – eventually bifurcated into two separate forms of communication that then went on to develop into music and language. As is often the case with such speciation events, each of the derived forms retained certain traces of the common ancestral form (Brown, 2000, pp. 274–277, Fig. 16.2). For a number of reasons, this fifth scenario – insofar as it can be distinguished from scenarios three and four – is arguably the most convincing, and it will be explored next.

2.7.2 The Musilanguage Model

Fitch (2010) divides protolanguage into three categories, *lexical*, *gestural* and *musical*. In brief, the first hypothesises a repertoire of semantically rich utterances – protowords – but without an organising syntax (2010, p. 401). The second suggests that, using "visual/manual" actions, "iconic, intentional pantomime" was deployed as a means of pointing to and representing objects and phenomena (2010, pp. 433, 466). The third proposes a model of "phonological generativity", assembling utterances from a set of "sonic primitives" (2010, pp. 466–467), which subsequently support semantics and, later, syntax. Owing to the "repeated convergent evolution of song-like systems in at least six vertebrate lineages" (2010, p. 470) (§5.4), and to the several structural parallels between music and language discussed above under the rubric of Hockett's design features, this third category is pursued here. Gestural protolanguage may nevertheless have preceded musical protolanguage and – given it is still a living feature of human communication – provided a scaffolding for it.

Advocated by Darwin himself (Fitch, 2010, pp. 397–399), musical protolanguage forms the basis of two recent hypotheses of language evolution: Brown's "musilanguage" model (2000, p. 277; Fitch, 2010, pp. 487–489) and Mithen's "Hmmmmm" model (2006; Fitch, 2010, pp. 486–487). Each aligns with the extant evidence; that is, they accord with what is known of the evolution of the human sound-producing apparatus (lung capacity, vocal-tract development; §2.3) and with the properties of the two domains themselves (their various levels of organisation, including the aforementioned structural and functional correspondences) (see, however, the final paragraph of this subsection). Capturing the essence of this form of vocalisation in the sound of its acronym, Mithen's Hmmmmm model argues that musilanguage was "Holistic, manipulative, multi-modal, musical and mimetic" (2006, pp. 138, 172). As with Brown, Mithen holds that Hmmmmm gradually bifurcated into the two modern forms, with music retaining the melodiousness of the original protolanguage while losing some of its (limited) referential capacity; and language acquiring stable semantic and syntactic content while losing many of the more overtly musical inflexions of its parent. In this way, he argues, the "singing Neanderthal" gave way to the speaking (but still musical) human; indeed, the evolutionary utility of developed language in *Homo sapiens* may explain, in part, the extinction of *Homo neanderthalensis* and our own species' survival.

Brown's (2000) and Mithen's (2006) models, while not identical in all particulars, correspond sufficiently closely to warrant the joint/integrated consideration they will be given here. I will generally refer to this common ancestor using Brown's term, musilanguage, unless referring specifically to certain details of Mithen's arguments. Not only does Bickerton (2003) prefer the term protolanguage, he uses it in a different sense to Brown and Mithen. Whereas the latter two endorse a view of *musical* protolanguage, Bickerton's is essentially a model of *lexical* protolanguage (Fitch, 2010, p. 404, Tab. 12.1). Aside from this key difference, the term protolanguage is generally avoided here – except when used either very generically or in specific reference to Bickerton's ideas (§2.7.6) – because it arguably privileges the linguistic over the musical, thereby downplaying the importance of music(ality) in the evolution of language.

Morley sees musilanguage as a form of universal "social-emotive vocalization" encompassing adult-to-infant (§2.5.4) and adult-to-adult communications. He argues that it

> was a form of communication that came to be used *throughout* the social group at a much earlier time [than the appearance of *Homo heidelbergensis*], without preference, both adult-adult and infant-adult, but is now perpetuated, in this predominantly non-lexical form, in adult-infant interactions and the prosodic content of adult speech. Furthermore, the shared prosodic pitch- and tempo-related properties of emotional vocalization (I[nfant]D[irected] and A[dult]D[irected]) and music are not borrowed from one to the other, in either direction, but are, and always have been, a shared fundamental component of both. (Morley, 2012, p. 127; emphasis in the original)

For Morley, as for Mithen (2006), social-emotive vocalisation originated towards the beginning of the *Homo* genus and not, with *Homo sapiens*, towards the end. Moreover, in broad alignment with Brown's (2000) and Mithen's (2006) positions, Morley argues that it "might gradually have evolved into music ..., or at least provided shared foundations, but it could also have been the basis for language amongst all of a population" (2012, p. 127). In considering musilanguage, music and language, it may in the end – despite my alighting upon the last of the five scenarios outlined at the end of §2.7.1 – prove impossible to reconstruct what came first and what evolved into what. But it is worth noting – to add to the discussion in §2.3.1 – that much greater lung capacity and more precise vocal control is needed for singing than for speaking (Fitch, 2006, p. 196; Merker, 2012, p. 232). Given that humans possess this complex cognitive-motor facility, and given that it is thought to have evolved not before the end of the *Homo erectus* line (Fitch, 2006, p. 196), then it is likely that musilinguistic vocalisation came first, and was presumably aptive, before elements of it developed into the arguably productionally less demanding incarnation of language. For this reason, "fossil indicators related to vocal biomechanics that traditionally have been taken to reflect the emergence of human spoken language may reflect the emergence of human song instead" (Merker, 2012, p. 232).

While Brown's (2000) and (particularly) Mithen's (2006) accounts are painstakingly outlined and convincingly supported, they can nevertheless be criticised on the grounds that they do not take their Darwinian focus to its logical conclusion. Mithen incorporates Darwinism into his consideration of the genetic basis of language – by way of an analysis of such interconnected aspects as bipedalism, the evolution of the vocal tract, and sexual selection (2006, pp. 139, 146, 176) – but he does not complement this by a consideration of Darwinism's operation in the cultural dimension. In this sense neither model offers a fully coevolutionary account of musilanguage (Durham, 1991), which would require considering the ways in which the selfish interests of each replicator, gene and meme, interact in this domain. The discussion of the evolution of music and language here and in subsequent chapters attempts to redress this imbalance by reconceiving the process of language evolution Mithen outlines in Universal-Darwinian terms, arguing that his "mimetic" can be replaced by Dawkins' "memetic" (Dawkins, 1989). Considering the self-interested replicated particle in culture as well as in nature offers a means of arriving at a unified cultural-evolutionary conception of music and language, one that understands their similarities and differences as a consequence of the evolutionary forces acting upon them. Moreover, it fosters a mediation between their phonological, syntactic and semantic dimensions (§2.7.3), and their neurological and psychological foundations.

2.7.3 The Music-Language Continuum

An element of the musilanguage hypothesis touched on in §2.7.1 is that traces of their common ancestor remain in music and language, such that the former has a clear (if non-specific) communicative potential, and the latter has a marked prosodic quality. Indeed, it is useful to think of the two modern forms as occupying the ends of a music-language continuum, rather than as absolute, closed categories. To help understand this it is useful to think in terms of the three basic levels, or dimensions, of music-language organisation: the *phonological* (the level of sound structure, not wholly synonymous with the *phonetic* (Fitch, 2010, pp. 95–96)); the *syntactic* (the level describing the recursive/hierarchic combination of elements at the phonological level); and the *semantic* (the level of meaning, which arises from the previous two levels, both via individual word-meanings and via the structure of a sentence as a whole) (Fitch, 2010, pp. 93–129; Fasold & Connor-Linton, 2014). It is clear that "modern" language[74] is well developed in all three dimensions, whereas music – as Fitch notes in §2.7.1 apropos Hockett's design features of language – lacks a coherent referential semantics. While music certainly "means" things – and a given piece of music may mean the same thing to many people and many things to the same person – it lacks the relatively fixed associations between sound-structure and meaning that are intrinsic to language and that arise from interaction between the phonological and syntactic levels. Of course, music has its own form of (often very highly developed) syntax, in that different musical styles ensure coherence by constraining the horizontal and vertical juxtapositions of sound-events in sophisticated ways. But this syntax is not normally implicated in referentiality, only in *affect*, where, for example, frustration of expected continuations gives rise to a broadly emotional response in the listener (Meyer, 1956; Narmour, 1990; Huron, 2006).

Brown incorporates these distinctions into a continuum that shows that, despite the hypothesised bifurcation, music and language share certain at-

---

[74] By this is meant all natural human languages, from the start of recorded history.

tributes that betray their common origin in musilanguage. Figure 2.2 (Brown, 2000, p. 275, Fig. 16.1) represents this continuum, which incorporates the two levels at which music and language operate, the "phonological" level and the "meaning" level.

- The phonological level, in language, concerns phonemes and their assembly into words and phrases.[75] In music the phonological level concerns pitches and their assembly into motifs (musemes) and phrases.

- The meaning level, in language, relates to "propositional syntax", which Brown argues "specifies temporal and behavioral relationships between subjects and objects in a phrase" and which "is based on relationships between actors and those acted upon" (2000, pp. 292–293, 296). In music, the meaning level relates to what Brown terms "pitch-blending syntax" (2000, p. 274), which correlates the structures formed by horizontal and vertical sound juxtapositions with their expressive effects.[76] In this sense, pitch-blending syntax is a hybrid of the "introversive" and "extroversive" forms of semiosis formalised by Agawu, after Roman Jakobson (Agawu, 1991, p. 23).

At the far left-hand side of this continuum (the top part of Figure 2.2), language is represented as the use of sound for referential meaning and, at its far right-hand side, music – certainly in what Brown terms its "acoustic mode" (Brown, 2000, p. 271) – is represented as the use of sound for emotive meaning. Being a continuum, there are naturally several intermediate states between these two extremes, and these may be taken as evidence that the bifurcation of musilanguage is not total, and that there are therefore modes of communication that, while primarily linguistic, retain traces of music, and vice versa.[77]

---

[75] The subject of phonology ("the study of the sound systems of languages"), phonemes are "those contrasts in sound … which make differences of meaning within language" (Crystal, 2019, p. 248)

[76] Essentially, patterns of openness/tension-closure/relaxation in music are correlated with their emotional/affective equivalents, so the music is an analogue of, and a stimulus for, the associated affect.

[77] Long after evolutionary bifurcations, traces of one lineage tend to remain in the other, and some very basic ground-plans – such as backbones – end up functionally unchanged across several otherwise very different descendant lineages.

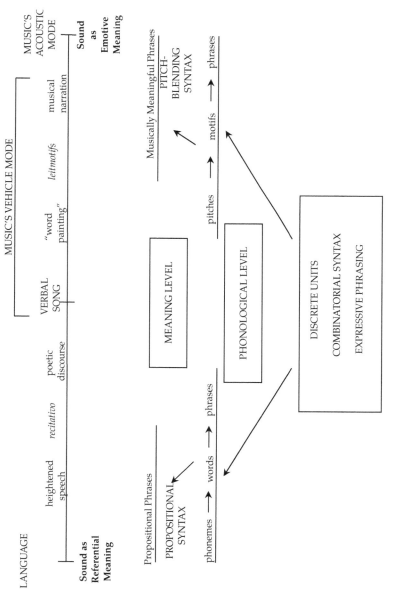

Figure 2.2: The Music-Language Continuum.

2.7.4 Echoes of Musilanguage in the Modern World

In accordance with Donald's "principle of the conservation of previous gains" (in Fitch, 2010, p. 433), the extant intermediate states in the middle region of the continuum of Figure 2.2 afford evidence for the past existence of musilanguage and its persistence in our own world. Might we be able to reconstruct this type of utterance, hearing once again the sounds that daily echoed around the locations of hominin communities? At first thought, this might seem impossible, because the hypothesised bifurcation of musilanguage is thought to have occurred after *c.* 0.200 MYBP (Mithen, 2006, p. 257) and the essence of the parent utterance (while surviving vestigially in music and language) might be thought to have been lost as a result of this division. But it might be possible to find a "living fossil" of it, analogous to the Coelacanth once long thought to have become extinct in the Late-Cretaceous period (100.50–66 MYA) but discovered alive in 1938. Four particularly suggestive intermediates might be identified: IDS, tone languages, mantras, and certain other forms of quasi-syllabic vocalisation, of which "scat" singing in jazz is one of the most salient examples, together with a provisional fifth candidate in the form of electroacoustic music.

IDS has already been covered in §2.3.4 and §2.5.4. Suffice to add here that Mithen asks "when we hear mothers, fathers, siblings and others 'talking' to babies, are we perhaps hearing the closest thing to 'Hmmmmm' that we can find in the world today?" (2006, p. 275). In raising this issue again, it is important to distinguish between IDS as a *clue* – on account of its "intermediate" status – to the (co)evolution of music and language, this being the concern here; and IDS as an *aptation* serving human survival, this being the concern of §2.5.4.

In a *tone language* meaning is communicated in part by the production of words at specific pitches, either fixed ("level tones") or mobile ("contour tones") (Patel, 2008, p. 39). While over half the world's languages are tonal (including most African and south east Asian languages), only a very small minority use the apparent maximum of five level tones (2008, pp. 40, 41). The Amazonian Ticuna language appears a strong candidate for the one most proximate to musilanguage, in having five level tones and seven "glides" from one pitch to another (2008, p. 42, Fig. 2.12). If tone languages are closer to music than non-tonal languages by virtue of their musical (prosodic) characteristics, non-tonal – inflected – languages are closer to what might be regarded as the essence of language. That is, they communicate meaning primarily by their word-forms and grammatical structures, not by their expressive-emotional flows, and so they are closer to artificial languages like computer programming languages. This distinction perhaps suggests that, in the future, human music will be increasingly intense emotionally, but with ever looser syntax; whereas human language will be increasingly neutral emotionally, but with ever tighter syntax.

Despite his assertion that IDS is the most likely contender for the persistence of Hmmmmm, Mithen later goes on to offer the mantras of eastern religion as an alternative, in his view stronger, candidate. He suggests that, "[a]s relatively fixed expressions passed from generation to generation, [mantras] are, perhaps, even closer than IDS to the type of 'Hmmmmm' utterances of our human ancestors" (2006, p. 277). Mantras exist in many different forms according to the specific religious tradition from which they spring, whether this be Hinduism, Sikhism, Buddhism or Jainism. But many align closely with the hypothesised attributes of Hmmmmm, in that they exist as melodic-melismatic elaborations of one or more syllables. Indeed, according to Mithen, "[t]he philosopher Franz [*sic*; *recte* Frits] Staal … concluded that these lengthy speech acts lack any meaning or grammatical structure, and are further distinguished from language by their musical nature" (2006, p. 277).

Various types of non-verbal vocalisations generally regarded as forms of music are also candidates for residual musilanguage. Scat singing is perhaps the most well known of these, being a prominent part of many jazz traditions, as exemplified particularly by Louis Armstrong and Ella Fitzgerald. Scat is a form of wordless vocal improvisation over some musical structure (a melodic line or chord progression, for instance) that assembles nonsense syllables associated with scale- and arpeggio-fragments, and other stereo-typical figures, into longer sequences.[78] Scat may have arisen as a result of the assimilation by singers of sonic fragments (musemes) originally played by instrumentalists, which seems a common and ongoing process in several

---

[78] Cognate traditions of such non-verbal musicking include central-European yodelling (Wey, 2020), the polyphony of African pygmies (Rouget & Buckner, 2011), and Tuvan overtone singing (Bergevin et al., 2020).

musical cultures. In this sense, it might represent a reversal of the (seemingly equally common and ongoing) process described in §2.6, whereby the earliest instrumental music may have assimilated figures from vocalisation and/or gesture.[79]

To these four categories, one might tentatively add a fifth, in the form of certain types of electroacoustic music. As a result of the nature of the medium itself, many works in this tradition lack clear segmental articulation; although they are not entirely beyond a memetic analysis when inter-opus, cross-stream mapping resulting from a transcendence of the medium's intrinsic constraints towards homogeneity occurs (Adkins, 2009). Such music is arguably a homoplasy, not a homologue, of musilanguage; but it might be predicted broadly to follow the course taken by musilanguage in its future evolutionary history, and therefore indirectly to afford evidence in support of the Brown/Mithen hypothesis outlined here.

2.7.5 The Power of Vocal Learning

One fundamental commonality shared by music and language – number (xiii), and arguably others, in the list Fitch (2006) derives from Hockett (1960) given on page 126 – is that while both stem from an innate capacity or aptitude, both also need to be *learned by cultural transmission* in order for an individual to acquire competence in them. While humans are innately musical, facility in this domain requires the assimilation of and practise with a repertoire drawn from an individual's culture; and while children are born with a capacity for language, they need to acquire the phonology, syntax and semantics of their native tongue from their parents and peers. This learning relies upon a form of imitation-assimilation, whereby what is heard uttered by others is then repeated by oneself. Merker argues that "the capacity to reproduce by means of the voice that which has been heard by ear" is "a competence that is lacking in other apes, and whose corresponding neural mechanism is, accordingly, a uniquely derived trait of the genus *Homo*" (2012, pp. 215–216). Such *vocal learning*, or *vocal imitation* (Fitch, 2010, p. 339),

---

[79] The Brilliant style topic – in which bravura vocal figures based on scales, arpeggios and leaps emulate those more idiomatic to instruments – and the Singing style topic – in which lyrical instrumental figures based on conjunct, narrow-tessitura motion emulate those more idiomatic to voices – represent these processes, respectively, in late-eighteenth-century music (Ratner, 1980, pp. 19–20).

is arguably at the heart of the constellation of interconnected phenomena underpinning music and language, and appears to have been a key driver of the evolution of modern humans. While occupying only a subsection of this chapter, this should not be taken as an indication of the relative (un)importance of the topic: the "vocal learning constellation" (Merker, 2012) is arguably the key to understanding why humans and certain non-human animals are musical, and how humans came to acquire language; so, directly or indirectly, it informs all parts of this book.

Merker's argument is complex and extended, but is worth outlining the elements of this "constellation" and their interconnections in full, as follows:

1. Biologists have often focused upon homology for answers to questions in human evolution, ignoring the insights that analogy (homoplasy) affords when used in comparative studies of the selection pressures driving the evolution of traits shared by humans and often distantly related species (Merker, 2012, pp. 216–217). One of these traits is vocal learning.

2. Most mammals and non-human primates communicate via innate vocalisations (§5.3), even though these can "undergo learned modification" to some extent in response to certain contextual motivations (2012, p. 217).

3. The vocalisations of *Homo sapiens*, certain birds and certain cetaceans are characterised by vocal learning, leading to the origin of two forms of culture in those animals: (i) *ritual culture*, which – driven by a "conformal motive" impelling high copying-fidelity (§1.6.3.3) – requires the acquisition, and adherence to in performance, of a correct form, or "canonical pattern"; and (ii) *instrumental culture*, which is guided by utility at the task undergoing imitation and is thus subject to natural selection in favour of those most adept at the "observational learning" and action-implementation characterising this form of culture (2012, pp. 218–221).

4. Certain vocal-learning species possess an "'open-ended' vocal ontogeny", i.e., the capacity of "'vocal emancipation' … by which vocal production is released from innate constraints to achieve genuine pattern novelty" (2012, pp. 221–222). These "paths to non-predictability" (2012, p. 222) are achieved variously by inter-species imitation, spontaneous invention/improvisation of new patterns, and a process of assortative recombination whereby "model patterns are disas-

sembled into phrases and fragments and reassembled into new unique song types" (2012, p. 222).

5. The biological motivation for the significant energy costs associated with vocalisation, especially the florid type characteristic of "emancipated" vocal learning species, is the "honest signalling" – be the audience for these signals "mates or rivals" (2012, p. 227) – of the handicap principle (§2.5.3) (2012, p. 224). Thus, "the level of song proficiency in effect sums up, in a single performance, the entire developmental history of the singer, and as such provides an all-round certificate of competence" (2012, p. 226), be that competence for fighting, mating, or offspring-nurturing – factors squarely associated with sexual selection.

6. Vocal learning capacity correlates strongly with encephalisation, measured in terms of brain : body and telencephalon : brain ratios,[80] as an *allometric* (body-ratio-related) trait (§2.3.4). Thus, the proportion of the brain occupied by the telencephalon in the African grey parrot (*Psittacus erithacus*), an emancipated learner, is similar to that in humans (2012, p. 228).

7. Beyond the correlation noted above, Merker hypothesises that vocal learning *drove* encephalisation (2012, pp. 229–230). He argues that, assuming a natural or sexual selection pressure for vocal learning, there would be an aptive benefit to an expansion of "telencephalic 'song nuclei'" (2012, p. 229). But the architecture and ontology of the brain impose "yoked schedules of neurogenesis", which militate against simply expanding one component or system in isolation (2012, p. 230). A more efficient process is "simple allometric expansion" – i.e., scaling everything up in proportion, so embryology and ontogeny do not have to be radically reconfigured (2012, p. 230). Thus, provided there were sufficiently strong aptive benefits to vocal learning – and these seem clear on the basis of both natural and sexual selection – then vocal learning seems to have had great power in pushing evolution towards favouring ever greater encephalisation. This claim is central to the issue of memetic drive, discussed further in §3.7.1.[81]

---

[80] The telencephalon is the part of the brain made up of the cerebrum plus certain sub-cortical structures, and deals with demanding tasks involving perception, cognition and memory, among other competences. Non-telencephalic brain structures, such as the cerebellum, tend to be evolutionarily older and concerned with more instinctive capacities.

[81] To consideration of encephalisation should be added the issue of brain plasticity (Harvey, 2017, pp. 60–62), a subset of the issue of phenotypic plasticity, which encompasses the malleability of body, brain and behaviour. Humans are thought to have undergone significant evolutionary changes in neural architecture, connectivity and chemistry that are involved in "shaping activity and influencing the computational power of the brain" (2017, p. 60). These

8. While vocal learning underpins human language, this does not necessarily mean that it evolved (primarily or initially) *for* language: for Merker, its most common function across the species in which vocal learning has evolved is learned song, which implies that language is a later capacity that built upon a (musilinguistic) song substrate (2012, p. 231). Thus, "[i]n a comparative perspective, song evolves far more readily than speech, so an unusual size or shape of [fossil indicators of vocal biomechanics] does not begin to bear on the issue of speech until the explanation 'song' has been eliminated" (2012, p. 232; see also §2.7.2).

9. The appearance of vocal learning in the *Homo* genus is hypothesised to have occurred within *Homo erectus*(/*Homo ergaster*) (Table 2.1); and, after further brain-expansion, the appearance of language is hypothesised to have occurred within *Homo sapiens* (2012, p. 233).

10. The arrival of *Homo erectus*(/*Homo ergaster*) is marked by the sexual non-dimorphism and male provisioning discussed in §2.3.3. Moreover, the mental aptitudes required for the kind of foraging involved in provisioning – "[c]uriosity, memory capacity, and strategic planning" – serve as additional selection pressures for encephalisation (2012, p. 234).

11. The "strategic partnerships" (2012, p. 236) between males and females intrinsic to colonial monogamy (§2.3.3) were cemented by vocality, specifically by the singing of duets. While "rare in terrestrial mammals", there appears to be a "latent functional coupling between monogamy and pair duets in primates", evidenced, for example, in gibbons (§5.3.3) (2012, p. 236). Nevertheless, non-human-primate pair-duetting, like that of other mammals, is "innately structured", and not – according to Merker's hypothesis – vocally learned (2012, p. 236). In a striking correspondence, the only other group of organisms aside from (early) humans where pair-duetting involves vocally learned patterning – birds (§5.4.1) – also demonstrates extended bi-parental offspring-care and male provisioning, a form of nurturing largely absent from mammals other than humans (2012, p. 236; see also the discussion of monogamy on page 400).

---

enhancements include the presence of astrocytes, a type of glial (non-neuronal) cell that "play a crucial role in plasticity associated with learning and memory, and perhaps also influence aspects of human cognition…. [they are] the 'yin' to the neuronal 'yang' …" (2017, p. 61). The issue of plasticity is relevant when one considers that the brain of *Homo sapiens* is, on average, actually slightly *smaller* than than of *Homo neanderthalensis* (Alan Harvey, personal communication; see also (Kochiyama et al., 2018)), so our superior plasticity may have been a factor in compensating for raw size differences. Note, finally, that certain aspects of brain plasticity appear to have an epigenetic (§1.8) as well as a genetic underpinning (Harvey, 2017, pp. 67–74; Harvey, 2020, pp. 9–10; see also Schaefer et al., 2021).

> In this sense, (early) humans, unlike our closest primate relatives, appear very similar to birds in terms of extended parental care in the context of colonial monogamy "underwritten" by vocal learning (2012, p. 236). This "underwriting" works according to the principle of honest signalling outlined in point 5, which marks out individuals as "precious repositories of experience" (2012, p. 237).

This is not the entirety of Merker's thesis, for it does not, as it stands, explain how vocally learned song in our hominin ancestors evolved into fully compositional language in modern humans. This is the topic of the next section, but I will end that section (page 147) with a summary of Merker's account of these remaining elements of the vocal learning constellation, thus picking up where the list in this section left off and completing it in order to offer a full account of Merker's argument.

2.7.6 Holistic *versus* Compositional Sound-Streams

Mithen understands hominin musilanguage (§2.7.2) in a different sense to Bickerton, the latter believing that what he terms (lexical) protolanguage was made up of "words, with limited, if any, grammar" (Mithen, 2006, p. 3; Bickerton, 2003). Mithen, by contrast, argues that: (i) the component gestures of his Hmmmmm could not, *contra* Bickerton, be decomposed into individual meaning-units (protowords), but were to be understood as constituting a single unified, holistic message; (ii) it was designed to affect and mediate the thoughts and behaviour of others, often to the advantage of the utterer; (iii) it drew not only upon sonic elements, but also upon physical gestures and movements, actions and facial expressions; (iv) it was what we today might easily regard as a form of vocal music, in that it consisted of interconnected melodic phrases that combined pitch, rhythm and, presumably, dynamics and timbre; and (v) it was often imitative of the sounds of the world of the utterer – those of the birds, animals and other natural phenomena that constituted the environment of the hominin species that utilised it. Aligning with point 9 of the list on page 139, Mithen argues that Hmmmmm was employed (to list the hominin line in hypothesised order of appearance) by *Homo erectus/Homo ergaster*, *Homo heidelbergensis*, *Homo neanderthalensis* and early *Homo sapiens* (Mithen, 2006, p. 7, Fig. 1; see also Foley, 2012).

If musilanguage constituted a form of holistic communication, then "modern" languages – that is, the discrete-word-based, syntax-governed, semantically precise form of communication that began to evolve in *Homo sapiens* after *c.* 200,000 years ago – are, by contrast, "compositional". Compositional languages "can use different symbols to represent different attributes of meaning and combine these symbols in a systematic way to form a message such that the meaning of the whole message is formed from a simple combination of the meaning of its parts" (Y. Ren et al., 2020, p. 12; see also Kirby et al., 2015). They are thus made up of relatively discrete sonic units that may be recombined (often recursively/hierarchically) according to the principles of some grammatical system, in order to assemble a near-infinity of potential utterances, thereby vastly exceeding the flexibility and communicative power of holistic forms of communication. While a sonic unit in a compositional language may have a fairly stable semantic content, this may change according to the grammatical function of the unit within the utterance, as exemplified by Truss's celebrated amphibology "eats[,] shoots and leaves" (2003). That *Homo neanderthalensis* never learned to shoot, despite eating shoots and leaves, might be a consequence of a lack of the expansion in thought and invention – the Cognitive Revolution – fostered by, and fostering, the evolution of compositional language in *Homo sapiens*.

Mithen argues that one of the principal factors that drove the evolution from Hmmmmm to compositional language was *segmentation* – "the process whereby humans began to break up holistic phrases into separate units, each of which had its own referential meaning and [which] could then be recombined with units from other utterances to create an infinite array of new utterances" (2006, p. 253). It is important not to let the much later appearance of written and printed language obscure the picture: while a word might appear discrete and self-contained on the printed page – the surrounding characters' worth of whitespace affording the necessary gestalt grouping clue to demarcate its group of letters from other groups – in spoken language a word is normally part of a continual, unbroken sound-stream, and so its isolation into a linguistically significant unit relies upon a number of segmentational factors.

There are a number of interrelated processes by means of which segmentation of musilanguage into discrete units could have occurred. Developing ideas of Wray (1998) – who earlier and similarly argued for the existence of a holistic and musical protolanguage (Fitch, 2010, pp. 496–498) – Mithen argues that the first of these processes was the result of "the recognition of chance associations between the phonetic segments of the holistic utterance and the objects or events to which they related. Once recognized, these associations might then have been used in a referential fashion to create new, compositional phrases" (2006, p. 253). While certainly a credible hypothesis, it appears to be predicated upon the existence of another, arguably prior, process to enable it: the presence of some innate psychological tendency that perceives (and imposes) segmentation boundaries at certain points of an ostensibly holistic sound-stream, in order to create the "phonetic segments" to which Mithen refers.

Generally considered under the rubric of gestalt psychology, it is well understood that certain phenomena in a sound-stream tend to impose a segmentation boundary (Deutsch, 1999), breaking it up into discrete units. As Narmour argues, "unlike the notoriously interpretive, holistically supersummative, top-down Gestalt laws of 'good' continuation, 'good' figure, and 'best' organization ... the [bottom-up] Gestalt laws of similarity, proximity, and common direction are measurable, formalizable, and thus open to empirical testing" (1989, p. 47). Thus, where similarity becomes difference, where proximity becomes distance, and where common direction becomes a change in (pitch) direction, a segmentation boundary is likely to be perceived. Moreover, this factor combines with the constraints of STM to impose a limit on the size of the "chunks" that lie in between segmentation boundaries (Snyder, 2000, pp. 53–56; Snyder, 2009, p. 108). In Miller's well known formulation, it is "seven, plus or minus two" units (1956; see also Simon, 1975); for Temperley, in music it is "roughly 8 notes" (2001, p. 69).

An additional, supporting, process at play in segmentation and meaning-assignment is what might be termed *coindexation-determined segmentation* (Jan, 2011a, sec. 4.1.2, para. 57). A *coindex* is a copy of a replicator, the extent of the similarity relationship between an *antecedent coindex* and a *consequent coindex* verifying the status of the two patterns as members of the same replicator *allele-class*, as opposed to each being an entity *sui generis*. In coindexation-determined segmentation, such "overlap" – arising when cross-mapping two sound-streams, wherein one coindex is stored in memory and the other is heard in real time – imposes a segmentation boundary at the start and end (the initial and terminal nodes) of the shared segment, provided it is not strongly contradicted by gestalt forces. This affords the common segment greater perceptual-cognitive salience than it would otherwise have possessed. In other words, as Calvin argues, "that which is copied may serve to define the pattern" (1998, p. 21). In music, coindexation-determined segmentation might be regarded as culturally (as opposed to genetically) mediated, and an example of the operation of what Narmour terms "extraopus style" (1990, pp. 35–38). As such, it is likely to be more malleable – and therefore more evolutionarily variable (even dialect-mediating (Meyer, 1996, p. 23)) – than genetically mediated (gestalt-psychological) segmentation.

Given the presence of gestalt grouping, STM-constrained "chunking", and coindexation-determined segmentation, Mithen's "recognition of chance associations between the phonetic segments of the holistic utterance and the objects or events to which they related" is eminently feasible. Assuming the alignment of these various processes, overlapping, gestalt-demarcated segments would have acquired a distinct identity, and the association with specific "objects or events" would have become ever more firmly established. Such associations may initially have been "iconic" (segmented verbal chunks acting mimetically as "signs that are motivated by similarity" to that with which they come to be associated; and so not strictly "chance associations"); but later they may have become "indexical" (chunks "motivated by contiguity or co-occurrence" with that with which they come to be associated; thus more properly "chance associations") (Tolbert, 2001, p. 88; see also Cross & Woodruff, 2009, p. 25). On the grounds, as Deacon argues, that "the criterial attribute of human symbolic thought is arbitrary reference displaced from its immediate context, and that displacement [point (ix) of the list on page 126; see also point 18 of the list on page 149] is a function of the hierarchical structure of symbolic thought" (in Tolbert, 2001, p. 88), one might assume the chronological priority of the iconic over the indexical.

Any tendency to stream-segmentation in hominins must presumably have relied upon genetic factors for its implementation, and so it is necessary to appreciate that those factors that are present in modern humans may not necessarily have been in place in earlier hominin species, such as *Homo erectus/Homo ergaster*. In this case, these earlier hominins may not have possessed the capacity to hear a holistic utterance as anything other than an undifferentiated sonic continuity. Implicated in the neurobiology of the perception and production of speech in modern humans, the Forkhead box P2 (FOXP2) gene may have played a role in musilinguistic stream-segmentation (Enard et al., 2002; S. B. Carroll, 2003). This gene is present in a number of species, including our primate cousins, but "[i]n humans, there is evidence for the positive selection of specific mutations in the FOXP2 gene .... [yet] this same FOXP2 variant is also found in Neanderthals and in another recently discovered archaic hominin, the Denisovan" (Harvey, 2017, p. 70). The human(-Neanderthal-Denisovan) allele "fulfills the criteria for a genetic difference that *makes a difference in speech ...*" (Fitch, 2010, p. 359; emphasis in the original), and presumably conferred some aptive benefit that fostered its replication and selection. Strictly, Fitch's point relates to a further mutation of this allele, one unique to our species, is believed to have occurred *c.* 0.060–0.050 MYBP (Harvey, 2017, p. 70). This dating, and that of *c.* 0.440–0.270 for the earlier allele-Denisovan, broadly aligns with the chronology of musilanguage bifurcation and with the flowering of the Cognitive Revolution outlined here.

Mithen cautions that "FOXP2 is not *the* gene for grammar, let alone for language. There must be a great many genes involved in providing the capacity for language, many of which are likely to play multiple roles in the development of an individual" (2006, p. 250; emphasis in the original).[82] Nevertheless, he hypothesises that "[p]erhaps the process of segmentation was dependent upon this gene in some manner that has yet to be discovered" (2006, p. 258); and he notes that studies suggest that those with a faulty version of the gene (such as the "KE" family, which he offers as an example)

---

[82] Indeed, FOXP2 codes for a "transcription factor" – a protein that regulates the expression (the "switching on and off") of other genes – that is important in the regulation of "the functionality of sensory and motor (sensorimotor) circuits between the cerebral cortex, cerebellum, and basal ganglia" (Harvey, 2017, pp. 69–70). This suggests a possible implication in the mCBGT (page 95) and thus a role in the vocal learning and rhythmic synchronization hypothesis (page 96).

encounter "difficulties … with the segmentation of what sound to them like holistic utterances" (2006, p. 258). The FOXP2 gene could therefore be hypothesised indirectly to underpin segmentation, in that it might subserve certain gestalt grouping principles in perception, it might mediate the length-constraints of STM, and it might support the recognition of similarity in cross-sound-stream mapping. If so, then perhaps its appearance in *Homo sapiens* – dated to *c.* 0.220 MYA, consistent with the appearance of anatomically modern humans (*c.* 0.200 MYA) (Fitch, 2010, p. 360) – facilitated the process of moving from holistic musilanguage towards segmented music and language, and thus helped to create the conditions necessary for the Cognitive Revolution. This hypothesis is supported by the fact that, while language and music are to some extent *lateralised* in the modern human brain (§2.7.7), FOXP2 is nevertheless expressed *bilaterally* (Harvey, 2017, p. 70).

One might term the discrete units resulting from the segmentation of musilanguage "protemes", in order to signify that they were the cultural-evolutionary precursors of both musemes (the sound patterns of music) and lexemes (the sound patterns of language). It seems reasonable to suggest that protemes, as self-contained units of information, were subject to the VRS algorithm – this driving the evolution of musemes and lexemes from them – and that, for a good deal of early hominin evolution, all three types of replicator formed a fuzzily overlapping and co-existing group. It is likely that the perceptual-cognitive salience of protemes-lexemes (perhaps in conjunction with their nascent syntactic and semantic attributes) correlated, and still correlates, with their replicative success. The perceptual-cognitive salience of protemes-musemes would similarly have correlated with their replicative-evolutionary fortunes (Jan, 2007). The most salient and striking extant musical patterns – perhaps those with the most interesting melodic contours or tonal structure – are normally those that are replicated most, that go on to appear in numerous musical works, and that therefore play the largest role in shaping the profile of a wider musical dialect. In this sense, musemes' perceptual-cognitive salience, however it is measured, is an index of their likely statistical prevalence in a given museme-pool and, ultimately, of their selfishness (Dawkins, 1989; Distin, 2005).

While lexemes replicate under tighter syntactic and semantic constraints than musemes (in the sense that their mutation rate is limited to a greater extent by the imperatives of communication), it appears likely that, as segmented sound-units, they warrant consideration in similar ways to musemes. As with the origin, florescence and senescence of musical genres, styles, and systems of tonal organisation (Jan, 2013, p. 152, Fig. 1; Jan, 2015b), the notion of linguistic speciation – recognised by Franz Bopp before that in nature (J. Miller & Van Loon, 2010, p. 100) and adopted by Darwin as a means of illustrating biological speciation (Darwin, 2008, p. 311) (§3.6) – might be understood as a system-level consequence of the operation of the VRS algorithm upon the relevant unit of selection, the lexeme (§7.5). Indeed, Dawkins gives a small but telling example of this in the mispronunciation of the second line of the chorus of "Rule Britannia" as "Britannia, rule[s] the waves". This, he argues, is the result of the greater salience of the sibilant ending of "rules" as against the original "rule"; and also the more grammatically comprehensible indicative mood of the "rules" version, as against the more nuanced imperative, or even subjunctive, implication of "rule" (1989, p. 324).

How does communal, rhythmically coordinated vocalisation (§2.5.2) relate to the model of the evolution of language outlined here? Specifically, what is the relationship between communal rhythmic vocalisation and the hypothesised bifurcation of musilanguage into music and compositional language? Comparing the vocalisations of gelada monkeys (*Theropithecus gelada*) with human speech (particularly rapid, interactive conversational speech), Richman notes that

> [i]n both cases, friendly vocalizing is produced in units averaging a total length of about nine or ten syllables, produced at a rate of about five syllables per second, organized by differentiation of strong and weak beats with about three or four strong beats per unit, and all under an intonation contour (melodic contour) where the end of the unit is signaled by tonal changes. Finally, both human conversational formulas and gelada vocal units are produced with no hesitation phenomena and no internal pauses as one continuous gushing-forth of a whole unit of activity. (Richman, 2000, pp. 301–302)

One must be careful in comparing these two kinds of vocalisation because human conversation is clearly learned-propositional whereas gelada vocalisations, while broadly communicative, are innate-emotional. Moreover, despite its rapidity, human conversation is segmented and compositionally re-combinatorial, whereas gelada vocalisations are presumably not. In aligning the two we are comparing the hypothesised beginning of a process (represented by pre-linguistic vocalisation in non-human primates) with what is held to be a later, or even terminal, stage of the process (represented by fully linguistic vocalisations in humans). Nevertheless, the similarities and differences are instructive. Richman's "units", as a "continuous gushing-forth", appear to lack strong segmentation boundaries in both species. In gelada vocalisations this is probably the case, but in humans there is the added infrastructure of language – the semantic and syntactic dimensions – that provides the necessary articulatory cues to parse the utterance into discrete units. This permits the kind of coindexation-determined segmentation that imposes "virtual" segmentation boundaries – articulation points of sense and structure – upon what is ostensibly an undifferentiated sound-stream. Richman's "units of activity" are in this sense broadly equivalent to musilinguistic utterances, except that in geladas they are truly holistic, whereas in human conversation they are merely "pseudo-holistic".

To conclude this discussion, I complete the outline of Merker's "vocal learning constellation" (2012) begun in §2.7.5. The final stages consider how vocally learned song evolved into modern language, and will be correlated with the processes outlined in this section.

12. The evolution of holistic, vocally learned song-strings in *Homo erectus/Homo ergaster* into fully compositional language in *Homo sapiens* relied upon cultural evolution in the context of a "learner bottleneck", whereby "a state of competition for access to the next generation [of utterers] exists among utterances" (Merker, 2012, p. 238). Discussed more fully in §6.3, computer simulations of this process have shown that it is possible to move a system, in an "iterated learning model", from "an initial state in which nonsense-strings are randomly paired with meanings on an individual basis to a state of semantic and syntactic organization exhibiting compositionality, lexical categories, constituent order, frequency-dependent coexistence of regular and irregular forms, and recursion, all shared by the population as a whole" (2012, p. 238).

13. Iterated learning in the context of a learner bottleneck has the power to break down a repertoire of communally shared musilinguistic song-strings into sub-repertoires characterised by "assortative linkages" between strings and "different behavioural, motivational, and environmental contexts" (2012, p. 239). This kind of "repertoire differentiation" has been observed in vocally learning birds, in this case differentiating between courtship and (even specific types of) rivalry, and is hypothesised to have also driven human language evolution (2012, p. 239).

14. For such differentiation to have functioned optimally, the (arguably) initial driver of vocalisation – sexual selection linked, like most mammals, to manifest oestrus (ovulation; see note 67 on page 106) – needed to have been blunted in order to admit of "causation" (i.e., epistemic domains) other than courtship and male rivalry (2012, p. 239). This was accomplished by the evolution of modern human sexual behaviour, which involves year-round fertility, concealed ovulation – which fosters "a more extended period of exclusive copulation" – and (usually) private mating (Fitch, 2010, pp. 246–247). The driver for these changes may have been the "enticement" of females from dominant males by food-bearing subordinate males (offering "non-monopolizable", "high quality nutrients") discussed in §2.3.3 (Merker, 2012, p. 239). Initial opposition to this provisioning (certainly its first, seductive, phases) from dominant males may have led to the evolution of such "furtive pair associations", which served as a further driver of colonial monogamy and of reduced sexual rivalry (2012, pp. 239–240).

15. Having freed learned vocalisation from time-specific reproductive imperatives, it could fill the daily lives of early *Homo* and thus be subject to the kind of functional and contextual differentiation discussed in point 13 (2012, p. 240). Much of this differentiation could have been accomplished by a form of *statistical learning*, whereby if a given context (for instance, a location or a behaviour) x was associatively linked – for whatever reason – with both string y and string z; and if there were more y strings in the association x–y than there were z strings in the association x–z; then encountering context x would enhance the replicative advantages of string y more than those of string z, thus favouring the association x–y over the association x–z, and causing "the learner bottleneck to perform assortative allocation of strings by context over the generations" (2012, pp. 240–241).

16. A feature of the learner bottleneck is that the evolutionary imperative of parsimony tends to eliminate redundancy. Assuming the string-segmentation into

protemes discussed above, the "V" element of the VRS algorithm will "ensure that some behavioural situations that share something in contextual terms also happen to share some substrings.... No more than a capacity to segment strings and to generalize is required for this to occur" (2012, p. 241). Yet "[c]ontinued long enough, its imperceptible multigeneration dynamic will eventually yield single phrases [protemes] matched to single generalized contextual abstractions (in effect concepts) amounting to a tacit lexicon with rich, implicit semantic content, along with the formal syntactic efficiency measures" evident in the iterated learning models (point 12) (2012, p. 242).

17. Such ever more precise context-substring associations are not, at this stage, used to communicate meaning. They are still driven by ritual-culture's conformal motive towards copying-fidelity (point 3 on page 137), as an "all-round certificate of competence" (point 5 on page 138) (2012, p. 242).

18. There is, however, a potential instrumental-cultural utility – a potential natural-selection advantage – to breaking, in certain circumstances, the linkage between a given string and its context. That is, Hockett's (1960) language design feature of displacement (point (ix) of the list on page 126), while it risks undermining the "statistical association between song-strings and contexts that gives the repertoire its entirely tacit conceptual content", may have sufficient utility to justify violating ritual-culture's conformal motive for specific instrumental purposes (2012, p. 242). In this way, strings are "situationally decoupled" and "natural selection [and cultural selection] is given a foothold to work on the conversion of the sexually selected song tradition to a form compatible with its use for ... spoken language proper" (2012, p. 243). The action of natural selection is this context might well also serve to augment learning and imitative capacity, as an additional factor in memetic drive (§3.7.1).

19. Displacement has a safety net, in that "every false start and failed solution to the decoupling problem" could fall back on the ritual tradition and the use of learned song as a sexually selected "certificate of competence" (2012, p. 243). Even if "corrupted" through over-use of instrumental decoupling, the "glacial" learner bottleneck would reinstate ritualistic associations in the same way that it initially formed them (2012, pp. 243–244).

20. As a further consolidation of instrumental decoupling, various communicative enhancements would have been foregrounded, including markers to differentiate "in-context" from "displaced" usage; "grammatical conventions related to communicative intent"; pragmatic factors, including physical gestures; and

a separate "mode of delivery", leading to a differentiation between song and speech along the music-language continuum (§2.7.3) (2012, pp. 244–245). This process – the appearance of fully compositional language and, therefore, also of separate vocal music – would not have been completed until after the appearance of anatomically modern humans (*c.* 0.200 MYBP), and perhaps even later, with the arrival of cognitively modern humans (after *c.* 0.100 MYBP?) (Table 2.1) (2012, p. 245).

The functional differentiation referred to in point 20, and thus the formation of the music-language continuum itself, would have been underpinned by structural changes in the hominin brain, which represent the key phenotypic consequences of the various selection pressures described above. These changes served to differentiate those neural substrates subserving musilanguage towards those more specialised to subserve musicality and those more specialised to subserve language. These evolutionary changes, as with so many others in our species' phylogeny, are inscribed in the very structure of the modern human brain. These specialisations – remnants of the ebb and flow of the evolutionary tide – are considered in the next section.

2.7.7 Structural and Functional Lateralisation

Results from brain imaging studies may be interpreted as implying that music and language are part of one large, vastly complicated, distributed neurological system for processing sound in the largest-brained primate. Both systems use intonation and rhythm to convey emotions, that is, affective semantics .... Both rely on partly overlapping auditory and parietal association cortices for reception and interpretation, and partly overlapping motor and premotor cortices for production.... Music and language can both be produced by mouths or by tools and each is processed somewhat differently by men and women. Each activity engages a frontal lobe-mediated ability to keep ideas in mind long enough to bring them to fruition, and recruits additional areas of temporal and parietal cortices for longer retention. Finally, humans are able both to speak and to hear music in their heads. (Falk, 2000, pp. 212–213)

Studying the structure and function of the brain in terms of the systems believed to be responsible for our musical and linguistic competences allows us not only to gain an insight into the operation of two of our most distinctive attributes, but also to make and test hypotheses for their evolutionary origins and the selection pressures that appear to have driven their appearance in our species. A rapidly developing field of research, cognitive neuroscience has two broad strategies for investigating music and language in the brain. The first is to use the standard paradigms of experimental psychology in order to test the nature of capacities in each domain – be they, as Falk (2000) distinguishes, in perception or production – and how one affects the other. That is, such experiments explore whether facility at a music-related task correlates in some way with competence at a language-related task. These often relate specifically to the phonological, syntactic or semantic dimensions and their interactions, but there are also other cognitive skills that are invoked, including memory. Positive correlations are often taken as evidence of some functional, and possibly structural, overlap. Some such studies (such as Thompson et al. (2012), discussed below) are undertaken with subjects who have suffered a brain lesion or a developmental disorder. A specific area of injury may be correlated with a deficiency in some musical or linguistic feature, the area in question therefore being understood to perform that function in a healthy individual. Other experimental paradigms involve the exploration of phenotypic plasticity in musicians; that is, whether musical training confers advantages upon an individual that might also accrue to aspects of language perception and/or production.

The second investigative strategy is to combine such studies with real-time brain scanning, in order to see which brain regions "light up" (are activated) when undertaking specific music- or language-related tasks, or tasks that require cross-modal integration. The resolution of brain scanning has improved significantly over recent decades owing to continual advances in imaging technology. The latest PET (Positron Emission Tomography) and fMRI (functional Magnetic Resonance Imaging) scanners permit visualisation of brain activation in subjects performing musical and linguistic activities with very fine resolution. As a consequence of this ever greater discrimination, knowledge of the implementation of music and language in the brain continues to be refined, and much older information is rapidly superseded.

As the foregoing indicates, an important topic in cognitive neuroscience is the structural localisation of specific brain functions – where the "wiring" for particular abilities is to be found. While the complexities of the brain will probably remain elusive for decades, perhaps centuries, to come, significant progress has been made over the last few decades in understanding the localisation of musical and linguistic function in the brain, and the basic picture, in the sense of the gross localisation of functions, has been broadly clear for a number of years (Sacks, 2011; Koelsch, 2013; Schulkin, 2013). This knowledge also aligns closely with the evolutionary account of musilanguage bifurcation discussed above. To summarise (and inevitably to coarsen) a complex picture, there is a degree of "hemispheric specialisation" in music and language functions, but also a good deal of overlap. At its very crudest, the right hemisphere of the cerebrum is orientated towards music-related functions, and the left hemisphere is orientated towards language-related functions (in right-handed individuals); but this first approximation is clearly an oversimplification because the deep commonalities observed between the two domains in §2.7.3 suggest a significant degree of functional and/or structural overlap.

More precisely, regions in the right hemisphere appear to dominate the processing and generation of contour, tonality and timbre of both melody and speech (the prosodic dimension); whereas regions in the left hemisphere appear to dominate the processing and generation of syntactic organisation and semantic content in language, together with rhythmic structure in both music and language (Morley, 2012, p. 118). As a caveat, however, Patel argues that hemispheric asymmetries are "more subtle than generally appreciated" (2008, p. 75). He notes that whereas the left hemisphere is activated when processing phonemes (which are temporally fine but spectrally coarse) and the right hemisphere is activated when processing pitch (which is temporally coarse but spectrally fine), this depends upon whether an input is categorised via learning as specifically linguistic: an unfamiliar language might be processed "musically" rather than "linguistically", drawing upon the resources of the "wrong" hemisphere (2008, pp. 74–75).[83] In Morley's summary,

> structures in both hemispheres are involved in the production and pro-cessing of both music and language; some of the fundamental elements of music and language production and perception are shared ... and some have subsequently become specialized. Musical functions are a whole are less clearly lateralized than language function, but tasks relat-ing to pitch and pitch discrimination do seem to be right-hemisphere dominated. Linguistic functions seem to be most detrimentally affected by left-hemisphere lesions; most musical functions seem to be impaired in some respect by damage to either hemisphere. (Morley, 2012, p. 118)

To expand upon this, and on the basis of PET scans of subjects engaged in sentence and (vocal) melody generation/completion tasks, Brown et al. (2006) argue for the following three categories of music-language implement-ation in the brain: (i) *shared* (and therefore co-localised) neural processing of certain music and language features; (ii) *parallel* processing and partial over-lap (and therefore some co-localisation) in brain systems for certain other features of music and language; and (iii) *distinct* processing (and therefore separation) in brain substrates for yet other music and language elements (2006, p. 2798, Fig. 5). While bearing in mind, apropos categories (i) and (ii), that "activation overlap [on an fMRI scan] does not necessarily imply computational overlap or even the involvement of the same neural systems at a finer-grained level of analysis" (Rogalsky et al., 2011, p. 3846), Table 2.2 summarises the hypothesised correlations between certain brain regions and associated music- and language-related functions from Brown et al. (2006, p. 2798, Fig. 5), adding additional information from Patel (2008, pp. 73–76), Norman-Haignere et al. (2015), Besson et al. (2017, pp. 42–45), and Bowden et al. (2020) (the last of these being the standard online resource for brain anatomy and function, incorporating the *NeuroNames* system of nomenclature) (the shaded cell is discussed further on page 281).[84]

---

[83] The extension of hemispheric localisation of certain functions to the notion of "left-brained" (analytical/logical/verbal) and "right-brained" (creative/emotional/visual) character/personal-ity types, according to which hemisphere is "dominant", lacks empirical support (J. A. Nielsen et al., 2013; see also Corballis, 2014).

[84] Regions of the cerebral cortex are identified in Table 2.2 and elsewhere using the numbering system devised by Brodmann (1909) at the turn of the twentieth century, which is still used in modern cognitive neuroscience. This system partitions the cerebral cortex – the gross structure

Category	Brodmann Areas LH: left hemisphere; RH: right hemisphere; BL = bilateral		Function		Interface Areas
Shared	Input:	BA 41, 42 (BL; primary auditory cortex).	Input:	Acoustic input (LH: phoneme perception/chunking; RH: pitch perception/chunking).	
	Output:	BA 4 (precentral gyrus).	Output:	Motor output.	
Parallel	Input:	BA 22 (LH = Wernicke's area).	Input:	Sensory phonological generativity (LH: language; RH: music).	Phonology/semantics interface area. Also implicated in fine-grained timing of music and language sounds.
	Output:	BA 44, 45 (LH = Broca's area).	Output:	Motor phonological generativity (LH: language; RH: music).	Syntax/phonology interface area. Broca's area is also implicated in processing phonological, lexical and semantic information, suggesting that syntax and semantics are co-processed in each domain.
Distinct		BA 20 (inferior temporal gyrus), 21 (middle temporal gyrus), 38 (superior temporal gyrus and middle temporal gyrus), 39 (angular gyrus), 40 (supramarginal gyrus), 47 (inferior frontal gyrus).		Parts of the superior temporal gyrus appear specialised in the LH for language processing; and the *planum temporale* (part of Wernicke's area in the LH) and the *planum polare* (located near the auditory cortex) are BL specialised for music processing.	Semantics/syntax interface area.

Table 2.2: Brain Regions and Associated Music and Language Functions.

Summarising the three categories of relationship, Brown et al. (2006) note that

> (i) ... *Shared* processing elicits overlapping activations between music and language in primary auditory cortex (BA 41 [and 42]) and primary motor cortex (BA 4). (ii) ... Phonological generativity is seen as the major point of *parallelism* between music and speech. Regions of BA 22 and BA 44/45 are seen as sensory and motor centres, respectively, for phonological generativity. These areas of parallelism may be localized such that *BA 22/44/45 of the left hemisphere is specialized for speech phonology and the corresponding right hemispheric areas are specialized for musical phonology.* The processes for phonological generativity in BA 22 and BA 44/45 may interface differentially with other functions, with BA 22 being a phonology/semantic interface area and BA 44/45 being a phonology/syntax interface area. (iii) ... *Domain-specific* [i.e., distinct] areas for music or language, with nonoverlapping activation profiles for melody generation and sentence generation, are interposed between BA 22 and BA 44/45 in a series of semantics/syntax interface areas distributed throughout the extrasylvian[85] temporal lobe (BA [20], 21, 38,

---

of which consists of two hemispheres, left and right, each with four lobes (frontal, parietal, temporal and occipital) – into over fifty "Brodmann areas" (BAs) based on cytoarchitectural (cell-/tissue-type) distinctions. While primarily a histological-structural scheme, BAs, individually or in adjacent groupings, correspond with functional distinctions. Each BA in the left hemisphere has a structural – *but not necessarily functional* – analogue in the right hemisphere. The associated anatomical names for some important functional areas for music and language processing include: BA 44 (*pars opercularis*) and 45 (*pars triangularis*) (together constituting Broca's area, in the *left* frontal lobe, involved in speech production); BA 22, 39 and 40 (Wernicke's area, in the *left* temporal lobe, involved in language comprehension); and BA 41 and 42 (primary auditory cortex, in the temporal lobe, responsible for frequency representation) (Bowden et al., 2020; Johns, 2014, p. 35, Fig. 3.12). The foregoing lateralisation relates to the *c.* 90% of humans who are right handed – where the left hemisphere is dominant. Of the *c.* 10% who are left handed – where the right hemisphere is dominant – *c.* 75% actually manifest "*left* hemisphere dominance for language [i.e., Broca's and Wernicke's areas are located in the left hemisphere, not the right], while the remainder process language function on the right side or bilaterally" (Harvey, 2017, p. 43; emphasis mine) (by contrast, *c.* 95% of right-handers manifest left-hemisphere dominance for language (2017, p. 42)); the auditory cortex, by contrast, is structurally and functionally *bilateral*. Note that there are complex and imperfect overlaps between intermediate-level structural features such as the gyri (the flat areas of "high ground") and sulci (the "valley floor" of the folds) that constitute the cortex, Brodmann areas, and functional regions, which often make localisation of music- and language-implicated regions difficult: Heschl's gyrus, for instance, is broadly, but not precisely, coterminous with BA 41 and 42 and with primary auditory cortex. There is also complex multifunctionality in certain areas: Broca's area, for instance, is also involved in bimanual coordination (Harvey, 2017, p. 111), and aspects of visuospatial cognition (Sluming et al., 2007).

[85] This term refers to regions of the temporal lobe located away from the Sylvian (or lateral) fissure, the large sulcus that separates the temporal lobe from the frontal and parietal lobes.

39, 40) as well as the inferior frontal gyrus (BA 47). (Brown et al., 2006, 2798; my emphases)

To condense this summary even further, hearing and producing the sounds of (vocal) music and language, perhaps unsurprisingly, *share* neural resources. Generativity (i.e., "assembling" utterances prior to their vocal-motor production) is conducted in *parallel*, with language occupying left-hemisphere and music occupying analogous right-hemisphere regions. The left-hemisphere BA 22 (part of Wernicke's area) implements connections between phonology and semantics,[86] whereas the same hemisphere's BA 44/45 (Broca's area) implements connections between phonology and syntax. Crucially, this functionality *includes musical as well as linguistic syntax* – understood as "the rules that structure sequences of events that unfold in time" (Besson et al., 2017, p. 42) – by means of connections between left-hemisphere language-orientated BA 44/45 and their right-hemisphere music-orientated homologues. This issue is revisited in §3.8.6, where a mechanism for the relationships between linguistic and musical syntax is discussed. Outside Broca's area and Wernicke's area, other regions mediate the semantics-syntax interface *separately* for music and language.

Nevertheless, it is important not to regard such regions as Broca's area and Wernicke's area as isolated "islands" of functionality: "the computations necessary for language and music processing are not performed independently from other cognitive functions and ... language and music are not modular and encapsulated systems" (Besson et al., 2017, p. 45). Indeed, the "multi-dimensional hypothesis" of music and language asserts that both domains "are processed in interaction with other cognitive, emotional, and motor functions" (Besson et al., 2017, p. 40). These include various "executive functions" associated, among other things, with working memory (Besson et al., 2017, p. 39), itself a component of consciousness, which are partly localised in the frontal lobes. More broadly, there is growing evidence that, as a *complex dynamic system* (Nolte, 2014, Ch. 7), the brain recruits structures

---

The "perisylvian" region, which surrounds the Sylvian fissure, encompasses Broca's area and Wernicke's area (Bowden et al., 2020; Johns, 2014, p. 28, Fig. 3.1).

[86] Wernicke's area is close to the visual cortex, and is also implicated in recognition of the graphical representation of language (writing) and, by inference, music (notation) (Johns, 2014, p. 36). Broca's area and Wernicke's area are connected by a bundle of white-matter (sub-cortical) nerve-fibres termed the arcuate fasciculus (Johns, 2014, p. 35, Fig. 3.12).

flexibly in order to implement functions that depend on connections with, and activation states of, other structures (Besson et al., 2017, p. 45).

Moreover, while there is growing understanding of the structure and function of the brain's systems for music and language, it is important to consider, in addition to these genetically driven design features, those that arise as a result of phenotypic plasticity (note 81 on page 138). This includes those changes to the "default" brain morphology that arise as a result of sustained musical training, and that help to confirm other types of data on brain structure and function. To give a brief indication of one such ontogenetic change, it is known that "enhanced phonetic discrimination [of speech and non-speech sounds] in musicians [is] correlated with enhanced cortical surface area of the left P[lanum]T[emporale] … and with increased structural connectivity between the right and left PT …, providing evidence that long-term intensive musical training is associated with anatomical and functional changes in speech-specific brain regions such as the PT" (Besson et al., 2017, pp. 42–43). That such changes have been observed in monozygotic – genetically identical – twins, where one is musically active and the other is not, indicates that "a significant portion of the differences in brain anatomy between experts and nonexperts depend[s] on causal effects of training" (Manzano & Ullén, 2018, p. 387).

To the centres responsible for the melodic/prosodic dimensions of music and language, one must add those responsible for their rhythmic dimension. Brain centres subserving rhythmic aspects of music and language are separate from those subserving their melodic, syntactic or semantic dimensions. As discussed in §2.5.2, the neural substrates supporting rhythmic entrainment and synchrony are located in various brain regions, but are connected via the motor cortico-basal-ganglia-thalamo-cortical (mCBGT) circuit. That humans can produce melodic and prosodic vocal utterances that are also rhythmically regular suggests the presence of connections between those brain regions discussed by Brown et al. (2006) for melody and speech production and those forming the mCBGT circuit discussed by Merchant et al. (2018). Indeed, this is the assertion of Patel's vocal learning and rhythmic synchronization hypothesis (2008), which, as noted on page 96, implicates the basal ganglia in "binding" – like Ixion to the fiery wheel – the inherently limber melodic and prosodic aspects of music and language to the regular "rotation" of the internal tactus and its physical manifestation via gestures controlled by the motor system. This binding leads to "similar activations of frontal and temporal regions of both hemispheres when processing the temporal structure of sentences and melodies, thereby arguing against a simple dichotomy between the left hemisphere for language and the right hemisphere for music and providing support for shared neural resources between music and speech" (Besson et al., 2017, p. 43).

The foregoing discussion is necessary in order to arrive at the central point of this section: how brain specialisms for music and language were shaped by evolution. As the quotation at the end of the previous paragraph implies, it is likely that the neural substrates for musilanguage were, as an essentially melodic-rhythmic phenomenon, initially bi-lateral; and as segmentation and compositionality evolved, the substrates responsible for language-primary elements (syntax and semantics) were increasingly focused and developed in the left hemisphere. As Marin and Perry (1999) argue, "[t]he close correspondence between the networks of regions involved in singing and [linguistic] speaking suggests that [linguistic] speech may have evolved from an already-complex system for the voluntary control of [musilinguistic] vocalization. Their divergences suggest that the later evolving aspects of these two uniquely human abilities are essentially hemispheric specialisations" (in Morley, 2012, 119; insertions are Morley's and mine).[87] Their assertion accords with Thompson et al. (2012), who determined that those with congenital amusia – a deficit in processing music – were unable to process emotion in language prosody, this finding further supporting the hypothesis of shared neural mechanisms and a common evolutionary history connecting the two domains back to musilanguage.

Hemispheric specialisation is conceived by Harvey in terms of the fundamental evolutionary principle of parsimony. He argues that

> during the emergence of our two communication systems, language and music, with subtly different processing requirements it became necessary to separate out some distinct circuitries for each mode of communica-

---

[87] While such differentiation appears to have characterised human phylogeny, the ontogenetic development of linguistic and musical competences in individuals might not necessarily rely (wholly) upon domain-specific processes (Patel, 2008, p. 77).

tion. Because the overall cellular and connectional organization of the two cerebral hemispheres is relatively similar, perhaps some left-right parcellation of function was the simplest and most conservative option in evolutionary terms.... links between [a predominant right-] handedness, tool use, gesture, and emergent language may have contributed to a left-sided bias for articulate speech, while the right ... may have been more suited to specializations associated with the development of interactive musical capability. (Harvey, 2017, p. 121)

If correct, this is another example of the VRS algorithm's arriving at an aptation by the most efficient and economical means, which, in this case, involved reorientation of a single-function/distributed system in order to perform two related functions via a degree of hemispheric differentiation/ specialisation. The alternative strategy – starting from scratch and rebuilding separate systems for music and language – would have been prohibitively costly in terms of time and resources, and would have contradicted the gradualism and parsimony inherent in cumulative selection. The evolution of music and language is therefore perhaps the classic example of how evolution does not go back to the drawing board, but rather makes do with what resources it has at hand.

With the proviso that this differentiation was a slow and gradual process in which the distinctions between musilanguage, music and language were fluid, these specialisations appear to have: (i) focused the primary control for emerging musilinguistic/linguistic syntax and semantics in the left hemisphere, in Broca's area and Wernicke's area, respectively; (ii) retained the deployment of these left-hemisphere areas for their already established musilinguistic/music-related functions, namely the phonology, syntax and affective semantics of musilanguage/music, the first of these being recruited to serve an additional musilinguistic/linguistic function; and (iii) retained right-hemisphere control over the prosodic dimensions of musilanguage/ language, and over melodic contour in musilanguage/music.

Summarising some of these changes, Levitin argues that

[c]rucial evolutionary changes that enabled the evolution of the musical brain in humans surely included those in the orbital and ventrolateral prefrontal cortex, [Brodmann] areas 47/12 [orbital gyri], 46 [middle

frontal gyrus], 45, and 44 [Broca's area in the left hemisphere] ..., and possibly area 10 [transverse frontopolar gyri and orbital gyri]. These regions are known to be involved in the representation of ideas and the maintenance of them in working memory .... Area 6 [precentral region], just behind 44, is part of the premotor cortex, and is involved in moving the lips, jaw, and tongue.... During 20 million years of evolution, it is not too difficult to imagine a new function evolving right here where these regions meet, gradually enabling the brain to report what it is holding in consciousness – to start talking or singing about what it is thinking about. (Levitin, 2009, pp. 291–292)

The functional-structural correlates of the bifurcation of musilanguage, with all their implications for music, language and consciousness, represent the most recent stage of a long evolutionary process. Having said on page 157 that "[b]rain centres subserving rhythmic aspects of music and language are separate from those subserving their melodic, syntactic or semantic dimensions", it is important to add that the former are evolutionarily older, being located in brain regions (particularly the basal ganglia) that were laid down earlier in our phylogenetic history. This is perhaps unsurprising given our timeline: our mammalian ancestors moved but could not rhythmically entrain, and had a repertoire of primitive calls; our hominin antecedents were perhaps capable of some degree of entrainment, and developed a richer repertoire of musilinguistic vocalisations; and cognitively modern humans demonstrate both entrainment and complex learned vocalisations. Every stage of this millennia-long process involved building upon extant brain structures, which, in the case of humans, included quite literally forming evolutionarily later structures on top of earlier ones.

Moreover – and this is perhaps the clincher in discussions of the evolutionary origins of music and language – the evidence discussed here suggests that brain structures primarily subserving music (strictly, those that might have subserved the prosodic dimensions of musilanguage and the capacity for rhythmic entrainment to a tactus) are, as has been implied here, *phylogenetically older* than those subserving language (see also point 8 of the list on page 138). This notion is supported by Podlipniak (2017b, 2020), who argues for the importance of tonal qualia – the emotional efferents of expectations bound up with statistically learned and motor-associated pitch hierarchies (see also

§3.5.2 and §7.2.1) – in understanding human evolution. Presupposing the existence of pitch-centre recognition (Podlipniak, 2016), tonal qualia have their roots early in the hominin line, perhaps appearing after the origin of the fine vocal control of the larynx required to produce pitch, which may have occurred after *c.* 0.6 MYA (2017b, p. 40) (and which may thus have arisen in *Homo erectus/Homo ergaster* and/or *Homo heidelbergensis*). The evolutionary antiquity of fine vocal control, and the fact that tonal qualia, and the pitch centricity and pitch hierarchy upon which they depend, are "unique, music-specific phenomena in the same way as the sensations of phonemes or words are unique and specific to speech" (Podlipniak, 2017b, p. 36), add further support to the argument that an ancestral melodic/prosodic musilanguage later bifurcated into music and language. Hemispheric lateralisation resulted from nascent language's motivation and recruitment of new left-hemisphere regions for its own partially independent syntax and semantics, this in order to compensate for language's attenuation of the predominantly pitch-based syntactic and semantic dimensions of musilanguage.

Podlipniak's thesis elegantly integrates tonal qualia with two other aptive factors in the evolution of music considered in §2.5 and §2.7.5, namely group synchronisation and vocal learning. In the former factor, the predominantly tactus-based/rhythmic nature of entrainment is linked to the melodic dimension by means of coupling with communally shared, pitch-structural hierarchies (and the tonal qualia they motivate) abstracted from shared song-melodies. The linkage gives rise to "brain-state alignment" between hominin conspecifics and a resulting "social consolidation" via rhythmic-melodic interaction (Podlipniak, 2017b, p. 39). This mechanism is broadly consonant with Patel's vocal learning and rhythmic synchronization hypothesis, discussed on page 157 in terms of the basal-ganglia-mediated, "Ixion-like" binding of rhythm and melody. Indeed, by analogy – and perhaps partially overlapping – with the mCBGT circuit hypothesised to underpin temporal anticipation and Patel's "online integration of the auditory and motor system" (2008, p. 410; §2.5.2), Podlipniak (2017b, p. 38) invokes "cortico-subcortical loops" as the basis for tonal qualia and for the hierarchic pitch structures that underpin them. In the latter aptive factor, "[b]ecause vocal learning is in fact a kind of learning by imitation that necessitates the motor control of the larynx, pitch class comprehension must be somehow related to motor schemata which mentally represent the production of pitches by the vocal apparatus. Therefore, [brain-state alignment] can be understood [after Cox's (2011) 'mimetic hypothesis'] in terms of 'mimetic engagement' …". This suggests that "vocal communication at least partly involves 'mimetic cognition', which is strictly related to imitation, not only as a method of learning, but also as a means of comprehending meaning" (2017b, pp. 39–40).

The argument of the evolutionary priority of music over language also follows logically from the foregoing discussion of specialisation, because if one accepts that hemispheric localisation of music and language was built upon extant, bilateral brain systems for musilanguage; and if musilanguage is understood as, at its origin, a form of song that (having arisen as a result of one or more of the reasons advanced in §2.5) only later acquired referential function; then it follows that the kind of vocalisations that we might now retrospectively regard as musical came before those we might regard as linguistic in our evolutionary and neurobiological history. This hypothesis is additionally evidenced, albeit circumstantially, by the fact that musicality – including memory for song-melody and its associated text – often persists in individuals with dementia long after language (in a form not associated with melody) is lost (Bannan & Montgomery-Smith, 2008). Owing to music's deep structural-evolutionary enmeshing in the brain, when the syntax and semantics of language are parasitic on musical melody, they are preserved, ghost-like in dementia patients. In this state they are essentially functionless simulacra, merely sustained by melody; when they have to function independently of music, as free-standing competences, they sadly falter.

From the perspective of the effect of nature on culture, the implications of these brain-structural changes on protemes would have been considerable. In particular, the tendencies towards segmentation and compositionality discussed in §2.7.6 would have been enhanced by the "binding" discussed on page 157 of melody/prosody to a tactus. While Stravinsky complained about the "tyranny of the barline" (Levitz, 2004, p. 81), the yoking of protemes to regular systems of metre and accentuation may have augmented their perceptual-cognitive salience and thus fostered their cultural transmission. This might have resulted, in part, from the tendency of a regular metre to foster anticipation (particularly the imagining of notes expected to occur on the next strong beat), which serves to heighten the attention of listeners and thus to augment the salience of associated protemes. From the perspective of the effect of culture on nature, it is not difficult to see increasingly segmented musilanguage, with its growing referentiality, driving the development of syntax-regulating centres in the left hemisphere (i.e., Broca's area), in order to prevent a profusion of incoherent meanings associated with unconstrained morpheme combination. This augmentation of cerebral substrates for syntax might have occurred via the process of memetic drive (§3.7.1), with protemes directing the evolution of genes in ways that primarily serve the former's replicative interests.

2.8 Summary of Chapter 2

Chapter 2 has argued that:

1. While the question of what constitutes music remains open, it seems likely that the range of competences that comprise musicality are, or were, individually or collectively, adaptive or exaptive. Thus, an evolutionary explanation for music and musicality appears more rational than one that sees them as merely side-effects of other, more fundamental, imperatives.

2. The journey from our earliest common ancestor with chimpanzees to modern humans is, while not long in evolutionary terms, certainly convoluted, with many environmental and social pressures acting upon those aspects of our physiology and psychology that are implicated in musicality. In short, we became savannah-dwelling hunter-gatherers whose social cohesion (and individual survival) appears to have been dependent, in part, upon the communicative vocalisations underpinning both music and language.

3. There are three principal candidates for the aptive benefits of musicality, namely fostering group cohesion through coordinated rhythmic movement and vocalisation, sexual selection, and infant-caregiver bond-formation. It is entirely possible that these are non-mutually-exclusive, indeed that they are mutually reinforcing. What is perhaps less clear is the sequence in which these uses evolved.[88]

---

[88] Much less tangible than these three candidates, and excluded from consideration here for this reason, is perhaps a fourth: the capacity of the propositional language, and perhaps consciousness, arising from musilanguage to structure our ancestors' conception of past and future time and of their own mortality. Likely then as now, the "modern human mind" served

4. Music and language are seemingly two sides of the same evolutionary coin, bifurcating from a common musilinguistic ancestor after *c.* 0.200 MYA. The evolution of segmentation gave musilanguage the potential to develop a compositional syntax that is also evident, albeit without the rich semantic content of post-bifurcation language, in post-bifurcation music.

5. The localisation of substrates for music and language in the brain aids in the reconstruction of their evolutionary history. This suggests a common neural basis for musilanguage, with increasing lateralisation – left hemisphere for language, right hemisphere for music – as the two forms became differentiated. Such re-purposing makes perfect sense from the standpoint of evolutionary parsimony. The likely sharing of left-hemisphere centres for both music and language syntax and semantics might be understood not only to caution against an excessively lateralised view of the two domains, but also to imply the parasitism of these dimensions of post-bifurcation language upon their musilinguistic antecedents.

On the basis of the principles discussed in §1.5, Chapter 3 will attempt to extend the scope of the discussion to encompass cultural replicators, now generally referred to as "memes". It argues that attempting to understand human musicality and music in purely biological/natural terms is inadequate, and that the cultural/nurtural perspective afforded by theories of cultural replication is essential for a complete picture. It will: argue why cultural replicators are necessary for the understanding of music and musicality; survey pre- and proto-memetic theories of cultural change; explore some key themes in memetics; consider some central issues in music from a memetic perspective; expand the consideration of biological taxonomies in Chapter 1 to encompass cultural categorisation; explore the issue of dual-replicator coevolution insofar as it affects musicality and music; and examine further the (co)evolution of music and language.

---

as a fortress to counter fatalism with optimism; and music was used as a balm to attenuate the fear of oblivion (Harvey, 2017, pp. 75, 162–163).

3. Music-Cultural Evolution in the Light of Memetics

'But it isn't Easy' [to make up a Pooh song about Owl's old house], said Pooh to himself, as he looked at what had once been Owl's House. 'Because Poetry and Hums aren't things which you get, they're things which get *you*. And all you can do is to go where they can find you'. – Winnie the Pooh. (Milne & Shepard, 2016, p. 146; emphasis in the original)

3.1 Introduction: Cultural Replicators, Vehicles and Hierarchies

One of the most difficult conceptual leaps to be made when understanding music in an evolutionary context is to move from considering – as Chapter 1 and Chapter 2 have done – the *evolution of humans* as musical creatures and the associated *role of music* in our individual development and daily lives, to considering *the evolution of music itself*. As will be argued in Chapter 4, the concept of evolution has played a largely metaphorical role in scholarly discourses on music, but my aim in this chapter is to take music's relationship with evolution literally. That is, I consider here *the evolution of music itself* from a systemic standpoint, arguing that its changes over time are driven by the same evolutionary forces, those of the VRS algorithm, that have driven evolution in the natural world (Jan, 2007). In this sense, I am again adopting a Universal Darwinian standpoint (§1.5.1), arguing that there is no meaningful distinction, on an algorithmic level, between biological evolution – as manifested, for instance, in the difference between a Flutist wren (*Microcerculus ustulatus*) and a Superb lyrebird (*Menura novaehollandiae*) – and cultural evolution – as manifested, for instance, in the difference between the style of Mozart and that of Beethoven (no avian analogy intended).

 https://doi.org/10.11647/OBP.0301.03

As the leading candidate theory of cultural evolution, the main focus of this chapter will be upon memetics (see Blackmore, 1999 for an overview and Dennett, 2017, Ch. 11 for rebuttals of criticisms). While the adherents of various theories of cultural evolution assert that there is clear blue water between them, for such a theory to be truly Darwinian – as memetics most certainly is – it would have to cleave to the notion that cultures evolve because they implement the VRS algorithm; that is, they change as a consequence of the variation, replication and selection of particulate chunks of cultural information. To this principle, memetics adds the epidemiological notion of cultural information moving through communities like a bacterium or virus (§3.4.1). Harari, for instance, argues that

> [e]ver more scholars see cultures as a kind of mental infection or parasite, with humans as its unwitting host.... [Analogously to organic parasites,] cultural ideas live inside the minds of humans. They multiply and spread from one host to another, occasionally weakening the hosts and sometimes even killing them.... [C]ultures are mental parasites that emerge accidentally, and thereafter take advantage of all people infected by them. (Harari, 2014, p. 242)

When engaging with memetics it is important not to accept the potential limitation of its scope that has arisen in recent years. As Figure 3.1a indicates, in contemporary popular and internet culture a meme has been reduced to the status of a comic image with a large-font caption, one usually mocking the hapless target of the latest online *faux*-outrage (Shifman, 2013). As Figure 3.1b indicates, even so-called "music" memes bear little relationship to the replicated sound patterns that are discussed in this chapter. While such images certainly testify to the infective power of memes – this considerably augmented in the digital world (§7.6.1) – to regard them as the only entities that exemplify the cultural replicator would significantly limit the scope and subtlety of Dawkins' (1989) original concept, which covers phenomena of great diversity. In music, a meme can encompass any replicable entity, from a short three-note pattern, to a structural archetype hidden from immediate perception but engendered by more tractable lower-level patterns, to an abstract idea for manipulating a particular class of musical patterns (what might be termed a "musico-operational/procedural meme" (Jan, 2011b, pp. 242–243)).

(a) Cat Meme.

(b) "Music" Meme.

Figure 3.1: Internet Memes.

This chapter continues by addressing the question of why cultural replicators are required in the first place (§3.2), arguing that biological replicators alone are insufficient to explain the origin and complexity of human musics. It then looks at certain precursor theories to memetics, in order to identify common threads in cultural-evolution models (§3.3). Thereafter, it turns to memetics itself, exploring certain key themes pertinent to the understanding of music and musicality as well as to other cultural forms (§3.4). The next section looks at certain specifically musical issues from the perspective of memetics (§3.5). The following section returns to the issue of taxonomy covered in §1.7, attempting to extend certain principles of cladistic taxonomy to music-cultural evolution (§3.6). Having covered music-memetic evolution, the issue of dual-replicator coevolution is addressed next, in order to explore how genes and memes affect each others' evolutionary opportunities (§3.7). Lastly, the chapter returns to the issue of music and language (co)evolution, exploring how semantics and syntax might have arisen from memetic processes and how the mechanisms of how these dimensions of music and language might be implemented in the brain (§3.8).

3.2 Why the Need for Cultural Replicators?

One can answer the question at the head of this section by referring back to the quotation by Harari on bee societies (page 3). In bee and many other insect species, most behaviours are genetically, not culturally, transmitted. In extreme cases, if an interconnected sequence of behaviours is interrupted, the animal will repeat the sequence of actions from the start, mechanistically. As a famous example, certain wasps of the genus *Sphex* deposit their prey (usually a paralysed insect) at the entrance of their nest and then enter the nest in order to check it. If the prey is moved away (by a human experimenter), the wasp will move the prey back to the nest entrance, but will also repeat the nest-inspection behaviour, a pattern that seems to be replicable *ad infinitum*. Indeed, the creature is truly enslaved by its genes – more specifically, by the patterns of behaviour-generating neuronal firing those genes motivate – to the extent that it is difficult to speak of it possessing any free will. This condition is aptly termed, after these gene-shackled wasps, "sphexishness" by Hofstadter (1985, p. 529).

Creature	Attributes
Darwinian	Those subject to the operation of the VRS algorithm, operating (only) upon genes (Dennett, 1995, 374; Fig. 13.1).
Skinnerian (after ideas of B. F. Skinner)	Those endowed with "conditionable (phenotypic) plasticity", such that *operant conditioning* (or instrumental conditioning) – a form of the VRS algorithm that acts upon genetically controlled behaviours – reinforces (i.e., favours for future deployment) actions that, on testing, result in benefits to the organism (1995, 374–375; Fig. 13.2).[89]
Popperian (after ideas of Karl Popper)	Those possessing an evolutionarily designed internal (virtual) selective environment able to preview and mentally pre-test candidate actions in order to determine, without risk, which would be most advantageous to deploy in specific real-world situations (1995, 375–377; Fig. 13.3).
Gregorian (after ideas of the psychologist Richard Gregory)	Those whose internal selective environment is able to draw upon culturally transmitted information, such as tool design/use and language (itself a higher-order, cognitive tool), in previewing and mentally pre-testing candidate actions. (1995, 377–378; Fig. 13.4).[90]

Table 3.1: Dennett's Four Types of Creature.

To speak of free will is to presume, if not a consciousness capable of self-reflection (§7.3), then at least a capacity for weighing up options and deciding upon alternative courses of action. While such decision-making can also be genetically determined – by means of hard-wired option-choice circuits – much of it in humans is driven by learning (nurture) rather than instinct (nature). That is, decisions are based on ideas of utility and correctness which, while they generally correlate with the genetic "good", are ultimately cultural, not biological. As summarised in Table 3.1, Dennett (1995) expands upon this notion, identifying four categories of "creature" that occupy concentric circles of increasingly smaller magnitude (see also Dennett, 2017, pp. 98–99). These represent a progression from the application of the VRS algorithm in the domain of nature towards its application in that of culture.

---

[89] In addition to the (Darwinian) operant conditioning theorised by (Skinner, 1953), there exists (non-Darwinian) *classical* (Pavlovian) conditioning, where a neutral stimulus elicits expectation of a reward, the former having previously been associated with the latter.

[90] Only this category of creature would appear fully able to deploy the intentional stance described in the quotation on page 64.

These creatures broadly correspond with, and are indeed products of, what Plotkin and Odling-Smee (1981) term the "four levels of evolution", characterised by different modes of "information gain and storage" (1981, p. 229). These are: (i) the level of the gene, where "the site of [information] storage is a population's gene pool", changes in gene frequencies being a function of interactions between phenotypes and environments (giving rise to Darwinian creatures) (1981, pp. 228–229); (ii) the level of "variable epigenesis",[91] where phenotypes are modifiable during epigenesis by environmental factors, leading to polymorphism, i.e., alternative-track phenotypes driven by specific alleles (giving rise to Skinnerian creatures) (1981, p. 229); (iii) the level of the "learning phenotype", where an individual is capable of transcending its inherited genetic information – and thus of solving the "uncertain futures" problem (Plotkin & Odling-Smee, 1981, p. 230; Plotkin, 1995, p. 144) – by acquiring additional, non-genetic, information via learning over the course of its lifespan, but where this information is confined to that individual (giving rise to Popperian creatures) (1981, pp. 229–230); and (iv) the level of "sociocultural" evolution, where non-genetic information acquired by an individual via learning can additionally be (memetically) transmitted to others (giving rise to Gregorian creatures) (1981, pp. 230–231).[92]

Gregorian creatures ostensibly have the greatest survival advantage, for not only do they have millennia of evolutionarily wired survival knowledge from their Darwinian, Skinnerian and Popperian heritage – Dennett's "Smart Moves" (1995, p. 374) – they can also draw upon various culturally transmitted tools for survival and problem-solving. In this sense a *coevolutionary* perspective (§3.7) is needed to understand them – to understand *us*, given that we are the prime exemplar of this creature on earth – one that attempts to reconcile gene with meme and nature with nurture, or at least to hypothesise which might have the upper hand in any particular context. As summarised in Table 3.2, the interactions between these two domains have been modelled by four main theories, broadly in terms of dominance hierarchies.

---

[91] Not to be confused with epigenetics (§1.8, §3.4.3 and §4.4.1.1), epigenesis is the "[o]rigin during ontogeny of structures from undifferentiated material" (E. Mayr, 1982, p. 958).

[92] Plotkin (1995) conflates levels (i) and (ii) into the "primary" – "genetic-developmental" – heuristic (1995, p. 138). Level (iii) is termed the "secondary heuristic" (1995, p. 149), and level (iv) the "tertiary heuristic" (1995, p. 206).

Discipline	Privileged Dimension	Precepts
Sociobiology (E. O. Wilson, 2000)	nature/gene	Culture is on the "leash" of the genes and serves adaptation; gene-based natural selection is all-powerful.
Evolutionary Psychology (Pinker, 1997)	nature/gene	Culture is determined and constrained by genetically evolved psychological predispositions.
Gene-Culture Coevolution-ary Theory (GCC) (Boyd & Richerson, 1985)	nature/gene and culture (re-produced cultural information)	Human behaviour is the result of subtle interactions between genes and inherited cultural information.
Memetics (Blackmore, 1999)	culture/meme	Culture is transmitted by memes that are partially independent of genes and sometimes in control of them.

Table 3.2: Four Perspectives on Nature and Culture.

Moving down Table 3.2, the four theories shift from a gene-centred to a meme-centred orientation. The extremes are demarcated by Wilson's famous dictum that "[t]he genes hold culture on a leash. The leash is very long, but inevitably [cultural] values will be constrained in accordance with their effects on the human gene pool" (1978, p. 167), and Blackmore's theory of memetic drive (1999), whereby meme replication is hypothesised to have shaped human genetic-cognitive development in the direction of ever greater imitative and culture-fostering ways (§3.7.1). The *via media* is perhaps best represented by (Richerson & Boyd, 2005, pp. 237–238), who, paraphrasing Dobzhansky (1973), assert that "nothing about culture makes sense except in the light of [biological *and* cultural] evolution".

As will be explored more fully in Chapter 4, the existence of cultural replicators is alluded to in the musicological literature, although rarely in explicitly evolutionary terms. One manifestation of this awareness is the idea of the composer ab/extracting a lexicon of patterns by exposure to the music of his/her culture and assortatively recombining elements of this lexicon in order to create "new" music (Ratner, 1970). A flavour of this tendency is given by Mattheson in his *Der vollkommene Cappelmeister* of 1739 (Mattheson

& Harriss, 1981), when he asserts that "[t]he composer, through much experience and attentive listening to good work, must have assembled something now and then on modulations, little turns, clever events, pleasant passages and transitions, which, though they are only isolated items, nevertheless could produce usual and whole things through appropriate combination" (1981, p. 283, para. 15; see also Ledbetter, 2013).

While it is necessary to be sensitive to the cultural situatedness of this view – the eighteenth century is a time when discussion of assortative recombination as a compositional principle reaches its zenith – it is arguably broadly applicable to most if not all human musics. This is on account of the fact, discussed in §2.7.6, human, that gestalt segmentation forces in conjunction with the limitations of STM will – from both a poietic and an esthesic standpoint, as Nattiez (1990) would frame it – impose strong (evolutionary-psychological) pressures in favour of music's existing as discrete particles. The latter attribute, together with the tendency of the VRS algorithm to "feed upon" such particles, mean that a purely sphexish explanation is both inadequate and unnecessary to explain the richness and diversity of human musics.

3.3 Pre- and Proto-Memetic Theories of Cultural Evolution

Given that the evolution of music – as distinct from the evolution of musicality – relies upon our status as Gregorian creatures, it is useful briefly to review the history of the concept of the cultural replicator, before examining in more detail what such a notion can offer to our understanding of music. The following subsections consider, necessarily selectively, three key stages in the development of cultural replicator theory since the early-twentieth century, seeing them as stepping-stones towards the modern theory of memetics. These theories generally focus on replication in verbal culture, but their precepts are applicable in principle to any medium of culture, including the visual and the sonic.

3.3.1 The Mneme

Dawkins maintained that the name for his cultural replicator, the meme, arose from a contraction of "mimeme" (Dawkins, 1989, p. 192), itself derived from *mimeisthai* ($\mu\iota\mu\varepsilon\iota\sigma\theta\alpha\iota$; to imitate) (Laurent, 1999, p. 1). Laurent argues that a "more straightforward source" for "meme" is "mneme", which he maintains derives from *mimneskesthai* ($\mu\iota\mu\nu\varepsilon\sigma\kappa\varepsilon\sigma\theta\alpha\iota$; to remember), and which is related to *Mnemosyne* (M$\nu\eta\mu o\sigma\upsilon\nu\eta$), the Greek goddess of memory (1999, p. 1). Laurent locates an appearance of "mneme" in Maeterlinck's entomological study *The life of the white ant* of 1927 (Maeterlinck, 1927).[93] He notes that the white ant (i.e., the termite) is regularly referred to by Dawkins (see, for example Dawkins, 1989, p. 171; Dawkins, 2006, p. 151), and hypothesises that this may have influenced Dawkins' development of the term "meme" (Laurent, 1999, p. 1).

Before Maeterlinck (and indeed Marais), however, and at the turn of the twentieth century, the German zoologist Richard Semon was also using the term "Mneme" (Semon, 1909; Semon, 1911; Semon, 1921; Semon et al., 1923). Despite the seemingly different etymology of Dawkins' "meme" (*mimeisthai*–mimeme–meme) and Semon's "Mneme" (*mimneskesthai*/*Mnemo-syne*–Mneme), the concepts are broadly similar. That is, both refer to a particulate unit of information that is stored in an organic form – in the substance of the brain. Dawkins makes this clear when he says – drawing on ideas of Delius (1989, 1991) (see also §3.8.3) – that memes are "self-replicating brain structures, actual patterns of neuronal wiring-up that reconstitute themselves in one brain after another" (1989, p. 323). This formulation aligns with Semon's belief that the experiences undergone by an organism lead to the formation of memory traces – engrams – that record the event and that can subsequently be re-activated. As Semon explains,

> I use the word *engram* to denote this permanent change wrought by a stimulus; the sum of such engrams in an organism may be called its 'engram-store', among which we must distinguish inherited from acquired engrams. The phenomena resulting from the existence of one or more engrams in an organism I describe as mnemic phenomena.

---

[93] On its first mention, Laurent (1999, p. 1) mistakenly gives the name of Maeterlinck's text as *The soul of the white ant*, which is in fact a work of 1925 by the ethologist Eugène Marais (Marais, 2017), from which Maeterlinck (1927) plagiarised his text.

> The totality of the mnemic potentialities of an organism is its 'Mneme'.
> (Semon, 1921, p. 24; emphasis in the original)

Aside from the fact that Semon is using the term Mneme here to refer not to a *single* stimulus-driven memory change but to the *totality* of an organism's engrams (i.e., what I term the memome; Table 1.3), there is a more significant difference between Semon's and Dawkins' conceptions. This is the former's Lamarckian belief that such memory structures can be transmitted biologically, from one generation to another – his "inherited engrams" – as well as culturally, from one person to another – his "acquired engrams". Dawkins, by contrast, maintains that memes are not transmitted biologically, but only culturally; and that the latter process is Darwinian, not Lamarckian. There are, nevertheless, what might be termed epimemetic complications relating to this point, discussed in §3.4.3.

3.3.2 Evolutionary Epistemology

Although nineteenth-century commentators – even before the publication of the *Origin of species* – made the connection between the development of living things and the growth of human intellectual constructs, Donald Campbell, developing ideas of Karl Popper's, was arguably the first to set such speculations on a firm footing (Popper, 1959; Campbell, 1960; Campbell, 1965; Campbell, 1974; Campbell, 1990). One of Campbell's important early contributions was to distinguish clearly between a number of contrasting approaches to the application of evolutionary theory to human culture. These fall into two broad categories.

The first category is concerned with the "interaction of culture and social organization with man's biological evolution" (Campbell, 1965, p. 19), which Campbell subdivides into: (i) "genetic influence upon culture" (1965, p. 19), in which cultural change is a manifestation of processes occurring at the genetic level; and (ii) its converse, "cultural influence upon genetics" (1965, p. 20), in which genes are affected by cultural changes. The second category is the most pertinent here, being concerned with "socio-cultural evolution of socio-cultural forms independent of changes in genetic stock" (1965, p. 20). This second category is also subdivided, into: (i) a number of "theories descriptive of the facts and course of socio-cultural evolution" (1965, p. 21);

and (ii) a "theory descriptive of the process of evolution: variation and selective retention" (1965, p. 22). It is this latter principle – variation and selective retention (the latter essentially a form of replication) – that forms the basis of Campbell's application of biological models to cultural change.

Asserting that this "evolutionary epistemology" is grounded on the "psychological and epistemological point that all processes leading to expansions of knowledge involve a blind-variation-and-selective-retention ["BVSR"] process" (Campbell, 1960, p. 397) – note the attenuation of agency and intentionality implied by the adjective "blind" – Campbell takes the mechanism of evolution by natural selection and applies it directly to the growth of human culture. He identifies that "[t]hree conditions are necessary: a mechanism for introducing variation, a consistent selection process, and a mechanism for preserving and reproducing the selected variations" (1960, p. 381). This closely parallels Dennett's, Calvin's and Plotkin's summaries of evolution given in §1.5.1, echoing their articulation of the three terms of the VRS algorithm. As the VRS algorithm ($\equiv$ g-t-r) in another guise, BVSR represents the same fundamental paradigm – subsumed under the aegis of Universal Darwinism (§1.5) – that underpins all increases in complexity in the universe.

While Campbell's illustrations – in keeping with their Popperian foundations – often focus upon the growth of verbally mediated scientific knowledge, any human conceptual system that can sustain complex mental constructs, irrespective of medium or symbolic system, is amenable in principle to evolutionary-epistemological processes.[94] Moreover, in emphasising the blindness of the process, Campbell foregrounds the lack of agency and intentionality – at best, the golden serendipity; at worst the hapless fumbling – that very often attends the inception of insights in both the scientific and the artistic realms, and that has a direct parallel in biological evolution's lack of "strategic" long-term goals (Dawkins, 2006).

Lastly, understanding Campbell's model in terms of the VRS algorithm challenges Sereno's assertion that evolutionary epistemology is an example of the organism/concept analogy (1991, p. 476) (§1.6.2). This is because

---

[94] Appendix I of Campbell (1974, pp. 457–458) lists sources on "trial-error and natural-selection models for creative thought"; see also Appendix II (1974, pp. 458–459), which lists sources on "natural selection as a model for the evolution of science".

replicators, and not vehicles, are subject to the operation of the VRS algorithm (§1.6.1), and thus evolutionary epistemology's focus upon discrete units of blind variation and selective retention – single ideas, albeit often organised into complexes – implies that the gene (as replicator), not the organism (as vehicle), is the appropriate analogue to the particulate unit of knowledge.

3.3.3 Cultural Ethology

Asking "is a cultural ethology possible?", Cloak (1975) anticipated many of Dawkins' (1989) precepts of memetics, and aspects of its later development by others. These precepts include: (i) the digital nature of cultural information, which Cloak maintained exists as "tiny, unrelated snippets" (1975, p. 167), or "corpuscles of culture" (1975, p. 168); (ii) a distinction between (in memetic terms) the memomic and the phemotypic forms of a meme, in Cloak's terms between "specific interneural instructions culturally transmitted from generation to generation" and their material products, or between "i[nstruction, internal]-culture" and "m[aterial, external]-culture" (1975, pp. 167–168); (iii) the control of m-culture by i-culture in order to foster the latter's replication ("the natural selection of instructions") (1975, p. 169); (iv) the assembly (or co-replication) of units of cultural information to form complexes, or "cooperating cultural instructions" (1975, p. 169); and (v) the view that a unit of i-culture is "more analogous to a viral or bacterial gene than to a gene of the carrier's own genome", so is at best symbiotic with and, at worst, parasitic upon, its human "hosts" (1975, p. 172).

Central to Cloak's thesis is the idea (point (iii)) that the human behaviour (leading to the production of m-culture artefacts) that is the concern of (cultural) ethology is controlled by replicators – corpuscles of (i-)culture – in ways that foster their replication. In a manner that is directly analogous to gene-based natural selection, Cloak argues that,

> [a]s a system of instructions [i.e., a memeplex] proliferates in a given environmental subregion, its several instantiations come into 'constructive' competition with each other. Any instantiation of the system which is fortuitously modified – usually by the acquisition of a novel component instruction – so that the m-culture feature it produces is better able to help determine the occurrence of the whole set in certain locations

will often thereby exclude the other instantiations from surviving or propagating in those locations. Then it is only a matter of time before the modified instantiation becomes typical of the system. As this competition process is repeated, of course, the system becomes more complex and, as a rule, the m-culture feature becomes more elaborate and more 'powerful' in terms of its particular environmental effects. (Cloak, 1975, p. 169)

Of course, to equate a unit of cultural information with a "corpuscle" is to align it with a cell and not, as Dawkins proposed, with a sub-cellular molecule (a gene; level seven of Table 1.4). Nevertheless, the reference is presumably metaphorical, being made to stress the indivisible, particulate nature of cultural inheritance: Cloak implies that, like "genetically programmed instructions", the units of cultural replication are "fixed and discontinuous", not "plastic [and] continuously variable" (1975, p. 166). Thus, the fundamental units of cultural information are the "specific interneural instructions" referred to in point (ii) above.

3.4 Key Issues in Memetics

For all their different origins, the pre- and proto-memetic theories of culture outlined in §3.3 have several features in common, generally hypothesising a particulate basis for culture in which variant forms of units arise quasi-randomly and are selected according to some set of (conscious or unconscious) criteria for further replication. In this sense, memetics – to the extent that it has been theorised – is not fundamentally different from its precursor theories. It does, however, appear to have greater traction, certainly in popular culture, compared with its antecedents. This is perhaps the result of Dawkins' wise formulation of the word "meme" as an analogue of "gene" (§3.3.1), and the arguable considerable sonorous appeal, concision (and similarity to "même", for francophones) of the word. In this sense, the acceptance of Dawkinsian memetics is not necessarily the result of its intrinsically greater explanatory power compared with, for example, Cloak's (1975) hypothesis. Rather, it arises, at least in part, from the kinds of cultural-saliency effects memetics predicts, this salience to some extent serving to validate the theory itself. In short, the "'meme' meme" (Costall,

1991) is a good replicator; the rest of the theory of memetics – the wider verbal-conceptual memeplex – piggybacks on the selfishness of this "index" term. In this section, I consider three aspects of memetics that seem key to the idea of cultural replicators, illustrating some aspects of them by reference to musical examples.

3.4.1 Qualitative *versus* Quantitative Memetics

Memetics celebrated its fortieth birthday in 2016, if the publication of the first edition of Dawkins' *The selfish gene* (Dawkins, 1989) is taken to be the inception of this particular incarnation of cultural replicator theory. How high is its intellectual capital at the time of writing, and how has this changed over the last four decades? Perhaps a more tractable question might be: "how widely replicated is the 'meme' meme and what might this tell us about the esteem in which memetics is (or is not) held"? Of course, any current salience of the term does not necessarily mean that memetics is an established academic discipline, nor, more importantly, that it necessarily captures some or all of the truth. Indeed, repeated citations of a term might indicate attempts to bury it, rather than to praise it, as Mark Anthony might have said.[95] Nevertheless, one way of measuring its changing impact, if not its veracity, is by tracking citations of terms such as "meme(s)" and "memetic(s)" (Jan, 2015a, pp. 71–72, Fig. 2). These occurrences serve as markers of the "meme" meme – as noted above, it is strictly a verbal-conceptual memeplex, indexed by "meme" – in the sense that their appearance is normally correlated with expositions, discussions and critiques – and even endorsements – of the concept(s) encompassed by the memeplex.

The justification for undertaking such tracking is that, as a verbal-conceptual memeplex, memetics is as subject to the operation of the VRS algorithm as any other memeplex. Tracking citations explicitly measures the "R" element of the algorithm and implicitly captures the "S" element. The "V" element is not directly measurable using such approaches, because the search terms are, as noted, merely markers of the larger memeplex and do not evidence internal structural changes within it – these occurring by means, as Cloak (1975,

---

[95] In some disciplines, such as anthropology, memetics is often cited in the context of criticism (Kuper, 2000), in part because memetics counters the holistic and static view of culture offered by anthropology with its own particulate and dynamic alternative.

p. 169) would have it, of "the acquisition of a novel component instruction". Only more detailed study of such sub-terms of the memeplex can allow one to track changes in its wider complexion and structure over time. The Mark-Anthony caveat notwithstanding, selection is often a marker of some level of acceptance of the concept selected.

To illustrate how this tracking might be accomplished, Figure 3.2 shows a visual representation of the chronological and conceptual-spatial distribution of a subset of publications containing the term "memetic" – in their title, abstract, keywords and (crucially) their references – from 1980–2020 listed in the *Scopus* research database (Scopus, 2020) and generated by the *CiteSpace* citation-analysis/visualisation software (Chen, 2019b; Chen & Song, 2019).[96] *CiteSpace*

> is designed to answer questions about a knowledge domain .... A knowledge domain is typically represented by a set of bibliographic records of relevant publications.... *CiteSpace* is designed to make it easy ... to answer questions about the structure and dynamics of a knowledge domain[, such as] ...: What are the major areas of research based on the input dataset? How are these major areas connected, i.e., through which specific articles? Where are the most active areas? What is each major area about? Which/where are the key papers for a given area? Are there critical transitions in the history of the development of the field? Where are the 'turning points'? The design of *CiteSpace* is inspired by Thomas Kuhn's [*The*] *Structure of Scientific Revolutions* [(Kuhn, 2012)[97]]. The central idea is that centers of research focus change over time, sometime incrementally and other times drastically. The development of science can be traced by studying their footprints revealed by scholarly publications. (Chen, 2014, p. 4)

CiteSpace essentially maps the forms of conceptual transmission described by the epidemiological "virus-of-the-mind" (Brodie, 1996) and "thought-contagion" (Lynch, 1996) formulations common in the memetics literature of the 1990s (see also Rosati et al., 2021). By "a visual representation of the

---

[96] "Scopus is the largest abstract and citation database of peer-reviewed research literature including ... [o]ver 24,000 titles, including 4,200 Open Access journals from more than 5,000 international publishers" (Scopus, 2020).

[97] Kuhn generally terms such "turning points" "paradigm changes" but "paradigm shifts" has become more common (2012, pp. xxiii, 52), perhaps because it is a superior meme.

chronological and conceptual-spatial distribution" in the paragraph before
the quotation above is meant a depiction of the cultural-transmission relationships between sources dealing with the chosen concept and the groupings
they form. Sources are termed "nodes" in *CiteSpace*, and are represented
by small coloured dots in the "visualisations" it generates. Groupings are
termed "clusters", and are represented by collections of nodes of varying
density connected by coloured lines emanating from one or two central
nodes, the latter being identified by associated author-date citations. Clusters
therefore arise when certain relatively discrete, highly interconnected constellations of nodes develop as a result of their drawing upon one or two seminal
(highly-cited) nodes at their notional "centre", creating a network of many
citers connected to few citees. In this sense, "[e]ach cluster corresponds to
an underlying theme, a topic, or a line of research" (Chen, 2020, sec. 4.2).

From a Darwinian perspective, the connections binding together clusters essentially trace replication relationships from intellectual antecedents to their
consequents. To map these epistemological spaces, clusters are identified by
a number (starting at "#0", in descending order of cluster size) and a verbal
label, these being associated with one or two node labels identifying the most
important sources in each cluster. Cluster labels are generated by *CiteSpace*
using title, index/keyword, or abstract terms, utilising specific statistical-
weighting models.[98] Cluster #0 in Figure 3.2, for instance, represents sources
linked by the noun-phrase "evolutionary ecology" and its cognates, the analysis extracting this label using a log-likelihood ratio (LLR) distribution from
node-titles (other statistical-analysis methodologies may alternatively be
utilised for this purpose). The analysis and representation of cluster distribution by *CiteSpace* is extensively configurable using a considerable array of
mathematical functions, and one could compare and contrast the outcomes
of several of them in order to understand more fully the cultural-transmission
dynamics of the knowledge domain in question. For present purposes, however, Figure 3.2 represents the results of employing the default settings of
CiteSpace and of following the guidance for use given in Chen (2019a).

---

[98] *CiteSpace* can minimise node- and cluster-label overlaps in visualisations, but this function
is not used in Figure 3.2 (or in Figure 4.10 (§4.6), which explores publications containing the
terms "music" and "gender"), in order to associate as closely as possible the centres of clusters
with their generative node(s). Sources obscured by overlapping labels are clarified in the text.

Returning to the dataset, using "memetic" as the search term will also locate "memetics", and will avoid confusion of "meme" with "même" in literature in French. At the time of searching, and using the search-parameters selected, the total number of publications containing this term was 4,158, the earliest being Ball (1984) and not Dawkins (1989). This is because Dawkins (1989) (the first edition of which was published in 1976), while it coins the term "meme", does not use the term "memetic" in its title. To constrain the search results to a reasonable size, *CiteSpace* analysed a subset of these 4,158 publications, namely entries in *Scopus*'s Arts and Humanities category, which, at the time of the query, contained 160 records. The justification for this constraint is that this subset represents a clear disciplinary boundary from other subsets, such as the Mathematics category (1,609 records), or the Biochemistry, Genetics and Molecular Biology category (93 records). The Arts and Humanities subset does not include Ball (1984) as a record because it is not assigned to this category, but this source is (as the citee) referenced in an article (as the citer) from 1998. The earliest record in this category of the *Scopus* database to contain the search term relates to an article dating from 1996.[99]

Having explained the necessary context, what does Figure 3.2 reveal about the chronological and conceptual-spatial distribution of the selected literature on memetics? Before examining the visualisation itself, *CiteSpace*'s analysis of the number of unique records (of the total 119 given in note 99 on page 181) per year, graphed in Figure 3.3, shows a halting but clear increase, indicating growing dissemination of the "meme" meme.

Turning back to Figure 3.2, and to summarise a complex set of relationships,[100] one might make the following observations:

---

[99] The report detailing the outcome of *CiteSpace*'s extraction of data from the .ris bibliographic citation file exported from *Scopus* states that "159 records [were] converted .... Total References [i.e., citations of literature within sources]: 6,880[;] Valid References: 6,859 (99.0%)". It should be noted that, as is often the case with Scopus records, there is a certain amount of duplication in the data (i.e., the same article is listed as two ostensibly separate records), and so a further stage of processing was undertaken, which reduced the sample size to 119 unique records.

[100] There is a risk in enumerating the analytical outcomes of programs such as *CiteSpace* that one ends up in the position of Borges' map-makers in his short story *On exactitude in science* (1946), who decided that only a map of scale 1:1 would be adequate; thus, "the Cartographers['] Guilds struck a Map of the Empire whose size was that of the Empire, and which coincided point for point with it" (1998, p. 325).

Figure 3.2: *CiteSpace Visualisation of Citations of "Memetic" per year 1980–2020 in Scopus.*

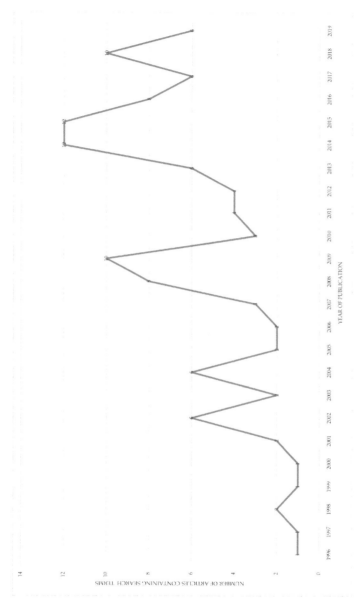

Figure 3.3: Number of Records Containing "Memetic" Per Year 1996–2019.

1. While there are 116 notional clusters and eleven clusters graphed in the default layout (#0–#6, #10, #14, #16 and #24), using *CiteSpace*'s facility to display only the largest of them reduces this number to eight principal clusters (#0–#6 and #10). The presence of a number of clusters, entirely typical of *CiteSpace* visual-isations, indicates that, as with most knowledge domains, transmission here does not occur in orderly concentric circles from a single central point in the manner of ripples in a pond, but rather in the form of various semi-discrete breakout "infections", which spawn their own local progeny. Another way to regard the non-concentric layout of Figure 3.2 is to invoke the concept of spe-ciation. While the verbal-conceptual memeplexes underpinning the different clusters are not, according to Figure 1.4, analogous to species (memeplexes occupy level six; species occupy level three), a similar process is at work in that once a cluster has broken away from its "parent", it tends not to re-aggregate with it.[101]

2. As might be expected from a nascent discipline, some of these clusters arise from sources that appear to have (co-)fostered the development of more than one cluster. Those sources are Boyd and Richerson (1985) (clusters #2 and #6) and Blackmore (1999) (clusters #1, #2 and #4). In addition to these highly cited *sources*, highly cited *authors* include (unsurprisingly) Dawkins, represented by Dawkins (1989) (labelled on Figure 3.2 by the date of publication of the first edition, 1976) (cluster #1), and Dawkins (1983a) (labelled by its first-edition date of 1982) (cluster #3); and Aunger, represented by Aunger (2000) (cluster #0), and Aunger (2002) (cluster #5). *CiteSpace*'s term for such pivotal sources is "centrality", which "quantifies the importance of the node's position in a network" (Chen, 2006, p. 362). The program's "narrative summary" of this network identifies the three most central nodes as (in decreasing order of centrality) Aunger (2000), Dawkins (1989) and Blackmore (1999). Moreover, the summary identifies, in its "citation count" ranking, the three most cited nodes as (in decreasing order of citations) Dawkins (1989), Blackmore (1999) and Aunger (2000).

3. As noted above, cluster #0 is associated with the concept of evolutionary eco-logy, and Aunger (2000) is the central node. Its intellectual focus is exemplified by one of the "hidden" nodes – i.e., one not explicitly labelled with an author-

---

[101] The standard layout of *CiteSpace* visualisations prioritises the conceptual-spatial over the chronological, in that clusters further away from the centre are not necessarily later in their formation (one can extract an average year for each cluster, which "indicates whether it is formed by generally recent papers or old papers" (Chen, 2020, sec. 4.2)). The program's "timeline view" inverts this prioritisation.

date citation – of Figure 3.2. On Blute's definition, evolutionary ecology "seeks a theoretical halfway house between the near-universal tautology of the fitness-selection nexus and the near-complete historical specificity of the myriad details of what is adaptive in locally prevailing circumstances" (2002, sec. 1; see also Tab. 1). In ways that are directly applicable to memetics (specifically the evolution of science, in the case of Blute (2002)), the discipline considers the effects on evolution of population density (i.e., fixed boundaries, variable energy) (Blute, 2002, sec. 2, sec. 3), and of growth rate (i.e., variable boundaries, fixed energy) (2002, sec. 5).

4. Cluster #1 relates to the extension of the "selfish gene" metaphor coined in Dawkins (1989) to cultural replicators, this "selfish meme" cluster being particularly distinct. As the layout of Figure 3.2 suggests, while the initial impetus for this cluster was provided by Dawkins (1989), it was further impelled by Blackmore (1999). The label of cluster #2 lacks the adjective "selfish" of cluster #1. This absence might account for the smaller size of cluster #2 in comparison with cluster #1 (as noted above, the lower the number, the larger the cluster), and might, indirectly, be taken as evidence of the selfish replicator concept itself.

5. Cluster #3 is concerned with the evolution of satirical cartoons of the catastrophic oil-slick caused by the sinking of the *Prestige* oil tanker off the coast of Spain in 2002. While exemplified by such sources as Domínguez (2015), and while perhaps the ultimate source of the phenomenon discussed apropos Figure 3.1, this cluster originates (as noted) from Dawkins (1983a) and also from Brodie (1996), the latter, as mentioned after the quotation on page 179, developing (as with Lynch (1996)) an epidemiological model of memetics. Associated with Aunger (2002) and Baudrillard (1988), cluster #5 relates to patenting and other intellectual-property issues understood in the light of memetics, and takes its label from the title of Bedau (2013).

6. The transmission of memetic ideas in the musicological literature is relatively peripheral to the main centres of transmission, but – at the risk of appearing immodest – the (sub)title of one of my own publications (Jan, 2012) figures as the label of cluster #4. *CiteSpace* extracts the phrase "Haydn chord progression", which might suggest that the whole cluster is concerned with this subject. It is worth remembering, however, that in this network of citers and citees (and indeed all networks analysed by *CiteSpace*), a wide range of sources may be referenced, and a significant portion of this literature may not necessarily be about Haydn, this specific chord progression, or even music theory more

generally. In this sense, and although potentially illuminating, a cluster label may often represent the tip, as opposed to the main body, of an iceberg.

7. Two clusters, #6 and #10, are marked by the appearance of the phrase "natural myside bias", which relates to issues of belief-transmission in knowledge communities. Cluster #6 (which develops as an outgrowth of cluster #2) is centred on a study of children's awareness and understanding of adult thought-processes (i.e., of children's possession of a "Theory of Mind"; §3.7.1, §3.8.2) in Cameroonian pygmies (Avis & Harris, 1991). Cluster #10 relates to issues of authority and controversy in science, represented by Hull (1988b) and Gould (1997), the latter node representing a specific skirmish in a protracted conflict between Dennett and Gould over Darwinism pitting "fundamentalists" (principally Dawkins and Dennett) against "moderates" (as Gould implicitly presents himself).

To recall the distinction made earlier, it seems that some of these 119 sources (and the 4,158 of which they form a subset) did indeed come to praise memetics and some came to bury it. Whether one believes the *pro* or *contra* sources, at the very least, as a hypothesis, memetics has had a successful replication history (although this is not to compare its replication with other theories of cultural evolution, let alone with other scientific theories more broadly). This history exemplifies a key precept of the theory, namely that transmission of an idea is independent of its veracity. Of course, undertaking a distributional analysis of a verbal-conceptual memeplex is only one form of what might be termed *population memetics*, one that aligns with, and is facilitated by such corpus-analytical/"big-data" approaches exemplified by *CiteSpace* (see also Sharma et al., 2014; Rose et al., 2015; Jeffries, 2019).

There is, moreover, an extant tradition of computer-aided intra- and inter-work pattern-analysis in music (§6.1), whose methodologies can be re-purposed to serve a specifically quantitative-memetic agenda. Indeed, some of this work – Savage (2017) is a good example – has essentially studied memetic evolution, albeit generally not explicitly under that rubric. Thus, while intra- and inter-work memetics has hitherto often been conducted *qualitatively* – certain patterns having been identified "manually" in candidate works and ascribed a memetic status on balance-of-probability grounds – there is considerable scope for applying the technologies represented by

CiteSpace to music "automatically", in order to garner *quantitative* data on museme prevalence and transmission.

3.4.2 Cultural Adaptation and Exaptation

Discussing the fact that the distinction between adaptations (aptations built by selection for their current role) and exaptations (aptations "coopted" for their current role) had not been fully recognised until their own article gave it an appropriate nomenclature (§2.5.1), Gould and Vrba argue that "the conceptual framework of modern evolutionary thought, by continually emphasizing the supreme importance and continuity of adaptation and natural selection at all levels, subtly relegated the issue of exaptation to a periphery of unimportance" (1982, p. 6). It is possible to understand this as an example of the replication of a particular verbal-conceptual memeplex (that defining exaptation) being constrained by the predominance of a more powerful memeplex (that defining "the [adaptation-focused] conceptual framework of modern evolutionary thought"). In this sense, the relationship between the two memeplexes is readily conceivable in terms of constraints on the selection of the weaker memeplex by the stronger.

What would constitute an adaptation in memetic terms, and how might it be distinguished from those phenomena that might more properly be regarded as exaptations? It is perhaps easier to find examples related to this issue in music than in verbal culture. Figure 3.4 shows candidates for these processes, Figure 3.4a showing the local subdominant of V (thus, a hint of the tonic, G major) in the dominant second half of an exposition; and Figure 3.4b showing the same inflexion but now as a *beginning* gesture, not as the arguably more normative *ending* gesture, to invoke Agawu's tripartite "beginning-middle-ending paradigm" (1991, pp. 53–54).

I make this claim of normativity without advancing any supporting evidence; but hypothesise that a statistical survey of the various binary forms antecedent to sonata form, and of sonata forms themselves (Rosen, 1988; Caplin, 1998; Hepokoski & Darcy, 2006), would probably show a significant

(a) Adaptation: Mozart, Piano Trio in G major K. 496 (1786), I, bb. 75–78 (after bb. 72–74).

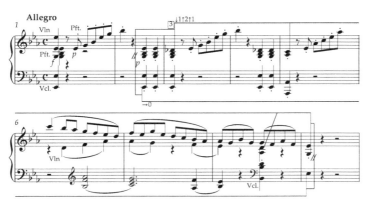

(b) Exaptation: Beethoven, Piano Trio in E♭ major op. 1 no. 1 (1795), I, bb. 1–9.

Figure 3.4: Adaptation and Exaptation of Musemes.

predominance of the "ending V/IV–IV" over the "beginning V/IV–IV".[102] This would suggest that the ending form evolved first (i.e., it was an earlier adaptation, perhaps for reasons of its alignment with various natural and nurtural constraints); and its "cooption", to use Gould and Vrba's (1982) term, as a beginning gesture was a later exaptation. Nevertheless, the use of the *quiescenza* schema – the archetype of this pattern – as a beginning gesture in some mid- to late-eighteenth-century music (Gjerdingen, 2007a, pp. 181–182, 460) might be taken as evidence against my "end-adaptive/beginning-exaptive" claim and in favour of its inversion, although Gjerdingen believes that "[a]s a framing device, it could also appear as an opening gambit ..., though this usage was less common" (2007a, p. 460).

3.4.3 Lamarckism *versus* Darwinism in Cultural Evolution

The key distinction between Darwinian and Lamarckian inheritance in biological evolution was discussed in §1.8. This section considers the extent to which the distinction is applicable to cultural evolution (see also Dennett, 2017, pp. 243–247). To summarise the earlier discussion briefly, while Lamarck believed in the inheritance of acquired characteristics, the Darwinism of the Modern Synthesis insists on the distinction between a germ line and a soma line, to recall Weismann's terms. This means that only changes motivated by the genetic "shuffling" that occurs at conception can be transmitted to an organism's offspring, not any modifications to a parent's body that occur during its lifetime. One apparent manifestation of Lamarckism is the phenomenon of epigenetic inheritance, which offers a set of mechanisms – perhaps most notably the chromatin-marking EIS – by means of which certain acquired attributes might not only be inherited by cells within tissues, but which might also be transmitted to an organism's offspring. As argued on page 60, this poses no threat to Darwinism – the Lamarckism is illusory – because genes are the only replicators on earth able to carry sufficient information to build vehicles; and, perhaps more fundamentally, because whatever mechanism carries information, the VRS algorithm does not depend upon a specific architecture for its implementation, only upon the presence of its three component processes.

---

[102] Note that these are essentially the same museme – strictly, all instantiations of either form of the pattern belong in the same *museme allele-class* (§3.5.2) – and that they differ primarily in respect of their structural location (Jan, 2010, pp. 11–13).

One point not made in §1.8 is that epigenetics is not universally accepted by evolutionary theorists, and is particularly controversial when applied to our own species. This is due not only to ongoing scientific debates about the nature and extent of epigenetic mechanisms (which remain imperfectly understood), but also because the theory has been hijacked by those who wish to use it in the service of social engineering in order to foreground nurture over nature. As Murray remarks, "[e]pigenetics seems to promise release from genetic determinism. It seems to offer new explanations for phenotypic differences and new possibilities for remediation. At the extremes, it seems to offer hope for greater equality of capabilities and outcomes across groups" (2020, loc. 5058). Yet, having considered such organisms as the mule, the hinny and the Toadflax – in which epigenetic inheritance appears to elucidate certain phenomena that defy a genetic explanation – it should be noted that the "involvement of epigenetic mechanisms in intergenerational transmission has been yet little documented in humans ..., and never across several generations" (Marcaggi & Guénolé, 2018, p. 6). Nevertheless, it is important to make a distinction between *epigenetic transmission / inheritance* – where some attribute is inherited by non-genetic means – and the *action of epigenetic factors* in brain plasticity – where some ontogenetic change occurs for reasons that are not directly genetic. Of these phenomena, the latter is more accepted than the former (see note 81 on page 138). Despite this, it is possible that epigenetics in the former sense might yet be relevant to some extent to cultural, if not to (human) biological, evolution, although not necessarily in ways its more extreme proponents might envisage. As Kellermann summarises epigenetics and his application of it,

> [e]pigenetics is typically defined as the study of heritable changes in gene expression that are not due to changes in the underlying DNA sequence. Such heritable changes ... often occur as a result of environmental stress or major emotional trauma and would then leave certain marks on the chemical coating, or *methylation*, of the chromosomes. The coating becomes a sort of 'memory' of the cell and since all cells in our body carry this kind of memory, it becomes a constant physical reminder of past events, our own and those of our parents, grandparents and beyond.... In the same way as parents can pass on genetic characteristics to their children, they would also be able to pass on all kinds of 'acquired' (or epigenetic) characteristics, especially if these were based on powerful

> life-threatening experiences .... Such environmental conditions would leave an imprint on the genetic material ... and pass along new traits even in a single generation. (Kellermann, 2013, p. 34; emphasis in the original).

Reiterating the caution that epigenetic markers can only be passed on to an organism's descendants if they affect gametes, the type of epigenetic inheritance hypothesised here concerns a different category of traits from those generally explored by "mainstream" epigenetics. While the latter consider the transmission of *morphological* and *physiological* changes acquired during an organism's lifetime, for Kellermann (2013) the traits in question are, it seems, primarily *psychological*; and they tend to result specifically from some form of violent trauma, rather than from some other environmental or idiopathic cause. Kellermann (2013) explores the specific case of the horrors suffered by holocaust survivors, which, he believes, are re-lived by first- and second-generation descendants of victims as a result of epigenetic transmission. As he claims in connection with such "transgenerational transmission of trauma" (TTT), "[i]t seems that these individuals, who are now adults, somehow have absorbed the repressed and insufficiently worked-through Holocaust trauma of their parents, as if they have actually *inherited the unconscious minds* of their parents" (Kellermann, 2013, p. 33; emphasis in the original; see also Franklin et al., 2010).

Kellermann asserts that epigenetic changes to parents' DNA resulting from trauma might be transmitted to their children and grandchildren who, as a result, would have a higher propensity to suffer from post-traumatic stress disorder (PTSD), despite not having directly experienced their parents' or grandparents' ordeals. PTSD is often manifested in such individuals in the form of nightmares whose specific content seems to replicate their ancestors' experiences (Kellermann, 2013, p. 35). Despite his caution that, "[whether] any *specific* past memory can be epigenetically transmitted or not ... must be left open to speculation and we should be careful not to slip from reasonable assumptions to fantastic and unsupported scenarios" (2013, p. 35; emphasis in the original), Kellermann appears to believe that there is indeed some mechanism whereby trauma-mediated methylation can be transmitted to offspring in ways that – and here is the leap – affect neurons in such a way as to reconstitute in the child the ancestral patterns of interconnection responsible for encoding the trauma – if not the specific details of the original memory from the parent or grandparent, at least some existential shudder caused by its epigenetic echo.[103] It should be clear that this claim goes well beyond what mainstream epigenetics would be prepared to countenance, adherents generally restricting themselves to considering such cases as the odd-shaped flowers of the peloric Toadflax. For harsher critics of epigenetics, or certainly of its populist appropriation, the evidence for such extended applications is "weak, circumstantial, observational, and correlative, and ... warrants circumspection and careful interpretation ..." (Mitchell, in Murray, 2020, loc. 5121) – this apropos a related study by Yehuda et al. (2016).

A memetic interpretation offers a different way of understanding what appears to be happening here, countering Kellermann's (2013) implication that memories can be biologically transmitted, whether genetically or, as he suggests, epigenetically. It seems more likely that the propensity to PTSD in the descendants of holocaust survivors results from their being influenced by the memetic transmission of imagery of horror, both within the affected family and also from the wider culture, to which affected individuals are unavoidably exposed. The effects of such cultural transmission would presumably be intensified in individuals who grew up with older family members with first-hand experience of such events, whose psychological scars – perhaps manifested in the form of high general anxiety levels or excessive risk-aversion – would be evident, even though often unspoken, and would heighten the force of culturally transmitted holocaust imagery as a result of the direct personal connections involved.[104]

A distinction, articulated in the form of two questions, now presents itself, which will be treated briefly, and at times somewhat speculatively, in the remainder of this section: (i) what epigenetic factors, if any, affect memetic

---

[103] A variant of this situation – the biological transmission of memory – features in an episode of the Paramount Television series *Star Trek: Voyager* ("Flashback", Season 3, Episode 2, originally broadcast 11 September, 1996). The Vulcan Tuvok suffers from distressing memories caused not by observation or learning (memetic transmission) but by a virus (parasitic transmission) that created a person-specific (false) memory so horrible its bearer represses it, allowing the virus to survive undisturbed.

[104] The same arguments might also be made in regard to claims of alien abduction: they are memeplexes acquired from others and from the wider culture, not repressed memories of traumatic past real-life events; and they are (sometimes) triggered by sleep paralysis, which heightens (by analogy with the family-unit repercussions of holocaust trauma) the susceptibility of individuals to the alien-abduction memeplex (Blackmore, 1999, pp. 176–178).

transmission?; and (ii) if the transmission of memes is held to be analogous to the transmission of genes, is there a memetic equivalent to epigenetic inheritance – what might be termed *epimemetic* inheritance?

On the first question, even if, *contra* Kellermann, a memory cannot be epigenetically (and thus neither genetically) *transmitted* – which, on the basis of the above discussion, seems very likely to be the case – it might be that the memetic transmission of the memory's information-content could still be *mediated* in some way by epigenetic factors. Might epigenetic modifications to the peripheral and central nervous systems, if they exist, differentially advantage (or disadvantage) certain m(us)emes? If so, is there a clear qualitative or quantitative difference between the *genetic mediation* of memetic transmission, where genes set the environmental "frame of reference" for memes; and the *epigenetic mediation* of memetic transmission, where some experience in an individual's life (or the life of one of their (grand)parents) affects their gene expression, which in turn specifically affects the kinds of memes that individual, and his/her (grand)children, are receptive (or averse) to and/or are more likely to remember and transmit?

To say that *genetic mediation* affects the transmission of m(us)emes is nothing new: our innate perceptual-cognitive attributes determine what may or may not be memetically replicated, and thus our cultural life is to a significant extent contingent upon what we can and cannot perceive, comprehend and remember (Lerdahl, 1992). As discussed in §3.2, this was framed by Wilson in terms of the metaphor of genes holding culture on a leash. Gene-imposed constraints are, however, often quite coarse-grained: they specify such generic restrictions as, in music, the duration of STM for phrases, or the normative pitch intervals of melodies; they do not, for instance, privilege precise sequences of intervallic contours, or specific rhythmic patterns. By contrast, *epigenetic mediation* is equivalent, to adapt Wilson's metaphor, to the (epi)genes giving the cultural dog specific commands, or eliciting certain behaviours, perhaps using particular rewards to do so. The difference between these two categories is therefore that genetic mediation inheres in the configuration and policing of the learner bottleneck; whereas epigenetic mediation inheres in the finer-grained "nudging" of movement through that bottleneck, together with a more selective degree of filtration.

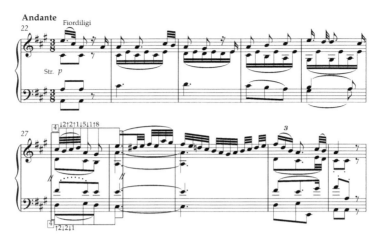

Figure 3.5: Dissonance-Consonance/Pain-Pleasure Museme: Mozart, *Così fan tutte* K. 588 (1790), no. 4, "Ah guarda, sorella", bb. 22–28.

Developing the latter point, and at the risk of abandoning the cautions around epigenetics advocated above, it might, at least in principle, be possible to correlate epigenetic mediation with specific m(us)emes. Could it be, for instance, that a profound emotional experience in the early life of an individual might lead to epigenetic changes in the emotion centres of their brain, such that they or their descendants are especially sensitive to certain m(us)emes, thus making them more likely to assimilate and transmit them (or, conversely, to reject them)? In music, this might perhaps be manifested in a heightened sensitivity to musemes that have a "pain-pleasure" emotional contour owing to underpinning dissonance-consonance patterns, such as that shown in Figure 3.5, with its 7–6 ($c\sharp^2$–b^1 over bass d) appoggiatura in b. 27.

The answer to this question is obviously very difficult to determine, because any increased (or decreased) propensity to replicate certain musemes differentially over others may be the result of one or more of the following four factors: (i) genetic ("culture on a leash"); (ii) epigenetic (altered-gene-expression mediating perceptual-cognitive propensities); (iii) memetic (multi-museme-mediated changes to a cultural environment); or epimemetic (see below) factors. Each could produce broadly similar results to the others, and all could operate in various forms of conjunction.

On the second question raised on page 192, and occupying the distant shores of speculation, if there is a meaningful distinction between the genetic and the epigenetic, is there also a parallel distinction between the memetic and the epimemetic? One of the main hurdles this question faces relates to the quite different mechanisms of genetic and memetic inheritance: the former relies upon the complex information-architecture of patterns of nucleic acids acting, via the proteins that build bodies, to ensure their replication; the latter relies upon the complex information-architecture of patterns of neuronal interconnection acting, via behaviours and the artifacts this behaviour gives rise to, to ensure their replication. Moreover, because there is not such a clear-cut (replicator-vehicle) distinction between the memome and the phemotype – between the germ line and the soma line – as there is between the genome and the phenotype, it is arguably more difficult to distinguish between the memetic and the epimemetic than it is to distinguish between the genetic and the epigenetic. Is there anything in memetics that is even remotely analogous – functionally, if not structurally – to the chromatin-marking EIS? A comparable phenomenon might perhaps be seen in the capacity of m(us)emeplexes to contain elements that are "expressed" in some instantiations and "silenced" in others.

In the verbal-conceptual realm, for instance, a given articulation of a particular constellation of ideas might include several or most of its independent memetic subcomponents; or it might restrict their expression, such that one meme stands for the whole (silenced) verbal-conceptual memeplex, as in the rhetorical trope of synecdoche. In music, a museme that forms a component of a musemeplex might stand alone, implying the other silenced musemes. As an example, Figure 3.6 shows a two-voice pattern that is also a constituent (specifically, Musemes 1 and 5) of the musemeplex shown in Figure 3.10a and Figure 3.10b on page 204 (see also Jan, 2004, p. 73). In Haydn's phrase, these two musemes form components of a different structure, itself possibly a musemeplex. This might be understood as suppressing the expression of those (three) other musemes, and thus the musemeplex as a whole, from the chronologically and possibly aetiologically antecedent Mozart phrases that are not shared with Haydn's phrase.

Figure 3.6: Musemes from "Silenced" Musemeplex: Haydn, String Quartet in F major, op. 74 no. 2 (1793), II, bb. 1–8.

A putative epimemetics is also tied up with the issue of mutation/variation. In the case of genes, mutations may confer advantages upon their possessor that may differentially affect their survival. The same is true of epigenetic changes that, while they do not alter a given gene, may nevertheless mediate its expression and thus have an aptive effect via the resultant phenotype. In the case of m(us)emes, a comparable situation might be found in the aptive benefits that accrue from the (eventual) expression of what might be termed "suppressed mutations". An intriguing passage in Narmour (1977), an early statement of his Implication-Realisation (I-R) model, serves as an illustration of this principle, and also affords an objective mechanism for certain processes often understood purely metaphorically in historiographic discourses on music (§4.3.3). Figure 3.7 (a much simplified version of Narmour, 1977, 127–129, Ex. 44, ignoring certain rhythmic aspects) hypothesises how implicative forces in musical patterns – a form of agency reinscribed in cognitive-psychological terms – can, if realised, become consolidated as new (historical-) stylistic norms that themselves, as a result of newly available implications, motivate further style-expanding realisations.

Here, pattern x arises from the realisation in Figure 3.7b of the implication for further upward motion from the g^1 in Figure 3.7a. Pattern x then carries within it the implication for further upward continuation from the a^1. All these implications are instances of the structure Narmour terms "Process", symbolised by "[P]" – i.e., they are step-wise (or small skip-wise) motions

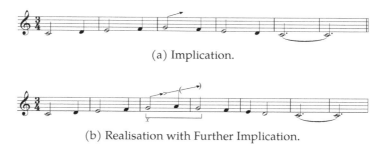

(a) Implication.

(b) Realisation with Further Implication.

Figure 3.7: Realisation of Implicative Forces as a Factor in Musical Style-Change.

that are continued in the same direction and by similarly small intervals (1990, p. 89). The opposite structure is termed "Reversal", symbolised by "[R]" – i.e., they are stepwise (or small skip-wise) motions that are interrupted by a large interval moving in the opposite direction (or vice versa) (Narmour, 1990, p. 151; see also Narmour, 1999). An epimemetic interpretation of this process of style-expanding mutation would see such changes as being initially suppressed by various closural forces, before eventually overwhelming those constraints and reifying that which was previously latent.

3.5 Memetics and Music

Although §3.4 included some consideration of music, this section considers in more detail three areas in which memetics might be brought to bear specifically on its evolutionary understanding. After a brief overview of some key precepts of "musicomemetics" (§3.5.1), the first area (§3.5.2) concerns the assemblage of musemes, a process that creates the large-scale hierarchic structures characteristic of most human musics. The second (§3.5.3) expands upon the first, regarding improvisation and composition as exemplifications of the processes discussed in §3.5.2. The third (§3.5.4) considers the relationship between musemes and what might be termed "gestemes" – the culturally transmitted gestures intrinsic to musical performance.

3.5.1 Overview of Musicomemetics

I have covered elsewhere various aspects of memetics as it relates to music (Jan, 2007; Jan, 2010; Jan, 2011a; Jan, 2011b; Jan, 2012; Jan, 2013; Jan, 2014; Jan, 2016b; Jan, 2015b; Jan, 2016c; Jan, 2016a; Jan, 2018a; Jan, 2018b). The following discussion will serve as a very concise summary of some of the issues covered in these publications, and as an attempt to relate them to some of the ideas covered in Chapter 1 and Chapter 2. By way of a starting-point, Figure 3.8 shows a candidate museme at various stages of its hypothesised evolutionary history.

Figure 3.8a (Mussorgsky, 1987, after) shows a passage that, over a dominant pedal, features the lower-auxiliary motion $\hat{2}$–$\hat{1}$–$\hat{2}$.[105] The middle element of this pattern, the $\hat{1}$, is harmonised by a chord that, if one assigns a local harmonic designation, is an implied vii^{4}_{2} – the "6", e^2, is not stated – within the local dominant prolongation of the auxiliary. Figure 3.8b (Tchaikovsky, 1900, after) shows a similar $\hat{2}$–$\hat{1}$–$\hat{2}$/V structure in which the middle element is harmonised by a full vii^{4}_{2} in which all components of the central seventh chord are present, giving the pattern a subtly different sonority – the "6", here b, markedly alters the effect – to Mussorgsky's version. Figure 3.8c (Stravinsky, 2006, after) has essentially the same progression as Tchaikovsky, save that the auxiliary motion is incomplete, being $\hat{2}$–$\hat{1}$–$(\hat{4})$. A schema is shown in Figure 3.8d, (i). An alternative method of harmonising such a $\hat{2}$–$\hat{1}$–$(\hat{2})$ auxiliary is shown in the abstract of Figure 3.8d, (ii), whereby the $\hat{1}$ is harmonised by, on one interpretation, a V_{11}, created by overlaying a IV chord over the dominant bass. The central "IV + V" element of this form is termed the "rock dominant" by Spicer (2004, p. 38), owing to its prevalence (not just in auxiliary structures) in rock and pop songs. If Figure 3.8d, (i) represents what might be termed the "Russian auxiliary" progression, then Figure 3.8d, (ii) might be termed the "Rock auxiliary".[106]

---

[105] This melody is based on the Russian folk song "Slava bogu" ("Praise to God [in the highest]") (Dearmer et al., 1928, 219, no. 107), used by Beethoven as a "Thème russe" in the third movement of his String Quartet in E minor op. 59 no. 2 ("Rasumovsky") of 1806, and by Rimsky-Korsakov in his Overture on Three Russian Themes op. 28 of 1880.

[106] Such parallel harmony over the dominant, here $\frac{6}{3}$ chords, are also found in the piano writing of Stravinsky's *Petrushka* of 1911, for example b. 1 of the Russian Dance (Rehearsal no. 33). I am grateful to Nicholas Bannan (personal communication) for this point.

(a) Mussorgsky: *Boris Godunov* (1872), Prologue, Rehearsal no. 28, bb. 8–13.

(b) Tchaikovsky: *The Sleeping Beauty* op. 66 (1889), Panorama, bb. 23–26.

(c) Stravinsky: *The Firebird* (1910), Tableau II, Rehearsal No. 200, bb. 1–4.

(d) Middleground Schema.

Figure 3.8: Museme in Three Russian Composers.

Naturally these two variants (three, if Mussorgsky's version is distinguished from Tchaikovsky's and Stravinsky's) of the auxiliary museme – like the "German", "French" and "Italian" augmented sixth chords – have different aural/phenomenological properties: their different note-structure, represented by different notational symbology and explicable using different theoretical terms, gives rise to different aural effects. While it is always difficult to use verbal language to capture musical effects, there is something, to my ears at least, very striking and singular about the Russian auxiliary. Even if cultural familiarity did not perhaps lead us to associate it with such extra-musical concepts as the onion domes of Saint Basil's Cathedral, the incense of Russian Orthodoxy, or the chill of a Siberian winter, it would perhaps impress itself upon our perception as something particularly vibrant and "colourful". Thus, it is potentially a good museme, because it inveigles its way into our memories as something pleasurable to recall and savour. However it arose – as a series of intersecting melodic schemata or as a distinct harmonic phenomenon – it exemplifies perfectly the tendency of musical material to engender its replication in direct proportion to its perceived/cognised salience, whether this is assessed qualitatively or quantified objectively.

Of course, I have not quantified the prevalence of this museme, merely hypothesised that it might be widely replicated in this repertoire, and possibly in French music, from which Russian music drew extensively at this time.[107] I have done this on the basis of the cultural context of these three composers and their use of a Russian folk melody (the direct source of Figure 3.8a) for inspiration. Naturally, one could indeed conduct a quantitative survey – a corpus-analytical investigation along the lines of that discussed in §3.4.1 – searching a dataset of (usually symbolically) encoded music using a pattern-finding utility such as the *Humdrum Toolkit* (Huron, 2002; Huron, 2022; see also Velardo et al., 2016). But there is room also for the kind of qualitative intuition represented by Figure 3.8 because in some ways it validates the hypotheses on which memetics rests: if one knows a passage such as Figure 3.8b, then hearing Figure 3.8a and/or Figure 3.8c, either for the first time or on re-hearing, will perhaps "cue" one's internal representation of the pattern, adding the new instance(s) to the extant (internal representation of the) museme allele-class.

---

[107] I am grateful to David Fanning (personal communication) for this point.

3.5.2 Musemic Hierarchies: Recursive-Hierarchic Structure-Generation via Allele-Parataxis

As an observed principle of pedagogy, composition, improvisation and analysis, discrete musical patterns may combine in a variety of ways in order to form longer musical sequences. In some musics, such as that based on the Galant schemata of the eighteenth century, a relatively small repertoire of clearly defined patterns combines in ways that are statistically predictable, in a Markovian sense[108] (Gjerdingen, 2007a, p. 372, Fig. 27.1). In other traditions, the nature of the units is more variable, and the range of combinations more extensive; but in presumably all musics there are certain more or less statistically likely, or unlikely, juxtapositions. Such concatenation is determined by two ostensibly opposing forces: the *bottom-up* attributes of the constituent musemes, specifically how their initial and terminal nodes (their first and last pitches) affect their patterns of (re)combination, what might be termed their *conglomerative grammar* (Jan, 2010, p. 13); and the *top-down* constraints of some structural schema, which, because such models recur consistently in cultures, are themselves musemes, at a higher structural-hierarchic level.

In terms of bottom-up forces, the harmonic and voice-leading attributes of a museme fit it for playing a particular role in a larger-scale musical structure – it might serve to modulate to a new key, to consolidate that key, or to fulfil any one of a number of other such structural/functional roles. These functions tend to occur in a specific order – a movement will not normally modulate in its final bars, for instance – and so a span of music can be thought of as a series of structural-sequential *loci* or nodes, each of which will tend preferentially to be filled by members of a certain set of musemes that are all broadly similar in their underpinning contrapuntal-harmonic and voice-leading framework, but which might be somewhat different in their surface details. In this sense, the set of musemes capable of occupying/instantiating a structural *locus l* can be thought of as *museme alleles* (or "allomemes" (Durham, 1991, p. 194)) of each other – they form an allele-class of (so to speak) same-shaped but different-coloured pegs that, by virtue of the first of these two properties, can fit securely into the same hole – in the same way that the class of DNA

---

[108] At its most basic, a Markov chain is one in which event *n* of a sequence determines the range of options for event *n*+1 (§6.5.1.3).

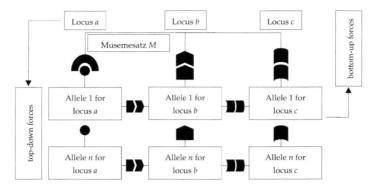

Figure 3.9: Recursive-Hierarchic Structure-Generation via Allele-Parataxis.

segments capable of occupying a *locus l* on a chromosome and controlling the expression of some phenotypic characteristic are genetic alleles of each other.[109]

The phenomenon of structural-sequential *locus*-instantiation means that certain types of museme-sequence will tend, all other things being equal, to recur, and certain others will not. As a consequence of this museme *parataxis*, certain "higher-order" structures will be repeatedly reinstantiated, bottom-up, from the recurrent patterns of "lower-order" museme concatenation. These higher-order structures are capable – as types of memes (see below) – of exerting a top-down regulatory role, by determining the nature and sequence of structural *loci* and thus biasing the likelihood of an exemplar of a particular museme allele-class appearing at a given *locus*. The interaction between bottom-up and top-down forces is represented in Figure 3.9 (Jan, 2010, p. 14, Fig. 1).

A higher-order structure may arise in one of two ways:

- They may arise from the repeated ($\geq$ 2 instances) recombination of (more or less) the *same* lower-order museme-sequence. Such paratactic assemblage of (broadly) the *same* set of musemes forms what might be termed a "real" musemeplex.

---

[109] Cope captures this idea with his notion of seemingly different "signatures" – formulaic, often cadential, patterns – that may be regarded as allelically equivalent because, when their embellishments are stripped away, their common structural core is revealed (2001, p. 48).

- They may be reinstantiated by configurationally *different* but allelically equivalent (*locus* to corresponding *locus*) sequences (≥ 2 instances) of lower-order musemes. Such paratactic assemblage of *different* but allelically equivalent musemes forms what might be termed a "virtual" musemeplex.

That two passages might contain a variable-proportion mixture of the same musemes and of museme alleles at each *locus* suggests that the real and virtual types are actually end-points on a continuum, and not two mutually exclusive categories. This proviso notwithstanding, the same higher-order structure will arise in each category for ≥ 2 instances of a given set of pattern-combinations. Figure 3.10 gives examples of these two scenarios, with Figure 3.10a, 3.10b and 3.10c (after Jan, 2007, 86–90, Ex. 3.12) representing the first (therefore showing a real musemeplex), and Figure 3.10d, 3.10e and 3.10f representing the second (therefore showing a virtual musemeplex).

The higher-order structures schematised in Figure 3.10c and Figure 3.10f form what might be termed – after museme and *Ursatz* – a *musemesatz* (Jan, 2010). This is an abstract, replicated (therefore memetic) structure of *loci*/nodes and their associated infill-types that, however represented, indexes a particular configuration of pattern (re)combination. It is the outcome of the process described by the somewhat unwieldy title of this section: *recursive-hierarchic structure-generation via allele-parataxis*, hereafter abbreviated to "RHSGAP" and represented in Figure 3.9. The process is recursive-hierarchical because it is not necessarily limited to the illustrative two levels here: a "higher-order" structure on a given level might, in combination with other structures at that level, become a "lower-order" structure in relation to the generation of an even more abstract structure at a yet higher level.

For this reason, it is not necessary to specify the number of levels in such a hierarchy, or to fix them absolutely (as opposed to relativistically). What matters is the underlying principle that a sequences of "level-1" musemes $a + b + c$ (or their alleles $a^n + b^n + c^n$) might, for instance, generate a more abstract "level-2" structure, *ABC*, which goes on to occupy the "*a*" (or the a^n) *locus* of the next-higher, "level-3", structure – and so on, ever "upwards". Here, levels 2 and 3 represent musemesätze, in a macrocosm of the microcosmic process by which, in Narmour's terms, sets of style shapes – the same or a different set of shape-alleles for each structure-instantiation – assemble to

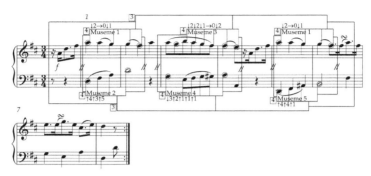

(a) Mozart: Flute Quartet in A major K. 298 (1787), II, Minuet, bb. 0–8.

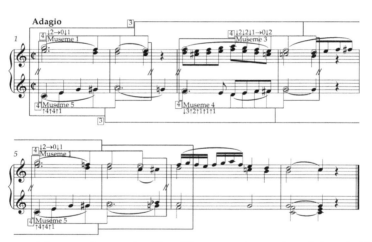

(b) Mozart: Adagio in C major for Glass Harmonica K. 356 (617a) (1791), bb. 1–8.

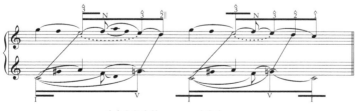

(c) Middleground Schema.

(d) Mozart: Piano Concerto no. 27 in B♭ major K. 595 (1791), I, bb. 107–112.

(e) Chopin: Piano Concerto no. 1 in E minor op. 11 (1830), II, bb. 63–67.

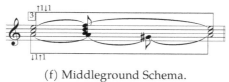

(f) Middleground Schema.

Figure 3.10: Musemes and Musemeplexes.

generate a set of instances of the same style structure (1990, p. 34) (levels seven and six, respectively, of Table 1.4).

Figure 3.10c and Figure 3.10f represent phrase-length examples of a musemesatz, exemplifying in this case the common antecedent-consequent pattern; but the concept can be extended to encompass more extended section- and movement-length structures. In the latter cases, the musemesatz *loci* may be instantiated not only by members of particular *museme allele-classes*, as seen in Figure 3.10c and Figure 3.10f, but also by members of particular *musemeplex allele-classes*. To illustrate the scope of this process – the power of large-scale structure-generation via interactions between bottom-up and top-down memetic forces – Figure 3.11 (Jan, 2010, 38, Ex. 8) illustrates a significantly more extended musemesatz than that in Figure 3.10, showing a musemesatz – aligned with a more normative Schenkerian *Ursatz* (Schenker, 1979) – common to three keyboard-sonata first-movement expositions.[110]

While Figure 3.11 does not necessarily verify the assertions made in this sub-section, these three movements offer suggestive evidence of its basic intuition: that musical material cannot appear in a random order in a composition, and that the tendency for what is essentially narrative (thus psychological) coherence is the result of coevolutionary interactions between "natural" human perceptual-cognitive constraints, including those of memory, and the "nurtural" evolution of musemes to optimise their survival by means of cooperative alliances with other musemes in large-scale structures. This cooperation presumably extends even beyond the scale of Figure 3.11, with a movement-length musemesatz presumably being abstractable from (and so operative in) a set of sonata-form movements, and therefore being able to represent key aspects of the form's configuration at a particular point in its evolutionary history.

---

[110] These movements are Haydn: Sonata in F major Hob. XVI: 23 (1773), I; Mozart: Sonata in C major K. 279 (189d) (1775), I; and Beethoven: Piano Sonata no. 3 in C major op. 2 no. 3 (1795), I.

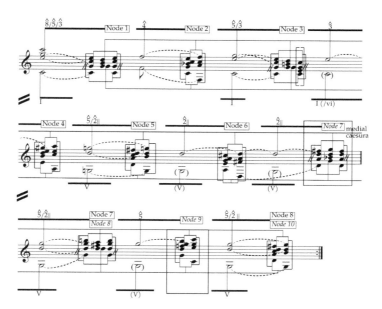

Figure 3.11: *Ursatz* and Musemesatz in Three Keyboard-Sonata First-Movement Expositions.

3.5.3 Improvisation and/as Composition

The model outlined in §3.5.2 is both synchronic and diachronic: it is synchronic in the sense that it offers a means by which the detailed hierarchic structure of a movement can be understood in terms of the memetic forces that gave rise to it; and it is diachronic in that it offers an account of the processes of music generation, in composition and improvisation. Well before the formalisation of Tinctoris's distinction, made in the late-fifteenth century, between *componere* (improvised music) and *compositor* (notated music) (Dunsby & Whittall, 1988, p. 15), improvisation occupied a central place in the world's musical cultures. Indeed, it is perhaps only in the post-Enlightenment West, with its fetishisation of the composer and of the notation that preserves his or her masterworks immutably for posterity, that *compositor* has attained (an increasingly unstable) primacy. The notionally "pure" and unmediated nature of improvisation is complicated by the extent to which it draws upon culturally transmitted models of structure and process. Thus, a third category, the transmission of common structures and associated rhetorical schemata, elaborated and varied by (group) improvisation, dominates many non-Western musical cultures. Yet the latter is difficult to separate from "pure" improvisation, which, as will be argued below, also draws upon inherited schemata. Given the similarity of many "traditional" musical cultures to the hypothesised earliest human musics (§2.5.5), the group-improvisatory embellishment of culturally shared and valued (ritualistic) formulae is likely to have a long ancestry in our species.

Whereas composition might be regarded as a process in which musical ideas organise themselves sequentially with the potential for subsequent reflective revision (whereby certain musemes in the sequence may be replaced by their alleles, or whereby the resultant/regulatory musemesatz may itself be mutated), clearly there is no scope for such editorial (synchronic) reworking in the real-time (diachronic) unfolding of an improvisation. Given this difference, it is legitimate to ask whether the process of (solo) improvisation operates broadly according the structural principles outlined in §3.5.2, or whether it requires a fundamentally different theoretical model for its explication. My contention is that, given the nature of musemic replication, the former is likely to be the case, despite the obvious complicating factors, in improvisation, of the constraints of real-time decision-making processes and the associated need to incorporate real-time sensory and motor feedback. It is nevertheless perhaps more realistic to conceive these issues in terms of a music-generative continuum, with composition and improvisation situated at the extremes and various hybrid stages located in between, orientated according to: (i) the degree to which prior planning and notation (or the lack thereof) are factors in generation; and (ii) the structural-hierarchic depth of the regulatory musemesätze – these being deep and all-encompassing in the case of composition, and relatively shallow and time-contingent in the case of improvisation.

To support this claim, I shall review Pressing's (1988) model of improvisation, arguably the most detailed extant formulation, which demonstrates certain alignments with the RHSGAP model, at the same time offering a critique of its most significant weakness: the lack of any notion of the role of replication in moment-to-moment pattern selection as a key feature of improvisation as much as it is of composition. Essentially, Pressing's elegant model describes improvisation in highly formalised detail, but does not fully explain the cultural-evolutionary processes underlying it. The heart of the model is the concept of the "event cluster" (Pressing, 1988, p. 153). Represented in Pressing's quasi-mathematical notation by E, this is a self-contained (but arbitrary length) section of an improvisation containing a number of musical events. An improvisation is therefore a sequence of such event clusters, as symbolised in Equation 3.1 (1988, p. 153).

$$I = E_1, E_2 \ldots E_n \tag{3.1}$$

While the two terms do not map onto each other precisely, the E seems broadly comparable to a museme or, depending on the extent of the E, to a musemeplex. For Pressing, each E "may be decomposed into three types of analytical representation: objects, features, and processes" (1988, p. 154). *Objects* are a "unified cognitive or perceptual entity" (1988, p. 154); they are, in my terms, a museme or a musemeplex. *Features* are "parameters that describe shared properties of objects" (1988, p. 154); they are an enumeration of the component elements (i.e., the "atomic" pitch and rhythm primitives) of a ("molecular") museme (level eight of Table 1.4), or the elements (i.e., the musemes) of a musemeplex (level seven). *Processes* are "descriptions of changes of objects or features over time" (1988, p. 154); they represent the musico-operational/procedural memes regulating intra-museme/musemeplex element-connections. These three descriptors are represented using "variable-dimension arrays O, F, and P" (Pressing, 1988, pp. 154, 156, Fig. 7.1), which map objects, features and processes against (somewhat arbitrary) "cognitive strength" ratings (Pressing, 1988, p. 155). Pressing argues that

> the fundamental nature of the improvisation process is … the stringing together of a series of 'event clusters' during each of which a continuation is chosen, based upon either the continuing of some existing stream of musical development (called here an event-cluster class [K]) by association of array entries, or the interruption of that stream by the choosing of a new set of array entries that act as constraints in the generation of a new stream (new event-cluster class). (Pressing, 1988, p. 168)

These two modes of continuation – associative generation (itself divided into similarity and contrast), and interrupt generation (Pressing, 1988, pp. 155–

157) – differ according to the number of array (museme/musemeplex) components changing from E_i to E_{i+1}, and the extent of the cognitive-strength changes as quantified by their respective OFP arrays.

Pressing's concept of the "event-cluster class" is analogous to the notion of the musemeplex allele-class (§3.5.2), in that it makes diachronic what, in memetics, is an abstract synchronic alignment; and it opens up the further theoretical possibility of the *musemesatz allele-class* – the recurrent parataxis of a set of musemes and/or musemeplexes (and/or their alleles) that engenders a common underlying structural framework that is nevertheless elaborated differently on each improvisation-instantiation. Thus, to summarise these mappings between Pressing's model and structures theorised in memetics, an *event* equates to a museme or a musemeplex; an *event cluster* equates to a museme-sequence or a musemeplex-sequence; and an *event-cluster class* equates to a musemeplex allele-class or a musemesatz allele-class.

Pressing understandably encounters difficulty in theorising the details of "how one continuation comes to be chosen over all other possible ones" (1988, p. 164). He wraps this problem into two abstractions: "a set of current goals", symbolised by $\mathscr{G}$; and the "referent", R, which is "an underlying piece-specific guide or scheme", these being held in long-term memory, M, for the duration of the improvisation. They are integrated in Equation 3.2, which represents the "process of event-cluster generation" and, as the arrow implies, event-cluster parataxis (1988, p. 153).

$$(\{E\}, R, \mathscr{G}, M)_i \rightarrow E_{i+1} \tag{3.2}$$

In acknowledging that improvisation may be guided by "a vast panorama of culturally and cognitively based musical processes and stylistic preferences" (1988, p. 164), Pressing admits the role of schemata (R) in shaping generation $(\mathscr{G})$ (1988, p. 152). Some of these schemata are cognitive but, to a significantly greater extent than in composition, others are motor: i.e., they are patterns of motor-control memes and memeplexes, discussed in §3.5.4 under the rubric of "gestemes" or "gesture-control memes". As an illustration of the role of schemata in improvisation, Pressing considers the work of Parry (1930, 1932) and Lord (1964, 1965) on "formulaic composition" in folk epics, a genre that "is created anew at each performance by the singer from a store of formulas, a store of themes, and a technique of composition" (Pressing, 1988, p. 146). He argues that

> [a] 'formula' is a group of words regularly employed under the same metrical conditions to express a given essential idea; it has melodic, metric, syntactic, and acoustic dimensions. By choosing from a repertoire of roughly synonymous formulas of different lengths and expanding or deleting subthemes according to the needs of the performance situation, the experienced performer is able to formulaically compose (in real-time, hence improvise) a detailed and freshly compelling version of a known song epic. As a result of the composition system, instances of pleonasm and parataxis are common.... In the words of Lord ...: 'the really significant element in the process is ... the setting up of various patterns that make adjustment of phrase and creation of phrases by analogy possible' .... In addition, the permutation of events and formulas may occur, as well as the substitution of one theme for another. (Pressing, 1988, p. 146)

This account affords clear parallels, in a different medium of memetic replication, to the operation of the RHSGAP model in music: (i) the notion of "a repertoire of roughly synonymous formulas" is equivalent to the idea of the museme allele or musemeplex allele; (ii) the concept of "expanding or deleting subthemes" is analogous to the modification, reordering, interpolation or deletion of structural *loci* that drives musemesatz mutation; and (iii) the "essential idea" corresponds to the musemesatz itself, generated by, yet also regulating, the lower-level processes it subsumes. That the literary process also appears analogous in several ways to musical improvisation – not least in their real-time unfolding – allows us to hypothesise that common processes of memetic conglomeration and structuralisation relate these realms, despite their different media and dissimilar phemotypic manifestations.

Within the broad structural constraints imposed by a musemesatz, those attributes of musemes and musemeplexes determining their parataxis affect their compatibility with other musemes and musemeplexes in both memomic and phemotypic forms. These factors partly decide which member of a potentially *locus*-generating museme allele-class or musemeplex allele-class is successful, *vis-à-vis* its rivals, in expressing that *locus* in any real-time instantiation of the improvisation's musemesatz. Yet invoking the operation of "formulaic composition" – or, in my terms, the RHSGAP model – in improvisation, as in composition, arguably still does not fully account for the "residual decision-making" of "how one continuation comes to be chosen over all other possible ones" (Pressing, 1988, p. 164). Pressing advances four hypotheses to explain the source of this continuity: "intuition", "free will", "physicalism" and "randomness" (1988, p. 165). While the first can be dismissed as mystical (or, more charitably, as devolving to the third and/or fourth), the RHSGAP model aligns most closely with the third, while admitting, in keeping with the precepts of the overarching VRS algorithm, the role of the fourth. In physicalism,

> complex decision making is seen to be an emergent property of the fantastically complex physical system known as a human being, in interaction with a series of environments. Free will in this perspective is either illusory, or simply a somewhat misleading metaphor for certain complex characteristics of the system. (Pressing, 1988, p. 165)

Recast in terms of the standpoint argued for in this book, physicalism suggests that memomic musemes and musemeplexes are in a state of constant competition for phemotypic expression – and thus for potential further replication – and therefore those that are most successful in this quest will, self-evidently, prevail (this being the "tautology" referred to by Dawkins in §1.6.2). Inherent in this is a tension between top-down and bottom-up factors: in the former, a musemesatz, often only dimly apprehended by the composer or improviser, "seeks" (in Dawkins' rhetorical language of selfish intentionality) to select those musemes or musemeplexes that will articulate its structural *loci*; in the latter, musemes and musemeplexes, "aware" of this constraint, "compete" with their rivals for the survival-enhancing benefits such "victory" brings. One element of this success is a propensity for cooperative interaction – coadaptation – between replicators, both synchronically and diachronically. In summary, the sequential ordering of musemes and musemeplexes, and the configuration of the resultant musemesatz, is arguably less the product of conscious intentionality or agency on the part of the composer or improviser and more an "emergent property" of blindly algorithmic/mechanistic lower-level processes – Pressing's notion of free will as an illusion. Indeed, Pressing's physicalism aligns closely with Dennett's

"Multiple Drafts Model" of consciousness, discussed in §7.3, which offers an algorithmic view of consciousness in which intentionality is framed as an illusion arising from the operation of the VRS algorithm.

3.5.4 Performance

The performance of music brings together a number of processes that can be understood in the light of evolution. Performance (including improvisation and conducting, and extending to include dance and drama) obviously utilises the body, and so depends upon, and illuminates, attributes – sensory/perceptual, cognitive and motor – shaped by millennia of evolution. Indeed, the evolutionary aspects of musical performance are predicated on the principle that the spatial movements of an organism in relation to its (geological) environment, or to another organism, are optimised to facilitate the imperatives of gene-survival, namely risk-avoidance (evasion of predators and other environmental hazards) and reward-garnering (securing shelter, food and mates). These have become hard-wired into brains so they are accessible at a split-second's notice. Such reflex actions modulate the movements underpinning musical performance, which have become stylised microcosms and re-playings of encounters and conflicts encoded into us in our distant evolutionary past. These propensities are covered by Crewdson (2010), who formalises them under the rubric of an "etiological perspective". Essentially, for Crewdson, when we listen to music we are transported back to our evolutionary prehistory, perceiving the virtual kinesis of music in a way analogous to that deployed when we perceive the real kinesis of an approaching predator or thunderstorm. Here, I attempt to apply this perspective to the motor actions of performance.

While innate (evolutionarily wired) movements are often preferred in nature, because they constitute optimum ways of quickly achieving certain physical goals, other movements, particularly the fine-grained actions involved in musical performance, are learned as specific motor skills, often as a result of years of painstaking practise, and often in defiance of what the body finds easy or natural.[111] Such learned body movements are types of memes or,

---

[111] The popularity of such therapies as the Alexander Technique (Woodman & Moore, 2012) among musicians testifies to the consequences of systematic deviation from natural body positions intrinsic to the mastery of certain instruments.

rather, they are the phemotypic effects of memes. One might term them "gestemes", or "gesture memes" (see also Gritten & King, 2006; Gritten & King, 2011). Like all other categories of meme, they are subject to the operation of the VRS algorithm, being varied in response to cognition or discovery of different strategies for executing the gestures in question; replicated, via visual and/or oral instruction from teacher to pupil or from peer to peer (who might take the form of a recording), as part of a pedagogic interaction; and selected according to their perceived utility and efficiency in rendering the music in question.

Recent research in the study of recorded music has indicated how tempi vary significantly within individual performances; and vary from performance to performance of the same work by the same performer and from performer to performer in the same work, over time; as have certain global baseline tempi in some repertoires (Leech-Wilkinson, 2009a). This fluctuation might be regarded as controlled, in part, by gestemes, which regulate the physical tendency to move the hands and fingers more or less quickly, or to pivot the torso in certain ways and in certain directions. One might also hypothesise that gestemes are coadapted with the musemes that code for the music performed, whether these are primarily score-based, as in the performance of notated music; or largely brain-based, as in the creation of improvised music (§3.5.3). Performance thus appears to rely on an interplay between culturally transmitted sound patterns (musemes) and culturally transmitted gesture patterns (gestemes); and a memetics of musical performance should therefore attempt to determine how this interplay functions and to understand how the evolutionary pressures affecting each domain reinforce or contradict each other.

Two questions arising from the issue of tempo-fluctuation are: (i) is such rubato the consequence of some attribute of musemes that might motivate intra-museme tempo changes (thus, are gestemes created in part by musemes);[112] and (ii) if so, once this tendency is realised in one performance, can the effect be consolidated, indeed augmented, on its cultural transmission to other performers by the synergy between the relevant museme(s)

---

[112] While the term "rubato" is often applied in a narrow sense to the performance of certain nineteenth-century piano repertoires, I am using it here more broadly, to refer to any deviation from "metronomic" tempo.

and the newly associated gesteme(s)? Extending this, if the attributes of musemes do motivate tempo changes, then presumably these might be co-ordinated when musemes assemble to form a musemeplex, engendering a parallel *gestemeplex*. Moreover, if a musemesatz is generated by the tendency of members of certain museme and musemeplex allele-classes to instantiate the structural-sequential *loci* of a movement (§3.5.2); and if members of each of these allele-classes are potentially coadapted/coaligned with members of allele-classes of gestemes; then a higher-order sequence of gestemes will arise, which might be termed a *gestemesatz*.

One might hypothesise that such gesteme-generating museme tempo fluc-tuations are driven partly by innate (natural) forces and partly by learned (nurtural) forces, in complex interactions. In the former category, the effect is partly the result of image-schematic factors (§4.2, §4.5) and partly the result of the I-R forces illustrated in Figure 3.7 (see also Narmour (1990, 1992)).[113] In the case of image-schematic factors, a quasi-gravitational force operat-ing in three-dimensional musical "space" upon the metaphorical "mass" of the constituent musemes might be assumed to affect certain aspects of their tempo. In the case of I-R forces, the various implications intrinsic to a museme might be understood to impel the tempo forward, whereas both realisations and frustrations might conceivably act to retard the tempo.

The operation of these natural, and certain nurtural, factors is summarised in the following two-part list. Beyond being incomplete (there are presum-ably many more factors affecting the dynamics of performance than are identified here),[114] this list is clearly over-simplistic, because: (i) the two domains cannot be entirely separated (the learned stabilities of pitch and rhythm hypothesised in the second part are underpinned by natural pre-dispositions shaped by acoustic and morphological regularities); and (ii) multiple factors within and between each category may reinforce and/or contradict each other in complex ways (nature is modulated by nurture, and

---

[113] The empirical testing of the I-R model in relation to performance is not advocated in the "twenty experimental questions suggested by the Implication-Realization Model" (there are actually twenty-one questions listed) that form the conclusion of Narmour (1990, pp. 418–423).

[114] These factors include, but are not limited to, the intrinsic constraints of musical instruments, such as the need, on many "non-pretuned" instruments, to hesitate/elongate whilst a pitch is consolidated (Nicholas Bannan, personal communication), an effect that might potentially trans-fer to other ("pretuned") instruments via a player's familiarity with both types of instrument, or even via hearing this effect.

vice versa). Moreover, the effect ascribed to a particular cause might be manifested *prospectively* (in anticipation of the cause) or *retrospectively* (after the cause has been processed in cognition). This distinction itself relies upon the difference between sight-reading and performance based upon practise and reflective engagement. In the "natural" sub-list, "IS" symbolises situations where (innate) image-schematic factors are hypothesised to be dominant; "IR" symbolises situations where (innate) implication-realisation forces are hypothesised to be dominant; and combinations of these symbols indicate that the tempo-altering effect results broadly from a synergy ("IS+IR") or a conflict ("IS-IR") between them.

1. **Natural**; primarily genetically transmitted factors:

   (a) If a museme segment or museme-museme interface is moving downwards in pitch, there may be a tendency to acceleration, in terms of shortening of inter-onset interval (IOI) and/or offset-to-onset interval (OOI) (Temperley, 2001, p. 68) (IS).

   (b) The effect of point 1a may be augmented if the museme articulates a [P] (IS+IR); and it may be diminished or counteracted if the museme articulates a [R] (IS-IR).[115]

   (c) If a museme segment or museme-museme interface is moving upwards in pitch, there may be a tendency to deceleration, in terms of lengthening of IOI and/or OOI (IS).

   (d) The effect of point 1c may be diminished or counteracted if the museme articulates a [P] (IS-IR); and it may be augmented if the museme articulates a [R] (IS+IR).

   (e) If a museme segment or museme-museme interface encompasses a decrease in note-length (e.g., from crotchets to quavers, or from "straight" quavers to triplet quavers), there may be a tendency to acceleration that exceeds the "measured" acceleration governed by the note durations (IS).

---

[115] To restrict this consideration to [P] and [R] is clearly to oversimplify Narmour's (1990) complex theory, but it nevertheless gives a flavour of how it might be applied to this issue. See also Jan (2007, pp. 129–133, Tab. 4.1).

(f) The effect of point 1e may be augmented if the museme articulates a [P] (IS+IR); and it may be diminished or counteracted if the museme articulates a [R] (IS-IR).

(g) If a museme segment or museme-museme interface encompasses an increase in note-length (e.g., from quavers to crotchets, or from triplet quavers to "straight" quavers), there may be a tendency to deceleration that exceeds the "measured" deceleration governed by the note durations (IS).

(h) The effect of point 1g may be diminished or counteracted if the museme articulates a [P] (IS-IR); and it may be augmented if the museme articulates a [R] (IS+IR).

(i) The octave may have a multivalent effect, sometimes increasing and sometimes decreasing tempo depending on the context. Rising octaves might impel a sense of "momentum-building" to surmount the "height" of the octave, whereas falling octaves might call upon a "precipice-avoiding" steadiness (IS).[116]

2. **Nurtural**; primarily memetically transmitted factors related to style-specific aspects of scale and chord degree and to metrical/rhythmic position:

(a) There may be a tendency to decelerate around/into relatively stable chord-notes (the root, third or fifth) of the locally prevailing triad.

(b) There may be a tendency to accelerate around/into relatively unstable non-chord notes sounding in conjunction with the locally prevailing triad.

(c) There may be a tendency to decelerate around/into relatively stable scale degrees ($\hat{1}$, $\hat{3}$ and $\hat{5}$) and/or triads (I|i, IV|iv, vi|VI and V *versus* $\mathrm{I}_4^6|\mathrm{i}_4^6$) of the locally prevailing key.[117]

---

[116] Narmour argues that, in terms of I-R theory, inexperienced listeners hear the octave as a large interval, implying *prospective* [R]; whereas experienced listeners hear it as a register transfer (i.e., as the "same" note), with the option of perceiving it as a *retrospective* [(R)] (1990, p. 234).

[117] Despite the ostensible stability of the tonic, Rosen gives an example (bb. 23–28 of the first movement of Beethoven's Piano Concerto no. 4 in G major op. 58 (1807)) where rhythmically accelerating tonic-dominant alternations mean that Beethoven "turns this most consonant of chords … into a dissonance. … almost by rhythmic means alone …, the tonic chord of G major *in root position* clearly requires a resolution into the dominant" (1997, pp. 387–388; emphasis in the original).

(d) There may be a tendency to accelerate around/into relatively unstable scale degrees ($\hat{2}$, $\hat{4}$, $\hat{6}$ and $\hat{7}$) and/or triads ($\text{I}_4^6|\text{i}_4^6$, ii|iio, iii|III, V|v and viio|VII) of the locally prevailing key.[118]

(e) There may be a tendency to decelerate around/into rhythmically strong/accented beats (beats 1 and 3 of a $\frac{4}{4}$ bar or beat 1 of a $\frac{3}{4}$ bar).

(f) There may be a tendency to accelerate around/into rhythmically weak/unaccented beats (beats 2 and 4 of a $\frac{4}{4}$ bar or beats 2 and 3 of a $\frac{3}{4}$ bar).[119]

(g) There may be a tendency to decelerate at phrase and sub-phrase endings (followed by a compensatory acceleration at the start of the following phrase or sub-phrase), this motivated in part by the (learned) closural force of imperfect or perfect cadences.

(h) There may be a tendency to return (via acceleration or deceleration) to the original tempo of a museme on its return, if the tempo immediately preceding the point of return has decreased or increased.

To illustrate how these factors might operate, a passage from Chopin's Mazurka in F minor op. 7 no. 3, shown in Figure 3.12a, will be examined. One outcome of the *Mazurka Project* (CHARM, 2019b), conducted under the aegis of the *CHARM* Research Centre (CHARM, 2017), was analyses of recordings of this mazurka performed by Ignaz Friedman, made in 1930, and by Charles Rosen, made in 1989, which graphed beat-to-beat tempo fluctuations (CHARM, 2019a; see also N. Cook, 2007a). The graphs of bb. 9–17 of these recordings are shown aligned in Figure 3.12b.[120] This phrase is chosen for analysis here over bb. 1–8 owing to the greater variety and movement of the later material – it is the main melody, compared with the more static introductory material of bb. 1–8 – which motivates more diversity in tempo than bb. 1–8. In the graphs, red dots indicate the beginning of the

---

[118] The status of chord V is problematic in that, despite being a major triad situated in close (psycho)acoustic proximity to the tonic, it is often (contextually) relatively unstable in many styles.

[119] Points 2e (decelerate around strong/accented beats) and 2f (accelerate around weak/unaccented beats) may reinforce points 2c (decelerate around/into relatively stable degrees) and 2d (accelerate around/into relatively unstable degrees) in this list, respectively, because there appears to be a correlation between the use of triads I, IV and V on strong beats and triads ii|iio, iii|III, vi|VI and viio|VII on weak beats (C. W. White, 2017).

[120] Perhaps more than most other composers, the works of Chopin exist in numerous versions (many sanctioned by the composer) and associated editions, so Friedman and Rosen may have been playing from different editions (N. Cook, 1998, pp. 84–85).

first beat of each bar and the following two blue dots indicate the beginning of the second and third beats, representing beat-onsets equidistantly on the *x* axis (the upper *x*-scale counts bars, the lower counts beats). Because of the tempo fluctuations, beats are not located equidistantly in performance: the position of the dots on the *y* axis represents the measured tempo of the time-slice demarcated by a beat, the left-hand scale representing beat-duration in milliseconds (ms) and the right-hand scale in beats per minute (BPM). Note that the layout of these scales means that the *lower* the dot on the graph, the *faster* the tempo, and vice versa. The various lines connecting the dots represent data from listener tempo-tapping trials that, being estimates of tempo (unlike the measurement-related dots), are not directly relevant to present concerns.

The intra-museme tempo fluctuations within and between bb. 9–17 of these two recordings are summarised in Table 3.3. While bars are not always necessarily coterminous with musemes, bar lines here do indeed demarcate perceptually-cognitively salient (melodic) units, and therefore can be taken as markers of initial and terminal museme-nodes.[121] Table 3.3a shows the antecedent phrase (bb. 9–12) and Table 3.3b shows the consequent phrase (bb. 13–16). The two-bar sub-phrases within each phrase are separated by double lines. The table also takes inter-museme tempo fluctuations into account, which occur in the context of the closural force of the musemes' terminal node (see the rows for bb. 9–10, bb. 10–11, etc.). The assessed magnitude of beat-to-beat tempo change is represented by "S" = small; "M" = medium; and "L" = large. Nevertheless, at times, it is not always easy to distinguish between equal- and small-, and small- and medium-sized changes. The direction of tempo change from beat to beat is indicated by "↑" = acceleration; "↓" = deceleration; and "=" = no significant change. An ellipsis (…) separates observations pertinent to the beat 1–beat 2 span from those pertinent to the beat 2–beat 3 span within a given bar/museme. Significant cross-recording overlaps of tempo-profile between parallel musemes or museme components are indicated in bold.

Number/letter combinations in brackets refer to those hypotheses in the list on page 216 judged most relevant to explain the observed tempo variation,

---

[121] This analysis focuses on the melodic line, while acknowledging that the arpeggiated left-hand accompaniment may have a potential (dragging) effect on the tempo in places.

(a) Chopin: Mazurka op. 7 no. 3 (1830–1832), bb. 1–17.

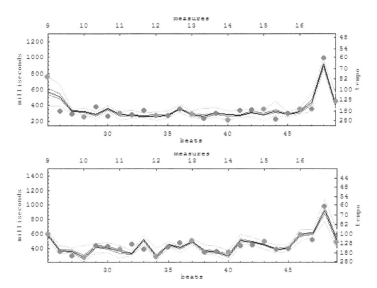

(b) Tempo Graphs of bb. 9–17: Friedman 1930 (upper); Rosen 1989 (lower).

Figure 3.12: Two Performances of Chopin, Mazurka op. 7 no. 3 (1830–1832), bb. 9–17.

adopting the most parsimonious interpretation in each case.[122] Sometimes these require nested brackets in order to clarify the combination of factors, thus demarcating combinations from the relationships between the combined forces and some other force or set of combined forces. For these higher-order relationships, a plus ("+") sign indicates synergistic augmentation, or contrastive neutralisation, of two factors or combination of factors; whereas the separator ">" indicates that, in the case of contradictory factors or combinations of factors, the former is judged to outweigh the latter in any particular instance of tempo change. If there is a change of tempo direction within a bar (an increase followed by a decrease, or vice versa), hypotheses pertinent to each are separated by an ellipsis.[123]

---

[122] Assigning a hypothesis to the equals sign (i.e., no significant tempo change at that point) is often problematic. In some cases, it represents a moment of stasis before a continuation of the tendency (acceleration or deceleration) represented by the immediately preceding symbol. In other cases, it is an apex point, before a subsequent movement in the opposite direction to that represented by the immediately preceding symbol (acceleration following deceleration or vice versa).

[123] In keeping with the principle of parsimony just outlined, not every possible hypothesis (and its opposing hypotheses) is enumerated as an explanation for each observation. The reader will hopefully be able to identify the nurtural opponent(s) to a given natural force, and vice versa.

Phrase, Bar	Friedman 1930	Rosen 1989
9	L ↑ ... S ↑ (1d > 1c)	M ↑ ... S ↑ (1d > 1c)
9–10	S ↑(1a + 1b + 1e + 1f + 2b)	
10	**M** ↓ ... M ↑ ((1g > 1h) + ((2a + 2c) > 2f) ... 1i)	**M** ↓ ... = ((1g > 1h) + ((2a + 2c) > 2f) ... 1i)
10–11	S ↓ (2g)	S ↑ (1e)
11	= ... S ↓ (1c > 1d ... 1c > 1d)	S ↓ ... S ↑ (1c ... 1d > 1c)
11–12	S ↑ (1e)	M ↑ (1e + 1f)
12	= ... S ↓ ((2a + 2c) > (1a + 1b) ... (2a + 2c) > (1a + 1b))	M ↓ ... S ↓ ((1g + 2a + 2c) > (1a + 1b) ... (2a + 2c) > (1a + 1b))
12–13	S ↑ (1a + 1b)	S ↓ ((2a + 2c + 2e) > (1a + 1b))

(a) Bars 9–12.

Phrase, Bar	Friedman 1930	Rosen 1989
13	S ↑ ... S ↓ (1d > 1c ... 1c > 1d)	M ↑ ... = (1d > 1c ... 1c > 1d)
13–14	S ↑ (1a + 1b + 1e + 1f + 2b)	= (2e > (1a + 1b))
14	M ↓ ... = ((1g > 1h) + ((2a + 2c) > 2f) ... 2f > (1c + 1d))	S ↓ ... = ((1g > 1h) + ((2a + 2c) > 2f) ... 2f > (1c + 1d))
14–15	= (1i > 1a)	S ↓ (1a > 1i)
15	M ↑ ... S ↓ (1d > 1c ... 2c > 2d)	S ↑ ... = (1d > 1c ... 2c)
15–16	S ↓ (2a + 2c)	M ↓ (2a + 2c + 2e)
16	= ... L ↓ (2c + 2d ... 2g > (1e + 2b + 2d + 2f))	S ↑ ... L ↓ (2d ... 2g > (1e + 2b + 2d + 2f))
16–17	L ↑(2h)	

(b) Bars 13–17.

Table 3.3: Intra- and Inter-Museme Tempo Fluctuations in Chopin, Mazurka op. 7 no. 3, bb. 9–17.

There is a good deal of data in Table 3.3, and, perhaps unsurprisingly, some of it is contradictory. For one thing, identical figures are not always performed in the same manner, even by each pianist, as in the case of b. 9 and b. 13, especially in Friedman's recording. Nor, indeed, are analogous figures, such as b. 9 and b. 11, rendered similarly, again particularly in the case of Friedman. More broadly, justifying the relationships posited in Table 3.3 between the tempo data and the hypotheses in the list on page 216 is beyond the scope of this chapter, so three examples from Table 3.3 must suffice for particular mention. These are outlined below:

1. In b. 9 of both recordings there is an acceleration, L ↑ (Friedman)/M ↑ (Rosen) ... S ↑. This suggests the counteraction of the potential deceleration motivated by an ascent (point 1c) by the countervailing "energy" of the [P] (point 1d). The museme in b. 9 ends with a (prospective) Intervallic Process ([IP]) (Narmour, 1990, p. 350), not with a [R]. Assuming it would have a tempo-mediating effect, albeit one weaker than a [R], the [IP] occurs after the start of the third beat of the bar, and so appears not to factor into the tempo calculation. Apropos points 1b, 1d and 1f, only [R]s where the change-of-direction note is the second or the fourth quaver (in $\frac{3}{4}$ time) are likely to affect the intra-bar tempo, unless there is in play the prospective cognition referred to on page 216. The effect of a [R] or an [IP] might be evident, however, on inter-bar/museme tempo, although this is not relevant in the case of bb. 9–10 here.[124]

2. Comparison of the analogous b. 10 and b. 14 shows illuminating differences. In Friedman, both bars decelerate into the second beat, perhaps motivated by the "trumping" by note-length increase (point 1g) of [P]-motivated acceleration (point 1h); and by the combined domination of harmonic stability factors (points 2a and 2c) over rhythmic factors (point 2f). Bar 10 has a compensatory acceleration on the f^1–f^2 ascent, whereas b. 14 has no change on the analogous f^1–c^2 ascent. The former (octave) change might be the result of image-schematic "aspirational" forces (point 1i), whereas the latter (fifth) change might be the result of the trumping by accelerative rhythmic forces (point 2f) of the decelerative [R]-related forces here (points 1c and 1d), this conflict motivating not an acceleration but tempo stability here. In Rosen, b. 10 also has a deceleration in the same place as Friedman (presumably motivated by the same factors), but no compensatory acceleration on the f^1–f^2 ascent; whereas b. 14 has a

---

[124] While many factors may break a sound-stream into discrete musemes – thus turning two adjacent pitches into initial and terminal museme nodes, respectively – often this juncture, and the resulting museme-parataxis, is articulated by I-R forces. See Jan (2010, pp. 19–22).

small deceleration (perhaps arising from weaker action of the forces attendant upon the Friedman segment) and, like Friedman, no change on the f^1–c^2 ascent (presumably motivated by the same factors). The significant difference in connection with the octave leap of b. 10 might be the result of the issues discussed in note 116 on page 217, with Friedman being motivated primarily by image-schematic factors and the arguably more cerebral Rosen hearing it as the "same" note owing to "Narmourean" octave-equivalence.

3. There is a large deceleration at the end of b. 16 in both recordings (they are the largest tempo changes in Figure 3.12b), followed by an acceleration into b. 17.[125] This deceleration suggests a strong (nurtural) phrase-ending effect here (point 2g), one that contradicts the (natural) implication of acceleration on rhythmic diminution (point 1e), even in the absence of any (natural) acceleration-inhibiting [R] here (point 1f). The deceleration would also appear to overrule the (nurtural) tendencies to accelerate around/into relatively unstable non-chord notes (point 2b), around/into relatively unstable scale degrees and triads (point 2d), and around/into weak beats (point 2f).

Constraints of space in this section have prevented my developing a fully developed evolutionarily grounded theory of musical performance. A few suggestive conclusions have emerged, although these need to be evidenced more substantively, perhaps using large-scale computer-aided correlation of tempo-fluctuation data with museme-contour analysis. Given the multiparametric nature of music, and the complex mixture of natural and nurtural factors involved in its performance, what are clear behavioural trajectories in the realm of biological actions often become entangled in musical performance. As a result, and in a parallel to the particulate nature of genetic inheritance, one might paraphrase Dawkins and suggest that "[t]his does not mean that the [natural and nurtural factors] concerned are not [discrete and] particulate. It is just that there are so many of them ..., each one having such a small effect, that they *seem* to blend" (1989, p. 195; emphasis in the original) when combined in the heat of the performance situation. Nevertheless, it seems the case that both biologically evolved patterns of physical movement and culturally evolved habits of nuancing those patterns play a significant role in shaping musical performance.

---

[125] The word *"rubato"* appears in b. 17 of the first edition and in subsequent editions, which might imply a suggestion to return to the baseline tempo towards the end of, rather than at the beginning of, b. 17, but which Friedman and Rosen, with their rapid return to the previous tempo-range at the start of b. 17, do not take up.

3.6 Music-Cultural Taxonomies

The discussion of taxonomy in §1.7 considered not only the great diversity of the natural world – as evidence by the number of taxonomic ranks (Table 1.5) and their internal richness – but also the conflicting views among biologists as to how sense might be made of this heterogeneity by systems of categorisation. As an approach that seeks strictly to trace evolutionary relationships, using the evidence of molecular biology as a validation of apparent connections suggested by morphological resemblances, cladistic taxonomy (§1.7.2) is arguably the optimal way of mapping the operation of Darwinism in nature.

On the logic of Universal Darwinism, cladism would appear also to be the optimal way of charting the operation of Darwinism in culture. Here the aspiration – one well beyond the scope of this book – would be the formulation of a complete taxonomy of human (and potentially animal and machine) culture to rival that assembled by biologists for the natural world (Jan, 2014, sec. 6). That this would in principle be possible – that there is an intrinsic connection between biological and cultural taxonomies – was recognised by Darwin, when he observed the similarities between language families and human genealogy. In a passage in which "musics" might readily be substituted for "languages", he argued that

> [i]t may be worth while to illustrate this [dendritic] view of classification, by taking the case of languages. If we possessed a perfect pedigree of mankind, a genealogical arrangement of the races of man would afford the best classification of the various languages now spoken throughout the world; and if all existing languages, and all intermediate and slowly changing dialects, had to be included, such an arrangement would, I think, be the only possible one. Yet it might be that some very ancient language had altered little, and had given rise to few new languages, whilst others (owing to the spreading and subsequent isolation and states of civilisation of the several races, descended from a common race) had altered much, and had given rise to many new languages and dialects. The various degrees of difference in the languages from the same stock, would have to be expressed by groups subordinate to groups; but the proper or even only possible arrangement would still be genealogical; and this would be strictly natural, as it would connect together all languages, extinct and modern, by the closest affinities, and

would give the filiation and origin of each tongue. (Darwin, 2008, p. 311; see also Sereno, 1991, pp. 471–472)[126]

Thus, a cladistic orientation appears to be the most logical basis upon which to develop music-cultural taxonomies, given the concern of memetics with the operation of the VRS algorithm at several structural-hierarchic levels and across various interconnected geographical domains over time. The most obvious musical implementation of cladism, and a good model for a more thoroughgoing cladistic memetics, is the tradition of musical text-criticism, one of the most venerated elements of the "old" musicology. Deriving from palaeography and classical philology, it offers a highly systematic and formalised methodology based on transmission and mutation for uncovering the filiation, as Darwin would say, of pieces, particularly music in manuscript sources, and for generating its own form of taxonomic trees, *stemmata* (Grier, 1996, Ch. 3).

While it is clear what are the significant taxonomic units of biology – of the levels discussed in §1.7, the most important from a cladistic perspective is arguably the species – it is not so clear what are the significant taxonomic units of culture. This ambiguity is the result of fundamental differences between the dynamics of biological and cultural evolution, and of the enormous variety of forms sustained by culture – both of which result from key mechanistic differences. For the former factor, and in biology, there is a clear separation between replicators and vehicles (§1.6.1); and the associated constraints of a fixed life-cycle (whatever its length) mean there is a clear rhythm of generations resulting from the time-lag between birth and the readiness of the vehicle to reproduce. In culture, no such rhythm occurs, and cultural replicators can be copied rapidly and "arhythmically". In short, this is the difference between the primarily periodic, "vertical" (parent-to-offspring) nature of biological transmission *versus* the primarily aperiodic "horizontal" (peer-to-peer) nature of cultural transmission.[127] "Oblique" transmission is sometimes used to refer to intergenerational transmission between adults and (unrelated) children, and is a significant mode of transmission in musical cul-

---

[126] A dendritic diagram, the only illustration in the *Origin*, is given in Darwin (2008, p. 90).

[127] In some traditional societies, much of culture is transmitted vertically, from parent to young adult, and this is certainly true for early-years enculturation in most societies; but it is not the norm in technologically advanced societies, where children generally assimilate culture-fragments from peers from a relatively early age.

ture, as well as in most other formalised educational systems (Shennan, 2002, pp. 48–51; see also Blute, 2006, pp. 156–157). For the latter factor, the absence in cultural evolution of a mechanism connecting replicators deterministically with vehicles analogous to that – DNA-mediated protein-synthesis – in biological evolution leads to the relatively unconstrained diversity of cultural phemotypes, as against the relatively constrained uniformity of biological phenotypes.

When pursuing the application of taxonomy to memetics, it is necessary to consider correspondences between comparable levels of the nature-culture analogy hypothesised in §1.6.2. As illustrated in Table 1.4, there are four main levels to the analogy. At the highest level, the correspondence operates between biological species and cultural dialects (Meyer, 1996, p. 23) (level three); below this, groups within a species might be mapped onto idioms (particular composers' styles (Meyer, 1996, p. 24)), genres, and formal-structural types (level four); at a still lower level, the equivalence is arguably between the individual organism and the individual movement or work (level five); and at the lowest level one might compare operons/genes with m(us)emeplexes/m(us)emes – I conflate levels six and seven of Table 1.4 here, given their structural and functional similarities.[128] At which of these culture-hierarchic levels might one most appropriately develop methodologies for a music-memetic taxonomy?

In the case of the approach mentioned above, the stemmata of musical text-criticism, the object of investigation and classification is usually the work,[129] which equates to the individual organism in biology. Clearly this is too low a level for biological taxonomy, which generally regards species ($\equiv$ dialect) – together with (sub)species, varieties, or other such "infraspecific" taxa – as the lowest manageable units of classification; and it does not appear useful for cultural taxonomy either, for there is arguably no meaningful sense in which a work can be equated to a parent lineage that bifurcates to create child lineages, even though particular works may well serve as inspiration, models even, for the efforts of later composers.

---

[128] In the quotation on page 226, Darwin equates a language with a "race", i.e., a group within a species.

[129] I am using this term here in its broadest, least historically and aesthetically/philosophically loaded sense (Goehr, 1992).

Mappings at the four levels are discussed in the following. Further implications of this issue are explored in §4.3.1.

3.6.1 Species-Dialect

In biology, cladistic-taxonomic discussion is primarily focused on the phenomenon of speciation, which might find its analogue in culture in the breaking-off of separate and distinct "child" dialects from a "parent" dialect. While this is a central area of cladistics in biology, the picture is somewhat more mixed in culture. Much depends upon how a dialect is defined: the options broadly devolve to some combination of the geographical/"horizontal"/synchronic ("Viennese Classicism", "the Mannheim School"); and the chronological/"vertical"/diachronic (the "style of the 1780s"). Nevertheless, music-cultural dialects have considerably greater musemic and configurational diversity than the potentially analogous genetic and morphological consistencies that are required for the determination of species: members of a species must manifest certain genomic and phenotypic regularities, which both result from and facilitate gene replication, regularities that are not required for the propagation of musical dialects.

For cultural speciation to occur, dialects require cultural-ecological "niches" within which potential child dialects could arise and flourish. The studies of bird-song transmission in §5.4.1 suggest that this can, in principle, be engendered by geographical separation and, certainly before the twentieth century, the predominant concentration of music in urban centres meant that distinct geographical dialects, each drawing upon their own subset of a wider museme pool, could survive and flourish. As an example, while there was a generic European Galant style, distinct French, German and Italian "subspecies" coexisted, each with its own subtle variants on standard practices (Heartz, 2003). Nevertheless, it seems that the force of the species-dialect mapping is primarily as a verbal-conceptual memeplex (i.e., it is metaphorical; §4.3.3), and not directly music-memetic.

3.6.2 Group-Idiom/Genre/Formal-Structural Type

The nearest cultural equivalent to cladistic taxonomy's study of speciation might be found in the study of evolving musico-structural types and categories within and across dialects – examples include the evolution of binary-form dance genres over the seventeenth and eighteenth centuries, and that of the various types of sonata forms and their associated multi-movement sequences over the eighteenth and nineteenth centuries – which corresponds with the group of organisms in biology. This of course breaks the level-mappings of Table 1.4 – which is not intended to be regarded as absolute and immutable – aligning level three in nature (species) with level four in culture (idiom/genre/formal-structural type). But given that a sub-group can form the basis of a new species, and given that the distinction between species and sub-species is not always clear, then the evolution of these particular cultural categories, might constitute a meaningful field for cultural taxonomy. As an example of potential bifurcation at this level, the often "monothematic" – or "P[rimary theme]-based S[econdary theme]" (Hepokoski & Darcy, 2006, pp. 135–136) – sonata movements of Haydn, for instance, might be regarded as a different branch to the often "bithematic" practice of Mozart and Beethoven. But – at the risk of oversimplifying a complex range of practices (there are various hybrid types) – the fact that Haydn also wrote bithematic sonata forms muddies these particular waters and separates this candidate cultural example of speciation from the more clearly demarcated lineages of biology.

3.6.3 Organism-Movement/Work

Cladistic taxonomy only considers individual organisms as *tokens* of the *type* represented by the species, recognising that to categorise them on an individual basis is meaningless in taxonomy (but not necessarily so in other domains of biology). The same holds true in culture: movements and works, as analogues of organisms, are tokens of higher-order categories, not types in themselves; and attempting to treat them cladistically, as akin to species, would again break the level-mapping of Table 1.4 by aligning, in this case, level three of nature with level five of culture. As argued in the discussion of the unit(s) of selection in §1.6.2, musemes, not whole works, are transmitted from composer to composer. There is therefore no sense in which a work itself is subject to the operation of the VRS algorithm: this mechanism applies only to (some of) the musemes that constitute a work. Thus, it applies only indirectly, via bottom-up forces, to the idioms, genres, and formal-structural types that a work tokens. Nevertheless, the attributes of these level-four categories might additionally be shaped via the action of musico-operational/procedural memes.

3.6.4 Operon/Gene-M(us)emeplex/M(us)eme

Most cultural change at the dialect ($\equiv$ species) level is perhaps due less to the geographical and/or chronological bifurcation of child dialects than to the evolution of the system itself brought about by internal musemic mutation, an issue covered more fully in §7.5. Some biologists assert that the ultimate driver of evolution is gene selection, yet this is always mediated by interactions between phenotypes and environments. While this probably also holds true for culture, measuring the effects of interactions between phemotypes and environments – human perceptual-cognitive constraints acting in conjunction with effects arising from the wider culture – is difficult, whereas measuring m(us)eme-level change is more feasible. In this sense, the level equivalent to that of the gene – the m(us)eme – is arguably the most tractable for cultural taxonomies. At this level, however, the configuration of a gene-pool is, strictly, the province of population genetics, not of taxonomy; and mutation, not evolution, is the appropriate concept when considering its reconfiguration (because genes mutate whereas species evolve). Similarly, a study of the constituents of a m(us)eme pool – a classification of antecedent forms and their mutational descendants in terms of their spatio-temporal position on what would be a vast tree of transmission relationships – is one that falls, strictly, within the purview of population memetics, even though one might ostensibly conduct it under the rubric of a memetic taxonomy.

Cope's concept of the *lexicon* is pertinent to this issue (Cope, 2001, p. 94; Cope, 2003, p. 20; Jan, 2016c). While he does not explicitly invoke memetics, a lexicon is essentially the outcome of assigning museme alleles – a set of structurally/functionally analogous musemes any of which might occupy a particular *locus* in an instantiation of a specific structural archetype (§3.5.2) – to their parent museme allele-class. Lexicons impinge on Cope's work in computer-generated composition – most notably in his *Sorcerer* and *Experiments in Musical Intelligence* (EMI) systems (§6.5.1.1) – in that a member of a given lexicon can be inserted interchangeably with other lexicon-members into a specific position in a composition, thus reconciling high levels of pattern richness with algorithmic parsimony. Mattheson suggests that composers perform such museme allele-class assignment semi-automatically. He advises that

> [t]hese particulars must not be taken so strictly that one would perhaps write down an index of like fragments, and, as is done in school, make a proper invention box out of them; but one would do it in the same way as we stock up a provision of words and expressions for speaking, not necessarily on paper nor in a book, but in one's head, through which our thoughts, be they verbal or written, can then be quite easily produced without always consulting a lexicon. (Mattheson & Harriss, 1981, p. 284, para. 17)

This indexing of "like fragments" is a function of the sophisticated sorting and comparison powers of the human brain to group patterns that are similar according to various criteria, and operates both consciously and unconsciously. It is argued in §3.8.4 to be a function of the "hashing" formalised in Calvin's Hexagonal Cloning Theory, whereby shared attributes of two or more cortically encoded patterns are connected by neural links to a "centrally located representation" (CLR) that serves to abstract and index their defining features. In this sense, hashing is a form of *cortical taxonomy*, because it creates higher-level categorical groupings that associate phenomena that are perceptually and cognitively similar in certain respects.

The phenomenon of one-way binary branching, while intrinsic to biological speciation, is difficult to apply to population memetics (as a proxy for a memetic taxonomy). While cladistic taxonomy takes as a cardinal principle the notion of strict hierarchic inclusion – the "perfect nesting" of monophyly (Dawkins, 2006, p. 367) – a taxonomy of culture must account for the hybridising interaction between members of different lineages, a phenomenon arguably applicable to several of the levels at which nature-culture alignments are hypothesised to exist. Hybridisation is evident, for instance, in the Galant schemata with which Gjerdingen (1988, 2007a) is concerned. The variety of changing-note patterns replicated by composers in the eighteenth century were presumably not the result of successive branchings in a lineage that began with a single primary schema; rather, they are more likely to have resulted from the intermixing (hybridisation) of initial and terminal schema-events from several coexistent schemata (Jan, 2013).

3.6.5 Distinguishing Homologies from Homoplasies in Music-Cultural Evolution

Having argued in §3.6.4 that m(us)emes are the most tractable units with which to construct cultural taxonomies, it is instructive to attempt to apply to them the three categories outlined in §1.7.2 used to organise biological similarities – namely, homoplasy, ancestral homology, and derived homology (page 50). To review these briefly, a homoplasy is "a character shared between two or more species that was not present in their common ancestor" (Ridley, 2004, pp. 427–428, 480), most often resulting from *convergent evolution* arising "when the same selection pressure has operated in two lineages" (2004, p. 429); an ancestral homology is "present in the common ancestor of the group of species under study" (2004, p. 431) and "found in some but not all of the descendants of the common ancestor" (2004, p. 480); and a derived homology "evolved after the common ancestor, within the group of species under study" (2004, p. 431) and is "found in all the descendants of the common ancestor" (2004, p. 480).

Like the palaeontologist with his or her fossil record, the musicologist has at his or her disposal the phemotypic forms of musemes, preserved as notated and recorded music. As with the fossil record, however, this account is incomplete; but whereas the palaeontologist can see slow-moving biological evolution reflected in exposed rock strata and build taxonomic trees from them (and from molecular-biological evidence), the speed of cultural evolution is so rapid, and the number of interacting individuals sustaining it so large and diverse, that only a comprehensive sequential account of all the interactions among all participants in a dialect over a given segment of geography and/or chronology can securely establish chains of museme transmission and, therefore, trees of cultural evolution. This constraint suggests that, while not impossible, developing musemic taxonomies will be difficult and time-consuming. As §6.1 and §7.5.3 suggest, computer technology may well expedite such research.

I consider here how homologies might be distinguished from homoplasies at the level of the museme, extending the discussion in Chapter 1 apropos Figure 1.1. One fundamental issue here is that biological phylogenies take account of both morphology and molecules, which, in cultural phylogenies, equate to structure and musemes, respectively.[130] This would imply an approach that attempts to identify different structural *loci* (analogous to morphology in biological classification), and the various museme alleles that instantiate those *loci* (analogous to molecules in biological classification) (§3.5.2). In this sense, one is recuperating the taxonomy of formal-structural types (§3.6.2) under the aegis of an ostensibly museme-level perspective.

Ridley lists three principal criteria by which homologies can be distinguished from homoplasies in biological evolution (2004, p. 430), and I list them here in order that inferences on the treatment of cultural homologies *versus* homoplasies might be made:

Structural Similarity: homologies have the same fundamental structure, not merely surface similarity. Bird and bat wings look superficially similar, but are structurally quite different, and are in fact homoplasious (Ridley, 2004, p. 428, Fig. 15.3).

Relations to Surrounding Characters: homologous features are usually related to surrounding structures, such as a given bone to its surrounding bones, in broadly similar ways.

Embryonic Development: homologies normally follow similar lines of embryonic development; similar adult characteristics arrived at by different embryological routes tend to be homoplasies.

How might these three criteria be applied in cases of similarity between musemes and between musemeplexes, in order to distinguish cultural homologies (ancestral and derived) from cultural homoplasies? Table 3.4 attempts to rework for application to musical contexts the criteria for these phenomena in biology just listed; and Figures 3.13a–3.13f provide candidate musical ex-

---

[130] The first elements of these pairs misalign the "Genetic-Structural" level five and the "Memetic-Cultural" level four of Table 1.4; and the second elements are aligned at the Genetic/Memetic-Structural level seven. See also §4.3.1 for a related issue.

amples (taken mainly from the Viennese classical repertoire) of homoplasies and homologies.[131]

Criterion	Homoplasy	Ancestral Homology	Derived Homology
Structural Similarity	(i) Foreground-level pitch similarity not supported by middleground-level similarity; and/or (ii) few rhythmic resemblances; and/or (iii) few contextual/poietic connections (Figure 3.13a).	(i) Foreground-level pitch similarity with some middleground-level similarity or vice versa; and/or (ii) some rhythmic resemblances; and/or (iii) some contextual/poietic connections (Figure 3.13b).	(i) Foreground-level pitch similarity underpinned by significant middleground-level similarity; and/or (ii) significant rhythmic resemblances; and/or (iii) significant contextual/poietic connections (Figure 3.13c).
Relations to Surrounding Characters	No or limited instantiation of a virtual musemeplex (after the distinction on page 202) and (thus) no or limited instantiation of a musemesatz (Figure 3.13d).[132]	Some instantiation of a virtual musemeplex or limited instantiation of a real musemeplex and (thus) some instantiation of a musemesatz (Figure 3.13e).	Significant instantiation of a virtual musemeplex or of a real musemeplex and (thus) significant instantiation of a musemesatz.[133]
Embryonic Development	No evidence of derivation from antecedent musemes in a composer's sketch materials or other poietic documents.	Some evidence of derivation from antecedent musemes in a composer's sketch materials or other poietic documents.	Strong evidence of derivation from antecedent musemes in a composer's sketch materials or other poietic documents.

Table 3.4: Criteria for Distinguishing Between Musemic Homoplasies and Homologies.

---

[131] It must be stressed that the criteria advanced in Table 3.4 are not hard-and-fast, and there are therefore many potential uncertainties. Moreover, examples are not given for the three categories of the Embryonic Development criterion, partly owing to space-constraints on presenting such evidence, and partly owing to the more fundamental issue – a challenge to this criterion in the case of its application to culture – that absence of evidence does not constitute evidence of absence.

[132] Recall that a real musemeplex arises from the re-assembly of (more or less) the same *museme*-sequence; and that a virtual musemeplex arises from the re-assembly of the same *museme-allele*-sequence.

[133] On account of this RHSGAP, this category overlaps, at a higher structural-hierarchic level, with "structural similarity/derived homology".

(a) Structural Similarity: Homoplasy. J. S. Bach: *Das wohltemperirte Clavier* Book II (*c.* 1740), Praeludium V, BWV. 874, bb. 1–2 (upper); Mozart: Symphony no. 41 in C major K. 551 ("Jupiter") (1788), II, bb. 28–29 (lower).

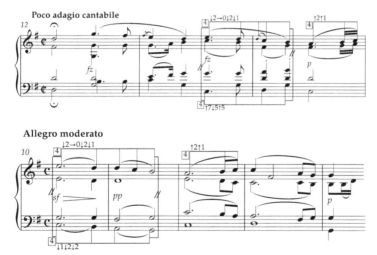

(b) Structural Similarity: Ancestral Homology. Haydn: String Quartet in C major op. 76 no. 3 ("Emperor") (1797), II, bb. 12–14 (upper); Beethoven: Piano Concerto no. 4 in G major op. 58 (1807), I, bb. 10–14 (lower).

(c) Structural Similarity: Derived Homology. Mozart: *La clemenza di Tito* K. 621 (1791), no. 7, "Ah perdona al primo affetto", bb. 44–46 (upper); Ferdinand David: Concertino for Trombone in E♭ major op. 4 (*c.* 1837), I, bb. 1–4 (lower).

(d) Relations to Surrounding Characters: Homoplasy. Mozart: *Don Giovanni* K. 527 (1787), no. 13, "Signor, guardate un poco", bb. 249–253 (upper); Schubert: String Quintet in C major D. 956 (1828), I, bb. 138–142 (lower).

(e) Relations to Surrounding Characters: Ancestral Homology. Beethoven: Symphony no. 9 in D minor op. 125 (1824), I, bb. 74–80 (upper); Schubert: Symphony no. 9 in C major D. 944 (1828), III, Trio, bb. 57–64 (lower).

(f) Relations to Surrounding Characters: Derived Homology. Haydn: String Quartet in E♭ major op. 9 no. 2 (1769), II, bb. 1–10 (upper); Mozart: Requiem K. 626 (1791), "Hostias", bb. 3–10 (lower).

Figure 3.13: Musemic Homoplasies and Homologies.

As might be expected from Table 3.4, Figures 3.13a, 3.13b and 3.13c relate to musemes, whereas Figures 3.13d, 3.13e and 3.13f relate to musemeplexes. Beginning with the "Structural Similarity" criterion, Figure 3.13a shows two patterns that, although spanning the melodic interval of a fifth, are structurally different in that the Bach passage prolongs tonic harmony whereas the Mozart outlines a $\hat{1}$/I–$\hat{4}$/V progression, the g^1 ($\hat{5}$) in b. 29^1 being an échappée from the preceding f^1 ($\hat{4}$). The rising-fifth line is an example of the kinds of "good tricks" (Dennett, 1995, pp. 77–78) (§5.5.1), or "commonalities" (Cope, 2003, p. 17), which form the generic connective tissue of much tonal music.

Figure 3.13b shows a more closely related pair of passages, the upper-line museme in the second half of the Haydn phrase appearing at the start of the Beethoven passage. The different harmonisation of the penultimate element ($V7$ in b. 14^1 of the Haydn; V^4_3 in b. 11^{1-2} of the Beethoven), the result of different coadapted lower-line musemes, is the motivation for assigning this relationship to the category of ancestral homology, rather than derived homology, on the assumption that both passages derive from a common ancestor, but have diverged to some extent from it. Nevertheless, Beethoven's museme is followed by another (b. 12) that occurs in the analogous position in the Haydn passage (b. 14^{3-4}), suggesting some "relation to surrounding characters".

Figure 3.13c shows less divergence between the two passages, with the outline of the Mozart phrase being replicated very closely in that by David. Both are instances of the *Romanesca* schema, which constitutes their common ancestor.[134] The two alleles in Figure 3.13c represent variants that mutate the *Romanesca*'s core (enclosed by a dashed-line box in both passages) by rising to the upper $\hat{1}$ followed by a descent to an imperfect cadence, further mutated in the David passage in its local emphasis on vi in b. 3^{3-4}. As a derived homology, these two passages "evolved after the common ancestor, within the group of species under study" (Ridley, 2004, p. 431), the group being these two examples and, possibly, others.

Turning to the "Relations to Surrounding Characters" criterion, Figure 3.13d shows a cadential figure given a minuet-topic (§3.8.5) treatment in Mozart

---

[134] The *Romanesca* schema consists of the melodic/bass scale-degree sequence $\hat{1}$|$\hat{3}$/$\hat{1}$–$\hat{5}$/$\hat{7}$–$\hat{1}$/$\hat{6}$–$\hat{1}$/$\hat{3}$ (Gjerdingen, 2007a, pp. 39–40, 454).

and a march-topic garb in Schubert (Ratner, 1980, pp. 9–11, 16; see also Monelle, 2006). Other than this museme, there are no further musemic-structural alignments, as the interpolated emphasis on E minor in bb. 139–140 of the Schubert passage – which has no parallel in the Mozart – might imply. Therefore, there is no musemeplex common to these two passages, no musemesatz, and thus there are no relations (certainly in terms of the parameters considered) to surrounding characters.

Figure 3.13e shows two passages that might initially seem as dissimilar as those in Figure 3.13d. Nevertheless, as the overlay indicates, their component musemes at each *locus* are allelically equivalent, and therefore a virtual musemeplex, and thus a musemesatz, is generated.[135] This suggests the passages are related in terms of an ancestral homology, although the close chronological proximity of the two works, and the clear cultural influence Beethoven had on Schubert, might afford counter-evidence in favour of a derived homology.[136]

Despite the greater chronological distance between the two works in Figure 3.13f compared with Figure 3.13e (twenty-two years as against four years, respectively), the passages in Figure 3.13f show greater structural similarities, hence the ascription of a derived homology rather than an ancestral homology. Not only does the Mozart passage reinstantiate the musemeplex, and thus the musemesatz, of the Haydn, but the generative foreground-level musemes in these two passages are more similar than is the case in Figure 3.13e, and these similarities are based upon a greater number of museme-museme correspondences. Thus, the passage is arguably closer to the "real" than to the "virtual" end of the musemeplex-type continuum identified in connection with the definitions on page 202.[137]

While the precepts outlined in Table 3.4 are ultimately subjective, and while Figure 3.13 applies them using relatively informal and intuitive judgements,

---

[135] To avoid clutter, certain musemes in Figure 3.13e and 3.13f are not given the analytical overlay-symbology used in other music examples (§2); instead, they are shown boxed.

[136] Whereas the "Structural Similarity" row of Table 3.4 has criteria related to contextual/poietic connections, the "Relations to Surrounding Characters" row does not. Such connections should, however, not be disregarded when considering the latter criterion.

[137] Figure 3.10a and Figure 3.10b arguably represent another instance of a derived homology, although it is debatable as to whether this category is tenable in the case of relationships between two passages by the same composer.

it is useful in some situations to be able formally to measure and quantify relationships between musemes. On this logic, above a certain similarity-threshold, two similar musemes might be held to be homologous, not homoplasious, and vice versa if they are below the threshold. Various computational approaches have been developed in order to quantify similarity in music (Velardo et al., 2016). Some of these aim to model perception and cognition, in that two passages ranked according to their underlying algorithms as closely related are also perceived as such by listeners. Müllensiefen and Frieler (2004) evaluated some forty-eight similarity-detection algorithms, comparing them with the responses of listeners in tests of melodic similarity (see also Müllensiefen & Frieler, 2006). Their findings suggest that some of the most psychologically robust metrics of melodic similarity are of the "edit-distance" type (Müllensiefen & Frieler, 2004, p. 168), whereby the cost of moving from one pattern-form to another is quantified.

A well established example of this type is the metric proposed by Damerau and Levenshtein (Levenshtein, 1966; see also Orpen & Huron, 1992). This assesses the notional costs, according to some predetermined scale of values, of the operations of *insertion* (adding a new component), *deletion* (removing a component), and *substitution* (replacing one component by another that is equivalent to the original), by means of which a source text is transformed into a target, or a target is understood to be derived from a source. A related approach, the *Earth Mover's Distance* (EMD) metric, first developed in the context of image-retrieval research (Rubner et al., 2000) and then applied to music (Typke et al., 2003; Wiering et al., 2004; Typke, 2007; Typke et al., 2007),

> determines the minimum amount of work that is needed for converting one set of weighted points into another.[138] The required work grows with the amount of weight that needs to be moved to different positions, and with the distance over which the weight needs to be moved. (Typke et al., 2007, pp. 154–155)

Put more simply,

---

[138] A set of weighted points is a group of discrete entities occupying multidimensional space, such as the notes of a museme, each assigned a relative weighting.

[o]ne pattern … is represented as heaps of earth, the sizes of which correspond to the weights of the dots; the other pattern … as holes with a certain capacity, likewise corresponding to the dots' weights. The task is to fill the holes with as little effort (that is, ground distance times weight) as possible. (Wiering et al., 2004, p. 117).

The EMD is defined by the following equation (Typke et al., 2007, p. 155):

$$EMD(A, B) = \frac{min_{F \in \mathcal{F}} \sum_{i=1}^{m} \sum_{j=1}^{n} f_{ij} d_{ij}}{min(W, U)} \tag{3.3}$$

Unpacking this,

A [source] and B [copy] are sets of weighted points. $\mathcal{F}$ is the set of all possible flows that would convert A into B …. Every flow consists of one flow element for each pair of points out of the m points in A and the n points in B. Every flow element carries a weight of f_{ij} over a ground distance of d_{ij} from one point in A to one point in B. W and U are the sums of weights in set A and B, respectively. Therefore, the EMD is the sum of distances in the optimum flow, weighted with the corresponding weights, normalized with the total weight of the lighter point set. (Typke et al., 2007, p. 155)

Such approaches align well with the mappings of levels seven and eight of Table 1.4, in that differences between genes and between m(us)emes can be represented in terms of edit-distance metrics used to quantify the operations of insertion, deletion and substitution (Hoeschele & Fitch, 2022; Savage et al., 2022; see also §3.6.6). As the mechanisms of replicator mutation, these three operations act on nucleotides – in a process termed "point mutation" (Ridley, 2004, p. 28, Fig. 2.4) – serving to move a gene away from other genes, including its alleles, in a multidimensional genetic *hypervolume*. The latter are vast conceptual-potential spaces encompassing, in this case, all possible genes and all their possible alleles (Jan, 2007, pp. 197–199; see also §5.5.2, §6.5 and §7.5.3). A genetic hypervolume is the biochemical equivalent of Borges' "Library of Babel" (1970; see also note 307 on page 611). The same three operations, acting upon pitches and rhythms, create museme mutations (Jan, 2007, pp. 116–117), these serving to move a museme away from other musemes, including its alleles, in a multidimensional musemic hypervolume.

3.6.6 Cultural Cladograms

Whether using informal judgement or formal similarity/difference quantification between musemes to distinguish between homoplasies and homologies, it is useful to represent the latter graphically, for just as the long-term outcomes of biological evolution can be represented in terms of branching lineages on (by convention) a tree diagram, so can those of cultural evolution. Applying the principles of cladistic taxonomy (§1.7.2), one might arrive at a representation, a cultural cladogram, not just of the evolutionary relationships between dialects (Savage, 2019, pp. 4–6), but also of those between musemes. As noted in §3.6.4, the latter enterprise, population memetics, is closer to population genetics than it is to the taxonomy of species.

As a first word of caution, attempting to calculate cultural phylogenies – what might be termed *phylomemies* – risks falling foul of what might be termed the distinction between *real* and *virtual* phylogen/memies.[139] A real phylogen/memy is one that is objectively evolutionarily correct, indicating the transmission relationships between the replicators at various positions on the cladogram. A virtual phylogen/memy is one that arrives – perhaps as a consequence of a restricted sample-size – at a "pseudo-cladogram". This, while a logical and parsimonious representation of the patterns under investigation, is nevertheless potentially *not* evolutionarily true, and is therefore not properly cladistic, because it does not take into account patterning outside the sample under consideration that, if included, might alter the relationships represented by the cladogram. It would appear considerably easier to arrive at a real phylogeny – where groups of potentially related organisms are often relatively geographically localised, morphologically distinct and, nowadays, genetically tractable – than it is to arrive at a real phylomemy – where groups of potentially related cultural forms are often scattered across space and time.

---

[139] At the risk of terminological explosion, it is potentially useful to identify – by analogy with ontogeny – the concept of *ontomemy*, which might be defined as the accumulation and development of an individual's meme complement/profile via education and enculturation over the course of their lifetime.

Yet this enterprise is worth pursuing, if only to illustrate the possibilities of the approach, one that C. J. Howe and Windram (2011) term "phylom-emetics", the cultural equivalent of phylogenetics. As they acknowledge (2011, p. 1), this is by no means a new methodology in the humanities, where philologists in both linguistic and musical research have long attempted to reconstruct stemmata showing relationships of transmission and mutation in sources as diverse as biblical texts and Medieval music manuscripts (K. M. Cook, 2015). Conducted under (or, some might fear, annexed by) the rubric of phylomemetics, such research can incorporate all the intellectual infra-structure of Darwinism – the notions of variation, replication and selection; concepts of fitness; and ideas of lineage bifurcation – in attempting to trace connections between the phenomena under investigation.[140]

Using the phylogeny-calculation software *Phylip* (Felsenstein, 2018) – which essentially performs edit-distance calculations on symbolic representations of genetic data – six versions of the folk ballad "The two brothers" are analysed (Jan, 2018a).[141] This analysis is based on the input data shown in Figure 3.14 (Jan, 2018a, p. 11, Fig. 3a), which is a date-ordered list of the melodies consisting of a sequence of their constituent pitches, grouped into two-bar-long museme alleles ("v" represents a variant form of the melody).[142] It should be stressed that this is an illustrative calculation only, designed to outline a methodology that might be adopted and developed in larger studies. The highly restricted dataset naturally limits the scope of the conclusions – potentially limited to a virtual phylomemy – that can be drawn.

The phylomemetic tree shown in Figure 3.15 (Jan, 2018a, p. 12, Fig. 4a) is generated using the *Phylip Pars* utility, which "is a general parsimony program which carries out the Wagner parsimony method [(Eck & Dayhoff, 1966)] with multiple states. Wagner parsimony allows changes among all states. The criterion is to find the tree which requires the minimum number of changes" (Felsenstein, 2018). For ease of comparison, the text-based output

---

[140] It might be argued that phylomemies differ from phylogenies in their potential for "cross-fertilisation", whereby two lineages may share material, or even rejoin, after bifurcation. But this is also true, to a lesser extent, in nature, where gene-transfer between recently bifurcated lineages remains possible for a limited time.

[141] The text of this ballad, and those of many others originating in the British isles, were collected by (Child, 1904); the associated melodies were collated by (Bronson, 1959).

[142] This method of encoding might be further developed by incorporating rhythmic values, whereby, for instance, "bbb" = ♩. and "b" = ♪.

```
6   26
15sept1916 0ccegagg cceed ddbcddb bggabc
15sept16-v 0ccegagg cceed bbgbddd deeabc
16sept1916 cccegaag ccegd ddbbddb bggabc
18sept1916 gccegagg ccegd bbddedd dggabc
18sept16-v gccegagg ccegd ddbbddb gggabc
03sept1918 0ccccaag ccegd ddbcddb bggabc
```

Figure 3.14: Input Data for Phylomemetic Tree.

of *Pars* (strictly, that of the *Phylip* graphics-generating utility *DrawGram*) is augmented in Figure 3.15 by images of the relevant melodies, in which boxed numbers distinguish museme alleles.[143]

Such cladograms represent Darwin's "descent with modification" (2008, p. 129), whereby items located to the left (bottom/past) are hypothesised to be evolutionarily earlier than those located to the right (top/present); and where proximity to points of bifurcation (branch-length) represents relative evolutionary distance. While parsimony is a powerful constraint on evolutionary possibilities, and is a key element of *Phylip*'s analytical algorithm, it does not invariably align with evolutionary reality, particularly in the case of cultural cladograms. Thus, a parsimonious cladogram – one that proceeds from left to right by minimal branching and short mutational distances – is not necessarily "real", in terms of the distinction made above. Moreover, as suggested in §2.5.1, evolution is fundamentally a process of *adaptive change* (Ridley, 2004, p. 4) and not necessarily one where that change leads to an increase in "the logarithm of the total information content of the biosystem (genes plus memes)" (Ball, 1984, p. 154).[144] In this light, musemic simplicity does not necessarily correlate with chronological anteriority, any more than musemic complexity corresponds with chronological posteriority.

As a second word of caution to add to the first given on page 244 – one that applies more broadly to any attempt to analyse music by means of the kinds of symbolic representations used in *Phylip* – in order to perform the phylomemetic analysis, the musical sounds of these melodies, already con-

---

[143] Note that these are "rooted" phylomemies: there is assumed to be an unidentified common ancestor to the left of the tree (Ridley, 2004, p. 439).

[144] This may often be the case with oral transmission, where the principle of *lectio difficilior potior* – "the more difficult reading is the stronger" (Robinson, 2001) – might support one in ascribing chronological anteriority to a more complex form.

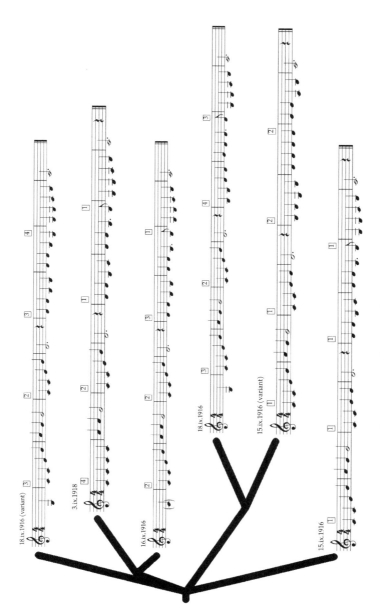

Figure 3.15: Output Phylomemetic Tree.

verted to their traditional western letter-name notation by (Bronson, 1959), was rendered as a series of ASCII characters to form the input to the *Pars* utility. In this way, the sounds of these extracts are treated as a text. This means that the analysis is operating on a representation two stages removed from a living performance: not only has a vocal rendition been regularised and shoehorned into western notation, a form of "lossy" compression; but this representation has itself been further divorced from its connection with sound by its reduction to an abstract symbol-set. Perhaps more fundamentally, while the *Phylip* software to some extent "understands" genetics, in that it is based on a formalisation of the dynamics of the biochemistry underpinning it, it has little conception of music and the dynamics of pitch and rhythm combination underpinning it. Nevertheless, the symbols offered as input bear at least some connection with their long-distant musical antecedents, and so permit a provisional phylomemetic analysis based on parsimony relationships to be conducted. This issue is considered further in §6.4.

§4.4.1 considers to what extent cladograms can be related to the prolongational trees in the Generative Theory of Tonal Music (GTTM) of Lerdahl and Jackendoff (1983) (see also §3.8.6).

3.7 Gene-Meme Coevolution

The evolution of *Homo sapiens* was driven by a number of selection pressures. Many of these, certainly initially, were *biological-environmental*: our species had to adapt to harsh and varied climates; we had to develop strategies to counteract predators, and rival hominin species; and we had to find means to communicate and cooperate as part of our communal lifestyle. These selection pressures acted upon our genes – for whom the evolution of *Homo sapiens* was ultimately in the service – causing us to become stronger, faster, more cunning and more sociable. In the process, our genes evolved to become more replicable (they coded for features that enhanced the statistical likelihood of their replication), and in some respects they shaped their wider environment in order to make it more conducive to them, for example by destroying rival species and by reshaping the world in favourable ways. But a second type of selection pressure, *cultural-environmental*, also operated upon us, certainly from the beginning of the Cognitive Revolution (§2.5.5), if not earlier in the hominin lineage. Here, the memes that populated our brains began to exert pressures on the biological systems that sustained them in order to create a better environment for themselves. In the process, our memes evolved to become more replicable (they became leaner, fitter, more memorable and more beneficial to their hosts; or they capitalised on their hosts' hopes and fears (see note 88 on page 163)), and in some respects they shaped their wider environment in order to make it more conducive to them, for example by leveraging three-dimensional space to provide opportunities for their aural and visual expression.

This short overview suggests that there are various ways in which intra- and inter-replicator-class relationships might operate. These are considered in this section, which encompasses some of the means by which musicality and music are shaped by gene-meme (as opposed to gene-gene or meme-meme) *coevolution*. Coevolution is an important topic in evolutionary theory – the key texts are Lumsden and Wilson (1981), Cavalli-Sforza and Feldman (1981), Boyd and Richerson (1985), Durham (1991), and Richerson and Boyd (2005) – even when only considering a single (genetic) replicator, not least because the evolution of complex organisms was a (intra-replicator-class) coevolutionary process. Moving from single-celled organisms to the complex multicellular structures of which we are perhaps the supreme example required collaboration between ostensibly selfish replicators. Over the course of evolutionary history, selection rewarded those replicators that joined forces to create a single, encompassing vehicle, one that served the interests of all the replicators it carried (§1.6.1). Typically, such coevolution was associated with the division of labour, such that certain replicators coded for vehicle-features that served one function, while others coded for features with a different, complementary, function.

Whether dealing with interactions between replicators of one class or of two, there are three fundamental categories into which their relationships fall: "*cooperation* or mutualism, in which both parties benefit from the inter-action (a plus/plus relationship); *competition* in which both parties lose (a minus/minus relationship); and *conflict* or antagonism, in which one party benefits and the other loses (a plus/minus relationship)" (Blute, 2006, p. 154; emphases mine). There are, moreover, two broad strategies by which

such coevolution has been formalised: population-genetics models and op-
timisation/game-theory models. "The essential difference is that population
genetics attempts to model underlying informational structures, whether
genetic or memetic, while optimization (for non-social situations) and game
theory (for social situations) model surface or observable characteristics,
including behavior, which are commonly called 'strategies'" (2006, p. 153).
It is game theory that perhaps offers the best means by which gene-meme
coevolution can be understood.

Developed in mathematics by John von Neumann – his contribution to computing is discussed in §7.3.1 – game theory is concerned with competitive
situations in which agents (replicator-driven vehicles) adopt a range of
strategies in order to maximise their share of a finite resource. The "Prisoner's Dilemma" game is a simple example of some of the ideas underpinning
Game Theory. Here, two players, A and B, can choose to "cooperate" or to
"defect" (i.e., to break an implicit trust, leading to competition or conflict, in
the terms of the first quotation from Blute (2006) above). The four outcomes
resulting from their combination are often represented in a two-by-two grid.
The outcomes (and their pay-offs in Dawkins' summary of the game) are:
(i) A: cooperate–B: cooperate (A and B both gain $300 as a "[r]eward for
mutual cooperation"); (ii) A: defect–B: defect (A and B both lose $10, as
"[p]unishment for mutual defection"); (iii) A: cooperate–B: defect (A (the
"sucker") loses $100 and B gains $500, reflecting the "[t]emptation to defect");
and (iv) A: defect–B: cooperate (in an inversion of (iii), A gains $500 and B,
now the sucker, loses $100) (Dawkins, 1989, pp. 203–204). There are many
variants of this game, some differing in the allocation of the pay-offs. More
fundamentally, some variants move away from the determinism of simpler
variants in favour of more complex-dynamic-system models (Blute, 2006,
p. 162).[145]

---

[145] A UK television game show, charmingly named *Shafted* (2001), hosted by Robert Kilroy-Silk,
was based on the Prisoner's Dilemma game (IMDb, 2019). Its brief life-span – it was cancelled
after only four episodes – was perhaps a result, among other deficits, of the nastiness of the
defections and the evident distress of those who, in seeking to cooperate, were "shafted" and
thus denied a monetary prize. Even in this manifestation, nature is revealed, in Tennyson's
phrase from *In Memoriam A. H. H.* (1849), as "red in tooth and claw" (Tennyson, 2007, 135
(Canto 56)).

Game theory was extended to evolutionary theory by John Maynard Smith (Maynard Smith, 1982), who considered the mechanics of the interactions between organisms in order to understand in what circumstances it is advantageous for them to be cooperative or to be antagonistic. Here the behaviours of cooperation and antagonism are understood as phenotypic manifestations of genes – "strategies of the kind that genes might preprogram" (Dawkins, 1989, p. 208) – so, as always in evolution, any real advantage arising from behaviours accrues to the replicator, not to the vehicle. Because cooperative and antagonistic interactions between individuals occur in the context of multiple factors, not least numerous similar interactions between other conspecifics, they – like the VRS algorithm that subsumes them – constitute a complex dynamic system, which, by nature, are intrinsically non-linear (i.e., variations in input and output are not proportional). Sometimes, such systems are constantly unstable, oscillating from one state to another. In other situations, however, they reach an equilibrium, in which one state prevails and becomes resistant to perturbation. Maynard Smith coined the notion of the *Evolutionarily Stable Strategy* (ESS) to describe such situations of equipoise in the evolution of interactive behaviour. This is

> a strategy which, if most members of a population adopt it, cannot be bettered by an alternative strategy.... the best strategy for an individual depends on what the majority of the population are doing. Since the rest of the population consists of individuals, each one trying to maximize his *own* success, the only strategy that persists will be one which, once evolved, cannot be bettered by any deviant individual.... once an ESS is achieved it will stay: selection will penalize deviation from it. (Dawkins, 1989, p. 69; emphasis in the original)

The types of dimorphism arising from sexual selection (§2.5.3) represent a category of ESS, although it is one that can be perturbed by those events subsumed by the third category of computer-simulation model of the Fisher process ("invasion analysis") on page 100.

While game theory was initially applied to model interactions between replicators of the same class (i.e., gene-gene), it has subsequently been extended to gene-meme interactions. The three categories of cooperation, competition and conflict outlined on page 249 work as follows in the case of such dual-replicator coevolution. In *cooperation*, genes and memes are "favored to match" (Blute, 2006, p. 155). That is, whatever circumstance or situation serves the interests of certain genes also serves the interests of certain memes: their interests match, or align (equivalent to Dawkins' outcome (i) of the Prisoner's Dilemma game in the list on page 250). In *competition*, genes and memes are "favored to unmatch" (2006, p. 155). That is, whatever serves the interests of certain genes does not serve the interests of certain memes, and vice versa (Dawkins' outcome (ii); "mutual defection"). In *conflict*, "one is favored to match and the other to avoid matching, two ways" (2006, p. 155). That is, there are two possible sub-scenarios, where: (i) certain memes are favoured if they match certain genes, but in this matching those genes are themselves *dis*favoured (so memes "chase" genes, which try to "run away", in an evolutionary sense); and (ii) certain genes are favoured if they match certain memes, but in this matching those memes are themselves *dis*favoured (so genes "chase" memes, which try to "run away") (Dawkins's outcomes (iii) and (iv), respectively, where his player "A" represents genes and his player "B" represents memes, and where one replicator gains and the other is the "sucker") (2006, pp. 155–156).

These scenarios are represented in Table 3.5, a Prisoner's-Dilemma-type two-by-two grid after Blute (2006, p. 155, Tab. 1; p. 156, Tab. 2), with Table 3.5a representing cooperation and competition and Table 3.5b representing conflict (and where "G" and "g", and "M" and "m" represent gene and meme alleles, respectively; and "h" and "l" indicate "high" and "low" pay-offs, respectively).[146]

An example of gene-meme coevolution has already been given in §2.3.5 and §2.5.4 – namely, the case of the invention of fire changing the types of food humans were able to eat, thereby shaping the evolution (directly) of our digestive tract and (indirectly) of our brain. To this example one might add that of dairy farming. Patel (2018, p. 116) notes that around

---

[146] Another issue inherent in dual-replicator coevolution is the seemingly greater speed of memetic *versus* genetic evolution. Blute argues that *evolution rate* (a function of fitness-enhancing variation) should not be confused with *generation time*; and that, for memes, the latter is significantly shorter in horizontal transmission than in vertical or oblique transmission (page 227) (2006, p. 160). For the latter two modes of transmission, "genetic and cultural generation times are necessarily equal, and all else being equal, rates of genetic and cultural evolution are necessarily identical" (2006, p. 160).

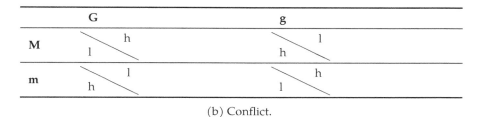

(a) Cooperation (pay-off shown to the left of the vertical line) and Competition (pay-off shown to the right of the vertical line).

	G	g
M	h / l	l / h
m	l / h	h / l

(b) Conflict.

Table 3.5: Pay-off Matrix for Gene-Meme Coevolution.

8,000–11,000 years ago humans began herding animals for milk production. Previously, humans predominantly drank milk from their mothers and, after weaning, the enzyme lactase, for the digestion of the milk protein lactose, was switched off. A genetic mutation for continued lactase production appears to have spread in human populations under the selection pressure of the cultural practice of dairying. In other words, without the memes for dairying, the genes for continued production of lactase would likely not have been replicated. In turn, the genetic support for lactose-digestion fostered the further cultural evolution of memes for dairying, leading to the evolution both of better technologies for farming and of more varied uses for milk (such as cheese, yoghurt, etc.).

3.7.1 Memetic Drive

Both of the examples of gene-meme coevolution given in the last paragraph of the previous subsection are relevant to the subject of this book, because anything that augments brain capacity (enhanced nutrition, in these cases) is likely to enhance musicality and thus provide an ever more fertile environment for musemes. This section considers an another example of brain-augmenting gene-meme coevolution, the hypothesis of *memetic drive* (or *memetic driving*), whereby encephalisation – the increase in absolute and/or relative brain size – is argued to have been fostered by the selection pressures imposed by memes (Blackmore, 1999, pp. 76–80; Blackmore, 2000a, pp. 31–33; Blackmore, 2001, pp. 243–245).[147] Specifically, memetic drive concerns the encephalising responses made by genes in response to the survival advantages conferred by memes, which result in memes acquiring ever greater autonomy from genes and eventually turning the tables on genes by driving genetically sub-optimal but memetically optimal additional encephalisation. Thus, memetic drive represents a variant of sub-scenario (i) on page 252, whereby memes "chase" genes to force them to provide an ever more conducive environment for their own replication. It is possible that memetic drive worked in conjunction with other encephalisation-driving processes, including the nutritional examples just given.

There are many factors limiting the indefinite expansion of brain size in an animal, but the two most important are the fact that the brain consumes a disproportionate amount of resources (it is *c.* 2–3% of the human body by mass but draws *c.* 25% of the resting body's energy (Harari, 2014, p. 9)); and the fact that, in humans, a large brain in the uterus makes passage down the birth canal difficult and risky for both mother and infant. The latter factor may account for the relatively long period of infant care in *Homo sapiens* compared with many other primate species: the human infant needs such protracted care, during which brain size increases, because an infant could not have been safely delivered at a more advanced stage of brain development (Dissanayake, 2008, p. 172) (§2.3.4).

Given these various constraints on brain size, it is necessary to account for encephalisation in the hominin line – not just the increase in the absolute size of the brain, but the increase in its size relative to the body as a whole (as measured by the encephalisation quotient), and its associated lateralisation in humans (§2.7.7). After all, many organisms survive perfectly well with much smaller brains, so why do humans have such large, complex and physiologically expensive brains? Blackmore argues that this may be explained in terms of memetic drive. In summary, the three-stage process she hypothesises is as follows (a concise review is given in §5.2; see also Jan

---

[147] In addition to encephalisation, it is not unreasonable to hypothesise that memetic drive also fostered increasing brain plasticity (note 81 on page 138).

(2007, pp. 242–244)). Note that, while animals can of course copy actions, the "capacity to imitate" in the account below is arguably most potent in the domain of sound, in the form of the *vocal* learning discussed by Merker (2012) (2.7.5).

Selection for Imitation: "Capacity-to-imitate" (hereafter "CtI") genes (those controlling the perceptual-cognitive and vocal-motor substrates for imitation) will tend to spread in a gene-pool because of the fitness advantages imitation confers on an individual compared with trial-and-error learning (Blackmore, 1999, p. 77). Those who are most adept at imitation – the quick learners – are termed "meme fountains" (hereafter "MF") by Blackmore (2000a, p. 32). This mechanism alone can explain an increase in brain size, because it binds encephalisation to survival advantage via Darwinian natural selection (Blackmore, 2000a, p. 32). This is because imitation is a cognitively demanding skill and therefore requires substantial brain capacity; those with the biggest brains will tend to be the best imitators and will tend, via the survival advantage imitation-transmitted knowledge confers, to have more viable offspring.[148] The mechanism for this process, an element of vocal learning (§2.7.5), is outlined in point 7 of the list on page 138, and in point 18 of the list on page 149.

Selection for Imitating the Imitators: A genetically controlled ability to identify and preferentially imitate MFs may confer a "borrowed" gene-fitness advantage on this ability-detector's possessor, leading to a differential increase of such "imitate-the-meme-fountains" (hereafter "ItMF") genes (Blackmore, 1999, pp. 77–78) – i.e., genes for knowing who is a good bet to imitate. Memetic evolution and the expansion of culture gathers pace in this phase (Blackmore, 2000a, p. 32), perhaps engendering, among other replicator-types, the protemes of musilanguage.

Selection for Mating with the Imitators: Here, advantages to genes and advantages to memes diverge. While the imitation described in the first and second points above would probably have been built on a substrate of innate primate capacities that arose initially via natural selection to fulfil a number of functions, it may subsequently have been augmented by sexual selection (Dennett, 2017, p. 266), leading to the appearance of *coevolutionary* sexual selection (§2.5.3).[149]

---

[148] Blackmore notes that this stage is "a version of the Baldwin effect [§1.8] ..., which applies to any kind of learning – once some individuals become able to learn something, those who cannot are disadvantaged and genes for the ability to learn, therefore, spread" (2001, pp. 243–244; see also Podlipniak, 2017a).

[149] Computer simulation broadly supports this hypothesis. While their model of song-evolution can be criticised for arguably not fully implementing clearly separate biological

As with all coevolutionary processes, there may come a point, as appears to have been the case here, where a replicator's interests are best served not by continued cooperation but by defection, to use the terminology of the Prisoner's Dilemma game.[150]

- From the point of view of genes: (i) it is advantageous for a female to mate with a male MF because of the fitness advantages (accruing from a high capacity to imitate memes) conferred on her offspring (and grandoffspring) by the CtI genes (Blackmore, 1999, pp. 78–79) (as predicted by the "sexy sons" hypothesis (page 101)). As an instance of sexual selection, this preferential mating process will tend to lead not only to a differential increase of CtI genes (the ornament), but also of "mate-with-the-meme-fountains" (hereafter "MwtMF") genes (the preference). Moreover, (ii) there will be an *enhanced* advantage for any alleles of the CtI genes that privilege replication of the most currently "favoured" memes (Blackmore, 1999, p. 80) – assuming such memes are initially gene-replication-enhancing – and, thus, an associated advantage for females to mate with those males with these specific alleles.

- From the point of view of memes, this initially gene-beneficial privileging of the most "favoured" memes will initiate a process whereby: (i) memetic evolution is further expedited, in the form of ever more diverse and extreme ornaments; (ii) the ornament-memome may give rise to an ornament-phemotype that is detrimental to the replication of genes (such as reckless behaviours); and (iii) such gene-detrimental ornaments will tend to evolve much more rapidly than genes can evolve to control them, meaning that memes, capitalising on genetically mediated preferences, are able to "outwit" genes (Blackmore, 1999, p. 78). In this sense, memetic

---

and cultural replicators, and (as they acknowledge) for not incorporating culturally acquired song-preferences, Werner and Todd (1997, p. 441) determined that "[w]ithout sexual selection, ... simulation models have evolved little diversity in communication signals [i.e., songs; the ornament]. When instead we replace natural selection with sexual selection, signal diversity within and across generations blossoms. Our simulations here lend strong support for the role of co-evolving songs and directional (surprise-based) preferences in maintaining diversity over time ...".

[150] In Blackmore (1999), this third stage of "selection for mating with the imitators" (1999, p. 78) is followed by a fourth stage of "sexual selection for imitation" (1999, p. 79), these two stages being conflated in Blackmore (2000a, pp. 32–33). The two phenomena are broadly equivalent, however, in that "selection for mating with the imitators" becomes "sexual selection for imitation" when one sex becomes established as the imitators (the bearer of the ornament) and the other sex becomes established as desirous of mating with them (the bearer of the preference).

evolution has escaped the genes' "leash" (Table 3.2) and is harnessing increased encephalisation to its own ends (Blackmore, 1999, p. 80).[151]

The advantage of Blackmore's memetic drive hypothesis, specifically its third stage, is that it instantiates the type of Fisher-process linkage disequilibrium underpinning sexual selection, albeit across two replicators rather than in terms of the single-replicator perspective underpinning classical sexual selection. While the alignment of memetic drive's proposed mechanism with a biological-evolutionary process that has been extensively modelled mathematically and computationally – using the approaches outlined on page 100 – does not in itself prove the existence of memetic drive, it is certainly suggestive that the process is credible. Indeed, to my knowledge, three studies broadly support the hypothesis, in different ways. First, a mathematical model of memetics confirms that ItMF genes can indeed spread within a population (Kendal & Laland, 2000, sec. 3). Second, adapting for a dual-replicator perspective the NKCS model of coevolving species (Kauffman, 1993), Bull et al. (2000) assert that

> for most degrees of dependence between the two replicators, regardless of the dependence within the populations, a phase transition-like dynamic occurs as the relative rate of replication is varied. Within our model, until the rate of meme evolution is $\frac{1}{30}$ that of genes, genes remain unaffected by their presence. From then on, until the memes evolve 10 times faster than the genes, the genes experience increasingly negative effects from the presence of the memes, *and thereafter are unable to evolve effectively* [i.e., auto-beneficially]. Conversely, the memes do not experience any benefit from increasing their rate of evolution until it is around $\frac{1}{10}$ that of the genes. From then on, until they evolve 30 times faster than the genes, they experience increasing benefit from increasing their rate of evolution. Thereafter they suffer no beneficial or detrimental effects from any increase. (Bull et al., 2000, p. 234; emphasis in the original)

Third, Blackmore argues that a study on mirror neurons by Iacoboni (2005) supports three memetic-drive-related hypotheses. Mirror neurons have been

---

[151] Note that this is not a zero-sum game: increased encephalisation can benefit both genes and memes, although the benefits to the former need to balance the advantages – greater cognitive flexibility, including "Gregorian" (Table 3.1) situational modelling – with the disadvantages – increased danger during birth, higher nutritional demands – of greater brain size. Memetic drive hypothesises that there is a *differential* benefit to encephalisation, in favour of memes.

reported in certain primates, including humans, and in song-birds. They are "multimodal association neurons that increase their activity during the execution of certain actions and while hearing or seeing corresponding actions being performed by others" (Keysers, 2009, p. 971), and have therefore been proposed as implicated in gestural and vocal imitation, social and emotional affiliation, and the capacities described by the Theory of Mind – that is, the ability to understand the motivations of others on the assumption that their mental processes are not dissimilar to our own (Fitch, 2010, p. 452; Harvey, 2017, pp. 56–58). The three hypotheses are as follows:

> [(i)] if brain size has been meme-driven, then within groups of similar species brain size should correlate with the ability to imitate.... More specifically, I predicted that [(ii)] brain scans of people either initiating or imitating actions should reveal that 'imitation is the harder part – and also that the evolutionarily newer parts of the brain should be especially implicated in carrying it out' [(Blackmore, 2000b, p. 73)]. This implies that the parts of the brain that differ most between chimpanzees and humans should be those involved in imitation (assuming that present-day chimpanzees are closer to our common ancestor than humans are).[152] Finally [(iii)], if memetic drive is responsible for the evolution of language, then we should expect the language areas in the human brain to be derived from areas originally used for imitation. This is what Iacoboni [(2005)] and his colleagues have demonstrated, thus confirming these predictions. (Blackmore, 2005b, p. 204)

Memetic drive is considered further in §5.4.1.3, in connection with learned bird-song.

3.8 The (Co)evolution of Music and Language II: Semantics, Syntax and Thought

Having outlined in §2.7 how musilanguage might have become articulated into discrete segments, and how any segments that became freighted with

---

[152] That humans and chimpanzees have followed *c.* six million years of separate evolution (Schaefer et al. (2021, pp. 7, 13) suggest a figure as high as *c.* 13 million years) might be regarded as making it impossible to triangulate the attributes of these three points – LCA, chimpanzee, human – in evolutionary time and space. Yet the clearly superior imitative abilities of humans in comparison with chimpanzees suggests Blackmore's point is valid.

meaning might have gone on to constitute the foundations of language, I now consider certain issues in the philosophy of language that have a bearing upon later stages of this hypothesised process. Because one selection pressure driving the bifurcation of musilanguage was the need to communicate thoughts and desires with ever greater precision, it follows that language is associated in some way with the thoughts it evolved to help communicate. Moreover, because much of human thought is conscious (a lot is not, shading into our automatic behaviours and reactions that, in a broad definition, are categories of thought), language is deeply implicated in the problem of consciousness (§7.2.1). I attempt to deal here, and in §7.4, with the thorny question of the relationship between language, thought and consciousness, insofar as they apply to the evolution of musicality and music. I take certain ideas of Peter Carruthers and integrate them with precepts from memetics and neuroscience. Building a synthesis between the two main dimensions of music and language – external sound structures and internal brain implementation of musemes and lexemes – allows one to explore deep structural and functional similarities between the syntactic and semantic dimensions of language and music.

3.8.1 Language and Cognition

Considerable debate surrounds the issue of how language and thought relate to each other (Dennett, 2017, Ch. 9). Is language the mechanism for thought, the medium through which it is (exclusively) conducted, the so-called "cognitive conception" of language; is it simply a vehicle for, or translation of, thoughts conducted more fundamentally, in some kind of brain-language or "mentalese", the so-called "communicative conception" of language; or does it occupy some intermediate position between these extremes (Carruthers, 2002, p. 657)? The cognitive conception of language, hereafter "cognitivism", is associated with the "relativism and radical empiricism" of Whorf's (Whorf, 1956) view of language – "the Standard Social Science Model", in Pinker's somewhat dismissive opinion (Carruthers, 2002, pp. 661, 664). By contrast, the communicative conception of language, hereafter "communicativism", is generally more strongly advocated by cognitive scientists and evolutionary psychologists.

In part, the distinction devolves to one of nurture (cognitivism) *versus* nature (communicativism). For cognitivists, such as Dennett (Dennett, 1995), the mind exists because the *tabula rasa* of the new-born child is shaped (bottom-up, inductively, *a posteriori*) by the nurtural power of language (indeed, in Dennett's view, by the power of memes themselves). For communicativists, such as Pinker (1997), much of the mind is naturally and innately pre-formed (top-down, deductively, *a priori*) at birth by natural selection, so memes, if they are implicated at all in cognition, do not do the heavy lifting; rather, they act merely as epiphenomena of more fundamental processes. Seen in these terms, cognitivism intersects partly with "constructionist" approaches to language, which assert that "[g]rammar does not involve any [innate] transformational or derivational component"; rather, "learned [memetic] pairings of form [lexemic sound-pattern] and function [meaning/concept]" constitute structures "in a network in which nodes are related by inheritance links" and in which "[s]emantics is associated directly with surface form" (Goldberg, 2013, p. 15; see also Goldberg, 2003; Boas & Sag, 2012; Gjerdingen & Bourne, 2015).

There is currently no consensus on this particular nature-nurture question, despite the two positions not being mutually exclusive; and responses to the issues involved tend, as suggested, to be split along disciplinary lines. A fuller understanding certainly requires an interdisciplinary integration of neuroscience, psychology and philosophy. The argument advanced in Carruthers (2002) (see also the peer commentaries, 2002, pp. 674–705, and Carruthers' response 2002, pp. 705–718) is perhaps one of the most convincing attempts to unpick the issues involved, and his preferred analysis of where on the cognitivism-communicativism continuum the most robust explanation for language and/as thought lies will be taken as the basis for much of what follows, not least because of its ready accordance with the memetic interpretation advanced in this book. Essentially, Carruthers, a moderate cognitivist, attempts to chart a *via media* between cognitivist claims of different strengths, ranging from weak (language is necessary for at least some kinds of thought) to strong (language is essential for all types of thought) and, by doing so, implicitly illuminates the communicativist inversion of this continuum.

3.8.2 Modularity, Language and Thought

Carruthers starts from the position that while *"some* thoughts are carried by sentences (namely, non-domain-specific thoughts which are carried by sentences of natural language), others [i.e., domain-specific thoughts] might be carried [non-linguistically] by mental models or mental images of various kinds" (Carruthers, 2002, p. 658; emphasis in the original). His hypothesis is that

> non-domain-specific [conscious and unconscious] thinking operates by accessing and manipulating the representations of the language faculty. More specifically, the claim is that non-domain-specific [conscious and unconscious] thoughts implicate representations in what Chomsky ... calls 'logical form' (LF). Where these representations are *only* in LF, the thoughts in question will be non-conscious ones. But where the LF representation is used to generate a full-blown phonological represent-ation (an imagined sentence), the thought will generally be conscious. (Carruthers, 2002, p. 658; emphasis in the original; see also p. 666)

To accept this, one has to endorse a modular view of mental structure similar to (but not necessarily in complete accordance with) the views expressed in, for example, (Fodor, 1983). In Carruthers' account, "besides a variety of input and output modules (including, e.g., early vision, face-recognition, and language), the mind also contains a number of innately channeled conceptual modules, designed to process conceptual information concerning particular domains" (2002, p. 663). These modules, for which strong selection pressures existed in early hominins, "include a naïve physics system ... a naïve psychology or 'mind-reading' system ... a folk-biology system ... an intuitive number system ... a geometrical system for reorienting and navigating in unusual environments ... and a system for processing and keeping track of social contracts" (2002, p. 663).

By LF is understood here the unconscious mentalese structures underpinning and motivating the various connections possible between the components of natural language, in particular the relationships between verbs and the other sentence-elements required to combine with verbs in order to make a sentence grammatical (the mechanism for which is considered in §3.8.4), which some grammarians discuss under the rubric of "valency" (Durrell et al., 2015, Ch.

8). As Carruthers argues, a LF, that is, "a non-conscious tokening of a natural language sentence would be ... a representation stripped of all imagistic-phonological features, but still consisting of natural language lexical items and syntactic structures" (2002, p. 666). Such "imagistic-phonological" features would appear to equate to the lexemes associated with a given LF. As discussed in §2.7.6, a lexeme is the imagined (internally heard) or spoken (physically produced) sound pattern of a word. While not framed by him in evolutionary terms, this category of replicator is broadly analogous to Saussure's notion of the "sound image"(§3.8.5).

While domain-specific thought operates independently of language (using mental models or images), non-domain-specific (i.e., domain-general) thought, in being *tokened* by language (Carruthers, 2002, p. 660), draws upon language's syntactic structure – mediated by the underlying Chomskyan LF – to *constitute* it, not merely to *express* it (Carruthers, 2002, p. 664). Essentially, LF impels the generative-transformational aspect of language (Chomsky, 1965; Lerdahl & Jackendoff, 1983), whereby a finite set of recursive and hierarchical syntactic structures can underpin an infinity of content-specific utterances (§3.5.2). In particular, Carruthers suggests that "distinct domain-specific sentences might be combined into a single domain-general one" by means of "multiple embedding of adjectives and phrases" (2002, p. 669), giving as an example "THE TOY IS IN THE CORNER WITH A LONG WALL ON THE LEFT AND A SHORT WALL ON THE RIGHT", produced initially in mentalese as a mental model or image by the geometrical module; and "THE TOY IS BY THE BLUE WALL", similarly produced by the "object property" module dealing, among other things, with colour.[153] These become integrated (unconsciously) by LF as the basis for the non-domain-specific/domain-general, and potentially lexemically (consciously) manifested, *"The toy is in the corner with a long wall on the left and a short blue wall on the right"* (Carruthers, 2002, p. 669).[154]

Figure 3.16 (a visualisation and extension of certain aspects of Carruthers (2002), after Jan (2016b, p. 478, Fig. 1)) hypothesises how the various

---

[153] I adopt here Carruthers' convention of using SMALL CAPITALS for concepts in mentalese and using *italics* for internalised and vocalised language utterances.

[154] The integration of domain-specific representations by domain-general LF is essentially the process of representational redescription discussed in the quotation on page 6.

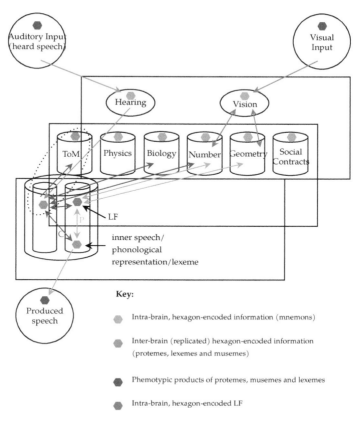

Figure 3.16: Modularity, Language and Thought.

language-related input and output systems, and their associated modules, might be organised and how they might interact.

The domain-specific modules – such as (naïve) physics, (folk) biology and (naïve) psychology, the latter termed here "ToM" (Theory of Mind) – are shown in the intermediate (middleground) layer.[155] While these and other modules are represented here as discrete "silos", they are presumably highly interconnected in neurobiological reality. Moreover, while conceived in terms of input-output connections, modules also store information and so involve memory, of varying degrees of volatility. This memory is hypothesised to

---

[155] Structures located at the background, middleground and foreground layers are somatic; those elsewhere are extrasomatic. This hierarchic representation (after Schenker, 1979) is for expository clarity and is not intended to represent the topography of these functions in the brain, insofar as this is known (§2.7.7).

be encoded in the brain in accordance with the precepts of the Hexagonal Cloning Theory, discussed in §3.8.3.

The domain-specific modules receive perceptual-sensory input processed by the hearing and vision centres (and also the centres responsible for taste, touch and smell), shown in the background layer; and they can also "back-project" to these sensory inputs, as in situations where aural and visual imagination is used to recreate or generate sounds and images (Carruthers, 2002, pp. 658, 666, 670). For clarity, not all linkages from sensory input to the domain-specific modules are shown in Figure 3.16. The language module, shown in the foreground layer, consists of comprehension and production sub-modules/sub-systems and it receives inputs from, and sends outputs to, the domain-specific modules. As Carruthers argues,

> [The] production sub-system must be capable of receiving outputs from the [domain-specific] conceptual modules in order to transform their creations into speech. And its comprehension sub-system must be capable of transforming heard speech into a format suitable for processing by those same [domain-specific] conceptual modules. Now when LF representations built by the production sub-system are used to generate a phonological representation, in 'inner speech', that representation will be consumed by the comprehension sub-system, and made available to central [domain-specific] systems. One of these systems is a theory of mind module.… perceptual and imagistic states get to be phenomenally conscious by virtue of their availability to the higher-order thoughts generated by the theory of mind system …. this is why inner speech of this sort is conscious: It is because it is available to higher-order [ToM] thought.[156] (Carruthers, 2002, p. 666)

In Figure 3.16, the production sub-system ("P", and the associated blue arrows) is shown receiving outputs of the Number and Geometry modules after the receipt of some visual stimulus (purple arrows).[157] These mentalese

---

[156] This relates directly to Levitin's assertion, in the quotation on page 159, that "[d]uring 20 million years of evolution, it is not too difficult to imagine a new function evolving … where [a number of] regions [controlling music and language] meet, gradually enabling the brain to report what it is holding in consciousness – to start talking or singing about what it is thinking about" (2009, p. 292).

[157] For the sake of expository clarity, the discussion suggests an element of unidirectionality; but in reality (and as implied by the double-headed arrows) it seems more likely that continuous bi-directional feedback loops connect structures at all three levels.

inputs are synthesised into a LF that potentially serves as the foundation and cue for a lexeme – in this case, perhaps one articulating some notion of the quantity of a certain environmental shape or regularity. Whether verbalised or not (the former indicated by the arrow to "produced speech"), the production sub-system may generate a phonological representation in "inner speech" (the lexeme sounding internally, perhaps by recruiting auditory-system neurons). Over time, and as a result of enculturation, the establishment of evolutionarily stable associations (coadaptations) between certain LFs and certain lexemes – in a kind of "lock-and-key" process – constitute language acquisition, both ontogenetically and phylogenetically. This phonological representation is "consumed" by the comprehension sub-system ("C", and the associated green arrows). Its availability to higher-order thought via the ToM module (indicated by the arrow from the comprehension sub-system to the ToM module) renders it conscious, even though (as Carruthers' remarks might be taken to imply) consciousness (and therefore language) is not necessary for comprehension.[158] This "zone of consciousness" is approximated by the dotted ellipse in Figure 3.16. In language reception, perceived speech (red arrows, initially from "Auditory Input (Heard Speech)") is directed towards the comprehension sub-system via the hearing centre and cognised by means of "deconstruction" of its inferred LF into the aforementioned "mental models or mental images of various kinds" (Carruthers, 2002, p. 658) and by reference to the relevant domain-specific modules necessary to understand it. In the case of Figure 3.16, these are Biology and Number – appropriate, for example, for a sentence articulating some notion of the quantity of a particular animal or fruit.

Having explained how underlying LF mentalese may be associated with an "imagistic-phonological" lexeme, I argue in §3.8.6 for a musical equivalent to this process: an association between LF mentalese and similarly"phonological" – but perhaps less overtly "imagistic" – musemes.

3.8.3 The Hexagonal Cloning Theory (HCT)

Is there a known mechanism of neural information encoding that might be consonant with Carruthers' hypothesis of language outlined in §3.8.2

---

[158] Blackmore also argues that consciousness presupposes a theory of mind and the associated capacity to ask "[a]m I conscious now?" (2005a, loc. 582; 2009, p. 41).

and also accommodate lexemes and musemes? One candidate is a family of related theories that stem primarily from Donald Hebb's work in the 1940s on the columnar organisation of neurons and the formation of representations via neuronal interconnections, the latter process sometimes called Hebbian Learning (see also §6.5.1.2). Hebb (1949) argued, and subsequent work has confirmed, that certain cells, the pyramidal neurons, are arranged within the cerebral cortex in discrete columns, each of which is implicated in the encoding and representation of an element of perception or cognition. Rather than being distributed randomly, these columns are, in certain brain regions, broadly equidistant, giving a cortical polka-dot pattern when viewed from above (Calvin, 1998, p. 29). Subsequent research confirmed this hypothesis (Mountcastle, 1978), determining that columns of pyramidal neurons tend to form interconnected, co-resonating arrays – "cell assemblies" (Calvin, 1998, p. 13) – in the geometrically optimal form of the triangle (Leng et al., 1990; Leng & Shaw, 1991).[159]

An extension of triangular-array models, Calvin's Hexagonal Cloning Theory (HCT) (1998; see also Jan, 2011a) asserts that coordinated pyramidal-neuron "minicolumns" (1998, p. 29) forming triangular arrays "interdigitate", allowing several attributes of a percept or concept to be represented, via association of each attribute with a specific array. Again the result of geometrical parsimony, coordinated triangular arrays are themselves optimally encompassed by (virtual) hexagonal zones of cortex, these encompassing some array-implicated and some "silent" minicolumns (1998, pp. 43–45, 62). While they are synchronic structures of relatively stable neuronal connectivity, cortical hexagons also have a diachronic dimension, in that they encode a "spatiotemporal firing pattern" (SFP) (1998, p. 47) – a characteristic sequence of array-activation. Borrowing a concept from chaos theory, Calvin argues that the minicolumns forming the vertices of the triangular arrays constituting a hexagon create "basins of attraction" in cortex, these representing sensitisation (learning) resulting from perceptual input (1998, p. 68). Encoded patterns are reactivated as the phenomenon of recognition if the same input is subsequently encountered, and they may be internally or externally triggered as recollection and memory, the latter albeit of varying degrees

---

[159] It should be stressed, however, that columns are not uniformly constructed across all brain regions, and that their architecture and connectivity differ substantially from region to region (Alan Harvey, personal communication; see also Tischbirek et al. (2019)).

of coherence and durability over time (Bonnici & Maguire, 2018; Gonzales et al., 2019). Multiple basins of attraction can be overlaid upon the same region of cortex, likened by Calvin to the layers of fish in sashimi; the deeper the layer, the more strongly encoded the pattern (1998, p. 107).

The cortical hexagons of the HCT afford a mechanism by which complex perceptual and cognitive information can be implemented and integrated at the neural level. The notion of integration is important here, because this architecture is particularly characteristic of "association cortex" – those regions of the brain where input from different sensory and motor areas is brought together and reconciled (Calvin, 1998, p. 42). This integration includes the parameters of musical pitch and rhythm, and presumably other attributes of music; indeed, Calvin often illustrates his theory using various musical concepts, seeing individual triangular arrays as "notes", hexagons as melody-playing "ensembles", and areas of co-resonating cortex as a "chorus" (1998, p. 39). Calvin's exposition makes it clear, however, that such alignments go well beyond metaphor: the synchronic and diachronic aspects of music are, in reality, implemented this way. Thus, a hexagon is the minimal cell-assembly – the "cerebral code" (Calvin, 1998) – for representing the neural encoding (the memome) of a museme.

For such encoded information to constitute a museme it must be: (i) perceptually-cognitively salient; and (ii) replicated. The first condition is readily satisfied, because incoming perceptual information is often pre-segmented into discrete units by gestalt processes operating at "lower" levels of the perceptual input system (represented by the background level of Figure 3.16). Thus music-auditory data encoded by cortical hexagons generally constitutes (but is not necessarily limited to) patterns that are at least potentially musemes (Jan, 2011a, sec. 4.1.1). The second condition is satisfied when the original brain-encoded hexagonal pattern is reconstituted in a second brain, via another individual's engagement with those phemotypic products to which the original memome gives rise (Table 1.3).

Alignment between input stimuli and extant basins of attraction leads to the activation and replication – "cloning" (Calvin, 1998, p. 40) – of a hexagon's pattern, forming territories of interlocking plaques – "mosaics of the mind" –

on the surface of the cortex. For this to occur, at least two abutting hexagons, representing the "minimal cell-assembly", are required (1998, p. 47). As the mechanism for recognition or remembering, cloning underpins another significant element of Calvin's theory, that of competition between rival hexagons – each form representing a candidate for the optimal encoding of a multi-component percept or thought – for the conquest of cortical terrain. Indeed, the HCT regards the architecture of the brain as enabling the operation of a Darwin machine in its connectivity (1998, pp. 33–34) (§1.5.4; see also the quotation from Calvin (1987b) on page 577). This neural Darwinism supports the VRS algorithm by means of: (i) the "variations on the cloned pattern" potentially arising from the failure of "error-correction" mechanisms (perhaps caused by "dead-key" missing notes, by hybridisation of two patterns that encounter each other in cortical "no-man's-land", or by hexagons attempting to pass through corrupting "barriers" in cortex) (1998, pp. 58–59, 88); (ii) the replication of successful hexagons across cortex; and (iii) their selection according to the criterion of fit between encoded/remembered information and incoming stimuli (see also McNamara, 2011; Fernando et al., 2012).

While the argument of this book is not contingent upon there being a specific topography of neuronal structures – it requires only that discrete phenomena in the world are encoded discretely in the brain – subsequent work on spatial location encoding in the entorhinal cortex has supported Calvin's model (Fuhs & Touretzky, 2006; Shrager et al., 2008; Burak & Fiete, 2009; Doeller et al., 2010; Mhatre et al., 2012; Killian et al., 2012; Stensola et al., 2012). Indeed, this research, together with accounts of the tonotopic organisation of the auditory cortex (Zatorre, 2003, p. 233), and of the phototopic/retinotopic organisation of the visual cortex (Braitenberg & Braitenberg, 1979; Reichl et al., 2012a; Reichl et al., 2012b), not only suggests deep similarities between brain representations of a variety of sensory inputs, but also indicates that, for all the astonishing complexity of neuronal interconnections, *a triangular-hexagonal disposition of cortical minicolumns activated in a SFP is a recurrent structural-topographical configuration.* Thus, while some twenty-five years old, a considerable time period when seen in the light of the rapid progress of neuroscience, more recent work has nevertheless supported the claims of the

HCT and evidenced its applicability to a number of areas of brain function of relevance to music and musicality.

Recalling Marin and Perry's (1999) assertion cited in §2.7.7 that language and music are "hemispheric specialisations" of a previously bi-lateral organisation of musilinguistic vocalisation (page 158); and understanding this differentiation in the light of the HCT, it might be hypothesised that, over the course of hominin evolution, right-hemisphere hexagonal plaques representing increasingly discrete (FOXP2-segmented?) sonic units (protemes) were yoked (by means of connections to be discussed in §3.8.4) to left-hemisphere hexagonal plaques regulating their syntactic interrelationship and semantic content – these perhaps even implementing a proto-LF – thereby engendering the lexemes of compositional language.

3.8.4 Implementation of Linguistic Syntax in the Light of the HCT

Carruthers' suggestion that "distinct domain-specific sentences might be combined into a single domain-general one" by means of "multiple embedding of adjectives and phrases" (2002, p. 669) (§3.8.2) – a means for the implementation of his central hypothesis – has a ready mechanism in the HCT. Calvin suggests that hexagons encoding certain kinds of mental data in one part of cortex are connected to others encoding different kinds of data in other regions. Moreover, and invoking an idea of Damasio's (1989), he argues that "there are specialized places in the cortex, called 'convergence zones for associative memories' [or 'association cortex'], where [representations in] different modalities come together" (Calvin, 1998, pp. 129–130; from Calvin, 1996, p. 117). Calvin speaks of "hashing" or indexing – abstracting the attributes of a "distributed [domain-specific] 'data base'" in order to create a "centrally located [domain-general] representation" (CLR) – the mechanism for which appears to be hash/index-hexagonal overlapping/interdigitation in association cortex (1998, pp. 17, 135, 207).

The connections between domain-specific hexagonal codes (a sub-committee, to adapt one of Calvin's metaphors (1998, p. 45)) and the fully "associated" domain-general LF code (a master committee) are achieved by certain types of "corticocortical projections" that go beyond the localised connectivity

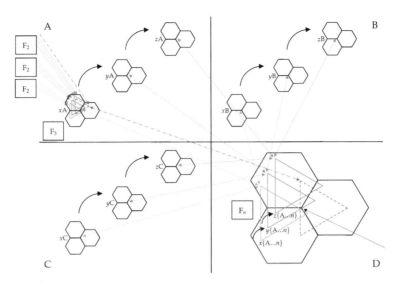

Figure 3.17: Calvinian Implementation of Structural-Hierarchic Abstraction/ Integration.

responsible for supporting triangular/hexagonal arrays and that involve links that "can go long distances, as from one hemisphere to another ..., though most only make a U-shaped passage through the white matter of one gyrus and then terminate in a nonadjacent patch of cortex that's only a few centimeters away" (1998, p. 131). Because such links are able to reconstitute the hexagonal plating of one area of cortex in another, Calvin terms them a *"faux* fax" and, writing in the mid-1990s, likens them to hyperlinks in the then nascent internet (1998, pp. 125, 131).

Figure 3.17 (Jan, 2011a, sec. 4.3.2, Fig. 13; see also Jan, 2016c, p. 459, Fig. 4) shows how the process might function in general terms. Note that the entities in the North-West, North-East and South-West quadrants might represent variously musemes, lexemes, or domain-specific thought; and that the structure in the South-East quadrant (the CLR) is a higher-level museme, musemeplex or a musemesatz (§3.5.2), or a domain-general LF.[160]

The following is an overview of how certain key aspects of language syntax are implemented by the HCT, *faux*-fax linkages, and abstraction to a CLR:

---

[160] The symbols "F_1"–"F_4" are relevant to a discussion in §6.5.1.2.

1. The adjectival modification of a noun may be accounted for by "simple border-line superposition of hexagons" (Calvin, 1998, p. 193). Beyond a certain point (several adjectives and, perhaps, prepositions), however, superposition runs the risk of creating an unspecific – Bickertonian lexical protolinguistic (1998, p. 193) – mix of words, the solution to the potential chaos of which is recursive hierarchical embedding (see point 4 below).

2. The binding of a pronoun to its referent may be accomplished by a *faux*-fax link that connects the representations of these two words, even if they are in different sentences (1998, p. 194).

3. The long-range dependencies of wh- questions are similarly implemented (1998, p. 194). The assumption for both point 2 and point 3 is that the *faux*-fax linkages are bidirectional. Using the metaphor of a choir, Calvin argues that "[b]ack projections ... can use the same code, and so immediately contribute to maintaining a chorus above a critical size .... A backprojected spatiotemporal pattern might not need to be fully featured, nor fully synchronized, to help out with the peripheral site's chorus" (1998, p. 194).

4. Recursive embedding – which is "at the very top of [linguists'] Universal Grammar wish list" (1998, p. 194) – is implemented by *faux*-fax links that allow higher-level concepts to connect representations of subsidiary parts of a sentence intelligibly.[161] According to Calvin, "if either subchorus [a discrete clause] falters, the top-level one [the integrity and sense of the sentence as a whole] stumbles" (1998, p. 194). Calvin gives the example of the sentence "I think I saw him leave to go home" (computationally/hierarchically, X://I think/ I saw him/leave/to go/home), wherein the Darwinian success of the hexagonal colonies representing the top-level *think* verb is dependent upon the survival of the *saw* and *leave* verb colonies connected to it via *faux*-fax links. In a process of "stratified stability", "[i]f the *leave* link stumbles, the *saw* hexagons might not compete very effectively and so the top level [*think*] dangles" (1998, p. 195). For this system to work, "[e]ach verb has a characteristic set of links: some required, some optional, some prohibited" (1998, p. 195) – termed valency in §3.8.2.

Such connections and their associated hierarchic relationships appear to be key to the nature of LF. Moreover, the various references to specific parts of

---

[161] These connections are encompassed by the issue of *perceptual binding*, which concerns the integration of information in different sensory modalities and brain regions into coherent representations (L. C. Robertson, 2005).

speech here arguably apply primarily to their LF representations, as functional encodings, and only secondarily to the associated (tokening) lexemes.

To summarise, the HCT (and with it *faux*-fax linkage and the Darwinian competition between cortical hexagons) is a candidate mechanism for Carruthers' central hypothesis of language as the medium for domain-general thought (§3.8.2). This is because it affords a means by which hexagons encoding domain-specific representations of "mental models or mental images" in various regions of the brain can be interconnected to (left-hemisphere-situated?) domain-general/LF conglomerations. These LF structures can then be similarly associated with those (right-hemisphere-situated?) hexagons encoding the coadapted lexemes that render the LF conscious.

3.8.5 Semantic Homologies between Language and Music

One might extend and support the discussion in §3.8.4 by considering how musemes might also bear semantic content by virtue of mechanisms analogous to those linking linguistic LF structures – which integrate domain-specific meanings to form a domain-general representation – to lexemes. Of course, many would argue that music has a semantic as well as an affective dimension (see, for example, Nattiez, 1990; Scruton, 1997; L. Kramer, 2002). What I am hypothesising here is that the mechanism by which this operates is parallel with that operating in language. In this sense, music is understood as acting as a kind of degraded language, retaining some of the semantic capacity of musilanguage by virtue of its ability, like the sound patterns of its antecedent, to become associated (sometimes arbitrarily, sometimes not) with extra-musical concepts, but lacking the kind of rich, semantically implicative syntax of language (point 13 of the list on page 147). Clearly music has its own highly sophisticated syntax, but this is, to recall Agawu's distinction from §2.7.3, generally more introversive than extroversive (1991, p. 23); so whereas the inversion of words in a sentence might have global syntactic and semantic effects, a comparable inversion in music might only perturb the local syntax (see also Patel, 2008, p. 259). I consider this issue further in §3.8.6, arguing, nevertheless, that the LF structures that lexemes token might have an analogue/parallel in music, their neural substrates perhaps being partially interconnected.

To help focus the discussion, I concentrate here primarily on the topics of late-eighteenth century music (Agawu, 1991; Ratner, 1991; Allanbrook, 1992; Caplin, 2005; Monelle, 2006; Mirka, 2014), which, in Meyer's terms, are broadly understood and widely held "connotations" afforded by musical patterns (1956, p. 258). Topics are abstracted and sustained by educated listeners from the historically contingent, indexical connections between certain musical patterns and specific extra-musical ideas. The former include dance-associated rhythmic sequences ("types"), together with more intangible associations of pitch and texture ("styles") (Ratner, 1980, p. 9); the latter include generic notions of social hierarchy and specific concepts and images. The mechanisms that afford semantic content to topics seem applicable in principle to more private associations, such as those individual composers and listeners might form between particular passages and pieces of music and certain extra-musical ideas, and so they may be generalisable beyond the frame of reference considered here.

One means of mediating between music and language in this respect is through classical semiology, specifically its association of a *signifier* with a *signified*. As Saussure argued in his celebrated definition,

> [t]he linguistic sign unites not a thing and a name, but a concept [the signified] and a sound-image [the signifier]. The latter is not the material sound – a purely physical thing – but the psychological imprint of the sound, the impression that it makes on our senses: the sound-image is sensory, and if I happen to call it 'material', it is only in that sense, and by way of opposing it to the other term of the association, the *concept*, which is generally more abstract. (in Nattiez, 1990, p. 3; emphasis in the original)

Mapping this onto the two conceptions of language and thought of §3.8.1 – communicativism and cognitivism – the following (mutually exclusive) assertions might be made:

1. In the communicativist view, which aligns elegantly with Saussure's definition, the "concept" is a domain-general, LF-implemented (unconscious) thought, whereas the "sound image" is one or more internally-heard (conscious) lexemes (and, it is argued, musemes).

2. In a cognitivist interpretation, which arguably aligns less well with Saussure's definition, the "concept" (broadly speaking the "function", in constructionist terms) would be regarded as existing purely (and simultaneously) in the shape of one or more (presumably) unconsciously active and consciously internalised lexemes (the constructionist "form"), and not as a LF.

Figure 3.18[162] generalises the topical association between a museme *m* and a lexeme *l* (or a "lexemeplex" or complex of lexemes). By this, I mean that *m* is functioning in a broadly equivalent manner to *l*, in that both are internal/ external sound-sequences that have the capacity to token LF-underpinned semantic associations. How one conceives the detailed operation of this process is nevertheless dependent upon whether one adopts a cognitivist or a communicativist standpoint; as noted earlier, the latter perspective is adopted here. Note the following:

1. From a cognitivist viewpoint, because most or all thought is understood to be conducted by means of the manipulation of language, any semantic content that might be possessed by *m* is wholly parasitic upon language, as the more fundamental medium.

2. From a communicativist viewpoint, *m*'s semantic content may:

   (a) draw *indirectly* – i.e., via or mediated by language – upon the *semantic* elements of LF mentalese; but it may also

   (b) draw *directly* – i.e., unmediated by language – upon the *semantic* elements of LF mentalese

As will be argued in §3.8.6, music might also draw directly upon the *syntactic* element of LF mentalese for its sequential structuring, in a manner that parallels language's recursive-hierarchical organisation by LF mentalese.

Figure 3.18 is organised according to three different dimensions. As will be evident as the discussion progresses, these relate in various ways to the hemispheric localisation of music's and language's neural substrates, discussed in §2.7.7. One of these three dimensions is semiotic, in that it attempts to represent three distinct meaning levels, termed "Level One", "Level Two"

---

[162] After Jan (2007, p. 104, Tab. 3.1) and Jan (2016b, p. 489, Fig. 2); the associated discussion is an extension of this earlier material.

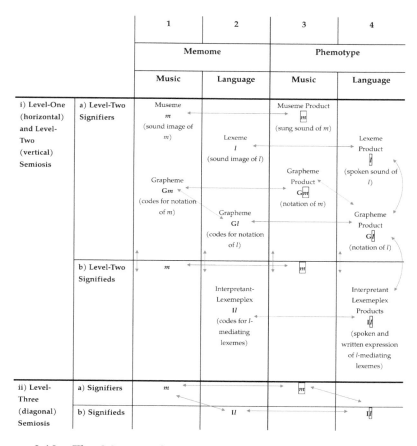

Figure 3.18: The Memetic-Semiotic Nexus of an *m-l* Music-Language M(us)emeplex.

and "Level Three". Another dimension represents the memome-phemotype (somatic-extrasomatic) distinction, whereby a (bold-type) formulation such as "m" refers to the memomic form of a museme m (§3.8.3) and where the boxed "$\boxed{m}$" refers to its phemotypic expression. Note that the memomic level is in principle conscious and is to be distinguished from the unconscious mentalese/LF structures with which it is associated and which it tokens. The third dimension makes a distinction between the two evolutionary outcomes of musilanguage, music and language.[163]

In Figure 3.18, (i) a, columns 1 and 3, and at the lowest level of referring, $\boxed{m}$ – the physical sonority, through which m, via the intercession of voices (or musical instruments), impinges upon us most directly – is represented, in a "horizontal" memetic-semiotic relationship, as the phemotypic (coded-for) meme-product of the memomic (coding-for) m. Thus, $\boxed{m}$ acts as a (somewhat abstract) signifier for m. $m\leftrightarrow\boxed{m}$ is often associated with a grapheme $Gm\leftrightarrow G\boxed{m}$, which partly governs the arguably superficial matter (from Carruthers' point of view) of notating m and which, while not essential for its existence, is nevertheless (in the case of literate cultures) often significant for its transmission. The same principle is true, of course, in the case of lexemes.

By analogy with $m\leftrightarrow\boxed{m}$, columns 2 and 4 of Figure 3.18, (i) a illustrate analogous relationships for the lexeme l, which codes for the spoken expression $\boxed{l}$. Paralleling $Gm\leftrightarrow G\boxed{m}$, Gl is a grapheme coding for the written expression $G\boxed{l}$. As with the music-related memes, the phemotypic forms $\boxed{l}$ and $G\boxed{l}$ act as signifiers (again somewhat abstractly) for the associated memomic signified forms l and Gl, respectively.

As represented in Figure 3.18, (i) b, columns 1 and 3, and at an intermediate level of referring, Gm also exists, now as a *signifier*, in "vertical" semiotic coadaptation with m, even though it is essentially independent of it (their relationship is "arbitrary" (Nattiez, 1990, p. 4)). $\boxed{m}$ is similarly associated, as signified, with the corresponding phemotypic signifier meme, $G\boxed{m}$.

---

[163] For clarity, Figure 3.18 ignores the motor-control memes (a subset of which are the gestemes considered in §3.5.4) that govern the muscular actions engendering writing, speaking, and the production of musical sounds, many of which are learned as "implicit memory" (Snyder, 2000, pp. 72–74) and which might also be regarded as memes.

Analogously, *l* and **G***l* function as signifiers of the signified language "interpretant-lexemeplex" **I***l*. By this is meant the wider network of cognate lexemes that provides the context for *l* and that anchors it in a broader web of signification.[164] The components of **I***l* ultimately devolve, in a communicativist view, to the "back-end" LF-integrated "mental models and images" for which *l* (and **I***l*) are the "front-end". In this sense, **I***l* is the essence of the "conscious propositional thought" (Carruthers, 2002, p. 664) tokened by *l*. As with the *m*-related memes, $\boxed{l}$ and **G**$\boxed{l}$ function as signifiers of the signified **I**$\boxed{l}$.[165]

As represented in Figure 3.18, (ii), and at the highest level of referring, the "diagonal" association between *m*↔$\boxed{m}$, as signifier, and **I***l*↔**I**$\boxed{l}$, as signified, forms a *m-l* m(us)emeplex, one either confined to a particular individual[166] or shared more widely (topically) within a cultural community. In such associations, the presence of the musical element triggers/cues the verbal in consciousness (or vice versa). In this sense, level-three semiosis corresponds not only to scenario 2a in the (second) list earlier in this subsection (page 274), but also potentially to scenario 2b – that is, the linking of musemes *directly* to the *semantic* elements of LF mentalese, displacing (or supplementing, in an intermediate state between scenarios 2a and 2b) their normal lexemic token. Such "semantic elements" are the meanings arising from the interconnected mentalese codes for nominal, adjectival, verbal, prepositional, etc. functions – the "natural language lexical items and syntactic structures ... stripped of all imagistic-phonological features" (Carruthers, 2002, p. 666) – that constitute LF.

This might be particularly the case with musemes that, on account of their strong image-schematic/embodied properties, link primarily *icon-*

---

[164] The term "interpretants" is Charles Sanders Peirce's (Nattiez, 1990, pp. 5–6). In Gottlob Frege's terminology, it aligns with the "sense" that qualifies and mediates the relationship between a term (a signifier/museme/lexeme) and its reference (a signified/object/concept) (Cross & Woodruff, 2009, p. 25).

[165] In language, *l*, **G***l*, and **I***l* give rise to an essentially unary product: the concept is effectively inseparable from its $\boxed{l}$, **G**$\boxed{l}$, or **I**$\boxed{l}$ manifestations, as symbolised by the curved brackets in column 4 of Figure 3.18, (i) a/b. In music, however, a separation is maintained, because **G***m* and *m* give rise to separate products: the notation (**G**$\boxed{m}$) and, separately, the sounds that the notation motivates and regulates ($\boxed{m}$). Thus, unlike language, these two musical replicators preserve the level-two signifier–signified dualism at the phemotypic level.

[166] Strictly, such an (initially, perhaps eternally) unreplicated complex should be termed a *mnemonplex*.

ically (§2.7.6) with LF representations deriving from one or more of the domain-specific modules of Figure 3.16. Nevertheless, in the case of topics, *indexical* linkages might also arise, because many topics have real-world (co-occurrent, albeit not always arbitrarily so) referents underpinning them, such as the emulations of horn and trumpet dotted rhythms that constitute the "military" style, or the bagpipe-like drones that define the "musette/pastorale" style (Ratner, 1980, pp. 18–19, 21; see also Monelle, 2006). In such cases, a context in which the instrument (or the dance rhythm, in the case of Ratner's rhythmic types) is used affords meaning to the topic.

The various cells in Figure 3.18 are connected by double-headed arrows, which represent the associations or linkages between phenomena in different domains and substrates by which understanding and meaning emerges. While the representation of patterns and their linkages on a two-dimensional page is useful to foster clarity of exposition and discussion, it also appears the case that this mirrors, to some extent, real functional and structural localisation and interconnection in the brain. As intra-brain linkages, all the vertical and diagonal connections linking columns one and two of Figure 3.18 (shown as red arrows) can potentially be accounted for by the HCT (§3.8.3). Naturally, the horizontal connections from columns one to three and from two to four, and the vertical and diagonal connection between columns three and four (shown as blue arrows) cannot be accounted for in this way, because they are not *intra*-brain linkages but rather somatic-extrasomatic (*inter*-brain) associations. In the case of columns one and two, however, the red double-headed arrows are the graphical equivalent of the *faux*-fax links that Calvin (1998) argues connect representations in one region or functional domain of the brain with those in another.

If the argument of this subsection is true, then one might ask why music is not as semantically specific as language. One reason might be that what might be termed an evolutionary "wedge" effect came into play after the bifurcation of music and language from musilanguage. That is, after separation their evolutionary paths diverged ever more widely because of the need for compositional language, as the information-communicating successor to musilanguage, to remain broadly coherent and specific to all members of a socio-linguistic group, and the concomitant relaxation of this constraint upon music once language had began to bear this burden.[167] Put another way, the Humboldtian nature of language – its compositional recombination of a relatively small number of component elements to form a near infinity of conceptual/propositional utterances (§5.6) – developed along more syntactically and semantically circumscribed lines than was the case in music.

Freed of its precursor's obligation to encompass referentiality, music was increasingly able to fulfil less tangible – but no less evolutionarily important – roles, particularly the fostering of group cohesion through (holistic and multimodal) communal physicality and pleasure (§2.5.2), still alive today in the throbbing beats of clubs or, virtually, in the speakers of an MP3 player. This observation accords broadly with critical views on non-vocal/non-texted music from the early-Romantic period, which celebrated it precisely because it lacked the conceptual precision of language and instead communicated more generalised, holistic phenomena. For E.T.A. Hoffmann (1776–1822), author of perhaps the most celebrated of such statements (Chantler, 2006), instrumental music

> is the most romantic of all the arts – one might almost say, the only genuinely romantic one – for its sole subject is the infinite. The lyre of Orpheus opened the portals of Orcus – music discloses to man an unknown realm, a world that has nothing in common with the external sensual world that surrounds him, a world in which he leaves behind him all definite feelings [and concepts] to surrender himself to an inexpressible longing [*Sehnsucht*]. (in Strunk et al., 1998, p. 151)

This is not to argue that music is a "universal language", even though there are clearly certain "musical universals" (§2.5.5) resulting from various evolutionarily shaped physical and perceptual-cognitive constraints (Lerdahl, 1992; Velardo, 2014). Nevertheless, whereas we can glean very little linguistic information from speakers of languages with which we are unfamiliar, the music of other cultures often speaks to us directly and powerfully, despite its initial strangeness to us and our unfamiliarity with the details of its semantic and syntactic conventions. Moreover, while we might be oblivious to the grammatical structure of an unfamiliar language, we can discern a good deal

---

[167] This is a general phenomenon in evolution, primarily observable in the inability of two species with a common ancestor to interbreed after a certain period of separate development has elapsed.

of emotional information from its specifically musical elements – from the musilanguage-derived intonation of the speaker in conjunction with their facial expressions and body language. In such situations, we are transported back to the world of our hominin ancestors and compelled to activate our capacity to engage with the holistic, the manipulative, the multi-modal, the musical and – perhaps most important – the memetic.

3.8.6 Implementation of Musical Syntax in the Light of the HCT

If the communicativist view of language is one of left-hemisphere LF tokened by imagined and spoken right-hemisphere lexemes, could introversive/ syntactic musical "thought" also be conducted in a form of mentalese – a left-hemisphere LF grammar of music – before association with the right-hemisphere musemes that give rise to imagined and vocalised (conscious) music? This question is an extension of point 2b – the potential for music to "draw *directly* – i.e., unmediated by language – upon the *semantic* elements of LF mentalese" – of the list on page 274, whereby not (just) the *semantic* but also the *syntactic* elements of LF is drawn upon. This extension is more problematic, because while these two dimensions are closely interconnected in language, they are clearly more independent in music.

It seems the case that processes covered under point 4 of the list on page 270 might also account for the representation of syntactic-hierarchic structure in music, such as that encompassed by the RHSGAP model (§3.5.2). In the same way that "*faux*-fax links ... allow higher-level concepts to connect representations of subsidiary parts of a sentence intelligibly" (to form a fully associated domain-general LF code), they might also connect subsidiary parts of a musical phrase together under some overarching "higher-level concept", which might be represented by such music-theoretical models as a framework harmonic progression, a "structural-melodic line" (Ratner, 1980, 89, Exx. 6–7), a Schenkerian *Zug* (Schenker, 1979, pp. 43–46), or some other schema (Leman, 1995; Byros, 2009). Moreover, in the same way that the structure of a clause is replicated recursively at the level of the sentence, and the multiply embedded clausal structure of a sentence is replicated at a higher level across a number of sentences, the same may be true for music. Deliège's notion of cue abstraction and/or Gjerdingen's concept of *Il filo* (the "thread", along which a discrete series of schemata are arranged) might be candidate psychological models of this neurobiological process (Delière, 2000; Cambouropoulos, 2001; Gjerdingen, 2007a, p. 369; see also Jan, 2010).

In this sense, music's syntax – which has been the subject of extensive language-orientated speculation ranging from the rhetorical schemata of the seventeenth century (Bonds, 1991) to the Chomskyan applications of the 1980s (Lerdahl & Jackendoff, 1983) (§4.5) – might, as suggested in §3.8.5, be to some extent dependent upon:

- Some degree of interconnection with (linguistic) LF (the two systems operating in *parallel*, to use the model of Brown et al. (2006) in the quotation on page 155); or upon

- A dedicated musical analogue to linguistic LF – musical LF – perhaps proximally located to linguistic LF in the brain (this notion going beyond the semantically orientated claims of §3.8.5) (*domain-specific*); or indeed upon

- Some hybrid (musilinguistic) LF-system (*shared*).

Thus, while music-language homologies were discussed in §3.8.5 in terms of *semantics*, it is possible that *syntax* might also be implicated, given the close alignment of the latter with the former in LF. While further research is needed – this being to some extent contingent upon ever finer resolution in neuroimaging technologies – there is some neurobiological evidence for a LF-underpinned syntax of music, in that Brodmann areas 44 (*pars opercularis*) and 45 (*pars triangularis*) – Broca's area in the left hemisphere – appear to implement a parallel "syntax/phonology interface area" subserving these functions in both domains (see the shaded cell in Table 2.2); and BA 22 – Wernicke's area in the left hemisphere – appears to implement a parallel "phonology/syntax interface area" (Brown et al., 2006, p. 2798, Fig. 5). Moreover, Patel goes so far as to propose a "shared syntactic integration resource hypothesis" (SSIRH), which asserts that language and music "have distinct and domain-specific [*parallel*] syntactic representations (e.g., chords vs. words), but that they *share* neural resources for activating and integrating these representations during syntactic processing" (2008, p. 268; emphases mine; see also Fitch, 2010, p. 477).

The argument for an LF syntax of music runs as follows, and requires three coordinated "ifs":

1. *If* music and language did share a common ancestor in the form of musilanguage; and

2. *If* sonically depleted but semantically rich language is a reflection of an underlying brain-language (the communicativist claim); and

3. *If* the latter attribute was present originally in musilanguage ...

... *then* sonically rich but semantically depleted music could have retained some element of this communicativist attribute. In this way, both evolutionary descendants of musilanguage might have retained certain elements of an ancestral, now to some extent shared, LF mentalese.

The third "if" is perhaps the most problematic in that, in its archetypal form, musilanguage (as discussed in §2.7.6) was likely a syntactically undeveloped form of communication, lacking the compositionality of fully developed language. As Carruthers argues, "it is natural language *syntax* which is crucially necessary for inter-modular integration" (Carruthers, 2002, p. 658; emphasis in the original). If his model is taken to hinge upon the underpinning and constitution of language by some form of mentalese-level, syntax-articulating LF, then perhaps the non-compositional musilanguage does not in fact implement it, and the argument for any evolutionarily persisting communicativism in music therefore falls. But if some form of communicativism does not require a *fully* developed syntax – if, in other words, it allows various shades of syntax, including the "protosyntax" potentially underpinning later, more developed forms of musilanguage (and, indeed, Bickertonian lexical protolanguage) – then musilanguage, and with it its evolutionary descendant, music, might indeed be amenable to a communicativist interpretation.

The latter would appear to be the more likely scenario, because – recalling the gradualistic reframing of Chomsky's "great leap forward" in §1.3, and Merker's account of the vocal learning constellation in §2.7.5 and §2.7.6 – musilanguage likely evolved into language and music over many millennia by means of gradualistic cumulative selection, and not by means of saltationist single-step selection. This accords with the general view in evolutionary theory that even a little bit of a good thing is preferable to none of it (Dawkins, 2006, pp. 125–126). One piece of evidence in favour of such "shades of syntax" might be derived from the earlier discussion on segmentation (§2.7.6). Once the processes engendering segmentation had started to have their effect on musilanguage, the medium would be in a transitional phase – one presumably lasting many hundreds of thousands of years – where attributes of both older musilanguage and newer compositional language were simultaneously present, musilanguage acting as a framework or scaffold for the newer form of communication before finally being supplanted by it (the "safety net" phenomenon discussed in point 19 of the list on page 149). The argument advanced here is that this "post-musilanguage" possessed just enough syntax – as a proto-LF – to give rise both to compositional language, communicatively understood, and to music *evolving on the basis of an underlying communicativist dualism between some form of perhaps partially shared LF mentalese and imagined (musemic) sound.*

If, on the basis of the above, the third "if" is held to be true, then both language and music would appear to draw upon some form of (partially shared) LF representation. In language, this can be represented in terms of Chomsky's generative-transformational grammar. In the literature of music theory, there are, as mentioned towards the beginning of this subsection, various music-theoretical representations of the syntactic basis of music, with one in particular, Lerdahl and Jackendoff's GTTM (1983), being the most explicitly (Chomskyan-)linguistic, although it is one that is in its very formulation chronologically and stylistically circumscribed. Despite the common parasitism of music theory upon models derived from language, and as the final part of §2.7.7 suggests, the likely evolutionary precedence of music over language suggests that linguistic syntax is derived from musical syntax, not vice versa.

Evidence for the SSIRH – as a corollary of a shared music-language LF representation – may be found in studies, some involving neuroimaging, of music-language co-processing, where violations of musical or linguistic syntax (and linguistic semantics) are observed to affect processing speed and/or acuity in the other domain (T. Collins et al., 2014, p. 51). The mechanism for this activation/integration in music might thus involve the same kind of (*faux*-fax) connections between right-hemisphere music centres and left-hemisphere semantic-syntactic LF centres discussed in §2.7.7. This reinforces the view articulated in connection with the quotation from Harvey (2017) on page 158 that, even after the bifurcation of musilanguage, both domains continued to retain significant structural and functional homologies, because it was evolutionarily inefficient for them wholly to implement a separation in their input, syntactic-semantic representation, or output systems.

3.8.7 Escaping Determinism via Evolution

As a final issue, and by way of drawing together some observations in the preceding subsections, there are clear alignments between Carruthers' (2002) model of the mechanism of thought and consciousness, its possible neural implementation via the HCT, and the "symbolic-representational system" (1991, p. 489, Fig. 6) underpinning Sereno's cell/person (1991, p. 478) discussed in §1.6.2. Proposing a common mechanism for protein synthesis and language reception/production, Sereno argues that

> a unique single-celled symbolic-representational system first arose from a prebiotic chemical substrate at the origin of life, permitting Darwinian evolution to occur. Subsequently, multicellular organisms evolved and they developed more and more elaborate humoral and neural control mechanisms. But … a similar, autonomous symbolic-representational system did not reemerge on any intermediate level until the origin of thought and language from the substrate of prelinguistic neural activity patterns in the brains of Pleistocene hominids. (Sereno, 1991, p. 484)

The motivation for this "reemergence" – which does not result from homology (evolutionary descent) but from homoplasy (convergent evolution) alighting upon another implementation of the same robust solution at a different structural-hierarchic level – is that

> the apparatus involved in cellular protein synthesis, and the neural patterns underlying human language comprehension are both mechanisms for escaping 'determinism'…. The pre-existing (prebiotic, prelinguistic) states can be described as complex, highly interactive, but deterministically evolving, 'soups' containing a number of different types of dynamically stable units (prebiotic molecules, prelinguistic neural activity

patterns). The problem is simply to encode, use, and reproduce information about how to make certain 'reactions' (chemical reactions, alteration
and recombination of neural activity patterns) in this soup happen. ...
In this sense, the resulting system is 'intentional'. (Sereno, 1991, p. 484)

The main elements of this "apparatus" in cell metabolism and language
processing are briefly summarised as follows, with key functions/structures
italicised: (i) a collection of *symbols* (DNA triplets; word-sounds) exist in a
chain (DNA sequence; word-sound sequence (lexeme phemotype)); (ii) this
chain is converted to a *symbol representation* (transfer RNA (tRNA) sequence;
secondary auditory cortex (Wernicke's area) activity pattern); (iii) a *chain
assembler* (ribosome; secondary auditory cortex activity pattern) builds a
parallel *"thing" representation* (amino acid; secondary visual cortex activity
pattern (objects and phenomena in the world represented in visual memory
and presumably in other memory modalities)); (iv) the *"thing" representation*
is linked to the *symbol representation* by a *3-D connector* (aminoacyl-tRNA
synthetase; secondary visual cortex activity pattern); (v) a *reaction controller* is built from the *"thing" representation* (enzyme; STM/working memory
pattern (internalised lexeme sounds)) in order to act on internal *objects* (various enzyme substrates; mental activity patterns in various domains and
modalities); and (vi) just as a non-arbitrary relationship connects *symbols*
with *symbol representations*, a similarly non-arbitrary relationship connects
"thing" representations to external *"things"* (prebiotic chemical compounds;
prelinguistic activity patterns in the primate brain) (after Sereno, 1991, p.
489, Fig. 6; p. 491, Tab. 1).

In this outline, the *"thing" representation* in language is implemented by LF
(the domain-general integration of domain-specific representations) and the
symbol representation is the lexeme-sequence (the tokening of LF by internalised word-sounds). All the various mental representations, as might be
expected, are able to be encoded according to the precepts of the HCT, with
the necessary *faux*-fax linkages providing longer-range connections between
brain regions (such as the communication between auditory and visual
cortex and inter-hemispheric connections). While Sereno (1991) does not
consider the finer details of neural organisation, such connections between
right-hemisphere lexeme-sound representations and left-hemisphere syntax
and semantic centres implementing LF appear to be key here, and subserve

the *chain assembler* and *3-D connector* functions (and presumably interconnect with the visual cortex centres identified by Sereno). As argued in §2.7.7, much of this neural infrastructure initially arose in response to the evolution of musicality. Sereno's model is thus also congruent with music as a phonological-syntactic-semantic system, and references to "lexemes" in the summary above can potentially be replaced by "musemes" as the original mechanism for escaping determinism in cultural evolution.

Sereno's is primarily a model of language *comprehension*, represented in biology by the "understanding" (translation) of the DNA code (*symbols*) in order to produce protein "meanings" (*"thing" representations*). The reverse process, language *production*, would contradict the Central Dogma (§1.8). If it obtained, a mechanism for Lamarckism would exist, because proteins could back-alter DNA, giving rise to "a more thoroughgoing, minute-to-minute Lamarckianism than has ever been conceived for biological organisms" (Sereno, 1991, p. 487). Production is, of course, fundamental in language and music, because communication is a two-way process requiring that *"things"* (prelinguistic, domain-specific meanings) can be used to generate *symbols* for them that are comprehensible to others. Thus, whereas comprehension is the exclusive mode in cells, both comprehension and production operate in language. Nevertheless, Sereno, following Sapir, emphasises what he regards as the primary motivation for language, namely comprehension via symbolisation (Sereno, 1991, p. 486). This motivates the question of how the symbolic-representational system of language evolved. The account presented here of the evolution of compositional language from musilanguage implies – *contra* Sereno – that (domain-specific) meanings were represented in hominin brains *before* a (musi)linguistic system evolved for integrating and symbolising them, initially via protemes and subsequently via musemes and lexemes.

3.8.8 Summary of Music-Language (Co)evolution

To summarise the main conclusions of §2.7 and §3.8, the following has been argued:

1. Music and language are two sides of the same evolutionary coin. The appearance in the hominin line of the capacity to produce and control vocalisations

was the result of numerous interacting aptive factors. Eventually, a holistic musilanguage arose that subserved a number of functions, initially aptive only for genes but increasingly also aptive for memes.

2. Once the neural substrates for the segmentation of musilanguage were in place, it was inevitable that the chunks of sonorous information resulting from this process would be subject to the operation of the VRS algorithm. Computer simulation of the mechanism, and of the ever tighter association of meanings with sound-segments, offers telling evidence of its likely validity.

3. The replicated sound patterns of language are arguably proxies of a more fundamental mental language, LF. Structures in this medium foster the integration of concepts in different domains to form multi-modal syntactic-semantic complexes that, in conjunction with sonic replicators, are not only amenable to consciousness but that also confer significant evolutionary advantages upon individuals who possess this facility.

4. Lexemes and musemes appear to be encoded in the brain in broadly similar ways – by means of hexagonal encoding, cloning and Darwinian competition – and they are predominantly right-hemisphere localised. This constitutes further evidence for their common evolutionary origin in musilanguage. The syntactic structures encoding LF appear to be predominantly left-hemisphere localised. *Faux*-fax links connect the two types of representation, allowing the cross-hemispheric tokening of LF by musemes and lexemes.

5. The mechanisms by which language acquires semantic content appear broadly replicated (albeit more loosely) in music, and might be understood in terms of multi-level semiotic process spanning different replicator domains (memome, phemotypic). Moreover, it may be the case that elements, or analogues, of LF structures might also subserve music's syntactic organisation.

3.9 Summary of Chapter 3

Chapter 3 has argued that:

1. To consider musicality and its products in purely biological terms is inadequate. A dual-replicator coevolutionary model is needed that takes account of both gene-based biological/musicality evolution and museme-based cultural/music evolution as instantiations of the VRS algorithm.

2. A number of theories of cultural change were developed in the twentieth century, in an attempt to find cultural equivalents to the gene and the structures it engendered. Of these, the memetics conceived by Dawkins and championed by Dennett arguably shows the greatest potential.

3. Issues relevant to the ongoing development of memetics include the nature and status of qualitative *versus* quantitative evidence; how the biological concepts of adaptation and exaptation might be applied to (music-)cultural evolution; and the extent to which the status of memetics as a Darwinian model is undermined by potentially Lamarckian factors.

4. A significant contribution memetics can make to our understanding of music is in its formalisation of pattern-replication at multiple structural-hierarchic levels. This is relevant to many dimensions of music, including the generation of recurrent higher-level structures, and to the creation of music in improvisation and to its recreation in performance.

5. While slavishly applying biological-taxonomic principles to music is unwarranted, the recursive ontology driven by the VRS algorithm leads to certain systemic-structural parallels between the processes and products of biological and cultural evolution that can illuminate a sensitive cultural taxonomy.

6. Coevolutionary accounts of human musicality and music attempt to reconcile the sometimes conflicting interests of each replicator system and to understand how their genomic/memomic levels interact with their phenotypic/phemotypic levels to produce the musical competences and products that depend on both replicators. More than any other species, humans are defined by the rich cultures encephalisation made possible, this brain-augmentation having itself perhaps been impelled by culture, via the mechanism of memetic drive. As a result, music's development has far transcended what might have been predicted on purely biological-morphological grounds.

7. Memetics fosters a deeper understanding of the structural-evolutionary relationships between music and language, arguing that both are made up of discrete, replicated sound-parcels that are amenable (language more so than music) to association with objects and meanings. A hypothesis for musical and linguistic syntax and semantics is afforded by the Logical Form of Chomsky and Carruthers, this perhaps being implemented by the Hexagonal Cloning Theory of Calvin.

Chapter 4 will build upon the extension of gene-based Darwinism to the meme-based Darwinism outlined in this chapter in order to explore how evolutionary metaphors have been employed in scholarship on music to explain the style and structure of music over time. Taking the implications of this chapter to their logical conclusion, Chapter 4 considers how discourses on music (evolutionary and indeed non-evolutionary) are themselves amenable – as music-historical and music-theoretical/analytical verbal-conceptual memeplexes – to the VRS algorithm. It will: explore the issue of metanarratives and metaphor in musical scholarship; examine evolutionary metaphors in music historiography and music theory and analysis; consider – as part of the ongoing discussion of music-language coevolution – how linguistic tropes have been used in music-scholarly discourses; discuss how the evolution of music-scholarly discourses can be theorised and quantified; and explore the complex coevolution of music, the socio-cultural structures that sustain it, and the discourses that seek to comprehend it.

4. Evolutionary Metaphors in Discourse on Music

> The origin of every life, whether of nation, clan, or individual, becomes its destiny. Hegel defines destiny as 'the manifestation of the inborn, original predisposition of each individual'.... The fundamental structure shows us how the chord of nature comes to life through a vital natural power. But the primal power of this established motion must grow and live its own full life: that which is born to life strives to fulfil itself with the power of nature. (Schenker, 1979, pp. 3, 25)

4.1 Introduction: Metanarratives in Musical Scholarship

This chapter continues to move away from the "nature" end of the nature-culture continuum covered in Chapter 1 and Chapter 2 and – the ground having been prepared by the consideration of memetics in Chapter 3 – turns to examine the deployment of evolutionary ideas in academic and scholarly discourse on music. Whereas the focus of Chapter 3 was on finding phenomena and processes in music that are structurally and functionally equivalent to those in biology, the emphasis here is on *metaphorical* connections between music and evolution. Nevertheless, the force of *non*-metaphorical connections between music and evolution, understood via memetics, will increasingly be felt – as a tension between *metaphor* and *mechanism* – as the chapter progresses.[168]

Metaphor, considered more fully in §4.2, has underpinned many of the wider frameworks humans have established in order to understand music,

---

[168] I initially considered using "scare quotes" to indicate metaphorical uses of evolutionary terms ("phylogeny", "species", etc.), but decided against this on the grounds that to do so would be cumbersome and visually distracting.

     https://doi.org/10.11647/OBP.0301.04

these *metanarratives* anchoring music historiography, music theory and music analysis to coherent and durable intellectual traditions. As well as being a cultural practice embedded in all human societies – a manifestation of its deep connection with our evolutionary history and identity as a species – music has been a persistent topic of intellectual speculation from the beginning of literate culture (and probably before). Musical metanarratives initially emerged in relation to theoretical issues, in order to explore the raw materials of music and their basis in natural acoustical phenomena. Only gradually – by the seventeenth century, perhaps – did the systemic focus on music *theory* widen to incorporate a consideration of specific pieces of music, what we would today regard as the beginnings of music *analysis*. The two domains are closely interconnected, both conceptually and historically. In the former, (general) theoretical models are assembled by means of the analysis of (specific) pieces of music; and pieces of music are analysed by reference to theoretical models. In the latter, analysis was initially motivated by the theoretical demands of compositional pedagogy: to draw on Spitzer's distinction, theory assumed the analytical study of "generic" (prototypical) exemplars in order to develop the understanding of musical structure necessary to support "generative" processes (2004, pp. 73–75, Fig. 2.8). Inverting Cook's dichotomy, the latter process represents "composition through analysis" (1996). The preconditions for the development of music analysis as a free-standing discipline would appear to have been the rising importance and systematisation of music notation; the greater permanence of certain (often Austro-German) compositions marking the beginnings of canonicity and the associated notion of the work concept (Goehr, 1992); the growing authorial presence of the composer, itself related to changing economic systems and associated career structures for creative musicians; the nascent aestheticisation of music; and the increasing desire to use analysis as a window into musical structure. The last of these, often achieved by means of composition, inverts its initial motivation and, restoring Cook's original formulation, affords "analysis through composition".

Some common threads have linked the pursuit of these two interconnected disciplines over the last two millennia, certainly in the west (Christensen, 2002). Music-theoretical and music-analytical metanarratives might be divided not just into their component disciplines, but also into two "bundles", one "cosmic", the other "human". The cosmic bundle relates to the fact that, for most of our history, we have believed that we are made in the image of a heaven-dwelling deity. As a consequence, music theory was initially conceived as affording an insight – as a metaphor, or a proxy – into the nature of our creator and the secrets, encoded in mathematics, of the cosmos that creator impelled (Clark & Rehding, 2001). This orientation characterises much Ancient Greek (Hagel, 2009; Nowacki, 2020) and Ancient Chinese writings on music theory (Thrasher et al., 2001, sec. II; Fang, 2019), although these are pre-dated by rich bodies of writing from such cultures as the Babylonians (Conner, 2014). From the perspectives of these cultures, the study of music offered a window into understanding the wider universe, the proportions and ratios of the former being a mirror and microcosm of the latter. This relationship between music and cosmology – most clearly evident in, and most intellectually influential via, the notion of the "harmony of the spheres" (Godwin, 1993) (§7.8) – persisted into the middle ages, with the seven-fold structuring of the Medieval university curriculum into a number-orientated *Quadrivium* of arithmetic, geometry, music and astronomy, and a language-orientated *Trivium* of grammar, logic and rhetoric (Leff, 1992; J. North, 1992).

The human bundle, which supplanted the cosmic during the Renaissance, relates to the use of music theory and analysis as endeavours conducted in order to understand our nature and place in the universe revealed by the cosmic bundle: we make music in our own image – in Jacobus of Liège's term, it is a mirror (Harne, 2012)[169] – so music theory and analysis have probed this simulacrum in order to glean insights into what makes us who we are. Again in the ancient Greek tradition, discussion of the (cosmic-)proportional structure of modes went hand in hand with consideration of their (human-)emotional effect upon us. In the European middle ages and later, theory and analysis were also used a key to understanding discourse, framing music as a form of non-verbal rhetoric partly in an attempt to illuminate the structure of thought and the wielding of influence (Bonds, 1991). In the European Enlightenment and ensuing Romanticism, models drawn from biology, most notably the concept of organicism (§4.4.1) – a persistent focus of this chapter

---

[169] The Latin *speculum* (mirror) is bifocal here, in that it could perhaps refer to the treatise's reflecting the nature of music; or to music's reflecting our own nature.

– became prevalent, partly as ways to understand ourselves in the context of continuities and discontinuities with other species. Twentieth-century developments in music theory and analysis brought to bear insights from cognitive science (Gjerdingen, 1999; Gjerdingen, 2010) and – in a reinvigoration of its Medieval focus – from linguistics (Lerdahl & Jackendoff, 1983; Patel, 2008) in order to co-illuminate music and its perception and cognition.

The study of music history – what in the UK is often termed "historical musicology" and, in the US, simply "musicology" (Kerman, 1985) – was the latest of the three major domains of "traditional" music scholarship to arise. It started to manifest itself in the early-nineteenth century with biographies of leading composers, such as those of J. S. Bach (by Forkel in 1802 (Forkel, 1920)) and of Haydn (by Griesinger in 1810 (Griesinger, 1810)). These were followed by surveys of musical history that attempted to integrate composers' biographies with such themes as style analysis (the *"Leben und Schaffen"* ("life and works") tradition); the waxing and waning of different chronological and geographical styles, often in relation to their political and socio-economic underpinnings; the development of musical forms and genres; and the aesthetic tenors of different ages. By the end of the nineteenth century, these two broad domains – the historiographic and the theoretical/analytical – had been assimilated into Adler's (1885) bipartite formulation of musicology as consisting of the "historical" and the "systematic" branches and their subcomponents.

The purpose of briefly rehearsing these well understood metanarratives is to provide some context for the consideration of music in terms of its relationship to the scholarly discourses surrounding it, particularly those that draw upon evolutionary metaphors. If the arguments of Chapter 3 are accepted, then musical style and structure are amenable to a memetic reading that sees them in Universal-Darwinian terms. That is, music can be understood in terms of a myriad of competitively replicating particles whose implementation of the VRS algorithm drives the evolution of musical style over time and gives rise to various higher-level structural archetypes. But music is only one element of culture, coexisting with patterning in the visual and verbal-conceptual domains. This means that musemic replication necessarily takes place in the context of the replication of other memes. There is therefore coevolutionary cooperation and competition (§3.7) between musemes/muse-meplexes and "non-musemes"/"non-musemeplexes" (i.e., non-sound-based memes/memeplexes), and this interaction between different cultural replicator-types shapes the evolution of music itself and that of discourse about music.

If one accepts Spitzer's view that "[t]o think, talk, or write about music is to engage with it in terms of something else, metaphorically" (2004, p. 1) – with its implication that non-metaphorical engagement with music is difficult if not impossible – then many of these music-discursive verbal-conceptual memeplexes constitute the cultural-evolutionary foundation of metaphorical writing on music, *whether they draw specifically on evolutionary thought or not*. In the case of music-evolutionary metaphors, the evolution of the verbal-conceptual memeplexes structuring these metaphors, and the evolution of the musemes to which the metaphors' verbal-conceptual memeplexes relate, serves as a real/hard exemplification of the process – the operation of the VRS algorithm – articulated virtually/softly via the metaphor.

As with gene-gene and gene-meme coevolution, it is not straightforward to understand how the type of museme/non-museme coevolution (as a subset of meme-meme coevolution) just described operates. For one thing, musemes and non-musemes occupy different domains of thought, so it is unclear how any cross-influence can be identified, either in terms of low-level implementation or higher-level outputs. Despite the hypotheses of §3.8.4, §3.8.5 and §3.8.6 – i.e., that brain substrates primarily associated with musemes may connect with the syntax- and semantics-implementing brain substrates primarily associated with lexemes – it is by no means straightforward to map how, for instance, a particular phenomenon in verbal syntax or semantics might influence a corresponding one in musical syntax or semantics, or vice versa. A further complication is introduced by incorporating visual culture – and the syntactic-semantic networks it draws upon – as a factor affecting verbal-conceptual memes and musemes. More often than not, influences upon music from the wider culture appear to inhere largely in quite broad-brush aspects, such as the oft-noted connections between imperial/militaristic politics and musical swagger (Rumph, 2004), that are inherently difficult to cross-map with a meaningful level of granularity. In general, music often tends to be seen as an epiphenomenon, not a driver, of culture: in the previous example, ceremonial music is primarily understood to reflect and glorify an extant swagger, even though a feedback loop might be assumed to have operated, whereby the music served further to embolden the swaggerers.

Beyond this general potential for the wider culture to affect the memetic evolution of music, and vice versa, my concern in this chapter is more limited and thus more tractable, being focused, as noted, upon those verbal-conceptual memeplexes constituting the academic/scholarly discussion of music – the metanarrative-underpinned traditions of music history, music theory and music analysis, with their, in Spitzer's view, unavoidably metaphorical dimensions. The chapter's threefold focus is thus on the following:

- *Within the domain of verbal-conceptual culture*:

    1. The use of evolutionary metaphors in scholarly discourses on music (i.e., with the uses of evolutionary thought as a prism through which to view music; §4.3, §4.4).

    2. The evolution of the verbal-conceptual memeplexes constituting scholarly discourses on music (§4.6).

- *Within and between the domains of verbal-conceptual and musical culture*:

    3. The tripartite coevolution of socio-culture, music, and scholarly discourses on music (§4.7).

As will be understood, the difficulty – which this chapter cannot claim to surmount – increases as one proceeds through this sequence: point 1 is tractable to some extent by surveying a sample of relevant literature; point 2 requires a more statistical approach, taking the appearance of certain key terms as phemotypic markers of cultural-evolutionary processes within music scholarship; whereas point 3 requires findings from the second enquiry to be correlated with data on extra-musical cultural evolution. From this it will hopefully be clear that, as noted at the beginning of the chapter, the metaphorical gives way to the mechanical, as the influence of memetics gradually increases over the course of the chapter. As a final point, it is worth noting that there is a dichotomy, on the one hand, between taking into account known influences of evolutionary ideas on the discourses discussed, and, on the other hand, reading into these discourses evolutionary ideas that may not have affected their origin and development. While my primary focus is on the former, there are occasionally cases where the latter can offer a fruitful strategy.

The chapter continues with a review of Spitzer's theory of metaphor, attempting to relate it specifically to evolutionary metaphors (§4.2). It continues with two related sections that examine the use of evolutionary metaphors in music historiography and in music theory and analysis (§4.3, §4.4).[170] Another return to the issue of music's relationships with language explores the use of linguistic tropes – specifically, those that see music as a form of ("universal") language – in music-scholarly discourse (§4.5). The following section moves away from the primarily metaphorical uses of evolutionary ideas in music-scholarly discourse considered hitherto in order to examine the cultural evolution of such discourses themselves (§4.6). Finally, the chapter expands the consideration of such cultural evolution to encompass coevolution: not gene-meme, or even meme-meme, but meme(plex)-museme(plex)-meme(plex); that is, between meme(plexe)s in the wider culture, those underpinning music, and those constituting music-scholarly discourses (§4.7).

4.2 Metaphor in Evolutionary-Musical Scholarship

Spitzer's rich overview (2004) argues that metaphor has played a key role in conceptualising music, in both historical and theoretical/analytical terms. He defines musical metaphor as

> the relationship between the physical, proximate, and familiar, and the abstract, distal, and unfamiliar. This relationship flows in opposite directions within the two realms of musical reception and production, and involves opposite concepts of 'the body'. With reception, theorists and listeners conceptualize musical structure by metaphorically mapping from physical bodily experience. With production, the illusion of a

---

[170] I should stress that in these two sections I have not undertaken a comprehensive review of all the scholarly literature in these fields that draws on evolutionary metaphors. Such a survey is well beyond the scope of this chapter, and would require both qualitative and quantitative (corpus-analytical) methodologies.

musical body emerges through compositional poetics – the rhetorical manipulation of grammatical norms. (Spitzer, 2004, p. 4)

The production-reception binarism here encompasses another dichotomy. The historical evolution of the application and conceptualisation of metaphor has moved from a poetic to a scientific orientation. In its Classical and Renaissance uses in literature and painting, metaphor is a poetic-rhetorical trope. It is linked with cognate tropes – such as metonymy (reference to something via one of its attributes) and synecdoche (the part standing for the whole) – concerned with the connection of two or more separate but related entities to form a nexus in which individual components are difficult to distinguish from each other. In its modern context, metaphor is increasingly understood as a powerful means of understanding perception and cognition, as a key to the operation of the mind (Spitzer, 2004, pp. 4–5). This is because the essential metaphorical act not of *seeing* or *hearing*, but of *seeing as* or *hearing as* – of comprehending something in terms of something else, in Wittgenstein's distinction (Spitzer, 2004, p. 9) – can be rationalised first in terms of elisions between psychological states and then, more fundamentally, in terms of interdigitation between neurological substrates (as in that occurring between the hexagon-encompassed triangular arrays theorised in the HCT (§3.8.3)). This dichotomy is thus a manifestation of that which underpins much of this book: between culture (metaphor as poetic-rhetorical trope) and nature (metaphor as cognitive-evolutionary function).

Spitzer argues that such hearing as allows us to hear music in ways ("modes of listening" or "listening types") that include the *visual* (as a quasi-pictorial experience, and motivating such images as a "line" of notes, a "decorative" passage, etc.); the *vocal* (as a quasi-linguistic utterance, with all the syntactic and semantic implications this entails); and the *organic* (as a living entity, at various biological-structural levels) (2004, pp. 11–12). Via "cross-domain mapping", he coordinates the first of these listening types with the musical parameters of *harmony* and/or *counterpoint* (on account of the quasi-pictorial tableau generated by a complex harmonic-contrapuntal texture);[171] the second with *rhythm* (on account of the linguistic-syntactic interconnection

---

[171] Spitzer initially coordinates the visual listening type with counterpoint, using the opening chorus of Bach's *St John Passion* as an example (2004, 16–19, Ex. 1.2); but, in a later figure (that adapted in my Figure 4.1), he aligns it with harmony.

of notes foregrounded by their alignment with the metrical structure); and the third with *melody* (on account of the "living" motion of melodic pitches – indeed, slipping from theorising metaphor to being seduced by it, Spitzer argues that in Beethoven's String Quartet in A minor op. 132, "scale steps … take on a life of their own … as organic motives. Beethoven's motivic cells seem to generate a life force that flows like blood or spirit through the living work") (2004, p. 27).

Figure 4.1 (after 2004, p. 59, Fig. 2.7; p. 100, Fig. 3.1) represents how these three listening types and their associated musical parameters fit into Spitzer's model of metaphor as a whole.[172]

As mentioned, and as represented by the connecting arrows in the lower left-hand part of Figure 4.1, the binary alignments posited between key musical parameters and extramusical phenomena are: (i) harmony-counterpoint/painting; (ii) rhythm/language; and (iii) melody/life. Moreover, each pairing is associated, to form a ternary "cluster", with a foundational image schema, as follows: (i) *centre/periphery* (articulating notions of two- and three-dimensional space, and of proximity and distance (2004, p. 57, Fig. 2.4)); (ii) *part/whole* (articulating notions of nested hierarchy and logical interconnection (2004, p. 58, Fig. 2.5)); and (iii) *path* (articulating notions of directed progression from origin to goal (2004, p. 59, Fig. 2.6)). As an additional set of associations, Spitzer reads an historical dimension to each of these clusters, arguing that in the history of metaphorical writing on music ("the archaeology of musical metaphor" (2004, p. 59)) during the common-practice period, metaphors of: (i) harmony-counterpoint/painting are predominant in the *seventeenth* century; (ii) rhythm/language are most common in the *eighteenth* century; and (iii) melody/life are central in the *nineteenth* century, thus forming a quaternary cluster associated with each mode of listening (visual, vocal, organic) (2004, pp. 59–60). Connected by its image-schematic foundations, the whole structure is partitioned into analytical metaphor (strictly metonymic part-whole relations within music) and

---

[172] Spitzer's theory is "bidirectional" (2004, p. 4), in that it encompasses a conceptual/cognitive dimension (body-to-text; left-hand part of Figure 4.1), and a poetic/literary dimension (text-to-body; right-hand part of Figure 4.1). Dotted lines connecting elements of the left- and right-hand parts of Figure 4.1 represent connections between analogous components of the two dimensions. For reasons of space and applicability, only the conceptual dimension is considered in detail here. See, however, note 173 on page 301.

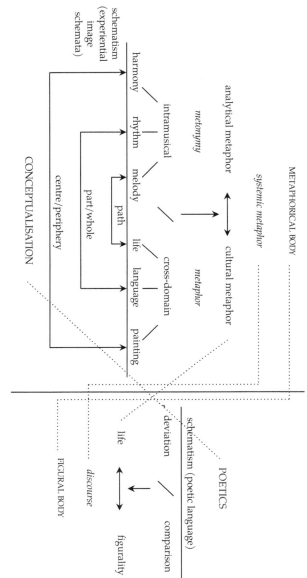

Figure 4.1: Spitzer's Model of Metaphor.

cultural metaphor (properly metaphorical cross-domain mappings between music and phenomena in other realms of culture).[173]

The last of these clusters – (iii) organic: melody/life; path image schema; nineteenth century – figures significantly in the deployment of evolutionary metaphors in discourse on music. As will be argued in §4.3 and §4.4, attempts to understand music in terms of organic-evolutionary concepts – conceiving music in terms of life-historical and life-structural processes of development and change, of survival and extinction – are primarily focused around the diachronic/horizontal dimension of music (its *melodic* aspects, and those proxies of melody such as harmonic progression and parametric change over time); they see this linear unfolding as a manifestation of a vital force (music as a form of *life*, seeking to ensure its ongoing survival); they are concerned with explicating "ontogenetic" and "phylogenetic" progression and change over time in the various dimensions of music (following a continuous *path* of development, as if the structure of musical works and the historical unfolding of musical style were a form of ongoing melody curving from bar to bar and leaping from work to work); and they are a particularly durable theme in the historiographic and theoretical/analytical literature impelled by the florescence of Darwinian evolutionary thought (from the mid-*nineteenth* to the early-twentieth centuries).

To understand the foundations of cluster (iii), one must return to Spitzer's reference to "the body" in the quotation on page 297. This notion draws, in part, on the aforementioned image-schematic coordination between music's parameters and the phenomenological experiences of individual listeners' bodies in three-dimensional, gravity-mediated space: the "up"/"rising" and "down"/"falling" of pitch (this *up/down* schema drawing on the centre/periphery schema), the "fast"/"accelerating" and "slow"/"decelerating" of rhythm, and the "light/thin" and "heavy/thick" of harmony and counterpoint (Spitzer, 2004, pp. 9–10). As mentioned in §2.5.2, all of these image

---

[173] In brief, the poetic dimension of Spitzer's model (right-hand part of Figure 4.1) is based on Paul Ricoeur's "tension theory" of metaphor, which "helps us to understand how the force of an aesthetic text impinges on our lives to the same, yet contrary, extent that we project our lives upon aesthetic texts through conceptual metaphor" (Spitzer, 2004, p. 100). Thus, whereas the conceptual dimension of the theory projects image-schematic experience metaphorically onto the "body" of a work of art, the poetic dimension projects various "figures" (often, in language, enacting a "grammatical impertinence" (2004, p. 97); and encompassing, in music, the *Figuren* of Baroque *Affektenlehre*) metaphorically onto the body of the reader or listener.

schemata have aptive motivations, because they arise from survival-related sensitivities to our location and movement in space and to the location and movement of potential environmental benefits and harms. But they are also activated in the perception and conception of art-forms that draw upon the sense modalities of vision and hearing, motivating a constant vigilance to the simulacra, intentional or not, of such benefits and harms in art, as formalised in the "etiological perspective" of Crewdson (2010) discussed in §3.5.4. Two operations foster the cultural-evolutionary origin and development of evolutionary metaphors of music via such image-schematic embodiment: inversion and pluralisation. First, by inversion, *music felt in the body* becomes *the body felt in music*: music and its components are rendered amenable to understanding as the whole and the parts of a living entity. Secondly, and building upon inversion, "the body" can also be understood not only as singular but also as plural, and with the latter the biological is foregrounded: the subjective individual becomes the objective species, and the life-history of its type-exemplars (ontogeny) and the evolutionary history of the wider collective of organisms (phylogeny) can thus be made tangible.

4.3 Evolutionary Metaphors in Music Historiography

When trying to conceive music in evolutionary terms, music historiography, and indeed music theory and analysis, generally frame evolution informally, seeing it as "[a] process of gradual change occurring in a system, institution, subject, artefact, product, etc., esp. from a simpler to a more complex or advanced state", rather than formally, as "the proposition that all living organisms have undergone a process of alteration and diversification from simple primordial forms during the earth's history; (in particular) a scientific theory proposing a mechanism for this process, now esp. that based on Darwin's theory of the natural selection of genetically inherited and adaptive variation" (Simpson & Weiner, 2018, Senses 7a, 8b). Thus, in adopting the informal sense, they generally eschew any explanatory model for this "gradual change"; or (as is explored in §4.3.4) they employ a model, but adopt a form of Lamarckism rather than the Darwinism underpinning more recent accounts of cultural evolution. Memetics' status as a formal model – a mechanism, not a metaphor, to recall the distinction made in §4.1 – will be understood as the reason why it is not itself considered here or in §4.4, even though it is invoked as a mechanism in §4.6. As will become apparent, however, the metaphor-mechanism distinction is not hard-and-fast, and discourses – and the accounts of them offered below – often slide, occasionally surreptitiously, from one side to the other.

Four of the key evolutionary metaphor-constellations invoked in music historiography to be considered here – the fourth to some extent encompassing and illuminating the first three – are:[174]

Ontogenetic Metaphors of Composers' Styles: whereby the progression in compositional technique and style (in Meyer's (1996) sense of idiom; §1.6.2) from apprentice to graduate and then to master is understood in terms of life-historical processes of growth, maturation, senescence and death.

Ontogenetic Metaphors of Historical Styles, Genres and Formal-Structural Types: whereby the origin, development, perfection and decline of music-historical styles (in Meyer's (1996) sense of dialect), genres and formal-structural types is understood in terms of individual life-historical processes of growth, maturation, senescence and death.

Phylogenetic Metaphors of Historical Styles, Genres and Formal-Structural Types: whereby the origin, development, perfection and decline of music-historical styles, genres and formal-structural types is understood in terms of species-historical evolution.

Lamarckism *versus* Darwinism in Music Historiography: whereby the development of a composer's style, or that of an historical period, genre, or formal-structural type, is understood as resulting either from intentional/directed processes of improvement (Lamarckism) or from the random operation of the VRS algorithm (Darwinism).

These four constellations are explored, respectively, in the following subsections.

---

[174] For reasons outlined in the Preface, this section, together with §4.4, is exclusively focused upon the western canon; but a parallel approach could, in principle, be undertaken based upon the historiographic and the music-theoretical/-analytical traditions of other cultures. Moreover, one could track syncretic fusions between western and non-western traditions (see, for example, McClary, 2004), the opposite of the bifurcation occurring in biological speciation (§1.7.3).

4.3.1 Ontogenetic Metaphors of Composers' Styles

Section 1.6.2 proposed certain structural-hierarchic analogies between nature and culture, summarised in Table 1.4. This and the following subsection (§4.3.2) cover music-historiographic traditions that draw upon some of the principles articulated in §1.6.2, but which deviate from the details of Table 1.4 in certain key ways. Table 1.4 hypothesised a broad correspondence between idiom (the level of individual composers' styles (Meyer, 1996, p. 24)) and the sub-group of organisms at the "Genetic/Memetic-Cultural" level four, because an idiom gives rise to, and is instantiated by, multiple discrete but related works – it implements a token-type relationship (§3.6.3). Works, each characterised by their own intraopus style, are equated with individual organisms at the "Genetic/Memetic-Structural" level five, and in this sense are more the province of theory and analysis (§4.4.1), or of style analysis, and less that of historiography. Table 1.4 also bundled genre and formal-structural type with idiom on the "culture" side of the analogy, thus also aligning the former two categories with the sub-group of organisms at the "nature" side at level four, on account of their representing, like idiom and the sub-group of organisms, types instantiated by multiple tokens; and it proposed a higher-level correspondence between dialect (the level of chronologically and/or geographically defined styles (Meyer, 1996, p. 23)) and the species – both, again, defined by token-type relationships – at level three.

While the latter analogy (dialect-species, the subject of §4.3.3) has often obtained in music historiography, the former (idiom/genre/formal-structural type mapped against the sub-group of organisms) has not acquired much currency. The issue discussed in this subsection – understanding idiom (composers' style-development) in terms of an individual-organism life-cycle model – has been rather more thoroughly explored. Yet it is clear that this particular trope, individual organism-idiom, misaligns two levels of Table 1.4, namely level five of nature (individual organism) with level four of culture (idiom); and, moreover, that this misalignment crosses the Genetic/Memetic-Structural-Genetic/Memetic-Cultural boundary. While there is no necessary reason that Table 1.4 is true – it is, as noted in §1.6.2, merely a hypothesis – it is arguably internally coherent and accords with observed structures in nature and culture. As with all analogies, the acid test is whether mappings between such diverse realms can elucidate meaningful similarities, either in support of "hard" scientific or "soft" music-scholarly inquiry. While the alignment-schema proposed in Table 1.4 appears logical in terms of the dynamics between replication hierarchies and the units of selection, music-scholarly discourse has, perhaps unsurprisingly, found the resemblances between a composer's life history (the composer as individual organism) and the "life" of that composer's personal style (his or her idiom as individual "idiom-style-organism", reified in the corpus of his or her works) to be more compelling.

Such life-history/idiom resemblances often seek to map the tripartite youth-maturity-old age sequence of the composer's life against corresponding stylistic phases or periods in his or her creative development. Perhaps not uncoincidentally aligning with the Aristotelian "rule of three" ("*omne trium perfectum*"; everything that comes in threes is perfect), it is common for accounts of composers' creativity to be framed in terms of notions of early, middle and late styles.[175] Commonly, early works are understood as derivative but imbued with a youthful and sometimes reckless audacity; mid-life works represent the consolidation of a distinct personal style in which stability and experimentation are balanced; and late works enter new realms of exploration and reinvention, often suffused with a profoundly spiritual glow.[176] In this trope, the life history of the composer is, moreover, understood as *motivating* the life history of his or her style, in that physical and intellectual development, maturity and decline are understood as in some way causative of analogues in musical style. Indeed, the trope might be understood as "anti-dualistic" (§7.2.2), in that mind and body are seen as tightly interconnected, as opposed to the clear separation insisted upon by dualism.

The outputs of the third and final phase have often provoked the most interest (Said, 2006), given the usual pinnacle of technical and creative achievement

---

[175] This scheme encompasses the third and fourth ("lover", "soldier"), the fifth ("justice'"), and the sixth ("pantaloon") ages, respectively, of the "seven ages of man" outlined in the Melancholy Jaques' "All the world's a stage" monologue in Act II, Scene VII of Shakespeare's *As you like it.*

[176] As Taruskin puts it, "[a]ll composers, even the ones who die in their twenties or thirties, seem to go through the same three periods – early, middle, and late. No prizes for guessing which period always seems to contain the freshest works, the most vigorous, the most profound" (2005, Vol. 1, p. 381).

reached, after a lifetime of experience and practise, towards the end of most composers' lives. As the body declines in later life, there may be an artistic decline, albeit one sometimes tempered by a slight lag, in that the final period of creativity often benefits from the richness of experience afforded by old age before – as in the case of Gluck and Haydn – its depredations rob the composer of the mental and physical vigour to create. Perhaps more so than the first two phases of the Aristotelian trinity, late style often motivates an additional organic-metaphorical alignment of the (three-stage) life-span of a composer and the associated progress of his or her idiom-style-organism with the (four-stage) passage of a year from spring to winter. Reflected, for instance, in the view of Strauss's *Vier letzte Lieder* as "autumnal, luminescent late songs, which contemplate the meaning of death" (Gilliam & Youmans, 2001, sec. 8), late works are often described in terms of a culminating fruitfulness, harvested before the onslaught of winter. Straus (2008) decouples this invernal chill from chronology, understanding it instead in terms of disability – which can, of course, affect composers at any stage of their lives – and arguing that

> in the end *there may be nothing late about late style* in the sense of chronological age, the approach of life's end, or authorial or historical belatedness. Rather, late style may in some cases be more richly understood as *disability style*: a perspective composers may adopt at any age, often in response to a personal experience of disability. (Straus, 2008, p. 6; emphases in the original; see also B. Howe et al., 2015)

Even when the ontogeny of the composer – which may be indeed be shaped by acute or chronic disability – is framed as the driver of music-stylistic development, the artistic outcomes are often conceived as existing quasi-independently of their corporeal foundations, as the products of self-contained organic growth processes. That is, the composer's idiom-style-organism, as the term implies, is depicted an *entity in its own right*, growing, flourishing and dying. Nevertheless, it should be stressed that the ontogeny of a composer's idiom-style-organism, like that of the composer as an individual, is *not in and of itself evolutionary* in the sense understood in this book. Just as Darwinism holds that a single organism cannot itself evolve – only its phenotype can change over time – any changes in a composer's idiom-style-organism are not strictly Darwinian-evolutionary.

Only when an idiom-style-organism is reconciled with the wider dialect – when the former's musemes are understood to be subject to the operation of the VRS algorithm shaping the latter – can idiom-level change be formalised in terms of mechanism rather than metaphor. In their framing in the music-historiographic literature as metaphorically evolutionary, intra-idiom-style-organism changes align most readily with Lamarckian models (§4.3.4). These, as noted in §1.8 and §3.4.3, assign the heavy lifting work of evolution to the active striving of organisms for betterment. Applied to ontogenetic metaphors of composers' styles, this approach sees the composer purposively reshaping his or her creative vocabulary, sometimes with and sometimes without the cooperation of their quasi-independent idiom-style-organism.

Of all western composers, Beethoven has perhaps been the most comprehens-ively discussed in terms of the three-phase life-history model of composer style, even though this division is clearer in some genres (such as the string quartet) than in others (such as the piano sonata), and even though the boundaries between the phases are (as the gradualism of musemic evolution implies) fuzzy rather than distinct.[177] The three-phase model in Beethoven has been consistently aligned with the Classical-to-Romantic *Zeitgeist*-shift encompassed by his life-span (albeit with the inherent problem of divid-ing three by two), with the early works seen as essentially derivative of the Classicism of Haydn and Mozart, and the second and third-period works un-derstood as increasingly Romantic. Despite these "morphological" changes, Beethoven's idiom-style-organism is nevertheless usually seen as possess-ing a unity that transcends the evident changes. As with Stravinsky – the "personality" of whose style is apparent from the Cantata (for the sixtieth birthday of Rimsky-Korsakov) of 1904 to the *Requiem canticles* of 1966 – the personality of Beethoven's style is similarly recognisable from the Cantata on the Death of Emperor Joseph II WoO 87 of 1790 to the String Quartet in F major op. 135 of 1826. While it is a supreme challenge to music theory/ analysis and music psychology to offer an explanation, the (metaphorical)

---

[177] Many commentators place the boundary between the first and second periods around 1802–1803 – coinciding with the acknowledgement of the seriousness of his deafness at Heiligenstadt (Solomon, 1998, Ch. 11) – and that between the second and third periods around 1815–1816 – coinciding with a range of personal crises that occurred around the time of the Congress of Vienna (Solomon, 2003, Ch. 17).

stylistic "DNA" of his idiom-style-organism appears to remain stable even as its "body" ages.

Naturally any alignment between personal and communal style change in Beethoven presupposes (in a crude tripartition): (i) that the composer's idiom-style-organism was (wholly) influenced by its environment of the wider culture (as historiographies of *Kleinmeister* composers generally assume); or (ii) that the converse was the case (a tall order, even for a cultural giant like Beethoven); or (iii) that some combination of the two influences obtained (as would tend to be assumed by most theories of cultural evolution). Again there is a tension here between metaphor and mechanism, in that the former orientation might ascribe disproportionate power to Beethoven's creative persona (scenario (ii)), whereas the latter might understand the composer as being as much influenced (and thus arguably less (r)evolutionary (R. Jones, 2014)) as influencing (scenario (iii)). In a strikingly ahistorical turn, however, Rosen (1997) attempted to overturn received orthodoxies of style-historical alignment between Beethoven's idiom-style-organism and its environment. His thesis was that a variously "classicising" and "proto-romantic" first-period style (1997, pp. 380, 381) gave way, at the onset of the middle period, to a return to full-blooded classicism. On this reading, "with the *Appassionata* he set himself firmly against the squarely organized and yet loose and apparently improvisatory structures of late classicism and early Romanticism, and returned decisively to the closed, concise, and dramatic forms of Haydn and Mozart, expanding these forms and heightening their power without betraying their proportions" (1997, p. 381).

For all its elegance, this interpretation arguably neglects the listener's phenomenological experience of Beethoven's music in favour of the analyst's logical interpretation of its abstract structure, because there is a dissonance between Rosen's insistence on the recuperation and consolidation of a cool and rational classicism and the increasingly intense and fractured subjectivity of the music. As Said insists, after Adorno (2002), "Beethoven's late works remain unreconciled, uncoopted by a higher synthesis: they do not fit any scheme, and they cannot be reconciled or resolved, since their irresolution and unsynthesized fragmentariness are constitutive, neither ornamental nor symbolic of something else" (2006, p. 12; see also Spitzer, 2006). Nevertheless, Rosen's analysis has the advantage of ascribing a quasi-biological unity and coherence to Beethoven's idiom-style-organism: after youthful Romanticist indiscretions, Classical order prevails in his work, even – *contra* Adorno – in the third period, where a Classical focus, via the rubric of the primacy of exploration over expression, is maintained. Thus, "Beethoven is perhaps the first composer for whom this exploratory function of music took precedence over every other: pleasure, instruction, and, even, at times, expression" (Rosen, 1997, p. 445). As will be argued in §4.3.2, this ahistoricism has a deeper motivation: it is the price that must be paid to sustain Rosen's notion of The Classical Style (capitalisations intentional) as *itself an organism* – a "dialect-style-organism" – at a higher structural-hierarchic level than the various idiom-style-organisms, including Beethoven's, that constitute it.

4.3.2 Ontogenetic Metaphors of Historical Styles, Genres and Formal-Structural Types

As implied in point 167 of the list on page 303, the concerns of this section represent a macrocosm of those considered in §4.3.1, in that the waxing and waning of a human life, and its literal and metaphorical connections with the development of a composer's idiom-style-organism, is writ large in accounts of the origin, development, apotheosis, senescence and death of musical styles, genres and formal-structural types as higher-order dialect-style-organisms. Thus, the definition of an idiom-type (idiom-style-organism) by multiple intraopus-style tokens – Memetic-Cultural/Structural levels four and five, respectively, of Table 1.4 – is replicated, at the higher structural-hierarchic level of a dialect-type (dialect-style-organism), by multiple idiom tokens and also by instances of the categories of genre and form-structure – Memetic-Cultural levels three and four, respectively, of Table 1.4.

Genre and formal-structural type are themselves partly contingent upon idiom – they exist concretely via intraopus-style instances in composers' works – and thus, while tokens of dialect, they are also types tokened by specific exemplars.[178] Thus, "sonata form" is a type-abstraction derived

---

[178] There is a conceptual problem with this distinction, one I shall skirt, in that whereas a concrete "car-token", for instance, may capture the abstract type "car" with adequate scope and specificity, an intraopus style-token of idiom, or an idiom-token of dialect, represent only partial (and therefore imperfect) exemplars of the complex higher-order categories they token. Thus, a

from a large class of movements of varying (proto)typicality (Gjerdingen, 1988, pp. 94, 103). Nevertheless, unlike idiom-style-organisms, which imply a distinct end-point at the close of the composer's life,[179] historical styles, genres and formal-structural types (as opposed to their tokens) have, as dialect-style-organisms, indistinct beginnings and endings. As with species, these three categories represent, as interlocking types, a "smeary continuum" (§1.7.3) and not, unlike their tokens, discrete objects whose existence in time is accurately definable.

Owing to this distinction, ontogenetic models of chronological and geographical styles, genres and formal-structural types are conceptually more problematic than ontogenetic models of composers's personal styles, even though the former type are represented in the literature, as illustrated by the dialect-style-organism of The Classical Style conceived by Rosen (1997) considered below. Indeed, only the phylogenetic models of these phenomena considered in §4.3.3 possess sufficient coherence to sustain meaningful analogies, this arguably lacking in the ontogenetic orientation outlined in this subsection. Of course, one must remember that the issues considered here and in the previous and following subsections relate to organic-evolutionary metaphors, not to mechanisms, and that the strength – or, indeed, the weakness – of a metaphor is that it need not be grounded (in whole or in part) in scientific facts. Yet there are two further reasons – in addition to the smeary-continuum issue – for preferring a phylogenetic over an ontogenetic interpretation of the three categories of style, genre and formal-structural type. The first is another instance of the problem of misalignment between hierarchic levels in Table 1.4 raised in §4.3.1. There is a mismatch in the present ontogenetic perspective between nature and culture that also fractures the cultural side of the hierarchy: level five of nature (individual organism) is aligned with both level four (genre and formal-structural type) *and* with level three (dialect, i.e., style) of culture. The second reason for preferring a phylogenetic interpretation is perhaps the more fundamental: as with an ontogenetic view of a composer's idiom-style-organism, the ontogenetic perspective applied to

---

sonata by Mozart, or Mozart's *oeuvre* as a whole, are not necessarily representative of Mozart's *oeuvre* or the classical style, respectively.

[179] A composer's idiom-style-organism may nevertheless persist, if later composers succeed in emulating it, as was the case with the Beethovenian gestures that echoed in much of the music of nineteenth-century composers.

these categories as dialect-style-organism is also *not in and of itself evolutionary*, whereas the phylogenetic view certainly is, both as a foundation of metaphor and – via memetics – in terms of mechanism.

In Rosen (1997), style, genre and formal-structural type are interconnected and seen in terms of a single-entity life-history – that of The Classical Style as dialect-style-organism.[180] The style, the genres it sustained, and the formal-structural types that underpinned these genres – principally sonata form – constituted an individual and indivisible unity, in that they were mutually supportive and self-sustaining. This is not to say that there is no trace of the phylogenetic metaphor in Rosen's narrative; rather, the ontogenetic is overwhelmingly predominant. Rosen's ascription of dialect-style-organism status to The Classical Style rests on his implication that it had sufficient identity for its attributes to be defined, although the smeary continuum issue means he is unwilling or unable to specify its start- and end-points. Instead, he identifies significant early flowerings (such as Mozart's Piano Concerto in E♭ major K. 271 (1777) (1997, p. 59)) and late fruitings (such as Schubert's Symphony no. 9 in C major D. 944 (1828) (1997, p. 521)) of the dialect-style-organism, painting the former, somewhat heroically, as breaking free of the outmoded constraints of the Baroque; and representing the latter, somewhat nostalgically, as resisting the enervating tide of the Romanticism of the 1830s (Rosen, 1995, see also). By such linkages, he implies that the significant differences between such works (certainly in their sound-content), and their very different socio-cultural contexts, are transcended by an overarching stylistic unity. This represents a higher-level manifestation of the unity evident in the early and late works of a single composer (as in the cases of Beethoven and Stravinsky discussed on page 307). Thus, as the works of composers are typical of their parent idiom-style-organism, so a dialect-style-organism can be understood to possess a similarly stable (metaphorical) stylistic "DNA", even though the sound-world, and the associated socio-cultural contexts, of the works of different composers may differ greatly.

---

[180] I should concede that, more so than in any other part of §4.3 and §4.4, I am to some extent constructing an implicit metaphor, rather than, as elsewhere in these sections, attempting to illuminate ones that are, to a large extent, made explicit by their authors.

In biology, one of the most important functions an individual organism must perform is to separate itself from its environment: it must draw a clear distinction between that which is part of itself and that which is not, because the regulation of "self", which is complex and demanding enough, must be distinguished from the regulation of "other", which, lying outside the boundaries of self, is vastly greater and more intractable. What comes across very strongly in Rosen (1997) is the sense of The Classical Style as a distinct entity with attributes that both defined it and, in doing so, that regulated its separation from those styles – framed as "other" – that bookended it. With this distinction comes identity, and with identity comes agency, in the sense that the dialect-style-organism is presented as regulating its existence, resisting and eliminating those elements that threaten its local chronological and geographical stability and its global unity. Such self-regulation in living organisms – homeostasis – acts when a system in a previously stable state is perturbed in some way. Corrective processes, in the form of negative feedback mechanisms (where movement in one direction is countered by balancing movement in the opposite direction), are initiated, which restore the system to its default, optimal state (Gonzaga, 2020). Homeostasis is an organism's way of resisting an increase in entropy. Formalised by the Second Law of Thermodynamics, entropy, from the Greek for "transformation", is a "quantitative expression of the degree of disorder or randomness" of a system (Ligrone, 2019, p. 478), and – as modelled by Information Theory (Shannon, 1948) – is therefore proportional to the amount of information needed to describe it. As a "non-isolated system" (Ligrone, 2019, p. 478), an organism's homeostatic regulation will eventually fail: the amount of entropy in the system will become too great for homeostatic mechanisms to counteract. Mortality reflects the grim certainty that there eventually comes a point of no return, resulting from a series of unmanageable cascade failures, that ultimately brings about an organism's death.

In Rosen's formulation of The Classical Style, the regulatory "quasi-homeostasis" is inscribed in certain musical processes that are taken as constitutive of the style. Specifically, the very survival of the dialect-style-organism is contingent upon its controlled accommodation of a tripartite process of stasis-tension-resolution. Tonal-harmonic tension is the source of the energy that drives the style, but it must be accommodated quasi-homeostatically within a context of stability, lest it break its bounds and give rise to chaos and disorder.[181] Stasis-tension-resolution processes operate at several structural-hierarchic levels of the dialect-style-organism, but they are found most axiomatically in sonata form. Perhaps more accurately, the sonata *principle* (Carter, 1987, p. 89) serves as a kind of container – a cell membrane, as it were – for a number of "music-chemical reactions". Chief among these is the tonic-dominant modulation found in the exposition of a sonata-form movement and the polarity, coded as both structural and expressive, that ensues. The sonata principle also effects the organismic interconnection between style, genre and formal-structural type intrinsic to this metaphor, in that it underwrites the most important formal scheme of The Classical Style, which is a default in all but a few (Baroque-residual) genres.

This music-chemical reaction – which engenders a music-dramatic "arc of beauty" – serves in Rosen's model variously as a high-level driver of the style's philosophical and technical motivations (in a top-down reading) and/or as a low-level generator of those motivations (in a bottom-up reading). The move-ment from an established tonic (stasis) to an unstable dominant (tension) and then back to the original tonic (resolution) is perhaps the most funda-mental gesture of the dialect-style-organism, whether it is encompassed by a short phrase (in which case the music may move, to recall Tovey's useful prepositional distinction, *on*(*to*) the dominant), or whether it governs the un-folding of a whole movement (in which case the movement is generally *in*(*to*) the dominant) (2015, p. 17). As the most elegant example of the symmetry underpinning this process, restoration of the tonic is usually associated with the subsequent introduction of the subdominant – the "antidominant", in Tovey's phrase (2015, p. 6; see also Rosen, 1988, p. 288; Rosen, 1997, p. 79) – before the final tonic closure, which renders the whole arc a zero-sum pro-cess: one step clockwise on the circle of fifths (seven semitones) is undone by one step of the same size anticlockwise, so 0 (stasis) $+7$ (tension) $+0 - 7 + 0$ (resolution) $= 0$. As Tovey puts it, "[s]tepping on to or into the dominant is

---

[181] Moving beyond this metaphorical use of these two concepts, and owing to their applic-ability to the issue of expectation (and all its structural and expressive correlates), entropy and Information Theory underpin a growing literature in music theory and analysis. See, for example, Knopoff and Hutchinson (1981), Margulis and Beatty (2008) and Febres and Jaffe (2017).

an active measure like walking towards the vanishing point [of a painting]; subsiding into the subdominant indicates recession and repose" (2015, p. 6).

Even movements written later in the dialect-style-organism's history, in the early-nineteenth century, and that deviate from this canonical form of the music-dramatic arc, can be understood as fundamentally conformant with it. The first movement of Beethoven's "Waldstein" Sonata of 1804, for example, modulates in the second subject group (b. 35) not to the then still normative dominant, but to the mediant (E major; four steps away from the tonic on the circle of fifths). Rosen accommodates this seeming anomaly via his concept of the "substitute dominant" – a harmony that, while not the true dominant, fulfils the same structural role as it (1997, p. 33). Owing to their relative remoteness from the tonic, such substitutes – the lexicon in Beethoven is (in major-key movements) III, VI (as in the first movement of the Triple Concerto) and (in minor-key movement) ♭VI (as in the first movement of the Ninth Symphony) – a more forceful process of resolution is needed.[182] In the "Waldstein", this resolution is accomplished by bringing the opening chorale-like theme of the second subject group (for which it stands metonymically) back initially in A major (b. 196) – a non-metaphorical exaptation of the "−7" V–I move, here from III to VI – before shifts to A minor (b. 200) and then C major (b. 203). The tonic is nailed down, and thus resolution clinched unequivocally, by a final statement of the chorale theme in the coda (b. 284).

Rosen's extended analysis of Beethoven's "Hammerklavier" Sonata of 1818 (1997, pp. 404–434), the longest segment in the book dedicated to a single work, identifies another key facet of the style, one intimately bound up with the tonic-(substitute) dominant polarity: its concern with motivic logic. As a general principle of this dialect-style-organism, a work's tonal-harmonic structure is usually integrated with, indeed impelled by, its motivic content, a phenomenon most clearly evident in the works of Haydn and Beethoven. In the "Hammerklavier", this integration is represented by a systematic motivic focus on the interval of a third, evident on the most cursory glance at its main themes, its connecting passages and its accompanying figures. Indeed,

---

[182] All the substitute dominants used by Beethoven are (sub)mediants, being a third, major or minor, above or below the tonic (Rosen, 1997, p. 33). As such, they are early symptoms of the growing importance of third-relationships in the nineteenth century and the concomitant gradual breakdown of diatonic organisation (Cohn, 1996). See also §7.5.

"the use of descending thirds is almost obsessive, ultimately affecting every detail in the work" (1997, p. 407). Following up the implications of this statement, Rosen goes on to connect the surface-level motivic third-patterns with the deeper tonal-harmonic structure, noting that the key-scheme of each movement is itself governed by sequences of falling thirds.[183] In this way, a connection is read between local and global structure that, while taken to its extreme in the "Hammerklavier", is framed by Rosen as broadly characteristic of the dialect-style-organism as a whole.

This brief summary of Rosen's account of the "Hammerklavier" Sonata is not to be taken as implying his straying into a narrative of the work as organism (§4.4.1), although this is certainly not an untenable interpretation in an entity as rigorously unified and systematic as this sonata. Rather, the intention is to see the "Hammerklavier" as fundamentally typical of (tokening) the style (the type), for all that it represents an extreme point of concentration. While it may not inhabit the same sound-world as a Mozart comic opera or a Haydn piano trio (both subjects of chapters in Rosen (1997)), it stems from the same impulses that sustain the "body", to adapt Spitzer's (2004) concept, of the dialect-style-organism more broadly.

As a final point, and just as the late works of composers have often received detailed critical attention, so the late phase of The Classical Style is given a particularly focused treatment by Rosen. He is especially concerned with certain of Beethoven's works from the middle of the second decade of the nineteenth century, such as the song cycle *An die ferne Geliebte* (1816) – "a sport among his forms" (1997, p. 379)[184] – and the Piano Sonata in A major op. 101 of the same year. To these works, Rosen imputes a quality of improvisatory poetic freedom, "a movement towards the open forms of the Romantic period", characterised by an "unclassical looseness" (1997, p. 403). Their impact on the Romantic Style (if it truly warrants the same nominalisa-

---

[183] The first movement's "structural" key-scheme is Exposition: I–VI; Development: IV–ii–♮I; Recapitulation: ♭I–♭VI–♮I–♭I. The Fugue moves through the key-scheme I–♭VI–iv–♮I–♮VI–IV–III–♭I (Rosen, 1997, pp. 430–433). As can be seen by comparing the emboldened Roman numerals, the predominantly falling-third key-scheme gives rise to large-scale semitonal conflicts between B♭ major and B♮ minor. See also Busoni (1894, Appendix 3) and note 182 on page 314.

[184] In botany, a sport is a spontaneous morphological variant, as exemplified by the peloric form of the Toadflax flower discussed in §1.8. As with the metaphorical sport represented by *An die ferne Geliebte*, true sports sometimes afford aesthetic benefits to our species, as in the case of the origin of the "Chicago Peace" rose as a pink variant discovered in Illinois of the earlier yellow "Peace" variety.

tion Rosen affords The Classical Style) is evidenced, in part, by citations of a melodic fragment from *An die ferne Geliebte* at key junctures in Schumann's Fantasie in C major (1838), an iconic work from perhaps the leading figure of the first generation of Romantics (1997, pp. 513–514).

While it adopts the same cyclic, unbroken movement-sequence of *An die ferne Geliebte*, Beethoven's String Quartet in C♯ minor op. 131 (1826) represents a kind of purging of the Romantic infection in his works of a decade earlier, although this reading is only hinted at by Rosen (1997, 403, note 1; p. 441). This purification is accomplished – in a virtuosic display of classical symmetry and logic – by relating, "Hammerklavier"-like, the key-scheme of the whole quartet to those tonalities implied by the opening fugue subject and its working out in the first movement. Perhaps such deviations from the architectural rigour of The Classical Style represented by Beethoven's op. 98*An die ferne Geliebte* and op. 101 might be understood, apropos Straus (2008), as a form of disability, or at least an illness, caused by the infection of the style with those corrupting forces that would eventually lead to its destruction. As with all living things, this is an entropic inevitability, only temporarily staved off by op. 131 and other late works of Beethoven that, via their concentration and logic, temporarily reassert the youthful vigour of The Classical Style as dialect-style-organism.

4.3.3 Phylogenetic Metaphors of Historical-Geographical Styles, Genres and Formal-Structural Types

As indicated in point 167 of the list on page 303, this category frames historical styles, genres and formal-structural types in terms of the multiple interconnected life-cycles constituting a species. That is, whereas the mapping considered in §4.3.2 attempted to understand these cultural entities in terms of the ontogeny of a single, unitary organism, the models considered here see them in terms of the phylogeny of multiple, connected organisms. A species might nevertheless be regarded as a "super-organism" (Hull, 1976): a group of independent agents (individuals) whose genetic and morphological similarities are sufficiently close to bind them together to form a reproductive-ecological community that exists as a higher-order entity. The super-organism that is a biological species may be equated to its musical analogues by virtue of certain mappings between part and whole. In the case of genres and formal-structural types, the parts (individual exemplars) are specific tokens of a particular type, for instance, string quartets or sonata forms. In the case of chronological and geographical styles, the parts may be specific works (intraopus style; themselves instances of particular genres or formal-structural types) and/or the idiom of a composer. In terms of the hierarchical alignments of Table 1.4, level three of nature (species, the whole whose component parts are the sub-group and the individual organism at levels four and five of nature, respectively) is equated with level three of culture (dialect, the whole whose component parts are the idiom/genre/formal-structural type and the intraopus style at levels four and five of culture, respectively). Thus, on the basis of Table 1.4, there is greater proximity between metaphor and mechanism when equating a dialect with a species than is the case with the mappings considered in §4.3.1 and §4.3.2.

As suggested in §4.3.2, the arguably greater coherence of a phylogenetic over an ontogenetic conception of these phenomena perhaps accounts for the seemingly greater predominance of the former metaphor over the latter in the literature (but see the qualification given in note 170 on page 297). Zon (2016) considers a number of nineteenth-century writers on music influenced by evolutionary thought in general and by the phylogenetic metaphor in particular. After considering Herbert Spencer's[185] speculations on the origin of music – in contrast to the views of Darwin and to the argument of §2.7, Spencer held that language *preceded* music evolutionarily (2016, p. 125) – Zon moves on to consider a number of "writers on music influenced by evolution" (2016, p. 126).

While those writers whose work is surveyed – in Zon's sequence, Edmund Gurney, Joseph Goddard, Hubert Parry, William Wallace and J. Alfred John-stone – have distinct academic and personal agendas, there are a number of common themes connecting their work that bespeak the influence of an organicist-evolutionary orientation. These themes include the evolutionary precedence of speech *versus* song (a tradition influenced by Spencer), this

---

[185] As an early Universal Darwinian, Spencer advocated the extension of Darwinism to other domains, most notably human society. He developed the notion of "Social Darwinism", now widely discredited as racist and eugenicist, which argued that the "survival of the fittest" (a term Spencer himself coined) should apply as much to social organisation as it does to interactions between competing organisms (M. Taylor, 2007).

being related to the more fundamental question of the distinction between sound/noise and music (2016, p. 127); the origin of the raw materials of music (such as scales and chords), and thus the evolutionary relationship between history and theory (2016, p. 128); the levels at which evolution might be understood to operate in music (2016, p. 132); the evolution of the human aesthetic/emotional faculty for music and its links with perception and cognition, understood in terms of the nature-nurture distinction (2016, p. 141); and, perhaps most pertinent to the concerns of this subsection, the historical evolution of musical styles as driven by the innovations of composers (2016, p. 152). Despite Zon's framing of their work, it should be stressed that many of these writers are not necessarily intending to pursue a metaphorical strategy; rather, they are often genuinely trying to elucidate music's production and reception in terms of unmediated evolutionary ideas because, it seems, they recognised the power of these ideas to elucidate the natural and cultural worlds. Perhaps it is because their approach is often largely speculative rather than rigorously scientific – their background is artistic rather than scientific; their methodologies are generally more qualitative than quantitative; and their available data-sets are limited – that their work lends itself to being understood today more as metaphor than as mechanism.

It is the last of the themes discussed in the preceding paragraph – the role of the composer as a semi-autonomous agent within a larger stylistic collective – that taps most clearly into the phylogenetic metaphor. Parry articulates this perspective clearly in offering a corrective to the cult of genius. He held, in Zon's digest, that

> [t]he great composer is … not simply a great individual, to be applauded by his age, but is to be understood as the sum of evolution to that point in time. He does not compose in splendid isolation, but exploits his gifts in the context of influences, antecedents, progressions, and developments. And as such he is in his own personal development, in microcosm, a metaphor for evolution's historical progress from simplicity to complexity, from limitation to license, from the 'small and insignificant beginnings' to the great masterpieces. In this respect the composer also gradually unshackles himself from the prescription of theory and frees his art from the trappings of conservatism, thus preparing the ground for further advances in evolution. (Zon, 2016, p. 152)

There are several interconnected ideas here that warrant a careful unpacking and comparison with their analogues in biology. First, and blending the two columns of Table 1.4 that have in my treatment been kept separate, there is a view of the composer forming part of a larger whole, engendering a super-organism or "cultural species" consisting of a multitude of distinct creative individuals pursuing broadly similar aesthetic goals – as idiom and dialect made flesh. Secondly, in biological evolution it is the appearance of advantageous variations in individuals (as a result of gene mutations) that are seized upon by selection, if aptive, and preserved into the future, leading to gradual evolutionary change. In cultural evolution, by contrast, such advantageous variations are understood here to arise from the innovations of composers, which – unless one adopts a memetic explanation favouring Campbellian blind variation and selective retention (§3.3.2) – implies a quasi-Lamarckian striving for improvement (§4.3.4). Thirdly, this striving is, in culture, presented by Zon in terms of the virtue of breaking free of certain constraints (variously imposed by tradition or, as discussed further in §4.6, by the prescriptions of theory), whereas in biology the only immutable virtue is replicator survival, which is enhanced by an ever greater fit of the organism to its environment.

Attendant upon the third point, and alluded to in the above passage, is the issue of simplicity *versus* complexity (see also the final point in the next paragraph). In biology, there is no intrinsic advantage accruing to the members of a given replicator system in the ever greater complexity of the vehicles they build; indeed, as noted in the discussion of memetic drive (§3.7.1), the pressure in favour of greater encephalisation is potentially disadvantageous to genes, even as it is potentially advantageous to memes. In culture, however, the verbal-conceptual memeplexes of post-Enlightenment art tend to favour complexity for its own sake – as an aesthetic virtue – which tends to create an evolutionary arms-race between composer-agents.[186]

---

[186] This last point relates to Dahlhaus's assertion that "[s]ome work of art flawed from the point of view of perfection may be significant from the point of view of greatness" (1982, p. 88). The significance, from an evolutionary perspective, inheres in the "great" work of art's "unshackling" itself (in the terms of Zon's account of Parry) from some set of constraints. This violation constitutes a "license" not accessible to the "perfect" work, which, as the price of its perfection, must conform to certain "limitations".

Fourthly, the reference to "preparing the ground for further advances in evolution" represents a (non-memetic) formulation of cumulative selection (§1.7.3): by analogy with the incremental variation driving the gradualism of biological evolution, the seeming innovations of composers build upon the achievements of their predecessors, and also lay the foundations for future developments. Finally, in seeing the composer as "in his own personal development, in microcosm, a metaphor for evolution's historical progress from simplicity to complexity", Parry's idea, via Zon (2016), is a paraphrase of the notion advanced by Haeckel that "ontogeny recapitulates phylogeny". The latter's "Recapitulation Theory" (§4.4.1.1) argues that the development of an organism (ontogeny) replays the evolutionary history (phylogeny) of the species to which it belongs. Put another way, the (ontogenetic) metaphor of the composer's creative life-history (§4.3.1) is itself a metaphor for the (phylogenetic) metaphor of a stylistic community as a cultural species.

While the latter, dialect-species, metaphor is broadly conformant with Table 1.4 and sustains the historiographic traditions to which the nineteenth-century authors identified above contributed, certain difficulties arise – as with the two ontogenetic metaphorical frameworks considered previously – when one moves beyond a merely cursory analogy. In particular, if the metaphor is is to be coherent and illuminating in conceiving a cultural species (as thought and/or as flesh)[187] in terms of its life-history (the chronological/diachronic dimension) and its location in a specific cultural-ecological niche (the geographical/synchronic dimension, this to some extent overlapping with the music-theoretical/-analytical issues considered in §4.4.3), then it is necessary for the metaphor to account for the circumstances of the cultural species' origin and demise, and for it to formalise the structural-hierarchic level-mappings of the species' constituent parts, respectively. In music historiography, these issues have been considered in terms of the rubric of style-periodisation (which has both a diachronic and a synchronic dimension), but they apply more broadly to genre and formal-structural type, and also to related domains such as the historical and geographical specificity of systems of tonal organisation, as

---

[187] It will be understood that framing a dialect in terms of thought (i.e., the transmission of ideas) gravitates towards a mechanistic (memetic) interpretation; whereas understanding it in terms of flesh (i.e, the actions of composer-agents) aligns more closely with a metaphorical reading.

dialect-related phenomena (§7.5).[188] Thus, and notwithstanding the proviso made on page 310 that a metaphor need not be grounded in scientific facts, it is legitimate to ask how phylogenetic metaphors of historical styles, genres and formal-structural types might be enriched by developing connections with phenomena in biology. Perhaps more so than the metaphor-categories considered in §4.3.1 and §4.3.2, this category gravitates strongly towards its own foundation in science. Indeed, such reification represents the rationalistic advance of mechanism over metaphor.

The issue considered at the end of §4.3.2 – the late phase of The Classical Style – serves as a microcosm of the diachronic and synchronic problems outlined above. When the previous ontogenetic model (the Style as dialect-style-organism) is reformulated in terms of phylogeny, the resulting "dialect-style-species" is just as mortal and transient as the dialect-style-organism, but the (metaphorical) manner of its demise must necessarily be different. Unlike the unequivocal end of an idiom-style-organism, both dialect-style-organisms and dialect-style-species dissolve slowly away, like the vanishing grin of the Cheshire Cat in *Alice's adventures in wonderland* (L. Carroll, 1993, p. 88). But whereas The Classical Style as dialect-style-organism might be understood as having metaphorically withered away owing to the entropic depredations of old age, it is not clear how the same entity as dialect-style-species met its fate. In the terms of the dialect-as-cultural-species metaphor (as thought not flesh), three possibilities (at least) suggest themselves. The style may have: (i) come to an end as the result of an extinction event, to be followed by the rapid historical and geographical ingress of a new cultural species (Romanticism) that occupied the same cultural-environmental niche; (ii) been challenged on its own "territory" by the new, external, species and eventually driven to extinction; or (iii) become transformed in response to environmental pressures into the new species through evolution.

---

[188] Even when considered without the intercession of (evolutionary) metaphors, periodic views of music history – Adler's *"Geschichte der Musik nach Epochen"* ("history of music according to epochs") (1885, p. 16) – are problematic. They are undermined, for example, by the existence of mutually dissonant parallel categories (contradictory paradigms), such as the galant style's (Gjerdingen, 2007a) coexistence, in the middle third of the eighteenth century, with the Baroque and the Classical styles (insofar as any of these three styles are discrete entities). Moreover, the tendency of style-periodic views to downgrade certain composers – such as Domenico Scarlatti and C. P. E. Bach – as essentially "transitional" risks skewing our understanding of their significance by subordinating them to an inflexible categorical frame. In the case of Beethoven, this tendency to categorise has the effect of undermining the genuine and powerful transitionality of his style.

Aside from the ever-present smeary-continuum issue, building meaningful phylogenetic metaphors for the diachronic and synchronic dimensions of music requires addressing the fact that there are different approaches to defining a species in biology, and so any metaphor that is parasitic on this concept must attempt, however, imperfectly, to come to terms with the implications of these approaches. In other words, phylogenetic metaphors can be finessed and buttressed by means of an appeal to mechanism, but only when the metaphor remains within the boundaries of a single definition, or is regulated by a coherent alignment of definitions. In Ridley's formulation, species may be defined in terms of: (i) *biology* (members of a species are capable of interbreeding with each other but not with members of other species); (ii) *ecology* (members of a species occupy a specific environmental-ecological niche); or (iii) *phenetics* (members of a species share certain physical characteristics, these potentially forming the basis of taxonomies; see the list on page 48) (2004, pp. 351–355). Critiquing the three metaphors for the demise of The Classical Style outlined in the previous paragraph – i.e., (i) extinction-replacement; (ii) challenge-extinction; and (iii) mutation – requires at least some mechanistic contextualisation. The following list offers a preliminary framework for this:

Biological: there is no direct cultural equivalent to the restricted breeding implied by biological conceptions of speciation. Provided composers have means of accessing others' works, such as are afforded by publishing and by more recent technologies of dissemination, then interbreeding – which can be coded metaphorically as the influence of often very different styles upon each other, and mechanistically as museme-transmission between individuals – can readily occur across cultural-ecological boundaries.

Ecological: the existence of national styles – most notably the Italian, French and German styles in the eighteenth century (Ratner, 1980, p. 335) – suggest that cultural-ecological niches in the form of urban centres and their associated musical infrastructures can sustain different cultural species, understood as schools or traditions of composition. The "migration" of a composer from one tradition-centre to another can create a metaphorical speciation event, such as in the case of those numerous eighteenth-century Italian composers who left their native cities and established stylistic "islands" in foreign lands and amid alien styles. This definition-category is perhaps more contingent than the other two upon socio-cultural and socio-economic factors – upon musico-operational/procedural memes and verbal-conceptual memeplexes mediating the production and reception, respectively, of native and foreign styles.

Phenetic: resemblances between the "individuals" of a cultural species depend, of course, upon how one defines these individuals and how one calibrates resemblance. The categories of genre and formal-structural type lend themselves, through the rubric of (proto)typicality, to this comparison; but the nuances intrinsic to music mean that superficial resemblances can often mask more subtle differences, such as the very different practices of composers who ostensibly all employ sonata form. As in biological taxonomy, a phylogenetic/cladistic orientation (§1.7.2) may help to finesse this category.

Seen in these terms, the three scenarios for the demise of The Classical Style as dialect-style-species might be understood as drawing on the categories of biology, ecology and phenetics, respectively: (i) extinction-replacement implies the lack of reproductive vigour and the inability to interbreed with, or the capacity to out-breed, insurgent challenger styles; (ii) challenge-extinction implies the ingress of a rival style better adapted to the prevailing cultural-environmental niche; and (iii) mutation implies a gradual *in situ* stylistic reconfiguration. The received historiographic formulation of the The Classical Style's late-historical context holds that Vienna, as the *locus* of the Style, became politically and culturally less important – because of the political and linguistic emancipation of its vassal states (and the associated rise of competing nationalisms), the decline of aristocratic patronage, a general coarsening of public taste resulting from (or leading to) the growth of more "socially" orientated genres, and the absence of a "great" composer based there between the death of Schubert in 1828 and the arrival of Brahms in 1862 – being supplanted in terms of esteem and vibrancy by Paris and by the German centres in which Romanticism flourished (Antonicek et al., 2001, sec. 5(i)). This reading perhaps tends to favour metaphors grounded on a predominantly biological-ecological interpretation: The Classical Style died out – in terms of thought and flesh – and newer, insurgent, traditions successfully filled the cultural niche it left behind.

Perhaps the overriding conclusion here, one relevant to phylogenetic metaphors drawing upon any of the above three species-definitions, is that the level of granularity a metaphor incorporates has a significant effect upon both its structure and the interpretations it motivates. In culture as in nature, what seems to resemble saltationism (single-step selection) when viewed telescopically becomes gradualistic (cumulative selection) when viewed microscopically (§1.7.3). Whether conceived in terms of biology, ecology or phenetics, the chronological-stylistic gap between The Classical Style and Romanticism might, on the former perspective, seem to constitute a form of metaphorical punctuated equilibrium; but at a finer level of resolution, the steps connecting these dialect-style-species become individually insignificant.

4.3.4 Lamarckism *versus* Darwinism in Music Historiography

Parallel distinctions have been made between Lamarckian and Darwinian models of evolution in nature §1.8 and between the same two models of evolution in culture §3.4.3. To contextualise their applications in music historiography, it is necessary to make a further sub-distinction within the latter (cultural) category, namely between:

1. the *non-metaphorical* (i.e., the real/mechanistic) operation of Lamarckian or Darwinian *processes* driving the observed cultural-evolutionary changes in music-historiographic discourses over time (§3.4.3); and

2. the *metaphorical* (i.e., the virtual/non-mechanistic) applications of Lamarckian and Darwinian tropes in music historiography in order to illuminate aspects of musical change over time.

The first of these two perspectives will be expanded upon in §4.6, whereas the second will be explored briefly here, albeit with some appeals to mechanism in order to provide a grounding for metaphorical applications of Darwinism and Lamarckism.

Like the giraffe elongating its neck in Lamarckian accounts of evolution by striving to reach the highest, juiciest leaves on a tree and then passing on this acquired characteristic to its offspring (see page 56), composers have often been understood to have striven to reach new heights of technical and expressive power. Perhaps more realistically – and foregrounding tactics over strategy[189] – they have striven to nibble away at specific technical challenges and then passed these acquired characteristics on to those who came after them. In this sense, music historiography, as with historiography more generally, has often adopted a loosely Lamarckian approach, albeit not always explicitly. Exemplified by the passage from Zon (2016) cited on page 318, it has framed the progression of musical styles, genres, and formal-structural types in terms of largely intentional processes of improvement, the fruits of which have then nourished later generations. While the question of agency is important – one cannot deny a desire on the part of composers, certainly those working in Europe after *c.* 1750, to develop and progress their art – also at issue, for metaphor as for mechanism, is the distinction between replicators and vehicles (§1.6.1), and the associated question of the relevant units of selection (§1.6.2). While the two evolutionary models often do not exist metaphorically as a stark binarism, the orientation in relation to these three issues – agency (tactical more than strategic) *versus* "blindness" (in Campbell's sense), replicators *versus* vehicles, and the units of selection – determines whether the historiographic account is broadly Lamarckian or whether it is more characteristically Darwinian.

In a mechanistic Darwinian view, there is a clear distinction between a transient vehicle – Weismann's soma line – and an immortal replicator – his germ line. In a memetic view of musical culture, this devolves to the distinction between a work – which is transient in the sense that the set of elements that comprise its physical manifestation will never again align in exactly the same way – and the musemes (the aforementioned elements) that comprise it – which are immortal in the sense of their surviving across time by inveigling themselves into the brains of composers, often ahead of those with whom they previously collaborated in a work (see also §3.4.3). This binarism accounts for both poiesis and progress, in the sense that it encompasses the assemblage of musemes in the former and their evolution, via the VRS algorithm, in the latter. As well as, in effect, ignoring the replicator (memome)-vehicle (phemotype) distinction, attempts to invoke Darwinism

---

[189] By this is meant that the composer may have a general sense of the specific technical problem that needs to be solved (akin to the Giraffe's apprehension of the fugitive leaves), and an idea of how the problem might be tackled (akin to the Giraffe's instinct or intuition that it must stretch its neck to reach them), but no clear sense of the wider historical-stylistic implications of finding a solution (akin to the Giraffe's lack of comprehension of the (Lamarckian) effect its exertions might have on its lineage in the future).

metaphorically in music historiography tend concomitantly to sit at an unrealistically high unit-level of selection, whereby works are presented as in some sense surviving in culture *en bloc*. That is, they are regarded as an irreducible whole influencing later composers owing to the fitness – their aptation to their cultural environment – arising from inherent expressive-stylistic attributes. Moreover, such quasi-Darwinian historiography is sometimes reluctant to make such metaphors more fully conformant with Darwinism's blindness, by framing the fitness of a work as relying on some degree of intentional (Lamarckian) striving on the part of the composer.

Aside from its certainty over agency, there is in a mechanistic Lamarckian view a confusion – perhaps more so than in metaphorical Darwinism – over the distinction between replicators and vehicles, and an attendant lack of clarity on what constitute the relevant units of selection. Thus, because Lamarck did not fully hypothesise a mechanism for evolution[190] there is arguably little substantive difference between mechanistic and metaphorical applications of Lamarckism to culture. In the metaphorical Lamarckism of some traditions of music historiography, the blurring of the replicator/vehicle distinction and the augmentation of the unit of selection is evident in the "body" of the "parent" style, genre, formal-structural type, composer or work itself being assimilated by the "child" generation, not any of the antecedent's particulate constituents. Indeed, the process is essentially inscrutable and mystical because what is assimilated is less a musical "body" and more its irreducible essence – its "soul" or "spirit" (a *Werkgeist*). Moreover, and assuming a distinction can indeed be made between tactical agency and blindness, both mechanistic and metaphorical Lamarckism involve a sighted process of intentional striving – either on the part of the composer or mystically impelled by the *Werkgeist* – not the blind accidents of mechanistic and metaphorical Darwinism.

---

[190] Darwin, pushed towards a more Lamarckian orientation by criticism of his theory of natural selection (see page 57), hypothesised the Theory of Pangenesis (after the Ancient Greek philosopher Democritus), ascribing a key role to acquired-characteristic-transmitting particles called "gemmules" (J. Miller & Van Loon, 2010, pp. 140–142).

4.4 Evolutionary Metaphors in Music Theory and Analysis

As implied in §4.1, music theory constitutes one of the largest bodies of human knowledge, having been pursued continuously for nearly three millennia. It is impossible to give a sense of its scale and breadth here, given that all major human civilisations have contributed to it, some – the ancient Chinese and Greek cultures, the European late-eighteenth to mid-twentieth centuries – with particular determination and rigour. As an implementation of music theory, music analysis is a rather more recent pursuit, coalescing in the mid-eighteenth century as a result of the socio-cultural factors considered in §4.1.

Three of the key evolutionary metaphor-constellations invoked in music theory and analysis to be considered here – the first itself encompassing three sub-constellations – are:

The Work as Organism: whereby (i) the *embryological* phase of ontogeny is taken as a model for the origin (in Nattiez's (1990) sense of poiesis) of a movement or work; (ii) the *diachronic unfolding* of a movement or work is framed as equivalent to ontogenetic processes of growth, maturation, senescence and death; and (iii) the *synchronic structure* of a movement or work is understood, by means of the principle of division of labour, as functionally analogous to that of a multicellular/multi-organ organism.

The Motive as Organism: whereby motivic-thematic development within a movement or work is ascribed agency and read in terms of evolutionary change.

Tones and Tonality as Organisms: whereby the governing tonic of a movement or work is seen as being engaged in a struggle for supremacy with other keys as the music unfolds.

These three constellations are explored, respectively, in the following subsections. As noted in §4.3 apropos ontogenetic models, because evolution is a process that connects several organisms in time – in a Darwinian (but not a Lamarckian) view, an individual organism does not evolve; rather, the species of which it is a member does – evolutionary metaphors have perhaps gained more traction in (phylogenetically orientated) music historiography than in music theory and analysis. In the latter two traditions, and particularly in analysis, evolution is often understood in terms of various alignments between ontogeny and phylogeny, and via a particular focus on organicism – and associated ideas of logic and coherence – which is often used metonymically to stand for evolution.

4.4.1 The Work as Organism

Organicism – understanding a movement or work of music (and indeed exemplars of other art-forms) in terms of analogies with or equivalences to living organisms – is a defining literary-critical and music-theoretical/analytical trope of the long nineteenth century, albeit one with roots stretching back to the late-seventeenth century and ultimately to antiquity (Solie, 1980, p. 147). Among its adherents, a fundamental distinction can be made between those who saw artistic works as *metaphorically* akin to living organisms, and those who regarded them as part of a more fundamental *continuity* with the world of biological entities. The latter category includes philosophers from the Idealist tradition, which maintained that "reality exists in the ideal realm and not in the finite world of objects.... the point of calling something 'organic' was not to describe the arrangement of its physical attributes but, on the contrary, to elevate it to a status transcendent of the physical" (Solie, 1980, pp. 149, 150).[191] Thus, while a living organism and a work of art are materially different in the "finite world of objects", they were held to share certain commonalities in the "ideal realm", and it is these commonalities – a sense of logical interconnectedness of parts and whole, the (synchronic) indivisibility of the whole, and the (diachronic) rationality of the work's unfolding in time – that the organicist tradition of criticism seeks to elucidate, particularly those who adopt the "second perspective" on organic unity discussed on page 333 below.

The preconditions for regarding the work as a quasi-living entity were a subset of those listed on page 292 as necessary for the development of music analysis itself, most importantly the appearance of the work concept and the development of the aesthetic perspective it sustained (Dahlhaus, 1982). A corollary to this is that non-notated musics – including folk musics and

---

[191] See §7.8 and the quotation on page 623 for further discussion of this idea.

improvised traditions – have not generally been understood in terms of organicist metaphors. Nevertheless, that we often speak of the performance of non-notated musics, of improvisation, and indeed of non-studio recordings of music as "live" suggests that an ascribed quality of organic agency or potentiality is not restricted to the canonic works of the common-practice period.[192] Those works most amenable to an organicist reading arguably first appeared in the mid-eighteenth century, a time when a functionalist view of art was giving way to one based upon the disinterested contemplation of aesthetic objects, each seen as distinct and individual, despite its drawing on common principles of structure and expression (Gjerdingen, 2007a).[193] The following Romantic age attempted to relate the organicism of the work to the genius of its creator by seeing the latter as "a kind of vessel for the life forces of art or inspiration" (Solie, 1980, p. 156), rather than as the rational, intentional craftsman of the eighteenth-century conception. While arising from a quite different intellectual tradition, the Romantic view of the artist as conduit is not dissimilar to that advanced by memetics, with its notions of the human brain as a repository for memes, and of human consciousness as itself a meme-product (§7.3).

Outside the Ideal realm, there are various issues for criticism generally, and for music theory and analysis specifically, that arise when attempting to understand music in terms of living organisms. First, difficulties often stem from a confusion between, or conflation of, the poietic level – i.e., organicism applied to illuminate the generative processes giving rise to a work of music – and the (for the purposes of this analysis amalgamated) neutral and esthesic levels – i.e., organicism read in the structure of a work in its finished form and the listener's response to it. Secondly, this poietic-neutral/esthesic dichotomy is sometimes associated with a separate confusion between the diachronic and synchronic dimensions of music. At the poietic level, a piece of music is often not assembled linearly (i.e., quasi-diachronically), because there

---

[192] Perhaps this is to conflate the notion of music's having organicism with its having agency. While related (§4.4.2, §4.4.3), they are nevertheless distinct concepts.

[193] Dahlhaus identifies five phases of European music history since the Renaissance: (i) functionalism (*c.* 1550—*c.* 1650); (ii) the doctrine of the affections (*Affektenlehre*) (*c.* 1650—*c.* 1750); (iii) the aesthetics of individual expression (*c.* 1750—*c.* 1850); (iv) formalism (*c.* 1850—*c.* 1950); and (v) the notion of works documenting the processes that led to their inception (*c.* 1950—) (1983, pp. 20–23). Associated with stages (iii) and (iv) is a move from musicians' "scripting performances" – stages (i) and (ii) – to their "composing concepts" (Emily Worthington, personal communication).

is usually some input to the generative process of an overall conception or model of the intended work, this often deriving from influences above the level of intraopus style. At the neutral and esthesic levels, musical works can exist diachronically, as real or imagined performances (the latter with or without the aid of a score), and also synchronically, as atemporal impressions ("seeing" the whole conception in one "take"). Thirdly, there are, as discussed in §4.3, differing views on the hierarchic alignment between nature and culture. Table 1.4 offers one scheme, and while acknowledging that it represents merely a hypothesis, it possesses a certain internal logic that is not always found in music-theoretical/analytical discourse, with its tendency, as with historiography, for often significant misalignments between levels. Examples of such mis-mappings include Schenker's equation of single notes (level eight of culture in Table 1.4) and Reti's correlation of musical patterns (musemes; level seven of culture) with the individual organism (level five of nature).

These issues, and the subsections below in which they are addressed, might be formalised as follows, which is organised according to the intersecting axes of poietic/neutral-esthesic and synchronic/diachronic. The latter axis is expanded to incorporate the structural-hierarchic; thus, the diachronic equates to the linear/sequential, the synchronic equates to the static/synoptic, and the structural-hierarchic integrates the diachronic and synchronic under the rubric of shallow/deep:

Poietic Level

- *Diachronic*: Aside from the case of improvisation (§3.5.3), composition is rarely a linear-sequential process (comparable to the real-time unfolding of a twelve-note row), and steps taken can always be reversed; so the generation of a movement is not analogous to the one-way ontogeny of living things (§4.4.1.1).

- *Synchronic*: A composer may plan a movement by (re)conceiving its abstract generalities before (re)formulating its concrete particularities, and may (re)develop its parts non-linearly before (re)assembling them sequentially into a whole; whereas ontogeny presupposes a strict commitment to implementing a pre-established developmental schema (§4.4.1.3).

- *Structural-Hierarchic*: The aetiology of specific pitches and pitch-groupings, and their structural-hierarchic location within a movement, aligns only imperfectly with the ontogenetic interconnection of the structural-functional units of an organism (§4.4.2, §4.4.3).

Neutral and Esthesic Levels

- *Diachronic*: A movement unfolds perceptually-cognitively in time in a developmental manner that is not directly analogous to the homeostatic stability of a living organism; nor is this unfolding directly analogous to the life-cycle of a living organism. The latter analogy presupposes, among other things, a temporal disparity, whereby an organism's life-cycle, often measured in decades, is equated with the "life-cycle" of a piece of music, often measured in minutes (§4.4.1.2).

- *Synchronic*: A movement has a synoptic configuration – a set of parts that exist to some extent abstractly and atemporally – that is only imperfectly analogous to the functional/systemic hierarchies of a living organism (§4.4.1.3).

- *Structural-Hierarchic*: The function of specific pitches and pitch-groupings, and their structural-hierarchic location within a movement, aligns only imperfectly with the morphology, physiology or behaviour of an organism (§4.4.2, §4.4.3).

A key tenet of organicism is the notion of (organic) unity, sometimes termed organic coherence. Like many elements of organicism, the concept is not without its complications, given that most works of art attempt to reconcile unity with diversity, lest unremitting one-ness renders the work anodyne. The unity-diversity dichotomy maps loosely onto that between coherence and incoherence, and also that between predictability and unpredictability, the latter two binarisms being as much perceptual-psychological (esthesic), and indeed information-theoretic, as they are artistic-generative (poietic). Of course, these three dichotomies are not restricted to intra-work factors, but are also mediated by extra-work (stylistic) considerations. Indeed, while they arise from the perception and cognition of individual works by natural constraints, the dichotomies are also calibrated with reference to nurtural factors, including those stylistic regularities abstracted through statistical learning of the works constituting a dialect.

As an epiphenomenon of modernism, it is perhaps unsurprising that organicism has come under sustained assault from postmodernism, even while the evolutionary theory upon which organicism is parasitic has, if anything, consolidated its position as the supreme metanarrative of human epistemology. Street notes, apropos music analysis, that "by supposing an organic link with both perception and external reality, [organicists hold that] music … might be understood as capable of converting culture into nature" (1989, p. 82). He offers a postmodern critique of organicism based on the premise that, "ubiquity apart, the unifying urge is by no means immune to doubt. Indeed, far from demonstrating its objectivity in every case, the same ideal constantly succeeds in exposing its own arbitrariness" (1989, p. 80). Morgan, reviewing a selection of analyses of music by a number of scholars whose work advances Street's "opposition to unity" by "asserting disunity" (2003, pp. 7, 42), attempts to recuperate organicism by arguing that these analyses

> draw a common false conclusion: that the compositions they consider contain unbridgeable conflicts and inconsistencies, defying rational explication.… I have attempted to uncover unifying elements that suggest they are wrong. I do not believe, however, that these elements reside 'objectively' in the compositions, or that they represent 'natural' attributes, but only that they are demonstrably linked to perceptible features of the music. (Morgan, 2003, p. 42)

It seems that many of the complications attendant upon organicism that Street (1989) attempts to unpick – and that Morgan (2003) subsequently tries to restitch – result from what the latter terms "predispositions" (2003, p. 42). That is one might undertake a "unity-oriented analysis" or, by extension, a "disunity-oriented analysis" (2003, p. 42), the multiparametric richness (Morgan's "perceptible features") of music sustaining a multitude of "plots" subsumed within these two strategies or situated on a continuum between them (Nattiez, 1985). In this sense, predispositions are verbal-conceptual memeplexes that articulate biases or, frankly, prejudices, of various kinds guiding what music analysis should attempt to "find". My purpose here is not, however, to assess the truth-content of the organicist claim – even though memetics contends that music, to invert Street's formulation, converts nature into culture – any more than it is to test the various theoretical and methodological alternatives to organicism that have been proposed by advocates of a more critically motivated musicology. Rather, I explore organicism here in terms of point 1 of the list on page 296. That is, I examine it in order to illuminate the influence evolutionary theory – for which, as noted at the start of this section, organicism serves as a metonym – has had on the conduct of musical scholarship; and not to assess the veracity – insofar as this is a meaningful concept in the arts and humanities – of that scholarship.

Solie (1980) identifies two philosophical perspectives on organic unity. The first – broadly eighteenth-century, Kantian, and bottom-up/inductive/*a posteriori* – relates to the reconciliation of contradictions within a work, whereby the artist's aim is "to create not the greatest possible amount of unity but the optimum amount consistent with preserving the separate character of the components – that is, to maintain the creative tension between whole and parts" (1980, p. 148). While first articulated by Coleridge (2014, pp. 210–214) apropos works of literature, this view is well suited to the music of his near contemporary, Beethoven, with its radical discontinuities and tensions between what A. B. Marx termed *Satz* (closed, regular, periodic phrases) and *Gang* (open, irregular, developmental passages) (1997, pp. 14, 45; see also note 210 on page 364). The second perspective – broadly nineteenth-century, Hegelian, and top-down/deductive/*a priori* – was characterised by "[a] gradual reorientation of philosophical and analytical attention … from a consideration of the part-to-whole construction of the world which prevailed in mechanistic pre-Romantic times to a construction in which the whole is primary and its constituent parts derived therefrom" (Solie, 1980, p. 150). This second, holistic perspective, is seemingly more strongly articulated than the first in the music theory of the nineteenth and early-twentieth centuries, perhaps owing to the predominance of the Hegelian over the Kantian during this period.

Key among theorists developing organicist metaphors of music was Heinrich Schenker, discussion of whose work will appear periodically in this section. A *locus* for a number of intersecting conceptual streams that flowed in nineteenth-century aesthetics, Schenker was instrumental in developing several of the metaphors outlined in the list on page 327 (N. Cook, 2007b; Kassler, 1983; Snarrenberg, 1997; but see Pastille, 1984). Perhaps more rigorously than any other theorist, he not only carried through the implications of Solie's second perspective on organicism but also infused holism with a mysticism that pervaded all his work.

As identified in point 4.4 of the list on page 327, there are three principal dimensions to the metaphor of the work as organism – namely, poiesis as embryology, diachronic unfolding as ontogeny, and synchronic structure as functional differentiation – and they are considered in turn in the following subsections. As will be understood from the foregoing, the focus here will primarily be upon theorists/analysts from the late-nineteenth and early-twentieth centuries.

4.4.1.1 Poiesis as Embryology

While often taken primarily to encompass the period from fertilisation to the attainment of the mature form of an organism, ontogeny strictly encompasses its whole life-span, including senescence and death. In this metaphor, however, the process of generating a work is aligned essentially with the first, *embryological*, phase of ontogeny, whereby the birth of the organism is equated with the completion of the work. Developing ideas of others, Haeckel claimed in his Recapitulation Theory that "ontogeny recapitulates phylogeny" (§4.3.3). By this he meant that the embryo of organisms of "higher" species passes through a series of stages (ontogeny) in which it resembles the adult forms of organisms of "lower" species, before moving on to attain a more advanced level of development, thus replaying in months the millennia-long evolutionary processes that separate these various species (phylogeny). Recapitulation theory aligns with the Platonic concept of the Great Chain (or Ladder) of Being (Lovejoy, 1976), which was incorporated by Lamarck into his evolutionary theory (§1.8). The Great Chain demarcated a graded sequence from the most lowly to the most exalted states of life, which organisms strove to ascend – their ontogeny recapitulating the climb, in Haeckel's terms – in search of ever greater perfection.

Haeckel's theory is now discredited – as a foundation for his own exposition of ontogeny and phylogeny, Gould (1977) offers an analysis of the traditions in which it has been misappropriated – and evolutionary theorists nowadays generally draw upon it with care (see, for example, Diogo et al. (2019)). Nevertheless, Recapitulation theory has certain parallels with what is known of the generative processes of some composers. These parallels are most evident in Beethoven, on account of his extensive sketching and the preservation and analysis of a significant body of these documents (Johnson et al., 1985, pp. 3–11). At the risk of being overly speculative, it is certainly possible that the "Haeckelian" processes outlined here might have been evident in composers such as Haydn and Mozart, were they to have sketched as prolifically as Beethoven – they very likely did not – and were such sketches to have been as well preserved as Beethoven's. Note that here I am referring to a memetic-Haeckelian *mechanism* – whereby the aetiology of aspects of a musical structure passes through phases that resemble earlier form-historical stages – that may have motivated a recognition, in the form of a *metaphorical* Haeckelianism, articulated in the literature.

A case in point are the four "continuity drafts" for the exposition of the first movement of the "*Eroica*" Symphony, found in the "Landsberg 6" sketchbook of 1803–1804 (Nottebohm, 1979, pp. 50–58; Lockwood & Gosman, 2013, Vol. 1, Part 3 (sketchbook transcription), pp. 10–21).[194] Here there is a clear sense that the ontogeny of the exposition – significantly longer and more sectionalised than most previous sonata-form expositions – recapitulates the phylogeny of this element of sonata form. The question relevant to the present issue is: do either Nottebohm (1979) or Lockwood and Gosman (2013) draw, implicitly or explicitly, on evolutionary-Haeckelian imagery in their accounts of the sketchbook? The answer is a tentative "yes", but surprisingly – and despite Nottebohm's general organicist claim that "[i]f we understand [a work] as an organic formation, we must assume that it arose organically and that it *developed outwards* into a unified whole" (1979, p. 7; emphases mine) – it is arguably Lockwood and Gosman (2013) (drawing on the support of Tovey) who is the more clearly Haeckelian.

---

[194] "Beethoven's sketchbooks fall into two categories: those in large oblong format, which he used at his desk at home [generally writing in ink], and those in smaller format, either upright or oblong, which he could carry about in his coat pocket [writing in pencil]" (Johnson et al., 1985, p. 12). Continuity drafts, which use sketchbooks of the first category, are extended melodic lines representing the gross structure of a major section of a movement, working out of the fine details occurring at a later stage. In addition to work on the "*Eroica*", the Landsberg 6 sketchbook contains sketches for the "Waldstein" Sonata and for *Leonore*, among other works. An overview of the location of the four continuity drafts in Landsberg 6, and associated shorter sketches, is given in Lockwood and Gosman (2013, Vol. 1, Part 2, p. 33, Fig. 11). The earliest recorded work on the "*Eroica*", including an expositional continuity draft for the first movement, is found on pp. 44–45 of the "Wielhorsky" sketchbook of 1802–1803 (Johnson et al., 1985, p. 134; Lockwood & Gosman, 2013, Vol. 1, Part 2, p. 29).

The first continuity draft (Nottebohm, 1979, pp. 50–51; Lockwood & Gosman, 2013, Vol. 1, Part 3, p. 11) appears after several pages of sketches for
the movement's development section (Lockwood & Gosman, 2013, Vol. 1,
Part 2, p. 32) and represents Beethoven's attempts to organise his thoughts
for the thematic-tonal sequence of the exposition.[195] In a bat's squeak of
Haeckelianism (Waugh, 1962, p. 74), Lockwood and Gosman (2013) note
that "[n]ot surprisingly, the initial continuity draft … has the elements of
traditional sonata form: a first theme group beginning at st[ave]. 1, m. 3; a
second theme group in the dominant key beginning at st. 4; and a closing
theme in the dominant key on st. 8" (2013, Vol. 1, Part 2, p. 33). Yet this first
draft is problematic, owing to various "untenable thematic assertions" (2013,
Vol. 1, Part 2, p. 34) that confuse the received tonal-harmonic and thematic
sequence of a "normal" sonata-form exposition. The two most significant of
these deviations are (i) a premature statement of the opening theme on the
dominant (2013, Vol. 1, Part 3, p. 11, st. 2, bb. 11–14), representative of "a
tiresome tendency [in the continuity drafts] of the main theme to appear on
the dominant before its proper third statement", the latter appearing in E♭
starting at b. 37 – still in the first-subject group – of the finished movement
(Tovey, in Lockwood & Gosman, 2013, Vol. 1, Part 2, p. 34); and (ii) a return
to the opening theme in the tonic key at the end of the exposition (2013, Vol.
1, Part 3, p. 11, st. 10, bb. 11–14), in the manner of a sonata-rondo form's
second entry of the rondo theme.

As the simplest solution, these two statements of the main theme – the "premature dominant" version and the "unwelcome tonic" form – needed to
exchange places with each other, but this was not exactly Beethoven's ultimate solution, nor was it arrived at easily, as Tovey's impatience suggests.[196]

---

[195] Lockwood and Gosman (2013, Vol. 1, Part 2, p. 32) note Wade's (1977, p. 272) identification
of a striking resemblance between Beethoven's early ideas for the main theme of the Symphony's
first movement and the main theme of the finale of Mozart's Piano Concerto in B♭ major K. 595
(1791) (2013, Vol. 1, Part 3, p. 5, st. 7b–8a):

[196] Leaving aside the various shorter sketches that are interspersed between the continuity
drafts, the second draft (Nottebohm, 1979, pp. 53–54; Lockwood & Gosman, 2013, Vol. 1,
Part 3, p. 12) relocates the premature dominant statement to a position *after* Tovey's "proper

The premature dominant statement in the first continuity draft in fact "generate[d] three separate passages for the final version of the first movement" (Lockwood & Gosman, 2013, Vol. 1, Part 2, p. 34, Ex. 6). The third of these passages – the dominant preparation (bb. 424–429) for the triumphant return of the main theme in the recapitulation (bb. 430–433) – represents an ontogenetic expansion of vast scale, whereby a part of the "embryo" is relocated to a different structural "limb", facilitating a substantive increase in complexity and "strength". In Tovey's words, and fusing Haeckelianism with psycho-Lamarckism (discussed below), the premature dominant statement is "quite unworkable in the exposition, but the probable reason why it was so importunate in Beethoven's consciousness is that it becomes *vitally necessary* long afterwards in the recapitulation" (in Lockwood & Gosman, 2013, Vol. 1, Part 2, p. 34; emphasis mine; the fate of the late E♭ entries of the main theme is discussed on pp. 34–35).

In this connection, there is what Nottebohm terms a "variant" of the first continuity draft on the page preceding it in the sketchbook (1979, pp. 52–53); Lockwood and Gosman (2013, Vol. 1, Part 2, p. 32; Part 3, p. 10) term it "supplementary" to the first draft. This "variant"/"supplement" is significant because even though "the number and key of the appearances of the exposition's opening theme entries remain in flux after page 10, [the "variant"/"supplement"] closely corresponds to the final version" (Lockwood & Gosman, 2013, Vol. 1, Part 2, p. 34). The relatively advanced state of development of the page-10 draft therefore raises a question as to its position in the chronological-developmental sequence of the continuity drafts. The issue arises, in part, because Beethoven often started a new phase of work on the *recto* page of a sketchbook, initially leaving the opposite *verso* page (and more before it) blank before subsequently returning to fill them at a later stage of sketching, when space became tight (Nottebohm, 1979, pp. 4–5). Thus, "when the page 10 revision of the page 11 [first continuity] draft was made must remain an open question" (Lockwood & Gosman, 2013, Vol. 1, Part 2, p. 34). Indeed, page 10 may not even be a (direct) revision of page 11; on the basis of the occurrences of the premature dominant statement of the main theme – admittedly an impoverished criterion when considered in isolation –

---

third statement", in which relative position it returns in the third (Nottebohm, 1979, pp. 55–56; Lockwood & Gosman, 2013, Vol. 1, Part 3, pp. 14–15) and fourth (Nottebohm, 1979, pp. 56–58; Lockwood & Gosman, 2013, Vol. 1, Part 3, pp. 20–21) drafts.

the "variant"/"supplement" might even *post-date* the *fourth* continuity draft, despite the greater extent and level of development of the latter. On this interpretation, the page-10 sketch would constitute a kind of *précis* of the exposition, one that implicitly acknowledges the intended translocation of the premature dominant statement to the recapitulation. Given the various advances and retrenchments evident in these drafts, it is nevertheless difficult – perhaps even impossible in principle – to identify a point when the Haeckelian recapitulation of phylogeny ended and its Darwinian-memetic development began.

There is a great deal more one could say about the structure of the four continuity drafts, but moving beyond form-historical echoes in the global outline of the exposition they attempt to crystallise, certain local figuration in the drafts is also amenable to a Haeckelian reading, in that it is itself reminiscent of patterns from earlier styles. That is – to pivot again from metaphor to mechanism – there are musemes in the continuity drafts that seem more typical of – more frequently replicated in – the music of Haydn and Mozart than that of Beethoven. As Beethoven worked further on the exposition, these musemes lost their by-then-generic, galant attributes and were mutated – in a process of micro-Haeckelianism – into more characteristically Beethovenian forms, or were replaced by such musemes. Figure 4.2 offers an example, showing the similarities between a cadential museme in Haydn, Figure 4.2a, and an allele of it from Beethoven's fourth continuity draft, Figure 4.2b (Nottebohm, 1979, p. 57; Lockwood & Gosman, 2013, Vol. 1, Part 3, p. 20, st. 13, bb. 5–8). By the final version of the exposition, this museme had evolved into the pattern shown in Figure 4.2c, with its more distinctive *sforzando* and syncopation on the g^2 of bb. 89^3–90^1.

In another application of the poiesis as embryology metaphor, Schoenberg's renunciation of tonality in the first decade of the twentieth century led him to rely – even after his development of serialism – upon ever more sophisticated motivic relationships and transformations, these processes being the culmination of tendencies that had existed in music since at least the time of Beethoven (N. Cook, 1994, p. 91). Some theorists have used Schoenberg's concept of the *Grundgestalt* – the "basic shape", from which all details of a composition spring (Schoenberg, 1995; see also Epstein, 1979) – as a rubric for

(a) Haydn: String Quartet in E major op. 17 no. 1 (1771), II, bb. 1–5.

(b) Beethoven: Fourth Continuity Draft for Symphony no. 3 in E♭ major op. 55 ("*Eroica*") (1804), I, p. 20, st. 13, bb. 5–8.

(c) Beethoven: Symphony no. 3 in E♭ major op. 55 ("*Eroica*") (1804), I, bb. 87–91.

Figure 4.2: Musemes in Haydn and Beethoven.

finding coherence in music by relating details at various structural-hierarchic levels and in different parameters to an entity that is variously conceived as a seed or a template. In this version of the metaphor, the embryological dimension inheres in the "germination" of the seed and the concomitant differentiation of its amorphous substrate into the different functional elements of the mature organism.

Drawing on Schoenbergian principles, and Rudolf Reti's notions of thematic unity (§4.4.2), Hans Keller hypothesised a two-level structure for music, consisting of "background" and "foreground" levels and arguing that "[f]unctional analysis" – his term for the analytical methodology arising from his theory – "postulates that contrasts are but different aspects of a single basic idea, a background unity" (H. Keller, 1994, p. 143). While turned to quite different uses by Keller, Schenker anticipates this notion, saying – in one of the "Aphorisms" that appear in the Introduction of *Der freie Satz* – that "[t]he whole of foreground, which men call chaos, God derives from His cosmos, the background. The eternal harmony of His eternal Being is grounded in this relationship" (Schenker, 1979, p. xxiii).

While assimilating elements of Schenker's hierarchic model (itself based on ideas of earlier theorists), there is nevertheless a significant difference:

Keller's background formed the *locus* of the atemporal, synchronic basic idea, whereas Schenker's background encompassed the temporal, diachronic *Ursatz* (Fundamental Structure). In this way Keller's background serves as a kind of Platonic arbiter and guarantor that, however disjointed the sequential unfolding of the foreground appeared, it could always be explicated and validated by reference to the background from which it originated. Thus, Keller asserted that the background ("which boils down to form") is "both the sum total of the expectations a composer raises in the course of a piece without fulfilling them, and the sum total of those unborn fulfilments"; and that the foreground ("the individual structure") is "simply, what he does instead – what is actually the score" (1994, pp. 123, 124).

The practical implementation of this theory, Functional Analysis (FA) (H. Keller, 1957; H. Keller, 2001), increasingly moved away from verbal description until the analysis was eventually represented wholly in music notation (starting with H. Keller, 1958; see also O'Hara, 2020). Keller justified this approach, his equivalent of the Schenkerian analytical graph, by arguing that "[a]ll conceptual thought about music is a detour, from music *via* terms to music, whereas functional analysis proceeds direct from music *via* music to music" (1994, p. 127). Unlike a Schenkerian graph, however, the FA is intended to be performed, being intercalated between the movements of the subject work. This rendition is intended to prime the listener's subconscious in order to facilitate the detection of the background coherence underpinning the work's seeming foreground contradictions (H. Keller, 1985). Keller asserted that from this interplay between the work and its analysis arose "musical logic", which inheres in the "tension … between what the composer does and what he makes you feel he was expected to do" – that is, between the "contradiction" of the foreground and the "unity" of the background (1994, p. 123).

While Keller did not, to my knowledge, draw an explicit connection between his model and embryology, it is nevertheless possible to see the basic idea as akin to an embryo (or to the genes controlling it), the former's unfolding over time giving rise to the outward shape of the movement while always maintaining the same underlying "genetic code", and thus retaining an inner unity. While it is beyond the scope of this chapter to speculate on the memetics of this process (given the primary focus before §4.6 on evolutionary metaphors, not evolutionary mechanisms), it is arguable that the basic idea acts as a kind of memome, regulating the unfolding and differentiation of the composition over time, as the genome of an embryo regulates its "unfolding" and differentiation. Perhaps more accurately, the basic idea is less a memome than a museme (or a musemeplex), because the kinds of patterns Keller sees as germinal to musical works are closer to motives (or to sequences of motives) than to the "form" to which, as noted above, he asserts the background "boils down". The regulation of musical unfolding and differentiation occurs in several dimensions, including not only the poiesis of the work, but also its esthesis: a work's embryology is reified by the composer, but it is also recreated by the listener.

Keller's conception of music also incorporated a strongly Freudian element, as the reference above to the subconscious priming effected by the performance of his analytical scores, and his view that FA supports a listener's "instinctive understanding" (1985, p. 73), might suggest. Moreover, Keller asserts that "the foreground is that which suppresses the background – often even represses it in the dynamic, psychoanalytic sense, so that the composer is unaware of what has happened and receives the analytic disclosure [afforded by a FA] like a revelation" (1994, p. 123). Keller's Freudianism inheres in the similarity between the basic idea and the id, the unconscious and instinctual component of the psyche (Freud, 1981, pp. 23–24, Fig. 1). Just as the id drives us in ways the ego sometimes struggles to control and rationalise, so the basic idea drives the composer to create music in ways that sometimes escape his or her conscious oversight.[197]

Freud maintained a keen interest in evolutionary theory, starting at the time of his medical studies in Vienna during the 1870s (Marcaggi & Guénolé, 2018, p. 3). While familiar with the work of Darwin, Freud was a stronger adherent of Lamarckism and of Haeckel's Recapitulation Theory, maintaining his

---

[197] There is a large literature, much of it anecdotal and some of it fabricated, discussing this "creative somnambulism" – Campbellian blind variation – of composers. Keller gives a hint of this in noting, somewhat immodestly, that "[w]hen I asked [Britten] what had made him so enthusiastic about my method, he replied that it was the only type of music analysis that interested him, because it confined itself to the composer's own pre-compositional thought, partly conscious, partly unconscious. He had thus learnt a lot about himself from my FA of his Second Quartet" (1985, p. 73).

belief in their ideas despite the increasing acceptance of Darwinism after the First World War (Marcaggi & Guénolé, 2018, p. 6). It is worth recalling that initial criticism of *On the origin of species* pushed Darwin to a more Lamarckian position in later editions of the book (§1.8), and so to some extent Freud may have been absorbing Lamarckian ideas via Darwin. The influence of Lamarck and of Haeckel on Freud (Gould, 1977, p. 156) led to his development of a "psycho-Lamarckism" – "the evolutionary theory according to which species adapt over generations by the effect on the body of individual will and resulting actions" (Marcaggi & Guénolé, 2018, p. 6).

This theory held, among other things, that: (i) there was "hereditary transmission of certain [ancestrally acquired] emotional complexes", including taboos, the latter resulting from survival-related pressures (Marcaggi & Guénolé, 2018, p. 4); (ii) in Freud's words, and offering a driving force for the inheritance of acquired characteristics and thus of his favoured mechanism for biological evolution, "[Lamarck's] concept of 'need' which creates and modifies the organs is nothing other than the power of unconscious ideas on the body" (in Marcaggi & Guénolé, 2018, p. 5); and (iii) in a "a massive recapitulationism, far exceeding the conceptions of Haeckel himself", Freud argued that the psychological/emotional ontogeny of an individual – the different stages through which he believed we passed as children – replayed the psychological/emotional phylogeny of our species (Marcaggi & Guénolé, 2018, p. 5). As discussed in §1.8, Lamarckism has been recuperated recently in theories of epigenetic inheritance. To recall, these hypothesise that certain *biological* changes to an organism acquired (via Lamarckism) during its lifetime are encoded in ways that allow them to "piggyback" the (Darwinian) processes underpinning DNA transmission. Given that epigenetics has also been advanced as a potential mechanism for the transmission of certain acquired *psychological* states – as in the notion of TTT discussed in §3.4.3 – it might thus additionally account for certain elements of Freud's psycho-Lamarckism, particularly points (i) and (ii) above.

Keller's work is suffused with a form of Freudian psycho-Lamarckism applied to music theory, in that not only does the basic idea engender a "need" (point (ii) in the previous paragraph) that "creates and modifies the organs" of the movement's foreground (which might then be inherited when later composers emulate aspects of the work in question); but certain musical techniques are ontogenetically recapitulated (point (iii) in the previous paragraph), having arisen phylogenetically in the music of earlier periods. An example of the latter principle is Keller's doubly Freudian concept of "Classical serialism". By this, Keller is referring to various late-eighteenth- and early-nineteenth-century antecedents of Schoenberg's practice he discerned in certain works of Mozart and Beethoven, and not to the canonical twelve-tone techniques formulated by Schoenberg in the early 1920s (Schoenberg, 2010, part 5). Binding the First and Second Viennese Schools in a Haeckelian-Freudian nexus, Keller maintained that "Schoenberg was Mozart's unconscious serial pupil [Haeckelian Recapitulation] .... [yet Schoenberg] repressed his knowledge of classical serialism because it would have injured his narcissism [Freudian repression]" (1955, p. 23).

4.4.1.2 Diachronic Unfolding as Ontogeny

As has been widely discussed in the literature, "Schenker's theory of Fundamental Structure regards the unified masterpiece as an example of organic growth from background to foreground" (Street, 1989, p. 78). While this statement might be understood in terms of the rubric of §4.4.1.1 – i.e., expansion of the latent, seed-like potentiality of the *Ursatz* being the driving force of poiesis, as with Keller's basic idea – it might also be understood in the sense of the present section; namely, that the sequential unfolding of a (completed) movement over time – in performance, through reading the score continuously from start to finish, or in episodic-memory recollection (Snyder, 2009, p. 108) – may be aligned with the *post*-embryology ontogeny of an organism. This is because to some extent *diachrony recapitulates (post-embryological) ontogeny*, to paraphrase Haeckel, in the sense that the "conceptual", top-down movement from background to foreground in poiesis is reified in the "kinetic" movement from beginning to end of a movement at the neutral and esthesic levels, giving, as represented in Figure 4.3, a curve linking the two dimensions.

Such a view naturally presupposes a hierarchic conception of music, one in which several structural layers exist simultaneously, the distance between them being traversable via – in the case of the theorist – reduction (analysis/esthesis) or – in the case of the composer – accretion (synthesis/poiesis). In

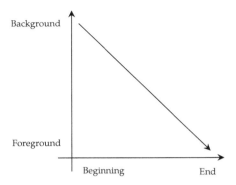

Figure 4.3: Intersection of Background-Foreground Movement with Diachrony.

converting the atemporal *Naturklang* ("chord of nature") (Schenker, 1979,
p. 10, Fig. 2) into the temporal *Ursatz* (1979, p. 4, Fig. 1), there is a need for
prolongation that is provided, in the first instance, by the $\hat{2}$/V (in a $\hat{3}$/I–$\hat{2}$/V–
$\hat{1}$/I *Ursatz*) (Schenker, 1979, Fig. 15). At lower structural-hierarchic levels, a
cascade of diminutions leads to ever more complex nested prolongations of
prolongations, until, all top-down forces being spent, the foreground in all
its detail and richness is arrived at.

The autotelic dimension of this process – i.e., the work striving through its
own will to attain a goal – is indicated in Schenker's assertion that,

> [s]ince it is a melodic succession of definite steps of a second, the funda-
> mental line signifies motion, striving toward a goal, and ultimately the
> completion of this course. In this sense we perceive our own life-impulse
> in the motion of the fundamental line, a full analogy to our inner life.
> Similarly, the arpeggiation of the bass signifies movement toward a spe-
> cific goal, the upper fifth, and the completion of the course with the
> return to the fundamental tone. (Schenker, 1979, p. 4)

As with similar elements in Keller's work, it is possible to discern a hint
of psycho-Lamarckism in these remarks. To recall Freud's assertion, cited
in §4.4.1.1, "[Lamarck's] concept of 'need' which creates and modifies the
organs is nothing other than the power of unconscious ideas on the body" (in
Marcaggi & Guénolé, 2018, p. 5). A mixture of three factors, it is debatable
the degrees to which (i) the physical (resulting from a natural law, such as

that governing the *Naturklang* (Schenker, 1979, p. 10)); (ii) the metaphysical (resulting from the forces described by Idealist philosophy, as Schenker acknowledges (1979, p. 3)); and (iii) the psychological (resulting from an innate, biological desire) contribute to make up the driving force – the "need", "striving" or "life-impulse" – impelling the "body" of the *Ursatz*. As in similar cases discussed here, resolving this issue depends to some extent upon which of the two main perspectives negotiated in this chapter is adopted. Understood wholly metaphorically – and thus freed of the constraints of scientific grounding – the explanatory force is largely metaphysical, indeed mystical. Understood in terms of mechanism, a solution may be found in a number of factors, already extensively discussed, that relate to the interplay between nature (the acoustic realities of the harmonic series and our innate psychoacoustic sensitivity to them) and nurture (the generation of musemesätze via processes described by the RHSGAP model (§3.5.2)).

4.4.1.3 Synchronic Structure as Functional Differentiation

In this metaphor, a movement is understood as consisting of several distinct sections or structural units, each of which fulfils a particular function – this necessarily contingent upon sequential-temporal location in a temporal art-form like music – and without which there would be some deprecation of the overall aesthetic effect. The metaphor is grounded in the nature of the eukaryotic cell – the cell-type found in plants and animals – which can differentiate in order to form tissues of widely differing forms and functions. As with such organic division of labour, "a cardinal assumption of organicist criticism [of art] is that the form as given is 'necessary' – parts cannot be removed, added, or rearranged without, as Pepper [(Pepper, 1945)] says, 'marring or even destroying' the whole" (Solie, 1980, pp. 148–149). This conception relates also to an embryological view (§4.4.1.1), given that structural differentiation – the formation of the core tissues of the body – is the primary outcome of this first stage of ontogeny. In the present metaphor, the undifferentiated "germ" of the music gives rise to components that, by virtue of their occupying a particular sequential-temporal location, fulfil a specific structural-functional role (and vice versa).

One means of representing structural-functional differentiation is the (inverted) tree-diagram, where binary or ternary branching underpins a model of

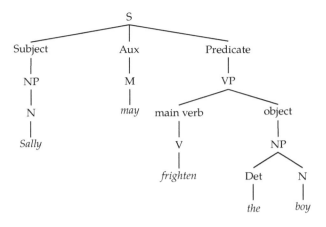

Figure 4.4: Generative-Transformational Tree.

strict hierarchic inclusion (Gjerdingen, 1988, 18–22, Ex. 2-6). This type of representation derives in part from the cladograms of cladistic taxonomy (§1.7.2,
§3.6.6); and it inspired the sentence-analyses of Chomskyan generative-
transformational grammar (§3.8.2). In the latter, and in the case of English-
language sentences, there is a correlation between sequential position and
syntactic-semantic function. In Figure 4.4 (Chomsky, 1965, p. 69, Fig. 6),
which replaces Chomsky's original (abstract) noun "sincerity" with the
(proper) noun "Sally", the sense depends on the first noun-phrase preceding
the second, and thereby being understood as the (nominative-case) subject. Were this to be translated into a highly inflected language, like Latin
or German, then the two noun-phrases could be inverted and still retain the
sense, because case-markers would indicate which noun-phrase constitutes
the subject and which the (accusative-case) object, so "den Jungen" (the
boy) could precede "Sally", the former still being understood as accusative,
without ambiguity.[198]

In some respects, music's structure follows the model of English grammar,
whereby sequential position indicates syntactic, and to some extent semantic,

---

[198] The situation is complicated in Chomsky's original, in that "sincerity" imposes restrictions
on inverting the sentence because (i) this noun does not normally function as an accusative
object in a transitive sentence; and (ii) there are semantic constraints that would render the
sentence nonsensical.

function.[199] In this vein, Schenker assigns structural-functional distinctions to specific prolongations, attempting to reconcile their synchronic role with the diachronic forces that impel them towards the closure of the *Ursatz*. Examples include initial ascents (*Anstieg*) to the primary tone (*Kopfton*) of the *Urlinie*, interruptions (*Unterbrechung*), and any prolongations situated in a movement's "structural" coda (i.e., the portion of the movement following the closure of the *Ursatz* (Cavett-Dunsby, 1988)). In the case of the interruption, while it can only occupy a certain diachronic position (i.e., after the first statement of $\hat{3}/I$ and before the restatement of the *Kopfton*), it also serves a specific synchronic function, namely the form-generating role of sustaining the development section.[200] Schenker's schemata for sonata form indicate that the development section can occupy the span from $\hat{3}/III\natural5-\hat{2}||/V\sharp3$ (1979, Fig. 26a), or serve as a prolongation of $\hat{2}||/V\natural3-\sharp3$ (1979, Fig. 26b). While not made explicit, it is clear that the penultimate $\hat{2}/V$ cannot fulfil the same function – is is structurally-functionally differentiated from the interruption-generating $\hat{2}||/V$.

As branching tree-diagrams, the graphical presentation of analyses conducted according to Lerdahl and Jackendoff's Generative Theory of Tonal Music (GTTM) (Lerdahl & Jackendoff, 1983; see also Temperley, 2001) resembles the cladograms of taxonomy and the linguistic trees of Chomskyan generative-transformational grammar, upon the latter GTTM being broadly based.[201] GTTM's reductions are of two forms: *time-span* and *prolongational*. The former identifies a salient pitch within each grouping-segment, arranging these in a hierarchy by identifying superordinate groups and the subordinate groups they encompass (Lerdahl & Jackendoff, 1983, p. 124); the latter identifies patterns of openness and closure, and thus tension and relaxation, in event-sequences (1983, p. 179). These reductions are guided by a system of *well-formedness rules* and *preference rules*. The former dictate what

---

[199] While music has no case-markers analogous to those of language, certain musical gestures nevertheless have "beginning", "middle" and "end" functions (Agawu, 1991, pp. 53–54), and so can – as in the opening of the second movement of Haydn's Symphony no. 100 ("Military") (1794) with a closing gesture (Meyer, 1996, 26, Ex. 1.3 (a)) – be repositioned for ironic or witty effect. This device was considered on page 187 under the rubric of exaptation.

[200] Schenker asserted that "[o]nly the prolongation of a division (interruption) gives rise to sonata form. Herein lies the difference between sonata form and song form: the latter can also result from a mixture or a neighboring note [but the former cannot]" (1979, p. 134).

[201] See Matsubara et al. (2018) for attempts to use the computer to automate music analysis according to the GTTM.

is permissible within the terms of the grammar, thus distinguishing the set of legal from illegal options; the latter take the set of legal options and rank them according to some set of criteria in terms of most- to least-preferred (1983, p. 9). The patterns underpinning prolongational reduction are of six fundamental types, representing the possible relationships that may inhere between two elements (structural nodes), x and y, at various structural-hierarchic levels. Three forms of relaxation-to-tension (y prolongs/repeats or progresses/departs from x), and three forms of tension-to-relaxation (x prolongs/anticipates or arrives/resolves onto y), are theorised, each with their associated linguistic-tree-based symbology (1983, p. 182, Fig. 8.6).[202]

While these six categories ostensibly derive from the structural descriptors of generative-transformational grammar, they are metaphorically and mechanistically music-evolutionary in the sense that their consequent components (y) arise from the associated antecedent (x) as part of functional differentiation, or division of musical labour: in the first three categories (Lerdahl & Jackendoff, 1983, p. 182, Fig. 8.6 a–c), y evolves from x synchronically (conceptually, structurally-hierarchically) as well as diachronically (intra-work-sequentially and inter-work-historically). Just as a limb requires a torso from which to evolve, so a departure (1983, p. 182, Fig. 8.6 c) needs a foundation from which to arise: the x/torso element (symbolised by a longer line) is often a tonic-orientated node (or, at a lower structural-hierarchic level, a dominant-orientated node); whereas the y/limb element (symbolised by a shorter line) is a dependent, non-tonic (or, at the lower level, non-dominant) node, which might be understood as a structural-evolutionary outgrowth – as it is graphically represented – of x. This principle is illustrated in Figure 4.5 (Lerdahl & Jackendoff, 1983, p. 209, Fig. 8.37), which shows a prolongational reduction of the St Antoni Chorale, used by Brahms as the theme of his Variations on a Theme by J. Haydn op. 56a of 1873.

The dominant chord of the imperfect cadence of b. 5 is represented as a local departure from the tonic chord of b. 1. Analogously, the diminished-seventh chord over the F pedal in b. 12 is a local departure from the dominant chord

---

[202] "Strong prolongations" (harmonic and melodic repetitions and anticipations) are symbolised by an open circle at branch-intersections (1983, p. 182, Fig. 8.6 a, d); "weak prolongations" (harmonic repetitions and anticipations) are symbolised by a closed circle at branch-intersections (1983, p. 182, Fig. 8.6 b, e); and "progressions" (departures and arrivals/resolutions) are symbolised by the absence of a circle at branch-intersections (1983, p. 182, Fig. 8.6 c, f).

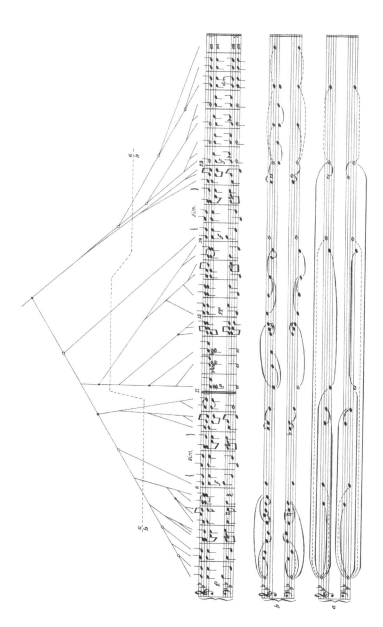

Figure 4.5: Prolongational Reduction of the St Antoni Chorale from Brahms: Variations on a Theme by J. Haydn op. 56a.

of b. 11, the return to which in b. 13 represents a weak prolongation of the chord of b. 11 – it is a return to the same harmony, but with a different upper-voice note (Lerdahl & Jackendoff, 1983, p. 182, Fig. 8.6 b). While it is the source of the latter prolongation, the dominant chord of b. 11 occupies a higher structural-hierarchic level in relation to the tonic of b. 1 than does the dominant chord of b. 5, in that the later dominant chord initiates the second phrase (bb. 11–18) of this "three-phrase binary" form theme. This second phrase might thus be regarded as a dominant-orientated limb growing, as a progression (Lerdahl & Jackendoff, 1983, p. 182, Fig. 8.6 c), from the tonic-orientated torso of the first phrase (bb. 1–10). The analysis reminds us that while the first (relaxation-to-tension) group of three x–y relationships (Lerdahl & Jackendoff, 1983, p. 182, Fig. 8.6 a–c) might be understood to represent Darwinian processes of structural-functional evolutionary aptation, the second (tension-to-relaxation) group (1983, p. 182, Fig. 8.6 d–f) are distinctly Lamarckian in their goal-directedness. The ii$^6_3$ chord of b. 17, for instance, aspires to realise – i.e., to effect a resolution to (Lerdahl & Jackendoff, 1983, p. 182, Fig. 8.6 f) – the dominant chord of the imperfect cadence of b. 18, after which appears the third phrase (bb. 19–29) as a strong prolongation of the first phrase (Lerdahl & Jackendoff, 1983, p. 182, Fig. 8.6 a). Indeed, at the very highest level, the B♭-major chord of b. 23 (the structural close of the third phrase and of the theme as a whole, followed by a coda, bb. 23–29) represents the *telos* of the whole theme: it is the superordinate harmony, demarcated by the longest branch of the prolongational tree, to which every preceding element ultimately strives as part of a deep-structural (tension-to-relaxation) weak prolongation (1983, p. 182, Fig. 8.6 e).

As a final point, and returning to the discussion before Figure 4.4, all such dendrograms – in biological or cultural taxonomy and in music analysis – have a dual nature. They are in one sense *structural-diachronic*, in that they represent design in terms of the passage of time. This is either the geological-evolutionary time over which a species branches to form offshoots; or the chronological-perceptual time in which a musical work or process unfolds in imagination or performance. But the dendrograms are also *structural-synchronic*, in that they represent design in terms of hierarchic relationships between elements that are in some sense understood to be related. These relationships are ones of derivation (and thus aetiological, morphological and genetic dependency) that obtain in the case of species that share a common ancestor; or relationships of prolongation and progression (and thus perceptual-cognitive and/or epistemological dependency) that obtain in music's event-sequences – including, as D. Clarke (2017) argues, in certain non-western musics.

4.4.2 The Motive as Organism

Despite also drawing inspiration from Schoenberg's concept of the *Grundgestalt*, Rudolf Reti developed a model of motivic similarity that differs from Keller's (§4.4.1.1) in several significant ways. In Keller's model, the focus is primarily upon the *movement or work as the organism* and how its organic unity arises from the overriding control of the basic idea, which functions, by analogy with the genome, as a kind of memome regulating its ontology. In Reti, by contrast, the focus is two-fold. On the one hand, styling the underlying idea of a movement the "prime cell" – Reti sometimes uses the term "prime motif", both allowing for other units to be identified – implies that it is functioning as a building block of a larger organism, the prime cell carrying the work's controlling "genetic code". On the other hand, there is also a metaphor of the *motive as the organism*, whose journey across a work not only acts as a unifying force but also represents a form of evolution in which, again to paraphrase Haeckel, *ontogeny is conflated with phylogeny*. That is, the genesis of the movement is interlocked with the evolution of the species of which type the motive is the token. Thus, the thematic elaboration of a work, the "thematic process" in Reti's phrase (Reti, 1951), is partly an evolutionary one – arguably more Lamarckian than Darwinian – because the prime cell is striving to adapt (or to exapt) to its "environment" in order to survive. Nevertheless, as with others considered previously, there is a hierarchic-level mismatch, indeed several, in the metaphor of the motive as organism. This is because the (prime) cell – which, in its biological form, is not assigned a level in Table 1.4 – is elided, intra-domain, with the organism (level five) on the nature side; and, inter-domain, with the motif/museme (the latter mapped to the gene at level seven) *and*, via the intra-domain cell-organism mapping, with the work on the culture side (level five).

While there is no formal division between background and foreground levels in Reti's theory (but see page 355), the hierarchic dimension of Keller's work – or, perhaps more methodologically, Schenker's – is also evident, in part, in Reti's acknowledgement – or, to those critical of his method, his escape clause – that the prime cell may encompass certain non-thematic notes interpolated between the functional motivic pitches. More fundamentally, Reti's concept of the "thematic pattern" (Reti, 1967) represents a relatively localised structure in which a shallow-middleground-level motive arises from the juxtaposition of several discrete component elements, one of which may be defined as the prime cell and each of which may potentially occur independently of the collection – a musemeplex, in memetic terms (§3.5.2). Figure 4.6 (after Reti, 1951, 11, Ex. 1; p. 12, Ex. 2; p. 13, Ex. 3; p. 14, Ex. 5; p. 16, Exx. 7, 8; p. 27, Exx. 31, 32) illustrates these principles, showing Reti's derivation of material in Beethoven's Symphony no. 9 from the main theme (bb. 16–27) of the first movement.

Reti divides this theme, or "shape", into "four motivic elements", a motif being defined as "any musical element … which, by being constantly re-peated and varied throughout a work or a section, assumes a role in the compositional design" (1951, pp. 11–12). As in many of Reti's analyses, the motivic material he sees as central in this work consists of short triadic or scalic patterns. Motif I is a falling D-minor arpeggio; motif II is a $\hat{3}$–$\hat{2}$–$\hat{1}$ scale-segment, which is inverted (or retrograded) to d^2–e^2–f^2 in bb. 21–22 and then transposed (in the inverted form) to g^2–a^2–$b\flat^2$ in bb. 23–24; motif III is a V7-implying arpeggio; and motif IV is a filled-in falling diminished seventh, with a distinctive musFlat$\hat{2}$. The second movement presents these four motives in the same order, although some sleight of hand is needed to accommodate motif III: as the fourth system of Figure 4.6 shows, whereas the first movement presented the sequence motif II (original)–motif III–motif II (inverted then transposed), the Scherzo broadly reverses this three-element structure, presenting the inverted form d^2–e^2–f^2 first and the original form in third position. Reti argues that the second-position e^2–f^2–g^2 pattern (b. 11) of the Scherzo represents motif III, stripped of its a^2. While "assuming simultaneously the shape of a[n] [inverted and] transposed motif II…., its appearance exactly between the two occurrences of motif II makes it certain that this E, F, G, is nevertheless meant as a corresponding substitute for motif

Figure 4.6: Four Motifs in Beethoven's Symphony no. 9 op. 125 (1824).

III" (1951, p. 13). Reti's primary motivation for this reading is to be able to slot motif III into its proper position in between two forms of motif II, this imperative trumping any concern for exact intervallic replication. Thus, not only are inversion and transposition permitted operations, but the internal intervallic structure of a motif may also be distorted – whether this be understood as the mis-transposition of the "pseudo-motif II" or as the omission of the a^2 in "motif III". The following iteration of motif IV evidences another interval-sequence distortion, containing a b♮ in b. 14 rather than the normative b♭ (marked by the asterisk in the third system of Figure 4.6), this adjustment motivated by constraints arising from the fugal treatment of the Scherzo's main theme. Here, the bounding scale degrees (the local ♭$\hat{6}$ and ♯$\hat{7}$) and interval traversed (nine semitones) serve as the guarantor of the motif's identity.

The third movement's opening theme is based on an intriguing reworking of motif I that clothes the falling D-minor arpeggio in a B♭-major garb, although this requires a downplaying of $\hat{1}$ and $\hat{4}$ in the theme (reflected in Reti's use of grace-note size for these pitches in his Ex. 5); in his formulation, it is a "D-minor theme in B-flat" (1951, p. 27). Indeed, Reti offers this as an example of the "method of *transforming a shape from one theme to another which is in a different key, but at the same time letting it sound at original pitch*" (1951, p. 15; emphasis in the original).[203] This tension between the tonic and submediant major – forged in the first movement's double statement of the main theme in D minor (b. 16) and B♭ major (b. 50) – erupts at the start of the finale, where Reti derives the opening harmony from a juxtaposition of the two forms (i and ♭VI) of motif I, "verticalising" what has hitherto been presented horizontally (the second statement of this gesture chord, in b. 208, adds the A-major form of motif I to the D-minor and B♭-major forms). Reti does not explicitly mark motifs I, II and III in the "joy" theme, identifying only motif IV in bb. 102–103 – which, in a far greater violation than that represented by his analysis of bb. 13–15 of the Scherzo, covers the "wrong" number of semitones on the "wrong" scale degrees. Nevertheless, as Figure 4.6 shows,

---

[203] Strictly, as Reti's Ex. 1 and Ex. 2 indicate, he means the *original pitch-classes* here, given that he abstracts the component pitches of motif I an octave lower than it is presented in the Violin I part of the first movement. In addition to this general insensitivity to register, Reti also variously indicates, and ignores, rhythm, as in his treatment of motifs II and III in Ex. 1 and Ex. 3 (1951, pp. 11, 13).

one can find motifs I, II and III in the first five bars of the melody, conjoined in a dense motivic nexus.

While this is an incomplete account of Reti's analysis of the Symphony (he finds various interesting derivatives of the first movement's second theme, bb. 80–87, among other things), it indicates numerous intriguing resemblances that perhaps tilt the scales towards some equilibrium when weighed against certain other, rather more speculative, analyses by Reti. Returning to connections with evolution, and in an echo of Keller's notion of background and foreground, Reti notes that Beethoven "strives toward *homogeneity in the inner essence* but at the same time toward *variety in the outer appearance*", these phenomena representing the two "form-building forces in music" (1951, pp. 13, 109; emphases in the original). To invoke the metaphor-mechanism distinction again, this binarism can be read in at least two ways. Metaphorically, "homogeneity in the inner essence" represents the persistence of the "personality" of the motive and its survival through the "journey" of the work, this notion drawing upon what I term Spitzer's "cluster (iii)" – melody as traversing the path of life (page 301). Under the rubric of "thematic evolution", Reti describes this journey as the process of "how a theme *moves by transformation toward a goal …*" (1951, p. 139; emphasis in the original), thus making an implicit distinction between motives/themes and the "substrate" (the rest of the music) through which they flow. In this sense, this metaphor invokes the romantic notion of The Wanderer. Exemplified by Friedrich's painting *Der Wanderer über dem Nebelmeer* (*The wanderer above the sea of fog*) (*c.* 1818) and by Schubert's songs of this name (D. 489 (1816), D. 649 (1819) and D. 870 (1826)), this trope concerns the journey of the solitary hero through life, confronting various adversities until arriving – to borrow the title of Strauss' tone poem – at the *telos* of *Tod* and, hopefully, *Verklärung*.

In terms of mechanism, the homogeneity-variety dichotomy can be readily accommodated in terms of the three related concepts of museme alleles, musemeplexes, and musemesätze. For the first of these, the composer, having selected a given museme, is arguably psychologically primed to select further patterns from the same museme allele-class, as opposed to patterns from other allele-classes, inevitably giving rise to various degrees of pattern-recurrence. For the second, the components of real or virtual musemeplexes (page 202) create phrase-level similarity-sequences, stronger (but perhaps less frequent) in the case of real than virtual musemeplexes. For the third, musemeplexes generate the more abstract framework of a musemesatz, which might account for generalised relationships (and perceptions) of similarity between corresponding sections at higher levels of organisation, and thus afford a means of answering Reti's question – if we accept its premise – "[w]hy is it that we cannot produce a convincing musical composition by taking a group or a section from one work and linking it to that of another ...?" (1951, p. 348). Understood in this light, Reti's metaphorical motivic evolutionism can readily be reconciled with the mechanistic musemic evolutionism of memetics.

4.4.3 Tones and Tonality as Organisms

Schenker's notion of the "will" or "egotism" of the tone (1980, p. 30; see also Morgan, 2014, Ch. 4) – made explicit in the title, *Der Tonwille*, of a ten-volume, sole-author periodical he wrote between 1921 and 1924 (Schenker, 2004; Schenker, 2005) – neatly encapsulates the notion covered in this section: that individual pitches (understood as scale-degree-aligned note-classes (Temperley, 2001, p. 115) or, more abstractly, as pitch-classes) are driven by an inner force that compels them to pursue their own advantage at the expense of other, "rival" tones.[204] For Schenker, the egotism (or "vitality") of the tone, as with that of a living organism, is "directly proportionate" to two factors: "the number of relationships" – systemic interconnections, as governed by the attributes of different mode/scale types – within which a tone is implicated and which it can leverage; and "the intensity of the vital forces lavished on [those relationships]" (1980, p. 84). Thus, framing the "biologic foundation of the process of [pitch] combination" in organism-level terms, Schenker asserts that

> [i]f the egotism of a tone expresses itself in the desire to dominate its fellow-tones rather than be dominated by them (in this respect, the tone resembles a human being), it is the system which offers to the tone the means to dominate and thus to satisfy its egotistic urge. A tone

---

[204] One might use the term "the selfish tone", but this would contradict the precept in memetics that a meme is a *network of relationships*: a single note cannot make a museme nor, normally, can two (Jan, 2007, pp. 60–61).

> dominates the others if it subjects them to its superior vital force, within
> the relationship fixed in the various systems .... (Schenker, 1980, p. 84)

In this equation of a tone with a human being, Schenker, and indeed also Schoenberg, understand the former as "living creatures driven by procreative urges" (Arndt, 2011, pp. 103–104, Fig. 4). Beyond such begetting of offspring of the tone itself, Schenker also believed that, "[o]bviously, every tone is possessed of the same inherent urge to procreate infinite generations of overtones.... [which] appears to be in no way inferior to the procreative urge of a living being" (1980, 28–29; see also p. 84), thus blurring the diachronic/horizontal and the synchronic/vertical dimensions of tone-propagation. While most of these overtones are, by definition, not of the same pitch-class as the fundamental – they are different tones, being implicated in relationships (in Schenker's sense above) within the system that are different to those that enmesh the fundamental – they were perhaps understood by Schenker as reproduction-enhancing proxies of the fundamental tone.

The organicist implication of the will of the tone is clear: aligning an individual note with an organism – thus mapping level eight of culture to level five of nature in Table 1.4 – sees each note as possessing a life-force that drives it forwards in fulfilment of its teleology. To speak of a tone's "egotism" is therefore to identify a quasi-Freudian "I" (ego) – this entity not, perhaps, a sexed "he" or "she", but a more bestial and cunning "it" (id). Beyond this individualistic and static organicism, there is a clear systemic and dynamic evolutionism evident in Schenker's notion of the self-interested tone. From a Lamarckian perspective, the tone strives for self-augmentation of its power and capacity across the course of its "life", i.e., its series of occurrences in a single movement or work. From a Darwinian viewpoint (and thus moving from metaphor towards mechanism), the tone fights for survival within a movement or work by engaging in ruthless competition for selection with the other eleven pitch-classes – perhaps by means of system-reconfiguring relationship-variation – in which struggle it is every tone for itself in the quest for system-dominating replication.

More so than by the intercession of the "overtone-proxies" referred to above, this domination, to which Schenker refers in the quotation above, is achieved by a pitch's achieving tonic-status. It becomes the keynote of a section of

Figure 4.7: The "Will of the Tone" in J. S. Bach: Concerto nach italiänischem Gusto BWV 971 (1735), I, bb. 30–34.

a piece of music, subordinating other pitches to its authority and therefore maximising its chances of reproduction – of proliferating within the system via replication. Perhaps one might mutate "dominating" into "dominanting", given that, very often, a tone forces other pitches to function as components of dominant-functioning harmonies and thus to act as auxiliaries in its service.[205] Schenker gives a clear example of this phenomenon, from J. S. Bach's Italian Concerto of 1735, shown in Figure 4.7. Here, thanks to its innate powers of agency, "the scale-step in question [B♭], without any ceremony, usurps quite directly the rank of the tonic, without bothering about the diatonic system, of which it still forms a part" (1980, 256, Ex. 219).

Shifting theoretical paradigms, we might understand this (metaphorically) in terms of the notion of basins of attraction from chaos theory (Gleick, 1998),[206] in the sense that the b♭[1] in the middle voice of b. 31 bends its local space (Lerdahl, 2001), pulling the upper-voice e(♮)[2] of this bar into its basin and distorting it into e♭[2]. This process serves the "will" of the b♭[1] – a token of the note-class type – because the e♭[2], as a local flattened $\hat{4}$, conforms to B♭'s key signature and, in conjunction with the middle-voice a[1] remembered from b. 30, creates the key-defining tritone a[1]–e♭[2] of B♭'s diatonic scale. Although fleeting – F reasserts its "will" in b. 32, restoring its servant e♮[2] and forcing the b♭[1] to act subserviently as $\hat{4}$ in the F-defining tritone b♭[1]–e(♮)[2] – the attempt at "usurpation" of the "rank of the tonic" is clear, indeed brazen.[207]

---

[205] Joseph Riepel's socio-spatial(-gendered) model of tonality makes this hierarchy of servitude explicit, styling the tonic as the *Meyer*, or landowner, lord and master of all those on his estate; and the dominant as the *Oberknecht*, or chief servant (Riepel, 1755, p. 66).

[206] Actually, there is no need for the white-flag defence of metaphor here: as discussed in §3.8.3, Calvin's HCT integrates the concept of basins of attraction with the neuronal mechanisms for museme-encoding (Calvin, 1998, p. 68).

[207] A memetic mechanism, one not incompatible with that suggested in note 206 on page 358, might assert that musemes associated with – in the case of Figure 4.7 – a B♭-major harmony would normally have an E♭ and so the force of schematic memory would bend any E♮ in a

Owing to his preference for mysticism over mechanism, and his essentially static, even Platonic, conception of major-minor tonality, Schenker was not readily inclined to make certain implications of *Der Tonwille* explicit, whether in metaphorically evolutionary terms or not, but they can be readily extrapolated. Despite the adherence in his mature theory to the notion of monotonality – the intraopus counterpart to his rule-level tonal Platonism contending that the (global) tonic of a movement is sovereign and thus any "modulations" are merely illusory phenomena at sub-background levels (Schoenberg, 1983, see also) – one can understand the will of the tone as a force impelling the breakdown of the diatonic order. This is because unrestrained will (egotism) leads to disorder and so – slipping from metaphor to mechanism – disorder, in the form of the anarchy of self-interested scale degrees increasingly disconnected from diatonicism, inevitably weakens the central authority of the tonic. Much has been written on this topic in the last few decades, often discussed under the rubrics of "extended common-practice" tonality (Kinderman & Krebs, 1996; Tymoczko, 2011) and neo-Riemannian theory (Cohn, 1997; Gollin & Rehding, 2011), although (metaphorically) evolutionary metaphors are, perhaps unsurprisingly, used very sparingly in this literature.

Thus, at a higher hierarchic level – that of the system, not the individual pitch – the will of the tone might be understood to have driven structural changes in the network of which it forms a microscopic part, even though Schenker could not bring himself to acknowledge the implications – whether in (metaphorically) evolutionary terms or otherwise – of this will. He could acknowledge the tone-will's effect on the diachronic unfolding of a work, as a phenomenon of prolongation, but could not accept an analogous, higher-level, diachrony (via a series of synchronic time-slices) in the structure of the major-minor tonal system itself. Despite Schenker's reticence to countenance it, there are two ways in which the evolution of tonal systems (broadly understood) has been framed in music-theoretical/analytical discourse – ontogenetically and phylogenetically – although these are not always clearly

---

Bb-major context to conform with the attributes of the parent museme allele-class. In a related explanation, Schubert and Pearce (2016, p. 358) argue that veridical ("case-based") memory accounts for the mental representation of music by means of "the chaining together of different, pre-existing veridical segments of music". On this model, the memory of a similar museme – that is, one from the same allele-class – from a different work might have supervened upon Bach's initial "intention" for e♮² in b. 31 of the Italian Concerto.

demarcated. In the former, the system is aligned with an individual organism and its life-cycle – the collective of tonal works constituting a super-organism or, to extend the terminology of §4.3.1 and §4.3.2, a "rules-style-organism" – thus mapping level three of culture to level five of nature in Table 1.4. In the latter, the system is aligned, often implicitly, with a species – each tonal work representing an instantiation (token) of that species (type), the whole making, to extend the terminology of §4.3.3, a "rules-style-species" – thus mapping level three of culture to level three of nature.[208]

Methodologically, the ontogenetic tradition is as much historiographic as it is music-theoretical/analytical, because charting the life-cycle of major-minor tonality as a rules-style-organism involves documenting its waxing and waning over time as much as – variously metaphorically and mechanistically – explaining the technical processes underpinning this progression. The same is true of the more recent phylogenetic tradition, which, unlike the often case-based methodology of the ontogenetic tradition, often takes corpus-analytical/big-data approaches to track systemic changes in the rules-style-species over time (Huang et al., 2017). Nevertheless, while bringing scientific rigour – and thus mechanism – to bear on the issues involved (Nikolsky, 2015; Nikolsky, 2016), the references to evolution in this tradition are often tenuous and insubstantial, because the mechanisms invoked are generally neither Lamarckian nor (more importantly) Darwinian; rather, they rely on other models, such as those deriving from neuroscience and cognitive psychology, to theorise the processes observed. This is not to say that these other disciplines do not play a significant role in understanding cultural evolution – neuroscience and cognitive psychology certainly do – but without a systematic invocation of the VRS algorithm as a guiding factor in their deployment, such models cannot be genuinely (Darwinian-) evolutionary.

As a final consideration here, it is worth noting that some have recently questioned whether the endeavours of music theory warrant the status of theories in the strict scientific sense of being amenable to verification or to falsification. Wiggins, for instance, argues the "obvious point" that

---

[208] The latter mapping is the basis for the memetic explanation for this process, discussed in §7.5.

> music theory, as it currently exists, is not a scientific theory. I propose that, instead, it is rooted in what psychologists call a folk theory of mind, or folk psychology, which allows each individual human to share naming of intersubjective phenomena that they see experienced by others; the same idea applies to colours, for example. (Wiggins, 2012, p. 137; see also Wiggins et al., 2010)

Aside from the probability that discrete phenomena in music can be categorised more precisely and in more detail than can colours, music theory arguably warrants the status when one considers its more explicitly mathematical branches (§4.1): much of the music theory of the ancient Greeks is largely a restatement of mathematical principles in terms of vibrating strings and columns of air, although their equation of modal scales with emotional states, the basis for later key characterisations, is clearly subjective (H. Keller, 1956; Steblin, 1996). Similarly, developments in late/extended-tonal and atonal theory – such as Babbitt's and Forte's pitch-class (PC) set theory (Babbitt, 1961; Forte, 1973; Rahn, 1980; see also §6.6.3), Lewin's interval-transformation model (2011), and Tymoczko's geometric models (2011) – convert pitches to a numerical representation and then subject them to operations that, to some, are very much more mathematical than musical – even though, in the case of PC set theory, others have questioned the objectivity of the operations the theory supports (McKay, 2015). Similarly, applications to music theory of linguistic models (Lerdahl & Jackendoff, 1983) and frameworks from cognitive psychology (Krumhansl, 1990) represent hypotheses for which there is a body of evidence to support them, or at least a coherent framework for empirical investigation.

But a substantial body of music theory in between these chronological-mathematical "bookends" – such as the phrase-structure assemblage of Koch (Sisman, 1982; Steiner, 2016) and Kirnberger, the voice-leading prolongations of Schenker, and the motivic transformations of Reti – occupies a more problematic status, and would appear vulnerable to Wiggins' dismissal of it as folk psychology. This does not affect the present discussion, which is focused on the use of evolutionary metaphors within the domains of music theory and analysis, not whether these domains are capable of supporting verifiable or falsifiable theories. Of course, even when a music theory uses evolutionary ideas in a metaphorical sense, as those outlined in this section largely do, this does not necessarily preclude it from being scientific, because the evolutionary metaphor might be a rhetorical device employed to elucidate a scientific mechanism.

4.5 The (Co)evolution of Music and Language III: Linguistic Tropes in Discourse on Music

As argued in §2.7 and §3.8, music and language are intimately connected across the sweep of hominin evolution. Thus, to understand music implies the need to understand language, and vice versa. Separate from such evolutionarily grounded (mechanistic) alignments – which extend, in music scholarship, to attempts to apply Chomskyan generative-transformational grammar to music (§3.8.2, §4.4.1.3) – there is also a rich stream of discourse that draws metaphorically upon the relationships between music and language, seeing the former as assuming some of the syntactic and semantic attributes of the latter – indeed, seeing music as in some sense parasitic on language. The durability of the "music-as-language" tradition in musical scholarship is perhaps not surprising given the evolutionary relationships between the two domains, hypothesised in §2.7 and §3.8 to be a function of their bifurcation from a musilinguistic precursor. Represented as stages on a continuum in Figure 2.2, these relationships arguably do not support the notion of evolutionary parasitism of music on language – indeed, the converse (language evolving from musilinguistic song) is more likely to be true – but they readily invite and sustain the formation of cross-domain metaphorical mappings, whether their scientific basis is acknowledged or (as is usual) not. What is perhaps more surprising is the lack of an equally developed parallel tradition in language scholarship that seeks to use music to illuminate language.

As discussed in §2.7.3, Figure 2.2 indicates that both music and language possess syntax ("propositional" in the former, "pitch-blending" in the latter) and semantics ("referential" in the former, "emotive" in the latter). The rhetorical tradition of music-as-language often inverts these categories, however, imputing to music syntactic propositionality and semantic referentiality: music, it holds, can articulate types of thought by virtue of its syntax; and it can convey often quite precise extra-musical meanings. While an expansion of the scope of musical syntax and semantics beyond that represented in Figure 2.2 is entirely tenable – structural commonalities between the neural implementation of musical and linguistic syntax and semantics that might form a basis for this expansion are discussed in §3.8.5 and §3.8.6 – the music-as-language tradition in musical scholarship draws upon the alignment not as a means of illuminating mechanism but rather as a pedagogical, an analytical, and a hermeneutic device. These approaches were pursued chronologically broadly in this order; indeed, "Ricoeur's poetics of word, sentence, and work maps onto the history of music poetics: word = baroque, sentence = classical, work = romantic" (Spitzer, 2004, p. 101).

Perhaps the oldest of these traditions is that which attempted to understand music in terms of classical rhetoric. The ancient Greek and Roman tradition of public oratory, formalised by Quintillian after the model of (among others) Cicero and Caesar,[209] in which a speech had to follow certain principles of structure and content, was taken as a model for the sequential ordering and expressive-dramatic pacing of a piece of music. As suggested apropos the discussion of the "human bundle" in §4.1, this modelling was initially synthetic – it was intended to form a pedagogical framework for composers to work within (composition through analysis) – but it later became hermeneutic, as music theory was increasingly turned not only towards providing composers the necessary intellectual frameworks to make new music, but also towards offering listeners (and composers-as-listeners) analytical strategies for the understanding and interpretation of extant, valued music.

Writing in the early-seventeenth century, Joachim Burmeister (1564–1629) represents a high point of this already centuries-old tradition, and his analysis of Lassus's motet *In me transierunt* (published 1562), part of Burmeister's *Musica poetica* of 1606, both confirms the reliance of seventeenth-century music theory on linguistic models and represents one of the earliest analyses of a complete piece of music (Bent & Pople, 2001, sec. II.1). In this approach, syntax inheres in the combination of short musical "figures" (*Figuren*; Spitzer, 2004, p. 101) to form longer segments, these basic units serving as "wordless" analogues to the rhetorical tropes that form a longer "oration" (Bonds, 1991).

---

[209] Quintillian's *Institutio oratoria* (*c*. 95 CE) had been rediscovered in 1416 (Bent & Pople, 2001, sec. II.1).

Global structure – essentially an articulation of Agawu's beginning-middle-ending paradigm (1991) – derives from the functional role each trope fulfils and thus integrates syntax with pragmatics. Burmeister accordingly divides Lassus's motet into nine "periods" (Bent & Pople, 2001, sec. II.1), each coded with terms from classical rhetoric such as *Exordium* (introduction) and *anadiplosis* (repetition of a unit from the end of one section at the start of the next) (Burton, 2007; Ratner, 1980, pp. 91–92), for which equivalences in musical figuration and technique were posited (Ratner, 1980, pp. 92–94). Semantics inheres in the relationship between the global structure and the local *Figuren*, the latter being not only music-syntactic but also music-semiotic units that render the sense of the associated text through expressive pitch-rhythm contours. The concatenation of *Figuren* into nested rhetorical-structural hierarchies provides the necessary syntactic sense within which the semantic sensibility is grounded. Implicit in this tradition is the equation of musical with linguistic units – a valid strategy, both metaphorically and mechanistically, in the light of certain of Hockett's design features of language (page 126) – such that musical figures represent words or short phrases, and longer musical segments are variously understood as more extended linguistic phrase-types, such as periods and sentences.[210]

A transitional figure linking the seventeenth-century "word" tradition to the eighteenth-century "sentence" tradition (in Ricoeur's senses referred to on page 363), Johann Mattheson's (1681–1764) *Der vollkommene Capell-meister* of 1739 (Mattheson & Harriss, 1981) codified the sequence of music-rhetorical tropes proper to a composition as *Exordium-Narratio-Propositio-Confutatio-Confirmatio-Peroratio*, in addition to hypothesising various equivalences between linguistic and musical punctuation (Agawu, 1991, p. 52). Both concerns, the former global, the latter local, exemplify the eighteenth century's interest in techniques for building musical form in terms of syntactic-semantic units understood via the prism of language, the syntactic tradition reaching its zenith with the work of Koch. The logical conclusion of Mattheson's work was his claim that purely instrumental music was a "language

---

[210] Spitzer distinguishes, perhaps too prescriptively, between periods and sentences by arguing that "[a] period is an eight- or sixteen-measure antecedent-consequent form", whereas a sentence is "an eight-measure theme characterized by internal development and acceleration of phrase rhythm …" (2004, p. 74). Understood this way, the former is symmetrical and poetic, and is characteristic of Marx's *Satz* material-type; and the latter is asymmetrical and prose-like, and characteristic of *Gang* (§4.4.1).

of tones". That is, he argued that music was capable of the communication of meaning, provided the listener was familiar with its syntax and semantics. This was particularly controversial in the early-eighteenth century because instrumental music was regarded as inferior to that which set or accompanied a text. This tradition assumed that ironic contradictions between text and musical setting were exceptional, so it was held, somewhat tautologically, that what the text said was what the music "meant". Instrumental music's "emancipation" from vocal models (Dahlhaus, 1982, p. 24) was only accomplished in the late-eighteenth century – partly thanks to the achievements of the Mannheim and Viennese schools – and consolidated in the early-nineteenth century tradition of "absolute" music (Chua, 1999). This emancipation is evidenced by Hoffmann's assertion – rooted in Ricoeur's nineteenth-century "work" tradition – that "instrumental music . . . , scorning every aid, every admixture of another art (the art of poetry), gives pure expression to music's specific nature, recognizable in this form alone" (in Strunk et al., 1998, p. 151).

As an adherent of the "doctrine of the affections" – *Affektenlehre*; broadly analogous to the theory of *Figuren*, *Figurenlehre* – Mattheson held the view that localised musical patterns were not only building blocks of syntactic structures at higher levels but were also able to communicate emotion and sketch out more concrete imagery, thus serving as figures of musical "speech". A memetic reading of *Figuren* would understand them as musemes whose extra-musical content inhered in the complex dialectic between the natural (image-schematic and Implication-Realisation forces) and the nurtural ("topical" associations between the figure and extra-musical content, underwritten by the identified natural affordances). In terms of image schemata, many *Figuren* represent "pathways leading to a goal" (Snyder, 2000, p. 110), this equivalent to Spitzer's "path" schema (§4.2). Relying on "motion-linkage-causation" and "linearity: paths and goals" (2000, pp. 113–115), such trajectories – whose arrival at a destination, or circumvention of it, give rise to emotional and/or intellectual satisfaction or frustration, respectively – align closely with structures theorised by the Implication-Realisation model,[211] specifically Process (Narmour, 1990, p. 89). The related schema of "'up' and

---

[211] For Narmour, frustrated expectations take the form of "tiny cognitive 'jolts' to the neuronal electrical system governing our subconscious cognitive expectations" (1990, p. 138).

Figure 4.8: *Figuren* from *Der vollkommene Capellmeister*.

'down'" (Snyder, 2000, pp. 111–112) aligns most naturally with Reversal (Narmour, 1990, p. 151).

Figure 4.8 illustrates a two-phrase passage of music from Mattheson's discussion of "melodic invention", representing an "example of a scornful saying [phrase 1, bb. 1–4] bursting forth in unexpected joy [phrase 2, bb. 5–8]" (1981, p. 299).[212]

The interaction of natural and nurtural forces referred to above is clearly evident here. On the natural forces, there is a clear series of image-schematic "pathways leading to a goal", in the form of the rising and falling patterns opening and closing each phrase (bb. 1, 3–4; bb. 5–6, 7–8), these being understandable in terms of the indicated [P] structures. The higher-level rising [P] in bb. 5^1–6^3 encompasses, and transcends, the Retrospective Registral Reversal – [(VR)] – in b. 5^{4-6}, whereas the [(VR)] at the analogous point of the first phrase, bb. 1^4–2^2, returns to the phrase's starting pitch, a^2, giving a less directional Duplication – [D] – in bb. 1–2 at the level equivalent to that of the [P] in bb. 5–6. Indeed, the rising and falling [P]s in the second phrase – essentially ascending from $\hat{1}$–$\hat{5}$ then descending from $\hat{5}$–$\hat{1}$ – are more strongly goal-orientated than those in the first phrase. Those in the first phrase, although encompassing the same boundary scale degrees ($\hat{6}$–$\hat{1}$) and interval as those in the second phrase (the minor sixth, bb^1–d^1 in the first phrase and f^2–a^1 in the second), are attenuated by the [R] of bb. 2^3–3^2, which represents a more strongly disruptive force than the analogous but weaker Intervallic Process – [IP] – of b. 7^{1-3}.

---

[212] The text here (after Psalm 144 in Luther's 1545 translation) is: "[phrase 1] *Wohl dem Bold dem es also gehet; [phrase 2] aber wohl dem Bold, des der Herr ein Gott ist!*" ("[phrase 1] Blessed are the bold of whom this is true; [phrase 2] but blessed are the bold, whose Lord is God!").

On the nurtural forces, there are several incursions here of what Narmour terms "intraopus style" ("os") and "extraopus style" ("xs") (1990, p. 38).[213] The latter encompasses the general influence of the minor mode, which perhaps augments the assertive effect of the instances of [P] and gives them a bleaker edge. A further artefact of the minor mode are the three occurrences of the $\hat{6}$–$\hat{5}$ dyad (bb. 3, 6 and, at a higher level, bb. 1–2), which is an expressive trope – the *"Seufzer"* (sigh) topic (Caplin, 2005, p. 115, Tab. 1), perhaps best understood as a component of the *empfindsamer Stil* (style of sensibility) (Ratner, 1980, p. 22) – common in minor-key music of the common-practice period and which possesses an affective/pathetic connotation. Other topical connotations include the "gay and lively" gigue rhythm of the second phrase (Ratner, 1980, p. 15). More broadly, the nurtural dimension encompasses those effects upon the music of the text and vice versa. The former include the emphasis on certain notes engendered (phonetically and semantically) by salient words of the text, such the additional foregrounding of the strong-beat a^1 of b. 2^{1-2} and e^2 of b. 6^{1-3} by *"Bold"* ("bold"), and the emphasis on the weak-beat b^1 of b. 7^{4-6} by *"Gott"* ("God"). The latter include the intensifying effect of the minor mode on the "scornful saying" of the first phrase,[214] and the converse dampening effect of the minor on the "bursting forth in unexpected joy" of the second phrase.

The late-Baroque tradition of *Figurenlehre* was recuperated in the 1960s by Cooke, who attempted to ground the intuitions of Baroque *Affektenlehre* more firmly on music-theoretical and music-psychological principles. By doing so, he ostensibly shifted the centre of gravity of the music-as-language tradition from metaphor towards mechanism, although one empirical study found "only very limited support for the specific details of Cooke's . . . theory" (Kaminska & Woolf, 2000, p. 151). Cooke argued that the intrinsic e/motional properties, to recall Levitin's concept (page 98), of certain musical patterns allowed one to speak with confidence of a "language of music" (1968). A

---

[213] The former – broadly equivalent to Meyer's concept of the same name, save for the latter's emphasis on the replication of patterning – concerns veridical expectancies set up by the work's ongoing unfolding. The latter concerns influences on a work imposed by its encompassing culture, understood here in terms of memetics.

[214] The scorn is directed towards those three situations abhorred in "that there be no breaking in [invasion], nor going out [captivity]; that there be no complaining [distress] in our streets" (Psalm 144, line 14; King James Version).

controversial and much critiqued work (Smoliar, 1994) – perhaps because it assumes to be true that which it sets out to prove – Cooke aimed

> to discover exactly how music functions as a language, to establish the terms of its vocabulary, and to explain how these terms may legitimately be said to express the emotions they appear to. Beginning with the basic material – notes of definite pitch – … musical works are built out of the *tensions* between such notes. These tensions can be set up in three dimensions – *pitch*, *time*, and *volume*; and the setting up of such tensions, and the colouring of them by the *characterizing agents* of *tone-colour* and *texture*, constitute the whole apparatus of musical expression (Cooke, 1968, p. 34; emphases in the original)

As befits a mechanistic explanation, Cooke's three dimensions of pitch, time and volume have broader evolutionary significance, in that they align closely with the "sentic" states – internal e/motional dispositions expressible via a range of output channels – common to humans and other species hypothesised by Clynes (1978). These states result from

> a general modulatory system involved in conveying and perceiving the *intensity* of emotive expression along a continuous scale. It expresses intensity by means of three graded spectra: tempo [time] modulation (slow-fast spectrum), amplitude modulation [volume] (soft-loud spectrum), and register [pitch] selection (low-pitched-high-pitched spectrum). This system appears to be invariant across modalities of expression in humans, such as speech, music, and gesture …. It also appears to function in a similar way in emotive behavior in nonhuman animals …. (Brown, 2000, p. 287; emphasis in the original)

Cooke's methodology was to hypothesise the likely emotional content of certain figures – "the emotions they appear to [express]" – using various music-theoretical and, implicitly, image-schematic intuitions, this perhaps undertaken in conjunction with consideration of the relevant segments of the texts of vocal music using those figures. Thus identified, such figures – Cooke's "basic terms of musical vocabulary" (1968, Ch. 3) – occurring in instrumental music allowed him to attach the identified emotion to those passages, in the absence of direct verbal correlation. Understood in terms of memetics, Cooke's basic terms represent museme allele-classes, defined by their common shallow-middleground-level scale-degree structure. There are clear examples of such vocabulary-items in bb. 5–8 of Figure 4.8. The pattern in bb. 5–6 is an instance of the "ascending 1–(2)–3–(4)–5 (minor)", which is "expressive of an outgoing feeling of pain – an assertion of sorrow, a complaint, a protest against misfortune ..." (1968, p. 122). It is elided with a second term, the "(5)–6–5 (minor)" – the aforementioned *Seufzer* – of b. 6, "giving the effect of a burst of anguish" (1968, p. 146). This in turn overlaps with the "descending 5–(4)–3–(2)–1 (minor)" of bb. 6–8, "which has been much used to express an 'incoming' painful emotion, in a context of finality ..." (1968, p. 133).[215] Of course, there is a dissonance here between the deployment of these three particular basic terms and the affirmative content of the text of this phrase, one that does not necessarily require one to assert that Mattheson had any ironic intentions in mind. More broadly, and as Figure 2.2 implies, the further apart two modalities are on the continuum between music and language – or, in this case, where there is evident tension between the explicit "verbal song" of "music's vehicle mode" and the implicit content of "music's acoustic mode" – the more problematic the "translation" between them.

4.6 The Evolution of Scholarly Discourses on Music

Nattiez is keen to maintain a separation between the object of musicological enquiry and the discourses that surround it.[216] He argues that

> [a]n analysis in effect states itself in the form of a discourse – spoken or written – and it is consequently the product of an action; it leaves a trace and gives rise to readings, interpretations, and criticisms. Although we find the tripartite dimension of all symbolic forms in analysis as well, analysis is nonetheless not merely a semiological fact comparable to others discussed so far. Analysis exists because it deals with another object – the musical fact being analyzed. In other words, discourse about music is a *metalanguage*. Consequently, an epistemological and semiological examination of analysis involves three elements: (a) *The object....* (b)

---

[215] The first and third of these terms, with their notions of "outgoing" and "incoming", respectively, draw upon the centre/periphery schema (§4.2).

[216] While Nattiez uses the term "analysis" in his account, it can readily be generalised to all forms of music-scholarly enquiry, including historical and critical study. Figure 4.9 should be understood in this light.

The metalanguage.... (c) *The methodology* of analysis. (Nattiez, 1990, pp. 133–134; emphases in the original)

Here, the object, while mediated by the observer's "analytical situation", represents the music under investigation (1990, p. 133). From a memetic perspective, the latter is not only the phemotypic product(s) of the composer's memome, but also that phemotype reconstituted as memomic neuronal interconnection in the brains of receivers. The metalanguage is, as its name implies, the higher-order (verbal-conceptual) language used to interrogate the lower-order language (musical "language"), which is the medium or substrate of the object. As is often the case with metalanguages, "translation" is needed between the "object language" (1990, 133, Note 1) and the metalanguage. With music this is inherently problematic for, as Keller argued, "the laws of [conceptual thought's] logic are far removed from the laws of musical logic" (1985, p. 73).[217] The methodology is made up of a series of procedures that connect the object to the analysis (Nattiez, 1990, p. 134).

Because scholarly discourses/metalanguages are verbal-conceptual memeplexes (§4.1), they are subject to the operation of the VRS algorithm; but they are not fully autonomous evolutionary systems (insofar as any such system can possess full autonomy). This is because they are shaped by an additional selection pressure beyond those generally attendant upon verbal-conceptual memeplexes – the latter including the lower-level pressures of euphony[218] and the higher-level pressures of internal coherence. This additional selection pressure is that of perceived alignment with (i.e., explanatory utility for) that which they attempt to model or explicate – hence their only partial autonomy. In other words, most music-theoretical/analytical verbal-conceptual memeplexes "aim" – in the same non-intentional, blindly algorithmic manner that characterises evolution in general – to adapt (or to exapt) to the music with which they coevolve.

---

[217] By "musical logic", and as discussed in §4.4.1.3, Keller is referring in part to the kinds of motivic relationships he detected in the music of Schoenberg and then extrapolated (as did Reti (Reti, 1951; Reti, 1967)) to the music of other composers. The argument of §3.8.6 is that linguistic and musical syntax ("logic") are not as "far removed" from each other as Keller implies. See also H. Keller (2001).

[218] That is, some music-theoretical/analytical concepts prosper not (just) because of their internal coherence and relevance to the music that is their object, but (also) because their terminology is striking – "GTTM", *Tonnetz*, "Meyer [Schema]", etc. – and memorable. See also the related discussion of "Rule Britannia" on page 146.

The evolution of the verbal-conceptual memeplexes that articulate cultural discourses often lags some way behind the evolution of the music that they are adapted to explicate, and this gap is sometimes particularly pronounced in the case of music theory and analysis. It is seen when certain phenomena that arise in the work of progressive composers often take decades to be assimilated by music theory and formalised by music analysis as valid compositional procedures. As this implies, such modelling, or *description*, often takes the form of regulations, or *prescription*, for what is permissible in some pedagogical or critical system. While there are exceptions to this principle of practice-theory asynchrony – perhaps most notably in traditions where continuity and craft are privileged, such as the school of sacred polyphony crowned by Palestrina and codified by Fux (Fux, 1965); and the Italian *partimento* tradition (Gjerdingen, 2007a; Gjerdingen, 2007b) – for much of post-Renaissance European musical history concerns have been raised by theorists about composers' perceived deviations from "correct" procedures and their alleged breaking of "rules".[219] In retaliation for this perceived intrusion, some composers have defended what they see as their right to set the terms of reference for their work, articulated perhaps most famously in the statement attributed by Varèse to Debussy, that "works of art make rules but rules do not make works of art" (in Albright, 2004, p. 185).

Perhaps the archetypal example of the initial disjunction between a laggard theory and the fleet-footed practice of composers is Beethoven, whose reception in the music-theoretical/analytical literature, crudely summarised, curves from incomprehension to canonisation over the course of the nineteenth century. This is also a model that aligns in part with much twentieth-century *avant-garde* music, the disturbances at notorious 1913 performances of Schoenberg's Chamber Symphony no. 1 (1906) and Stravinsky's *Le sacre du printemps* (1913) establishing a durable trope (also evident with Beethoven) of audience alienation.[220] While a considerable generalisation, we might in summary invoke Lyotard's dictum that "a work can become modern only if it is first postmodern" (in J. D. Kramer, 2016, p. 6); that is, it must not

---

[219] Conversely, some composers – most notably in the case of Scheibe's critique of J. S. Bach (Maul, 2013) – have been accused of excessive, stultifying conservatism.

[220] There are numerous caveats here, however. For one thing, the two concerts failed, in part, owing to intrigue, not aesthetics. Moreover, some twentieth-century music, perhaps most notably that based on serialism (and, later, "total" serialism), is the product of an antecedent theory, not its precursor, thus foregrounding prescription over description.

only transgress stylistic boundaries (as a result becoming postmodern) but must also become accepted as a contribution to artistic development (thus becoming modern).

The radicalism of such advances in compositional practice has occasionally been matched by paradigm changes/shifts in the verbal-conceptual meme-plexes/metalanguages of music scholarship, which to some extent parallel those in the sciences (Kuhn, 2012; see also note 97 on page 179). In these reorientations, one theoretical or methodological model is supplanted by another, such as the movement from positivistic to critical musicology in the 1980s and the incursion of geometric models into music theory and analysis in the 1990s. While such reorientations may – like those in musical style – sometimes appear to be saltational, the logic of Darwinism implies that they in fact arise gradualistically from the operation of numerous interacting "microhistorical" (Herbert, 2003) processes. As in biological evolution, it is the factors of "(time)scale, perspective and granularity" (page 54) that give the illusion of saltation in cultural evolution. As a form of the latter, metalinguistic paradigm shifts appear to operate in accordance with the model to be discussed, apropos music-systemic paradigm shifts, in §7.5, whereby low-level (microhistorical) musemic changes are understood to feed upwards and cumulatively reshape global systems of tonal organisation.

Figure 4.9 shows Nattiez's representation of the interplay between music and the scholarly discourses associated with it (1990, p. 135, Fig. 6.1). He hypothesises two parallel trajectories of (evolutionary) development, one of the object (music) and the other of the metalanguage, each strand interacting, as a selective force, with the other.

Here, "P" and "E" represent the poietic and esthesic levels, respectively; and the "work" is located at the neutral level. The "methodology of analysis" represents "a transition, controlled by implicit or explicit *procedures*, from the work to the analysis" (Nattiez, 1990, p. 134; emphasis in the original). The "influence on the music" represents the closing of the feedback loop, in that certain concepts abstracted from a work (or from several works) and sustained by a metalanguage – which includes pedagogical traditions of composition – may, as noted, go on to influence the practice of later composers. This model is returned to and extended in §6.6.3, which attempts to formalise

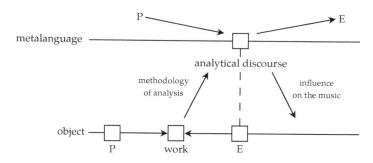

Figure 4.9: Nattiez on Object, Metalanguage and Method.

more explicitly the operation of the evolutionary processes involved, and to accommodate music produced not only directly by humans (Figure 6.13) but also indirectly by means of quasi-autonomous generative computer systems (Figure 6.14).

Tracing the evolution of the verbal-conceptual memeplexes constituting music-scholarly discourses is complex. One way to do so is to track citations of certain key terms, as was done in the case of the term "memetic" in §3.4.1, using them as markers of the wider memeplex encompassing the network of concepts constituting the discourse/metalanguage. Repeating the methodology represented in Figure 3.2, Figure 4.10 uses *CiteSpace* to graph co-occurrences of the terms "music" and "gender"[221] from publications in *Scopus*'s Arts and Humanities category, which, at the time of the query, contained 1,538 records. The earliest record in this category of the *Scopus* database to contain the search terms is an article dating from 1981.[222]

What does Figure 4.10 reveal about the chronological and conceptual-spatial distribution of the selected literature on music and gender? Before examining the visualisation itself, and by analogy with Figure 3.3, *CiteSpace*'s analysis of the number of unique records (of the total 1,242 given in note 222 on page

---

[221] This is not the place to enter into the increasingly controversial debate over (biological) sex *versus* (psychological) gender. Suffice to say that the literature in this category generally uses the latter term to encompass concepts related to the former.

[222] The report detailing the outcome of *CiteSpace*'s extraction of data from the .ris bibliographic citation file exported from *Scopus* states that "1,535 records [were] converted .... Total References [i.e., citations of literature within sources]: 104,247[;] Valid References: 102,943 (98.0%)". By analogy with the data discussed in note 99 on page 181, elimination of duplicates reduced the number of unique records to 1,242.

Figure 4.10: *CiteSpace* Visualisation of Citations of "Music" and "Gender" per year 1980–2020 in *Scopus*.

373) per year, graphed in Figure 4.11, shows a generally steady and steep increase, indicating fairly rapid dissemination of the "music and gender" verbal-conceptual memeplex.

Turning back to, Figure 4.10, and subject to the same Borgesian constraints as were articulated in connection with the list on page 181, one might make the following observations:

1. While there are 254 notional clusters and fifteen clusters graphed in the default layout (#0–#5, #7–#10, #12, #15, #24, #43 and #45), using *CiteSpace*'s facility to display only the largest of them reduces this number to eleven principal clusters (#0–#5, #7–#10 and #12).

2. There are two interconnected clusters, #0 and #1, each labelled with the identifier "gay music". Cluster #0 is associated primarily with Hebdige (1979) and Green (1997) (who examine music and gender in relation to their roles in subcultures and education, respectively); whereas cluster #1 is associated with Butler (1990) and Walser (1993) (the first of these being a seminal text in the field). Both clusters are connected by the widely cited McClary (1991); and cluster #1, via Walser (1993), gives rise in part to cluster #3, with its coverage of issues of gender and sexuality in heavy metal music.

3. Cluster #4 is centred around Frith (1981) (the node label "Frith S (1981)" is largely obscured by the cluster label "#4 social harmony" in Figure 4.10), and while covering similar ground to cluster #3 – both explore subcultural niches articulated by specific popular-music genres, metal in cluster #3 and rock in cluster #4 – the layout of the visualisation suggests a separate aetiology for each cluster. That is, clusters #3 and #4 represent, by definition, coherent bodies of interconnected research, each of which traces a distinct approach to the study of ostensibly similar repertoires and comparable social functions.

4. While clusters #0, #1, #3 and #4 arguably encompass the main focus of literature orientated around the two search terms – i.e., on questions of individual and group identity and sexuality as they pertain to music and gender – other distinct areas of research exist based upon concepts related to these terms. Cluster #9, for instance, relates to literature that explores them from a psychological perspective,[223] even though one of the key nodes identified – Juslin and Laukka

---

[223] While there is a separate Psychology category in *Scopus* (consisting of 150 records containing the present search terms at the time of searching), some psychology literature is included in the Arts and Humanities category.

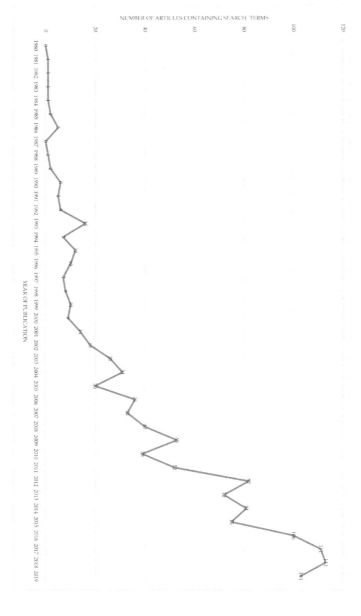

Figure 4.11: Number of Records Containing "Music" and "Gender" Per Year 1980–2019.

(2003); another node in this cluster is Chamorro-Premuzic and Furnham (2007) – uses the word "gender" only once in its main text. The article is concerned, however, with implicitly gender-specific aspects of vocal production, such as frequency and intensity (2003, p. 790, Tab. 6); it also considers evolutionary issues relevant to vocalisation that are pertinent to the discussions in §2.3 and §2.5.

5. Another area of music psychology represented in Figure 4.10 grows out of cluster #9. Cluster #2 is concerned with the subject of music and emotion, and includes as key nodes Gabrielsson and Juslin (1996) and A. C. North et al. (2000), both of which consider gender as a factor mediating the emotional affects/effects of music.

6. While having different antecedents, clusters #8 and #10 concern the relation-ships between music, gender and education (the title of a text, Green (1997), central to cluster #0). Cluster #8 is centred on Abeles (2009) and Freer (2010), which consider reasons for instrument-choice among young people of relev-ance to music educators, including socialised associations between instruments and the learner's sex (Abeles, 2009), and the pursuit of "possible selves" via instrument-choice (Freer, 2010). Cluster #10 is centred on Bandura (1997) and S. G. Nielsen (2004), the latter node examining the effect of gender on the instrument-practise strategies deployed by degree-level music students in terms of the concept of "self efficacy" articulated in the former node. While of separate aetiology, cluster #5 is broadly cognate with clusters #8 and #10. Centred on Barber et al. (2001), it analyses the educational (and general life-success) outcomes of participation in music, among other activities.

7. Cluster #12 is something of an outlier, perhaps on account of its relative infancy as a research field. In the context of music technology being a field generally regarded as male-dominated, indeed sometimes distinctly sexist, for all but its most recent history, Rodgers (2010) considers the experiences of women in electronic music, in terms of their specific modes of creativity and more broadly in the light of feminism.[224]

8. *CiteSpace*'s narrative summary (see point 2 of the list on page 184) of this network identifies the three most central nodes as (in decreasing order of centrality) Bourdieu (1984), Butler (1990) and McClary (1991). Moreover, the

---

[224] The *Scopus* used for this analysis does not contain some of the most recent work in this field, such as Dobson (2018), which addresses the specifically educational implications of a "digital audio ecofeminism".

summary identifies, in its citation count ranking, the three most cited nodes as (in decreasing order of citations) Butler (1990), McClary (1991) and Green (1997).

Of course, *CiteSpace* primarily tracks replication of the verbal-conceptual memeplexes that constitute an academic discourse and that therefore define and "underwrite" its metalanguage. Variation of these memeplexes is implicitly represented by the "speciation" events forming clusters. Selection, while generally regarded as a form of endorsement, can instead be negative, for two reasons. Firstly, as argued in Bloomian intertextuality theory, an "anxiety of influence" may motivate evasion (non-selection) – as part of a "paradoxical 'including/excluding' movement" – rather than emulation (Korsyn, 1991, p. 8). In such evasion, the notions articulated by a memeplex are essentially accepted but, in a Freudian sense, repressed. Secondly, writing an article on some academic subject can (in an oversimplistic binarism) be an attempt either to endorse or to refute the precepts of its antecedent literature – the "praise versus bury" dichotomy discussed in §3.4.1.

The latter is illustrated, at its most extreme, by a recent hoax by Boghossian and Lindsay (2020) against gender studies and, its perpetrators would argue, the subject's postmodernist, left-wing underpinning. This deception was itself inspired by the "Sokal hoax", whereby the physicist Alan Sokal had a parody article published (and then, on discovery of the hoax, retracted) by the journal *Social Text* (Sokal, 1996). Sokal's article incoherently juxtaposed complex mathematics with an opaque postmodern vocabulary and convoluted writing style. In the view of Boghossian and Lindsay (2020), "[t]he publication of this nonsense paper, in a prestigious journal with a strong postmodernist orientation, delivered a devastating blow to postmodernism's intellectual legitimacy".[225] The later hoax took the form of "an absurd paper ['The conceptual penis as a social construct'] loosely composed in the style of post-structuralist discursive gender theory" (Boghossian & Lindsay, 2020), which was published (under pseudonyms) by the journal *Cogent Social Sciences* (Lindsay & Boyle, 2017). The authors took the view – which they held to have been vindicated by the acceptance of their paper – that "[t]he most potent among the human susceptibilities to corruption by fashionable non-

---

[225] Sokal's article motivated the development of the *Postmodernism generator* website (Bulhak, 1996), which assembles random, postmodern-sounding text using recursive grammars.

sense is the temptation to uncritically endorse *morally* fashionable nonsense. That is, we assumed we could publish outright nonsense provided it looked the part and portrayed a moralizing attitude that comported with the editors' moral convictions" (2020, emphasis in the original).

Amusing as all this might be to those critical of "grievance studies" (Pluckrose et al., 2018), and of the broader "woke" agenda that sustains them, there are important evolutionary points to be made in the light of these hoaxes. For one thing, to parody a metalanguage, the verbal-conceptual memeplex that defines it must, as with all memeplexes, be: (i) sufficiently internally consistent (i.e., conceptually and structurally coherent) to exist as a reasonably stable and durable entity (the replicator attributes of copying-fidelity (§1.6.3.3) and longevity (§1.6.3.1), respectively); and (ii) sufficiently perceptually-cognitively salient for it to be transmitted widely enough to be recognised as something relatively current and significant in culture (the attribute of fecundity (§1.6.3.2)). The profusion of literature in the arts and humanities dealing with music and gender visualised in Figure 4.10 – perhaps only a subset of which is concerned with the "post-structuralist discursive gender theory" mocked by Boghossian and Lindsay (2020) – suggests that these two conditions have been met in the case of this particular memeplex. Moreover, as Figure 4.11 indicates, the increasingly rapid acceleration in transmission of the memeplex starting in the early 2000s is perhaps evidence of its growing evolutionary success. Of course, this conquest of intellectual territory, as with any verbal-conceptual memeplex, is not necessarily an index of veracity.

4.7 Culture-Music-Discourse Coevolutionary Models

If cultural evolution is driven by the VRS algorithm (§1.5.1), and if the evolution of music is understood as a subset of cultural evolution more broadly, then the question arises as to the relationship between the non-musical and the musical dimensions of cultural evolution.[226] Do evolutionary

---

[226] By "non-musical dimensions", I refer to the interaction between phenomena in the domains of politics, economics, philosophy (broadly defined) and other domains sustaining verbal, graphical and imagistic patterning, whose replication gives rise to memes and memeplexes. While cultural evolution encompasses two domains – crudely, the structural and the ornamental – they are treated as closely related here.

processes in music in some sense follow those of culture more generally – is music a mere epiphenomenon of more powerful cultural forces that buffet and shape it? – or does music have to capacity to feed back into other dimensions of cultural evolution to influence it? Even accepting the possibility of two-way interaction between non-musical culture and musical culture, one would perhaps have to concede that the direction of travel – of the arrow of causation – might be primarily from non-musical to musical culture, and that countervailing pressures would be less substantive; and one would also have to concede that there is an inherent translation problem, because the medium of music (sounds and their associated phemotypic products) is incommensurate with those media through which non-musical culture (verbally expressible concepts, images) is propagated. This is the same issue that Keller identified in §4.4.1.1, when he asserted that "[a]ll conceptual thought about music is a detour, from music *via* terms to music ..." (1994, p. 127). Perhaps one interface between these domains might lie in discourse on music, scholarly and journalistic, which channels the reception of music through conduits shaped by the *Zeitgeist* of society, and which – while not claiming that verbalisation about music possesses significant cultural power – affords at least some potential for the reciprocal (re)shaping of non-musical culture. More directly, the texts of popular musics – such as protest songs of various kinds (Friedman, 2013; Martinelli, 2017) – can have powerful effects on non-musical culture, given their capacity to motivate mass-action. These possibilities notwithstanding, my interest here is primarily on less tangible, non-verbal connections between the nature of music and the nature of the wider society of which it forms a part.

In this regard, some of Susan McClary's most seminal writings explore the possibility that changing socio-economic structures are in some senses inscribed in music – thus considering at least a one-way influence – the latter domain serving variously as avatar, mirror or simulacrum of the cultural and economic forces that gave rise to it (McClary, 1986; McClary, 1993; McClary, 1994). McClary's focus on the music of the late-eighteenth to the late-nineteenth centuries in several of her writings motivates her to read well understood socio-cultural issues of that century – arguably the most dynamic phase of the transition from a feudal, agrarian and aristocratic system to a bourgeois, industrial and capitalist model – in terms of their effects on music. Several themes recur in the social and cultural history of this period, most notably tensions between masculinity and femininity and the functional roles these imply; and the dialectic between the individual and society. The first of these dichotomies transcends issues of time and place, even though its implications are socially mediated. While McClary does not formalise it in evolutionary terms – the implications of patriarchy, to use her preferred formalism, are not traced back to their evolutionary motivations – the dichotomy might nevertheless be understood in terms of effects resulting from sexual selection (§2.5.3). The second dichotomy engages not only the political, economic and legal obligations attendant upon the individual *vis-à-vis* the collective (the price that must be paid for the benefits afforded by society), but also the individual's internal trajectories of self-actualisation – their struggles with "problems of identity and alterity" (McClary, 1986, p. 137). This dichotomy is perhaps the more relevant to the concerns of the present section: one of McClary's most consistent claims in this literature is that individual fulfilment and social coherence were broadly compatible in the late-eighteenth century, but became increasingly irreconcilable in the nineteenth; and that these tensions were played out via certain key features of musical structure and style.

While several facets of McClary's work have faced often strident criticism – the preface to McClary (2002) and the introduction to McClary (2007) ("The life and times of a renegade musicologist") take stock of some of the responses to her writings – she hypothesises certain suggestive alignments between social and musical structure that are amenable to an evolutionary reading, despite her not explicitly pursuing this approach. Discussing the second movement of Mozart's Piano Concerto in G major K. 453 of 1784, perhaps her most thorough working-out of the musical consequences of the second of the above dichotomies, McClary contends that three elements of the movement work to articulate a dialectic of the individual *versus* society. These elements – tonality, "sonata procedure" (what is termed the sonata principle in §4.3.2), and "concerto format" – work synergystically to shape a narrative in which the soloist – understood as a representation of the individual, and possibly of Mozart himself – first opposes and is then reconciled with society. For McClary,

> [t]onality emerged in the seventeenth century in direct opposition to a
> musical language that (like the church and aristocracy that nurtured it)
> articulated a static worldview in which notions such as radical progress
> and destabilizing goal-seeking were threats. Likewise the rationality
> of the eighteenth century was called into question by the nineteenth-
> century Romantics who rejected what they regarded as 'instrumental
> reason' in their celebrations of the irrational: in music, this rejection
> was manifested in unconventional narrative plans and in an increasingly
> individualistic, convoluted, deviant harmonic language. (McClary, 1986,
> pp. 135–136; see also McClary, 1994, pp. 69–70)

Sonata procedure, she contends, takes the goal-seeking of tonality – the
dramatic arc represented by the initial stable tonic, its usurpation by the
second key, and its triumphant closing return – and aligns it with a narrative
dichotomy of protagonist and antagonist, or Self and Other, represented by
the first and second subjects, respectively (1994, pp. 70–73). Appearing in an
alien key, the second subject must be forced back into conformity with the
tonic in the recapitulation. Not only does McClary present the two subjects
as polarised agents but she often reads them as gendered, drawing upon a
distinction evident in some of the earliest discussions of sonata form (Marx,
1997, p. 133) and arguably underwritten by image-schematic alignments
with stereotypical sex-differences. In this trope, the first subject is coded as
"masculine", by means of a loud dynamic, uneven (thus perhaps "assertive") rhythms, and a wide pitch-range; and the second subject is coded as
"feminine", by means of a soft dynamic, even (thus perhaps "submissive")
rhythms, and a narrow pitch-range. These various dichotomies encompass a
palpable tension, for while

> [t]he outcome [of a sonata-form movement] is invariable, predetermined
> – the first key and its theme *have* to prevail if this is truly to count as a
> piece of tonal music – yet the threat must always appear genuine so
> that we can repeatedly celebrate the triumph of the tonic protagonist
> and the appropriation of the 'Other'. And it is, finally, only by virtue of
> the encounter with the second theme and key that the identity of the
> first seems able to affirm itself narratively. It depends on its 'Other' for
> extension and self-definition. (McClary, 1986, p. 137; emphasis in the
> original)

Indeed, this "triumph" is often accomplished ruthlessly, as McClary's controversial account of the first movement of Beethoven's Ninth Symphony in terms of sexual violence maintains – for her, the opening of the recapitulation represents "the throttling, murderous rage of a rapist incapable of attaining release" (McClary, 1987, the passage being excised in the article's reprint in McClary, 2002, p. 128; see also Jan, 2016a). Yet in some cases, the Self-Other dichotomy, whether gendered or not, is a mere foil to the more fundamental quest for identity undertaken by the first subject. Thus, in the case of the first movement of Brahms's Symphony no. 3 of 1883, the subjugation of the second subject – read by McClary as not only feminine but also alluringly exotic (1993, pp. 337–338) – is relegated to the status of a side-narrative, subordinate to the movement's fundamental problem of reconciling the personality-defining but tonally deviant A♭ of the first subject (b. 4) with the A♮ required by the social order and represented by the work's tonic key of F major.[227]

Combining tonality and sonata procedure with concerto "format" – the third of these being a "subspecies" of the first two (McClary, 1986, pp. 137, 138) – brings in a further dimension, for in its *solo-tutti* distinction the concerto articulates a dialectic of individual *versus* society. Inverting the Self/protagonist/tonic-Other/antagonist/non-tonic configuration of sonata form, the opening tonic-key ritornello of a concerto movement (the orchestral exposition) represents not the individual, as in the case of a non-concerto sonata form, but the social group, articulating its shared norms and values. In contrast, the soloist, in its dominant-striving first entry (the solo exposition), represents not just Otherness, as would be expected in the context of sonata procedure, but also individualism and the quest for self-determination. In this way, it

> enacts as a spectacle the dramatic tensions between individual and society, surely one of the major problematics of the emerging middle class.... The individualistic 'violation' is itself socially encoded. In an eighteenth-

---

[227] A serious critique of McClary's analytical work is that, despite foregrounding the importance of narrativity in ostensibly absolute music (1994, pp. 66–67), some of her accounts are often highly selective, omitting significant chunks of the "story" in order to focus on those elements that support the overriding hermeneutic agenda. In the case of the discussion of Brahms's Symphony no. 3 (McClary, 1993), for instance, the second, third and fourth movements do not figure significantly in her account.

century concerto, whatever antagonisms were manifested between individual and society appear to have been resolved by the end: the stable
community has withstood the adventures and conflicts of the soloist,
and they have been reconciled to co-exist in mutually beneficial bliss.
(McClary, 1986, p. 138)

In the second movement of Mozart's K. 453, this "reconciliation" is cemented
by the soloist's presentation of a consequent phrase (bb. 127–130; outlining
the progression IV–I) at the end of the movement that finally completes
and, at a great remove, balances the movement's opening antecedent phrase
(bb. 1–5; outlining I–V), a passage McClary terms the "motto". The ante-
cedent/motto phrase recurs several times in the movement, but its closure
is repeatedly deferred until this final serene apotheosis (1986, pp. 154–155).
To what extent the alleged utopia represented by the closure of the motto
aligned, in Mozart's case, with the realities of Josephinian Vienna; and how
the relationships between the myriad individual experiences and any "ag-
gregated" social reality operated, is difficult to divine. But we nurture an
ideal of this particular time and place, perhaps naively, as a golden age in
European history, where social stability and individual liberty coexisted
happily (Wangerman, 1973). Assuming that the arrival at "mutually beneficial bliss" in both socio-cultural and musical structures and processes is not
coincidental, the challenge to an evolutionary view of culture lies in determining the reasons for the observed dialectical convergence. As suggested
at the start of this section, the options for the direction in which the causal
arrow of influence points are, essentially, non-musical-to-musical, musical-
to-non-musical, and two-way interactive. We can rule out the first (musical
culture is surely not *exclusively* influenced by non-musical culture), and the
second (non-musical culture is surely not *exclusively* influenced by musical
culture), and admit the existence of the third, albeit highly asymmetric and
non-music-to-music dominant.

It is worth stressing that McClary's alignment between the two domains
is not metaphorical: while she does not state it explicitly, she strongly implies that, in such cases, correlation results from causation. For example,
she suggests that "[c]onflict and struggles for dominance for purposes of
establishing and maintaining all-valued self-identity become essential preoc-
cupations in [late-eighteenth-century] style (and, one might argue, *at this*

moment in history)" (1986, p. 137; emphasis mine). Moreover, while the direction of causation is not specified here, it becomes clear from her assertion that musical style can be "understood as a kind of trace of European ideological history" (1986, p. 136). Expanding upon these purported alignments between socio-culture and the musical styles it motivates, McClary compares aspects of baroque music, specifically that of J. S. Bach, with the tonality-sonata-concerto model of classical music, specifically that of Mozart, in terms of the rubrics of scope (the latter is more expansive and tonally adventurous than the former); melodic material (the former uses a single unifying motivic pattern, the latter two clearly demarcated themes or theme groups); and form (the former encodes unity, the latter diversity) (1986, pp. 136–137). Informing this comparison is the implicit hypothesis that these musical distinctions are the consequence of quite different foundational socio-cultural structures. Nevertheless, while the baroque and classical styles are presented in binary terms, there is also the implication that, just as their associated socio-cultural structures evolved relatively slowly in order to connect one era with the other, the same holds true for the musical structures that somehow "tracked" them over time. For this reason, McClary's (1993) account of Brahms's Symphony no. 3 foregrounds the increasing tensions between individual aspiration and social constraints, the former aligned with the chromatic forces rupturing tonality in the late-nineteenth century, the latter with the still-prevailing diatonic order. These tensions, while sustainable in 1780, were not so in 1880: socio-culturally and musically, they had become an "untenable fairytale" (1993, p. 343).

While eschewing metaphor, McClary nevertheless does not offer any mechanism for this hypothesised causation: music internalises society – somehow – but the nature of the causal linkages is not spelled out. This is understandable, given the enormous body of data-points involved in socio-cultural evolution; the complexity of identifying and mapping the arrows of causation between phenomena in non-musical culture and musical culture; and the difficulty in understanding how subconscious and/or conscious processes in musical production and reception, individually and/or collectively, engender the observed correlations. Constraints of space permit the consideration of only one example – correlations between social structure and the evolution of sonata form in eighteenth-century Europe (see also §5.5.2) – which might at least shed some light on the mechanisms involved. Understanding baroque binary forms as evolutionary antecedents of sonata forms, a possible mechanism of causation for the observed correlation – a mechanism for "McClaryism" – might be as follows:

- A loose alignment existed between the structure of a simple binary form – the A–B thematic/tonal sequence of the first reprise returning as A–B (thematic)/ B–A (tonal) in the second reprise, thereby presenting both theme-clusters in each key – as effect, and the Newtonian world-view of the early-eighteenth century, as cause. Both arguably constitute mechanistic and deterministic systems (perhaps represented in music by the motivic uniformity and consistent rhythmic drive suggested by McClary's comparison of Baroque and Classical styles on page 385) in which the intercession of free will (perhaps represented in music by the association of tonal and motivic/rhythmic diversity) is restricted (Heylighen, 2006).

- Some binary forms, notably those associated with the minuet genre and eventually becoming the three-phrase type, were "deviant" in relation to the simple binary form archetype. By means of selection-favoured variation, the child forms extended the second reprise to encompass an initial non-tonic area, this already evident in the parent but without its associated restatement of the A thematic material; and, more significantly, they reorganised the second-reprise thematic structure so that the A material of the first reprise returned not only later, but also in the tonic key and not, as in simple binary form, in the second key.

- While the processes discussed in the previous point had proximate memetic causes – the evolution of lower-level musemes gave rise to new modes of parataxis that fed into the emergent structures of musemeplexes and musemesätze (§3.5.2) – they were shaped not only by musical but also by socio-cultural (non-musical) selection pressures.

- These selection pressures included a broad criterion of alignment with the perceived *Zeitgeist*: in an age – the Enlightenment – when technological progress had led to the questioning of authority and the economic emancipation of certain members of society, the nature of individualism (of freedom *versus* responsibility) was actively discussed and would have been understood by most creative artists of the time. The appositeness of an alignment between human individualism and the individuality and dynamism of musical materials (as avatars of that individualism) would not perhaps have gone unnoticed by composers. Indeed, this recognition characterises the shift between phases (ii; music articulating generalised affective states in a formulaic manner) and (iii; music articulating the affective states of the composer in an increasingly idiosyncratic manner) in note 193 on page 329.

- Whether composers rationalised this reorientation consciously or merely intuited it, there were musical means by which investment in notions of individualism might have fed into music and thus generated positive selection pressures in favour of certain musical-structural/stylistic changes. One of these is via the intercession of musico-operational/procedural memes (page 166), which essentially function as an interface between the domains of music and language: they are verbal-conceptual memeplexes (some feeding into and deriving from music theory, as represented by the "methodology of analysis" and "influence on the music" arrows, respectively, in Figure 4.9) articulating and regulating certain operations that can be performed on musemes. The replication of musemes can lead to reconstitution (by inference) of the musico-operational/procedural memes that shaped those musemes and their concatenation.

This account is intrinsically difficult to falsify, and it is subject to the criticism that the key stage (point 220 of the list above) is wrapped up in the "black box" – a virtual space in which the operation of an algorithm or process is not directly accessible or observable – of musico-operational/procedural memes; but it might nevertheless be verifiable by means of dual-replicator agent-based computer simulation (§273). The process is also potentially reversible, and can therefore account for influences from musical culture to non-musical culture, the aforementioned issue of asymmetry notwithstanding. At the risk of invoking a further *deus ex machina*, the mechanism for this process might inhere in the "reconstitution (by inference)" (point 220) of musico-operational/procedural memes via the replication of musemes. While this reconstitution normally facilitates museme replication in relatively circumscribed professional collectives – and indirectly serves the replicative advantages of the associated musico-operational/procedural memes themselves – it might also give rise to less formal ways of understanding musical patterning and processes. In contrast to detailed formulae for mutation and recombination, these more accessible ways of engaging with music – observing and responding to its general ebb and flow, its affective tenor and its internalisation of agency – might be more extensively transmitted to a wider segment of a society and thus might to some extent be consequential on the configuration of the non-musical culture, and potentially the socio-economic direction, of that society.

Note, finally, that this asymmetric-but-bidirectional model of influence further supports my conflation of the psychological and socio-cultural categories of the recursive ontology model (§1.5.5) discussed on page 32. As Figure 1.2 indicates, higher categories are emergent from lower ones, this process being driven by the complexity-building engine of evolution (as indicated by the arrow at the left of the figure labelled "complexity"). While the process is not necessarily exclusively bottom-up unidirectional, this is clearly the case between the physical and the biological categories (the actions of living things cannot change the rules of physics), and probably also the case between the biological and the psychological categories (attitudes of mind *per se* cannot directly change – in Lamarckian fashion – an organism's biochemistry, physiology or morphology). It is clearly not the case, however, between the psychological and the socio-cultural categories, because the top-down mediation of the former category (specifically, the practice of composers) by forces from the latter proposed by McClary's thesis is almost indisputable, even if one takes exception to her specific claims regarding the nature, extent and consequences of this mediation.

4.8 Summary of Chapter 4

Chapter 4 has argued that:

1. Since its foundation in the eighteenth century, modern scholarly discourse on music has been guided by various metanarratives, these often reflecting the prevailing world-view and thus seeing music as a reflection of it.

2. Underpinning these metanarratives are constellations of metaphors. In Spitzer's (2004) formulation, one class of metaphor encompasses "organic" alignments between melodic motion and the striving of living beings, but many more such nature-culture associations have been employed in music scholarship. The evolutionary metaphor of music's changing in ways that mirror the changes in living things has been one of the most persistent and has profoundly affected music historiography and music theory and analysis.

3. The discourses of music historiography have drawn upon ontogenetic models to account for the progress of individual composers' styles and for the developmental trajectories of historical styles, genres and formal-structural types; and they have also understood the latter trio of phenomena in phylogenetic terms. The last of these models, the metaphor of the dialect-style-species, is perhaps the closest to biological reality.

4. The discourses of music theory and analysis have viewed the intricate structures of musical works as reflections of the inner unity and coherence of living beings. In particular, they have understood the aetiology, the dynamic and static aspects, the local and global organisation, and the constituent tones and tonal systems of the work in the light of the structural-hierarchic levels and functional processes of organisms.

5. In addition to the "mechanical" (evolutionary) relationships between music and language that obtained in our early evolutionary history, there is also a metaphorical alignment between the two domains articulated in the various traditions of music scholarship that (inverting their likely evolutionary sequence) regard music as a form of language.

6. As verbal-conceptual memeplexes, the discourses of music scholarship, whether they draw upon evolutionary concepts or not, are themselves subject to the VRS algorithm. The resulting evolution may be modelled by citation-analysis software in order to understand the spatiotemporal distribution of discourses as interconnected ecologies of ideas.

7. Given that musical culture is a subset of human culture more broadly, then just as genes coevolve with other genes, and with memes, so memes in one domain of culture can coevolve with those in another. This results in a three-way coevolutionary dynamic between the verbal-conceptual memeplexes of the parent culture, the musemes and musemeplexes sustained by that culture, and the verbal-conceptual discourse-memeplexes that are contingent upon both. This dynamic is not equally balanced, being skewed by the asymmetric influence of non-musical culture on musical culture.

Chapter 5 will consider to what extent non-human animals possess musicality and music. If these attributes arise in humans from the coevolution of biological/natural and cultural/nurtural forces, to what extent are they also present in certain animal species, and to what extent might animal behaviours and the products of these behaviours be related to human musicality and music? Such a discussion inevitably raises questions as to the uniqueness of human music and the status of our creativity. It will: consider the extent to which animal vocalisations are shaped by sexual selection; examine the two main categories of animal vocalisations, namely those that are primarily innate and those that are primarily learned (the latter via consideration of bird-song and whale-song); explore the relationships between musicality, music and creativity in humans and non-human animals; and revisit the issue of music-language coevolution in the light of insights gained from the study of animal vocalisations.

5. Animal "Musicality" and Animal "Music"

> Listen to them – the children of the night. What music they make!
> (Count Dracula, in Stoker, 2003, p. 25)

5.1 Introduction: What Makes Us Unique?

We readily anthropomorphise other living creatures, seeing them variously in terms of our own nature and characteristics. Conversely, we tend to assume that only humans are truly musical and so only we produce "real" music. Indeed, while we may shudder at Dracula's pleasure at hearing the wolves howling outside his castle – a line uttered with chilling ecstasy by Bela Lugosi in the 1931 film version of Stoker's novel (Browning & Freund, 1931) – we accept that only he and his fellow vampires could regard these creatures as truly musical.[228] Thus, we reserve these attributes as some of the precious things that define us and make us unique among the earth's living creatures. The assumption that only humans are musical might be understood in the wider context of the process started in 1859, when Darwin suggested that the distinction between humans and the rest of "creation" – the notion of human *exceptionalism* – was illusory, and that we therefore differ only in degree, not kind, from other living things. Since the publication of *On the origin of species*, advocates of evolution have sought to emphasise continuities with the rest of the animal kingdom, whereas proponents of creation have sought to emphasise disjunctions. Perhaps unsurprisingly, I adopt the former position here and so by "animal" in this chapter I mean "non-human animal", thus seeing our own species in anti-exceptionalist terms.

---

[228] Nevertheless, it is likely that hominin musilanguage, as social-emotive vocalisations (§2.7.2), shared certain attributes with such animal cries, which eventually found their way into human music. For example, the descending glissando of the wolf-howl, following a rapid ascent to the apex-pitch, aligns broadly with the "tumbling strains" for which Sachs "coined the term 'pathogenic' or 'passion-born'" (1962, p. 68).

   https://doi.org/10.11647/OBP.0301.05

While humans like to think that we alone among animals are musical, music is only part of that which makes us different from the rest of the animal kingdom, namely the wider phenomenon of culture, which is of course disproportionately developed in our species. Nevertheless, music is itself only a component – albeit, as Chapter 2 argued, an evolutionarily very significant one – of human culture. As is the case with music, a clear definition of culture is problematic,[229] but understanding it as the collection of beliefs, ideas and behaviours transmitted between members of a community accords well with the Universal Darwinism adopted here. Thus, and in nods to sociobiology and to evolutionary psychology (Table 3.2), while some elements of culture are indeed to some extent under the "leash" of genetic control, the majority of culture is governed by a separate, memetic, replicator system. On the same basis, animal "musicality" and "music" form components of the wider domain of animal "culture", which involves those aspects of their lives that are *learned* and shared memetically (by imitation) between conspecifics, as opposed to those aspects that are *innate* – "hard-wired" by biological evolution – and not significantly culturally modifiable (Laland & Galef, 2009). Innate behaviours may be understood in terms of Tinbergen's (1951) hierarchical model of instinctive animal behaviour, being regulated by an "Innate Releasing Mechanism" (Schleidt, 1962) that automatically unlocks an action in response to the build up of neural impulses motivated by some environmental stimulus (Pirger et al., 2014). In contrast to humans, however, innate behaviours regulate the majority of most animals' actions – the genetic leash is shorter and tighter – and so the domain of animal culture determines a significantly smaller proportion of their behavioural repertoires than is the case with our species.

The inverted commas around animal "musicality" and "music" are intended to indicate that, while most humans can distinguish between musical and non-musical sounds – we have a fairly stable sense of what is and is not music, whether or not we ascribe aesthetic value to those sounds that we concede are musical – when it comes to animal sounds it seems the case that: (i) there is often little agreement between humans on the musicality

---

[229] Unsurprisingly, definitions of culture differ according to disciplinary orientation, giving insights into the world-views of anthropologists (Bernard & Gravlee, 2014), sociobiologists (E. O. Wilson, 2000), sociologists (Inglis & Almila, 2016), psychologists (Cohen & Kitayama, 2019), evolutionary psychologists (Barkow et al., 1992) and memeticists (Blackmore, 1999).

of certain animal sounds (i.e., on their status as potentially musical), save perhaps for the "songs" of certain birds (H. Taylor, 2017); and (ii) science has a very poor understanding of whether animals *themselves* have any sense or intention that the sounds they or their conspecifics make, or the sounds other species make, are heard aesthetically, as opposed to ways that are survival- or territory-related. Thus, while this paragraph is the last in this chapter to enclose "music", "musicality" and "song" in "scare-quotes", they can be understood to hover invisibly above such uses of these terms, by way of a reminder of these two points, in what follows. Because the status *as music* of the sound patterns that make up animal vocalisations is contingent, I term such patterns "sonemes" here, in order to distinguish them from musemes, and from nearly verbal protemes and clearly verbal lexemes. As well as being gestalt-demarcated chunks of sound transmitted by replication among members of a cultural community, musemes are also readily *heard as musical*. Sonemes, by contrast, while possessing many or all of the functional and structural attributes of musemes, may lack this last attribute from the perspective of a human observer.

This chapter explores a range of animal sounds in order to understand how they relate to evolutionary forces, genetic and memetic, and to consider to what extent such potential animal music possesses an attribute held to be central in human music, namely creativity and the aesthetic values this implies. Having just spoken of animal "sounds", the vast majority of can- didates for animal music are in fact *vocalisations* of one form or another, and these are the primary focus of this chapter. As such, they constitute "signals emitted to influence the behavior of other organisms" (the lead-in to Miller's fourth question in the quotation on page 89) and thus may be assumed to have an aptive function (§2.5). Indeed, as suggested above, the majority of such vocalisations are innate (shaped by biological evolution) rather than learned (shaped by cultural evolution), whereas the opposite is the case in human musicality. The predominance of vocalisation in human and animal communication, whether innate or learned, is due to the fact that, while touch, vision and smell are inherently spatially constrained, sound patterns have the advantage of being able to travel long distances, day or night, and they are not wholly impeded by objects located in between the sender and the intended recipient(s) (Slater, 2000, pp. 49–50). There are other means by which animals – generally non-human primates – can produce sounds other than through vocalisation, principally by using their bodies or, prosthetically, by employing external objects as percussive devices. These – again largely innate – phenomena, which relate primate behaviour to human instrumental music, are considered in §5.3.4.

Having said that candidates for animal music are vocalisations, it is important to stress that: (i) such vocalisations are primarily a form of *communication* between a sender and one or more receivers; (ii) that other sense-modalities are also used for communication (particularly vision and smell, primarily for reception as opposed to production); and (iii) that the primary functions of such communications are territorial demarcation and mate-attraction, these two being to some extent interdependent (Slater, 2000, pp. 49–51). Additional, related functions – namely creating and maintaining dominance hierarchies, fostering group cohesion (including via danger-alerting), pair-bond consolidation, and infant nurture – are also found, as is the case in humans (§2.5). Given their communicative underpinning, and in parallel with Chapter 2, this chapter considers the relationship between animal vocalisations and language because, if music and language have a shared evolutionary history in humans (§2.7), then it may be the case that certain animal vocalisations are not only *communicative* (which is indisputable) but are also to some extent (*musi*)*linguistic* (which is not indisputable).

The vocalisations considered here are certain (innate) non-human primate and bird calls, and certain types of (learned) bird-song and whale-song. The innate category has arguably little substantive in common with human music and language, although some such vocalisations are to our ears perhaps more musical than linguistic, despite their essentially communicative motivation. The learned category appears to align much more clearly with certain attributes of human music and language, not only on account of its acquisition through cultural transmission but also because of various structural commonalities. Indeed, there is a clear distinction between the "holistic" unity of innate vocalisations and the "compositional" diversity of learned vocalisations (§2.7.6), with strong evidence of memetic replication in the latter that aligns closely, in terms of structures and mechanisms, with that underpinning human music and language. Nevertheless, while seemingly linguistic-*structural*, learned animal vocalisations are not necessarily linguistic-*syntactic*, let alone linguistic-*semantic*, in the same ways as human language, certainly when considered in terms of Hockett's design features of language (§2.7.1).

When discussing whether animals possess musicality and to what extent their vocalisations constitute music, one must consider a number of issues. The most fundamental of these is the degree to which the sound patterns they produce bear any structural and/or functional homoplasies or homologies to human musics. That is, do animal vocalisations have similarities to human vocal melodies or their instrumental derivatives? These similarities might inhere in the realms of: (i) vocal style (do animal songs have the relatively narrow tessitura and small melodic intervals typical of most human vocalisations?); (ii) melodic segmentation (do songs fall into museme-like – sonemic – chunks, as a result of the constraints of the animal's perceptual-cognitive architecture); and (iii) structural organisation (are animal vocalisations patterned at a number of recursive-hierarchic levels to form higher-order entities?). These issues will be considered in §5.4, in connection with the discussion of specific animal groups and their vocalisations.

The chapter continues by considering the extent to which animal vocalisations are artefacts of sexual selection (§5.2). It then examines innate animal vocalisations, focusing on certain non-human primate species (§5.3). Thereafter, the more pertinent issue of learned vocalisations is considered, with particular reference to certain bird and cetacean species (§5.4). The relationships between musicality, music and creativity – the latter often taken to be a purely human attribute, but arguably amenable to a broader, Darwinian analysis – is then explored (§5.5). Finally, a continuation of the discussion of music and language explores the similarities and differences between musilinguistic human vocalisations and those learned vocalisations of certain animals that appear to have musilinguistic properties (§5.6).

5.2 Animal Vocalisations and Sexual Selection

Given their foundation in natural selection, it is perhaps unsurprising that the functions of innate vocalisations include the primarily gene-benefiting activities of territorial demarcation, mate-attraction, dominance hierarchy formation, group cohesion, pair-bond consolidation and infant nurture out-lined in §5.1. It makes good sense for these calls and cries to have been hard-wired by natural selection, because there are many situations in the lives of animals where an immediate and automatic vocal response is needed to some pressing stimulus-situation, most often the arrival of a predator or the incursion of a territorial and/or sexual rival. The second of these threats, and the less pressing imperatives of pair-bond consolidation and infant nurture, may be capitalised upon by sexual selection (§2.5.3), resulting in often very marked sex differentiation in vocalisations, some evident in human vocal behaviours.

To summarise briefly the outline of sexual selection given in §2.5.3, the VRS algorithm works to advance the replicative agendas of not one but two ostensibly separate genes or gene-complexes: those for an ornament, expressed (usually) by a male; and those for a preference for that ornament, expressed (usually) by a female. To recall part of the summary of Fisher's mechanism for sexual selection given on page 99,

> [o]rnamented males will have a mating advantage if sufficiently many females mate preferentially with such males.... Because females with a strong preference tend to mate with males with a pronounced ornament, preference and ornament alleles often co-occur in the offspring of such matings, leading to a statistical association among these alleles. As a consequence, [direct] positive selection on the ornament will induce correlated [indirect] positive selection on the preference. Hence, pref-erences induce the evolution of ornaments and subsequently become selected owing to their association with the ornament. (Kuijper et al., 2012, p. 290)

While often arising from a random perceptual-cognitive-aesthetic prefer-ence, the runaway, sexually dimorphic (§2.3.3) augmentation of ornaments driven by sexual selection – whether these be "calls, odors, ornaments, and conspicuous behaviors" (Kuijper et al., 2012, p. 288) – is taken by females as an index of genetic capital and thus of potential paternal contribution to the viability of offspring and grandoffspring. Of this suite of ornament-categories, vocalisation is naturally the principal concern here. Given its arguably greater utility as a signal than many other ornament-domains, for the reasons given in §5.1, it is unsurprising that, having been consolidated by natural selection, vocalisation was subsequently seized upon and augmented by sexual selection in several species.

Despite its gene-benefiting motivations, sexual selection is not incompatible with learned vocalisations, in the sense that the latter evidence two interrelated genetic capacities: not only the *physical* capacity to sustain the costly – and therefore probably "honest" (Zahavi & Zahavi, 1997) – utterances characteristic of innate vocalisations; but also the *psychological* capacity to learn, memorise and produce inventive song, argued by G. Miller (2000, pp. 339–340) to have been in humans, and possibly in other vocal-learning species, a particularly reliable ornament. Yet sexual selection alone appears insufficient to explain the richness and diversity of certain animal vocalisations: the complex song of many birds, the extended melodies of certain whales and, most notably, the dazzling array of human vocalisations, musical and linguistic, seem to go well beyond what might be advantageous to genes, not least in their significant demands upon the resources of time and energy.

The process of memetic drive is a candidate explanation for the richness and diversity of learned vocalisations. To summarise briefly the account given in §3.7.1, the three stages of the process are: (i) *selection for imitation* (the naturally selected survival advantage of being adept at something – imitation – that keeps the organism alive long enough to pass on those genes for imitation); (ii) *selection for imitating the imitators* (the naturally selected advantage of an organism's knowing that copying the best imitators will keep it alive long enough to pass on those genes for being discriminating in this regard); and (iii) *selection for mating with the imitators* (the sexually selected advantage of an organism's knowing that by mating with a good imitator it will pass on an ornament to its offspring that, in the case of sons, will make them sexy enough to give the organism a reasonable chance of having grandoffspring and that, in the case of daughters, will make them discerning enough to choose the most ornamented – therefore likely the most genetically robust – males). Because the aptitude (ornament) upon which selection is working in this model is imitation, then the third stage becomes coevolutionary sexual selection, in which cultural replicators – sonemes, and then musemes, protemes and lexemes – capitalise on the gene-built capacity to imitate in order to aid their own replication and to bend biological evolution (often via increased encephalisation) to their own cultural-evolutionary advantage.

While the capacity for imitation upon which memetic drive builds can operate in many domains and substrates, in animals it is most often evident in actions and/or "words",[230] with the latter affording the most informationally rich – phonologically and later syntactically and semantically – medium for replication. In early humans the repertoire of innate vocalisations we inherited from our closest primate ancestors presumably served this foundational purpose, as did analogous (strictly, homoplasious) repertoires in more distantly related species that appear to have evolved learned vocalisations before humans. Thus, the innate vocalisations of some of our closest primate ancestors help to illuminate the nature and function of the platform upon which memetic drive may have operated in our own species; and the learned vocalisations of prolific vocal learners afford examples of this process that may have operated in species other than our own.

5.3 Primarily Innate Vocalisations

Perhaps the most significant forms of innate vocalisations, and the ones focused upon here, are those of non-human primates, i.e., those of monkeys and apes. I discuss a number of examples here – and an instance of innate *non*-vocal sound production (5.3.4) – concluding by considering another significant category of such vocalisations, innate bird-song. As suggested in §5.1, very few non-human primate vocalisations have elements that are learned and transmitted between conspecifics by imitation.[231] That is, such vocalisations have evolved and been selected for over time as a result of exclusively biological evolution, whereas modern human vocalisations (music and language) are a coevolutionary product of biological and cultural evolution, the latter working on the foundation provided by the former. This difference between humans and non-human primates is stark, especially con-

---

[230] In birds and cetaceans the lack of functional arms and hands imposes constraints on the quantity and granularity of information that can be conveyed using gestures, hence the high level of development of their vocal signals.

[231] One exception is the marmoset, a New World monkey that is reported to manifest vocal learning by offspring from parents (Harvey, 2017, pp. 100–101).

sidering the relative evolutionary proximity of *Homo sapiens* to monkeys and, particularly, to apes (but see note 152 on page 258). Conversely, considering the relative evolutionary distance between our species and those prolific vocal learners discussed in §5.4, it is notable that certain characteristics of human music – particularly the recursive-hierarchical recombination of discrete sound patterns (§3.5.2) – are found not in our closest evolutionary relatives but in parts of the animal kingdom from which we are evolutionarily remote. This would suggest that the substrates for musicality arise as a result of homoplasy rather than of homology.

Primate taxonomy is complex owing, among other reasons, to tensions between the *monophyletic* arrangement that conforms to the precepts of cladism and various *paraphyletic* alternatives (§1.7.2), these particularly affecting the status of orangutans (Groves, 2017, p. 2). Primates are categorised into two suborders (Table 1.5), the *Strepsirrhini* ("wet-nosed") and the *Haplorhini* ("dry-nosed"). Species in the second suborder produce the most interesting and significant vocalisations from a music-evolutionary perspective. Those considered here include: (i) certain of the Monkeys, which are divided into "Old World" (superfamily *Cercopithecoidea*) and "New World" (parvorder *Platyrrhini*) types (§5.3.1); (ii) the "Lesser Apes", family *Hylobatidae* (gibbons) (§5.3.3); and (iii) the "Great Apes", family *Hominidae*, which includes chimpanzees and bonobos (genus *Pan*) (§5.3.2), gorillas (genus *Gorilla*), orangutans (genus *Pongo*), and humans (genus *homo*). The Lesser Apes and the Great Apes form the superfamily *Hominoidea*, which, together with the Old World monkeys (superfamily *Cercopithecoidea*), are members of the parvorder *Catarrhini*, which sits at the same taxonomic-hierarchic level within the *Haplorhini* as that of the New World monkeys (parvorder *Platyrrhini*) (Groves, 2017, Tab. 1; see also Fitch, 2010, 235, Box 6.1). The vocalisations of the (Old World) gelada monkey were considered in §2.7.6.

A distinction needs to be made between calling and singing in non-human primate vocalisations. While they are not unambiguously separate, the former category encompasses those cries, grunts, howls and barks found in the majority of primate species; the latter encompasses those more rare quasi-lyrical vocalisations that, to a human observer, appear almost song-like in their fluidity. Indeed, singing is found in only four primate genera, *Indri* (the only genus of the four that is a member of the suborder *Strepsirrhini*), *Tarsius*, *Callicebus* and *Hylobates*, equating to only *c.* 11% of primate species (Geissmann, 2000, p. 112). The evolutionary distance between these genera suggests that singing evolved independently (as a homoplasy) in each (Geissmann, 2000, p. 112), indicating strong selection pressures in favour of the aptive benefits it conferred. In these singing species both males and females sing, and *duetting* – coordinated singing within a bonded pair – occurs in most of them. Contrary to this aesthetic-anthropomorphic interpretation, it should be noted that Fitch defines song as "complex, *learned* vocalization" (2006, p. 182; emphasis mine; see also Harvey, 2017, p. 100), and so from his perspective only humans among the primates possess this capacity to any significant degree.

Just as singing is rare in primates, so is monogamy. Indeed, monogamy is relatively rare in the animal kingdom as a whole: only *c.* 3–5% of mammal species are monogamous, although *c.* 90% of bird species are; of the primates, only *c.* 15% are monogamous (Geissmann, 2000, p. 104; Díaz-Muñoz & Bales, 2016, p. 283). It should be stressed, however, that that "social monogamy" is not always matched by "genetic monogamy", on account of surreptitious mating outside established pair-bonds (Fitch, 2010, p. 245; Díaz-Muñoz & Bales, 2016, p. 283; see also page 43 above). The attribute of singing, and specifically duetting, is thought to be correlated (as cause or effect) with monogamy: it appears to have played this role in humans (point 11 of the list on page 139); and in birds, arguably more vocal than any primate other than humans, (duet) singing is similarly correlated with (social) monogamy (Geissmann, 2000, p. 112). Nevertheless, aside from duetting – which in some species, such as Gibbons (§5.3.3), is an innate attribute – there is evidence that vocal learning in (male) birds is correlated with extra-pair mating (i.e., genetic *non*-monogamy) in both sexes (§5.4.1.3) and so, on this basis, such vocal-learning-correlated/facilitated infidelity might be hypothesised also to have characterised early hominin pairings. If there were singing Neanderthals (Mithen, 2006), there were perhaps also cheating ones. Thus, while duetting is *positively* correlated with (social) monogamy, the (genetic) fidelity/stability of that monogamy may be *negatively* correlated with the degree of vocal learning in males of that species. The discussion below is organised broadly according to the calling-singing distinction, moving from species manifesting the former behaviour to those exemplifying the latter. Where appropriate, linguistic elements of vocalisations are discussed.

5.3.1 Vervet Alarm Calls

Vervet monkeys (*Chlorocebus pygerythrus*), a species of Old World Monkey, produce "alarm calls" in response to certain significant predators such as big cats, birds of prey and snakes. Each call is specific to the particular predator-class involved, and each motivates a different response in those vervets receiving it (Hauser, 2000, p. 78). For calls associated with big cats, the reaction is to climb a tree; for calls associated with birds of prey, the behaviour is to hide under a bush; and for calls associated with snakes, the response is to stand erect and to survey the surrounding ground intently (Hauser, 2000, p. 78; Manser, 2013, p. 492). Motivating a "domino effect" of responses among conspecifics, all these behaviours make good evolutionary sense, and their automatic nature suggests that they arise from a largely innate capacity, albeit with some evidence, discussed below, of a learned component in their deployment.

Study of this behaviour in vervets in the 1980s helped to motivate a change in ethology's understanding of animal vocalisations. This involved moving from seeing certain animal calls as broadly communicative of *affect* (thus occupying a position to the right of the top part of the music-language continuum of Figure 2.2) to regarding them as potentially communicative of *meaning* (thus occupying a position to the left of the top part of Figure 2.2). As affect, a vocalisation offers a window into the "internal motivational state of the signaller and/or the behaviour in which the signaller was likely to engage" (Manser, 2013, p. 492). As such, it constitutes a signal from a sender (the vocaliser) to one or more receivers (the vocaliser's conspecifics or members of other species) that may be honest or dishonest (§2.5.3): the vocalisation could be a genuine expression of e/motion, to recall Levitin's point in the passage cited on page 98 ("I don't like you: keep away!"); or it could be a ruse, a display of synthetic e/motion, to scare away rivals in order to allow selfish monopolisation of some resource ("Run! I can see a lion!").

Rethinking vervet alarm calls as being not (just) affective but also as "functionally referential" – i.e., semantic – (Hauser, 2000, p. 79), motivates considering them in the light of human (musi)language. It also raises the question as to whether functional referentiality involves "a simple association between a specific call type and the external event, allowing the receivers to show the appropriate response (perceptual semanticity), or whether the mental representation of the eliciting stimulus induces the response in the receiver (conceptual semanticity)" (Manser, 2013, p. 493). In other words, is the response the result of evolved operant conditioning; or does it evidence some form of innate mental representation of the stimulus and of the consequences of disregarding the call, respectively. If the former, then the vervet – and comparable species – would represent an example of a Skinnerian creature (one capable of reinforcing certain innate behaviours by post-testing evaluation); if the latter, it would constitute an example of a Popperian creature (one capable of pre-testing candidate behaviours via innate (gene-built) mental simulation), as defined in Table 3.1.

Evidence in support of the referential role of vervet alarm calls comes from the fact that some vervets have been observed to behave deceptively in certain alarm situations for reasons of self-interest. This dishonesty takes the form of: (i) "deception through silence" (Cheney & Seyfarth, 1991, p. 132), whereby, for instance, a vervet jeopardises the safety of a conspecific group rival by withholding an alarm call in the face of a real danger; and (ii) deception through giving false alarms, when no predator is present (sometimes, aptively, in the face of an incursion by an extra-group immigrant male) (1991, p. 137). What vervets do not seem to be able to undertake is: (iii) deception through "mislabelling" a given danger with the "wrong" call-type (1991, p. 137). The behaviours in (i) and (ii) have led, as part of an evolutionary arms-race, to "scepticism" in vervets (and in other species manifesting comparable behaviours). As a result, they attend not just to a signal but also to its producer (1991, p. 144). This safeguard is activated only after a certain threshold is crossed: receiving vervets seem inclined initially to regard deception as an error on the part of the signaller, as opposed to an intentional act (1991, p. 148).

The dishonesty involved in scenarios (i) and (ii) above indicates that vervet alarm calls are to some extent dissociable from those environmental contexts in which they originally evolved. Without this dissociation necessarily indicating that calls are in some sense linguistic – determining this depends upon the presence of not one but a constellation of features – such "situational decoupling" is at least a step towards the language design feature of displacement (point (ix) of the list on page 126 and point 18 of the list on page 149), although it is strictly only fully represented by scenario (iii) (mislabelling) above. Nevertheless, to speak of a call functioning honestly or, particularly, dishonestly might be taken to imply at least some basic level of intentionality on the part of the calling animal (Manser, 2013, p. 494), even though this attribute is not one of Hockett's (1960) design features. Intentionality in respect of truth or falsehood might only be the preserve of a Gregorian creature (one capable of pre-testing candidate behaviours via innate and learned (gene- and meme-built) mental simulation), although additionally to ascribe consciousness to such intentionality arguably requires the operation of the processes described in §3.8.2.

Returning to the music-language continuum of Figure 2.2, and in terms of their affective content, vervet alarm calls possess only a limited protomusical quality. While the intensity of their calls correlates with levels of arousal (Manser, 2013, p. 492), their vocalisations lack the expressive range of certain other primates such as gibbons, and they certainly lack the fine vocal control – a prerequisite of the melodic vocalisation fundamental to musilanguage – thought to have been present relatively early in the genus *Homo* (page 130). In terms of meaning, the functionally referential nature of vervet alarm calls suggests a greater protolinguistic than protomusical quality although, seemingly also lacking our species' advanced capacity for vocal learning, the potential for the linguistic bootstrapping of a vervet musilanguage by cultural evolution seems limited.

5.3.2 Chimpanzee Pant-Hoots

In addition to producing "barks" (Notman & Rendall, 2005, p. 185), male (predominantly) and female chimpanzees (*Pan troglodytes*) utter vocalisations termed "pant-hoots", some of which last over twenty seconds (Geissmann, 2000, p. 115). Their close kin the bonobo (*Pan paniscus*) utter similar (presumably homologous) vocalisations, termed "hooting complexes" (Geissmann, 2000, p. 116). Typically, pant-hoots have four "phases": (i) a short introduction, characterised by the production of low-frequency sounds; (ii) a crescendo-like section whose components are shorter than those of the introduction and that may continue to diminish in duration, these being produced both on exhalation and inhalation; (iii) a climactic section, generally absent in females, made up of one or more scream-like outbursts and that, as in the analogous phase of gibbon duets (i.e., the climax of the "great call", §5.3.3), involves piloerection (hair standing on end) and extravagant physical displays including "drumming" behaviours, where the animal will strike trees with its hands and feet (§5.3.4); and (iv) a concluding section, or "let-down" (Notman & Rendall, 2005, p. 180), in which energy dissipates and low-frequency sounds are produced, analogous to those in the introductory phase (Geissmann, 2000, pp. 114–116, Fig. 7.7 f; Notman & Rendall, 2005, p. 180, Fig. 1). A broadly similar structure is found in Gorilla (*Gorilla gorilla*) "hoot series", although these vocalisations tend to be shorter and generally less structurally demarcated than chimpanzee pant-hoots (Geissmann, 2000, p. 115).

The normal absence in females of phase (iii) of the above sequence implies that some element of sexual selection has led to this differentiation in the structure of the pant-hoot. Indeed, Fedurek et al. (2013) found that males preferred to coordinate these vocalisations – to form pant-hoot "chorusing" – with other males, and that this "joint pant hooting is a flexible affiliative behaviour reflecting short-term bonds between both neutral and preferred long-term social partners" (2013, p. 195). Such chorusing is often associated with similar bonding behaviours, such as grooming (§2.3.5) and coordinated non-vocal displays, and appears to function as a "mutual signal of positive or benign intent" in what is a "fluid fission-fusion social system" (2013, p. 194). This behaviour appears a homologue of the communal synchronous chorusing and dancing hypothesised in early hominin societies (§2.5.2), where, as in present-day chimpanzees, social relations were probably fragile (owing to their potential conflict with self-interest), and affiliations needed to be tentatively established and vigilantly monitored.

There is little that is protomusical about these vocalisations, although pant-hoots "produced while resting or feeding were more tonal and 'wail-like'" than those "roar-like" calls made when chimpanzees are travelling (Notman & Rendall, 2005, p. 185). As for their protolinguistic content, Notman and Rendall (2005) found that the general structure of pant-hoots described above, while subject to individual variations, also manifests certain generic alignments with specific contexts such as the two just identified. They argue that such patterns "reveal significant call variants or subtypes that reflect selective diversification in the structure of chimpanzee calls to support a system of referential communication about important features of the environment" (2005, p. 185), even though this referentiality does not appear to have the clear sound-context specificity of vervet alarm calls. Moreover, Notman and Rendall (2005) qualify their assertion of referentiality by suggesting that the generally limited acoustic differences between the putative hoot-context associations they studied might in fact mean that pant-hoots serve only a "generalised social function", which is "to clearly signal identity (and all the subsidiary social dimensions that flow from it, such as status, alliance relationships, etc.) in order to coordinate social activities and relationships at a distance" (2005, p. 186). If so, it is likely that hoot-context associations have a primarily genetic underpinning, as evidenced by their alignment with survival- and reproduction-critical contexts. Nevertheless, there is some evidence of very limited vocal learning affecting the configuration of pant-hoots (M. Wilson et al., 2018), even though chimpanzees' capacities in this regard are trivial compared with the prolific vocal learners discussed in §5.4.

Moving beyond pant-hoots, there is evidence of certain commonalities between human speech-rhythms and the phenomenon of chimpanzee "lip-smacks". These are "affiliative signals typically produced by groomers during social grooming", equivalents to which occur in several other primate species (Pereira et al., 2020, pp. 1–2). Speech-rhythm is a product of

> the fast open–close mouth cycles characteristic to each and every spoken language in the world .... This rhythm is inherent to speech and universal across spoken languages because it expresses the production of syllables, where the opening and closing of the mouth roughly correspond to vowel and consonant production, respectively .... This rhythm typically exhibits a rate of 2–7 Hz, i.e., 2 to 7 open–close mouth cycles per second ..., and is a visual and acoustic signal of speech that appears to be critical to its intelligibility. (Pereira et al., 2020, p. 1)

Pereira et al. (2020) found that "chimpanzees produce lip-smacks at an average speech-like rhythm of 4.15 Hz", which they regard as "offering clear support for the hypothesis that [human] speech-rhythm has deep origins within the primate lineage ... and was built upon existing signal systems" (2020, p. 3). Moreover, the association of lip-smacking with (physical) grooming in chimpanzees supports Dunbar's (2017) hypothesis for the role of vocal grooming in the evolution of human (musi)language (§2.3.5). As argued in Chapter 2, various adaptations and exaptations in biological and cultural evolution – of which vocal learning' was surely central – built upon these "existing signal systems" in humans in ways that led to the evolution of musilanguage and then, via music and language, to the Cognitive Revolution.

5.3.3 Gibbon Songs and Duets

Gibbons live in monogamous family groups consisting of the two parents and up to three offspring. They occupy, and defend, exclusive territories (Geissmann, 2000, p. 104) and thus are to some extent "culturally" isolated from other such groups. As discussed on page 400, this monogamy is seemingly correlated with the fact that, unusually for primates, their vocalisations involve not only solo singing but also (in almost all gibbon species) duetting between the members of a mated pair (Geissmann, 2000, p. 105). Their utterances consist of "a series of notes, generally of more than one type, uttered in succession and so related as to form a recognizable sequence or pattern in time" (Thorpe, in Geissmann, 2000, p. 104). This note-series gives rise to "a succession of phrases with nonrandom succession probability" (Tembrock, in Geissmann, 2000, p. 104). Gibbons engage in extended bouts of duet-singing, normally in the hours around dawn, the duration of these performances ranging from *c*. 10 minutes to over an hour (Geissmann, 2000, pp. 104–105). Not only are singing times species-specific, but so is the structure of duets, which include distinct and closely coordinated male and female contributions, this confirming the essentially innate basis (but see below) of gibbon-song.

The innate foundation of gibbon duets allows evolutionary relationships between species to be analysed in terms of song morphology (Geissmann, 2000, p. 105; Thinh et al., 2011). The phylogenetic inheritance of song characteristics is reinforced by the fact that, ontogenetically, female "hybrid" offspring of two different gibbon species mix the attributes of female song from their parents' species. If such offspring learned their song from the female parent – because male and female elements of duets are quite distinct, a female infant could not learn its song from the male parent and vice versa – then such miscibility would not occur and the song would conform strictly to the female parent's type (Geissmann, 2000, pp. 108–110).[232] Despite its innate basis, song development in gibbons is nevertheless facilitated and to some extent shaped – in a seemingly vestigial form of vocal learning – by parental contact, certainly in the case of mother-daughter interactions (Merker & Cox, 1999; Koda et al., 2013). This facilitation appears to parallel the ontogenetic development – our superior vocal learning capabilities not-withstanding – of human vocal capacities by means of IDS (§2.5.4). Koda et al. (2013, p. 9) identify other similarities between humans and gibbons – including certain neurobiological overlaps relating to rhythmic control, aspects of lifestyle (ancestrally, in the case of humans), and the extended period of nurturing – that might explain comparable forms of "motherese" in gibbons and humans.

While different in each species, gibbon duets involve males delineating a crescendo of activity, with their constituent short phrases becoming increasingly more complex in terms of note number, note types and frequency profile as their contribution progresses. At regular intervals, females interpolate a series of rhythmic long notes of increasing pitch and/or tempo, an interjection termed a "great call", this being the attribute inherited from both species that is mixed in hybrids. The onset of a great call usually leads the male to stop singing, and the call's eventual termination is followed by a male response or "coda", before the male returns to its previous short-phrased declamations. The great-call-plus-coda unit is termed a "great call sequence" and each iteration climaxes with animated physical gestures by both participants that often involve the shaking of tree branches and piloerection, as in the analogous phase of chimpanzee pant-hoots. This unified collection of distinct events – alternations of male short phrases, great calls and codas – may be repeated *en bloc* multiple times during a single session of duetting (Geissmann, 2000, p. 107).

---

[232] Geissmann discusses sonograms of such inter-species hybrids, which clearly indicate intermingled vocal attributes, whether the offspring of species A and B results from A ♂ × B ♀ or from A ♀ × B ♂ (2000, p. 109, Fig. 7.6).

While clearly protomusical, gibbon duets are arguably also protolinguistic. Terleph et al. (2018) studied the coda of the song of the White-handed gibbon (*Hylobates lar*), which, as outlined above, is a recurrent male-only structural unit in a song-bout. Some of their main conclusions are that: (i) codas are complex structures made up of a sequence of distinct multi-note phrases (the latter equivalent to a soneme in my terms), each phrase conforming to one of four types (Type I = one or two "wa" sounds; Type II = a "trill"; Type III = a series of "quavers"; Type IV = two or more "wa" sounds (2018, p. 652, Fig. 1)); (ii) the full four-phrase structure is arrived at by phrase-addition during the course of a song-bout and, as part of this process, phrases themselves become more complex, by means of note-addition (in Type-II and Type-III phrases) and as a result of various other pitch and rhythmic changes (2018, p. 656); (iii) "the transition order between phrases was highly stereotyped" (2018, p. 655), meaning that the phrase-type sequence I–II–III–IV was over-whelmingly predominant (2018, p. 656, Fig. 3); and (iv) the parataxis of phrase-types during the course of a song-bout requires a capacity for hier-archical structuring also observed in certain other species, implying that gibbons possess neural substrates equivalent to the "hierarchical organiza-tion of motor pathways in the songbird brain [that] includes separate nuclei for not only the production of individual song syllables, but also for syllable sequences …" (the latter termed "strophes" in §5.4.1.2) (2018, p. 656).

Moreover, Terleph et al. (2018) found that: (v) phrase parataxis as a gen-erative principle, and Type-II and Type-III phrases as specific sonemes, are exclusive to male contributions to gibbon duets, suggesting a sexual-selection component to their origin, one that shaped the neural substrates referred to in (iv) (2018, p. 656); (vi) this observation is reinforced by the fact that Type-I phrases carry long distances, and Type-II and Type-III phrases are physically demanding to produce and sustain (Type-II-like (trill) vocalisations are a common indicator of male dominance and of health in a number of animal species), and thus they may function as territorial boundary-markers and as honest signals, respectively (2018, pp. 656–657); (vii) Type-II and Type-III phrases feature note-onsets that occur at a frequency close to that of human speech (human syllable production occurs at a rate of 3–8 Hz (2018, p. 649)), and that are produced using a single exhalation in coordination with facial movements (2018, p. 657); and (viii) these similarities with human speech suggest they are homologous – i.e., that this feature in gibbon-song fed into the human line via our last common ancestor with gibbons, even though it appears not to have been retained in the other Great Apes[233] – and they offer some evidence against a contrary hypothesis for human speech origins, namely the lip-smacking that occurs in a number of primates, including chimpanzees (§5.3.2) and geladas (§2.7.6; perhaps uniquely, geladas vocalise their lip-smacks), whose production-rate is similar to human syllable-rhythm (2018, p. 657). These similarities with human speech will be taken up again in §5.6.

5.3.4 Ape "Drumming"

While not an example of vocalisation, the phenomenon of "drumming" in certain Great Apes – chimpanzees, bonobos and gorillas, but seemingly not orangutans – represents an aspect of innate musicality, in the form of the production of organised rhythmic and timbral patterning, that warrants treatment in this section. By drumming is meant the various manual (one-handed) or bimanual (two-handed) beating behaviours by which an ape produces sounds by striking its own body or an external object – which can even include a conspecific. While often quite brief – the most extended beating displays are performed by bonobos (Fitch, 2006, p. 195) – this drumming is rhythmically fairly regular, like the tactus of human music. Having said that our closest primate relatives lack the vocal-learning skills of more distantly related bird and whale species, Great Ape drumming nevertheless represents a behaviour in non-human primates that aligns closely with human musicality, given the likely deployment of similar behaviours as part of the communal vocal-motor synchrony hypothesised to have been central to the integrity of early hominin communities (§2.5.2) and the continuing importance of rhythmic percussion in most modern-day musical cultures, western and traditional (see the quotation from Savage et al. (2015) on page 117).

---

[233] Nevertheless, the point of separation is thought to have been *c.* 16–20 MYA (Carbone et al., 2014, p. 198), and so, as in other comparable cases, it is difficult to reconstruct the attributes of the LCA and thus to understand the evolutionary distance traversed by each lineage after separation.

Chest-beating displays – often aped, as it were, by title-role actors in the numerous film versions of the Tarzan stories, and also by boxers and wrestlers – are a common manifestation of drumming behaviour and are generally signals of aggression and dominance in silverbacks (i.e., adult male gorillas) (Wright et al., 2021). The aptive nature of this behaviour is suggested by the fact that "silverbacks sometimes increase the resonance of this drumming display by inflating their remarkable laryngeal sacs" (Fitch, 2006, p. 194). Moreover, "females also produce chest-beating displays, as do immature gorillas, in a more playful context" (2006, p. 194), suggesting, in the latter case, that play in this species, as in humans, is a preparation for behaviours relevant to success in adult life (see the quotation from Cross (2012) on page 112). In chimpanzees, drumming most often takes the form of striking trees (particularly their resonant buttress roots) with hands and feet (2006, p. 194). Given that the object being struck here is external to the animal (unlike gorilla chest-beating), this might be regarded as a vestigial form of instrumental music. In this species, drumming is often linked with vocal and motor production as part of a suite of behaviours (2006, p. 194). Indeed, chimpanzees are also capable of rhythmic entrainment, in the form of a swaying motion made both to regular and irregular beats, more pronounced in males than females. This behaviour, manifested in both quadrupedal and bipedal postures, suggests that "[t]he effect of sound in inducing rhythmic swaying is likely to have existed in the common ancestor shared by chimpanzees and humans ~6 million years ago" (Hattori & Tomonaga, 2020, p. 940).

It seems the case that all non-human primate drumming involves one or more hands and/or feet and either the body or an external object – thus, the drumming does not involve a separate "beater", as is often the case in human percussion musics. Indeed, "[t]he only attested form of instrumental music involving more than one [external] object is by palm cockatoos [*Probosciger aterrimus*], who drum against hollow trees with sticks" (Fitch, 2006, pp. 183, 195). Aside from this species, the only other avian example of drumming is the pecking behaviour of woodpeckers (*Picidae*), which, aside from using their beak to excavate bark in order to locate food, sometimes drum against resonant trees for reasons of territorial demarcation and mate-attraction (2006, p. 195). As for invertebrates, examples are as scant as in birds, but certain spiders manifest analogous behaviour: the Wolf spider (*Hygrolycosa rubrofasciata*) "drums" using dry leaves as the resonator and its abdomen as a beater, producing vibrations in the leaves and also in the air as sound waves (Parri et al., 2002, p. 615). This appears to be a sexual-signalling, and a sexually selected, behaviour because – on the basis that "females could use the magnitude of male advertisement as an indicator of male phenotypic or genetic quality" – this study found that "female preference increased steeply with drum duration across the natural range of drum duration variation" (2002, p. 620).

As a final point on innate primate calls and drumming, the discussion here indicates that many have a broadly arched shape at a higher structural-hierarchic level. They begin and end softly, and they climax in their middle with often violent utterances of high pitch and dynamic, associated with vigorous physical displays. This design is common in nature, reflecting the waxing and waning of energy flows typical in the physical universe. Its broadly Gaussian-curved shape might be seen, and heard, in a number of natural phenomena ranging from annual seasonal cycles, animal migrations, the primate calls described here, and the progression of infections in organisms. It is one of those seemingly intrinsic constraints that, according to a recursive ontology (§1.5.5), should affect the behaviour not only of the natural but also the cultural realm. In the latter, it is a common image schema in art – encapsulated by Agawu's beginning-middle-ending paradigm (1991), it is arguably a fusion of the centre/periphery, up/down and path schemata (§4.2) – and is manifested, for instance, in the structure and pacing of texts (§4.5), stage drama, the dynamic curve of a sonata-form movement, and in the integration of the latter media in the musico-dramatic forms of certain genres of opera (Carter, 1987, pp. 89–90; Rosen, 1997, p. 296).

In summary, this evidence indicates that while non-human primates are capable of producing structured vocalisations through calls and duets and of creating and to some extent entraining to rhythmic sounds through drumming, only humans are able to marry these aptitudes to prodigious vocal learning in order to form the substrate for full-blown musicality and language. Indeed, in advance of the discussion in §5.6, it seems clear that while several of the elements of musilinguisticality are present in the species surveyed in this section – vervet quasi-referentiality, vestigial chimpanzee vocal learning, gibbon phrase-structuring (a form of chunking), and rhythmic production and entrainment in chimpanzees – no non-human-primate species has the capacity to integrate them synergystically in the ways that we, and those species considered in §5.4, manifest so virtuosically and to such powerful culture-building effect.

5.3.5 Innate Bird-Song

Of all animal vocalisations, bird-song has perhaps been the most enduringly fascinating to humans. That it has been regarded as a form of singing is, of course, testament to its perceived musical qualities: its lyricism, the graceful arch of its phrases, and its rhythmic and timbral vitality. Indeed, of all the animals on earth, birds are often held to be the most musical, being richly praised for the beauty, diversity and stamina of their singing. For this reason, bird-song has been celebrated in art and literature for its ability to move and inspire us. While certainly incorrect from an evolutionary perspective, Lucretius captured the human fascination with bird-song by suggesting, in his *De rerum natura*, that "[m]en whistled to imitate the warbling notes of birds a long / Time before they could lift their voices in melodious song / Pleasing to the ears." (Lucretius, 2007, 192, lines 1379–1381). As the most closely connected art form, music celebrates birds' vocalisations, as in the output of composers such as Messiaen, whose work draws extensively from, and attempts in part to replicate, bird-song (Kraft, 2000; Schultz, 2008; H. Taylor, 2017, pp. 55–61). A theme in human discourse from our earliest civilisations (Head, 1997), bird-song has been extensively studied in recent decades in an attempt to understand animal cultures and the evolution of music and language in humans (Bolhuis & Everaert, 2013).

Within the class *Aves* (birds) there are *c.* 10,100 species, but their taxonomy is even more complex than is usually the case (§1.7.1). For present purposes, suffice it to say that over half (*c.* 5,700) of bird species occupy the order *Passeriformes*, the perching birds (Storer et al., 2020). Within the *Passeriformes*, a further distinction can be made between the suborder *Tyranni*, or the "suboscines" (*c.* 1,250 species), which produce innate vocalisations; and the suborder *Passeri*, or the "oscines" (song-birds; *c.* 4,500 species), which produce learned vocalisations (Heimerdinger Clench et al., 2020). Beyond the *Passeriformes*, only two other bird orders have species that demonstrate vocal learning: the *Apodiformes* (hummingbirds; *c.* 425 species) and the *Psittaciformes* (parrots; *c.* 370 species) (Storer et al., 2020; Ríos-Chelén et al., 2012, p. 2171). On these numbers, approximately half of birds produce song they learn from parents and conspecifics.[234] The other half – those bird species outside the *Passeriformes*, *Apodiformes* and *Psittaciformes* – produce vocalisations that are largely genetically controlled, in the sense that they require no learning in order for them to occur, and that are essentially invariant (in the same functional context) between conspecifics. In Kroodsma's phrase, "[s]ome species learn their songs, just as we humans learn to [sing and] speak, but others seem to leave nothing to chance, encoding the details of songs in nucleotide sequences in the DNA" (2004, p. 108).

It is impossible, and not directly relevant to the main (vocal-learning) focus of this chapter, to survey all innate bird-song. To give just one example, however, the call of the corncrake (*Crex crex*) is produced nocturnally during the breeding season (Budka & Osiejuk, 2017, p. 652). Like much innate bird-song, the call is simple and repetitive, consisting of iterations of a pair of "syllables", S1 and S2, separated by an inter-syllable interval, I1, each syllable consisting of a rapid burst of (*c.* 15–22) high-amplitude pulses (2017, p. 653, Fig. 1).[235] Calls – i.e., S1 + I1 + S2 groups – can vary within an individual corncrake in terms of the duration of each syllable, the length of the inter-syllable interval I1, and the interval between successive calls (i.e., that between the end of S2 and the start of S1 in the following call, I2), these factors defining the "rhythm" of the vocalisation (2017, p. 653). By contrast, the intervals between successive intra-syllable high-amplitude pulses are specific to and fixed for each bird, and so are tightly controlled by the bird's genes (2017, p. 653).

According to a study of "microgeographic" call variation in the corncrake by Budka and Osiejuk (2017), differences in syllable rhythm are broadly re-

---

[234] Kroodsma cautions us to be clear on the distinction between "learning" and "imitation", noting that "a bird could still learn but not imitate", on account of improvising on songs heard in its environment, thus learning something it has made and that is new to it (and different from the model(s)). Moreover, as in humans, "[a] bird can learn to recognize a song, such as that of a neighbor, but never attempt to reproduce it …" (2004, p. 114).

[235] Bird-song syllables are discussed more fully in §5.4.1.2. Suffice to say here that the syllables of learned bird-song exceed those of innate song in complexity.

lated to territorial-aggression and honest-signalling displays, and thus they vary, as response strategies, according to social interactions between (male) conspecifics (2017, p. 653). Their results were mixed, however, showing a number of contradictory findings for the relationships between call configuration (as measured by various rhythm-related metrics) and use-contexts. Varying according to specific call components, they found some evidence for: (i) greater call similarity among neighbouring than between distant males (suggesting competition within a population and/or a "neighbour-stranger" differentiation effect); (ii) the opposite, i.e., greater call similarity between distant than among neighbouring males (suggesting competitive differentiation of individuals within populations); (iii) no differences between neighbouring and distant males (suggesting the greater effect of local environmental factors, such as patterns of vegetation growth); and (iv) opposite spatial distributions of the same call configuration in two different populations and/or different years (2017, pp. 656–657). These somewhat mixed findings suggest that, despite corncrake calls being essentially innate, they are still capable of being modified – for a variety of primarily territorial and mate-attraction reasons – according to context. While it is risky to extrapolate this general finding, it is not unreasonable to infer from it that many other innate-vocalising species, avian or otherwise, may have the capacity to modulate their calls to some extent – beyond the seemingly universal correlation between arousal and call intensity – in order to optimise them for specific aptive purposes. Nevertheless, such optimisations might readily be accounted for in terms of a genetic basis – perhaps one regulating an "if-input … then-output" algorithm – rather than from any capacity for vocal learning, let alone cultural transmission.

As the corncrake illustrates, innate vocalisations do not attain the lyrical and combinatorial virtuosity of those that other birds learn by imitation. Nevertheless, whether innate or learned, all bird vocalisations initially evolved to serve one or more of the gene-aptive purposes noted in §5.1. The reasons why the extra investment of time and neural resources to support song-learning have evolved in some but not all bird species are considered in §5.4.1, but suffice to say at this point that Dennett's question *cui bono?* – who (which replicator) benefits? (1995, p. 325) – is relevant to this question. There is a clear aptive benefit to birds' genes from calling, otherwise they would not have evolved this behaviour: the sound-patterns of innate bird-song are thus extended-phenotypic products of the birds' genes (§1.5.3). There is also a potential aptive benefit to birds' genes arising from the capacity for vocal learning. But there is also an obvious benefit to birds' sonemes, whose very existence is enabled by this capacity. Sonemes capitalise on it, engaging in sometimes runaway replication that, by drawing heavily on birds' time and energy resources, often serves the sonemes' interests ahead of those of the birds' genes and thus attenuates any aptive benefits song-learning confers upon birds' genes. As independent replicators, the sound-patterns of learned bird-song are not extended-phenotypic products of genes; rather, they are phemotypic products of memomic sonemes.

5.4 Primarily Learned Vocalisations

This category of vocalisation encompasses those cases where a genetic predisposition to imitation leads to the transmission of sound-patterns between conspecifics by means of vocal learning (§2.7.5). As in the analogous process in humans, and on account of innate perceptual-cognitive constraints operating across species, learned vocalisations tend to be composed of discrete units – musemes and lexemes in humans, sonemes in animals – that are seized upon by the VRS algorithm as the raw materials of an evolutionary process. As with those underpinning human music and language, animal-cultural replicators are transmitted between members of a community, sometimes undergoing mutation; and they are assortatively recombined to form longer sequences that are often structured at a number of recursive-hierarchical levels. The songs that result differ in various ways between conspecifics and these distinctions coevolutionarily serve both the interests of the vocaliser's genes – via territorial demarcation, mate-attraction, dominance hierarchies, group cohesion, pair-bond consolidation and infant nurture – and, perhaps more importantly, those of their sonemes – by filling the vocaliser's cultural-ecological niche with sound-information. Indeed, such coevolution may go further, in that the operation of the VRS algorithm in the socio-cultural ontological category (§1.5.5) may bootstrap that in the biological category, driving an expansion in brain size – and thus fostering a greater capacity for imitation – in the vocaliser's species (§3.7.1).

5.4.1 Learned Bird-Song

As outlined in §5.3.5, those bird species that possess the capacity for vocal learning are to be found in the orders *Passeriformes* (specifically the suborder *Passeri*), *Apodiformes* and *Psittaciformes*. The discussion below is organised thematically, rather than in an attempt to survey the most vocally prolific species, and tries to draw connections between the identified features of bird-song and corresponding phenomena in human musics.[236]

5.4.1.1 The Acquisition of Learned Bird-Song

The acquisition of song in vocal-learning bird species often takes place in two phases. In the first phase, song is acquired during a bird's early development from the (usually) male parent. Merker notes that

> [t]hough there is no standard trajectory for the developing bird's duplic-
> ation of adult song ..., it typically includes an initial period of auditory
> learning[237] resulting in memory storage of the learned pattern of song
> produced by a conspecific model, followed by a protracted period of
> production learning. An initial practice phase called subsong features
> highly variable jumbles of low-intensity sounds.... This is followed by

---

[236] It is now widely accepted that birds evolved from dinosaurs (Xu et al., 2014, p. 2; see also G. Mayr, 2016). Low (2016) argues that Australia was one of the main focal points of this evolution, on account of the relative distance of the continent's geological ancestor – part of the supercontinent Gondwana – from the site of the asteroid impact – the Chicxulub crater in Mexico – hypothesised to have led to the extinction of the dinosaurs *c.* 66 MYBP. Indeed, "Australian birds appear to be more cooperative and bonded, longer lived, and perhaps even more intelligent than Northern Hemisphere temperate zone birds" (H. Taylor, 2017, p. 273). In the commonly accepted classification scheme by Benton (2015), all extant bird species arose from the *Theropoda* suborder of dinosaurs, which also encompasses such large terrestrial carnivores as *Tyrannosaurus rex*; specifically, birds evolved from the infradivision *Maniraptora* (Benton, 2015, pp. 209–210, Box 8.1; see also Xu et al., 2014, p. 4, Fig. 2). This view is sometimes termed the "BMT hypothesis" – that "birds are maniraptoran theropods" (Xu et al., 2014, p. 2). It is therefore interesting to speculate whether the vocal learning evident in certain bird species was present in their dinosaur ancestors (and that it was subsequently lost in those bird species without the capacity for learned song); or whether it evolved in certain birds after their evolutionary separation from dinosaurs. The nature of dinosaur vocalisation has been theorised, and it is believed that some were able to produce (closed-mouth) sounds (Riede et al., 2016). Nevertheless, some evidence suggests that the bird syrinx – the source of its vocal virtuosity – was a relatively late evolutionary development (J. A. Clarke et al., 2016; but see Habib, 2019 for a contrary view). As Levitin says in the quotation on page 74, however, vocal learning is more a matter of cognition than of vocal-organ mechanics. If vocal learning were present in the ancestors of birds, one might imagine communities of singing dinosaurs using learned song to defend their territory and to woo their mates.

[237] Recent research has suggested that, in some species, this process may even begin *in ovo*, before hatching (Colombelli-Négrel et al., 2021).

> so-called plastic song, in which the animal produces increasingly competent and elaborate song, but without adhering closely to the pattern of the model.... The model template stored in memory is nevertheless in the background throughout, because plastic song eventually issues in 'song crystallization' and full adult competence .... (Merker, 2012, pp. 220–221)

Having learned how to learn in the first phase, in the second phase, the young bird, having left the nest, is exposed to the song of conspecifics other than its father and begins song learning in earnest. This often occurs – as in the case of the Indigo bunting (*Passerina cyanea*) – when the young male returns from its first migration and occupies a breeding location (Kroodsma, 2004, p. 115). An adult neighbour in this location becomes a "tutor" for the young "student", resulting in the appearance of a two-bird "micro-dialect" within a particular territory (2004, pp. 115, 116, Fig. 4.6).

Both of these phases of song-learning appear to be guided by an *auditory template* (Marler, 1970), or model template, in Merker's (2012) terms. In Soha's summary of Marler (1970),

> a young bird possesses a crude auditory specification of species-specific song. This crude template guides song development if a bird is raised in isolation; otherwise, it acts as a filter to focus attention on the songs of conspecific adults. As the young bird hears conspecific adult song during the sensitive phase, the template is modified and becomes more precise (i.e., it comes to represent the memorized song models). Finally, when the young bird himself later begins to sing, his vocalizations will be matched to this template. In other words, during motor rehearsal, *the template is the internal representation of song* to which the bird compares his own vocalizations.... Thus, over the course of development, the template serves three functions: to focus attention on conspecific songs, to facilitate the memorization of those songs and to guide motor development of the bird's own song. (Soha, 2017, p. 247; emphasis mine)

From this account, it appears that the auditory template is a form of *sonemesatz* – an avian equivalent of the musemesatz of human music (§3.5.2) – governing the structural-hierarchic configuration of bird-song: it regulates both the higher-order structure of the song and the nature of the lower-order patterning (the sonemes) that instantiates it. Unlike a musemesatz, which – notwithstanding the genetic constraints that govern human musical pattern perception and cognition – is by definition essentially memetic/nurtural, the auditory-template sonemesatz is primarily genetic/natural. Nevertheless, as Soha's references to the template's being "modified and [becoming] more precise" and coming "to represent the memorized song models" make clear, it is also malleable: the initial innately configured structure is adjusted as a result of memetic/sonemic forces – from learning interactions with conspecifics – acting upon it. It is possible that this balance between natural and nurtural contributions to the auditory template varies according to bird species.

5.4.1.2 The Structure of Learned Bird-Song

While it is difficult to generalise the structure of the songs of vocal-learning birds – of which, as noted in §5.3.5, there are *c.* 5,000 species – the observations here attempt to capture the key features of the songs of the most virtuosic species. Bird-song structure, as with human speech, relies partly on the morphology of the sound-producing organ, the syrinx, counterpart to the human larynx, and partly on the neural substrates controlling it. Unlike the larynx, the syrinx of songbirds has an inverted Y-shaped structure consisting of two independent sound-producing chambers that connect to the lungs via the bronchi and that join at the base of the trachea (Düring et al., 2013). This enables the bird to divide rising and falling motions between the two chambers (often seamlessly at the point of crossover), and also to oscillate rapidly between relatively high and relatively low pitch registers in order to create the kind of pseudo-polyphony found in monophonic Baroque music (Slater, 2000, p. 50; Suthers, 2004, pp. 272–273).[238]

These rapidly rising and falling motions distinguish bird-song from human music and language. Humans have a tendency to categorical perception (Fitch, 2010, pp. 325–326), partly innate, partly learned, in that a frequency experienced in the context of others (or by itself, in the case of individuals with absolute (perfect) pitch) is assigned to a relative or absolute pitch category (which may or may not be associated with a standardised pitch-name),

---

[238] Bars 22–23 of the first movement of J. S. Bach's Concerto for Two Violins in D minor BWV. 1043 (*c.* 1731) are a case in point.

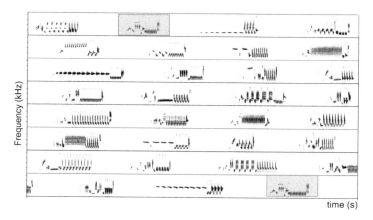

Figure 5.1: The Hierarchic Structure of Nightingale Song.

within which a range of frequency variation is tolerable. Exceeding that range forces re-categorisation of the frequency into an adjacent pitch category (and an associated renaming) (Patel, 2008, pp. 24–26). Birds' vocalisations, by contrast, are characterised by, among other sonic events, legato "glides" across a wide pitch-range, so whereas human musics (especially those preserved and transmitted using standard western notation) are understood in terms of discrete, categorical "notes" and their groupings, some components of bird-song are heard by humans as a series of portamenti (but see below and Figure 5.3). Of course, as gestalt psychology has demonstrated, in human musics, a sequence of discrete note-events is often perceived as connected – by means of the *phi-phenomenon* and the *beta movement* (Ekroll et al., 2008) – to form a single unit in cognition, the mind "joining the dots" to create a virtual line of pitch. Glides in bird-song are evident in Figure 5.1, which shows a spectrogram of the song of the Nightingale (*Luscinia megarhynchos*) (Zuidema et al., 2018, p. 256, Fig. 11.1 A).

Several different levels of organisation are evident in Figure 5.1. According to Große Ruse et al. (2016), and apropos the Great reed warbler (*Acrocephalus arundinaceus*) (GRW), the main structural units of bird-song – which Große Ruse et al. (2016) detect and classify using an automated analysis algorithm – are as follows:

> [A] *song* … is usually 3–10 min[utes] long and includes typically 25–40
> song *strophes*, each of which is composed of approximately 10–20 smaller
> sound units, the *syllables*. Subsequent strophes are separated by a period
> of silence/no singing in which only [background] noise is perceptible.…
> Syllables are more or less continuous sound sections separated by short
> silent periods and are the building blocks of a song strophe. A syllable
> in a GRW song has a duration of about 50–300 ms. Within a song strophe
> of the GRW, a syllable of [a] certain type is usually repeated 1–10 times
> in a row. (Große Ruse et al., 2016, p. 41; emphases mine)

Discussing the Singing honeyeater (*Meliphaga virescens*), Baker defines a
syllable as a "single or multi-note sound that is the unit of recombination in
a population of songs; [syllables are] the building blocks from which songs
are composed. Multi-noted syllables are not fragmented but are inherited as
units" (1996, p. 854; see also Jan, 2007, pp. 246–249). He explicitly equates
syllables in bird-song with memes (in my terminology, sonemes), and he
regards them, owing to their indivisibility, as the optimon – the "the unit of
[cultural] selection" (Dawkins, 1983a, p. 81) – of bird-song cultural evolution
(§1.6.2). As an example of a syllable, Figure 5.2 shows a transcription of
seven alleles, labelled (a)–(g), of a soneme from the song of a Common
Blackbird (*Turdus merula*), heard in my garden in Manchester, UK, at 03.00
on 12 April 2020. They are taken from a recording of 1':20" in duration and
are listed here in order of increasing complexity, not order of appearance in
the recording.[239]

While Figure 5.2 offers a particularly coherent set of closely related patterns
– all alleles have a common "core", which is varied (before the axial f^2 of
b. 2^1; Figure 5.2 (f) and (g)) and/or extended (after the axial f^2; Figure 5.2
(b)–(g)) – it is in the nature of bird-song syllables that they are sometimes
difficult to identify by means of the coindexation or coindexation-determined
segmentation (§2.7.6) that are effective in tracing museme replication or in
demarcating musemes in a sound-stream, respectively, in human music.
This is because whereas musemes have, perhaps more so in notated than
in sonic form, a digital quality – as discussed on page 419, they are able to
be represented by clearly demarcated symbol-groups on the page – bird-

---

[239] See H. Taylor (2017, pp. 129–136) for a detailed discussion of syllable – termed there variously "phrase" and "motif" – structure and combinatoriality in the song of the Pied butcherbird
(*Cracticus nigrogularis*).

Figure 5.2: Soneme Alleles from Common Blackbird Song.

song syllables appear to us as essentially analogue, certainly at their natural tempo. Their various glides, trills and "glitches" – somewhat "ironed out" in Figure 5.2 – therefore make segmentation and cross-comparison difficult, certainly for the human ear, both within a single song and also between two or more songs, be they by the same bird or by different birds of the same or of different species. Nevertheless, a spectrogram representation expedites this process, allowing visual comparison of replicated patterns (but see the discussion of syllable classification below): as the two shaded regions in Figure 5.1 indicate, the same soneme is clearly visible at the beginning and end of the extract.

Despite the analogue nature of bird-song syllables, they nevertheless possess a degree of harmonicity. That is, they include patterns that, to a human, are arpeggio- or scale-like. This feature, the recurrence of certain syllables at the same pitch level, and a sensitivity to the octave evident in such species as the Pied butcherbird ((H. Taylor, 2017, 156–157; Ex. 6.4); see also §5.4.1.3), suggests a sensitivity to pitch and, perhaps, to long-range tonal connections on the part of birds. While such tonal interpretations might be an artefact of human perception and cognition – we hear bird-song, as with other an-imal vocalisations, through the filter of our own innate and learned mental frameworks – it might also result from constraints imposed by the harmonic series, which, in various ways, has also made its mark upon human musics as the superordinate acoustical law, in Meyer's (1996) sense (but see also Nattiez, 1990, pp. 204–207). Similar constraints appear to operate in the case of whale-song (§5.4.2), which, while essentially anchored to harmonic-series pitches arising from a low fundamental, creates variety by means of the production of a range of glide-reached intermediate pitches (Nicholas Bannan, personal communication). The latter perhaps arise in a manner akin to the "stopped" notes produced by the hand-stopping technique of eighteenth-century horn playing, and/or by the alteration of the fundamental, as in trombone technique.

With greater sophistication than is deployed in Figure 5.2, there have been attempts by scientists, musicologists and composers to transcribe bird-song using conventional western music notation (H. Taylor, 2017, Ch. 3). These efforts are driven by a desire to understand it more fully – western notation, for all its shortcomings, offers the clear, digital perspective referred to above – and to draw upon it as a stimulus to musical creativity. The most important figure in the creative tradition, as suggested in §5.3.5, is Messiaen, whose works such as *Catalogue d'oiseaux* (1958) both incorporate (via transcription) and expand upon patterns from bird-song. But many other musicians have drawn inspiration from bird-song, including Hindley (1990, 1995), and they have therefore often attempted to capture it notationally (see also §5.4.1.4). Figure 5.3 shows Hindley's transcription of a passage of Nightingale song (1990, p. 30), taking part of what he terms phrase fourteen (i.e., strophe fourteen, in the terminology of the passage from Große Ruse et al. (2016) cited on page 419).[240]

In such notation, the syllables of bird-song become more tractable as sonemes, and the inter-soneme intervals – demarcated by rests or by register changes in notation – are made visible. What is clear from such transcriptions is that, relative to human music, bird-song appears significantly "speeded up". That is, when slowed down (to *c.* 50% of their natural speed), the "glides, trills and glitches" of bird-song syllables referred to above take on more of the character of musemes in human music (British Library, 2010), particularly those in the kind of rhythmically complex, richly chromatic and registrally wide-ranging music of twentieth-century western composers like Messiaen,

---

[240] Figure 5.3 is re-typeset here from a poor-quality scan of the article. While this is largely faithful to the original, a few minor aspects are necessarily conjectural.

Figure 5.3: Hindley's Transcription of Nightingale Song, Phrase 14, bb. 114–120.

which perhaps helps, in part, to explain their fascination with it. Conversely, such human music, when speeded up, takes on some of the character of bird-song.

Notwithstanding the potential clarification afforded by such transcriptions, and discussing the problem of formal syllable classification, Große Ruse et al. (2016) note that

> [t]he hitherto standard methods to classify song entities (syllables) [have] been by means of the audial and visual comparison of syllables …, where the latter is often conducted based on syllable spectrograms …. Unfortunately, these approaches are often time consuming, prone to observer bias and subjectivity, non-numerical (making statistical analyses problematic) and perform less well on songs with large syllable repertoires or with complex structures of song strophes/syllables ….
> (Große Ruse et al., 2016, p. 40)

As noted apropos the quotation on page 419, Große Ruse et al. (2016) outline an automated analysis algorithm for "syllable detection, representation and comparison" in order to rectify this imprecision (2016, p. 40). Passing over the technical details of the algorithm, their results appear to show improved performance, compared with previous techniques, in determining similarity relationships between syllables. They present the results of three experiments in which a large set of syllables is, in the first experiment (based on thirty-nine syllables), divided (forced) into two categories, a difficult task given the high "within-class variability" of the sample (2016, p. 45). The second

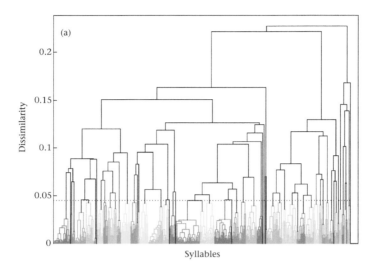

Figure 5.4: Dendrogram of Syllable Clustering in a Song of the Great Reed Warbler.

and third experiments represent examples of *clustering problems*. These involve the comparison and sorting into groups – soneme allele-classes, in my terminology – of a large number of syllables whose category-properties, and the number of resulting categories, are not (unlike in the first experiment) specified in advance (2016, pp. 43–44). Thus, in clustering, the sorting is conducted according to certain extracted features of the syllables.[241] In the second experiment, the algorithm assigns the set used in the first experiment into five categories, reifying latent subclasses evident from the first experiment (2016, p. 45). In the third experiment, the algorithm analyses a complete Great reed warbler song, four minutes in duration, and assigns its syllables, four-hundred and thirty-three in number, to fifty-seven categories (2016, p. 46). Figure 5.4 shows the dendrogram representing this clustering (2016, p. 49, Fig. 11a).

One of many fascinating aspects of this dendrogram is the fact that the algorithm incorporates hierarchical clustering techniques (2016, p. 44): different levels of resolution affect the numbers of soneme allele-classes identified. The

---

[241] In contrast to clustering problems, *classification problems* are those, such the first experiment, in which the properties and/or number of the groups are specified in advance (Große Ruse et al., 2016, pp. 43–44).

fifty-seven identified categories arising from the third experiment are based on the resolution indicated by the dotted line in Figure 5.4, this representing an optimality threshold (2016, p. 44). Raising or lowering this line would affect the "granularity" of the results, decreasing or increasing the number of syllable-categories, respectively. This situation is likely also to obtain when dealing with museme allele-classes, because that which, at one level of resolution, appears to be a homogeneous allele-class might be divided into two or more sub-classes at a higher resolution, the relationships between them being represented by intersecting Venn diagrams (Jan, 2016c, p. 451, Fig. 1). As in human music, the features employed to assign a museme to an allele-class determine the configuration of the resulting clustering. Adding to, deleting from, or changing the "feature vector" (2016, p. 41) would therefore give rise to other categorisations of the sonemes. Moreover, while the dendrogram in Figure 5.4 does not indicate it, it may be the case that certain syllables, while replicated separately, are also replicated as a group between two or more birds of this species (or even across species, as in the case of the Marsh warbler (*Acrocephalus palustris*), discussed in §5.4.1.3), thus forming (after ideas outlined in §3.5.2) a *sonemeplex*.[242]

5.4.1.3 The Aptive Benefits of Learned Bird-Song

Given that bird-song, innate and learned, is a form of vocalisation serving various (gene-) aptive purposes (§2.5.1, §5.1), it is pertinent to ask – further to the *"cui bono?"* discussion on page 414 – whether there are any particular features of learned bird-song that make it more effective than innate bird-song for these purposes. Is the former, in other words, more (gene-) aptive than the latter? Given that approximately half of bird species are vocal learners and the other half use innate vocalisations (§5.3.5), it might be thought that there is no particular genetic advantage (or disadvantage) to vocal learning, otherwise all species would have aligned in response to selection pressures favouring (or disfavouring) it. This is arguably over-simplistic, given that organisms evolve in order to align with specific, fluid environmental niches, these including selection pressures imposed by other species. Moreover, certain bird species appear to have relatively recently acquired vocal learning

---

[242] This concept is already implicit in the notion of a "double syllable[, which] is a syllable containing two (usually repeated) or three parts (kack-a-kack) and is a common phenomenon in the song structure of GRWs" (Große Ruse et al., 2016, p. 41).

(from innate song) and others appear to have, also relatively recently, lost it (reverting to an improvisatory mode of vocalisation; see below).

Kroodsma discusses certain species in the former category, and others in the latter (2004, pp. 109–112, 113–114). He correlates these category shifts with changes in two aspects of social/reproductive behaviour, noting that the acquisition of vocal learning is generally associated with: (i) the evolution of lekking behaviours – i.e., a system where male animals form a group, a lek, and compete against each other for female attention; and/or with (ii) the evolution of non-genetically-monogamous mating systems, where females in pair-bonds mate surreptitiously with males other than their established partner. As an example of both these phenomena, "[a]mong hummingbirds [*Apodiformes*] … it seems that [vocal] learning has been documented only in lekking or non-monogamous species" (2004, p. 112). Moreover, whereas the North American Marsh wren (*Cistothorus palustris*) is a vocal learner (with communities manifesting clear local song "dialects"), its close relative the Sedge wren (*Cistothorus stellaris*) improvises its repertoire "on the fly". The motivation behind this distinction appears to be the fact that members of the former species "tend to be resident or highly site-faithful" (and thus males compete to outperform each other in the learning and rendition of the songs of their shared dialect), whereas members of the latter have a "semi-nomadic lifestyle" (2004, p. 113).

These observations suggest that that learned bird-song represents a phenomenon resulting from sexual selection: it is a male ornament, sustained by a female preference (§2.5.3). Strictly, it is the genetic *capacity* for such song that is sexually selected, given that this phenomenon relates (at least initially) to the differential selection of genes, not the sonemes that capitalise on this capacity. As an extravagant display of virtuosity demonstrating the ability to memorise a large song repertoire and the stamina to perform it for extended periods of time, the capacity for vocal learning and its associated performative behaviours suggest a solid genetic endowment and good physical health. Of course, only memorisation is directly relevant to vocal learning, in that stamina can also be demonstrated by the performance of innate song repertoires, and by means of other physical activities. Beyond the abstract mathematical-theoretical support for the evolution of mechanisms for sexual selection, there is a good deal of circumstantial evidence supporting the hypothesis that song learning is a sexually selected trait in birds. This includes certain telling correlations between song repertoire size and a set of other variables related to reproductive success, such as harem size, offspring hatching date, number of extra-pair matings, and survival rates of offspring (Kroodsma, 2004, p. 125).

The difficulty with using such evidence to support an interpretation of sexual selection is that, as is often noted, correlation does not necessarily imply causation (the *"cum hoc ergo propter hoc"* fallacy). Despite Miller's assertion that "Darwin's idea that most birdsong functions as a courtship display to attract sexual mates is fully supported by biological research" (2000, p. 329), there is, according to Kroodsma, little hard evidence that – apropos learned as opposed to innate bird-song – "females actually use repertoire size in making mating decisions", not least because of the logistical difficulties of verifying it experimentally (2004, p. 125). Moreover, Fitch cautions that while "most of the birdsong in temperate regions is performed by males, female song and duetting is much more common in poorly studied tropical species. Since most bird species live in the tropics, our perception of the frequency of female song in birds may be somewhat skewed for accidental historical reasons" (2006, p. 184). Thus, "the traditional assumption that birdsong is always a [male-ornament/female-preference] sexually selected trait, dating back to Darwin ..., may need to be reevaluated in such [rare] cases [as female display (ornament) and male choice (preference) in certain species]" (2006, p. 187). Note that this does not constitute an argument against sexual selection *per se*; indeed, in indicating that preference and ornament can be decoupled from their predominant sex-associations, it emphasises the generalisability of the underlying mechanism of sexual selection.

While sexual selection is an elegant hypothesis, and while its operation has been more strongly supported by other categories of ornament – not least the tail-feathers of the Indian peacock – until more conclusive evidence is available, it must remain a candidate explanation, albeit a strong one, for vocal learning in birds (as it is in humans) and not a definitive cause. Nevertheless, and offering what might be regarded as a supply-side (male-advantage perspective), rather than a demand-side (female-advantage perspective) methodology, Geberzahn and Aubin (2014) have observed increased vocal performance in the Skylark (*Alauda arvensis*) in male-male competitive situations. This is manifested in the demanding compression of time intervals between adjacent syllables in which there is a large pitch distance between the end of one syllable and the beginning of the following one. The provisos above notwithstanding, such resource-depleting (thus honest) displays are, if not proof, then certainly a hallmark of sexual selection.

There must be an advantage to genes from innate bird-song or the capacity to produce it would have been eliminated by *natural* selection. As indicated above, these advantages may inhere in any or all of the aptive motivations for vocalisation listed in §5.1 (i.e., territorial demarcation, mate-attraction, dominance hierarchy formation, group cohesion, pair-bond consolidation and infant nurture). Whether innate bird-song is additionally a *sexually* selected trait, building upon a naturally selected antecedent substrate, or whether it arose from any or several of the other imperatives – and this is to oversimplify the issue by assuming similar cause-configurations for all instances of innate bird-song – it may be the case that it was *also* subject to memetic drive in some species by means of the process that Blackmore hypothesises underpinned the origin of the human capacity for imitation (§3.7.1; see also point 7 of the list on page 138).[243] That is – and again apropos the "*cui bono*?" discussion on page 414 – an extant capacity, naturally and perhaps also sexually selected, for innate bird-song might have been subsequently co-opted by memetic drive (the third stage in the sequence on page 255), as may also have happened with innate human vocalisations. This would have triggered coevolutionary sexual selection and allowed nascent sonemes to advance their own replicative advantage. Consequently, and as discussed on page 425, innate bird-song would gradually have evolved into learned bird-song, this occurring coevolutionarily with the origin of lekking and of non-monogamous pair-bonding (Kroodsma, 2004, pp. 109–112). If this hypothesised sequence aligns with evolutionary reality, it suggests that sonemes initially served the interests of the genes in learned song, as well as beginning to advance their own. The posited input of memetic drive to

---

[243] Note that memetic drive does not need sexual selection to operate, and sexual selection does not need memetic drive: memetic drive can operate on the basis of the first two stages in the sequence on page 255 without the third (sexual-selection) phase; and sexual selection can act without the involvement of cultural replicators.

the aetiology of vocal learning in birds implies that its advantages, initially accruing primarily to the bird's genes, would tend increasingly to favour the songs' sonemes, inasmuch as this advantage can be meaningfully assessed.

An explanation for Kroodsma's converse situation, where learned bird-song is *lost* over time in some species (2004, pp. 113–114), might paradoxically support the argument just advanced for the memetic-drive-based acquisition of learned bird-song. An example of such reversion can be found in the aforementioned differences between the Marsh wren and the Sedge wren. The Sedge wren's loss of vocal learning appears to be related to its evolution of a peripatetic way of life, which meant that learning a new repertoire of songs in each locale (for the lekking/male-competitive purposes used by its territorial cousin the Marsh wren) became impossible. As a result, in the Sedge wren "selection for imitation is reduced or lost, and instead males improvise, using some shared rules for generating species-typical songs" (2004, p. 114). Whereas in modern humans improvisation involves the assortative recombination of discrete, learned fragments in a balance between top-down and bottom-up constraints (§3.5.3), the equivalent behaviour in the Sedge wren appears to consist of a more mechanistic process of innate sound-unit assembly, and thus does not involve the VRS-mediated propagation of sonemes in communities of conspecifics. Thus, having perhaps powered the acquisition of vocal learning, memetic-drive might be put into reverse and even switched off if a system of soneme-based cultural evolution it helped to establish is subsequently constrained by certain biologically evolved factors – a now itinerant lifestyle, in the case of the Sedge wren, this coming into conflict with the bird's naturally finite memory capacity for song-acquisition. In this situation, gene-based natural and/or sexual selection might have to wrest back sole control, put sonemes back on the genetic leash (or even euthanise them), and reinstate a previously abandoned, but presumably latent, hard-wired solution to the problems of territorial demarcation and mate-attraction, namely innate song.

Perhaps the clearest example of learned bird-song serving the replicative advantages of sonemes is provided by the Marsh warbler, referred to in §5.4.1.2. On its migration between its summer breeding grounds in Europe and its wintering grounds in south-east Africa, males of this remarkable bird

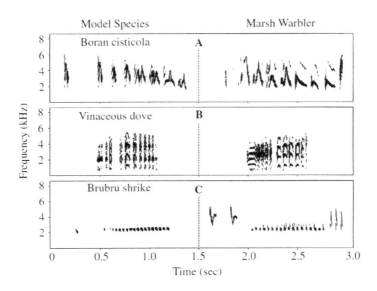

Figure 5.5: Cross-Species Soneme Replication in the Marsh Warbler.

acquire fragments of songs from a range of other bird species encountered on its journey south (Kroodsma, 2004, pp. 129–130). So far, "ninety-nine European and one-hundred and thirteen African species have been identified" as those whose song is imitated, while "[i]ndividual [Marsh warbler] repertoires contain hundreds of motifs [sonemes] belonging to eighty or more species, with about a fifth of entire songs still unidentified, perhaps consisting of imitations of unfamiliar species" (Dowsett-Lemaire, in Kroodsma, 2004, p. 129). Figure 5.5 (Dowsett-Lemaire, in Kroodsma, 2004, p. 129) shows three sonemes from the song of a Marsh warbler imitated from the songs of the Boran cisticola (*Cisticola bodessa*; eastern Africa), the Vinaceous dove (*Streptopelia vinacea*; Sahel and Sudan regions of Africa), and the Brubru shrike (*Nilaus afer*; Sub-Saharan Africa).

While the configuration of the sonograms in Figure 5.5 indicates that the replication is imperfect, the model-copy pairs are clearly homologous (Marler and Slabbekoorn (2004) includes a CD with recordings of these species), and the algorithm of Große Ruse et al. (2016) (§5.4.1.2) might well assign them to the same syllable category. Of course, imperfect replication is a feature of cultural-evolutionary systems, the copying of musemes in human musics often deviating significantly from the model owing to a range of factors. What seems clear is that the Marsh warbler gains no immediate genetic advantage from this prodigious imitation, unless the acquired sonemes serve as a kind of auditory camouflage to offer itself some protection around potentially hostile indigenous species on its journey: it is assimilating these sonemes *after* leaving its summer European breeding grounds (although they may possibly be retained in memory for female-wooing use in the following summer's breeding period). It would appear that the sonemes have, via memetic drive, hijacked the Marsh warbler's naturally and possibly sexually selected propensity for imitation to serve their own selfish ends.

The Marsh warbler is a *locus classicus* of dual-replicator coevolution in vocal-learning birds, wherein sonemes are hypothesised to have leveraged genes to their own advantage. Indeed, beyond the "primary" expansion of avian cognitive and memory capacity impelled by memetic drive, it is not inconceivable that a "secondary" augmentation of the physical capacities of the syrinx and its associated neural-control structures might have been driven by the same processes, genes being manipulated to produce an ever more complex vocalisation-generating infrastructure in order to serve the replicative interests of sonemes. In summary, and as with the human analogue of this process, the genes of those birds that acquired a vestigial propensity for vocal learning on top of an innate substrate would – assuming such a propensity was aptive for them – have been disproportionately represented in the next generation. Iteratively, sexual selection would tend to build upon this naturally selected foundation, favouring a capacity for vocal learning in males and a sensitivity to it in females. A conflict of interest between genes and sonemes is almost inevitable when memetic drive subsequently energises this process.

The Superb lyrebird (*Menura novaehollandiae*) that featured in Sir David Attenborough's documentary series *The life of birds* (B. White, 1998), imitating with uncanny accuracy the sounds of chainsaws, is a telling example of this conflict between replicators. While the demonstration has attracted some controversy – the bird in question was kept in captivity, so its rendition was not strictly "natural" – the fact that it possessed a capacity to mimic human-made objects, including ones so perilously destructive of its own environment, indicates at the very least that there is a dissonance between the replicative interests of the bird's genes and those of its sonemes (see also note 253 on page 449). While such high-fidelity mimicry is one manifestation of the power of sonemes, extraordinary musical virtuosity is another. Perhaps an extreme point of this latter capacity is represented by the Pied butcherbird, another Australian species (see note 236 on page 416). Taylor recalls that

> out of the blue I hear a leisurely, rich-toned phrase. It's a jazz flutist in a tree. An explosion of sound in another tree answers – a long, bold rattle descends sharply and swiftly, and a duet ensues – no, a trio. Twenty otherworldly seconds pass: low, slow, and enticingly familiar.... 'It's the pied butcherbird', [my companion] explains to me later. 'They get their name from snatching other birds' babies right out of a nest. Then they'll wedge their prey into the fork of a tree or skewer it on a broken branch'.... I notate several irresistible melodies .... Hard to put together this songster's name and savage reputation with this angelic voice. Won over by blue notes, hip riffs, and syncopated chimes, I've fallen head over heels for a convict. (H. Taylor, 2017, p. 2)

The Pied butcherbird is an apparent outlier even among vocal-learning birds. Beyond its extreme virtuosity and capacity for song-acquisition, females of this species are thought to be as prodigiously vocal as males, although this trait seems to be generally more common in southern hemisphere than in northern hemisphere bird species, with the repertoire of females in some species even exceeding that of males (H. Taylor, 2017, p. 25). This apparent equity suggests that the power of vocal learning in the Pied butcherbird, and in other Australian birds, is great enough even to attenuate the classical dynamics of sexual selection – ornamented/chosen male, preferring/choosing female – certainly in terms of vocalisations. In fact, the Pied Butcherbird is also sexually monomorphic: females are very similar in form and size to males. While this aligns with the notion of vocal learning's attenuation of classical sexual selection in vocalisation it simultaneously makes it difficult to verify experimentally (H. Taylor, 2017, p. 123), owing to the lack of vocal-range sexual dimorphism such as is found in humans. Thus, soneme-driven encephalisation – perhaps it should strictly be referred to as "sonemic drive" – appears to have captured female as well as male brain-space in this and other

Australian bird species as a further expansion of the capacity for storage and replication of such "blue notes, hip riffs, and syncopated chimes".

5.4.1.4 Learned Bird-Song and Human Music: *The Bird Fancyer's Delight*

The capacity of certain birds to memorise, assortatively recombine, and transmit songs to their conspecifics was capitalised upon by musicians in the eighteenth century, who attempted to train such birds to learn human-composed melodies. Books of tunes were published – perhaps most famously John Walsh's *The bird fancyer's delight* (Walsh, 1717; Angliss, 2011) – with the intention that they be played on wind instruments in the presence of caged birds in order to train them to reproduce the played melodies.[244] This is not the *imitation of bird-song by or in music*, often using (woodwind) instruments, which has a long tradition in western music as part of an aesthetics of imitation of the natural world.[245] Rather, it is the *imitation of bird-song-like music by birds*, the practice of using the bird as a sound-production device, after training by a human, in order to provide diversion and entertainment in genteel drawing rooms. Nevertheless, the two approaches are related, because the training melodies of *The bird fancyer's delight* and other such publications attempted to follow what the authors believed to be the contours and rhythms of the birds' own natural vocalisations – the "lessons" were "properly compos'd within the Compass and faculty of each Bird" (Walsh, 1717, p. 1) – in an attempt to facilitate efficient learning of the melodies.

While *The bird fancyer's delight* is written, and in part serves as a tutor, for the flute and the "flagelet/flagellet" (i.e., the flageolet; small versions of this instrument were specifically made for the purpose of bird-training), another favoured instrument for songbird training was the recorder, which was also often used in music to reproduce the sound of birds. Angliss (2019) observes that "[t]he word 'record' comes from Latin (*re*: again; *cordi*: from the heart).... When a songbird has memorised and can sing back its song,

---

[244] While at its peak in the eighteenth century, this tradition began in the seventeenth century and continued until the nineteenth, and there are even vinyl discs from the 1950s that claim to allow bird owners to train their pets to sing the melodies recorded on them (Bates & Busenbarn, 1958).

[245] The invocation of the Nightingale (*Luscinia megarhynchos*; learned song; flute), Quail (family *Phasianidae* and *Odontophoridae*; innate song; oboe), and Cuckoo (*Cuculus canorus*; innate song; clarinet) at the end of the second movement of Beethoven's "Pastoral" Symphony (bb. 129–136) is perhaps the best known example in this tradition (Jander, 1993). see also Preston (2004).

it's said to 'record' [the melody]".[246] This sense of copying and transmitting sound (and the associated emotions) perhaps explains the (re-)use of the word "recorder" in modern sound storage and reproduction technologies. Apropos the latter, and concerned to determine the relationship between innate and learned aspects of bird-song, Thorpe (1958a, 1958b) attempted to replicate this tradition of bird-training in experiments with the Chaffinch (*Fringilla coelebs*) he conducted in the 1950s, but with limited success. As the more fruitful experiments of Baptista and Petrinovich (1984) with the White-crowned sparrow (*Zonotrichia leucophrys nuttalli*) indicate, an important element in the success of this training – one neglected by Thorpe, who used tape-recorded sounds – was interaction with conspecifics in a process of "social tutoring" (1984, p. 176). This model – which of course naturally obtains in the wild – is to some extent (imperfectly) replicated in the human training of birds.

To make a fairly obvious point, books like *The bird fancyer's delight* are only able to train vocal-learning species: innate-vocalisation species produce stereotypical calls in response to certain stimuli, so are unsuitable for the kind of approach *The bird fancyer's delight* and related books offered. Given the range of vocalisations evident in the most virtuosic vocal-learning species, composers of such melodies had a degree of artistic flexibility. Indeed, Figure 5.6 shows the variety of melody ascribed to – and thus held to be capable of learning by – a single species, the Canary (*Serinus canaria* forma *domestica*). Figure 5.6a and Figure 5.6b show two (the first and the sixth, respectively, of seven) melodies presented as "proper tunes" for the "Canary Bird" from *The bird fancyer's delight* (Walsh, 1717, pp. 7, 17), the differences between them being far greater than can be found in instances of innate bird-song from the same species. Figure 5.6c, a depiction of *"Der Kanarienvogel"* ("The canary bird") from Mozart's Sechs Deutsche Tänze K. 600 (1791), is different again from these two Walsh examples, and indeed from the other five Canary melodies in *The bird fancyer's delight*. While not a training melody – it is part of a series of light pieces Mozart wrote for Viennese dance-halls – it is

---

[246] This usage is reminiscent of Beethoven's famous inscription at the head of the *Missa Solemnis* op. 123 (1823): *"Von Herzen – Möge es wieder – Zu Herzen gehn!"* ("From the heart – may it again – go to the heart!").

(a) Walsh: First "Canary Bird" Melody from *The bird fancyer's delight*.

(b) Walsh: Sixth "Canary Bird" Melody from *The bird fancyer's delight*.

(c) Mozart: Sechs Deutsche Tänze K. 600 (1791), no. 5, Trio ("Der Kanarienvogel"), bb. 1–8.

Figure 5.6: Three Canary-Song Melodies.

presumably intended as a representation of a typical song of this species, or certainly as something a canary could learn.[247]

Attempts by composers in this tradition at ornithological verisimilitude are largely superficial. Such melodies have much more in common with eighteenth-century European musical style than any type of natural (or naturally learned) bird-song: after all, those who sought to train their birds wanted to hear music with which they were broadly familiar, in a stylistic sense. For example, both Walsh's and Mozart's canary show a solid understanding of eighteenth-century phrase-structure: Walsh's bird (in Figure 5.6b) has great facility in modulating from C minor to E♭ major and back,

---

[247] Among other pets, Mozart kept a pet Canary and, most famously, a pet Starling (*Sturnus vulgaris*), the latter being apparently capable of singing, almost correctly, the melody of the finale of the Piano Concerto in G major K. 453 (1784) (bb. 0–4) (Solomon, 1995, p. 319).

and its end-cadence (bb. 15–16) is entirely idiomatic for the period. Subject to the degree of conformity to natural patterns in training melodies, any (re)use or (re)imagining of bird-song by human musicians is: (i) aptive for sonemes when humans replicate real bird-song sonemes; and (ii) aptive for musemes when humans, and possibly birds, replicate musemes from human music. That is: (i) a soneme ostensibly derived from bird-song and intended to train other birds may go on to have a life of its own, as a museme, in music other than training melodies; and (ii) a museme derived from human music and successfully assimilated by a songbird via a training melody becomes a soneme, which might subsequently be learned by others of its species. In the second category, perhaps some eighteenth-century canaries, taught musemes derived from the music of contemporary composers such as J. S. Bach and Handel via training melodies, might have escaped from their gilded Georgian cages and gone on to teach these newly sonemic patterns to wild birds. Some of these might have been of migratory species, like the Marsh warbler (§5.4.1.3), which might have carried these sonemes far from Europe and perhaps had them assimilated by native African species on the journey (the species in Figure 5.5 might have learned from, as well as been copied by, the Marsh warbler). Perhaps the music of these composers, or rather certain replication-stable fragments of it, would have been known to south-east Africans from hearing the song of their native birds well before it was taken to that part of the continent by Europeans.

5.4.2 Learned Whale-Song

Cetaceans are divided into two large groups (parvorders): the *odontocetes*, which includes smaller, toothed, species, such as dolphins and porpoises (and the large Killer whale (*Orcinus orca*) and Sperm whale (*Physeter macrocephalus*)); and the *mysticetes*, which includes larger, baleen-feeding,[248] species, such as the Bowhead whale (*Balaena mysticetus*) (Fitch, 2006, p. 191). As with birds, a distinction can be made between innate and learned song in whales, with some species demonstrating the former and others the latter. In general, the most complex (learned) vocalisations are found in *mysticetes* species, although certain *odontocetes* species are also capable of vocal learning

---

[248] Baleen is a keratin-based, sieve-like filtration system in these whales' mouths that is used to separate food such as Krill from water.

(2006, p. 191). Owing to the superior sound-conducting properties of water in comparison with air, cetacean vocalisations can travel considerable distances, measured at *c.* 10 km for smaller whales and, remarkably, at *c.* 1,000 km for Blue whales (*Balaenoptera musculus*) (Janik, 2009, p. 110; see Adam et al., 2013 for a discussion of Humpbacks' sound-production apparatus). This supports the point made in §5.1 regarding the superior communicative potential of sound over other modalities of animal communication.

Unlike innate bird-song (§5.3.5), innate whale-song will not be considered here. Instead, the focus will be on the learned song of a particular and much studied species, the Humpback whale (*Megaptera novaeangeliae*), which is known for the complexity and richness of its vocalisations. The Humpback is a migratory cetacean found in all the major oceans of the world. According to differences not just of geographical location but of song content, there appear to be nine different large population groups of Humpback in the world (Janik, 2009, p. 111). The Humpback has separate feeding and breeding seasons. The feeding season is in summer, spent in colder waters (Alaska, in the case of the North Pacific Humpback); and the breeding season is in winter, spent in tropical or semi-tropical regions (the Caribbean, in the North Pacific humpback). The breeding season is spent mating or, in the case of females, and after a gestation period of eleven or twelve months, giving birth. It is during the breeding season, of approximately five months' duration, that their long, elaborate vocalisations are produced, exclusively by males (Payne, 2000, p. 135).[249] Given the close aetiological, structural and functional correspondences between learned bird-song and learned whale-song (certainly as far as the Humpback whale is concerned), this section follows the layout adopted in §5.4.1.

5.4.2.1 The Acquisition of Learned Whale-Song

Because of the constraints of experimental methodology – birds in the air are significantly easier to study than whales in the sea – relatively little is known of the acquisition of song by juvenile Humpbacks, certainly in comparison with the detailed knowledge of this process in birds discussed

---

[249] Katharine Payne, her husband Roger Payne, and their collaborators undertook pioneering research in whale-song, publishing the results of decades of work on Humpback song in three seminal papers (Payne et al., 1983; Payne & Payne, 1985; Guinee & Payne, 1988). See also note 251 on page 447.

in §5.4.1.1. As a learned vocalisation for which the organism is genetically primed, Humpback song is acquired by imitation between conspecifics, but this seemingly lacks the early father-son learning that occurs in bird-song – albeit perhaps for want of evidence. The majority of song learning in Humpbacks, certainly in terms of the acquisition of song variations, appears to occur during the breeding season, via interactions between males within the same social group. Song-types learned during one year's breeding season are preserved accurately in Humpbacks' memories until the following year's breeding season, whereupon fresh variations are introduced and themselves learned (§5.4.2.2). While specific Humpback social groups occupy their own discrete breeding areas, they often share their feeding waters with other Humpback groups. These geographical and chronological overlaps afford the opportunity for inter-group song transmission: males from one social group sometimes acquire during the feeding season certain patterns from songs developed by a separate social group in the previous breeding season, and go on to transmit them within their own group (§5.4.2.3).

5.4.2.2 The Structure of Learned Whale-Song

The vocalisations of the Humpback have much in common with learned bird-song, and with human music and language, in that (i) they are built up of discrete sound-segments – referred to as syllables in the bird-song literature and, often, as "subphrases" in Humpback-song studies – that function as sonemes. Subject to the operation of the VRS algorithm, songs are (ii) transmitted between conspecifics and manifest change over time in a clear process of cultural evolution (Whitehead & Rendell, 2014). Songs' component sonemes are (iii) assortatively recombined, as in bird-song, and form patterning at a number of structural-hierarchic levels, in a direct analogue to the RHSGAP model of human music discussed in §3.5.2. Moreover, (iv) these shared attributes are homoplasies, not homologies – the structural and functional commonalities arose independently in the three lineages as a result of similar selection pressures. Lastly, (v) these commonalities build upon a genetic foundation, this imposing, in humans and presumably the other two groups, various gestalt perceptual-cognitive constraints that impose the chunking identified in (i) above (Lerdahl, 1992). In all three lineages, vocal learning appears to drive sexual selection, cultural evolution and – in principle in all three groups – memetic drive, which further optimises the organisms' psychology and morphology for the benefit of sonemes.

The hierarchic structure of Humpback song (point iii above) is arguably more stratified than bird-song, consisting, in Payne's (2000) formulation, of no fewer than six distinct levels. The basic building block is the *unit*, a single sound parcel – a Humpback-song "note" – that may vary extensively in pitch shape, timbre and duration.[250] Units are combined to form *phrases* (around fifteen seconds' duration; normally consisting of between six and nine units), which may themselves be divided into two *subphrases* (around seven seconds' duration; normally consisting of a minimum of three units) (Payne, 2000, p. 136). As noted in point (i) above, a Humpback subphrase or phrase might be taken to constitute a soneme in this species. Phrases are combined, sometimes by repetition, into *themes* (around two minutes' duration; normally consisting of a number of phrases). Themes assemble to form the *songs* themselves (around twelve minutes' duration; normally consisting of up to ten themes). If a song is repeated without a significant pause, it forms a *song session* or *song cycle*, the longest recorded example of which is over twenty hours in duration (2000, pp. 136–137, Fig. 9.1). These song components, and their structural-hierarchic relationship, are represented in Figure 5.7 (after Payne, 2000, p. 137, Fig. 9.1).

In contrast to the homogeneity of songs *within* a Humpback social group, *between* different Humpback social groups songs are heterogeneous, owing to variations in the configuration of their intermediate-level components. As Payne observes, "[w]hen we separated out the various voices in [a whale] chorus we discovered all the whales were repeating *the same phrases and themes in the same order*, but not in synchrony with one another"; yet "the songs in different populations were *similar in structure but quite different in content*" (2000, p. 138; emphases mine). This suggests that an aptive function of Humpback song, to add to those to be considered in §5.4.2.3, is *intra*-group sociality and, concomitantly, *inter*-group differentiation, akin to that hypothesised in §2.5.2 to have bound together, and demarcated, early human social groups. In addition to inter-group (synchronic) song differences, there

---

[250] Payne describes certain units image-schematically in terms of letter-shapes, defining "r's" as "rising units with a sustained final tone" and "j's" as "quick upward-sweeping units" (2000, p. 139).

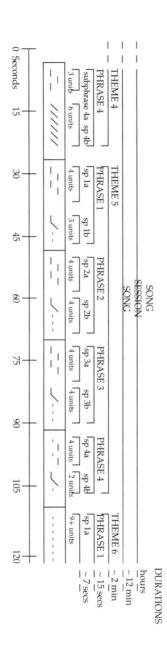

Figure 5.7: The Hierarchic Structure of Whale-Song.

is intra-group (diachronic) variation. Songs within the same social group are mutated over time, and these changes largely occur during the active winter singing/breeding period, and not as a result of any inter-migration forgetting during the summer feeding period: as noted in §5.4.2.1, song variants arising in the breeding period of one year are usually faithfully preserved in Humpback's memories until the following year's breeding season, when a further series of variants is introduced (2000, p. 139).

Changes observed in Humpback song bear a close methodological resemblance to processes evident in human music and language and in bird-song. This is perhaps not surprising, given that a system built from hierarchically nested and vocally learned chunks – and all systems amenable to the VRS algorithm have, and augment, this property – has a fixed number of operations by means of which those chunks can be manipulated. In human music, a museme can be altered by one or more of a number of mutational operations acting upon one or more of its constituent elements, namely insertion, deletion and substitution, these being discussed under the rubric of edit-distance in §3.6.5. These processes are evident in the mutation of Humpback phrases, as evidenced by a sonogram of a four-unit phrase recorded by Payne that, over the course of five years, modifies (by substitution of the original entity with a different form) the pitches and durations of certain units and inserts other units – the latter process sometimes occurring as a result of the division of a single unit into two separate entities (2000, pp. 138, 142, Fig. 9.3). The position of this phrase within its parent theme, and within the song as a whole, allows for tracking of the replication of these and other such phrase-level, unit-driven mutations between conspecifics over time.

At a higher hierarchic level, this principle of phrases occupying specific structural-sequential *loci*/nodes within a theme – as per the RHSGAP model – allows one to regard certain theme-level mutations as having been driven by allelic competition between structurally and/or functionally analogous phrases or subphrases. In another sonogram, Payne shows four "alternate forms" of a subphrase in the seventh theme of a song (2000, p. 145, Fig. 9.7). Each subphrase is distinct from the others, primarily in its first half, but all four variants were clearly regarded by the whales singing them as analogous and interchangeable for this particular *locus*, perhaps by virtue of their ending with two sustained low notes, and so they were variously substituted for each other in songs. Thus, while the overall configuration of Humpback songs remains constant – in the abstract sense of a generic multilevelled hierarchic structure and in the concrete sense of the specific allelic organisation of a particular song – there is considerable opportunity for internal variation. As always in memetics, and while guided by top-down archetypes, such mutational processes are bottom-up, in that unit-level changes reconfigure phrases, and phrase-level changes reconfigure themes.

Allelic competition is also relevant when considering the issue of Humpback song phrase-parataxis, one also relevant to large-scale structuring in human music and bird-song. Payne hypothesises (and her statistical studies corroborate this) that Humpbacks remember songs by utilising *rhyming*: the most complex songs have a number of themes whose subphrases begin or end similarly (2000, p. 147; p. 149, Fig. 9.10). While this is, as Payne argues, a mnemonic device, it also affords evidence for allelic competition because the invariant rhyming element (the first or second subphrase) is associated with a variant non-rhyming element (the second or first subphrase, respectively), such that the invariant element motivates the allelic substitutability of the phrase (2000, p. 148, Fig. 9.9). Moreover, this necessity to rhyme also imposes certain constraints upon which phrases may or may not be utilised in a theme and this, perhaps indirectly, mediates their parataxis. This attribute of Humpback song aligns closely with certain structural characteristics of orally transmitted epic poetry (as a category of song), whose rhyme-schemes, together with other structural features, have also been understood as memory-optimisation devices (Levitin, 2009, p. 156; see also the quotation on formulaic composition on page 211 above). Song-rhyming might be ascribed primarily to cultural-evolutionary rather than biological-evolutionary factors: whale genes having built a framework for vocal learning to serve their aptive interests, it is then in the interests of whale sonemes to build higher-order structures that, by virtue of their configuration (including rhyme-schemes), serve to foster the sonemes' own replication. This phenomenon is discussed in §5.5.2 under the rubric of the evolution of evolvability.

5.4.2.3 The Aptive Benefits of Learned Whale-Song

Humpback songs, like those of birds, are believed to serve the functions of territorial demarcation and mate-attraction (Herman et al., 2013). A third aptive benefit, that of group sociality (page 439), seemingly sits uneasily with the other two – as it does in other communal-living species – but reflects the fact that many animal groups are often (uneasy) coalitions, wherein individual interests are paradoxically sometimes advanced by being subsumed within those of the collective. A group of Humpbacks singing the same song is effectively like a sports team: players are wearing the same kit to emphasise their common purpose (analogous to group sociality), but individual players also keep their distance from each other (territorial demarcation), so as to optimise their opportunities for acts of personal success (mate-attraction). The latter, while indirectly benefiting the team, ultimately accrues directly to the individual.

On the second of these functions, Payne argues that Humpback song "innovation" is driven by a sexually selected propensity for males to use vocalisations in mate-attraction (2000, p. 146). That is – as always with the vocal learning constellation (§2.7.5) – those whales that possessed the capacity not just for song-learning but for intra-phrase and intra-theme variation (the ornament) would be more successful in mate-attraction and would pass on the controlling gene(s) to their offspring. Naturally this requires a corresponding sensitivity in females (the preference), which takes fecundity in song "composition" as an "all-round certificate of competence" (point 5 of the list on page 138). While not distinguishing between the genetic substrates for vocal learning and the cultural evolution that they facilitate, Payne argues that,

> [l]ike improvisation in human music, changes seem to be generated by an internal process [i.e., intra-brain, sonemically driven mutation], and as in music, the imitation that then occurs reveals [inter-brain] listening and learning. Song changing in whales seems to be a clear example of cultural evolution in a nonhuman animal.... Drift [i.e., cultural evolution] in whale song proceeds at a much faster rate than linguistic drift [in humans]. Most changes originate as modifications of preexisting material, but within one decade a population's song may undergo so much change that one can no longer recognize its relation to the earlier version. (Payne, 2000, pp. 142, 147)

As with "emancipated" bird-song (to recall Merker's (2012) term from §2.7.5), there comes a point in discussions of learned vocalisations when it is necessary to move away from consideration of the aptive benefits to genes – which may potentially diminish as a result of their fostering soneme-based cultural evolution – and to consider the interests of the sonemes that make up the vocalisations. That the operation of the VRS algorithm on sonemes can outpace that on genes is perhaps most clearly evident in certain cases of rapid cultural evolution in bird- and whale-song – changes that exceed even the speed of the "drift" referred to in the quotation above. An example of the latter – alluded to in §5.4.2.1 – is shown in a study by Noad et al. (2000). They observed that the song of a population of Humpbacks in the Pacific Ocean off the East Coast of Australia was rapidly invaded by (in my terms) sonemes from a different population from the Indian Ocean off the West Coast of Australia such that, after only a few years (1995–1998), the song of the eastern population, a community of over one hundred individuals, was completely transformed (via an "intermediate" type) into that of the western (Noad et al., 2000, p. 537, Fig. 1; see also Eriksen et al., 2005, p. 306, Fig. 1). The fact that this transformation was achieved by the incursion of only a few "foreign" singers is ascribed by Noad et al. (2000) to the effect of the novelty of the invading sonemes. While they attribute this change to cultural *revolution* (2000, p. 537), there is nothing in their results that suggests any kind of saltationism (§1.3). Rather, this is an example of transmission in the eastern population being affected by the perceptual-cognitive salience of the western population's sonemes in a way that is normative for the VRS algorithm, even if it occurred in this case at a speed that may be atypical for this species. In saying this rate of change is "unknown in the vocal cultural tradition of any other animal", Noad et al. (2000, p. 537) perhaps too readily discount similarly rapid changes in the repertoires of other prolific vocal learners, such as the Marsh warbler, discussed in §5.4.1.3.

Mcloughlin et al. (2018) undertook a study that attempted to model this kind of cultural evolution using an agent-based computer simulation – a form of AI in which virtual "agents" interact with each other in some conceptual space, often driven by evolutionary processes. As discussed in §273, the most sophisticated of these studies move beyond single-replicator systems to model dual-replicator (gene-meme) coevolution. A prior music-creative use of this agent-based approach by some of the same researchers, which subsequently underpinned Mcloughlin et al. (2018), is discussed in §5.4.2.4. Mcloughlin et al. (2018) modelled the interactions between a number of virtual Humpbacks assigned to two separate social groups. In this environment, and as often in nature, the animals shared the same summer feeding ground, but they migrated to separate winter breeding grounds. The size of the feeding ground was variable, allowing the simulation to explore the effect of different distances between conspecifics. Mcloughlin et al. (2018) ran simulations based on four separate models, within which further parametric variation was tested: (i) incorporating only the effect of distance between individuals; (ii) incorporating distance plus a vocalisation novelty-perception factor; (iii) incorporating distance plus a vocalisation production-error factor; and (iv) incorporating distance plus novelty-perception and production-error factors (2018, pp. 5–6).

While the study represents a necessarily limited model of Humpback cultural interactions – for one thing, the system's vocalisation-representation only included songs and themes (Figure 5.7), with no modeling of any structural elements below the level of the theme – Mcloughlin et al. (2018) nevertheless arrived at several interesting conclusions. To summarise some of their main findings, and related to the model-numeration in the previous paragraph, they determined that: (i) as observed in studies of real whale populations, similarity between vocalisations was a factor of distance, with smaller feeding grounds promoting greater and more rapid song-convergence owing to forced cultural interchange (2018, p. 13); (ii) while the proximity factor of model (i) was still evident, the way the model encoded novelty perception eventually resulted in all songs becoming increasingly unpredictable and thus (if novelty is regarded as a function of predictability and thus of the violation of expectation) as equally novel (2018, p. 13); (iii) again as observed in studies of real Humpback populations, songs maintained a variable degree of dissimilarity related to the model's probability of production errors occurring (2018, pp. 13–14); and (iv) the novelty-perception factor interacted with the production-error factor and, as in model (ii), "resulted again in unrealistically variable song sequences" (2018, p. 13).

From a cultural-evolutionary perspective, the main issue here is the difference between models (ii) and (iii), both of which involve an element of song-variation. In model (ii) the variation relates to a *perception*-side bias, whereby males show a preference (observed in real-world studies, including that of Noad et al. (2000)) for novel song. This is presumably because doing so affords them the opportunity to acquire an augmented advantage (via currency or fashion) in the domains in which complex vocalisation is advantageous, namely territorial demarcation and mate-attraction, the latter because it serves as a male ornament that is associated with a female preference for novelty. In model (iii), by contrast, the variation arises from a *production*-side bias. Specifically, it results from the edit-distance operations of insertion, deletion and substitution (Mcloughlin et al., 2018, p. 6) (§5.4.2.2) that underpin all replicator mutation. Beyond the fact that the findings of Mcloughlin et al. (2018) happen to support it (and remembering that this study is only a partial simulation of cultural evolution in Humpbacks), model (iii) appears to be a more realistic representation of the operation of the VRS algorithm in Humpback song, and perhaps in all learned animal vocalisations. This is because of its formalisation of a relatively stable culture that is nevertheless capable of being perturbed, and thus gradualistically transformed, by a propensity for production error that is intrinsic to vocal learning.

In real Humpback groups, Payne relates the latter scenario to the concept of "optimal mismatch" from psychology (2000, p. 142). Just as memetics suggests is the case in human music, a "goldilocks" range of mutation – not too conservative, not too radical – constrains the introduction of Humpback phrase- and theme-level variation. If assumed to be reasonably accurate representations of reality, the aetiological/evolutionary priority of models (ii) *versus* (iii) might initially seem to be a chicken-and-egg problem: did a production-error factor (model iii) arise before a novelty-perception factor (model ii) in evolution, or vice versa? It makes greater logical sense to assume the former: that the ornament (the biologically evolved ability of male Humpbacks to produce complex songs, and the culturally evolved complexity that builds upon it) arose before the preference (the biologically evolved tendency of female Humpbacks to perceive favourably certain novelties in those songs). This is because it is easier for coevolutionary sexual selection to track local innovations in a relatively static space than it is to build a preference for novelty when there is no consensus on what constitutes novelty – or when everything is novel so nothing is novel – and on what constitutes normativity. This might therefore be understood as a microcosm of a wider issue in evolution: that the gradualistic reconfiguration of a complex system is the norm on account of its being significantly safer than the system's saltational reconception.

5.4.2.4 Learned Whale-Song and Human Music

While bird-song has inspired musicians for centuries, whale-song has had less of a cultural presence, perhaps on account of its only relatively recent accessibility. By the nineteenth century, however, whalers were referring to the creatures as "singers" (Janik, 2009, p. 109), in recognition of the lyricism of their vocalisations. In recent decades the whale has been seen as a symbol of the environmental movement, its cruel destruction by whaling nations encapsulating human rapacity and our callous disregard for the natural world that sustains us. Perhaps for this reason, Humpback song, with its expressive and mournful tones, has come to represent the voice of nature, drowned out by the clamour of humanity's unfeeling technology. Moreover, for those who do not follow organised religion, these animals' vocalisations are often heard as spiritual and consoling, as if – as might well be the case – a profound, but very different, intelligence is calling out. Naturally, humans have sought to profit from this interest, and a number of commercial recordings of Humpback song have been released, marketed not only for their environmentalist credentials but also in terms of their resonance with "New Age" values (CRM Records, 2008).[251] On a more elevated level, the "golden records" sent into space in 1977 on the two Voyager probes contain, in addition to various human musics, recordings of whale-song together with other animal vocalisations. In several of the commercial recordings, there is an appeal to the aesthetic sensibility: whales' vocalisations are presented as a form of music, an aesthetic object to be approached with the kind of disinterested contemplation often characterising the listening experience of art music from the mid-eighteenth century onwards (Dahlhaus, 1982, p. 5).

---

[251] Unlike some later, frankly derivative recordings in this vein, (CRM Records, 2008) is a reissue of a seminal 1970 vinyl disc, perhaps the best selling of all natural history recordings, produced by Roger Payne, which helped to foster the global "save the whales" movement.

As outlined in §5.4.1.4, animal vocalisations have inspired composers to write music that in some way incorporates or responds to them, either by various degrees of mimesis, or via idiomatic, stylistic or structural assimilation. Recent innovations in digital sound technologies have facilitated this practice, as demonstrated, for instance, by *Fast Travel* (Kirke et al., 2011).[252] This work models vocalisations of Blue whales and Humpback whales using a multi-agent simulation. In *Fast Travel*, the agents represent individual whales, these being "seeded" with electronic samples of the real creatures' songs; and the conceptual space, in which the audience is metaphorically immersed along with the interacting pseudo-whales, is a virtual body of water. As a primarily artistic artefact, as opposed to a scientific model, *Fast Travel* incorporates a saxophone solo, positioned in the centre of the "ocean", which to some extent directs the evolution of the whale-song repertoires by means of a pre-determined musical score. The work represents "an unusual example of an artistic project being the inspiration for a hard science project, rather than the other way round" (2011, p. 353), having led to the research reported in Mcloughlin et al. (2018) discussed in §5.4.2.3.

If *Fast Travel* constitutes an example of a "hybrid" work, using natural whale vocalisations, digital sounds and an acoustic instrument, then perhaps ("pure") electroacoustic music represents a genre of human music closest in structure and sound to unalloyed whale-song (N. Collins & D'Escriván, 2017). While it is neither possible nor desirable to generalise a medium as diverse as electroacoustic music, many of the canonic works of the genre – such as Stockhausen's *Gesang der Jünglinge* (1956) and Varèse's *Poème électronique* (1958) – are perhaps not wholly dissimilar to whale-song. As with the vocalisations of whales, electroacoustic music often features low-pitched sonorities that, like whale-song units, may consist of static pitches or glides; its gestures have a sense of agency, in that the music, perhaps by virtue of a sonic analogue to the visual gestalt phi-phenomenon and beta movement (§5.4.1.2), appears to represent dynamism and goal-orientation; and, as a result of spatialisation techniques, it incorporates similar antiphonal/call-and-response effects to those audible in recordings of whale-song in ocean environments.

---

[252] An example of a work using bird-song and digital technology is Jonathan Harvey's *Bird Concerto with Pianosong* (2001). See also Gilmurray (2013).

5.5 Musicality, Music and Creativity

Having now reviewed a number of innate and learned animal vocalisations, it is useful to consider the extent to which such putative animal musicality and music, particularly that of the learned category, is *creative*. This is relevant because creativity is held to be a defining feature of human music-making, surpassing the mechanical practices and sonorous products intrinsic to musicality and moving the whole endeavour to the realm of the sublime and transcendent. This is a view perhaps more prevalent in the west than in other parts of the world; but even in traditional musical cultures, where the ritualistic preservation of established practices is particularly valued (Merker, 2012, pp. 219–220), there is very often the kind of "flow-state" of play and innovation that some take to be a defining characteristic of creativity (Csikszentmihalyi, 1996). One might therefore regard creativity in music as a phenomenon afforded by musicality and realised, to a greater or lesser extent, in various musical cultures. Creativity is also sometimes regarded as a barrier that must be crossed in order for something to be seen as human or human-like. In making such determinations, it is as if one is asking the candidate to pass a form of Turing Test (Turing, 1950) – i.e., can it produce music that would make a human think was by another human? – except that the object under scrutiny is an animal, not a computer.[253] Associated with creativity is the notion of aesthetic value (Scruton, 1997), given that regarding something as creative also implies that it has artistic worth. This value may be discerned by receivers even if the producer is not aware of it, so it seems reasonable to assert that creativity, as poiesis, is distinct from the taste-cultures that, as esthesis, assess, validate and rank it. That creativity can exist without any external arbiter deciding that it is present is also evident from the fact that, for billions of years, evolution was creative without any conscious assessment of the fruits of its labours, the only evaluation being the "red-in-tooth-and-claw" test of survival itself, the fundamental creative problem in evolution (§5.5.2).

The following subsections consider creativity, human and animal, in its evolutionary context, seeing the VRS algorithm itself as intrinsically creative,

---

[253] See §6.1 for discussion of certain caveats on the use of the Turing Test in such situations. These notwithstanding, the discussion of the Superb lyrebird's (§5.4.1.3) capacity to mimic the flute in Powys et al. (2013) amounts to a kind of Turing Test.

and attempting to outline a framework by which the studies of specific animal vocalisations in §5.4 can be assessed in terms of the degree to which (if at all) they possess this attribute.

5.5.1 Conceptions of Creativity

As implied in §2.1, humans decide what does and does not constitute music, and what is and is not creative, generally reserving both attributes, wholly or substantially, to our own species. While the former issue has primarily been considered hitherto – by means of the investigation of certain animal vocalisations in terms of their potentially musical attributes and affinities with human musics – the latter is considered here. In many ways it is the more difficult issue, because asking a group of humans – who else could one ask? – whether something is music(al) or not is likely to elicit a fair degree of uniformity, whereas asking the same group whether (or to what extent) something agreed by them to be music(al) (or to be painting or literature) is also creative is likely to call forth more nuanced responses. In this sense, determining if something is music is an objective/statistical question – "does the entity have attributes x, y and z?"; see also the discussion apropos Figure 2.1 – whereas determining if something is creative is an essentially subjective question.

By "creativity", and after Wiggins et al. (2018), is meant here the origination of something – a product of the process of creativity – that is in some sense *novel*, and to whose novelty is ascribed some *value*. Creativity is ultimately a function of the VRS algorithm, which, as has been argued extensively here, operates in several domains. Thus, while often understood as a cultural/memetic phenomenon, creativity also operates more fundamentally in biological/genetic evolution (§5.5.2), the latter providing the substrate for the former. In the cultural domain, value is accorded owing to the novelty either affording some *aesthetic* interest (in the arts) or serving some *functional* purpose (in the sciences and technology); in the biological domain, value is accorded primarily on the novelty serving a functional purpose. In both domains, novelty is an outcome of variation. The requirement for value means that novelty *per se* is not necessarily constitutive of creativity; rather, there has to be, in addition, some *assessment*, some (e)valuation, of the worth of the novelty in a particular context. In culture (both human and animal), such assessment requires mechanisms whereby the novelty can be perceived and cognised, a process that is initially individual (psychological) but that often requires the "tempering" effect of a collective (a system-level taste-culture). In biology, the value of a novelty (a potential adaptation or exaptation) is assessed – in a kind of system-level perception and cognition – in terms of its survival-enhancing benefits. In both domains, the judgement of value constitutes a form of selection; if the novelty passes the test of selection, it may then go on to be replicated.

The novelty that is a necessary but not sufficient condition of creativity often inheres in the interplay between the satisfaction and violation of established expectations, which may be defined in terms of "probability distributions over the set of symbols allowed" (Wiggins et al., 2018, p. 293). This interplay is generally taken to be the source not only of music's structural characteristics, but also of its affective content (Meyer, 1956; Huron, 2006). Distributions of symbol-sequences generally arise from innate constraints of the substrate, such as those described by Narmour's I-R model, and tend to be propagated by replication. As culturally disseminated phenomena, probability distributions are abstracted by receivers via a process of statistical learning, which builds up a basis for prediction and thus detection of expectation-violation. Such violations affect the perceptual-cognitive salience of musemes, which – if the violation is clearly aptive or clearly not aptive – in turn affects their replicative success and their population footprint, and thus potentially leads to the reconfiguration of the probability distributions that encompass them. Whether in nature or culture, "[t]wo quantities, entropy and information content, model uncertainty and unexpectedness, respectively" (2018, p. 293) (§4.3.2). These quantities have been modelled, in the domain of musical melody, by the IDyOM (Information Dynamics Of Music) model, which builds on the seminal work of Shannon (1948) in offering a representation of melodic expectation built, bottom-up, by means of unsupervised learning and encoded in Markovian terms (§6.5.1.3) (M. T. Pearce & Wiggins, 2012, pp. 630–632). As such, it offers not only a perceptual-cognitive model of melody but also, to some extent, an insight into what constitutes creativity in this domain.

Boden's (2004) model of creativity offers a number of useful perspectives for an evolutionary account of musicality and music. She makes a distinction between innovations, insights and novelties – concepts intrinsic to but not necessarily wholly constitutive of creativity – specific to an *individual* ("P[sychological]-creativity"; levels four and five of Table 1.4); and such phenomena in a global *chronological context* ("H[istorical]-creativity"; levels two and three of Table 1.4) (2004, p. 2). These two categories are loosely analogous, respectively, to Cohen's notion of "Little-C" and "Big-C" creativity (in Wiggins et al., 2018, p. 288), where the former represents personal triumphs and the latter events of historical moment. Thus, if one arrives at the four-note motif opening Beethoven's Fifth Symphony having never heard that work, one has demonstrated a remarkable feat of P-creativity; nevertheless, Beethoven deserves the H-creative credit. In addition to the P-creativity/H-creativity distinction, Boden (2004) identifies three further categories (in fact, processes (Wiggins et al., 2018, p. 290)) of creativity, listed here in ascending order of radicalism: *combinational creativity*, the origination of new ideas by reassortment of extant ideas; *exploratory creativity*, the origination of new ideas by traversal of regions of knowledge hitherto unexplored; and *transformational creativity*, the origination of new ideas by the inception of a new style of thinking (2004, pp. 3–6). Transformational creativity "is formally exploratory creativity at the metalevel, where the conceptual space of artifacts is replaced by the conceptual space of conceptual spaces" (Wiggins et al., 2018, p. 289).

It is still far from clear what makes certain pieces of music highly original. Understanding a work – if the memetic paradigm is accepted – as a (re)assemblage of mutated versions of patterns found in various earlier works does not begin to account for the compelling singularity of great music or, more broadly, that of any great art. While a comprehensive treatment of these weighty issues of creativity in art is beyond the scope of this book, and while even a detailed understanding of their style and structure (in the light of memetics or otherwise) does not necessarily make pieces of music, and music more generally, any less ineffable, a few observations on originality might be made in the light of memetics. Firstly, if originality is a marker of creativity, then imagination might be said to drive originality (N. Cook, 1990). Yet musical imagination cannot be divorced from the broader intellectual resources – the verbal-conceptual memes – of an individual. These ideas and beliefs define, in part, the personality of the composer, the fertility of his or her imagination, and (for instance) whether he or she is broadly conservative or progressive in respect of musico-stylistic innovation. Secondly, musical imagination is fostered by contact with other people and their ideas – by exposure to a diversity of memes, verbal-conceptual and musical. The more m(us)emes available to a musician, the greater the range of possible recombinations and mutations, and the richer his or her imagination, in improvisation or composition. Thirdly, there is the thorny and controversial issue of intelligence (Herrnstein & Murray, 1994). Put crudely, some musicians have greater mental processing power than others, and this ability to understand and act upon the potential of the available memetic resources perhaps explains, in part, the differences between conservative and radical composers. All these issues are further complicated by the varied socio-economic contexts, themselves memetically shaped, within which musicians find (or choose to situate) themselves.

Blackmore asserts that modern humans have brains that are "designed to remember, hum, sing, play, and pass on music; they are skilled at mixing up all the fragments they hear to make new ones and at using the schemes and musical tricks they come across to develop them further" (2007, p. 71). Contingent to some extent upon the issues outlined in the previous paragraph, "[t]his is what it means to have a musical imagination" (2007, p. 71). The notion of "mixing up all the fragments" relates to the often mechanistic issue of museme parataxis – those attributes of musemes that mediate their capacity to assemble and form longer sequences (musemeplexes and musemesätze, as "schemes and musical tricks") §3.5.2 – that might be understood under the rubric of Boden's combinational creativity. Owing to certain innate and learned attributes, the final element(s) of a museme (its terminal node) may create an implication for a specific museme or member of a specific museme allele-class as the next pattern. It follows that the Markovian richness of a museme-sequence – and arguably the imaginativeness, however quantified, of the resulting music – depends in part upon the combinatorial attributes of each museme and thus the number of potential links it can create, which might be described in terms of the museme's valency (§3.8.2).[254] Furthermore, to adapt Boden's (2004, pp. 43–44) distinction between P- and H-creativity, certain musemes ("H-musemes", some of which are the "good tricks" identified by Dennett (1995, pp. 77–78)) are not only generic, historically/stylistically normative, and relatively resistant to mutation, but they are also arguably of relatively circumscribed valency. Others ("P-musemes") are more specific, historically/stylistically deviant, and relatively mutable, and possess a greater range of valencies. It may be that the most radical composers' verbal-conceptual meme-complement motivated them to draw more extensively on P- than on H-musemes and thus to maximise the attributes of imagination, originality and creativity in their works.[255] Seen in this light, they exemplify Blackmore's dictum that "those of us who are the most creative are those who are best at accurately copying and storing the memes we come across, recombining them in novel ways, and selecting appropriately from the myriad new combinations created" (2007, p. 76).

5.5.2 Darwinism as Creativity

To reiterate yet again the key principle underpinning this book, Universal Darwinism holds that the VRS algorithm operates in numerous domains of information and knowledge, broadly defined (§1.5). Not only does it regulate gene-level processes in biological evolution, but it governs intra-organism functions as well, such as those regulating homeostasis and immune response. As the extension of the algorithm beyond biology in Chapter 3 has argued, human culture itself has a Darwinian foundation, in that the differential selection of the varied and replicated particles constituting it – the m(us)emes and m(us)emeplexes – can help to account for its synchronic organisation and diachronic reconfiguration. Thus, when the raw materials of a domain tend to assemble to make discrete particles, and when those particles can somehow be copied by reassembling more raw materials in certain ways, then the Darwinian engine almost cannot fail to fire up and start bootstrapping complexity.

---

[254] Gjerdingen considers the issue of valency in terms of the statistically most common sequences formed by the assemblage of Galant schemata (2007a, p. 372, Fig. 27.1).

[255] This is a very loose adaptation: in Boden's (2004) original sense, a distinction is drawn between H-/P-creative *ideas* and H-/P-creative *people*; and there is a certain elision of combinatoriality and mutation, kept separate in memetics, in her formulations.

As indicated on page 449, evolution's overriding imperative is to ensure survival. The variations generated in the course of replication undergo selection and those "fittest" forms may go on to be replicated in the future. This occurs at multiple hierarchic levels, from that of the replicator (gene or meme, the fundamental units of selection) to that of the complex vehicles (organisms, works) that replicators regulate and/or constitute, and even beyond, to that of higher-level, distributed entities (species, genres). In some respects, survival by means of evolutionary aptations boils down to exploring a *problem space* in order to find solutions that facilitate the replicators' (via the vehicles') opportunities for further replication (P. Todd, 2000, p. 367). Evolution as a means of problem-solving – logically, the only means – is made explicit in the g-t-r heuristic (§1.5.1). To give a biological example, a species living in an increasingly cold environment will need to adapt in order to survive, and so if gene variants for denser hair coverage appear (randomly, of course) in a particular organism, then that organism will stand a greater chance of survival, relative to that of its conspecifics that do not possess the adaptation. The fortunate bearer of the adaptation may go on, thus protected, to transmit the variant gene(s) to the next generation. In this scenario, the problem of a colder and more inhospitable climate is solved by the VRS algorithm's driving an exploratory-creative traversal, in Boden's sense, of the space of possible morphologies, and alighting upon the area of that space occupied by body forms with denser hair coverage.

In human culture we often speak of intellectual and practical problems in a variety of domains requiring creative solutions. By analogy, one way of regarding the kind of biological-evolutionary problem-space exploration just described is to see it, as suggested on page 449, as *a form of creativity*. As Bentley and Corne argue,

> [e]volution is not a person. It is an unthinking, blind process, a relentless procedure, a harsh and unconscious fact of life. How can we possible call something so inhuman, so brutal, *creative*? .... Evolution has been hard at work creating the myriad forms of life that have lived and died on our world for billions of years. In that unimaginably vast amount of time, designs of life wholly beyond our current comprehension have emerged.... Examples of aesthetic, lovely, poetic, and beautiful evolved solutions surround us, are contained within us, and are us. Every living

thing cries out proficiency, elegance, inventiveness, and skill in design. The abilities of natural evolution far surpass our most creative problem solvers. Moreover, ... many 'human' solutions [to creative/design problems] have existed in nature long before they were thought of by any human .... (Bentley & Corne, 2002, p. 56; emphasis in the original)

It is tempting to term this process *Darwinian creativity* (Kronfeldner, 2014), but because, in an evolutionary world-view, *all* creativity – biological and cultural – is ultimately Darwinian, the term is tautological (see also the quotation at the start of Chapter 6, which expands the frame of reference to incorporate creativity in computer systems). If creativity is a process of bringing about novelty, such that: (i) new ways of connecting existing things within a problem space are found; or (ii) new areas of a problem space are probed; or (iii) a problem space is reshaped in order to find more radical solutions, then these three categories – Boden's combinational, exploratory and transformational creativity, respectively (§5.5.1) – readily describe processes occurring in Darwinism. Human creativity is simply one form of the Universal-Darwinian problem-space searching driven by the substrate-neutral VRS algorithm. In cultural evolution, intermediate- and high-level novelty – and thus an expansion of the conceptual and expressive vocabulary residing in its replicators and vehicles – is generated by means of these three creative processes operating via meme-based Darwinism. In biological evolution, low- and intermediate-level novelty – and thus an expansion of the survival-related "vocabulary" residing in its replicators and vehicles – is generated by means of these three creative processes operating via gene-based Darwinism.

A Universal-Darwinian view of combinational creativity sees it operating in those situations where replicators are reassorted and juxtaposed in new configurations that have specific effects on vehicles. In biology, the most obvious example of this is the "crossing-over" occurring in *meiosis* (cell division), whereby genes on maternal chromosomes exchange places with their alleles on paternal chromosomes (Griffiths et al., 2015, pp. 155–157). Depending upon the genes concerned, this may lead to phenotypic effects in the offspring that appear to combine those of the parent phenotypes. In culture, combinational creativity is found in those situations where juxtaposition of entities (including musemes) not previously so juxtaposed occurs, giving rise to new effects and, potentially, to new higher-order structures. As noted at the end of §3.5.4, the *seeming* blending in biological evolution is, in reality, the result of the combination of a multiplicity of genes, each contributing a small effect towards the whole; and, as suggested in that section, a similar mechanism might be hypothesised to operate in cultural evolution.

Exploratory creativity, in a Universal Darwinian sense, constitutes the traversal of an *n*-dimensional space, a genetic or memetic hypervolume (§3.6.5, §6.5, §7.5.3), each dimension of which represents some gene/meme and its corresponding phenotypic/phemotypic expression. In terms of ideas discussed in §1.7.3, evolution is the cumulative motion through this space by small, incremental steps (gradualism), not by large discontinuous leaps (saltationism); and the various regions of a hypervolume represent virtual replicator niches analogous to the real environmental niches that evolution equips organisms or cultural products to occupy in the physical world. In biology, exploratory creativity is seen in the subtle adaptations made by organisms to survive in particular environments, such as the divergent but still recognisably related forms of finches observed by Darwin in different Galapagos islands (Lack, 1983). In culture, it might be found in the evolution of certain subtypes of formal models, such as sonata form, fitted to various functional and socio-cultural contexts. These subtypes, despite their aptation-motivated differences, remain essentially recognisable from Sammartini to Shostakovich in terms of their relationship to the parent type.

In both these domains, exploratory creativity involves searching a hypervolume in order to locate a specific object appropriate to meet the aptive demands of a specific situation, these being survival-related in nature and aesthetically motivated in culture. Puy (2017) understands musical works – specifically the composition *Nasciturus* (2010), generated by the *Iamus* computer (§6.5.3.2) – in this light, but the principles apply to all art-objects. Having surveyed a number of candidate ontological categories for (computer-generated) music-as-work – namely idealism, Aristotelianism, nominalism, perdurantism, nihilism, historical particularism, performance theory, and phenomenological theory (2017, sec. 5.1–5.7) – he rejects them all in favour of a radical platonic view. This holds that "[m]usical works are types, i.e., abstract objects that can be exemplified in particular performances" (the realist position), and that "[i]f musical works are types, they are not the sort of thing that can be brought into existence" (2017, sec. 3). They are therefore eternal and unchanging, waiting to be located in the hypervolume. In this sense, "to compose a musical work is to make a *creative-evaluative discovery*" of a timeless and unique entity (2017, sec. 3; emphasis in the original). It is not difficult to understand this process of creative-evaluative discovery as applying not only to cultural but also to biological objects: while the VRS algorithm is an intrinsically dynamic mechanism, it allows for the location of an infinity of static objects in a hypervolume, each of which, in biology, is suited to serve some aptive purpose.

To understand transformational creativity in a Universal Darwinian sense, one has to look for situations in which evolution finds analogies to, in Boden's terms, a new "style of thinking" (2004, p. 6). Transformational creativity in biology can clearly be seen in cases of exaptation (§2.5.1), where features evolved for one function are pressed into the service of another. Insect wings, it has been hypothesised, arose originally as raised nodules either for improving heat absorption (on account of their increasing the surface area of the insect's body) (Harari, 2014, pp. 147–148), or (and not incompatibly) as structures for heat dissipation (Bickerton, 2000, p. 160). Once these structures had reached a certain size, they allowed the insect to move more quickly by means of controlled jumping or wind-borne floating. Having assumed a new function – locomotion, not thermoregulation – selection could work to augment this capacity on account of its clear aptive benefit. A comparable situation is found in the exaptation of proto-feathers, also thought to have evolved for thermoregulation, for aerodynamic enhancement in birds (Patel, 2018, p. 117). In culture, transformational creativity inheres in radical changes in conceptual or expressive vocabulary and syntax – a paradigm change/shift, in Kuhn's terms (2012). The latter can be seen in structural changes in systems of tonal organisation, which evolve over time by the incremental expansion of inter- and intra-museme relationships and potentialities (§7.5). While intrinsically gradualistic, the cumulative weight of such changes often results in the system's eventually reaching a "tipping-point", whereupon new creative possibilities are catalysed, and some theoretical reorientation is necessitated (§4.6).

Another category of transformational creativity in biological evolution is the *evolution of evolvability* (Dawkins, 1988; see also Pigliucci, 2008; Valiant, 2009). As its name implies, evolvability is the capacity of or propensity for an entity to evolve. Strictly, genes mutate, while populations (however defined) evolve as a result of the differential spread of certain gene-variants; thus, individuals cannot evolve genomically, only change (*vis-à-vis* their ancestors) phenotypically. While evolvability is not always straightforward to separate from normal differences between populations in ability to evolve – these sometimes resulting from differences in the amount of variation that is heritable (Sniegowski & Murphy, 2006, p. 831) – it relates to "the capacity of populations to produce new selectable variation, rather than on the amount of standing variation already present in populations" (2006, pp. 831–832). There are, however, a number of conceptual problems with the notion of evolvability, including its inherent teleology (natural selection is only concerned with the here-and-now, not with laying down attributes that might be useful at some unspecified point in the future (2006, p. 832)); and the issue of whether evolvability is itself an adaptation. On the latter, and while variability over and beyond the level of "standing variation" of a population might potentially be adaptive, gene recombination and the normal "prevalence of deleterious mutations over beneficial mutations" tend to militate against the proliferation of the "variability alleles" necessary for evolvability to arise as an adaptation (2006, p. 832).

While the "evolvability-as-adaptation" hypothesis suffers from these potential population-genetic problems (i.e., gene recombination and deleterious mutation), the "evolvability-as-byproduct" hypothesis argues that "populations can differ in variability for reasons unrelated to selection on their capacities to adapt and evolve" (Sniegowski & Murphy, 2006, p. 833), although such reasons may themselves be subject to selection. An example is that "modularity in gene regulatory networks may have contributed evolutionary flexibility to development and facilitated the diversification of animal body plans" (2006, p. 833). Dawkins (1988) illustrates this principle using a (now quite dated) computer program – *Blind Watchmaker* (Dawkins, 2020; see also Dawkins, 2006, p. 73) – that draws two-dimensional virtual creatures, "biomorphs", whose embryology, and ultimate phenotype, is controlled by a number of virtual genes. He discovered that, having introduced "symmetry" and "segmentation" mutations, whole new phenotypic vistas – novel "body plans" – were opened up. This is because these changes are the computational equivalent to the third of three types of mutation Dawkins hypothesises. The first type concerns "ordinary changes within an existing genetic system", achieved by "normal allele substitution" (Dawkins, 1988, p. 217). The second type encompasses "changes to the genetic system itself", such as those changes in chromosome number that marked the separation (in Dawkins' example) of humans from elephants and that play a role in the normal "evolutionary divergence" of lineages (1988, p. 217). The third type are (transformationally creative) "evolutionary watersheds", which, while they "may or may not have coincided with a change in the genetic system … [,] open floodgates to future evolution" (1988, pp. 217–218). Examples of such "watersheds" – whether arising from evolvability-as-adaptation or evolvability-as-byproduct – include the "segmentation" mutation in Dawkins' biomorphs, this echoing events in biological evolution that "may have occurred only twice in history" (1988, p. 218).

There are various direct music-cultural equivalents to the evolution of evolvability hypothesis. One of these is the general modularity of musical forms, which permits localised expansions. While ostensibly self-contained, these tend to drive the expansion of other sections of the form in order to maintain structural balance. This phenomenon is not dissimilar to the process discussed in point 7 of the list on page 138, where expansion of avian song nuclei in response to selection pressure in favour of vocal learning drives encephalisation by motivating a general up-scaling in brain size, for reasons of embryonic efficiency. The evolution of simple-binary dance forms in the late renaissance seems a key ("watershed") development in this process (§4.7). The subsequent arrival of a phemotype consisting of two halves opened up new possibilities for formal evolution, one of which was the further, arguably more radical, innovation of an expanded second half with two distinct subsections: the three-phrase binary form, upon which sonata form was subsequently built. There is a real sense in which such design triumphs as the start of the recapitulation in the first movement of Beethoven's Symphony no. 9 (bb. 301ff.), with its apocalyptic reinvention of the opening of the movement, could not have evolved without the segmentation of the formal archetype upon which the movement is based into a recursive – (‖:A … B:‖: … (A … B):‖) – design. As Cook insists, "three into two will go" (1996, p. 157), and when it did, the "floodgates" of formal-structural evolution were flung open.

5.5.3 Can Animals be Creative?

This section briefly summarises several of the themes considered so far in this chapter. To determine if animals can be creative – that is, to ask if they can generate novelty and complexity in their vocalisations – it is necessary to ask whether this attribute is to be judged according to one of two frames of reference: (i) on human-specific criteria; or (ii) on separate, animal-specific – perhaps even species-specific – criteria. The second of these primarily de-volves to the notion of Darwinism as itself intrinsically creative. In terms of the first frame of reference, then certainly most innate animal vocalisations will probably be judged to fall significantly short of their human equivalents of music and language. As assessed in §5.3, the alarm calls of vervets, the pant-hoots of chimpanzees, and the calls of corncrakes lack the phonological, syntactic and semantic richness of human vocalisations, musical or linguistic. However, among vocal learners (§5.4), the combinatorial virtuosity and multi-hierarchic structural complexity of certain bird and whale vocalisa-tions, is arguably not far from human music, not least because it appears to arise from analogous (strictly, homoplasious) processes of cultural evolution building upon a biologically evolved substrate. Their similarities with human language are also telling, and are assessed in §5.6. Nevertheless, beyond these structural and functional commonalities, comparisons between learned animal vocalisations and those of humans are, if not odious, then potentially meaningless from an aesthetic perspective because it is intrinsically very dif-ficult to verify or falsify the notion that animals gain the kinds of intellectual and affective stimulation from vocalisation that humans gain from them, and from our own music. This last point – of value being necessary in addition to novelty for something to be deemed creative – thus needs to be considered from both human- and animal-centric perspectives. From the former, there is certainly an aesthetic dimension to learned animal vocalisations: we find them valuable to us on account of their complexity and beauty; from the latter, the evidence that animals vocalise because they find the process and its products pleasurable is too fragmentary to make a determination.

In terms of the second frame of reference, and more radically, one could embrace the notion that the three types of creativity identified by Boden – combinational, exploratory and transformational – are intrinsic to Universal Darwinism and the multifaceted complexity (novelty) engendered by the VRS algorithm (§5.5.2). Seen in this way, human aesthetic standards fall away and creativity is understood as arising from the same fundamental processes, whether they are manifested by our species' extraordinary survival abilities, a whale's singing a song to a prospective mate, or in a lymphocyte's attacking an invading bacterium. The value of this second type of creativity is that of survival and it must be judged according to the perspectives of the replicators involved. From that of genes, novelty (mutation) might afford aptive benefits and thus have survival-related value, whether the vocalisations supported are innate or learned. In this sense, the calls of the corncrake are as creative as those of the Marsh warbler in that both serve the advantages of the genes that underpin them, even though the novelty of the former's vocalisations advances at a glacial pace compared with those of the latter. Indeed, while hard to quantify, corncrakes are not necessarily less evolutionarily successful than Marsh warblers for not having learned vocalisations. From the perspective of sonemes, their faster mutation and replication rates permit them to slip the leash of genes, to some extent, by capitalising upon the innate perceptual-cognitive attributes of producing and receiving animals in order to spread more salient variants within a soneme-pool. These two frames of reference – the culture-centric/ aesthetic and the nature-centric/aptive – represent two sides of the same evolutionary coin: if aesthetic value inheres in the novelty and salience of memes (and potentially sonemes), then survival is essentially a kind of biological aesthetics, measured in terms of the same attributes of genes.

5.6 The (Co)evolution of Music and Language IV: Relationships between Animal Vocalisations and Hominin Music and Language

The eighteen statistical-universal features common to a broad sample of human musics identified by Savage et al. (2015) and represented in Figure 2.1

> have possible parallels in nonhuman animals. In particular, the learned
> songs of birds are often compared with human music. Like human
> music, birdsong tends to use discrete pitches (although there is debate
> about how analogous they are to human scales), descending or arched
> melodic contours, small intervals, short phrases, modal register, and to
> be performed predominantly by males .... (Savage et al., 2015, p. 8989)

The same observations might easily be made of whale-song, certainly that
of Humpbacks, so it is relevant to explore the musilinguistic aspects of
learned bird- and whale-song, and to ask to what extent they might relate
to the hypothesised development of human music and language from their
musilinguistic antecedents (§2.7).

In an elegant synthesis of the relationships between human music and language and animal vocalisations, part of which was quoted on page 400 above,
Fitch argues that "animal 'song' can be defined simply as complex, learned
vocalization. Almost coincidentally, this definition of 'song' (based on findings in ethology) also applies to humans, with one caveat – that music lacks
composite, propositional meaning – necessary only to distinguish it from
spoken language" (2006, p. 182). Thus, the three types of vocalisation have
a "shared formal core" of design features (2006, p. 173) (§2.7.1), differing
principally in terms of the nature of their semantic content. While human
music and animal vocalisations are indisputably meaningful, only human
language appears to possess the propositional meaning that allows for the
precise description of objects, the logical sequencing of events, and the formulation and elaboration of concepts. Fitch (2006) identifies five points of
correspondence between these three categories of vocalisation:

1. All are learned, possibly on the basis of similar genetic-neural mechanisms
   (2006, p. 189).

2. Vocal-learning species pass through a "sensitive period" during which they
   must be exposed to conspecific vocalisations in order to develop auditory-
   motor competence. Achievement of mastery is preceded by practise/imperfect
   vocalisations (subsong in birds, babbling in humans) (2006, p. 189).

3. The generation of vocalisations "involves the recombination of learned or innate
   notes (individual vocal units shared by all members of the species) into more

complex syllables and songs that are differentiated by which notes are selected and the order in which they are arranged" (2006, p. 190).

4. "Vocal-unit" recombination often occurs at multiple structural-hierarchic levels (2006, p. 190).

5. Vocalisations change over time and different geographical "dialects" arise in sub-populations of the same species (2006, p. 190).

6. While not specifically acknowledged by Fitch, the changes in point 5 are the result of cultural, not biological, evolution, driven by the operation of the VRS algorithm on the cultural optimon (§1.6.2) of the vocally learned substrate in question.

Apropos points 3, 4 and 6 above, Table 5.1 correlates organisational patterns at the different structural-hierarchic levels of the learned vocalisations considered in §5.4, matching them with corresponding patterns in human music and language in order to indicate structural and functional commonalities. For comparison with a non-vocal-learning animal, gibbons – arguably closest to the others in apparent musicality – are also indicated.

Perhaps the most important of these levels is the second – this being broadly analogous to level seven of Table 1.4 (as the third level of Table 5.1 is to level six of Table 1.4) – because patterns at this level form the meaningful building blocks, the optimons, of their respective cultures. By themselves, the entities at level one (equivalent to level eight of Table 1.4) are isolated sonic parcels, un-anchored and free-floating. When brought into alignment with each other in replicated, perceptually-cognitively discrete, particles they form patterns with sufficient identity and memorability to be captured by the VRS algorithm and used as the building-blocks of culture. Nevertheless, there is a clear difference between level-two units in animal vocalisations and human music, on the one hand, and those in human language, on the other – namely Fitch's "caveat", in the passage quoted on page 463, that human language has "composite, propositional meaning" and the other forms of learned vocalisation do not (or at least they do not in a way that is evident to human investigators).

Level	Gibbon-Song	Bird-Song	Whale-Song	Human		Language
				Music		
1	Note	Note	Unit	Note		Phoneme
2	Phrase	Syllable	Subphrase	Uniparametric museme (style shape)		Word
3	Great call/Coda	Strophe	Phrase	Multiparametric museme (style structure) / musemeplex		Phrase
4	Great call sequence	Group of strophes	Theme	Musemesatz/theme/ phrase		Sentence
5	n/a	Song	Song	Section/movement/ work		Sequence of coordinated sentences
6	Duet	Singing session	Song Session/Song Cycle	Performance/concert		Conversation/ dialogue/ritual

Table 5.1: Structural Correspondences Between Animal Vocalisations.

Marler (2000) makes an analogous distinction between what he terms "phon-ological syntax" and "lexical syntax". The former concerns the "[r]ecombi-nations of sound components (e.g., phonemes) in different sequences (e.g., words), where the components themselves are not meaningful. I call this 'phonocoding'" (Marler, 2000, p. 36). He contrasts this with "[r]ecombi-nations of component sequences (e.g., words in the lexicon) into different strings (sentences). Here there is meaning at two levels, the word and the sentence. The meaning of the string is a product of the assembled mean-ings of its components. I call this 'lexicoding'" (2000, p. 36). Merker (2002) understands the concept of phonocoding in terms of Abler's (1989, 1997) notion of the "particulate principle of self-diversifying systems", itself de-riving from Wilhelm von Humboldt's model of language. The particulate principle maintains that analogue continua such as the sound patterns of language are discretised, via categorical perception, into digital entities. A finite set of such particles are then (re)combined to form a near-infinite set of higher-level patterns. Merker (2002) argues that music is "the missing Humboldt system", arising from the discretisation of the pitch and dura-tion continua into sets of pitches and note-lengths (level eight of Table 1.4). When arranged in chunked combination, these form the optimons I term sonemes and musemes (these being phonocoded), and lexemes (these being lexicoded) (level seven).

While phonocoding encompasses learned animal vocalisations and human music and language, it appears that human language is the only unambigu-ous example of, additionally, lexicoding in the natural world. Only humans, it would seem, are able to associate gestalt-partitioned and hierarchically rep-licated sound-patterns with semantic content that inheres – as engendered by the mechanisms hypothesised in §3.8 – in the patterns themselves and in their syntax of (re)combination. Note that both non-phonocoded (i.e., most (innate) non-human primate vocalisations, with the possible exception of gibbons) and phonocoded (i.e., vocally learned) utterances may nevertheless be *affective*, as indeed might lexicoded ones: they may signal feelings and desires (honestly or dishonestly), including those "groans of pain" under-pinning Griffin's "GOP" concept (in Marler, 2000, p. 32). As Fitch observes, music – in common with other phonocoded vocalisations – has a "capacity to be *a-referentially expressive*" (2006, p. 180; emphasis in the original). But only those phonocoded utterances that are *also* lexicoded – i.e., human language – can be truly communicative in the fully symbolic-semantic-syntactic sense that impelled the human Cognitive Revolution (§2.5.5).

Perhaps understandably, given her decades of close intellectual and emotional involvement with the creatures, Payne wishes she could somehow get into the minds of Humpbacks, saying that "[i]t would be nice to know ... whether whales are aware of intentions as they compose and sing, and how they experience their own and other whales' songs" (2000, pp. 147–150). While the most speculative part of this chapter, it is not inconceivable that such awareness and intentionality might arise as a result of the learned vocalisations of birds and Humpbacks somehow motivating a form of (proto-)consciousness – whether of the "hard" or the "easy" type (§7.2.1) – driven by the power of imagined and/or heard sonemes. In Carruthers' (2002) model (§3.8.2), it is the *tokening of Logical-Form (LF)-integrated thought by the lexemes of language that renders it conscious in humans* (2002, pp. 658, 666). Might this mechanism also apply in certain avian and/or cetacean species? To translate Carruthers' model into the non-human vocal learners considered here, the sonemes of the vocalisation would serve as quasi-linguistic tokens of some mentalese structure – some avian and/or megapterine equivalent of LF – perhaps one encoding some persistent feature of its or arboreal or aquatic environment, the location of a food source or, in the case of Payne's query, introspection on the sound patterns it produces and receives. In humans, LF is a domain-*general* integration of domain-*specific* (modular) thought, this linkage underpinning syntax and semantics; but in birds and/or whales LF might conceivably encode domain-*specific* thoughts only. If so, then (proto-)consciousness would have to arise from the soneme-tokening of domain-specific thought in these creatures, even though, in Carruthers' model, this is not the case in humans, even though it might have been in our prehistory. Whatever the nature of the LF in these creatures – this being contingent upon the neural architecture of the animal – its tokening by sonemes might, as Carruthers hypothesises is the case in humans, potentially render it conscious: beyond the easy-consciousness phenomena of perception, cognition and behaviour, the animal might then experience the hard-consciousness phenomenon – the qualia – of "hearing" its thoughts.

In Carruthers' model, human LF is fully linguistic: by means of processes discussed in §3.8.4, it encodes the syntactic-semantic structure of language, which is rendered conscious by lexemic tokening. If one accepts in principle: (i) the extension in the previous paragraph of Carruthers' model to certain birds and/or whales; and if one accepts that (ii) any avian or megapterine LF might even encode domain-*general* thought (which appears to be a precondition of syntax); then it is logical to consider a further possibility. This is that (iii) these species *might also use their sonemes as (proto-)lexemes*, using them *linguistically* and therefore not just as free-floating tokens of domain-specific thoughts but also as "words" in a form of lexicoded syntactic-semantic medium of domain-general communication. Even if one accepts the hypotheses of this and the previous paragraph – and the arguments in §3.8 that underpin them – it is clear that verifying (or, indeed, falsifying) them is immensely difficult. This is not least because consciousness in humans, let alone in other species, is itself imperfectly understood (Blackmore & Troscianko, 2018), and any comparable phenomenon in animals has to be inferred – certainly given current experimental methodologies – from their behaviour. Moreover, in terms of the potential for incipient lexicoding, it is difficult to envisage how one might even begin to translate between human and avian and/or megapterine "language(s)".

The case of the African grey parrot Alex nevertheless suggests that the "Carrutherian extension" – the hypothesis that language and (proto-)consciousness arise via the sonemic tokening of LF-integrated domain-general thought in vocal-learning non-human animals – may indeed be tenable in principle. Seemingly the realm of the *Doctor Dolittle* stories, Pepperberg has trained this bird to go beyond the "simple mimicry" at which its species is virtuosically adept and to acquire a level of facility with English that proves that "parrots can be taught to use and understand human speech" (1998, p. 35). Owing to her "model/rival (M/R) protocol" training method – which is characterised, tellingly, by the bird's observing social interactions between two humans (Pepperberg, 1998, pp. 35–36), rather than a simple action-reward methodology (the analogous issue of "social tutoring" is discussed on page 434 above) – Alex has developed the ability to communicate what is an evident understanding of materials, number, shape and colour (1998, pp. 37–38). That is, he is able to represent objects and concepts using "displaced" sounds (point 18 of the list on page 149), the fundamental basis of symbolisation and thus of language. Note that, in Alex's case, it is the lexemes of human language that are perhaps being yoked, via this training, to some form of psittacine LF, one that appears to be able to integrate domain-specific thought into a domain-general representation. That the latter might be true is evidenced by Alex's ability to distinguish between objects that "possess properties of more than one category – a green triangle, for example, is both green and three-cornered" (1998, p. 36), an integration analogous to Carruthers' "*the toy is in the corner with a long wall on the left and a short blue wall on the right*" (2002, p. 669), discussed on page 262.

Perhaps this psittacine LF inheres to some extent in – or is connected as a parallel, intercommunicating, structure to – the auditory template by means of which vocal-learning birds acquire and regulate their song (§5.4.1.1). This aspect of the Carrutherian extension, and indeed the wider issue of animal "language",[256] highlights the difference, covered more fully in §7.4.1, between Chomsky's and Skinner's theories of language acquisition in humans. Subsequently given an evolutionary-psychological twist by Pinker (2007), Chomsky's "Language Acquisition Device" (LAD) (1959) proposed – in opposition to Skinner's *tabula-rasa* empiricism (2014) – an innate basis for the acquisition of human language syntax, although Chomsky nevertheless abjured any evolutionary explanation for its origin (Dennett, 2017, p. 277). As a genetically regulated framework for pattern configuration and combination, the avian auditory template (and any such megapterine equivalent) might serve as a candidate for such a LAD, constituting and/or subserving LF for the domain-general integration fostering domain-general thought in vocally learning animals; and, via homoplasy or homology, forming the basis – as proto-LF (§3.8.3) – of LF, as a form of generative-transformational template, in humans.

The example of Alex, powerful as it is, nevertheless does not constitute a "pure" instance of the Carrutherian extension. Its canonic form envisions the yoking of the bird's *natural* repertoire of sonemes to LF, not to the lexemes of the – to the bird – *artificial* language taught to it by humans. In the case of

---

[256] See Pepperberg (2017) for a survey of research in this area.

Pepperberg's studies, Alex is in effect assimilating the rudiments of a second language: he is learning how to associate the lexemes of English with a presumably extant LF, perhaps in the way that humans do when we acquire a first and subsequent languages. If such a canonic form of the Carrutherian extension exists, it may be the case that what humans think of as bird- and whale-song is in fact a form of musilanguage in those animals, one that is already well advanced, in certain species, along the developmental trajectory of the vocal learning constellation outlined in §2.7.5 and §2.7.6.

5.7 Summary of Chapter 5

Chapter 5 has argued that:

1. Non-human animals produce vocalisations largely for the same reasons as early hominins would presumably have, although most non-human animals have not reached the level of structural complexity and informational richness of human music and language.

2. Sexual selection is a factor in animal vocalisation as it may well have been in hominin evolution. The likely yoking, via learned vocalisations, of sexual selection to memetic drive in humans suggests the possibility of a similar coupling existing in animals.

3. The innate vocalisations of our nearest relatives, the non-human primates, despite their similar sound-producing apparatus to ours, are not close to human music or language. These animals appear to lack the cognitive infrastructure that would allow the segmentation and assortatively recombination that underpins these competences in humans. As a result, their vocalisations are neither truly musical or linguistic.

4. The learned songs of certain birds and whales have a number of common structural features, namely the recursive-hierarchic nesting of discrete units (sonemes) that are culturally transmitted within a group and, as part of this, mutated and assortatively recombined. These features support cultural evolution in these species, which, at its most advanced, appears certainly to approach, if not actually to cross, the threshold of what humans would regard as musical.

5. Music is one of the most fertile domains for the exercise of our creativity, which, in Boden's formulation, involves our combining what we know in novel ways,

exploring the limits of possibility afforded by a given system, and expanding possibilities by changing systems themselves. Seen in these terms, the VRS algorithm is itself creative, in its traversal and reconstitution of the space of all possible patterns, and there are strong reasons to believe that animal vocalisations should not be excluded from this domain.

6. The ostensibly quasi-linguistic nature of some animal vocalisations raises profound questions of intelligence and consciousness that are intrinsically difficult to answer. Nevertheless, the songs of certain birds and whales appear to be capable of carrying more than purely "musical" content, and they may thus, musilinguistically, communicate "linguistic" information using an architecture analogous to that hypothesised to operate in humans.

By analogy with the extension of musical culture to certain animal species attempted in this chapter, Chapter 6 will broaden the frame of reference further to incorporate the ostensibly non-living world of artificial intelligence. It explores attempts to use computers to create music and, most importantly, to simulate musical change in ways that are evolutionary to varying degrees. While some of these systems are Darwinian in only a limited sense, others are able to generate considerable musical complexity by implementing the VRS algorithm. It will: discuss the differences between analytical and synthetic approaches in music technology; frame approaches to synthesis in terms of a continuum of ever greater machine autonomy; review language-generative computer systems as analogues to music-generative ones; consider how the synthesis of music, as with its analysis, is bound up with issues of representation; give an overview of a number of music-generative systems based upon a range of algorithm-design strategies; and assess the extent to which machines might be understood to be creative.

6. Computer Simulation of Musical Evolution

Evolutionary computing (EC) may have varied applications in music. Perhaps the most interesting application is for the study of the circumstances and mechanisms whereby musical cultures might originate and evolve in artificially created worlds inhabited by virtual communities of software agents. In this case, music is studied as an adaptive complex dynamic system; its origins and evolution are studied in the context of the cultural conventions that may emerge under a number of constraints, including psychological, physiological and ecological constraints. Music thus emerges from the overall behaviour of interacting autonomous elements. (Miranda et al., 2003, p. 91)

6.1 Introduction: Computer Analysis and Synthesis of Music

The growth of computer technology in recent decades has made possible the understanding of a number of complex physical, biological and cultural phenomena and processes, such as weather patterns, evolutionary processes and economic cycles. In the third of these domains, culture, music has figured quite prominently in such research, not least because of its inherently high degree of complexity and the associated, and seemingly irresistible, challenge it poses for computer science. The application of computers to the study of music comes in two basic, sometimes overlapping, forms: *analysis* and *synthesis*. The analytic tradition deals with using computers to break music down into its component parts, primarily the more tractable aspects of harmony, melody and rhythm, with the aims of arriving at segmentations that are in some senses compositionally, music-theoretically or cognitively meaningful (Meredith, 2016). The object of such research is generally *symbolic music* – i.e., music encoded in some text-based or numeric representation format (§6.4).

https://doi.org/10.11647/OBP.0301.06

A separate field – exemplified by the *Shazam* song-identification software (Shazam, 2019) and the *Sonic Visualiser* recording-analysis software (Sonic Visualiser, 2021) – is audio-based analysis, which aims to identify patterns in sound files. Yet these must still be converted into some form of internal symbolic representation, upon which the analytical engine operates.

The parameter of melody has arguably received the most sustained attention in symbolic music analysis, the field being particularly concerned with sequential pattern-finding and similarity-matching (see, for instance Conklin & Anagnostopoulou, 2006; Janssen et al., 2017). Some of this research is conducted under the broader rubric of Music Information Retrieval (MIR) and is assessed via the MIREX (Music Information Retrieval Evaluation eXchange) organisation and its associated competitions designed to determine optimally performing systems (MIREX, 2020). The technologies for analysis are variously *offline* (Lartillot, 2019; this application using both audio and symbolic approaches) or *online* (Kornstädt, 1998; Huron et al., 2021); and they are orientated either toward broad usability by non-specialist musicologists (Wheatland, 2009), or for expert investigation of focused problem-spaces, such as building and testing hypotheses in music cognition (M. Pearce & Müllensiefen, 2017). Aligning with the growing accessibility of big data (§3.4.1), online pattern-finding utilities are often front-ends for music databases allowing, for example, large-scale searches for incipits and the location of common patterns in a particular corpus (RISM, 2021). While generally not explicitly conducted in such terms, the concerns of the computer-analytic tradition are well suited to locating the types of pattern replication – for finding musemes by virtue of what is replicated – encompassed by memetics.

The synthetic tradition – which arguably started in 1957 with the *Illiac Suite* (Hiller & Isaacson, 1957) – deals with using computers to generate music that conforms to a particular style or that is felt by a human observer to be convincing (as music) to some extent.[257] The degree to which this latter attribute is upheld is a form of Turing Test (TT) (Turing, 1950), in that the programmer is (sometimes) attempting to convince a human listener that the outputs of his or her program are the unmediated creative products of

---

[257] Perhaps the origin of this tradition is rather earlier, in the musical dice-games (the dice being a random-number generator) of the late-eighteenth century (Ariza, 2011; Moseley, 2016; Tesar, 2000).

another human intelligence. Nevertheless, Ariza (2009) offers a critique of applications of the Turing Test to music, arguing that a test that was designed by Turing to discern the existence of thought as articulated via natural-language interlocution has often been applied uncritically to music. He argues that "the TT employs natural language discourse to represent the presence of thought; its spirit is not preserved in either the MOtT [Musical Output toy Test] or the MDtT [Musical Directive toy Test]" (2009, p. 61). The MOtT attempts to distinguish between two musical outputs, one human-generated, the other computer-generated (2009, p. 55). The MDtT replaces "Output" with "Directive", whereby the interrogator requests (and attempts to distinguish between) music from a human and from a computer, generated according to some specification or input style (2009, p. 55). Some might argue – apropos the point above on "unmediated creative products" – that computer-generated music (hereafter "CGM") is in reality human-generated music (hereafter "HGM"), albeit at one degree of remove: they might assert that "[t]he computer can be seen not as an autonomous author but as a system that executes or reconfigures knowledge imparted to it by its programmers" (Ariza, 2009, p. 64). By contrast, genuine creativity, according to the "Lovelace Test" of Bringsjord et al. (2001), can be identified "when [a] H[uman architect] cannot account for how [an artificial] A[gent] produced [an] o[utput]" (2001, p. 4) (§6.6). Nevertheless, understanding the production of an o is not necessarily straightforward, given that some systems' generative operations occur, intractably, in a black box. Thus, the adherents of CGM might argue that their algorithms produce os that, because they cannot be "accounted for", are therefore potentially creative.

The analytic and the synthetic approaches are often conducted reciprocally: to generate music effectively it is necessary to understand its nature and structure analytically; and such understanding is itself deepened by the synthetic process of designing music-generative algorithms. Moreover, as discussed in §6.3, the music analysis-synthesis distinction also applies to cognate research in the computer simulation of language's structure and evolution, which – as the persistent focus in this book on the close evolutionary connections between music and language might suggest – has numerous overlaps with the computer simulation of music's structure and evolution.

The chapter continues by considering how music-synthesis systems occupy a continuum from minimally to maximally autonomous, and reviews the terminology associated with research on primarily autonomous systems (§6.2). It moves on to explore how computer systems for simulating language evolution relate to analogous technologies in music, both domains presenting to algorithm designers the problem of creatively evolving a Humboldtian medium in a virtual environment (§6.3). Before turning to examine examples of music-generative systems, it is necessary to consider how music might be represented in ways that are meaningful to machines (§6.4). The main body of the chapter is concerned with an overview of a number of different strategies for music generation – some evolutionary, some not – by means of the examination of one or two systems selected as representative of each approach (§6.5). Finally, the issue of machine creativity is considered, partly in the light of the discussion of animal creativity in Chapter 5 (§5.5), focusing on philosophies and strategies for evaluating CGM (§6.6).

6.2 The Continuum of Synthesis and Counterfactual Histories of Music

The focus of this chapter is, naturally, on the synthetic tradition. Research in this field occupies a continuum, or "spectrum of automation" (Fernández & Vico, 2013, p. 516). At one end of this continuum of synthesis are *augmentation systems*, which use the computer to expand the extant potential of a human composer or improviser; this technology is sometimes also termed Computer-Aided Algorithmic Composition (CAAC) (2013, p. 515). At the other end of the continuum are *fully automatic generative systems*, which aspire to the kind of autonomy typical of radical AI. Framed in this way, "CAAC [represents] a low degree of automation, algorithmic composition a high degree of automation" (2013, p. 516). The continuum of synthesis might be expanded to encompass the whole creative range, from (fully) HGM at one end to (fully) CGM at the other, with CAAC therefore occupying some mid-point. Apropos the point on mediation made in §6.1, one should nevertheless remember that (fully) CGM is, at least partly, HGM, because the underlying algorithms that give rise to CGM are the product of human intelligence, albeit arguably not the specifically musical domain of that intelligence, and albeit an intelligence that – in a manner analogous, for instance, to aleatoric HGM – delegates most or all of the decision-making to the computer.

One of the principal aims of research in CGM is to create computer systems that are capable not only of *generating* music – either in the form of augmentation/CAAC systems or of fully automatic generative systems – but also of *evolving* it over time. Specifically, systems with an evolutionary dimension, the main concern of this chapter, not only (i) model the "local" cognitive-evolutionary processes of the individual musician (as composer or improviser) – Velardo's psychological ontological category of being; but they may also (ii) model "global" structural-systemic processes of musical change over time – Velardo's socio-cultural category (2016, p. 104, Fig. 3) (§1.5.5). From a Universal Darwinian perspective, both processes operate by "translating" the VRS algorithm into the specific generative algorithms of the system, the latter modelling – insofar as these domains can be meaningfully separated – intra- and inter-brain Darwinism, respectively. Some of the explicitly evolutionary systems considered in §6.5 fall under the ambit of (ii), which – on account of its connection with processes operating in biological and cultural evolution – forms the centre of gravity of the discussion. Their implementation of evolutionary modelling potentially allows for the "replaying" of musical history, starting from generally accepted beginnings and evolving alternative, or counterfactual, histories of music – music not as it was in the past, but as it might have been, or might at some point in the future become. Nevertheless, whenever computers are used to model analytical or synthetic processes that occur fundamentally in the human mind, one needs to remember – as expressed in Temperley's double-negative formulation – that

> the mere fact that a [computer] model performs a process successfully certainly does not prove that the process is being performed cognitively in the same way. However, if a model does *not* perform a process successfully, then one knows that the process is *not* performed cognitively in that way. If the model succeeds in its purpose, then one has at least a hypothesis for how the process might be performed cognitively, which can then be tested by other means. (Temperley, 2001, p. 6; emphases in the original)

Given that many systems for the generation of music are based on Darwinian principles, and given that several of these are at least able to produce recognisably musical outputs of increasing complexity over time, then it can be said, to paraphrase Temperley, that if such a Darwinian model *does* perform the process successfully, then one knows that the process *might* be (or might have been) performed cognitively – and thus socio-culturally – in that way.

The music-synthetic research programme has been conducted under variously rubrics, including (alphabetically listed): *AI Music Creativity* (AIMC, 2021; Miranda, 2021);[258] *Algorithmic Composition* (Nierhaus, 2009); *Algorithmic Music* (Dean & McLean, 2018); *Computer Composition* (Miranda, 2001); *Computer Simulation of Musical Creativity* (CSMC) (as a subset of the field of computational creativity (McCormack & D'Inverno, 2012; Bown, 2021)); *Computer Simulation of Musical Evolution* (CSME) (Gimenes, 2015); *Evolutionary Computer Music* (Miranda & Biles, 2007); *Evolutionary Computing* (EC) (Miranda, 2004); *Generative Music* (N. Collins & Brown, 2009); and *Musical Metacreation* (MuMe) (Eigenfeldt et al., 2013),[259] among others (§1.4). Apropos two of these rubrics, the term "simulation" is often used interchangeably with "emulation", but there are important methodological differences inherent in the terminology. Here, *simulation* is understood as an attempt to duplicate/replicate the (external, perceived) *behaviour* or *outputs* of a system, as it appears to an observer; whereas *emulation* is understood as an attempt to duplicate/replicate the system's (internal, functional) *mechanisms* (and thus, *pace* Temperley, also its behaviour or outputs). Given these definitions, and while the term "CS[imulation]MC" has become current,[260] one might argue that "CE[mulation]MC" is a more appropriate acronym to encompass those systems that implement (emulate) specific mechanisms – here, the VRS algorithm – that are held to underpin the phenomena – here, cultural evolution and human creativity – being modelled.

Of the above rubrics, the acronyms CSMC and CSME align most closely with the concerns of this chapter, not least because, apropos the first, Darwinism has been framed as a form of creativity (§5.5.2). By virtue of this connection,

---

[258] See also the *Journal of Creative Music Systems* (https://www.jcms.org.uk/).

[259] Metacreation applies to a range of creative domains in addition to music, and encompasses a number of competences in addition to generation. See Pasquier (2019).

[260] This may be partly due to the arguably greater euphony and ease of pronunciation of "CSMC" as against "CEMC".

and as is indicated in some of the rubrics listed above, machine creativity often draws upon evolutionary mechanisms. Nevertheless, not all systems that generate music do so by means of (emulating) evolutionary mechanisms: many use ostensibly non-evolutionary processes in producing (simulating) music, so they are seemingly creative without being evolutionary. Thus, it is important to distinguish between means and ends in the realm of music generation: an evolutionary means might produce unsatisfactory musical ends; while satisfactory musical ends might be produced by non-evolutionary means – and vice versa. Some might argue that – despite the potential for unsatisfactory outputs – evolutionary mechanisms are more "authentic" from a Universal-Darwinian perspective, not least because the notion of what is "satisfactory" can only emerge from a taste-culture that – like the music being appraised – is generated by the VRS algorithm (§6.6.2). As a further complication, some systems that are not ostensibly or primarily evolutionary might nevertheless implement certain evolutionary processes. A neural network (§6.5.1.2), for instance, essentially takes an often highly varied input and selects regularities within it in order to replicate them in its output. In this sense, and to adapt the formulations above, such systems are both creative and implicitly evolutionary (CSMC+E). At the most fundamental level, and as explored in §6.6.3, the origination of non-evolutionary systems is nevertheless invariably the result of cultural-evolutionary (memetic) processes, hence my use above of "ostensibly".

6.3 The (Co)evolution of Music and Language V: Computer Simulation of Language Evolution

Discussing "chance associations between the phonetic segments of the holistic utterance [constituting Hmmmmm] and the objects or events to which they related" (§2.7.6), Mithen (drawing on Wray (1998)) argues that "a learning-agent mistakenly infers some form of non-random behaviour in a speaking-agent indicating a recurrent association between a symbol string [proteme] and a meaning, and then uses this association to produce its own utterances, which are now genuinely non-random" (2006, pp. 253, 256). Mithen's remarks echo an element of the argument for the vocal learning constellation made by Merker (2012) in §2.7.5 and §2.7.6 (point 12 of the list on page 147), and both he and Merker refer specifically to computer simulations of this hypothesised process conducted by Kirby and his colleagues (Kirby, 2001; Kirby, 2007; Kirby, 2013; Kirby et al., 2015; Scott-Phillips & Kirby, 2010; Y. Ren et al., 2020; see also Oudeyer & Hurford, 2006; Fitch, 2010, pp. 501–503) – a field that might be termed the Computer Emulation/Simulation of Linguistic Evolution (CE/SLE). These models are motivated by the desire to understand how compositionality evolved in language, using computers to replicate in minutes processes that occurred over many thousands of years and that are therefore not directly accessible to us. As "proof of concept" (Fitch, 2010, p. 502), they suggest that the Wray-Mithen hypothesis for the evolution of language from Hmmmmm – the fragmentation of musilanguage into fully compositional language and its associated bifurcation into music and language – may well reflect evolutionary reality.

In an iterated learning model (ILM) study, Kirby (2001) used agent-based simulation (§273) to model the transmission of language between an adult (teacher) agent and a learner agent. He made a distinction between meaning (expressed here simply as a two-component pattern a, b, each component of which had a value between 0 and 5 (e.g., a_0, b_3)) and signal (here a character string drawn from the letters a–z) (2001, p. 103). After the first fifty utterances by the adult, it became evident that a form of protolanguage had evolved (2001, p. 105). By a later stage of the simulation, the system had converged on a fully compositional language (2001, p. 106) in which meaning and signal had aligned closely under the aegis of a controlling grammar. Further refinement of the system allowed it to generate "stable irregularity", of the type common in natural languages where, for example, some of the most common verbs are highly but stably irregular (2001, p. 107). Kirby sees this outcome as a vindication of Wray's (1998) "associations ..." hypothesis, arguing (apropos a later ILM simulation) that

> similarities between strings that by chance correspond to similarities between their associated meanings are being picked up by the learning al-gorithms that are sensitive to such substructure. Even if the occurrences of such correspondences are rare, they are amplified by the iterated learning process. A holistic mapping between a single meaning and a single string will only be transmitted if that particular meaning is ob-served by a learner. A mapping between a sub-part of a meaning and a

[segmented, protemic] sub-string on the other hand will be provided with an opportunity for transmission every time *any meaning is observed that shares that sub-part*. Because of this differential in the chance of successful transmission, these compositional correspondences tend to snowball until the entire language consists of an interlocking system of [meaning-proteme] regularities. (Kirby, 2013, pp. 129–130; emphasis in the original)

Merker elegantly summarises the process as it is thought to have occurred in real hominin communities and as it has been modelled in computer simulations of these early, language-forming interactions. He argues that

[t]he [song] repertoire ... is launched on a process of progressive string-context assortative and hierarchical decomposition from holistic strings *downwards*. Taking place as an unintended side effect of intergenerational transmission through the learner bottleneck, the process is entirely passive and automatic, and takes place [initially] for no reason of instrumental utility whatsoever. (Merker, 2012, pp. 241–242; emphasis in the original)

In an implicit Universal Darwinism, Kirby is at pains to stress that his system is focused "less on the way in which we as a species have adapted to the task of using language [biological evolution] and more on the ways in which languages adapt to being better passed on by us [cultural evolution]" (2001, p. 110). Languages themselves have to adapt (towards greater compositionality) because "[h]olistic languages *cannot* be reliably transmitted in the presence of a [learner] bottleneck ..., since generalisation to unseen examples cannot be reliable" (Kirby, 2013, p. 129; emphasis in the original). Thus, in his model "there is no natural selection; agents do not adapt, but rather we can see the process of transmission in the ILM as imposing a cultural linguistic [i.e., memetic] selection on features of the language that the agents use" (Kirby, 2001, p. 108). While Kirby focuses on the power of cultural evolution as the driver of Merker's "string-context assortative and hierarchical decomposition", he nevertheless acknowledges the importance of the coevolutionary relationship between biological and cultural forces in language evolution (2013, p. 136). Indeed, as Fitch argues,

> [g]iven the importance of linguistic communication to human children,
> and given a pervasive change in the nature of the ambient communica-
> tion system, biological selection will still occur, favoring 'segmentation-
> prone' infants who master the new analytic [compositional] system more
> rapidly [than other infants] (in contrast to previous generations, where
> selection would favor the learning of holistic systems ...). (Fitch, 2010,
> p. 502).

The biological evolution of "segmentation-proneness" – perhaps fostered
by the effects of the FOXP2 gene (§2.7.6) – might also have been a factor in
memetic drive (§3.7.1). Segmentation (hierarchical decomposition) would
have optimised the capacity for imitation (point 140 of the list on page 255)
by means of a "divide-and-conquer" chunking mechanism that – by fostering the replication of memes, with its attendant aptive benefits to genes
– would have facilitated, directly or indirectly, the differential selection of
Blackmore's Capacity-to-imitate genes. Moreover, while the lack of a relatively stable meaning-component distinguishes music-cultural evolution from
language-cultural evolution – but see §3.8.5 – the former process has also
been successfully modelled by agent-based systems. Given its appearance
in the CGM outputs of such simulations, it is possible that the "compositional"/recursive-hierarchic structure of HGM arose from musilanguage via
the same mechanisms as the computer-generated language (CGL) simulations of Kirby suggest occurred in human-generated language (HGL). This
is indeed the implication of a study involving iterated learning, Miranda et al.
(2003), discussed in §273.

6.4 Music and/*versus* Its Representations

Before turning to the evaluation of a sample of music-generative systems
in §6.5, it is necessary briefly to address an issue that affects them all and
that indeed is relevant to many of the topics considered in this book more
generally, albeit sometimes only indirectly. As outlined in §6.1, most analytical and synthetic systems, however categorised, normally deal not with
music but with *representations of music* (Selfridge-Field, 1997). Putting aside
the complications attendant upon the ontology of music – which, in a hard
memetic view, exists fundamentally as patterns of neuronal interconnection,

potentially as hypothesised in the HCT (§3.8.3) – such systems convert what humans experience as sounds, plus their associated physical movements, into some form of cold numerical representation, which inevitably attenuates their richness. Such representations might be MIDI note-numbers, the "**kern" representation of the *Humdrum Toolkit* (Huron, 1997), or some other essentially abstract system, such as the text-based museme-representations in Figure 3.14.[261] This "representation problem" is closely connected to the issue of conscious experience (§7.3), for while music (and phenomena in other sensory modalities) is presumably encoded in our brains in an essentially abstract manner, it is somehow rendered powerfully vibrant in conscious experience and, through embodiment, is made visceral for us. In the case of CGM, while the systemic representations of music are comparably abstract, we can be quite sure that the machines running the simulations are not conscious, in the sense of their being capable of experiencing the resulting music as a human does.

Philosophically, the representation problem, and the poverty of experience it motivates, might be regarded as a significant flaw of music-generative systems, one that militates against their utility in demonstrating, for instance, the operation of the VRS algorithm in cultural evolution. How, one might argue, can a machine be used to explore the evolution of music through Darwinian processes in human societies if that machine is incapable of experiencing the emotions and physicality central to musicality in our species? These vibrant and visceral sensations of music and movement can be understood as qualia – the specific experiences that form a component of consciousness – the explanation of which constitutes the essence of the "hard problem" of consciousness (§7.2.1). One might counter this by saying that as long as the machine has some way of encoding (abstract) representations of emotional states and physicality as a component of its algorithms for determining fitness – the latter, on the "museme's eye view" (Blackmore, 2000a; Dennett, 2017, Ch. 10), an index of its selfishness – then the specific phenomenological experiences a museme engenders in humans are incidental to the operation of the VRS algorithm *in silico*, even though this is not the case *in vivo*. This circumvents the hard problem of consciousness insofar as the machine gener-

---

[261] This also holds true for robotic systems (Miranda, 2008), which, even though they utilise physical movements, represent these gestures as symbolic codes.

ation of music is concerned, by decoupling qualia – which themselves arise from (higher-level) evolutionary processes (§7.3) – from the (lower-level) evolution of musemes. By extension, the non-necessity of qualia to the operation of the VRS algorithm might also be held to apply to systemic views of consciousness arising in electronic networks (§7.6), without necessarily precluding the (eventual) evolution of qualia therein.

6.5 Overview and Critique of Music-Creative Systems

As outlined in §6.1, the aim of this section is to survey a number of different strategies employed by music-generative systems, each approach being illustrated by the consideration of one or two representative systems, in order to examine the underlying design philosophies and to evaluate their outputs. It should be evident that, owing to the rapid progress being made in digital technologies, it is likely that this survey will rapidly become out of date – perhaps at a greater rate than that of the scientific data drawn upon in this book – with once cutting-edge systems soon becoming obsolete and thus only of historical value. While the evaluation of music-generative systems is complex (§6.6.2), the aim here is to get a general sense of how similar the selected systems' outputs are to HGM, to determine if this alignment relates to their underlying algorithms, and to ascertain if those systems that produce music using explicitly evolutionarily approaches are able to "outperform" those that do not. Naturally this is highly subjective – the criteria for assessing the similarity of CGM to HGM and those for determining one system's outperformance of another are intrinsically contingent, fluid and relative – and there is not room here for a fully comprehensive and systematic survey; but the working hypothesis is that the VRS algorithm is, almost by definition, the best way to bootstrap quality (however evaluated), whether that be in human-generative or computer-generative environments.

CSMC (or whichever of the rubrics in §6.2 is used to describe it) is a relatively new field – momentum in it began to build significantly in the 1990s – and, as represented in Figure 6.1, necessarily incorporates several related disciplines beyond the purely computational.

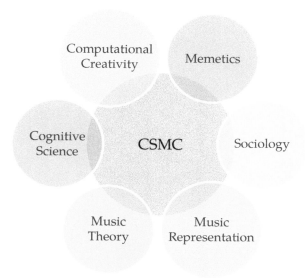

Figure 6.1: The Ambit of Computer Simulation of Musical Creativity.

Figure 6.2 shows a possible taxonomy of extant systems, arranged according to the AI techniques employed; apropos the continuum of §6.2, augmentation systems, fully automatic generative systems, and those in between, can in principle belong to any of the taxonomy's categories. It is partly guided by the magisterial surveys undertaken by Fernández and Vico (2013), which offers a taxonomy "structured by methodology" – i.e., by the operational mechanism of the underlying algorithm (2013, pp. 518–519, Fig. 1);[262] and (to a lesser extent) by Herremans et al. (2017), which presents a "functional taxonomy" based on the range of musical domains – melody, harmony, rhythm and timbre – in which generative systems have been developed to operate (2017, p. 3, Fig. 1).[263] The present section does not, however, attempt to rival Fernández and Vico (2013) or Herremans et al. (2017) in scope or depth – both have a number of subtle subdivisions and both survey a larger body of

---

[262] Fernández and Vico (2013, p. 519, Fig. 1) also list methods for music generation that fall outside the scope of AI – i.e., approaches that are "not based on models of human creativity" – such as cellular automata.

[263] Herremans et al. (2017) is complemented by an online repository (Herremans, 2022) of generative systems and their outputs in order "to provide a place for music researchers to exchange their results and make their works more visible".

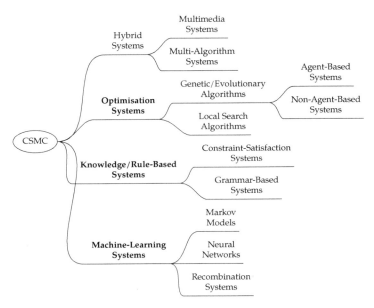

Figure 6.2: Taxonomy of Computer Simulation of Musical Creativity Systems.

literature – mine being focused primarily on those music-generative systems based on evolutionary models.[264]

Under their schema, Fernández and Vico (2013) posit three high-level categories: (i) *Machine Learning* systems (those abstracting statistical regularities from a dataset and using this information to generate further data in accordance with those regularities); (ii) *knowledge/rule-based* systems (which they also term *Symbolic AI*) (systems incorporating extant grammatical/syntactic knowledge/rules about the target domain that is used to generate new, grammar-conformant outputs); and (iii) *Optimisation* systems (those finding the best solutions to problems, often using the most powerful means of achieving this, the VRS algorithm), these categories being indicated in bold on Figure 6.2. Two broader points made by Fernández and Vico (2013) offer useful context for these three categories: (i) by virtue of the operation of their algorithms, many systems undertake *analysis* before they proceed to *synthesis*, reminding us that the distinction made between them outlined in §6.1 is not hard-and-fast (2013, p. 526); and (ii) several systems deploy

---

[264] I am grateful to Valerio Velardo for his thoughts on taxonomies of music-generative systems, which have also informed Figure 6.2.

not one mechanism (algorithm type) but several, therefore utilising a hybrid generative methodology (2013, p. 561) (§6.5.4). As might be evident from comparable endeavours in biology, the taxonomy in Figure 6.2 is only one of many possible arrangements: those systems surveyed could also have been classified chronologically by date of implementation, or aesthetically by perceived/assessed success of outputs, among other criteria; but the broadly "categorical" approach used here is intended to distinguish clearly between the philosophies underlying each system and, concomitantly, the basic mechanisms by which that philosophy is put into practice via algorithm-design. As noted in §6.2, the primary focus here is upon systems based upon evolutionary principles – in terms of both categories (i) and (ii) on page 477 – although not all represent a thoroughgoing implementation of the VRS algorithm. Including non-, partly-, and wholly-evolutionary systems in this consideration allows for at least a preliminary assessment of the issue of means *versus* ends in music generation raised in that section.

The taxonomy in Figure 6.2 does not establish separate categories for those systems that produce their outputs *offline*, as code that may subsequently be converted to score notation for later human performance or audio files that can be played later; and those that generate music *online*, in real time (Tatar & Pasquier, 2019, pp. 62–63), the latter sometimes in the context of human-machine interactive live performance and/or improvisation (termed "interactive reflexive musical systems" by Fober et al. (2019, p. 1)). Clearly those of the latter type must demonstrate rapid intelligent interaction with the ideas produced by their human colleagues, whereas the former are under no such restriction, being limited only by the constraints of their internal dynamics. Nevertheless, advances in computer processing power may sometimes result in the human being the drag in such systems, not the machine, even though the human often has the edge when it comes to fecundity of invention. While synchronic (offline) and diachronic (online) outputs represent very different ends, the underlying means are often very similar, and so their treatment is integrated here. A bridge between these two realms is afforded by systems that output their generated music in real time not as sound but in the form of western notation, such as that developed for Eigenfeldt's work *An unnatural selection* (Eigenfeldt, 2014b), which represents a "continuation of research into expressive performance within electroacoustic music by incorporating instrumentalists rather than synthetic output" (Eigenfeldt, 2014a, p. 276). Here, human performers play, or rather they sight-read, music created by a computer that is both generated – using a combination of Markov models (§6.5.1.3) and genetic/evolutionary algorithms (§6.5.3.2) – and notated on a tablet-device display in real time (2014a, p. 283).

6.5.1 Machine-Learning Systems

This category encompasses systems that are trained on some domain-specific dataset in order that they can subsequently reproduce what they have learned in their own outputs. They internalise the regularities of the target domain by means of statistical learning – essentially a process of noticing patterns and remembering them (see point 15 of the list on page 148). In music, this learning involves the extrapolation of the various recurrences that define musical styles and that, because they are constrained by perception and cognition, also foster comprehension. In the terminology of this book, such recurrences, as culturally transmitted phenomena, are by definition memetic. Subsequent to this analytical stage, machine-learning approaches in music generation simulate the concatenation of abstracted musemes to form musemeplexes and musemesätze in ways that align with those in the training repertoire. Thus, such systems need to be capable of learning high- and intermediate- as well as low-level pattern-regularities in order to generate convincing music.

6.5.1.1 Recombination Systems

A machine-learning approach is found in a number of systems designed by David Cope. One of the first pioneers of computer-composed music, his first attempts in this direction were motivated by a desire to use the computer as an augmentation system to help generate ideas for his own compositional work and act as a stimulus to his creativity. Conducted under the rubric of *Experiments in Musical Intelligence* (EMI; colloquially, "Emmy") (Cope, 1996; Cope, 2015) – which is both the name of a research project and the computer program that implements it – an important principle underpinning his research is recombination. In such systems a lexicon of musical patterns is learned, generally by the decomposition of one or more source works into units whose identity is afforded by, among other factors, their recurrence;

and the resulting units are then (re)assorted in ways that produce music that aims to be both syntactically correct and aesthetically satisfying. Cope argues that

> [m]uch of what happens in the universe results from recombination. The recombination of atoms, for instance, produces new molecules. Complex chemicals derive from the recombination of more rudimentary particles. Humans evolve through genetic recombination and depend on recombination for communication, since language itself results from the recombining of words and phrases. Cultures thereby rely on recombination to establish and preserve their traditions. Music is no different. The recombinations of pitches and durations represent the basic building blocks of music. Recombination of larger groupings of pitches and durations ... form[s] the basis for musical composition and help[s] establish the essence of both personal and cultural musical styles. (Cope, 2001, p. 1)

In Hofstadter's summary – "an accurate account of the fundamentals of the program's processes", in Cope's view (2001, p. 83) – EMI operates by means of two processes: "(1) chop up; (2) reassemble" (in Cope, 2001, p. 44).[265] *Chopping up* is achieved by searching for regularities – composers' style-specific "signatures" plus more generic material (Cope, 1998; Cope, 2001, pp. 48–49; Cope, 2003) – in some input, a corpus of music whose style EMI is intended to imitate in its own outputs. Chopping up – coindexation-determined segmentation – is accomplished by parsing extant HGM for recurrences of the well-formed units that tend to result from gestalt-psychological processes of pattern-formation. To reiterate Calvin's phrase from §2.7.6, "that which is copied may serve to define the pattern" (1998, p. 21). Essentially, the units arrived at in this stage are musemes, although Cope does not use this term, nor does he invoke memetics to describe them. *Reassembly* is arguably more problematic and, again according to Hofstadter, consists of two sub-processes: "([2.]1) Make the *local flow-pattern* of each voice similar to that in source pieces; ([2.]2) Make the *global positioning* of fragments similar to that in source pieces" (in Cope, 2001, p. 44; emphases in the original). These two sub-processes are coded as "syntactic/formal meshing" and "semantic/content meshing", respectively, by Hofstadter (in Cope, 2001, p. 44).

---

[265] Hofstadter's summary is given in Chapter 2 of Cope (2001) ("Staring Emmy straight in the eye – and doing my best not to flinch"), of which he is the author.

Chopping up and reassembly naturally result in the recombination of patterns central to the operation of EMI. They also engender replication, because the resulting patterns are subsequently redeployed in generated works. Not only is the latter phenomenon central to Universal Darwinism, it is also key to the notion of *style* in music, at least in the conception of Meyer: he argued that "[s]tyle is a replication of patterning, whether in human behavior or in the artifacts produced by human behavior, that results from a series of choices made within some set of constraints" (1996, p. 3).

The first of the reassembly sub-processes ([2.]1; local flow-pattern) again devolves to two (sub-sub-)processes: "([2.1.]1) voice-hooking; [and] ([2.1.]2) texture-matching" (in 2001, p. 45). Voice-hooking requires voice-leading continuity in the output piece between a museme, x^1, and that, y^1, chosen to follow it sequentially.[266] Voice-hooking is broadly analogous to the museme parataxis underpinning the RHSGAP model (§3.5.2), which, in my formulation, is partly contingent upon the strength of implication-realisation pressures spanning museme segmentation boundaries. For instance, a Process (Narmour, 1990, p. 89) initiated at the end of one museme, if continued in the following museme, will tend to bind the two together, attenuating the force of the segmentation boundary separating them and tilting the balance between openness (connection) and closure (disconnection) typical of most linear/diachronic art-forms towards the former. Texture-matching, perhaps more simply, requires the adjustment of the (accompaniment) texture of an input museme so that it conforms with that of its new context in the output composition (2001, pp. 45–46). The second of the reassembly sub-processes ([2.]2; global positioning) is arguably the more complex element. In brief, patterns at a number of hierarchic levels – in my terms, musemes, musemeplexes, and musemesätze, moving recursively upwards – are given a functional designation by Cope drawn from a set represented by the acronym "SPEAC". These functions – Statement, Preparation, Extension, Antecedent and Consequent – are intended, as Hofstadter conceives them, to represent the "tension-resolution status" of the pattern (in Cope, 2001, p. 46). Thus, as Hofstadter notes, "any local fragment of an input piece winds up with a set of labels – its own label, that of the larger fragment inside which it sits, then

---

[266] Specifically, voice-hooking requires that the cross-pattern juxtaposition of pitches in EMI's output, x^1–y^1, should match that which obtained in the original input, x–y (2001, p. 45).

that of the next-larger fragment in which that one sits, and so on, and so on" (in Cope, 2001, pp. 46–47).

Having outlined the nature of the algorithm underpinning EMI, one might wonder how closely it relates to what is known of the processes driving the generation of music in human brains and cultures, compositionally and improvisationally – and thus how convincing are its outputs. In Cope's view, "composers compose *recombinantly*. I use this term deliberately, since I believe Experiments in Musical Intelligence uses processes of recombinance similar to those that human composers use to compose" (2001, p. 89; emphasis in the original). In saying this, Cope is arguably asserting, albeit not in these terms, that the hypothesis of §3.5.2 – that competition between members of an allele-class of musemes to instantiate a structural *locus*/node of a mus-emeplex, which then, as a member of an allele-class of musemeplexes, itself competes to instantiate a component of a musemesatz – is the fundamental mechanism underpinning human composition (and improvisation), this conception therefore guiding the algorithmic basis of EMI. As a note of caution, we might nevertheless recall Temperley's comments on modelling cited on page 477 – that "the mere fact that a [computer] model performs a process successfully certainly does not prove that the process is being performed cognitively in the same way" (2001, p. 6). Thus, even when EMI *does* perform the process of composition successfully – as is suggested is the case below – this does not necessarily mean that the RHSGAP model actually underpins human perception and cognition during the music-generative process, despite its elegance and parsimony.[267] In its defence, the final paragraph of this section argues that there are significant differences between EMI's (partly Darwinian) functionality and the (fully Darwinian) RHSGAP model that to some extent ameliorate Temperley's caution.

On the question of its producing convincing music, many people are evidently "fooled" by the outputs of EMI. That is, they hear the music it produces and they come to the conclusion that it is the work of a human composer. This is attested by the success of EMI in what Cope terms "The Game". This

---

[267] This is perhaps naively to assume that all composers work, and have worked historically, in the same way. While they clearly have not – as evidenced by the enormous variety of past and present musics – the argument of this book is that there are a number of common (natural) cognitive processes underpinning the generation of music (on account of *Homo sapiens'* shared genetic heritage), despite their often highly varied cultural (nurtural) manifestations.

is played by presenting to a sample of listeners a variety of music, some by human composers, some by EMI, and asking them to differentiate between the two categories (2001, p. 13). According to Cope, "[r]esults from previous tests with large groups of listeners, such as 5000 in one test in 1992 ..., typically average between 40 and 60 percent correct responses" (2001, p. 21). Here the lower the rate of correct responses, the more convincing are the outputs of EMI: a score of 0% indicates that EMI is entirely convincing, in that listeners cannot distinguish its music from that of human composers – and vice versa for a score of 100%. This suggests, on the most positive interpretation, that EMI is capable of passing what is effectively a Turing Test – Ariza's (2009) caveats in §6.1 notwithstanding – at least in the estimation of a significant proportion of its listeners. Nevertheless, further research is needed on the correlations between musical knowledge and training and the ability to resist being fooled by EMI, or indeed any other music-generative system – which are presumably directly proportional.

To what extent can EMI be regarded as Darwinian? Certainly recombination is a feature of both biological and cultural evolution, in that, in the former, sexual reproduction involves the assortative recombination of gene alleles from both parents in the offspring, as occurs during the crossing-over phase of meiosis; and, in the latter, the RHSGAP model hypothesises, in a form of abstract crossing-over, the allelic substitution of structurally and functionally analogous musemes and musemeplexes. But Darwinism requires more than mere shuffling. Indeed, reassortment is itself only one aspect of the variation component of the VRS algorithm. Cope's model seemingly does not encompass the mutation that is essential for the creation of potentially aptive information-diversity – the low-level novelty-generation underpinning the higher-level processes of pattern shuffling in reassortment. Moreover, while EMI, as noted above, implements replication – by virtue of the recombination of identified patterns – it is not entirely clear from Cope's accounts how selection operates, namely how EMI decides which patterns among a set of candidate alleles to favour for a given structural *locus*. On this basis, and while certainly partly Darwinian, Cope's program cannot – to the extent that its detailed operation is understood – be regarded as a fully Darwinian-evolutionary system.

6.5.1.2 Neural Networks

This section will explore the generative power of *Artificial Neural Networks* (ANN), focusing on a system developed to assimilate and replicate stylistic regularities in folk music (for systems emulating rock and jazz, see (Dadabots, 2021)). First developed in the mid-twentieth century, an ANN, sometimes called a "connectionist" system (P. M. Todd & Loy, 1991), is a program that attempts to simulate networks of neurons in the animal brain, using virtual/functional equivalents of biological structures (Zou et al., 2009; Rosa et al., 2020). Their basic function is to *learn* – usually understood as the capacity to form stable *categories* from some set of input data – and thus they have been a key architecture in the field of machine learning. ANNs have their basis in the notion of Hebbian Learning (Hebb, 1949), the principle, discovered in the 1940s, that understanding of the world, as mediated by sensory stimuli, is represented by the brain in the form of connections between neurons of differential strengths.

As outlined in §3.8.3, the Hexagonal Cloning Theory (HCT) (Calvin, 1998) formalises the neuronal connections underpinning Hebbian Learning in terms of interdigitating triangular arrays in the cerebral cortex, these organised into hexagons with a characteristic spatiotemporal firing pattern. The cloning of a particular configuration across the surface of cortex represents its competitive (selective) success over rival candidates for alignment between incoming data and patterns stored by basins of attraction in the connectivity. The HCT offers a robust model of brain function, able to account for pattern learning and recall via operation of the VRS algorithm in a neuronal Darwin machine. While ANNs only loosely approximate the two- and three-dimensional structures proposed by the HCT (but see below), they nevertheless replicate its operating mechanism: they detect and encode uniparametric components of multiparametric input data; they learn statistical regularities (multiparametric association frequencies) in such data; and they separate learned patterns from surrounding "noise". In short, they are also a Darwin machine.

An ANN is a "sandwich" consisting of several *layers* of virtual neurons, usually represented two-dimensionally as columns of neurons arranged from left to right or bottom to top. The *input layer* (far left/bottom) and the *output layer* (far right/top) are separated by at least one intermediate "hidden" layer. Above (to the right of) the input level, each neuron receives several *inputs* via connections from neurons in the layer below (to the left of) them. Using a *propagation function*, the value of each input is multiplied by some *weight* before being summed to form a combined input. This input may be further adjusted by an *activation function*, which serves to restrict the value of the summed input to conform to some scale. Neurons may be retrospectively re-weighted by *backpropagation* in the light of an assessment of the fit of the output category to the input data (Arnx, 2019). As a categorisation device, an ANN seeks certain statistical regularities in the input and outputs its "understanding" of the configuration of these recurrent patterns. In *supervised* learning tasks, a desired output category, such as the configuration of a specific musical pattern, is pre-specified and the occurrences of the sought pattern in the input data are given in the output. In this sense, supervised learning is an example of a classification problem, to recall the distinction made by Große Ruse et al. (2016) in §5.4.1.2. In *unsupervised* learning tasks, the network is allowed to alight upon regularities it detects in the input, forming its own categories according to the strength (encoded as network weights) of features in the input data. In this sense, unsupervised learning is an example of a clustering problem.

The power of ANNs to categorise has been explored in the music-analytic tradition, perhaps most notably in four seminal articles by Gjerdingen (1989a, 1989b, 1990, 1992) that explored the use of *adaptive-resonance-theory* (ART) networks (an architecture developed by Grossberg (1987)) in (unsupervised) music-clustering problems. In brief, these studies show that a multi-layered network can abstract individual pitch elements (level "F_1"; level eight in Table 1.4) from a set of pieces; it can detect the stable associations of pitches in this set that constitute musemes ("F_2"; level seven); it can recognise the replicated sequences of musemes that generate musemeplexes ("F_3"; level six); and it can develop high-level representations of similarity such as are embodied by a musemesatz ("F_4"; level five) (Gjerdingen, 1990, p. 360, Fig. 8; see also Jan, 2011a, sec. 5, Fig. 14). These levels are also marked on Figure 3.17, to indicate how they relate to the operation of the HCT.

ANNs exist in a variety of different architectures appropriate to the task at hand. A type that has been developed extensively in recent years is the *Deep Neural Network* (DNN), which has more than one hidden layer and which is particularly suited to complex unsupervised learning tasks. These tasks are often subsumed under the rubric of *deep learning*, which concerns the application of machine-learning algorithms to data-rich domains (Schmidhuber, 2015; I. Goodfellow et al., 2016; Briot, 2021). Subtypes of the DNN include *Convolutional Neural Networks* (CNN), which are well suited to applications involving static data, such as images (Cireşan et al., 2011), as seen in Google's *DeepDream* image-manipulation software (Mordvintsev et al., 2015); and *Recurrent Neural Networks* (RNN), which are effective in applications involving dynamic data, such as the sequentially/temporally organised information to which music can be converted (Sturm et al., 2016, p. 3).[268] A RNN

> is any neural network possessing a directed connection from the output of at least one unit [neuron] into the input of another unit located at a shallower layer than itself (closer to the input). A deep RNN is a stack of several RNN layers, where each hidden layer generates an output sequence that is then used as a sequential input for the deeper layer. With deeper architectures, one expects each layer of the network to be able to learn higher level representations of the input data and its short- and long-term relationships. The recurrence (feedback) present in an RNN allows it to take into account its past inputs together with new inputs. Essentially, an RNN predicts a sequence of symbols given an input sequence. (Sturm et al., 2016, pp. 2–3)

While initially developed as *learning* devices, ANNs can redeploy what they have learned to *generate*, in the case of music, "new" pieces by reassembling certain of the abstracted attributes of some training sample. To this end, Sturm and Ben-Tal (2017) and Sturm et al. (2015, 2016) developed a related pair of RNN systems called *char-rnn* and *folk-rnn*, training them on a corpus of some 23,635 melodies of Irish folk music contributed by users of the online folk-music community *The Session* (Various, 2021) and generating some 30,000 output tunes (Sturm & Ben-Tal, 2017, p. 7). Specifically, the training sample consisted of transcriptions of that repertoire (Korshunova, 2016) into the text-based ABC symbolic music notation language (Walshaw,

---

[268] Related deep-learning architectures include the *Generative Adversarial Network* (GAN) (I. J. Goodfellow et al., 2014) and the *Variational AutoEncoder* (VAE) (Guo et al., 2020).

2019) (and is therefore subject to the "representation problem" raised in §6.4). In terms of the difference between the two systems, *char-rnn* "operates over a vocabulary of single characters, and is trained on a continuous text file"; whereas *folk-rnn* "operates over a vocabulary of transcription tokens, and is trained on single complete transcriptions" (Sturm et al., 2016, p. 4). Essentially, *char-rnn* builds up its understanding of the repertoire from the atomic level (single ABC characters); whereas *folk-rnn* builds it from the molecular level (groups of ABC characters). The latter includes the melodic patterns that, on account of their recurrence in the training set (and that are detected by *folk-rnn*), constitute musemes.

For various complex reasons, RNNs sometimes struggle to alight upon regularities in the input, an issue that can be solved by using a *long short-term memory* (LSTM) architecture. This modifies the activation function in ways that help to foster convergence (Sturm et al., 2016, p. 3). Both *char-rnn* and *folk-rnn* use three hidden layers with five-hundred and twelve LSTM "cells" or "blocks" each (2016, p. 6). Having said on page 493 that ANNs only loosely approximate the structures proposed by the HCT, LSTM cells nevertheless appear to be the closest functional equivalent to the hexagonally coordinated triangular arrays of the HCT. An LSTM architecture "increases the number of parameters to be estimated in training, but controls the flow of information in and out of each cell to greatly help with convergence ..." (2016, p. 3). In terms of Calvin's model, the parametric increase relates to the association of multiple feature-encoding triangular arrays within the constraints of a hexagonal plaque; and convergence pertains to the formation of the basins of attraction within the connectivity that stably encode regularities in the input.

Figure 6.3a shows an example of one of *folk-rnn*'s training inputs, the jig "Thank God we're surrounded by water" (melody no. 2611, second version, in *The Session*'s database);[269] Figure 6.3b shows one of the system's generated outputs (melody no. 2857, as transcribed in Sturm, 2017b, p. 2871); and Figure 6.3c shows an improved version of the melody of Figure 6.3b, with

---

[269] Sturm and Ben-Tal (2017) and Sturm et al. (2016) assembled their training sample in 2015, so any melody listed on *The Session* at that time would have been included. *The Session* website indicates when tunes were added to its database, so those melodies included in/excluded from the training sample can be identified.

suggested harmonisation, by Sturm (2017a), transposed to the "Ddor" of the original version in Sturm (2017b, p. 2871).[270] Of the system-generated melody (Figure 6.3b), Sturm says "I can't remember how I came across this tune, which appears in *The folk-rnn Session Book Volume 1* ... [(Sturm, 2017b), a collection of the system's generated compositions], but I do remember falling in love with it immediately" (2017a).

One can understand Sturm's affection for Figure 6.3b: it certainly has a pleasing lilt to it, and the dorian implications unfold effectively. There is also a degree of musemic "logic" here, in that the arpeggio pattern $b^1-g^1-e^1-e^1$ (b. 4^{1-5}) is answered by its transposition $a^1-f^1-d^1-d^1$ (b. 16^{1-5}, second time-bar).[271] There are some infelicities, however, the most grating among which are the circumvention of the strong D-minor implication in b. 10 by the following abrupt C major in b. 11 (corrected in Figure 6.3c as per the description in note 270 on page 497), and (paradoxically) the D-minor-implying b♭ of b. 7^{4-6}, which does not integrate smoothly with the melody's prevailing dorian mode.

While Figure 6.3a is but a small fraction of the input corpus assimilated, and while Figure 6.3b is an even smaller fraction of the system's output, there are nevertheless interesting similarities between the two, which suggest that certain attributes of Figure 6.3a were shared by other input tunes, were therefore abstracted by *folk-rnn*, and were redeployed in Figure 6.3b (and presumably in other output melodies), just as happens in human-only neural networks. At the highest structural-hierarchic level, and by means of a comparative statistical analysis of the training sample and all the generated outputs, Sturm and Ben-Tal (2017, pp. 7–8, Tab. 2, Tab. 3) determined that most of *folk-rnn*'s output melodies follow "the conventional structure AABB, with each section being eight bars long, with or without pickup bars, or explicit repetition tokens at the beginning of sections". This "tune (A)–turn (B)" form, typical in Irish traditional music (Sturm et al., 2016, p. 9), is evident in Figure 6.3b, which indeed follows the AABB structure of Figure 6.3a. Moreover, and as with Figure 6.3a, the generated melody

---

[270] I have made a few further modifications to Sturm's version in Figure 6.3c, correcting some odd harmonisations and, most significantly, changing the c^2 of b. 11^{1-2} to d^2.

[271] More broadly, the system seems to have assimilated this tradition's stylistic convention of a repeated ♪–♪ or ♪–♩ pattern with the second duration being approached by falling motion that is evidenced by this museme and by musemes in other generated outputs.

(a) Example of *folk-rnn*'s Training Input: Melody no. 2611, "Thank God we're surrounded by water", Second Version.

(b) Example of *folk-rnn*'s Generated Output: Melody no. 2857, Original.

(c) Example of *folk-rnn*'s Generated Output: Melody no. 2857, Version 2, as Modified by Sturm.

Figure 6.3: Examples of *folk-rnn*'s Training Input and Generated Output.

also incorporates an antecedent-consequent periodicity in the tune section (bb. 0–4; bb. 5–8), again indicating the system's "understanding" of another presumably corpus-wide aspect of large-scale organisation (unlike Figure 6.3b, however, Figure 6.3a also has an antecedent-consequent periodicity in the turn section).

Beyond these musemesatz- and musemeplex-level similarities, museme-level alignments between Figure 6.3a and Figure 6.3b – as manifestations of regularities in the training corpus assimilated in the generated corpus – include the d^1–c^1–d^1 museme (Figure 6.3a, b. 1^{4-6}; Figure 6.3b, b. 1^{4-6}), and the Ionian-mode-defining segment g^1–a^1–b^1–c^2 (Figure 6.3a, bb. 2^2–3^1; Figure 6.3b, b. 2^{2-6}). The latter pattern in Figure 6.3b is an example of a pitch-sequence recurrence that does not conform to gestalt principles (even though it arguably does in Figure 6.3a). A RNN might alight upon such potentially "invisible" sequences – those that might not be able to function as a candidate museme because they do not constitute a perceptually-cognitively salient unit for humans – on the basis of brute recurrence alone; and it might redeploy them in a similarly invisible manner (as is the case in Figure 6.3b). Beyond this example, the fact that a particular pitch sequence occurs in a training sample in significant numbers for it to be learned by a system suggests that it must nevertheless satisfy gestalt chunking criteria to a sufficient extent to constitute a museme and thus to be replicated by humans in the tradition from which that system learns. The issue is more complex than this, however, because *folk-rnn* appears to build its knowledge, in part, from musemic half-bar and whole-bar segments, so certain "invisible" – half-bar- and barline-straddling – patterns, such as the g^1–a^1–b^1–c^2 of Figure 6.3b, might arise indirectly as artefacts of the repeated parataxis of certain "visible" (musemic half-bar- and whole-bar-aligned) segments.

6.5.1.3 Markov Models

A Markov Chain (MC) represents a series of choices where the likelihood of a particular choice being made depends only on the outcome of the previous choice. More formally, "Markov sequences represent stochastic processes having the 'Markov property' .... This property says that the future state of the sequence depends only on the last state ..." (Pachet & Roy, 2011, p. 150). A Markov system uses statistical learning to internalise the rules

	C+	D-	F+	G+	A-
C+	1–5	6–20	21–50	51–80	81–100
D-	1–18	19–20	21–60	61–85	86–100
F+	1–30	31–48	49–50	51–81	82–100
G+	1–20	21–43	44–73	74–75	76–100
A-	1–30	31–48	49–65	66–98	99–100

Table 6.1: Transition Probability Table for Rock-Style Harmonic Progressions.

underpinning such progression-related probabilities in some domain. Thus, while Markov models might also be considered under the rubric of knowledge/rule-based systems (§6.5.2), they are included here under the present category of machine-learning systems because they often embody knowledge acquired by means of the analysis of some training corpus. In music, Markovian principles have been utilised by systems that generate sequences of events such as melodic pitches, rhythm values, chord progressions, etc. – discrete entities in these domains representing one of the "states" referred to above – each of which follows probabilistically from its antecedent.

Learned regularities in a domain are commonly represented in Markov systems by means of a table of *transition probabilities* that expresses the likelihood that a state S_n will be followed by a state S_{n+1} (Pachet & Roy, 2011, p. 149). Table 6.1 shows one such table – assembled from a number of *probability vectors*, where entries, all of which are positive, sum to 1 – suitable for generating chord progressions in the style of rock music. Here, each chord-type – corresponding to Roman numerals I, II, IV, V and VI in the key of C major – represents a state. Starting with the chord of C major in the left-hand column, a randomly generated number determines the second chord in the progression, this being the one in the top row that corresponds with the selected number. The size of the chosen chord's encompassing number-range represents the progression's transition probability. Having generated the second chord, the process is repeated, starting from whichever row the second chord occurs in on the far left-hand column, and so on.[272]

---

[272] I am grateful to Valerio Velardo for these transition probabilities.

As the top row of Table 6.1 indicates, there is a 5% probability (5-0 = 5/100) of the initial C major chord's being followed by another C major chord, but a 29% probability (80-51 = 29/100) that the second chord will be a G major chord. If G were indeed selected, then the next iteration of the algorithm would start on the fourth (G+) row and generate a third chord by means of a second random number, etc. Some progressions have a probability of zero because the chords of E minor (III) and B diminished (VII) are not even admitted as harmonic possibilities in Table 6.1, so they cannot occur in progressions. Thus, Table 6.1 is implicitly adopting a theoretical position on chord and chord-progression frequency that hypothesises the non-occurrence of these two chords in the style emulated by the table. As the corpus analysis conducted by De Clercq and Temperley (2011, p. 60, Tab. 2) indicates, this reading is (intentionally) erroneous: the actual predominance of III and VII in the corpus they studied – one hundred rock songs, made up of the top twenty per decade from 1950–2000 – is 0.019 (i.e., the chord-type is that of 19% of all chords in the corpus) and 0.004 (4%), respectively. Corpus analysis also helps to arrive at a more nuanced transition probability table: according to De Clercq and Temperley (2011, p. 61, Tab. 3), the transition I–III occurs on forty-four occasions in their corpus, so its probability can be calculated as a proportion of all the transitions within the corpus.

Such "first-order" MCs generate locally coherent musical sequences, on account of their embodying the low-level statistical regularities of the underlying style, but they are notoriously prone to producing a meandering output, one lacking any medium- or large-scale sense of direction. "Higher-order" MCs offer a partial solution to this problem, because they group "atomic" elements into larger, "molecular", chunks to form a state. If a given unit – such as the single chords in Table 6.1 – formed a state in a first-order MC, then two such units are considered to constitute a state in a second-order MC, and three in a third-order MC, etc. (Shamshad et al., 2005, pp. 694–695). In this sense, a state in a first-order MC is equivalent to an entity at level eight in Table 1.4, whereas in a third-order MC it is equivalent to an entity at level seven. Thus, higher-order MCs afford an opportunity to internalise regularities in terms of musical patterns made up of note sequences – musemes, as opposed to solitary "verticals" – that are, *en bloc*, the objects of the stochastic process. Nevertheless, higher-order MCs are also prone to the non-developmental circularity of first-order MCs, but at a higher structural-hierarchic level: a pattern might recur, but without the developmental modifications to which a human composer might subject it. As a partial solution, "variable-length Markov Models" (VMM) are able "to capture statistical correlations of different length scales in a single probabilistic model" (Pachet & Roy, 2011, p. 151), affording the opportunity to generate patterns learned from inputs containing "overlapping" and "nested" structures (Jan, 2011a, sec. 4.1.2, para. 57).

Further refinements are afforded by "hidden Markov Models" (HMM), where "hidden (not observable) states are added, as a way to better represent the context. Observable states can be considered as specific control properties" (Pachet & Roy, 2011, p. 152). To reconfigure Table 6.1 as a HMM would require n sets of some or all of the chord-types in the top row to be "stored" in "containers", one for each set, the latter encapsulating the hidden states. The algorithm would first select a container and then select a chord from within it. The next chord would also be selected from a container, but all these choices would be constrained by transition probabilities: container x might, for example, be more likely to be chosen than container y; and within the selected container, chord p might be more likely to be chosen than chord q. The sequence of generated/output chords would not be hidden (it is "observable"), but the sequence of containers that gave rise to it would (it is "not observable"), because the same chord might be stored in two or more containers. In music, an HMM might be used to restrict the set of chords (the contents of a container) available to be chosen at any specific point in a sequence, in order to align with some model of chord progression. This model might either be one arrived at via statistical learning – of which the corpus analysis of De Clercq and Temperley (2011) discussed above is a subset – or one based on some (presumably empirically grounded) theory – such as that of Piston (1962, pp. 17–18), which represents "generalizations ... based on observation of usage ...".

François Pachet's *Continuator* system (Pachet, 2003) learns musical style from input music using a Markov model in order to continue phrases played by a human performer. In interaction with the system,

> a user typically plays a musical phrase using a MIDI instrument (e.g., a keyboard). This phrase is then converted into a sequence of symbols, representing a given dimension or *viewpoint* [parameter; (Conklin & Witten, 1995; Conklin, 2013)] of music, such as its pitch, duration, or velocity. The sequence is then 'learnt' by the system by computing a model of the transition probabilities between successive symbols. When the phrase is finished (typically after a certain temporal threshold has passed), the system generates a new phrase using the Markov model built so far. The user can then play another phrase, or interrupt the phrase being played, depending on the chosen interaction mode. Each time a new phrase is played, the Markov model is updated. (Pachet & Roy, 2011, p. 149; emphasis in the original)

Thus, the *Continuator* combines analysis with synthesis (§6.1), parsing an input style by statistical learning into a set of transition probabilities, and then generating outputs according to those probabilities.[273] Moreover, the *Continuator* incorporates aspects of constraint-satisfaction systems (§6.5.2.2), in that it permits the user to specify certain conditions the output must satisfy, such as – in the case of a blues chord progression – stipulating certain starting, finishing and intermediate chord-types or – in distortions of normative blues style – the appearance of certain non-standard chords (Pachet & Roy, 2011, pp. 155–156). To achieve this, it uses an *Elementary Markov Constraints* (EMC) model, which "explore[s] the set of sequences that satisfy exactly the control constraints, and … define[s] the Markovian property as a cost function to optimize" (2011, pp. 158–159).

As with many leading music-generative systems, there are many online videos demonstrating their capabilities. In the case of the *Continuator*, Sony CSL (2012) shows the composer Gjörgy Kurtág improvising with the program, the latter responding – to my ears – in a congruent and engaging manner to Kurtág's sophisticated inputs. In a similar style to this interaction, Figure 6.4 (Fober et al., 2019, p. 1, Fig. 1) shows a transcription of part of another dialogue between a human (upper stave) and the *Continuator* (lower stave).

---

[273] The interactive design of the *Continuator*, and indeed other interactive augmentation systems (§6.2) such as *GenJam* (§6.5.3.2), makes it well suited to use in educational contexts (Ferrari & Addessi, 2014).

Figure 6.4: Sample Output of the *Continuator*.

While such freely atonal music as the user's input phrase – and those extemporised by Kurtág – might be thought easy to simulate using any number of approaches, including the quasi-random (see the discussion on page 525 following Figure 6.10), the *Continuator* has clearly abstracted the gross contour and aspects of the rhythmic structure of the input as a basis for its answering output phrase. It has first taken the user's opening d^1–eb^1 (b. 1) and mutated it to bb^1–$b\natural^1$ (b. 4); it has next matched the user's following wide-interval zig-zag eb^1–bb^1–c^1 (b. 1) with $b\natural^1$–$g\sharp^2$–c^1 (bb. 4–5); and it has then reworked the user's rising fifth–falling sixth pattern e^1–b^1–d^1 (b. 2) as $c\sharp^1$–$g\sharp^1$–bb (b. 5). Put another way, the *Continuator* has analysed a set of musemes and then explored the multidimensional hypervolume (§3.6.5, §5.5.2) encompassing them in order to locate other patterns occupying the regions of that hypervolume that define the musemes' allele-classes. It has then concatenated these museme alleles in a manner that creates a musememeplex. While the concept of the museme allele, and indeed those of the musememeplex and the musemesatz, have been defined primarily in terms of replicated pitch frameworks (§3.5.2), there is no reason why the looser, contour-based, similarities evident here cannot also be understood in terms of these three categories. Moreover, given the *Continuator*'s evident ability to abstract transition probabilities from the input phrase, it is reasonable to believe that the arguably greater challenge of a tonal input phrase would also be successfully learned and replicated.

Note, finally, that neither a first-order nor (normally) a second-order MC in themselves embody a Darwinian system. While the motion from an "prefix" state P to a "continuation" state Y (Pachet & Roy, 2011, p. 151) involves an element of fitness – a statistically more probable continuation is selected over a statistically less probable one, and thus is in this sense fitter – there is no complete VRS algorithm at work. This is because there can be no true variation nor any meaningful replication of such an information-poor unit as a state consisting of a monad or a dyad (assuming those monads or dyads themselves consist of a single entity, such as a note or a chord). This situation potentially changes, however, with third-order MCs because the level of information richness is sufficient to sustain the VRS algorithm, in the sense that discrete patterns in an input may be captured and then subjected to replication and selection (see also note 204 on page 356). Nevertheless, there is still little scope for variation here, unless a three-element state were to be replaced by another state that, on account of similarity, constituted an allele of it. Even so, this would only represent the substitution of museme x^2 for museme x^1, not the mutation of x^1 generating x^2. Moreover, and as its name implies, the mono-linear strand of an MC is at odds with the poly-linear nexus of intersecting strands characteristic of true Darwinism in biological and cultural evolution. Yet these limitations can be transcended when a Markov system is integrated with a human collaborator – as is the case with the *Continuator* – because this provides the missing ingredient of true variation of the patterns the system outputs. Thus nourished by human-driven variation, the system may then go on to replicate and select those human-generated musemes by encoding them via statistical learning and incorporating them in its outputs.

6.5.2 Knowledge/Rule-Based Systems

In contrast to the methodology of machine-learning systems (§6.5.1), which self-/soft-encode their knowledge as a result of the statistical learning resulting from exposure to the target domain, knowledge/rule-based systems – sometimes called "expert" systems Ebcioğlu (1988) – are hard-encoded by the programmer. They are explicitly taught what they know, and therefore they reflect the programmer's conceptions of the domain in question, generating music in the image of that conception. Machine-learning and knowledge/rule-based approaches are not mutually exclusive: a system can be given a framework of knowledge and rules – the basic epistemological building blocks of its domain – that it can then use to guide its statistical learning; conversely, the analytical and/or synthetic outcomes of a process of statistical learning can be filtered through a framework of knowledge and rules that constrains the learned abstractions in terms of some desired epistemological structure (§6.5.4).

6.5.2.1 Grammar-Based Systems

As has been argued throughout this book, statistical regularities in musical styles arise from the interaction between nature and nurture. Nature provides the perceptual-cognitive constraints that define which musical patterns can and cannot pass through its filter; whereas nurture transmits between members of a cultural community those viable patterns (memes) that can traverse the perceptual-cognitive filter, the most salient or useful of these increasing in predominance as per the mechanism of the VRS algorithm. These bi-causal regularities can be described or prescribed by a grammar (§4.6), that assigns functions to discrete entities – like words (noun, verb, determiner) or chord-types (tonic, subdominant, dominant) – and that formalises sequential-combinatorial rules, descriptive or prescriptive, for their concatenation. The use of the word grammar recognises the structural and functional commonalities between language and music that have been addressed throughout this book and that are crystallised in generative-transformational and other grammar-based accounts of musical structure (Quick & Hudak, 2013, p. 59) (§4.4.1.3). Music-generative systems can encode grammatical formalisms and use them to produce music that, on account of its conformity to a grammar, is in alignment with the style described/prescribed by that grammar; and that is perceptually-cognitively accessible to those who, by virtue of nature and/or nurture, can parse the music described or prescribed by the grammar.

Young (2017a) applies the concept of *categorial grammar* to the task of music generation. Unlike generative-transformational grammars, categorial grammars "not only describe the syntax of a sentence, but also how the meanings of the individual words combine to create the meaning of the entire sentence" (2017a, p. 2). Young argues that

> [c]ategorial grammars describe how 'objects' (computational expressions) of various types combine to form larger expressions.... Categorial

grammars lend themselves to automatic generation of music. Combinators can be used to derive new musical objects, including melodies, from pre-existing musical objects. There are a set of valid musical objects and functions, and they can be put together in such a way as to result in an expression that is a melody. By automatically generating valid lambda expressions, we generate small musical pieces. (Young, 2017a, pp. 1–2)

Lambda calculus allows the components of a sequence, such as words in a sentence or discrete musical objects, to be represented in terms of concatenation, predicate logic and nested hierarchy (2017a, p. 2). As an example, the expression

$$\lambda x, y, z.\text{combine}(x, y, z)$$
$$(\text{rhythm}, [0.5, 0.5, 1.0]) \ (\text{start\_pit},(5, 0)),$$
$$(\text{contour}, [1, 3, 2])$$

describes the set of possible musical objects – the museme allele-class – of three elements whose first element is c^1 and is the lowest pitch, whose second element is the highest pitch, and whose rhythm is $\frac{2}{4}$ ♪ ♪ ♩ (2017a, pp. 3–4, Fig. 3). Young (2017a) used categorial grammars to formalise and generate more extended musical entities than those constituting this allele-class. Figure 6.5 (2017a, p. 7, Fig. 6) shows a short piano piece based on the following grammatical rules:[274]

Chords are created by combining diatonic scales starting on different keys with chord types, namely triads, ninth, seventh, and eleventh chords. Each chord X is then made into a sequence of the chords X IV/X V/X .... The resulting chords are combined with a rhythmic figure with 3 notes and a total length of 2 beats. The resulting melody is manipulated in several ways, namely diminution with repetition, the addition of an appoggiatura, and inversion. (Young, 2017a, p. 7)

While only six bars in length, this piece is afforded considerable coherence by its grammar's specification of a limited number of permissible musical objects and their concatenation. The recurrence in every bar of the ♪. ♪ ♩ rhythmic museme and – apart from the triplet rhythm of the inversion-based b. 4 – its duple diminution, gives the piece a distinctive character.

---

[274] Young (2017b) gives other examples of music produced by this method.

Figure 6.5: Sample Output of Categorial Grammar.

The left-hand augmented-second/minor-third dyads ground the harmony, instantiating the "X–IV/X–V/X" sequence that results from application of the lambda expression's "[id , fourOf , fiveOf ,]" function (2017a, p. 7). While the grammar conceives these chords in terms of diatonic operations, the dyad spellings (and the associated upper-stave pitch) encourage reading the harmonic museme associated with the ♪. ♪ ♩ rhythmic museme as traversing the three diminished-seventh chords F–G♯–B(–D), B♭–C♯–E(–G), and C–E♭–F♯(–A), and therefore exhausting the chromatic collection. These attributes give the piece a flavour of the late/post-tonal music of the last quarter of the nineteenth century, the closest examples of similar HGM perhaps including – albeit of much greater scope and technique – such pieces as Liszt's *Sospiri!* S. 192 no. 5 of 1879 and his *Bagatelle ohne Tonart* S. 216a of 1885.

6.5.2.2 Constraint-Satisfaction Systems

A constraint-satisfaction system, as its name implies, attempts to find a solution to a problem by satisfying a number of constraints that delineate the problem. More formally, solving the problem involves locating the set of points within a hypervolume whose coordinates satisfy the constraints of that problem. These points – permissible values for a set of variables – define a "feasible region" for the location of a constraint-satisfying output. In music-generative systems, this approach amounts to encoding style rules as constraints in a number of parameters that the output music must satisfy.

In this sense there are significant overlaps between constraint-satisfaction systems and grammar-based systems (§6.5.2.1), in that the constraints are grammatical rules that must be satisfied. In terms of the VRS algorithm, the satisfaction of constraints represents a form of selection, one that filters out those configurations that do not meet the "survival" criteria represented by the constraints.

Quick and Hudak (2013) outline a (unnamed) grammar-based system that generates chord progressions in "classical" and jazz styles. Their program uses a *probabilistic temporal graph grammar* (PTGG). This overcomes certain limitations of other types of grammar – such as a *context-free grammar* (CFG) – in that: (i) it is able to capture phrase repetition; (ii) it can account for the probabilistic dimension of musical style; and (iii) it allows the temporal element in musical hierarchies to be accommodated (for instance, the generation from a minim-value I chord of a V–I progression assigns both the V and the I the value of a crotchet) (2013, p. 59). The first of these attributes, in particular, helps overcome certain limitations of other generative approaches – most notably Markov models, but also neural networks – which generally struggle to render convincingly the hierarchic patterns of phrase- and section-repetition evident in even the most simple instances of HGM (Quick & Hudak, 2013, p. 67).

Quick and Hudak (2013, p. 60, Fig. 1) use a two-phase design in their system. In the first ("abstract/structural generation") phase, a generative algorithm outputs the harmonic progression of a piece – the system deals only with harmony, and does not in this version feature a specific melody-generation facility – as an abstract sequence of Roman numerals. The generative algorithm proceeds by progressively expanding a "start" symbol – i.e., the highest hierarchic level, such as a sentence in linguistics or a Schenkerian background-level tonic in music theory – until a "terminal" symbol – i.e., a word or a foreground-level chord – is reached. This expansion is regulated by grammatical rules that are implemented as functions and that are deployed probabilistically by the generative algorithm based on stylistic precepts and regularities extracted from external statistical data (2013, p. 62). These "[r]ules can create repetition as well as exhibit[ing] conditional behavior, yielding complex structures with even a very simple generative algorithm" (2013, p. 61). In the second ("musical interpretation") phase, the system uses the "abstract" chords generated in the first phase to produce "concrete" chords, by voicing the former in musically meaningful ("perform-able") ways (2013, p. 63). This is achieved using a constraint-satisfaction algorithm informed by the "OPTIC" model of Tymoczko (2006) and Cal-lender et al. (2008) (see also Tymoczko (2011)). This model aims to expand and unify extant harmonic and voice-leading theory, proposing the form-ation of equivalence-classes of "objects" (sequences or sets of pitches) by disregarding the five categories of transformation: Octave equivalence, Per-mutation, Transposition, Inversion, and changes of Cardinality. Quick and Hudak (2013) use "OPC space" to move from the "block trichords" implied by the Roman-numeral output of the system's first phase to an expanded voicing suitable for mapping to the output music's four voices in the second phase (2013, p. 63; p. 64, Fig. 2; Callender et al., 2008, p. 346).

Both the generative and the constraint-satisfaction algorithms draw upon the syntax of "let expressions" (Quick & Hudak, 2013, p. 62). These allow for the replacement of the abstract terms x, y, etc., with concrete Roman-numerals, and for the recursive-hierarchical embedding of chord progressions. For instance, the let expression

$$\textbf{let } x = (\textbf{let } y = V^{t1}\ I^{t2} \textbf{ in } y\ y) \textbf{ in } x\ IV^{t3}\ I^{t4}\ x \tag{6.1}$$

– where the superscript "t" refers to the time duration of the chord – expands to the chord progression

$$V^{t1}\ I^{t2}\ V^{t1}\ I^{t2}\ IV^{t3}\ I^{t4}\ V^{t1}\ I^{t2}\ V^{t1}\ I^{t2} \tag{6.2}$$

(Quick & Hudak, 2013, 65, Eq. 14, Eq. 15).

A sample output of the system is shown in Figure 6.6 (after Quick & Hudak, 2013, p. 69, Fig. 8), the system's four-stave output being compressed here to two staves.

Figure 6.6: Sample Output of PTGG System.

The capacity of a PTGG to implement phrase repetition is evident in the extract's ABA structure, marked on Figure 6.6, the B section itself containing internal repetition (bb. 3–4, bb. 5–6). Yet while Quick and Hudak (2013, p. 60) assert that "our system's output sounds similar to a classical [i.e., Bach?] chorale", the passage has many shortcomings if held strictly to this claim. For one thing, the voice-leading is clearly very poor, with many awkward, unvocal intervals in all four parts. Despite its aspirations to chorale style, the system, as mentioned, does not claim to be able to generate melody. Perhaps this arises from a misunderstanding of the nature of melody: in the best Bach chorales, all four voices are independent melodies, smooth and interesting in themselves. Even though the constraint-satisfaction algorithm aims to "[r]egulat[e] voice-leading smoothness by restricting the range of movement in the voices" (2013, p. 66), tighter constraints on the range of permissible note-to-note intervals would have improved the melodic sense of all parts. This lack of voice-leading parsimony is presumably an artefact of the use of OPC space: in expanding from chord to chord, as opposed to voice-note to voice-note along a complete part, the constraint-satisfaction algorithm lacks the sensitivity to long-range voice-leading parsimony intrinsic to chorale styles, J. S. Bach's and others (such as "Classical hymn texture" (Rosen, 1997, p. 319)). Returning to the issue of means *versus* ends raised in §6.2, Bach's voice-leading parsimony seems to have resulted from his writing chorales by taking the extant melody, adding a bass line, then composing the tenor voice, and finally inserting the alto part (David et al., 1998, p. 399; Mabley, 2015). In short, each part arises from the linear concatenation (parataxis) of musemes in ways that respect the museme-concatenation of the other parts. The present system, in its chord-to-chord constraint-satisfaction search, behaves more like a university undergraduate student's composing "vertically" than like Bach's composing "horizontally". While using different means does not necessarily preclude alighting upon similar ends, adopting Bach's means would appear to make the end of an "authentic" – smoothly contrapuntal – chorale style more likely, in both HGM and CGM.

To add further criticism, the harmony of Figure 6.6 lacks a sense of direction, with some odd treatments of $^6_4$ chords (b. 2^{3-4}, b. 3^1, b. 5^1, etc.). Quick and Hudak (2013, p. 68) acknowledge this, noting that "the transition between the first instance of part A and the beginning of part B is a jarring transition that is not very suitable for the target genre. Similarly, the first measure of part B sounds rather odd with an unexpected major-minor transition in the middle of the measure". To understand these discontinuities, it is useful to refer to the Roman-numeral labels shown under the bass line of Figure 6.6, which result, as noted above, from the expansion of let expressions encoding probabilistic aspects of the grammar. While most of these progressions are within Bach's vocabulary, that at the start of the B section (b. 3) seems at the very distant periphery of probability in his style. The segment "M7(V M7(VII) VI V ...)" translates as: "chord V in relation to the seventh degree of C major (i.e., F♯ minor (not major) in the context of B minor); followed by chord VII in relation to the seventh degree of B minor (i.e., G♯ diminished – the root ungrammatically spelled here as A♭ – in the context of A major); followed by chord VI in relation to the seventh degree of C major (i.e., G major in the context of B minor); followed by chord V in relation to the seventh degree of C major (i.e., F♯ minor (not major) in the context of B minor)". I know of no Bach chorale that deploys this progression; and if any did, one would imagine his voice-leading would be very much smoother.

Judged as a chorale – as Quick and Hudak (2013) invite us to do – the output in Figure 6.6 is inferior to that produced by the significantly earlier *CHORAL* system of Ebcioğlu (1988, p. 50, Fig. 1, Fig. 2), one of the first successfully to generate music in this style. This is not to compare like with like, however, because – despite their broadly common knowledge/rule-based approaches – *CHORAL* is designed to harmonise extant chorale melodies (which serve to facilitate style-emulation), whereas the system of Quick and Hudak (2013) is not subject to this constraint, being primarily a melody-independent, chord-progression generator. In the domain of Bach-chorale generation, *CHORAL* is itself arguably trumped by the *DeepBach* system (Hadjeres et al., 2016; Hadjeres et al., 2017), which learns the style of chorales using a neural network. Their system is "steerable in the sense that a user can constrain the generation by imposing positional constraints such as notes, rhythms or cadences in the generated score" (Hadjeres et al., 2017, p. 1). Thus, in a hybrid methodology (§6.5.4), *DeepBach* combines a neural network learning-generative model with a constraint-satisfaction filter to refine the network's outputs.

6.5.3 Optimisation Systems

Optimisation systems, as this category's name suggests, seek to determine the optimum solution to a given problem. Similar to constraint-satisfaction systems, optimisation systems search a notional problem-space, but the latter attempt to trace the shortest and/or easiest route to a given solution. As with constraint-satisfaction systems, the problem space may be represented as a hypervolume in which the parameters of the problem are represented by the axes and various candidate solutions sit at their intersections. As has been argued on several earlier occasions, evolution by natural selection, driven by the VRS algorithm, is a means of searching a problem-space in order to locate an optimal solution to the problem of survival (§5.5.2); it is arguably the optimal optimisation algorithm. Nevertheless, it is a proximity-weighted algorithm, in the sense that it will alight upon the closest acceptable solution, not the best overall. That is, evolution does not search the whole hyper-volume, because it cannot see all that the hypervolume encompasses, and because leaping to the best solution involves too much genetic and ontogenetic risk. Instead, evolution moves gradualistically by the shortest possible (lowest-risk) distance to the nearest acceptable solution. Clinging stubbornly on to the cliff-face of life, it short-sightedly searches for the nearest aptive foothold able to prevent falling to oblivion; it does not risk the saltationist lunge to a secure, but more distant, ledge.

Even if an optimisation system avoids untrammelled saltationism, as it surely must if it is to be evolutionarily authentic, the combinatorial explosion that arises from parametric interaction in even short spans of music means that it must still search a large space in order to locate optimal solutions to a particular set of desired criteria. Herremans and Sörensen (2013, pp. 6427–6428; emphases in the original) identify three categories of *"metaheuristic optimization algorithms"* able to accomplish this searching: (i) *"population-based* metaheuristics"; (ii) *"constructive* metaheuristics"; and (iii) *"local-search* algorithms"* (sometimes also called neighbourhood search algorithms). The first of these approaches is considered in §6.5.3.2; the second, which "construct solutions from their constituting parts", will not be considered here owing to their relative underdevelopment for music-generative tasks; and the third is considered in §6.5.3.1.

6.5.3.1 Local Search Algorithms

Local search algorithms "iteratively make small changes to a single solution" (Herremans & Sörensen, 2013, p. 6428) in order to find the optimal solution within a relatively constrained search-space. Herremans and Sörensen (2013) developed a music-generative system, *Optimuse*, capable of composing instances of fifth-species counterpoint (Fux, 1965),[275] which they extended in the Android app *FuX* (Herremans et al., 2015, p. 85). In *Optimuse*, based on a *variable neighbourhood search* (VNS) algorithm, conformity to the principal melodic and intervallic/harmonic rules of the species (as formalised in Salzer and Schachter (1989)) is represented by a weighted *subscore* (where zero represents perfect conformity) relating to each rule. Weighting allows for increasing the emphasis of certain rules deemed to be particularly significant to the style. Some of these rules are inviolable ("hard"), implemented as strict constraints (i.e., they must score zero), whereas others are flexible ("soft"), allowing scope for partial conformity. An *objective function $f(s)$* sums the subscores and thus arrives at an overall assessment of how well a candidate fragment of fifth-species counterpoint accords with the style, where the lower the value, the greater the degree of conformity (2013, p. 6429).

---

[275] See Z. Ren (2020) for a contrasting – genetic/evolutionary algorithm-based – approach to the composition of first-species counterpoint.

In outline, *Optimuse* first generates a candidate fragment s – consisting of a *cantus firmus* plus a counterpoint – using the hard rules. In this sense, the program is functioning as a knowledge/rule-based system (§6.5.2; indeed, Herremans and Sörensen (2013) appears in a journal devoted to expert systems), because the hard rules used to arrive at an exemplar of fifth-species counterpoint represent its understanding of the style. The local search itself operates within three "neighbourhoods". In the first, "swap neighbourhood", *Optimuse* explores the set of proximate variants that may be generated by swapping any two notes in s, populating the neighbourhood by applying this swap to all notes in s. Having used $f(s)$ to find the optimum in this first neighbourhood, the system then takes this best version, $s\prime$, as s and uses it as the basis for populating and searching for an optimum in the second, "change1 neighbourhood", wherein the pitch of one note in the new s is changed to another pitch permissible in the key. Then, having found the optimum in this second neighbourhood, the best version, $s\prime$, is again taken as s and is used to populate and search for the optimum in the third, "change2 neighbourhood", wherein the pitch of two adjacent notes in the new-new s are changed to other pitches permissible in the key. Taking the best version, $s\prime$, from the third neighbourhood as s, the search then moves back to the first, swap, neighbourhood, and the cycle is repeated until no other candidate scoring closer to $f(s) = 0$ than the optimal form, s_{best}, can be found. Beyond this basic mechanism, *Optimuse* implements other strategies designed to prevent the search from becoming "trapped" around local optima, and to avoid an aggregate low score arising from the combination of several low and a few high scores (2013, pp. 6430–6431, Fig. 3, Fig. 5).

An example of *Optimuse*'s output (Herremans & Sörensen, 2013, p. 6433, Fig. 8) is shown in Figure 6.7.

Herremans and Sörensen (2013, p. 6434) say of this passage that "[i]t is the subjective opinion of the authors that the generated fragment sounds pleasing to the ear"; but they also acknowledge "its lack of theme or sense of direction". This is perhaps a fair assessment, and one that invites comparison (by analogy with the discussion of Bach chorales in §6.5.2.2) with the work of undergraduate students learning the basis of Fux's approach. Such beginners often manage to satisfy most or all of the rules, and in doing so arrive at

Figure 6.7: Fifth-Species Counterpoint Example Generated by *Optimuse*.

broadly agreeable solutions; but reconciling conflicts among the "soft" rules, in particular, often leads to a degree of short-term thinking – local problem-solving – that prevents the kind of coherent melodic flow and inner unity found in the work of Fux's models, particularly Palestrina. The melody in Figure 6.7 also arguably suffers from an under-specification of the rules: while their nineteen "horizontal" and nineteen "vertical" rules (Herremans & Sörensen, 2013, pp. 6435–6436, Tab. A.7, A.8) are certainly essential to the definition of the style, they do not capture the granularity of detail found in some specifications of practice, such as the detailed profile of Palestrina's style offered by Jeppesen (1992). In particular, the repeated notes in bb. 4, 8 and 12 are prohibited in Jeppesen's account (1992, pp. 111, 114, 136).[276] Nevertheless, Herremans and Sörensen (2013, p. 6434) acknowledge that future iterations of *Optimuse* could implement such sensitivity to composer-specific style features in the objective function.

While sometimes set apart from systems based on genetic/evolutionary algorithms as not truly evolutionary, local search algorithms nevertheless potentially implement the VRS algorithm. Variation is provided, in the case of *Optimuse*, by the swaps and changes – the edit-distance operations of insertion, deletion and substitution (§3.6.5) – made to the candidate fragment *s* that define the three neighbourhoods; replication is found in the copying

---

[276] Jeppesen would also dismiss as unidiomatic to Palestrina's style the upward skip from an accented crotchet (i.e., the first and third in a bar of four) in b. 7^{3-4} (1992, p. 120).

of a neighbourhood's optimal variant, *s*/, to serve as the starting point for the configuration of and search in the next neighbourhood; and selection is accomplished by the objective function $f(s)$, which assesses, by way of the subscores and their weights, the "fitness" of the generated melodies according to their conformity with the rule-set defining the style, and thereby locates *s*/. Nevertheless, the final two stages are inverted here compared with the algorithm's normal sequence – selection in *Optimuse* (of *s*/) occurs *before* replication, whereas in biological evolution (if not in cultural) it occurs after it. Perhaps, however, this is to take a too rigidly linear view of the arguably bidirectionally circular VRS algorithm, as is discussed in the third point of the paragraph (on algorithm-sequencing) on page 549.

6.5.3.2 Genetic/Evolutionary Algorithms

Invented by Koza (1992), and enabling "population-based metaheuristics" (to recall the categories identified by Herremans and Sörensen (2013, p. 6428) listed on page 514), the paradigm of genetic programming instantiates evolutionary processes by implementing the VRS algorithm in computer code. Systems based on genetic/evolutionary algorithms (GAs) both "generate" and "test", to use Dennett's distinction (1995, p. 373): they engender the necessary variation, often by dividing patterns in the relevant domain and recombining their subcomponents; they replicate the varied patterns; and they select from the resulting population using some *fitness function* (akin to *Optimuse*'s objective function) that determines the desired attributes of the successful patterns and/or their fit to some environmental or functional constraint. Suitable for exploring evolutionary scenarios in a number of domains, genetic programming has proved fruitful in music-generative tasks, allowing for the rapid replaying of the memetic processes hypothesised to have underpinned "real" music-cultural evolution. Beyond music synthesis, GAs have been used for music-analytical purposes (Rafael et al., 2009; Geetha Ramani & Priya, 2019); and for emotion-, genre- and piece/song-recognition tasks (Gutiérrez & García, 2016). In some music-generative systems – such as *DarwinTunes* (MacCallum, Leroi et al., 2012; MacCallum, Mauch et al., 2012) – selection is devolved to human choice, the power and reach of the internet making such crowd-based evaluations of candidate patterns relatively easy to solicit. The discussion below is divided into systems that do not associate the workings of the GA with interactions between virtual agents and those that do.

Non-Agent-Based Systems

One of the most successful music-GA systems is Biles' *GenJam* (*Genetic Jammer*) software (2007, 2020). It is a "real-time, MIDI-based, interactive improvisation system that uses evolutionary computation to evolve populations of melodic ideas (*licks*, in the jazz vernacular), which it uses to generate its improvisations in live performance settings ..." (Biles, 2013, p. 20; emphasis in the original). In a sense, it offers the same functionality as Pachet's *Continuator* (§6.5.1.3), except it uses a GA rather than the Markov model of the *Continuator*. *GenJam* has two modes of operation, "interactive" and "autonomous". In the interactive mode, the system supports: (i) "trading fours and eights" (i.e., human-machine alternation of four- or eight-bar phrases (Biles, 2007, p. 156; Biles, 2013, p. 22)); (ii) "collective improvisation" or "intelligent echo" (i.e., simultaneous human-machine improvisation (2007, p. 157, 2013, p. 22)); and (iii) "interbreeding" or "evolving ... in the direction of the human's playing" (i.e., hybridisation of human- and machine-generated bars (2007, p. 158, 2013, p. 23)). Essentially, in its interactive mode *GenJam* draws upon a vocabulary of musical patterns and, before and during live jazz human-machine co-improvisation, subjects them to the operation of the VRS algorithm in response to ideas devised by the human soloist. In the autonomous mode, the software runs this process with no interaction with a human colleague (2007, p. 159).

Aligning with ideas discussed in §1.6.1, *GenJam*'s architecture is typical of GA systems in that it ostensibly maintains a distinction between, in my terms, a memome and a phemotype, although Biles uses the corresponding terms (genotype and phenotype) from genetics (2007, p. 142). While this is a binarism inherent in all systems where computer code gives rise to musical sounds (§6.6.3, §7.6.1), in GA systems it is explicitly formalised in the architecture, as reflected in the organisation of the memotypic elements in conformity to the structure and function of DNA. Nevertheless, the issue is not straightforward because, in my conception, the memome aligns with the system's music-representing source-code memes – strictly, with the electronic impulses associated with the executable file derived by compilation from the source-code memes – and not (as is the convention in genetic programming) with on-screen representations of the source-code memes, which are the phemotypic products of the plain-text files encoding the source-code memes. In §7.6.1 these electronic-impulse replicators are termed "*i*-memes" or, using a term of Blackmore's, "tremes" (2015).

In contrast with the memome, the phemotype is not formalised explicitly by Biles. Indeed, there is a degree of slippage between replicators and vehicles in Biles' accounts of *GenJam*'s design and function that is indicated by his referring to the members of the phrase population (explained below) as both "chromosomes" and as "individuals" (2007, p. 142). While it is unnecessary to draw slavish comparisons between natural and cultural replicators, it is certainly incorrect to regard an entity as both a replicator and a vehicle, for this erodes the key distinction between the germ line (that which is replicated) and the soma line (that which facilitates replication) (§1.8). A memetic interpretation of the phemotype in *GenJam* would thus regard it as consisting of the sound patterns motivated by the tremes manipulated by the program, running on a silicon-based hardware; to which must be added the sound patterns generated by the human co-performer motivated by memes and musemes, running on a carbon-based hardware.

At the memomic/genotypic level, "genes" occupy slots in a "measure [bar] chromosome" and then – in one reading of Biles (2007, 2013) – at a higher structural-hierarchic level, measure chromosomes in effect themselves serve as genes occupying slots in a "phrase chromosome".[277] Measure chromosomes are members of a set of sixty-four one-bar units (the "measure population"), whose original members may be replaced by variants. Phrase chromosomes are members of a set of forty-eight four-bar phrases (the "phrase population") built from concatenation of members of the measure population (Biles, 2007, pp. 142–145; Biles, 2013, p. 21). This design essentially implements the RHSGAP model (§3.5.2), whereby bars (musemes) assortatively recombine to generate phrases (musemeplexes). At a higher

---

[277] Thus, Biles regards each note of a measure chromosome as a gene (2013, p. 21), not each complete ($\frac{4}{4}$) bar of eight quaver-value slots. This is perhaps on account of each slot's being coded for by four bits (see note 278 on page 520). Thus, a bit might be regarded as analogous to a nucleotide. In music, and as discussed on page 505 apropos third-order MCs, a single note is not normally sufficient to function as a museme, so there is some disanalogy between (pseudo) nature and culture here.

Repeat
    Select 4 individuals at random to form a family (*tournament selection*)
    Select 2 family members with the greatest fitness to be parents
    Perform *crossover* on the 2 parents to generate 2 children
    Mutate the resulting 2 children until they are unique in the population
    Assign 0 as fitness for both children
    Replace the 2 non-parent family members with the new children
Until half the population has been replaced with new children

Figure 6.8: *GenJam*'s Genetic Algorithm.

structural-hierarchic level is situated the "soloist" (broadly analogous to a musemesatz), this being Biles' term for "a collection of tunes that *GenJam* will perform during the training process", set up by the program's human "mentor" (2007, p. 145).

Figure 6.8 (Biles, 2007, p. 146, Fig. 7.5) represents in "pseudocode" – a natural-language statement of the operation of the algorithm – the GA under-pinning *GenJam*. The GA is deployed during a "training" phase, which draws upon the measure population and the phrase population and uses them to generate variants. This mutation is followed by human-driven selection: the mentor listens to variants and codes them as either "g" (good) or "b" (bad). This assessment determines, via a "fitness" value (2007, p. 142), the likelihood of the variant's use (its replication) in an improvisation.

In many GAs, the mutational operations are often "mindless", sometimes involving "flipping a random bit" of the data encoding (2007, p. 147).[278] Biles found that using this approach did not work well in *GenJam*, one of the reasons for this being that "while random changes will make measures and phrases different, they are unlikely to make them sound better" (2007, p. 148). While this perhaps underestimates the power of the "blind watch-maker" (Dawkins, 2006) to build complexity by seizing on small, random variations, Biles – keen to develop a system that would produce music that sounds recognisably like jazz – developed a number of "musically meaning-ful mutations", operators that implement the familiar motivic-development devices of transposition, retrogression and inversion (2007, pp. 148–149).

---

[278] As outlined in note 277 on page 519, each note is coded in *GenJam* by four bits, and each bar has eight quaver notes (which may be joined to form longer note values or rendered as rests), making thirty-two bits per bar.

Figure 6.9: Sample Output of *GenJam*.

Similarly, the "intelligent crossover" operations (deployed at measure- and phrase-level) attempt to avoid "unfortunate" crossover points, whereby a bar or a phrase is divided in ways that create a new museme or musemeplex with excessively large intra- or inter-museme intervals, respectively (2007, pp. 152–153). "Intelligent note-level measure crossover" is illustrated in Figure 6.9, which shows a transcription of a passage of *GenJam*'s output generated by this operation (2007, 153–154, Figs. 7.12, 7.13).

Here bb. 1 and 2 are the two "parent" bars and bb. 3 and 4 are the two resulting "child" bars. The crossover points are marked by vertical lines in Figure 6.9, showing that the parent bars have been split after the fifth quaver-event, leading, for example, to the preservation of the segment c^2–a^1–g^1 (segment 4) from quavers 6–8 of Parent 2 in the corresponding segment of Child 1. This crossover also results in the retention in Child 1 of stepwise melodic movement into segment 4, now from the $b\flat^1$ at the end of segment 1; and in melodic stasis on the d^2 (equivalent to segment 2) in Child 2. The underlying chord of this phrase is C major seventh throughout, but normally chords change once or twice per bar, as pre-specified in a "chord progression" file (2007, pp. 140–141; p. 145, Tab. 7.2) that constrains the number of available melody notes for each chord. This is in accordance with Biles' safety-first "design philosophy that starts with simple, robust choices and tries to avoid complex solutions to specific situations. I want *GenJam* to always sound competent and never sound 'wrong'" (2013, p. 22). As a calculated risk, however, *GenJam* is able to insert chromatic passing notes outside the specified note-list for each chord, as exemplified by the $e\flat^2$ on quaver four of Parent 2 (2007, pp. 144–145).

As a result of – or perhaps despite – these operations, the phrase in Figure 6.9 sounds idiomatic and characterful as jazz; but the real test of an interactive system is of course a live performance situation using a challenging piece. As demonstrated by Biles' and *GenJam*'s rendition of the jazz standard "You go to my head" (Biles, 2019), the system picks up smoothly at *c.* 0:50 and again at *c.* 1:20, and develops melodic ideas with some stylistic sensitivity, although perhaps without Biles' flair. At the very least, the improvisation demonstrates the power of the VRS algorithm to latch onto the musemes and musemeplexes constitutive of this style and to manipulate them in ways that align with the deployment of musico-operational/procedural memes in human-only jazz improvisations.

Arguably the most radical use of GAs in music generation is the *Iamus* computer (Diaz-Jerez & Vico, 2017), developed by a team led by Francisco Vico at the University of Málaga. Named after the prophet of Greek mythology – the offspring of Apollo and Evadne, who was able to understand birds – the system is designed to compose music for orchestra and traditional acoustic instruments in an avant-garde "classical" style, evoking the late- and post-modernism cultivated by many contemporary human composers. Its outputs are MusicXML files, which can be readily converted to musical scores using a score-editing program; and the developers' intention is that these scores then be performed by professional musicians, with all the nuances of expression and interpretation that they would bring to bear on human-composed music. Indeed, a commercial recording of some of *Iamus*'s compositions, performed by the London Symphony Orchestra, is available (Iamus, 2012). Another design motivation for *Iamus* is that its repository of generated materials are available to composers to draw from and adapt in order to stimulate their own compositional practice. Thus, beyond its arguably primary function as a fully automatic generative system, *Iamus* serves additionally as an augmentation system, to recall the terminology of §6.2. In its primary role, a co-developer, Gustavo Díaz-Jerez argues – and perhaps one needs a somewhat liberal interpretation of his word "intervention" – that *"Opus one* (generated by *Iamus* on 15 October 2010) is a good example of the quality of the resulting compositional process and, to our knowledge, the first musical fragment ever conceived and written in professional music notation by a computer without human intervention" (Diaz-Jerez, 2011, p. 14).

A computer cluster housed in a striking tigerprint-patterned case (Sewell, 2012), the underlying mechanism of *Iamus* is presented under the rubric of *Melomics* (Melodic Genomics) (Sánchez-Quintana et al., 2013). While the technology is commercially sensitive, it is possible to understand its algorithmic basis from published literature (Puy (2017, sec. 2) offers the most comprehensive overview). It operates on *evo-devo* (evolutionary-developmental) principles (S. B. Carroll, 2005), whereby (in biology) "evolutionary changes are interpreted as small mutations in the genome of organisms that modulate their developmental processes in complex and orchestrated ways, resulting in altered forms and novel features" (Sánchez-Quintana et al., 2013, p. 100). Thus, the system incorporates not only the traditional genomic/memomic aspects of systems based on GAs, but also an ontological-phenotypic/phemotypic element of embryology, whereby the "self-organized choreographies of precisely timed events, with cells dividing and arranging themselves into layers of tissues that fold in complex shapes, resulting in the formation of a multicellular organism from a single zygote" (Sánchez-Quintana et al., 2013, p. 100) of biological embryology is emulated in code.[279]

Using the Melomics algorithm,

> *Iamus* implements the evolution of complex musical structures, encoded into artificial genomes (resembling multicellular living organisms, which develop from a genome, and [which] also evolve in time). These genomes represent the musical information in an indirect and very compact way: each genome encodes the specifications to generate a music piece following a complex developmental process. (Sánchez-Quintana et al., 2013, p. 101)

Leaving aside the conflation of replicator ("artificial genomes") and vehicle ("multicellular living organisms") here, in memetic terms one might take this summary to indicate that the artificial genome functions as a musemesatz, in that it encodes a series of source-code memes (or source-code meme allele-classes), and/or the structural *loci*/nodes in which they are to be situated. By contrast, Puy (2017, sec. 2) equates the genome with a "'generating cell' or

---

[279] In biological evolution, embryological processes are "phenotype-side", not "genome-side". In the "digital embryology" of the Melomics algorithm, insofar as it can be reconstructed and understood from published accounts, the distinction appears blurred. This embryology is implemented by means of *indirect encodings* ("formal abstractions of developmental processes that define complex mappings between genotype and phenotype" (Sánchez-Quintana et al., 2013, p. 100; Puy, 2017, sec. 2)), in contrast to the *direct encodings* (which "straightforwardly map genotypes (representations of solutions) to phenotypes (the solutions themselves)" (Puy, 2017, sec. 2)) often used by other GA-based systems.

'musical motif"', akin to the Schoenbergian Grundgestalt/basic shape or the Kellerian basic idea (§4.4.1.1). On the former interpretation, the (memomic) source-code memes whose configuration and sequential structure is specified by the artificial-genome musemesatz provide – via the resultant executable – the instructions to generate a sequence of MusicXML-code memes. These, in turn, provide the instructions to a score-editing program to generate a series of (phemotypic) graphemes, delineating the generated musemes via western musical notation. These graphemes provide the instructions, to human performers, to generate sound sequences, which subsequently result in the (memomic) encoding of *Iamus*-generated musemes in the brains of their listeners.

The artificial genomes are subject to mutational operations, the resulting variant structures being evaluated by a fitness function (Sánchez-Quintana et al., 2013, pp. 101–102) that defines the "conditions" that must be satisfied by the selected music. These conditions are organised into the six categories of instrumental feasibility, notational correctness, form-type, instrument-specific expressive nuance, user-criteria (specifically, piece-duration and instrumentation), and aesthetic factors (encompassing dissonance levels and timbre) (Puy, 2017, sec. 2). The fitness function encodes almost 1,000 rules of music theory (Sánchez-Quintana et al., 2013, p. 102) and thus *Iamus* – in common with other GA-based systems whose fitness functions encode theoretical precepts as selective criteria – also represents a knowledge/rule-based system (§6.5.2). "Recombination operators" permit the merging of genomes encoding different musical styles and thus "offspring might show combined features of the parental genomes", this giving rise to "[n]ew fusion genres" (Sánchez-Quintana et al., 2013, p. 101). Again insofar as the detailed operation of *Iamus* can be understood, this suggests that the unit of selection (§1.6.2) in the Melomics algorithm is in effect the whole piece – strictly, the musemesatz underpinning its artificial genome – rather than any lower-level unit, such as the individual source-code memes constituting that musemesatz, or their resultant MusicXML-code memes, graphemes and musemes.

One of *Iamus*'s compositions is the piano piece *Colossus* (2012), named after the computer built during World War II to decrypt German codes by Tommy

Figure 6.10: *Iamus: Colossus* (2012), bb. 1–8.

Flowers with contributions from Alan Turing. Figure 6.10 shows the first eight bars of the score.[280]

On first hearing, this music seems technically and stylistically convincing, having, perhaps, a flavour of the style of Messiaen in its mystical and evocative textures. Cynics might argue that such a freely atonal avant-garde style is not difficult to pastiche, because musical surfaces generated by, for instance, a quasi-random approach to composition may not differ markedly from those generated by strict, logical and intentional processes, such as those seemingly underpinning the operation of *Iamus*. In a similar way, it is arguably not beyond the ability of most artistically untrained people to simulate, at least superficially, the visual style of an abstract painter like Jackson Pollock through random application of paint to a canvas. Of course, such "informed randomness" is part of the working methods of a number of composers and painters. Presumably on account of the music-theoretical rules encoded in its fitness function, the sound-patterns of *Colossus* tend to form chunks that are consonant with the perceptual-cognitive grouping criteria governing most HGM. Being thus coherent to a human listener, these segments are likely perceived, and may function, in terms of the musemes of HGM. Moreover, there is a good deal of stylistic consistency here, with the exploration of the high registers of the piano; the use of left-hand chords that are tied across the bar line and introduced by glissandi and acciaccature;

---

[280] See also Díaz Jerez (2012) for a performance with Díaz-Jerez on piano.

and a right-hand melody that mixes triplet and "straight" quavers. Yet the overall structure seems somewhat diffuse and lacking a clear developmental trajectory: while there is no obligation, or consistent tradition in such a style, for an arch-shaped tension-curve (page 411), the piece lacks a clear narrative, such as might be expected in the work of a human composer. This deficit is partly because, for all the chunking, there is little of the motivic development that might sustain such a narrative. In short, this piece is clearly music, but it is not particularly musical, as judged from an unavoidably biased human perspective.

Agent-Based Systems

In implementing the VRS algorithm, a GA is essentially concerned with generating a variety of patterns, copying them and then selecting them using some fitness function. This can happen in an "open"/unbounded way, by creating a (virtual) workspace within which the algorithm operates. In this way, the evolutionary processes are running abstractly, without any explicit representation of the contexts and structures within which the replicators are usually situated in "real-world" evolution. A more thoroughgoing implementation of evolutionary methodologies would represent both the replicator side *and* the vehicle side of the dynamic (§1.6.1), and would thus preserve the distinction between the germ line and the soma line. This model is implemented in certain *agent-based* systems that have been developed to simulate evolution in a number of domains (Bonabeau, 2002). In the most explicitly evolutionary of these, the agents constitute vehicles in which the replicators reside. Echoing the nature of biological and cultural evolution, the survival of the replicators in such systems is generally contingent upon that of the vehicles, and vice versa.

Tatar and Pasquier (2019) present a comprehensive survey of seventy-eight agent-based systems developed for music-related tasks (2019, pp. 57–60, Tab. 1), which they organise into a nine-dimensional typology (2019, p. 63, Fig. 2).[281] This overview indicates that the purposes for which such systems have been developed – the "musical tasks" dimension (2019, p. 63) –

---

[281] These nine dimensions are "agent architectures, musical tasks, environment types, number of agents, number of agent roles, communication types, corpus types, input/output (I/O) types, [and] human interaction modality (HIM)" (2019, p. 63).

are highly diverse and not always related to the autonomous, evolutionary-generative purposes that are the focus of this chapter. Some programs, for instance, serve as augmentation systems to facilitate the work of human composers (§6.2) (2019, pp. 63–64); while one system surveyed performs arrangement (2019, p. 64). Importantly, Tatar and Pasquier (2019, p. 65) make a distinction between "mono-agent" and "multi-agent" systems. On this criterion, certain systems I have considered under other rubrics – such as the *Continuator* (§6.5.1.3) and *GenJam* (§6.5.3.2) – would be regarded as (mono-)agent-based. Moreover, the inclusion of the *Continuator* in the mono-agent category indicates that agent-based systems (of both mono- and multi-agent types) use a range of generative methodologies, including those discussed in previous sections, and not just genetic/evolutionary algorithms. Given this considerable variety, and in order to maintain the evolutionary focus of the chapter, my concern in this section is with GA-based multi-agent systems that attempt to simulate evolutionary changes in musical cultures. These often draw upon memetic concepts, albeit rarely explicitly.

Agent-based systems of the latter type may themselves be divided into two categories: *single-replicator* and *dual-replicator* architectures. The former category is concerned solely with either cultural evolution (Lumaca & Baggio, 2017; see also Mcloughlin et al., 2018, discussed in §5.4.2.3), or with biological evolution (Jõks & Pärtel, 2019). The latter category attempts a coevolutionary simulation of replicator interaction (§3.7), such as the modelling of genetic and language-cultural (lexemic) coevolution in Azumagakito et al. (2018), or the modelling of genetic and music-cultural (musemic coevolution in Miranda et al. (2003), discussed below. Dual-replicator systems simulate not only the idea of generations of agents, common to many agent-based systems, but they also allow for the exploration of horizontal (cultural), oblique (cultural) and vertical (biological and cultural) transmission between agents (§3.6). By modelling socio-cultural interactions, dual-replicator systems thus allow for memetic factors to be yoked to genetic factors, in order to test, in microcosm, cultural evolution's role in mediating biological evolution, and vice versa.

Miranda et al. (2003) developed an agent-based system to simulate three interconnected music-evolutionary scenarios: (i) the sexually selected origin of musical preferences (§2.5.3); (ii) the transmission of musical patterns within a community owing to imitation; and (iii) the emergence of musical grammars that combine syntax and semantics (see also Miranda (2003)). In the first of these simulations, agents have a biological sex, with males attempting to woo females using melody. Thus, the simulation encodes a quasi-genetic and a quasi-memetic dimension. Females internalise a set of Markovian transition probabilities (drawn from a training corpus of folk songs) and they use these as criteria to rate the desirability of the male singer (2003, pp. 92–93). The female "mates" with the male producing the most highly rated melody and "has one child per generation created via crossover and mutation with her chosen mate" (2003, p. 92). As with sexual selection in biology, "[t]his child will have a mix of the musical traits and preferences encoded in its mother and father" (2003, p. 92), where "musical traits" is analogous to the "ornament" of sexual selection and "preference" is equivalent to the concept of the same name in biology. A particular variant of this simulation is worthy of mention, one where females rate most highly those males who *violate* the expectations encoded by the transition probabilities of the training corpus. In fact, "in order to get a high surprise score, a tune must first build up expectations, by making transitions to notes that have highly anticipated notes following them, and then violate these expectations, by not using the highly anticipated note" (2003, p. 93). While this simulation does not, to my knowledge, attempt to incorporate the theory of memetic drive (§3.7.1), this would illuminate the issue – not clear from the discussion in Miranda et al. (2003) – of whether the ornament is transmitted (in the terms of the simulation) via genetic or memetic means: is the ornament the capacity to vocalise (equivalent to peacock tail-feathers) or is it the vocalisations themselves (as in bird-song)? Strict adherence to sexual selection theory would require the former, but the dual-replicator coevolutionary orientation of memetic drive expands the focus in order to make a distinction between a genetically controlled preference (including for the aspect of expectation-violation in the ornament) and a memetically transmitted ornament that can reflexively mediate that preference (including the aspect of expectation-violation).

In
simulation is explored using robots – each the physical manifestation of an

agent – capable of hearing and reproducing sounds via auditory analysis, auditory-motor association, motor-control mapping, and voice-synthesis (2003, p. 95, Fig. 2). While an agent-based approach is capable in principle of representing interaction between autonomous creative entities, and of incorporating both memetic and genetic dimensions, the operation of the VRS algorithm occurs covertly within the system, and the principal manifest-ations of the system's processes are often its output logs – in some cases, data constituting the "compositions" produced by the agents at various stages of a cycle. From these, the changing museme-pool of the agent-community might be determined and the nature of the evolutionary changes understood. To make the processes involved more tractable, several agent-based systems employ robots capable of perceiving and generating – "singing" (Miranda & Drouet, 2006; Gimenes et al., 2007) – musical patterns. While such systems, obviously enough, tend not to implement analogues to biological reproduc-tion, their musemic replication is evident in a way that is not the case with more "virtual" systems. Genuine communities of social robots (Miranda, 2008) may be built, and aspects of vocal production and perception may be simulated more directly than is the case with virtual (non-robotic) agents. Nevertheless, it could be argued that, at worst, such systems are "gimmicky", in that all their functionality, and more, could be implemented using virtual agents. Moreover, and as might be inferred from §6.4, the seeming close-ness of such robotic systems to the dynamics of human music-making is arguably illusory, and thus their apparent physicality and vocality is just as "symbolic" – as opposed to "vibrant and visceral" (page 483) – as that of virtual-agent-based systems.

Despite these concerns, the use of robots in the second simulation does expedite the exploration of the vocal learning that is hypothesised to have played a key role in the evolution of music and language (§2.7.5). Here, "expectation is defined as a sensory-motor problem, whereby agents evolve vectors of motor control parameters to produce imitations of heard tunes" (2003, p. 94). While the use of robotic technology in this simulation is not strictly required – one could internalise the processes of listening and repro-ducing in a system – it does allow exploration of the constraints imposed by physicality when listening to and reproducing musical patterns, factors surely mediating memetic (mis)transmission.[282] The simulation indicated that "agents learn by themselves how to correlate perception parameters (analysis) with production (synthesis) ones and they do not necessarily need to build the same motor representations for what is considered to be perceptibly identical .... The repertoire of tunes emerges from the interactions of the agents, and there is no global procedure supervising or regulating them; the actions of each agent are based solely upon their own evolving expectations" (2003, p. 97). The strong tendency towards convergence on a shared repertoire of melodies evident in this simulation is not only driven by social interactions but is also an index of social bonding. In this sense, it supports hypotheses asserting the importance of group sociality cemented by shared musical practice in human evolution (§2.5.2).

In the third (purely cultural-evolutionary) simulation, Miranda et al. (2003) extend the iterated learning approach discussed in §6.3 in order to apply it to music. They simulate the evolution of syntax in short "compositions" based on the concatenation of members of a set of nine melodic "riffs" transmitted through a bottleneck between "teacher" and "learner" agents. The association of two riffs arbitrarily engenders one of twenty-four "emotions" (i.e., "*emotion(riff,riff)*"), which can be recursively embedded (e.g., "*emotion(riff,emotion(riff,riff))*"). Two such "emotion-structures" give rise to one of eight "moods" (2003, pp. 101–102). The outcomes of the simulations using this model were consistent: it was observed that

> [t]he learners are constantly seeking out generalizations in their input. Once a generalization is induced, it will tend to propagate itself because it will, by definition, be used for more than one meaning. In order for any part of the musical culture to survive from one generation to the next, it has to be apparent to each learner in the randomly chosen 200 compositions each learner hears. A composition that is only used for one meaning and is not related to any other composition can only be transmitted if the learner hears that composition in its input. Musical structure, in the form of increasingly general grammar rules, results in a more stable musical culture. The learners no longer need to learn each composition as an isolated, memorized piece of knowledge. Instead, the

---

[282] The second simulation is described as being based on a "mimetic" model (§3.3.1). While Miranda et al. (2003, p. 92) invoke the concept of memes only once, all three simulations draw implicitly on the concept of particulate, culturally transmitted replicators.

> learners can induce rules and regularities that they can then use to create
> new compositions that they themselves have never heard, yet still reflect
> the norms and systematic nature of the culture in which they were born.
> (Miranda et al., 2003, p. 106)

This simulation thus offers further support for the hypothesis that sound-systems move from holism towards increasing compositionality as a result of cultural transmission through a learner bottleneck. To reiterate Kirby's central point in the passage quoted on page 480, it shows that "[a] holistic mapping between a single meaning and a single string will only be transmitted if that particular meaning is observed by a learner. A mapping between a sub-part of a meaning and a [segmented, protemic] sub-string [a riff, in the case of Miranda et al. (2003)] on the other hand will be provided with an opportunity for transmission every time *any meaning is observed that shares that sub-part*" (2013, pp. 129–130; emphasis in the original). Unlike Kirby's models, of course, the third simulation in Miranda et al. (2003) uses music as its substrate for the association with meaning-states and not language – a distinction that seems to dissolve in the light of such ILM simulations. In fostering the origin of compositionality in any type of sound-stream, whether one chooses to conceive of it as musical or linguistic, such simulations afford evidence for Merker's (2012) account of the evolution of compositional language from musilinguistic vocalisations (points 12 and 13 of the list on page 147). Moreover, while post-bifurcation music indicates that compositionality is not necessarily associated with referentiality, the third simulation supports the notion of a semantic association between the resulting compositional protemes and specific extra-musical phenomena, in this case, emotions (points 15 and 16 of the list on page 148). As discussed in §3.8.5, this association might also obtain with musemes as the sonic replicator.

These three simulations arguably do not generate particularly interesting music: their outputs are short, often disjointed, melodic phrases with little musical character (Miranda, 2003, pp. 104–105, Fig. 8, Fig. 9). This often seems to be the case with agent-based systems, perhaps because their primary purpose is less the creation of interesting music – unlike *folk-rnn*, the *Continuator*, or *GenJam* – and more the testing of hypotheses on the cultural evolution of musical and linguistic patterns and structures. Thus, while aesthetically limited, such simulations nevertheless offer strong evidence for the operation of the VRS algorithm and the associated phenomenon of emergence. As Levitin explains, "[w]hen biological complexity arises from simpler forms in small steps, we call it evolution. When a wholly unexpected property – such as human consciousness – arises from a complex system, we call it emergence" (2009, p. 269). Links are made between evolution and consciousness in §7.3.2, which argues that consciousness is a form of evolution and that evolution is a form of consciousness. Agent-based simulations of music and language evolution not only afford evidence in support of these links – rendering them tangible in a relatively short time-scale – but they also suggest that, contrary to Levitin's implicit saltationism, the distinction between evolution and emergence is gradualistic, one of degree, not kind.

6.5.4 Hybrid Systems

This category encompasses two main sub-categories: (i) the combination of two or more of the techniques considered in the previous sections, which, in the systems discussed so far, were deployed in isolation; and (ii) the combination of one or more music-generation algorithms with phenomena in other media (usually the visual realm), these non-musical elements sometimes also being generated algorithmically.

6.5.4.1 Multi-Algorithm Systems

By this category is meant those systems that combine two or more of the generative approaches considered separately above, the output of one algorithm becoming the input to another. This is a common strategy in music generation, the rationale being that quality-enhancing synergies may result from the yoking of algorithms. Two recent multi-algorithm systems adopt essentially the same strategy: they generate music using a GA (§6.5.3.2) and then they filter the GA's output a using a neural network (§6.5.1.2). Specifically, the network is trained on a dataset of HGM in order to act as the fitness function.

Mitrano et al. (2017) uses a GA based on that underpinning Biles' *GenJam* (§6.5.3.2) to generate monophonic solos using a MIDI representation. They then utilised a RNN that forms a component of Google's *Magenta* software – an open-source project exploring deep learning techniques in visual art and music (Google, 2021) – as the fitness function. Specifically, they used *Magenta's Improv RNN*, which is pre-trained on a large dataset of melodies, in order to use what it had learned as a filter for the melodies generated by the GA component of their system. In studies comparing human-judgement fitness functions with the *Improv RNN*-based fitness function, Mitrano et al. (2017) found that the latter offered a more consistent, efficient and parsimonious assessment of fitness (Mitrano et al., 2017, pp. 4–6). Indeed, "although the conventions of functional tonal harmony are not explicitly encoded in *Improv RNN*, it is able to recognize basic triadic and diatonic hierarchical weightings that correspond to those conventions" (2017, p. 4). *Improv RNN* was thus able to assess (select) music in terms of the kinds of learned but innately shaped pitch representations that are formalised, for instance, in Krumhansl and Kessler (1982) and Krumhansl (1990) and that, as humans do, it had abstracted from its training set.

In an analogous approach, Farzaneh and Toroghi (2020) present a melody-generation system that filters the output of a GA, seeded with a database of folk melodies in ABC representation, through a LSTM acting as the fitness function. Specifically, their network is a *bi-directional LSTM* (Bi-LSTM), which is "an LSTM whose parameters represent the forward and backward correlations of the adjacent notes or frames of the musical signal ..." (2020, p. 2). Whereas Mitrano et al. (2017) run and test human-based and RNN-based fitness functions in parallel, in a two-stage process, Farzaneh and Toroghi (2020) deploy them in series, in a three-stage process: the outputs of their GA are first evaluated by human judges, and then the most highly rated melodies are fed into the Bi-LSTM in order to train it to serve as a fitness function. Thus, unlike the use of *Improv RNN* in Mitrano et al. (2017), which has already been trained on a musical dataset, the Bi-LSTM in Farzaneh and Toroghi (2020) learns what (some) humans find desirable on the basis of their "training" on a musical dataset. This means that, in the former system, the ANN-as-fitness-function indirectly captures human preferences (as they have played out over extended time-frames in the production and reception of music) whereas, in the latter, they are more directly (but perhaps more narrowly) represented.

An issue taken up again in §6.6.2, it is clear from both these studies that significant quality enhancements accrue from using what are essentially Darwinian algorithms in tandem: a GA is explicitly Darwinian, because it operationalises the VRS algorithm in code; an ANN is implicitly Darwinian, because (as noted in §6.2) it takes varied input data and selects certain of the patterns detected therein for replication in its output. A further extension of multi-algorithm systems – perhaps one implicit in the approach pursued by Mitrano et al. (2017) – is that suggested by Collins, whereby, in a "future feedback loop, … output algorithmic compositions are created by systems trained on real musical examples, and algorithmic outputs may in turn become the next generation of available music [for training]" (2018, pp. 11–12, Fig. 1). In this way, machines might be able to escape the constraints of human taste-cultures and establish their own independent frameworks for evaluation.

6.5.4.2 Multimedia Systems

This category refers to a generative algorithm that produces music to accompany another medium, most usually moving images, that carries some form of narrative. Such systems have primarily been developed to provide music to accompany video games (Plut & Pasquier, 2020), but virtual reality (VR) and augmented reality (AR) are other candidate application domains.[283] In such environments the system is not simply generating music as a stand-alone output, as in *folk-rnn* or *Iamus*. Rather – in a significant augmentation of the interactive performance dynamic of systems such as the *Continuator* and *Gen-Jam* – it is generating music in response to a rapidly changing context whose twists and turns result from the user's responses to real-time situations and myriad choice-points. Clearly such systems must not only produce internally coherent music, but they must also respond to the kinetic and affective states implied by the visual dimension and its objects and protagonists.

An example of a system in this category is *Kantor*, named after the pioneer of set theory, Georg Cantor (Velardo, 2019). *Kantor* is an interactive

---

[283] Such systems have not yet gained a secure foothold in film music, perhaps because of the higher status and greater economic muscle of film-music composers (certainly when speaking of the leading figures) compared with composers of video-game music. The increasing cultural prominence of video-game music (as evidenced by concerts and recordings of this music) suggests this imbalance may not be permanent.

system, partly inspired by ideas of Xenakis (2001), whereby the music for nine "islands" is produced by a generative algorithm. Each island is a three-dimensional space based on a two-dimensional image synthesised using geometrical-graphical elements – graphemes – derived from the style of the late abstract paintings by Kandinsky. Using a VR headset, a user moves through the dissociated elements of the *faux*-Kandinsky 3D-painting – as if the painting had been shattered into fragments by an explosion – each geometrical-graphical element being associated with a specific instrumental line of the complete generated composition. Movement towards and away from these floating painting-elements produces a corresponding adjustment in the configuration of the music, because

> [t]he different islands have unique sonic profiles, achieved through different arrangements of instrumental ensembles. Each geometrical pattern in an island is an audio source that broadcasts an instrumental part. The sound in the experience is spatialised and surrounds the player. The polyphonic music emerges through the interaction between the music associated with each shape and the player's position. By flying across an island, the player can experience infinite, slightly different implementations of the same piece. The music isn't static. It's a living being that evolves as a function of the player's position and the dynamic distances between the geometrical shapes. (Velardo, 2019, sec. 3)

This form of intra-game "evolution" is more metaphorical than literal: a piece is assembled extra-game in the initial generative process, and then the player experiences different sonic perspectives on that piece – its meta-morphoses – during their "flight" within the image. In fact, *Kantor* does not use an evolutionary algorithm, relying instead upon "stochastic (random) mathematical functions to generate musical sequences" – i.e., upon a Markov model (Velardo, 2019, sec. 3). Nevertheless, a true form of evolution is to be found in the extra-game, post-generation adjustments undertaken by the programmers before the music is deemed finalised. These "re-appropriate the creative process by polishing the generated material". At a more sys-temic level, the programmers "take an educated guess of what might not be working in the generative system, based on its creative output. As a result of this diagnostic phase, we change the initial instructions. In more radical circumstances, we tweak the code of the system to implement our *desiderata*"

(Velardo, 2019, sec. 1). These extra-game processes afford the variation (via "polishing", reconfiguration and recoding), selection (via determination of the optimum "tweaks"), and replication (via re-incorporation of the selected elements into the system) at the work level and the system level necessary for the VRS algorithm to bootstrap quality in this domain (see also Figure 6.14 and the associated discussion).

One significant dimension of *Kantor*'s operation is its invocation of a graphical equivalent to the linguistic principle of compositionality, whereby "[t]he meaning of a Kandinsky painting emerges through the interaction ... of single patterns, such as lines, circles and squares. When considered individually, these patterns don't display much artistic quality.... However, when enough patterns are wisely composed together, an aesthetic quality emerges" (Velardo, 2019, sec. 2). In linguistic compositionality, structures and meanings arise from the assembly of lexemes in syntactic-semantic configurations; in musical compositionality, musemes assemble to generate musemeplexes and musemesätze; and in image-based compositionality, the wider structure and sense of a painting emerges from the association of its component graphemes. In *Kantor*, the image-based compositionality gives rise to a form of musical compositionality in which sound-layers recombine horizontally-polyphonically – as when one hears the ever-changing combinations of sounds in a cityscape as one moves through it – as opposed to the vertical-paratactic recombination hypothesised to underpin musical generation in the RHSGAP model (§3.5.2).

Figure 6.11 shows a human-generated image in the style of late Kandinsky (Figure 6.11a), and the associated *Kantor*-generated music ("Kantor #8", subtitled "mystery") (Figure 6.11b).

The transcription in Figure 6.11b – a notation of the two-part stratum/track "mystery_1" does not do the music justice because, as noted, it is only one stratum – a graphical-object-associated instrumental part – of a complex polydimensional texture. In combination, the lines comprising Kantor #8 create a Gamelan-like texture, with subtly shifting and luminously oscillating tuned-percussion sonorities. The extract shown rises chromatically through a major third from a (mis-notated) implied tonic A♭ major to its mediant C major. This is usually accomplished here by a straightforward semitonal

(a) *Faux*-Kandinsky Image.

(b) Associated Output of *Kantor*.

Figure 6.11: Sample Output of *Kantor*.

ascent connecting the stages from I to III, but there is a neo-Riemannian L-operator (*Leittonwechsel*) shift that breaks the pattern. Enabled by resolving the A major of b. 4 to its local tonic, D minor, b. 5, the fall of a major third to the mid-point of the ascent, B♭, implements the L-operator (D⁻→<L>→B♭⁺); with an implied upper-voice motion from a¹–b♭¹ across bb. 5–6), from which point the semitonal ascent to C major resumes. Heard in conjunction with the other instrumental strata, however, there are certain contradictions to the progression just outlined. In fact, the harmony of b. 5 is, *en bloc*, B♭ major, not D minor (a B♭ is added to the D and F by other strata), and so there is no global L-operator, only a local, stratum-specific one, and therefore only a more conventional chromatic ascent. Nevertheless, as an antidote to this relatively uninventive harmonic framework, the B-minor harmony implied for most of b. 7 is in fact subsumed into a diminished-seventh chord. Its f♯ therefore implies a half-diminished-seventh chord (G♯-B-D-F♯) abutting dissonantly with the full-diminished-seventh (G♯-B-D-F♮) of the complete texture. A trace of this more complex harmony is afforded by the g♯ of b. 7^4. Another example of harmonic blending is the elision of the two final chords (the half/full-diminished-seventh and the C major), with elements of the former seventh chord persisting into b. 10. The same process of juxtaposition explains the g♯¹ in b. 4, which, while only appearing in this stratum on the third beat, is present throughout bb. 3–4 in the full "picture", as a suspension of the root of the previous G♯/A♭ harmony.

6.6 Machine Creativity

In addition to its advancement of computer science, the computer analysis and synthesis of music is an important tool for music psychology, offering a powerful means of developing and testing models of music perception, cognition and generation. Boden (2004) has explored the last of these, considering to what extent machines might possess the faculty of creativity – and thus give rise to processes or outputs that manifest it – and how this might illuminate our understanding of human creativity. In this sense Boden's model is orientated squarely around human creativity, and – while a formulation challenged to some extent in §6.6.2 – machine creativity is understood as to some extent parasitic on it. However, as §5.5 has argued, creativity can be understood in (Universal-)Darwinian terms, and thus while it is seen by many as a purely human attribute, there is a case for extending its reach to encompass the "outputs" (the vocalisations) of animals and – as is implicit in much of the foregoing discussion – those of machines. Thus, beyond using machines to shed light on human creativity, the generative power of the systems surveyed in this chapter, together with the many others that constraints of space meant could not be considered, implies that their outputs should be judged on their own terms, as potentially aesthetic objects. If this is accepted, it follows that there is a need for the *evaluation* of the outputs of music-generative systems, and indeed of systems designed to generate artistic outputs in other domains. Moreover, there is a higher-level need for a *meta-critical evaluation of the methodologies for evaluation* of the outputs of music-generative systems.

6.6.1 Can Machines be Creative?

The issue of computational creativity relates to the second and the fourth of the four "Lovelace-questions" – named after the nineteenth-century mathematician Lady Ada Lovelace (1815–1852) – identified by Boden:

> The first Lovelace-question is whether computational ideas can help us understand how *human* creativity is possible. The second is whether computers (now or in the future) could ever do things which at least *appear to be* creative. The third is whether a computer could ever appear to *recognize* creativity – in poems written by human poets, for instance. And the fourth is whether computers themselves could ever *really* be creative (as opposed to merely producing apparently creative performance whose originality is wholly due to the human programmer). (Boden, 2004, pp. 16–17; emphases in the original)

Questions two and four are, respectively, what might be termed "hard" and "soft" versions of the Turing Test. Question two relates to the ability of a computer to fool a human observer that a piece of music (for instance) it produced is the work of another human, as in the case of tests of Cope's EMI via The Game discussed on page 491 (but see again the critique of applications of the TT to non-natural-language media by Ariza (2009) in §6.1 and raised again in connection with The Game). Question four relates to the same ability, but replaces the "smoke and mirrors" of question two with real magic. Even though these two questions concern putative examples of non-human creativity, they aim ostensibly to model processes and perceptions operative in human music-making.[284] Whether the fruits of computers' electronic labours deserve credit as "honorary" human music, whether we consider them relativistically as a kind of extended "animal music", or whether we consider them as *sui generis*, is nevertheless a moot point.

While Boden's (2004) approach is admirably rigorous, it is impeded by the fundamental problem that whereas the development of algorithms for the machine-generation of music is objective, scientific and tangible, creativity is, by contrast, subjective, humanistic and intangible, and thus there is a fundamental dissociation between the two domains. There have been several attempts to define creativity (Runco, 2014), including Boden's own categories of P- and H-creativity and, within these, combinational, exploratory and transformational creativity (2004, pp. 3–6) (§5.5.1). All are compromised, however, by the slippery intersubjectivity of creativity: no two people will necessarily agree on what constitutes creativity, and there is no fixed standard by which someone's experience or qualifications allow them to trump the assessments of others. Moreover, this intersubjectivity combines both analogue (graded) and digital (all-or-nothing) judgements: one can deem something (or some component part of something) to be creative or not; and one can also entertain judgements of something's (or some component part of something) being more or less creative than something else.

The title of the following section implies that the answer to the question at the head of the present section is in the affirmative but, as the foregoing discussion indicates, the issue is not clear cut: leaving aside the problem of (inter)subjectivity, one could develop and test methodologies for the evaluation of machine creativity and find that, judged in their light, there is no such creativity evident in the sampled processes or outputs. While this does not necessarily verify that there is no such thing as machine creativity (or falsify its existence) – the evaluation methodology, or the interpretation of its outcomes, might be at fault; or the chosen sample might not demonstrate creativity, however defined – it at least gives one a starting point for develop-

---

[284] Lovelace indeed believed that computers might eventually be able to generate music, arguing that if "the fundamental relations of pitched sounds in the signs of harmony and of musical composition were susceptible of such [numerical] expressions and adaptations, the [computer] might compose elaborate and scientific pieces of music of any degree of complexity or extent" (in Herremans & Sörensen, 2013, p. 6427).

ing models for evaluation and for reflexively refining the generative systems themselves. Adopting the standpoint on creativity articulated in §5.5.2, if Darwinism represents a form of creativity (defined as combinational, exploratory or transformational operations conducted to locate solutions within a problem space); and if a generative system wholly or partly implements the VRS algorithm (whether because of its evolutionary architecture or in spite of its ostensibly non-evolutionary architecture); then that system has at least the potential to be creative and thus its resulting CGM embodies (or tokens) that creativity, whether or not the latter manifests itself in ways that align with the more circumscribed notions of creativity – shaped by culturally evolved notions of musical style, structure and genre – that generally attend HGM.

6.6.2 The Evaluation of Machine Creativity

There are several dimensions according to which machine (and human) creativity might be evaluated. While constraints of space prevent a comprehensive treatment, Jordanous (2012, Ch. 2), Loughran and O'Neill (2017) and Meraviglia (2020, pp. 16–17) offer overviews of issues and literature in this area.[285] The principal issues in this field are summarised under the following three rubrics and discussed more fully in what follows. Note that the terms of each rubric are non-exclusive, existing as points on a continuum rather than as binarisms.

1. *The Ontology of Evaluation*: Should evaluation focus upon some abstraction of the creativity of the system's processes, or instead upon one or more of its concrete outputs, as tokens of those processes? If the latter, does their ontology affect their evaluation? To what extent is the creativity of a system or its outputs an analogue or digital property?

2. *Qualitative versus Quantitative*: Should system outputs be judged qualitatively or quantitatively, both according to a set of evaluation criteria? While they are not coterminous, qualitative assessments imply the predominance of subjective over objective factors, whereas the converse is the case for quantitative assessments.

---

[285] Oft-cited evaluation methodologies include Ritchie's criteria for creativity (2007), Colton's "creative tripod" model (2008), the FACE and IDEA models (Colton et al., 2011; Charnley et al., 2012), Jordanous's own SPECS framework (2012), considered below, and the Apprentice Framework (Negrete-Yankelevich & Morales-Zaragoza, 2014).

3. *Intra- or Extra-Human Perception and Cognition*: Should only those outputs of music-generative systems that accord with the constraints of human perception and cognition be evaluated, or should those outputs that transcend those limits also be admitted?

Apropos point 1, it may be the case that a system demonstrates localised or generalised instances of creativity in its *processes*, but that its generated *outputs* are themselves of limited creative value – however system- or output-level creativity is defined, captured and assessed. This issue inheres, partly in the wider question of the ontology of the outputs of music-generative systems. That is, evaluation is partly contingent upon the extent to which a system's outputs align with the two dominant models of music in human culture: *music-as-work* and *music-as-process* – Taruskin's (1995) distinction between *text* and *act* (§1.3, §2.1, §5.1). In the former (musicological) case, a minority of human music ("classical" or "art") is organised into objects (works), is preserved and transmitted by elaborate notational systems, and is aestheticised in a canonic discourse. In the latter (ethnomusicological) case, the vast majority of human music ("world" and "popular") exists as a process, is preserved in memory and transmitted orally, and serves an array of social functions, religious, political and personal. When the outputs (as distinct from the generative processes) of machines are assessed as potentially creative, criteria of value may differ according to whether these outputs exist as texts or acts, in Taruskin's sense. When outputs come under the category of music-as-work (texts), and whatever specific ontological model one applies to them (Puy, 2017; §5.5.2), there is a predominant focus upon the synchronic factors of large-scale (global) structural coherence, carefully controlled handling of repetition and variation, and long-term/cumulative effect. As with early analytical and critical responses to Beethoven's music – which attempted to discern an overarching order that transcended the local moments of seeming discontinuity – evaluation of CGM in this category reads it in the light of criteria and values derived from the reception of the canonic masterworks of HGM (§4.4.1). When outputs come under the category of music-as-process (acts, this distinct from the generative-creative acts/processes of the parent system), the focus is upon the diachronic factors of moment-to-moment (local) narrative coherence, appropriateness of consequents in relation to their motivating antecedents, and short-term, hedonic affect/effect. Criteria of value for music in this category might also include the extent to which the system motivates a desire in a human musician to collaborate with it (Kalonaris, 2018, p. 2).

Apropos point 2 of the list on page 541, extant approaches to creativity-evaluation may be variously qualitative or quantitative. One very widely used qualitative approach is the Consensual Assessment Technique (CAT) (Amabile, 1982; refined in Hennessey et al., 2011). This is used "for the assessment of creativity and other aspects of products, relying on the independent subjective judgments of individuals familiar with the domain in which the products were made" (Hennessey et al., 2011, p. 253). At the risk of oversimplification, the CAT essentially relies on intersubjective expertise as the arbiter of judgements on creativity. This majoritarian-relativist view is understood in Darwinian terms at the end of this section; but a minoritarian-absolutist might argue against it, on the grounds that the wisdom of (educated) crowds might nevertheless be trumped by the greater wisdom of the (even more educated) individual. The majoritarian-relativist counter-argument to this stance is that the evaluation of creative artifacts is not scientific, and thus the aesthetic value of an art-object is a function of what the majority view finds valuable, just as the economic value of a commodity or a service inheres in the what the majority of purchasers would be prepared to pay for it.

Perhaps the most widely cited quantitative methodology of recent years is the Standardised Procedure for Evaluating Creative Systems (SPECS) framework developed by Jordanous (2012, p. 138, Tab. 5.1), which identifies fourteen "components" or "building blocks" of creativity in terms of which a system's processes and outputs might be judged. The components of this "ontology of creativity" are (in Jordanous's alphabetical listing): (i) "active involvement and persistence"; (ii) "generation of results"; (iii) "dealing with uncertainty"; (iv) "domain competence"; (v) "general intellectual ability"; (vi) "independence and freedom"; (vii) "intention and emotional involvement"; (viii) "originality"; (ix) "progression and development"; (x) "social interaction and communication"; (xi) "spontaneity/subconscious processing"; (xii) "thinking and evaluation"; (xiii) "value"; and (xiv) "variety, divergence and experimentation" (2012, pp. 118–120, Fig. 4.7). Processes and outputs need not score highly all these components in order to qualify as creative; indeed, two components in particular are difficult to align with generative systems: component (vii) ("[p]ersonal and emotional investment, immersion, self-expression, involvement in a process; [i]ntention and desire to perform a task, a positive process giving fulfilment and enjoyment" (2012, p. 119)) implies a degree of physicality lacking in computer systems; and component (x) ("[c]ommunicating and promoting work to others in a persuasive, positive manner; [m]utual influence, feedback, sharing and collaboration between society and individual" (2012, p. 119)) is only possible in facsimile via agent-based systems (§273). The two criteria minimally constitutive of creativity (the necessary conditions) given on page 450 – novelty and value – correspond to Jordanous's components (viii) ("originality")/(xiv) ("variety, divergence and experimentation") and (xiii) ("value"), respectively.

While broadly framed as a quantitative approach, it is nevertheless clear that determining the degree to which a particular component of Jordanous's framework is satisfied in a system's processes or outputs is inherently qualitative and thus subjective. Given this, it is arguably not possible to verify or falsify a claim made apropos a process in or object of HGM or CGM in relation to a specific framework component (2012, pp. 36–37). Jordanous sidesteps this objection by maintaining that "[t]here are ... a number of differences between SPECS and scientific method, largely due to how SPECS handles the non-scientific and dynamic nature of computational creativity" (2012, p. 157). Thus, both computational creativity and the SPECS framework are a complex mixture of scientific and non-scientific components, and the latter's subjectivity obscures the objective treatment of the former. While their own claims to objectivity are arguably overstressed – see the "final consideration" of §4.4.3, on page 360 – music theory and analysis offer a means by which the evaluation of the processes and outputs of music-generative systems might be supported. Specifically, they can add a quasi-scientific backstop to Jordanous's criteria (iv), (v), (viii), (ix), (xiii) and (xiv) in ways that might indeed allow for specific claims to be verified or falsified (§6.6.3).

Apropos point 3 of the list on page 542, another difficulty with the evaluation of machine creativity is the potential for computers to transcend human psychological constraints (Lerdahl, 1992). This may lead to the production of music that is partly or wholly beyond the perceptual-cognitive grasp of humans, such that the music is regarded, in the extreme, as noise.[286] This potential has already been realised by some human composers: the "New Complexity" school, as represented by the music of Brian Ferneyhough and Michael Finnissy, arguably illustrates the tendency most clearly. Such music, human- or computer-generated, would occupy what Velardo terms "Region Three" of the "Circle of Sound" (2014, pp. 15–17). As represented in Figure 6.12, after (Velardo, 2014, p. 16, Fig. 1), this circle contains everything that might be regarded as "music" – in itself a problematic concept. "Region One" contains low-complexity music that entirely respects human perceptual-cognitive constraints (2014, pp. 15–16). "Region Two" encompasses higher complexity music that requires some degree of training or knowledge – implying, therefore, a "competent, experienced listener" (Meyer, 1973, p. 110) – to appreciate its complexities fully (2014, p. 16). Region Three encompasses music that, on account of its violation of our perceptual-cognitive constraints, is too complex for the human mind to perceive and cognise – if not (*pace* Ferneyhough and Finnissy) to generate – and that might reasonably be assumed to be an inevitable product of computer, as opposed to human, creativity (2014, p. 17). Separated from Region Two by a "Horizon of Intelligibility" represented by the thick black line in Figure 6.12 (2014, pp. 16–17), Region Three is potentially the largest, on account of its freedom from the relatively tight constraints operating upon human perception and cognition (Figure 6.12 is not drawn to scale; the dotted line at the outer circumference represents the potentially infinite size of Region Three).

From this model Velardo and Vallati (2016, p. 11) derive the notions of *anthropocentric* and *non-anthropocentric* creativity. The former, occupying Region One and Region Two of Figure 6.12, encompasses creativity that is by and for humans. The latter, crossing the Horizon of Intelligibility and occupying Region Three, encompasses creativity that is beyond human appreciation and that is therefore restricted to non-human auditors (machines and perhaps intelligent aliens). Region Three might be accessible to humans if we could be genetically re-engineered in order to restructure our perceptual-cognitive apparatus to allow us to process its contents; or – more organically – if we were to evolve in the light of the selection pressures this music imposes. The

---

[286] For the issue of "noise in and as music", see Cassidy and Einbond (2013).

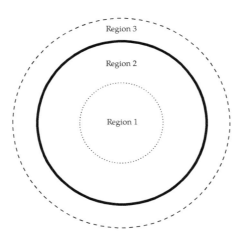

Figure 6.12: The "Circle of Sound".

latter is perhaps unlikely, given that competences deployed in the processing of Region One and Region Two (anthropocentric) music are likely an exaptation from capacities evolved in response to more urgent, survival-related demands; and given that, conversely, the inability to perceive and cognise very complex music is unlikely to put us at a significant survival disadvantage in the modern world. Nevertheless, memetic drive might be able to push genes in the direction of computer-analogous competences, in order to serve the interests of very complex, Region-Three (non-anthropocentric) musemes.

Expanding upon the categories of anthropocentric and non-anthropocentric creativity, Velardo and Vallati (2016, pp. 11–12) arrive at the framework summarised below:

- Anthropocentric Creativity

    Humans for Humans (2H): encompasses the bulk of human creativity and its entirety before the invention of computers.

    Computer-Aided for Humans (CH): relates to the use of computers as an augmentation system to support human creativity (§6.2).

    AI for Humans (AIH): involves technology able to motivate an affirmative answer to at least the second Lovelace-question (i.e., "whether computers (now or in the future) could ever do things which at least *appear to be* creative") and ideally the fourth (i.e., "whether computers themselves could ever *really* be creative (as opposed to merely producing apparently creative performance whose originality is wholly due to the human pro-grammer)") (Boden, 2004, pp. 16–17; emphases in the original) (§6.6.1).

- Non-Anthropocentric Creativity

  AI for AI (2AI): encompasses all creativity that is by machines and that is comprehensible only to other machines.

Non-anthropocentric creativity presupposes (i) non-anthropocentric dis-crimination and (ii) non-anthropocentric taste: (i) is the ability of machines to distinguish between functional uses of their competences and artistic/aes-thetic uses – akin to the ability of humans to distinguish between the skills required to solve a crossword puzzle and those required to write a sonata; and (ii) is the ability to value their creative outputs (in the light of (i)).[287] Taste, as the product of cultural evolution, is itself creative, because it is a verbal-conceptual memeplex (§3.4) that, like all memes, selfishly "seeks" its own survival by arriving at solutions that have the effect of expediting its rep-lication. One way of achieving this is for it to evolve a fit, via coevolution, with other memes and memeplexes, such as those constituting a particular cultural phenomenon or product. It is surely no accident that the growth of a public musical culture in Europe in the late-eighteenth and early-nineteenth cen-turies was associated with a rise in music criticism (Hoffmann, 1998): both replicator types – musemes/musemeplexes and verbal-conceptual memes/memeplexes – were mutually interdependent, because without the musemes of the musical culture there would be no motivation for the verbal-conceptual memes of the critical culture; and without the latter the former would not have been so extensively replicated.

A mechanism for this coevolution was proposed in connection with the discussion of sexual selection in §2.5.3, offering an account of taste-formation that does not depend upon the existence of absolute standards of value. To reiterate as a statement this mechanism, outlined as a question on page 108,

---

[287] Indeed, machines might value the creative outputs of other machines more highly than those of humans – which they might perhaps regard as hopelessly banal – preferring instead to dream of electric sonatas (Dick, 1968).

"a culturally transmitted ornament – a particular complement of musemes …
– [might] have been associated with a culturally transmitted preference – a
taste-related liking for the ornament represented by those musemes … – such
that they existed in a cultural linkage disequilibrium, i.e., in an alignment that
is more consistent than would be expected on the basis of random association
alone". One implication of this mechanism is there are no absolute standards
of taste, only relative ones; and thus the judgements that are sustained by a
taste-culture – the "acts" sustained by its "texts" – are subjective, not objective.
One therefore does not necessarily have to be a postmodernist to endorse
relativism: in Universal Darwinism, all assessments are local, contingent
and, ultimately, selfish.

In general, most approaches to the evaluation of machine creativity assume an
anthropocentric perspective, specifically (apropos the framework of Velardo
and Vallati (2016) on page 546) an AIH orientation. This is perhaps not
surprising, given that: (i) humans, for the various reasons outlined above,
aspire to develop systems that can organise sounds in ways that are recognisably musical (i.e., to be as close as possible to HGM); and (ii) 2AI is not,
by definition, subject to the constraints attendant upon (i). Having reviewed
a number of different categories of generative system, is it possible to determine which is/are the most likely to score well on AIH-based rubrics? In
other words, which algorithm type, or which combination of algorithms –
recombination systems, neural networks, Markov models, grammar-based
systems, constraint-satisfaction systems, local-search algorithms, or genetic/
evolutionary algorithms, to recall the categories of §6.5 – is able to produce
the most "realistic" music (according to comparison with some stylistic ex-
emplar(s) of HGM) and/or the most "convincing" music (from a quasi-TT
perspective), from the perspective of a human listener?

While resolving this question depends largely upon which of the approaches
to evaluation discussed above one takes – and how one operationalises it
and assesses its outcomes – it seems that, on balance, a generative strategy
that assimilates music-stylistic norms and pattern vocabularies from extant
corpora and that then bootstraps the outcomes of this learning using selective
processes would likely stand the best chance of producing "AIH-compliant"
CGM. I say this simply because this is how – certainly in the view articulated

in this book – music is generated in human cultures, as formalised by the operation of the VRS algorithm on musemes. A broad mechanistic alignment between generative processes might therefore reasonably be assumed to give rise to a close structural and perceptual-cognitive alignment between CGM and HGM, leading to a positive evaluation of the former. Thus, neural network models whose statistical learning of a corpus is subsequently refined by means of a GA seem, on this logic, the most well suited to producing "realistic" and "convincing" CGM. But the two systems (admittedly a very small sample) discussed in §6.5.4.1 – Mitrano et al. (2017) and Farzaneh and Toroghi (2020) – take the *opposite* approach: they refine the output of a GA using a neural network (GA → ANN); indeed, I know of no system that works the other way round (ANN → GA).

There are three reasons why this apparent sub-optimal sequencing of algorithms is insignificant from a cultural-evolutionary perspective. First, and as argued in §6.5.4.1, the VRS algorithm is intrinsic to both architectures, explicitly in the case of the GA and implicitly in the case of the ANN, and so it is perhaps irrelevant which is invoked first. Secondly, in the systems developed by Mitrano et al. (2017) and Farzaneh and Toroghi (2020) the ANN is tightly integrated into the GA as the fitness function, so the architecture is fundamentally a GA if one regards the fitness function as a "slot" that can be filled by a broad range of possible mechanisms for fitness-determination. Thirdly, and most fundamentally, the VRS algorithm is perhaps best understood as a bidirectional circle, not a line: while the initial impulse of the algorithm perhaps came from replication – this resulting from the appearance of "an entity ... capable of behavior that staves off, however primitively, its own dissolution and decomposition ..." (Dennett, 1993a, p. 174) – any one of variation, replication and selection can be the starting (or entry) point of an evolutionary process in an already established system, such as those musical (sub)cultures drawn upon and simulated by music-generative programs.

6.6.3 The Theory and Analysis of Computer-Generated Music

Whether CGM is realistic or convincing – to recall the two anthropocentric evaluation criteria from §6.6.2 – depends upon certain factors that music theory and analysis are well suited to model. While much attention has been given to methods for generating music using computers; and while almost as much thought has been given to strategies for evaluating the outputs as music, little consideration has been given, to my knowledge, to the music-theoretical aspects of CGM or to strategies for analysing it – but see Various (2012) for the broader context and methodology – analysis being understood here as a *species of evaluation*, even as a means for the verification or falsification of evaluative judgements (page 544). Nor, indeed, has the more fundamental issue of developing a philosophy to determine whether such music (collectively or in individual instances) warrants, by analogy with HGM,[288] such theoretical/analytical treatment in the first place.

The human-centricity of music theory and analysis (§4.4) poses certain problems for those wishing to extend it from HGM to CGM. This is partly because the motivations for music-related computational creativity are (non-exclusively) binary: from a scientific perspective, and as noted in §6.1, the inherent complexity of music, resulting from its multiparametric combinatoriality, makes it an irresistible challenge for computer science; from a humanistic perspective there is strangeness and beauty in experiencing music made by a non-human entity, when that music is not presented to listeners in the form of a Turing Test. The aesthetic frisson of the latter is not dissimilar to that arising from hearing the vocalisations of certain non-human animals (§5.4). Whichever motivation drives the application of music theory and analysis to CGM – the former might use it to verify the efficacy of an algorithm, the latter might use it to illuminate similar phenomena appearing in HGM – there are inevitably thorny philosophical issues, one of which is encompassed by the question of how should music theory and analysis approach CGM, and what does CGM have to offer ("as a goal or as a goad", to recall Kerman's phrase (1994b, p. 61)) to theory and analysis?

In terms of affecting the conception and practice of music theory and analysis as it applies to both HGM and CGM, it is useful to consider how the VRS algorithm relates to the three poles of the semiological tripartition. Figure 6.13

---

[288] As this book has stressed, HGM comes in a dazzling variety of forms according – to give just two constraints – to the cultural background and level of training of the composer/producer. My focus in this section is primarily on HGM produced by trained professional composers and written (as opposed to improvised) in broadly western art-music traditions.

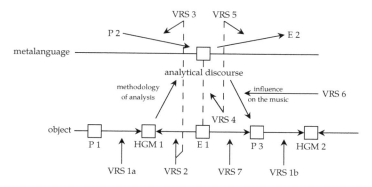

Figure 6.13: Theory and Analysis in HGM.

and Figure 6.14, after Figure 4.9, adapt Nattiez's model of "object, metalanguage and method" discussed in §4.6 in order to represent this interaction.

In Figure 6.13, the VRS algorithm drives seven stages of the process. It should be noted that this is a considerable oversimplification, and that there are, in reality, multiple connections between the nodes identified, these forming a highly complex and dynamic nexus:

VRS 1: VRS 1a drives the first poietic stage (P 1), by means of intra- and inter-brain memetic processes, resulting in the production of an object (i.e., a work) and/or a process (i.e., an improvisation) constituting HGM and situated at the neutral level (as score and/or sound), both forms being represented by the element labelled "HGM 1" in Figure 6.13.

VRS 2: mediates the esthesic stage (E 1), in that the extant memetic and musemic complement of a listener acts as a filter for the input musemes of the products of VRS 1a. There are numerous modes of listening, so while (primarily or secondarily) listening for aesthetic/subjective pleasure, the listener may, as a theorist/analyst, may attend to the music (secondarily or primarily) by deploying this more "intellectual" mode. Using the mental representation formed from HGM 1 (and potentially many other instances of HGM), in addition to knowledge of various theoretical/analytical discourses, this "bifocal" listening may serve: (i) to develop a theory (VRS 3); and/or (ii) to guide its analytical application, or the application of another theory (VRS 4).

VRS 3: receiving input from VRS 2 and from other instances of VRS 2 processes (represented by the left-hand vertical dotted line), this drives the poiesis (P 2) of a theoretical/analytical discourse – a metalanguage – that is reified in the form of a published text, or several (inter)texts (Allen, 2011), that constitute the phemotypic form of the theoretical/analytical verbal-conceptual memeplex.

VRS 4: mediates the connection between the theoretical/analytical discourse and the esthesis (E 1) of HGM 1 (represented by the central vertical dotted line). On occasions, the analyst may engage both modes of listening referred to apropos VRS 2, and so there are two, difficult-to-separate, sources for E 1: (i) that arising from an aesthetic/subjective response to HGM 1 (VRS 2); and (ii) that arising from a theoretical/analytical response to it – i.e., one related to the application of a particular discourse pertaining to it (VRS 4).

VRS 5: drives, analogously to VRS 2, the reception (E 2) of the theoretical/analytical discourse within the community that engages with it, in the light of: (i) its perceived alignment with, and development of, its intellectual tradition (including its potentially heightened explanatory power *vis-à-vis* its antecedent models); and/or (ii) its perceived alignment with its target HGM, this mediated by interaction with processes encompassed by VRS 4 (represented by the right-hand vertical dotted line).

VRS 6: mediates (by way of its effects on composers and improvisers) the "influence on the music" of one or more theoretical/analytical discourses, this being particularly evident in certain conservative traditions. It acts in conjunction with a re-iteration of VRS 1 (VRS 1b), giving rise to a consequent/child (HGM 2) of the antecedent/parent (HGM 1) arising from VRS 1a.

VRS 7: mediates the influence of esthesic (E 1) responses to HGM 1 on the poiesis (P 3) of a consequent HGM (HGM 2). In some cases, such as Rameau and Babbitt, the composer may also be a theorist (beyond the general understanding of theory, formal or otherwise, evident in most accomplished musicians). While the layout of Figure 6.13 is intended to indicate that such VRS 6-related responses are distinct from those pertaining to VRS 7, in reality they may well blend, and so there are, by analogy with VRS 4, two difficult-to-separate sources for P 3: (i) that arising from aesthetic/subjective responses to HGM 1 (VRS 2/VRS 7); and (ii) that arising from responses mediated by a theoretical/analytical discourse (VRS 6).

In Figure 6.14, there are two distinct tripartitional processes operating, one for the generative system and the other for the resulting music. They are shaped

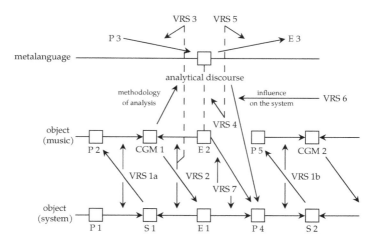

Figure 6.14: Theory and Analysis in CGM.

by VRS processes that are analogous across the two domains of technology and music. To adapt and supplement the points made apropos Figure 6.13:

VRS 1:   • Down-arrow: P 1 drives the design and coding of the music-generative system itself (S 1), leading to the production of a program that is situated, as electronically stored code and executables, at the neutral level.

   • Up-arrow: S 1 – in the case of those systems using genetic/evolutionary algorithms – then generates (diagonal arrow from S 1 to P 2) the output CGM (CGM 1), a process broadly analogous to the operation of VRS 1a in Figure 6.13.

VRS 2:   • Down-arrow: broadly analogous to VRS 5 in Figure 6.13, this mediates the reception (E 1) of S 1 itself, in terms of: (i) its perceived alignment with, and development of, its intellectual tradition (including its potentially augmented generative power *vis-à-vis* its antecedent systems); and/or (ii) its efficacy in generating music according to its specified design aims (diagonal arrow from CGM 1 to E 1).

   • Up-arrow: analogously to VRS 2 in Figure 6.13, mediates the reception (E 2) by humans of CGM 1. While CGM 1 can at present only motivate aesthetic/subjective and/or theoretical/analytical responses in a human listener (VRS 2 in Figure 6.13), such responses may also (eventually) be possible – as forms of consciousness – in another machine, as might, of course, responses to the HGM (HGM 1 and HGM 2) resulting from VRS 1 in Figure 6.13. The theoretical/analytical mode of interaction in computers is exemplified by the operation of such analytical programs as the *Humdrum Toolkit* (Huron, 2002; Huron, 2022), or the *Tonalities* prolongation-analysis software (Pople, 2002) (for the latter, see §7.5.3). Despite their being products of the VRS algorithm, these and other current music-analysis programs are arguably merely non-autonomous "prosthetic'" extensions of human theorists/analysts and are therefore not currently fully autonomous of our control.[289] Nevertheless, and apropos the category of "AI for AI" in point 279 of the list on page 547, at some point in the future one AI might conceivably be capable of "hearing", both aesthetically/subjectively and/or theoretically/analytically, the outputs of another.

VRS 3: as with VRS 3 in Figure 6.13, and also receiving input from VRS 2 and from other instances of VRS 2 processes (represented by the left-hand vertical dotted line), this drives the poiesis (P 3) of a theoretical/analytical discourse. This poiesis may formulate a model that (assuming those using the model are aware of CGM 1's status as CGM): (i) treats CGM in the same terms as HGM; or that (ii) takes account of the fact that the discourse relates specifically to CGM.

VRS 4: as with VRS 4 in Figure 6.13, this mediates the connection between the theoretical/analytical discourse and the esthesis (E 2) of CGM 1 (represented by the central vertical dotted line). On occasions, and extending VRS 2 in Figure 6.13 to encompass "trifocal" listening, the aesthetic/subjective perspective, the theoretical/analytical perspective, and the perspective of the generative system's programmer may be employed by the same observer, and so there are three, difficult-to-separate, sources for E 2: (i) that arising from an aesthetic/subjective response to CGM 1 (VRS 2, up-arrow); (ii) that arising from the application of a particular theoretical/analytical discourse pertaining to it (VRS 4); and (iii) that arising from understanding how specific features of CGM 1 may have arisen as a result of the operation and interaction of S 1's algorithms (VRS 2, down-arrow).

VRS 5: as with VRS 5 in Figure 6.13, this drives, analogously to VRS 2, the reception (E 3) of the theoretical/analytical discourse within the community that engages with it, in the light of: (i) its perceived alignment with, and development of, its intellectual tradition (including its potentially heightened explanatory power

---

[289] As McLuhan argued, "[a]ll media are extensions of some human faculty – psychic or physical" (1969, p. 26).

vis-à-vis its antecedent models); and/or (ii) its perceived alignment with its target CGM, this mediated by interaction with processes encompassed by VRS 4 (represented by the right-hand vertical dotted line). E 3 is contingent, among other factors, upon knowledge of the CGM-status of the target music, for should a model developed for use on HGM prove ill-suited to a work not known to be CGM (or vice versa), then the model might unreasonably be regarded as being at fault when the error lies, in reality, in its (mis-)application.

VRS 6: mediates (by way of its effects on programmers) the "influence on the system" of one or more theoretical/analytical discourses. It acts in conjunction with a re-iteration of VRS 1 (VRS 1b; diagonal arrow from S 2 – a child of the parent S 1 – to P 5) to engender a child (CGM 2) of the parent (CGM 1) arising from VRS 1a. As with HGM 1 and HGM 2, the connection between CGM 1 and CGM 2 may be indirect, especially if (in the case of CGM), S 2 represents a radical reworking of S 1, made after generating CGM 1.

VRS 7: extending VRS 7 in Figure 6.13, there are three inputs to the poiesis (P 4) of the second iteration of a music-generative system. While the layout of Figure 6.14 is intended to indicate that the two VRS 7-related inputs are distinct from the theoretical/analytical-discourse-mediated input deriving from VRS 6, in reality the three form interconnected sources for P 4:

- Down-arrow: that arising from understanding how specific features of CGM 1 may have arisen as a result of the operation and interaction of S 1's algorithms (E 1).

- Up-arrow/diagonal arrow from E 2 to P 4: that arising from the aesthetic/subjective responses to CGM 1 (E 2).

- That arising from the influence of theoretical/analytical discourses mediated by VRS 6.

As this discussion suggests, every element of these two analogous processes in HGM and CGM is made up of and driven by replicators, either in their memomic (brain-stored) or their phemotypic (physical-world) forms (Table 1.3), sustaining the VRS algorithm in a number of domains and substrates and operating at various levels of different ontological categories (§1.5.5).

Eschewing the *Ultima Thule* of Region Three of the Circle of Sound, and thus 2AI creativity (§6.6.2), one might argue that CGM is tractable using current (and historical) theoretical/analytical approaches *to the extent to which it reflects (or appears to reflect) the operation of human-like perceptual-cognitive constraints* on its generation. Specifically, if an instance of CGM respects the hierarchical-grouping structure of most HGM, then it is likely to be amenable to the same analytical methodologies that are applicable to HGM. Conversely, if an instance of CGM violates these constraints, then – depending upon how comprehensively they are rejected – it is less likely to be a meaningful object for HGM-focused analytical methodologies. This second scenario poses a significant challenge to attempts by theory and analysis to arrive at methodologies that are able to engage with such CGM, and it might indeed be deemed meaningless for a human-centred theory and analysis even to attempt to cross the Horizon of Intelligibility in order to attempt an encounter. As just suggested, this distinction is not necessarily clear-cut: an instance of CGM might *mostly* adhere to human perceptual-cognitive constraints, abandoning them only occasionally.

By hierarchical-grouping structure I mean – apropos the RHSGAP model (§3.5.2) – the perceptually-cognitively driven tendency of most HGM to be composed of musemes satisfying STM constraints; the tendency for these units to follow on from each other in coherent ways; and the tendency for this chunking to be replicated at multiple structural-hierarchic levels, such that there exist higher-order units that themselves relate logically to each other in the diachronic unfolding of the music. Much music theory and analysis has, unsurprisingly, attempted to understand music in these psychologically ori-entated terms, ranging – to briefly consolidate the accounts given in §4.1 and §4.4 – from sixteenth-century linguistically/rhetorically motivated analyses of vocal music by Burmeister; to eighteenth-century models of phrase- and cadence-concatenation in Koch and Kirnberger; to Schenkerian voice-leading models; to Schoenbergian and Retian theories of motivic transformation; and, in more recent times (and perhaps going full-circle), to applications to music of Chomskyan generative-transformational grammar (see also Bent & Pople, 2001, sec. II).

To illustrate this principle, it is useful to discuss a short case-study. An example of CGM considered in §6.5.3.2 – the *Iamus* computer's composition *Colossus* – is a good candidate. An analytical methodology appropriate for attempting to understand this music – one not listed in the above historical review – is PC set theory (Forte, 1973). In summary, this approach identifies salient pitch-collections drawn from the chromatic set ranging from three to nine notes (of which there are 4,096 in total) and reduces them, via the operations of transposition and inversion, to one of 208 fundamental set-classes. Transposition and inversion thus give rise to various members of each set-class, with 3–11, for instance, having 24 distinct forms (the twelve major and twelve minor triads). PC set theory affords the opportunity to relate seemingly unconnected pitch-collections using their membership of specific set-classes (each of which has a characteristic internal interval complement or interval-class (IC) vector) as a common denominator. In HGM, two patterns of the same set-class – or, alternatively, having a Z-relation, where two different set-classes share the same IC vector (Forte, 1973, p. 21) – are perceived, and may have been conceived, as having stronger synchronic and diachronic connections than patterns lacking such relationships. Thus, PC set correspondences may be taken as affording evidence of compositional intentionality and higher-order pitch-content planning in HGM, although there are certain cautions, to be discussed below, in this regard.

Four criteria seem appropriate to organise an analysis of *Colossus*. Firstly, as the boxes on Figure 6.15 – an annotated version of Figure 6.10 – suggest, and on the basis of the inevitably subjective segmentation adopted here,[290] there is a degree of ("vertical") recurrence of PC sets evident in this extract, in the form of three appearances of set-class 4–19 (bb. 1, 5 and 6) and two appearances of set-class 3–11 in b. 8. Nevertheless, and secondly, while there is a degree of motivic unity engendered by the recurrent 1 × ♪–4 × ♪ units in bb. 1 and 3, these motives are not related by membership of a common set-class. Thirdly, there is no Z-relationship evident between the PC sets identified, although alternative segmentations might reveal such relationships. Fourthly, identifying certain registrally salient pitches, as marked by the arrows, indicates that the lower-voice pitches (D♯ (b. 1), A♯ (b. 4), B♮ (b. 6), and G♮ (b. 7)) spell out ("horizontally") set-class 4–19, this

---

[290] Segmentation is a highly controversial topic in PC set theory (Hasty, 1981), given the arguably greater propensity of the method to circularity and to confirmation bias than is the case with approaches for analysing tonal music. The segmentation of *Colossus* utilised here attempts to respect motivic and gestalt-psychological grouping principles. See again the "final consideration" of §4.4.3, on page 360 and also Lalitte et al. (2009).

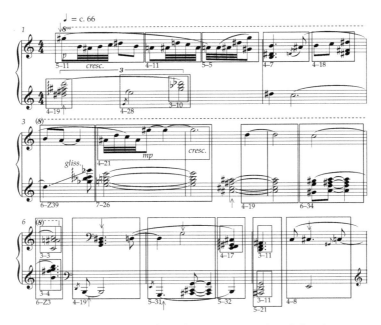

Figure 6.15: *Iamus: Colossus* (2012), bb. 1–8, with PC Set Annotations.

set-class, as noted apropos the first criterion, being significant vertically. No such registral connections are evident, however, in the upper-voice line.

It is not at all straightforward to assess the significance of these findings, which might be quasi-random, in the "pseudo-Jackson-Pollock" sense discussed on page 525. This is to assume, as PC set theory does, that in the case of HGM such set-theoretical phenomena are *not* random – i.e., that they are at some level intentional, and therefore significant and valuable because they represent a manifestation of the composer's agency and intelligence. The evidence for such intentionality in HGM might exist not directly but rather at some degree of remove: as with all theoretical systems and analytical methodologies, the phenomena theorised by PC set theory might themselves be epiphenomena – second-order intentional – of some more fundamental – first-order intentional – process, such as, in the case of PC set theory, a focus on the intervallic structure of harmonies and melodies. Some might argue that this focus is indeed the primary motivation behind Viennese early atonality, as opposed to the implicit (Fortean) set-class recurrence such intervallic structures motivate.

Intentionality in CGM is, as the discussion of Figure 6.14 implies, distributed, in that theory and analysis has to take into account both the "real" intentionality of the programmer (to some extent analogous to first-order intentionality in HGM) and the "virtual" intentionality of the generative system (to some extent analogous to second-order intentionality in HGM). An extreme point on the continuum of automation/autonomy discussed in §6.2, programmer *non*-intentionality in CGM inheres in the appearance of phenomena in the resulting music that are not explicitly coded for – or even broadly anticipated – in the generative algorithm. Given that the VRS algorithm itself cannot account for all the output possibilities of any given input, this does not necessarily undermine the significance of a given phenomenon, either in biological or cultural evolution. As in second-order intentionality in HGM, certain programmer-non-intentional aspects of CGM might be theoretically and analytically interesting even if they are not wholly controlled for via the underpinning algorithm. This autonomy – perhaps supporting an affirmative answer to the fourth Lovelace-question – thus represents the triumph of a system's virtual intentionality over the programmer's real intentionality.

One aspect of this intentionality inheres in the extent to which *Iamus* uses – or does not use – human-analogous perceptual-cognitive constraints when manipulating note-patterns. Some of these patterns in *Colossus* are, in Lerdahl's phrase, "cognitively opaque" (1992, p. 118). Nevertheless, the evo-devo algorithm underpinning *Iamus* might be sustaining the selection and replication of certain note-groups that, owing to their analogous interval-class content, leads to the vertical and horizontal set-class recurrences identified, even when note-order and rhythmic structure is subject to levels of variation that militate against explicit organisation on the basis of pitch- and rhythm-stable musemes situated at a number of structural-hierarchic levels. Thus, there is potentially memetic replication of certain intervallic structures – in the form of PC sets functioning as unordered, interval-defined musemes – in *Iamus*'s computer-algorithmic implementation of cultural evolution, even though there is little of the explicit pitch-plus-rhythm museme replication characteristic of HGM.

While comparisons are, in some cases, odious, it is perhaps instructive to relate *Colossus* to an example of free-atonal HGM. Figure 6.16 shows the

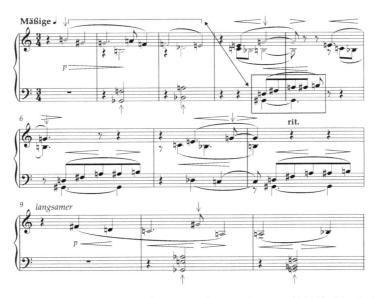

Figure 6.16: Schoenberg: Klavierstück op. 11 no. 1 (1909), bb. 1–11.

opening section of Schoenberg's Klavierstück op. 11 no. 1 (1909), which one
might compare with *Colossus* in terms of the four criteria outlined on page 557:
(i) recurrence of certain set-classes; (ii) alignment of set-class structure with
motivic/musemic structure; (iii) Z-relationships between significant sets;
and (iv) higher-order, registrally salient ("middleground"-level) set-class
structure.

On criterion (i), the red-coloured pitches in the right hand of bb. 1–2 (G♮,
G♯, B♮), the blue-coloured pitches in b. 3 (D♭, E♮, F♮), the green-coloured
pitches in bb. 4–5 (G♮, B♭, B♮), and the purple-coloured pitches in b. 10 (G♯,
A♮, C♮) are all members of set-class 3–3 (Straus, 2005, pp. 45–47), Schoenberg
relating set-class membership with motivic recurrence, criterion (ii), in ways
not evident in *Colossus*. Moreover, the bracketed melodic pitches in bb. 1–
3 (upward-facing note-sticks) are a member of set-class 6–Z10; and the
following pitches, boxed, in the left hand are a member of set-class 6–Z39.
On criterion (iii), these two set-classes are Z-correspondent with each other,
sharing the IC vector 333321 (2005, pp. 92–93). Finally, on criterion (iv), the
highest melodic pitches (G♮, G♯, B♮) and the lowest bass-voice pitches (G♭, G♮,
B♭) (marked, respectively, by down and up arrows) are themselves members

of set-class 3–3, forming an expression of this set-class at the middleground level (2005, pp. 104–105).

On this admittedly very limited body of comparative evidence, it would appear that, in terms of the aspects considered here (including the four specific criteria), *Colossus* possesses to some extent the hierarchical-grouping structure identified on page 556 as a key factor in the amenability of CGM to HGM-orientated analytical methodologies. This mode of organisation is clearly evident in the local and higher-order set-class structure of Schoenberg's op. 11 no. 1, whereas its deployment in *Colossus* arguably lacks the surface-level clarity and rigorous motivic logic of the Schoenberg piece. This potential deficiency is not necessarily to be taken as evidence that *Colossus* lacks aesthetic or intellectual value, or that is necessarily to be regarded as inferior to the Schoenberg piece. Rather, it is to acknowledge that CGM does not always conform as closely to certain perceptual-cognitive constraints as HGM despite, in this case (and from what we know of its operational principles), *Iamus*'s using a broadly Darwinian algorithm. Thus, it may potentially score less highly on rubrics deriving from analytical methodologies that have evolved to describe and explicate HGM. Of course, the notion of scoring on rubrics implies a quantitative methodology, whereas a largely qualitative approach was adopted in the present comparison. Perhaps more fundamentally, there is a wider (VRS-driven) general intelligence, strategic planning, embodiment and cultural memory underpinning HGM that, at present, is not sufficiently well implemented in computers to allow for the generation of fully human-convincing CGM. At the risk of sounding glib, and as Levitin might say (apropos the quotation on page 74) of computers, at the moment "they just don't get it".

Given the foregoing discussion, and in summary, one might make the following points:

- Music theory and analysis have developed alongside the HGM they seek to explicate, so it is perhaps inevitable that these two processes have become coevolutionarily self-reinforcing: theory and analysis evolve to model a target that is itself constantly evolving, change in both domains resulting from the action of the VRS-algorithm on memes and musemes; and much music, to ensure coherence (and thus replication), evolves to align with certain constraints of organisation consolidated in theory.

- While much CGM is to some extent convincing in comparison with HGM, its lack of – or perceived deficiencies in – the multilevelled hierarchical-grouping structure that engenders coherence for humans is a significant difference, often leading to the lower perceived (teleo)logical drive of CGM in comparison with HGM.

- This deficiency often renders CGM problematic when exposed to theoretical frameworks and analytical approaches evolved for HGM, and it leads to a methodological tension: should generative algorithms be modified in order to generate music that is more tractable to theory and analysis (and therefore, by extension, more comprehensible to human perception and cognition); or should theory and analysis expand its Horizon of Intelligibility, in order to accommodate the challenges of this new category of music, as it has done in the case of radical HGM for centuries?

- While it has been assumed that an analyst is normally aware that the object of investigation is an instance of CGM, it should be acknowledged – in what might be regarded as a theoretical/analytical Turing Test – that the outcome of an analysis may well be affected by knowledge of the non-human origins of CGM. If the analyst were unaware of the music's provenance, one might (perhaps cynically) hypothesise that certain elements regarded as deficiencies in *known* CGM might be regarded as creative – i.e., as novel and valuable – in *assumed* HGM.

Some of these issues arise from the the attributes of HGM's antecedent musilanguage, from the biological- and cultural-evolution-shaped nature of HGM, and from the perceptual-cognitive and embodied foundations shaping human musicality and music. They currently separate HGM from CGM, but it is not inconceivable that in the future cultural-evolutionary pressures might build human-analogous aptations in machines; or, conversely, that biological evolution might reshape human musicality along the Region-Three-unlocking lines discussed on page 545.

6.7 Summary of Chapter 6

Chapter 6 has argued that:

1. The power of computers makes them well suited to emulating/simulating processes that, in real time, are difficult to observe or analyse. At the most autonomous end of the continuum of synthesis, the machine generation of music can, when conceived and implemented in Darwinian-memetic terms, facilitate both the modelling of human perceptual-cognitive and creative processes, and the rendering of counterfactual histories of music.

2. Evolutionary change in replicator systems has been modelled by simulations of language evolution. The simulation of music evolution is in some ways less complex than that of language, because the semantic dimension central to language need not necessarily be incorporated for validation of the hypothesised mechanisms in music; yet in other ways it is more complex, owing to the arguably greater combinatorial and structural complexity of music.

3. A number of music-generative systems have been developed using a range of algorithms. While some of these are not strictly Darwinian, and while all must address the distinction between music and its representations, those modelling the operation of the VRS algorithm are certainly capable of evolving convincing outputs. Some of these systems simulate musical societies in which their virtual agents represent vehicles within and between which a rich nexus of replicators evolves. The most sophisticated of them also simulate gene-meme coevolution and thus represent the nearest machine equivalent to the dual-replicator coevolution operative in human – and potentially in animal – societies.

4. Just as certain species of non-human animals might be regarded as potentially creative, engendering novelty and perhaps value in their outputs, the same issue arises in connection with music-generative systems. The existence and nature of machine creativity is to some extent contingent upon the evaluation of the operation and outputs of such systems, approaches to which remain the subject of ongoing debate. A resolution depends, in part, upon whether one is prepared to consider the machine-generated denizens of the Circle of Sound's Region Three, whether existing as work or process, as constituting examples of music or not.

Chapter 7 will summarise the issues covered in Chapters 1–6 in the course of an exploration of certain similarities between evolution and consciousness. In particular, it will use Universal Darwinism to understand evolution (including music-cultural evolution) as a form of consciousness, and vice versa. It will: review current theories of consciousness, endorsing those that conceive it as not only shaped by evolutionary processes, but also as itself an implementation of the VRS algorithm; frame consciousness as a form of fast-acting evolution, and evolution as a form of slow-acting consciousness; revisit the discussion of music-language coevolution in Chapter 3 to explore further some of the issues pertinent to consciousness raised there; use the phenomenon of tonal-system change in music as an example of music-historical/structural consciousness; and assess the extent to which the new forms of information storage and transmission afforded by computer technology and the internet motivate an expansion of the ontology of replicators and, more fundamentally, constitute nascent forms of evolution.

7. Conclusion: Music, Evolution and Consciousness

[Consciousness is] a consequence of biological processes that humans share to some extent with other species, and that give a competitive advantage to those species that have it. One of the chief manifestations of these processes in humans is an expansion of memory function, including a diversification of working memory which made it possible for our species to keep track of a number of different domains of experience simultaneously. These domains include those focused on tactile and visual images, on movement, on emotions, on sound, on the sort of abstract symbolic structures basic to language, and on thought itself. (Zbikowski, 2011, p. 187)

7.1 Introduction: Why Is Music?

I borrow the title of this introductory section from Dawkins, who asks "why are people" (1989, p. 1). I shall not – apropos the same author's arguably most controversial and polemical work (Dawkins, 2007) – argue that music disproves the existence of God, although a case could be made to this effect, if one were to take music as an exemplar of the evolutionary processes that provide the foundations upon which Dawkins builds his refutation of theism. Instead, my aim here is to revisit certain earlier arguments about the aptive benefits of music to humans' survival (§2.5), and about the aptive benefits of humans to music's survival (§3.2), seeing both in terms of the phenomenon of consciousness. The latter topic has been discussed extensively in recent decades, but despite advances in cognitive science, an understanding of the nature of consciousness still proves elusive. I cover this issue here not in order to offer new insights into consciousness, or to elucidate that which has hitherto confounded far greater minds than mine: the literature is simply too extensive and the issues too complex and controversial to make this possible.

 https://doi.org/10.11647/OBP.0301.07

Rather, I consider consciousness – specifically, certain evolutionarily motivated theories of consciousness – in order to understand how the mechanisms they hypothesise underpin it mirror those of biological and cultural evolution and thus to demonstrate how the VRS algorithm links the two dimensions of our humanity that perhaps most clearly define us: our consciousness and our musicality.

The chapter continues with discussion of the importance of consciousness in an evolutionary account of music and musicality, offering a brief overview of different categories of theories of consciousness in order to provide the context for the arguments of following sections (§7.2). The next section considers consciousness in evolutionary terms, discussing how the operation of the VRS algorithm might account for its origins and mechanisms and, inverting the terms of the argument, framing evolution as itself a form of slow-motion consciousness (§7.3). Thereafter – in the book's final consideration of the evolutionary relationships between music and language – the cognitivism-communicativism distinction explored in §3.8 is reconciled in the light of the memetically inspired theory of (evolution-as-)consciousness considered in the previous section (§7.4). Turning to a musical application of the concept of evolution-as-consciousness, the following section considers the phenomenon of tonal-system evolution in music (§7.5). Next, the chapter considers the ontological implications of technologies of electronic storage and transmission on music and musicality, examining how the units and processes of the VRS algorithm exist and function when they leave the biological and the human-cultural realms and move to the vast proto-consciousness of the internet (§7.6). Lastly, after a summary of the chapter, the ideas explored in the chapter, and the book as a whole, are drawn together in a freely speculative, improvisatory Epilogue (§7.8).

7.2 Consciousness, Musicality and Music

Consciousness – and *mind*, as a superset of consciousness – might seem a somewhat abstract notion to consider in a book about music and evolution. It is nevertheless relevant because – leaving aside the issue of music's evolutionary relationships with language (§2.7), and the connections between language, thought and consciousness (§3.8) – most higher forms of musicality require consciousness for their operation. While the rhythmic synchrony (§2.5.2) and expressive vocalisations (§2.7.1) that underpin musicality are partly innate, to shape sounds compositionally and performatively into structurally coherent and aesthetically satisfying sequences, and to respond appropriately to them, requires the higher-order attribute of consciousness. Moreover, as well as motivating and directing the acquisition of these competences, consciousness also integrates self- and other-awareness and the richness of (inter)subjective experience with the perception, cognition and generation of music's pattern-structures.

7.2.1 The "Easy" and "Hard" Problems of Consciousness

> The hard problem of consciousness ... is that of explaining how and why physical processes give rise to phenomenal consciousness. A solution to the hard problem would involve an account of the relation between physical processes and consciousness, explaining on the basis of natural principles how and why it is that physical processes are associated with states of experience. (Chalmers, 2010, p. 105)

The "hard problem" of consciousness concerns what is arguably the most complex phenomenon and problem in the known universe. While the (plural) "easy problem(s)" of consciousness relate to such matters as perception, cognition and behaviour – which are largely tractable using the resources of cognitive science, specifically theoretical and empirical psychology and neuroscience (Chalmers, 2010, p. 4) – the (singular) hard problem relates to the causes of *subjective experience* (2010, p. 5). This is made up of the ineffable, externally inaccessible, internal subjective states – the qualia; Chalmers' "states of experience" – in and through which individuals experience their lives. Examples include "[t]he feel of the wind on your cheeks as you ride your bike .... [t]he sight of the bluey pink of the sunset sky .... [t]he indescribable chill of delight you experience every time you hear that minor chord ..." (Blackmore & Troscianko, 2018, pp. 35–36). At the heart of the hard problem is the question of whether qualia can be accounted for by a purely materialistic (or mechanistic) explanation – "how qualia relate to the physical world, or how *objective* brains and bodies produce *subjective* qualia" (2018, p. 36; emphases in the original) – or whether they require the intercession of something additional, something by definition non-materialistic and therefore mysterious.

Assuming the former, as most scientists do, the hard problem boils down to the question of how the biochemical processes of the brain are able to give rise to the subjective experiences of consciousness: how can a particular sequence of neuronal electrochemical "firing" engender the experience of colours, tastes and more abstract phenomena? While there are robust, mechanistic theories as to how the internal structure of the brain, particularly its low-level wiring, might process sensory inputs and generate appropriate motor outputs – the HCT (§3.8.3) is a strong candidate – a solution to the hard problem nevertheless remains elusive because of the wide gap between physical phenomena and subjective experience – between the biological and the psychological ontological categories (§1.5.5). A first step to tackling the hard problem is to divide the various candidate theories designed to address it into categories, so that within- and between-category comparisons, and with them a determination of the most epistemologically coherent category, might potentially be made.

7.2.2 Metatheories of Consciousness

For Blackmore, there are three categories of explanation – three overarching metatheories – for the hard problem of consciousness. These are: (i) *dualist*: consciousness is separate from the body, an occupant of it, being conceived by science in terms of mind and by most religions in terms of a spirit or soul, and formalised in the *Cartesian Dualism* of Descartes; (ii) *monist*: consciousness is inseparable from the physical realm, and thus any mind/spirit/soul-body dichotomy is illusory; and (iii) *materialist*: consciousness is a product or epi-phenomenon of physical (electrochemical) processes occurring in the brain (Blackmore, 2005a, loc. 271, 277, 279). Synthesising aspects of categories (i) and (iii), Dennett identifies the notion of *Cartesian Materialism* (1993a, p. 107), whereby the mystical aspects of (Cartesian) dualism are rejected, but the notion of a "Cartesian Theater" is upheld. The latter is a virtual, materi-alistically driven focus of consciousness, wherein an individual, in the form of a "homunculus" inside their head, observes the events and experiences of their lives running sequentially as if projected like a film on the screen of an imaginary cinema.

In Chalmers' formulation there are four broad categories of explanation. These are: (i) *reductive*: consciousness is entirely explicable using physical principles; (ii) *materialist*: consciousness is regarded as a physical, as opposed to a metaphysical, process; (iii) *nonmaterialist*: consciousness is seen as non-physical, even if its causes might be held to be physical; and (iv) *nonreductive*: consciousness itself constitutes an element of the explanation (2010, p. 105). Chalmers' categories (i) and (ii) are broadly subsumed by Blackmore's materialist category; his category (iii) corresponds broadly to Blackmore's (and Dennett's) dualist category; and his category (iv) corresponds broadly to her monist category. Chalmers (2010) further subdivides his four categories into six derived types, summarised in Table 7.1. This categorical expansion relies, in part, on invoking a further distinction, between the *epistemic* – what we know, or think we know, about consciousness – and the *ontological* – what does or does not exist in relation to it (2010, p. 109).

Chalmers (2010) attempts to unpick the complex intersections between materialist, dualist and monist theories, which are not as clear-cut as Table 7.1 implies. His arguments illustrate that while the subject of consciousness has been addressed from a number of disciplinary perspectives, it has primarily been seen as the purview of (initially) philosophy and (more recently) cognitive science. Subdividing the latter, psychology has attempted to address the phenomenological aspects of consciousness, and neuroscience their ostensibly mechanical foundation (from a materialist perspective). Given the conceptual and methodological differences between these disciplines, it is perhaps not surprising that the harshest critiques of models of consciousness developed by philosophers have tended to come from cognitive scientists, and vice versa. Beyond these two disciplines, some theories of consciousness – specifically, Type-D Dualism and Type-F Monism – have drawn on explanations from physics, particularly quantum mechanics. Most notably, Penrose's "Orchestrated Objective Reduction" (Orch OR) theory (1989, 1994, 1997) "attributes consciousness to quantum computations in microtubules inside brain neurons" (Hameroff, 2021, p. 74). While perhaps more controversial than most theories of consciousness, because Orch OR is

Category	Definition
Type-A Materialism	"[T]here is no epistemic gap between physical and phenomenal truths, or at least any apparent epistemic gap is easily closed" (2010, p. 111). Thus, the hard problem dissolves as one solves the easy problems.
Type-B Materialism	"[T]here is an epistemic gap between the physical and phenomenal domains, but there is no ontological gap" (2010, p. 115). Thus, while there appears to be a distinction between the hard and the easy problems, this is not based on any objective reality.
Type-C Materialism	"[T]here is a deep epistemic gap between the physical and phenomenal domains, but it is closable in principle" (2010, p. 118). Thus, while seemingly intractable, the hard problem is "solvable in principle" (2010, p. 118).
Type-D Dualism	"[M]icrophysics is not causally closed, and … phenomenal properties play a causal role in affecting the physical world" (2010, p. 126). Thus causation runs both ways: not only from the physical to the phenomenal (as argued by materialism), but also in the other direction.
Type-E Dualism	"[P]henomenal properties are ontologically distinct from physical properties, and … the phenomenal has no effect on the physical" (2010, p. 130). Thus, while the phenomenal is different in kind from the physical, causation is unidirectional, from the physical to the phenomenal.
Type-F Monism	"[C]onsciousness is constituted by the intrinsic properties of fundamental physical entities: that is, by the categorical bases of fundamental physical dispositions" (2010, p. 133). Thus, the physical and the phenomenal are indistinguishable.

Table 7.1: Chalmers' Six Types of Theories of Consciousness.

fundamentally materialist – it is, moreover, arguably not incompatible with the VRS-algorithm-based hypothesis outlined in §7.3.1 – Penrose's theory is in principle falsifiable (2021, p. 75).

The "physical processes" underpinning consciousness referred to in the quotation from Chalmers (2010) on page 567 are not exclusively located in the brain. Damasio (2000) sees consciousness as a three-layered phenomenon deeply rooted in brain-body connections. In his model, the first layer, the "protoself", represents the body's internal state in relation to its environment and its homeostatic regulation (2000, p. 154). The second layer, "core consciousness", "provides the organism with a sense of self about one moment – now – and about one place – here" (2000, p. 16). It "operates in stable fashion across the lifetime of the organism; and it is not dependent on conventional memory, working memory, reasoning, or language" (Damasio & Meyer, 2009, p. 6; see also Bosse et al., 2008). The third layer, "extended consciousness", "provides the organism with an elaborate sense of self – an identity and a person … – and places that person at a point in individual historical time, richly aware of the lived past and of the anticipated future, and keenly cognizant of the world beside it" (2000, p. 16). It "evolves during the lifetime of the organism; it depends on memory; and it is enhanced by language" (2009, p. 6). While arguably a Type-A Materialist, in Chalmers' terms, Damasio builds his theory on the basis that "the organism in the relationship play of consciousness is the entire unit of our living being, our body as it were; and yet, … the brain holds within it a sort of model of the whole thing" (2000, p. 22).

7.3 Consciousness as an Evolutionary Phenomenon

Having outlined at the start of §7.2 the importance of consciousness in any evolutionary account of musicality and music, this section considers systemic similarities between the mechanisms driving evolution and those driving consciousness. It argues not only for the status of consciousness as a *product* of biological- and cultural-evolutionary processes, but also as a microcosmic *instantiation* of those processes.

7.3.1 Evolution and The Hard Problem of Consciousness: The Multiple Drafts Model

To which of the theories of consciousness listed in §7.2.2 should an evolutionary view of music cleave? This question arguably devolves to two more fundamental questions: (i) how did the human brain itself evolve to the stage where it is able to support consciousness; and (ii) what is the mechanism by which this consciousness operates in this brain? From the argument of this book up to this point, it should be clear that the logical answer to (i) is that the brain evolved by means of the VRS algorithm, building up ever greater complexity by means of gene-meme coevolution (§3.7). Indeed this process – and specifically its subset, memetic drive – partly suggests the answer to (ii), namely that the main reason the brain is so large, complex and plastic in humans (see note 81 on page 138, and note 147 on page 254) is that it has evolved to sustain the large population of cultural replicators that in some way impels consciousness, certainly in cognitivist theories of language and cognition (§3.8.1, §7.4). In this view, once the aptive utility of the capacity for imitation had helped push the brain to a certain size, a critical mass was reached whereby those replicators that capitalised on this capacity helped in some way to engender consciousness.

As for question (ii), for Darwinism, monism and dualism are inherently mystical because – quantum-mechanical theories in these two categories aside – they rely upon the intercession of phenomena external to the various categories of being formalised by recursive ontology (1.5.5). That is, they generally invoke numinous spirits or immortal souls that exist apart from the normal laws of physics and that are therefore not measurable or quantifiable. Only materialism posits the existence of entities amenable to the action of the VRS algorithm and thus capable of supporting the kind of complexity – in terms of both questions (i) and (ii) above – of which consciousness is perhaps the supreme example, the pinnacle of evolution on earth. Thus, from a Darwinian perspective, only the three types of materialism – and perhaps specifically Type-B Materialism or Type-C materialism, in order to recognise the black-box or "evolved user-illusion" aspects of consciousness (Dennett, 2017, Ch. 14) – are sustainable, despite Chalmers' view that "consciousness seems to resist materialist explanation in a way that other phenomena do not"

(2010, p. 105). In many ways the argument around question (ii) is parallel to certain debates attendant upon Darwinism at its inception, still rumbling on today, that question whether the VRS algorithm does all of the work of building aptive complexity in nature; or whether something additional is involved, such as a supernatural agent, either to initiate the process, or to moderate and regulate its progress, as a benevolent overseer. Just as Darwinism renounces the superfluous and non-parsimonious explanations of such Creationism in the *evolution* of the human brain (question (i) above), it also rejects Creationism – in its incarnations as monism and dualism – as an explanation of the *function* of the brain (question (ii) above).

Having suggested that a Darwinian orientation can, on the basis of present understanding, only sustain a materialistic explanation of consciousness, one theory in particular – Dennett's "Multiple Drafts Model" (Dennett, 1993a; Dennett, 1993b), hereafter "MDM" – warrants fuller consideration here. It has been widely influential, certainly in illuminating the differences, alluded to in §7.2.2, between what constitutes valid explanations of consciousness in those models derived from philosophy and those derived from cognitive science; and, for some, in offering a plausible and full-blown Darwinian account of consciousness. Dennett's "Thumbnail Sketch" of his theory is worth quoting in full:

> There is no single, definitive 'stream of consciousness', because there is no central Headquarters, no Cartesian Theater where 'it all comes together' for the perusal of a Central Meaner. Instead of such a single stream (however wide), there are multiple channels in which specialist circuits try, in parallel pandemoniums, to do their various things, creating Multiple Drafts as they go. Most of these fragmentary drafts of 'narrative' play short-lived roles in the modulation of current activity but some get promoted to further functional roles, in swift succession, by the activity of a virtual machine in the brain. The [apparent] seriality of this machine (its 'von Neumannesque'[291] character) is not a 'hard-wired' design feature, but rather the upshot of a succession of coalitions of these specialists.

---

[291] John von Neumann (1903–1957) was an early pioneer of digital computing whose basic design, the now-ubiquitous (serial) "von Neumann architecture", articulates the distinction between immutable hardware and mutable memory. The memory provides an environment for the programs that, in their operation, engender *virtual machines*. These subsist on the computer's hardware, the underpinning *real machine* (Dennett, 1993a, p. 211).

The basic specialists are part of our animal heritage. They were not developed to perform peculiarly human actions, such as reading and writing, but ducking, predator-avoiding, face-recognizing, grasping, throwing, berry-picking, and other essential tasks. They are often opportunistically enlisted in new roles, for which their native talents more or less suit them. The result is not bedlam only because the trends that are imposed on all this activity are themselves the product of design. Some of this design is innate, and is shared with other animals. But it is augmented, and sometimes even overwhelmed in importance, by microhabits of thought that are developed in the individual, partly idiosyncratic results of self-exploration and partly the predesigned gifts of culture. Thousands of memes, mostly borne by language, but also by wordless 'images' and other data structures, take up residence in an individual brain, shaping its tendencies and thereby turning it into a mind. (Dennett, 1993a, pp. 253–254)

To reduce this thumbnail sketch to a "Little Finger Nail Sketch", one might summarise the MDM as follows:

1. Distinct brain systems (Dennett's "channels"; termed "modules" in some theories (§3.8.2)) process incoming information and regulate functions – as a biological-evolution-shaped *parallel real machine* – in autonomous, automatic and massively distributed ways.

2. Most of these "drafts" – the result of the brain's ability, in the passage by Zbikowsky cited at the head of this chapter, "to keep track of a number of different domains of experience simultaneously" (2011, p. 187) – are fleeting, and unconscious, but some fall under the control of, and subserve, a cultural-evolution-shaped *serial virtual machine*, which organises the parallel channels into a single flow (Dennett's "coalitions").

3. The virtual machine is constituted and coordinated by memes, primarily verbal-conceptual, but also those in other substrates.

Clearly the MDM draws heavily upon computational metaphors (see note 291 on page 573), just as the design of the first digital computers drew upon understanding of the workings of the brain, to the extent that this was known at the time, and insofar as this is ever reliably accessible by means of introspection (Dennett, 1993a, p. 215). The MDM also captures the central difference between the brain – massively parallel in architecture (performing many functions simultaneously), but giving the "user" (the conscious individual) an illusion of a serial focus in the form of the unitary Cartesian self; and the computer – largely serial in architecture (performing one operation at a time), but giving the user an illusion of parallel, multitasking functionality (Dennett, 2017, pp. 155–156). Moreover, in its explicit incorporation of Darwinian mechanisms – via the invocation of memetics – the MDM has the virtue of aligning with the key thesis of this book: that musicality and music, like other forms of complex organisation in the universe, result from the mindless operation of the VRS algorithm. While this alignment does not, of course, necessarily mean that the MDM – or the book's thesis as a whole – is valid, hypothesising the operation of Universal Darwinism in yet another substrate affords further evidence in favour of an evolutionary ontology and epistemology. These alignments between the MDM and other key phenomena discussed in this book are considered further in §7.3.2 and §7.4.

There have been several critiques of the MDM, many coming – as suggested in §7.2.2 – from philosophers. For these critics, the model is too mechanistic and reductive in that, for one thing, it fails to deal convincingly with qualia – the subjective experiences that constitute a central component of consciousness. Carruthers (2005, 32, note 7), for instance, notes that "[m]any have alleged that Dennett's [*Consciousness explained*] should really have been entitled, *Consciousness Explained Away* ...". For Dennett, however, the notion of qualia is dissolved by his model, because all such subjective states are illusory products of the algorithmic processes described by the MDM. In his view, qualia arise as a result of various "discriminative states" that supervene on biological-evolution-wired "innate dispositions" and on cultural-evolution-shaped "learned habits" (1993a, p. 372). "That 'quale' of yours", Dennett argues, "is a character in good standing in the fictional world of your heterophenomenology,[292] but what it turns out to be in the *real* world in your brain is just a complex of dispositions" (1993a, p. 389; emphasis in the original).

---

[292] Heterophenomenology refers to the rejection of first-person subjectivity in research on consciousness in favour of "the *neutral* path leading from objective physical science and its insistence on the third-person point of view ..." (1993a, p. 72; emphasis in the original).

In the case of the discriminative state of colour perception, for instance, Dennett argues that colour qualia have their origins in plant-pollinator co-evolution: the colour of a flower or fruit did not exist until an insect or bird evolved the ability to see the colour of the flower or fruit in order to pollinate or eat it; the colour was fixed by gene-gene coevolution because, "[i]n the beginning, colors were made to be seen by those who were made to see them" (1993a, p. 378). A similar argument might be applied to the evolution of "music-ness"; that is, the propensity of a sequence of sounds to be under-standable as music – as opposed to as any other type of sound-sequence – by a human listener. Unlike Dennett's example of the evolution of colour per-ception, however, this phenomenon requires the invocation of dual-replicator coevolution for its explanation. To paraphrase Dennett: the music-ness of a sequence of musilinguistic sounds did not exist until a human – one en-dowed with a specific meme- and museme-complement – evolved the ability to hear the music-ness of the sounds in order to comprehend them as an emotion-mediating, social-bonding (etc.) entity (§2.5); the music-ness was fixed by gene-meme coevolution because, in the beginning, music-ness was made to be heard by those who were made – who had evolved the mental competences, hard- and soft-wired – to hear it. Perhaps such music-ness – or some other "-ness" – might eventually evolve in computers, as they ac-quire the ability to perceive, cognise and perhaps even appreciate AI for AI creativity (§6.6.2).

To those who claim that the MDM is not a theory of consciousness – owing, for many critics, to its reduction of qualia to artefacts of coevolutionary processes – Dennett responds by asserting his restriction of consciousness to possessors of the virtual machine central to his theory. In a further elaboration, he styles this virtual machine a "Joycean machine", representing the MDM's analogy to "the meandering sequence of conscious mental contents famously depicted by James Joyce in his novels", this sequence being akin to William James' "stream of consciousness" (Dennett, 1993a, p. 214; James, 1950, p. 180; see also Calvin, 1987b; Calvin, 1987a; Rice, 1997). In a ringing declaration, Dennett states: "I hereby declare that YES, my theory is a theory of consciousness. Anyone or anything that has such a virtual machine as its control system is conscious in the fullest sense, and is conscious *because* it has such a virtual machine" (1993a, 281; capitalisation and emphasis in the original). Put another way, his theory draws upon the status of a Joycean machine as a subtype of Darwin machine (§1.5.1). Machines make or generate things: in the case of the MDM, the thing the brain's Darwin-Joycean machine makes is the user-illusion of consciousness itself (§7.4).

7.3.2 Consciousness as Evolution and Evolution as Consciousness

As argued in §1.5.5, mind is a property of the psychological category of a larger recursive ontology that unites a number of disparate realms by virtue of the operation of Universal Darwinism. If one accepts that consciousness – as a product of the psychological category – is somehow a consequence of the operation of the VRS algorithm – arising from the variation, replication and selection of brain activity in the form of triangularly and hexagonally organised neuronal activations (§3.8.3) – then one can regard *consciousness as a form of rapid (cognitive) evolution* and, vice versa, one can regard *evolution as a form of slow (systemic) consciousness*. If this interpretation is accepted, and if the VRS algorithm is indeed taken to be substrate-neutral, then all evolution, including cultural evolution in music, represents a species of consciousness, just as is the case with the origin of musicality thorough biological evolution. In this sense – and by analogy with the distinction between (biological) I[nternal]-language/I[nternal]-music and (cultural) E[xternal]-language/E[xternal]-music (§1.3) – the I-consciousness of myriad individuals drives the E-consciousness of the collective, "E" here representing "Evolution" as well as "External".

This alignment between evolution as consciousness and consciousness as evolution is articulated clearly by Calvin (1987b). Writing before his elaboration of the mechanism by means of which the brain functions as a Darwin machine – the HCT (§3.8.3) – Calvin argued that

> a series of [parallel] selection steps that shape up candidates [drafts, in Dennett's (1993a) terms (§7.3.1)] into increasingly more realistic sequences … is more analogous to the ways of darwinian evolutionary biology than to the 'von Neumann machine' serial computer. One might call it a Darwin Machine instead: it shapes up thoughts in milliseconds

rather than millennia, and uses innocuous remembered environments
rather than the noxious real-life ones. (Calvin, 1987b, p. 33)

The notion of aptation (§2.5.1) helps to illustrate the alignment further. If
the environment of an organism changes significantly – perhaps the climate
begins to warm or to cool markedly, or a new predator enters its ecosys-
tem – then those individuals whose genetic complement best suits them to
cope with the new reality will, self-evidently, survive and go on to pass the
advantage-conferring genes to their progeny. In this sense, evolution has
responded to the environmental change and made what amounts to a *decision* – one framed as creative in §5.5.2 – that will potentially have short-term
consequences for the viability of the organisms concerned and long-term
consequences for the species to which they belong. In human perception and
cognition, and faced with some response-motivating situation, an individual
will consider options and select the most appropriate response, a process that
devolves to the Calvinian selection of rival hexagons and the victory of the
configuration – Dennett's draft – that constitutes the best fit to the situation
at hand. Sometimes such decisions are processed so quickly that they do not
"enter" consciousness, being (evolution-driven) thoughts but not conscious
ones. This is the case in the common situation of possessing no memory –
which generally retains events of which one has been consciously aware – of
having driven a car some distance (the "unconscious driving phenomenon"),
with all the decision-making that involves (Blackmore, 2005a, loc. 749).[293]
Again, an evolutionary process has, via the selection of replicated variants,
made a (creative) decision.

In attempting to account for human forms of creative decision-making,
memetics draws upon the notion – intrinsic to the MDM – of consciousness as
a complex dynamic system consisting of myriad independent processes that
arrive at representations of the world and at solutions to problems (Blackmore & Troscianko, 2018, pp. 233–236; Dennett, 1993a, pp. 210, 218). The
crane- (not "skyhook"-) powered elevation (Dennett, 1995, pp. 74–75) of

---

[293] In some situations, there is insufficient time for any kind of considered evaluation, and an
instinctual response is triggered. Such responses are genetically, not memetically, mediated,
representing a kind of evolutionarily hard-wired thought. For all their seeming irrationality,
emotions arguably represent another form of these evolutionarily fixed rationalisations, motivating rapid and appropriate responses in order to short-circuit longer and thus more risky
reflection (Levitin, 2009, pp. 90–91).

complexity in a number of such ostensibly different systems is driven by inter-connected Darwin machines, imparting to them a fundamental equivalence: only their scope or frame is different (§7.8). It is in the nature of complex dynamic systems to be chaotic: as with all other forms, music-cultural evolution is, to adapt Lorenz's formulation, a phenomenon where "the past determines the present, but the approximate past does not approximately determine the present" (Danforth, 2013). Such chaos, in the formal sense, encourages a radically decentred view of musical creativity, one where the unitary self – and with it the sense of agency – dissolves (Herwig, 2010). This is because, in seeking the lowest level and unit of selection (§1.6.2), namely the m(us)eme, higher levels of organisation are bypassed. One such level is the "selfplex" (Blackmore & Troscianko, 2018, p. 234), the array of memeplexes responsible for our sense of identity and intentionality that, on a moderate-cognitivist view (§7.4.1), is implicated in Damasio's extended consciousness (§7.2.2). Taking a memetic view of consciousness and musical structure requires a renunciation of the idea – understandably often defended most strongly by improvisers and composers themselves – of the creative artist as lord and master/mistress of his/her realm. The latter view arises, according to Campbell (§3.3.2), because, in contemplating the "mystique of the creative genius and the creative act", "the causal-interpretative biases of our minds make us prone to such over-interpretations, to *post-hoc-ergo-propter-hoc* interpretations, deifying the creative genius to whom we impute a capacity for direct insight instead of mental flounderings and blind-alley entrances of the kind we are aware typify our own thought processes" (1960, pp. 390, 391). While this is a "view [that] may seem depressing or dehumanizing, with its emphasis on selective imitation and away from the power of consciousness" (Blackmore, 2007, p. 76), it nevertheless aligns with the precepts of the VRS algorithm – because "selective imitation" itself helps to drive consciousness – and with what is known of the practices of several creative musicians (Levitin, 2009, p. 93).

7.4 The (Co)evolution of Music and Language VI: Memetics, Cognitivism and Communicativism, and Consciousness

In the final treatment of the issue of music-language coevolution, I consider here the relationship between musemes, lexemes and consciousness. In the materialist-mechanistic MDM, consciousness is the most complex virtual machine running on the most complex physical machine in the known universe.[294] But it is necessary to understand, apropos the discussion on page 577, how the brain's Darwin-Joycean machine uses musemes and lexemes in order to generate the user-illusion of consciousness, insofar as this can be determined.

7.4.1 Cognitivism and/*versus* Communicativism Revisited

One way to address this issue is to invoke the distinction between cognitivism and communicativism, as outlined in §3.8.1. In summary, does language, as a complex of lexemes, *drive* thought – and, by extension, consciousness – being the medium through which thought is (exclusively) conducted (cognitivism; prioritising nurture); or is language simply a *vehicle* for thought conducted in some form of brain-language/mentalese (communicativism; prioritising nature) (Carruthers, 2002, p. 657)? This distinction aligns with the debate between Skinner and Chomsky touched upon in §5.6, whereby the former took an *a posteriori* (broadly cognitivist) view of human language, arguing for its assimilation via behaviourist (operant-conditioning-reinforced) mechanisms that presuppose an innate capacity for vocal learning; whereas the latter argued for an *a priori* (broadly communicativist) basis to language (via the Language Acquisition Device (LAD) and LF), particularly its generative-transformational structure.

In Carruthers' moderate cognitivism (2002), the internalised sound patterns of language (lexemes) – and, as I argued in §3.8.5, to a lesser extent those of music (musemes) – token the unconscious, domain-general Logical Form

---

[294] Perhaps benevolent (or malevolent) aliens are looking down on us and marvelling at our solipsistic arrogance; but until they make themselves known to us, we shall have to take this statement as provisionally true.

(LF) representations generated by the integration of unconscious domain-specific thought and, by this tokening, make them accessible to the theory of mind (ToM) module and thus to consciousness (Figure 3.16). In this model, the syntax of language is central to thought, and lexemes are fundamental to consciousness. By contrast – and Schenkerising consciousness – strong cognitivism might be taken to hold that there is no "background" LF and indeed no brain-language; rather, the "foreground" lexemes take on an even more fundamental role, undertaking the heavy lifting of thought and consciousness. Dennett's MDM is clearly strong-cognitivist, relying upon Darwinian processes of memetic variation, replication and selection to constitute the engine that drives consciousness. Thus, in one of his most striking passages, he contends that

> [h]uman consciousness is *itself* a huge complex of memes (or more exactly, meme-effects in brains) that can best be understood as the operation of a [serial] virtual machine *implemented* in the *parallel architecture* of a brain that was not designed for any such activities. The powers of this *virtual machine* vastly enhance the underlying powers of the organic *hardware* on which it runs, but at the same time many of its most curious features, and especially its limitations, can be explained as the byproducts of the *kludges* [*ad hoc* software bug repairs] that make possible this curious but effective reuse of an existing organ for novel purposes. (Dennett, 1993a, p. 210; emphases in the original)

Here, enculturation and education install the memomic forms of the software-analogous verbal-conceptual memes arising from cultural evolution that augment the biological-evolution-derived capacity of the underlying gene-phenotypic neural hardware. In fact, in a twist of ontology, the biological hardware *becomes* the cultural software by means of selective interconnection. While not denying that some kinds of thought are possible without language (Carruthers, 2002, p. 661), Dennett's strong cognitivism holds that a whole new vista was opened up by the lexemes that he contends are the raw materials whose manipulation constitutes – as opposed to communicatively expresses – the substantial majority of conscious thought.

Given that the MDM rejects the notion of background LF, and of brain-language more broadly, how does syntax arise? The implication of Dennett's theory is that this attribute derives (solely) from foreground memetic processes: that which – in communicativism, and in Carrutherian moderate cognitivism – is implemented by background LF is, in the MDM, accomplished by foreground meme-linkages. The latter are broadly equivalent to the schema-sequences discussed in §3.8.6 under the rubric of Deliège's notion of cue abstraction and/or Gjerdingen's concept of *Il filo*. In that earlier account, these sequences were hypothesised to be underpinned by either: (i) some degree of (parallel) interconnection with (linguistic) LF; or (ii) a dedicated (domain-specific) musical LF; or (iii) some hybrid (shared) musilinguistic LF-system (page 281). In Dennett's strong cognitivism, however, the hierarchic communicativist binarism between an abstract, unconscious LF background and a concrete, conscious lexemic foreground – the former tokened and made conscious by the latter – is flattened and attenuated in ways that arguably leave the issue of syntax, musical and linguistic, hanging. The next section considers how this issue might be resolved by invoking memetics and its neurobiological mechanism, the HCT.

7.4.2 Rehabilitating Memetics in Communicativism

Shifting the focus from the cognitivism *versus* communicativism debate to the role of memetics in thought and consciousness, it is arguable that adopting some flavour of communicativism does not – *contra* Dennett – necessarily mean abandoning a role for memes in thought and consciousness or, consequently, a memetic view of culture. It simply means accepting that some types of mental content are not *directly* amenable to the lexemic variation, replication and selection upon which memetics, and the MDM, are predicated; and therefore acknowledging that the operation of the VRS algorithm in brain function – the neural Darwin machine – and in the wider culture is only part of the picture. The remaining elements, reasonably enough, are to be found in those areas of mental functioning shaped most strongly by the VRS algorithm's phylogenetic operation over the course of biological, as opposed to cultural, evolution – by nature as opposed to nurture.

From this standpoint – and assuming a distinction is maintained between domain-specific mentalese (representing, as noted, "mental models or mental images of various kinds" (Carruthers, 2002, p. 658)) and domain-general, LF – it is the latter that not only facilitates a synthesis of the former, but that also offers a means of (memetically) transmitting the integrated information content between individuals by means of its tokening by lexemes and their subsequent dissemination. So not only may we admit of: (i) the traditional inter-brain *transmission* of classical memetics; but also (ii) an intra-brain process of *translation* between (a) those (unconscious) mental structures that encode domain-specific mentalese and domain-general LF mentalese – each instance of either category being a mnemon/mnemonplex, or item/complex of (initially unreplicated) brain-stored information (Lynch, 1998; see also Table 1.3); and (b) those (conscious) mental structures that encode domain-general lexemes/lexemeplexes. This distinction is represented in part by the differently coloured meme-symbols in Figure 3.16. On this basis, even a strong communicativist position is not incompatible with memetics because, even though thought is not taken to be *implemented* by language in this view, lexemes are still the medium by which certain (integrated) thoughts are *transmitted* between individual brains (with concomitant reconstitution back to LF mentalese in the receiving brain). Thus, for memetics, the differences between cognitivism and communicativism – strong, moderate or weak – tend to devolve to what exactly is translated into, and reconstituted from, language.

While memes are perhaps most readily sustained, as lexemes, in the realm of language (on the grounds that linguistic utterances are relatively easily and widely imitated),[295] and while Carruthers' model hypothesises language as the medium for the articulation and rendering conscious of LF-integrated/ domain-general thought, certain domain-specific thoughts might nevertheless be memetically transmitted. In Carruthers' example of "THE TOY IS IN THE CORNER WITH A LONG WALL ON THE LEFT AND A SHORT WALL ON THE RIGHT" (page 262), a mentalese-encoded mnemon/mnemonplex produced by the geometrical module and encoding the spatial information as a specific conceptual entity might be transmitted from one individual to another by the use of gestures and facial expressions in the context of a sensory stimulus (a visual input of the long and short walls), potentially bypassing any linguistic formulation entirely. If this information is successfully transferred, then a meme will, essentially, have been engendered. Further cross-domain/modal-

---

[295] For Kirby, "language appears to have adapted simply through the process of iterated learning in such a way as to become more learnable" (2013, p. 129).

ity connections made in the receiving brain – a memory of a similarly shaped blue wall, for instance – might render this domain-specific concept fully domain-general. In this way, the mnemon/mnemonplex becomes a meme/memeplex by virtue of its reconstitution in another brain by means, if not strictly of imitation, then certainly of a form of social learning. This process is broadly analogous to the "stimulus enhancement" found, for example, in tits (*Paridae*), who have been observed to notice others of their species pecking at milk-bottle tops (this behaviour being reinforced by the acquired cream) and then, their attention thus directed to the bottle (the stimulus), themselves repeating the behaviour (Blackmore, 1999, p. 48). This action suggests that the observer bird builds analogous mental structures in relation to this behaviour to those of the observed bird.

As was argued in §3.8.4 and §3.8.6, the neurobiological structures encoding the various types of mental content formalised in the HCT are not necessarily different in *kind*, only in the *type* of information – mentalese domain-specific thoughts, mentalese domain-general LF, protemes, lexemes, sonemes, musemes – they encode. The distinction between (i) predominantly soft/culturally wired cognitivism and (ii) predominantly hard/biologically wired communicativism in part devolves, respectively, to the difference between: (i) the localised connections that permit the propagation of resonating hexagons over adjacent regions of cortical territory; and (ii) the "*faux*-fax" links (point 4 of the list on page 271) that, by connecting more distant hexagons, implement the recursive embedding that is a key element of LF and that is thus central to linguistic syntax. This distinction is broadly coterminous with that articulated at the end of §7.4.1 in connection with the theorisation of syntax in the MDM, namely that between: (i) a conscious foreground sustained by lexemic tokening; and (ii) an unconscious background LF. Crucially – and suggesting a key role for cultural evolution in this attribute – some of the background *faux*-fax links may have started off as relatively plastic – memetic – foreground connections, but later became consolidated by selection to form relatively stable – genetic – background structures. This malleability may be hardened over the course of ontogeny (or ontomemy), or may have been hardened over the course of phylogeny (or phylomemy), the latter perhaps involving Baldwinian processes (§1.8).

Thus, a degree of reconciliation between cognitivism and communicativism might be arrived at via a gene-meme coevolutionary perspective, which of course maintains that cultural evolution can exert significant pressure upon biological evolution, and vice versa. Thus, despite saying that "strong cognitivism", such as is articulated in the MDM, "might be taken to hold that there is no 'background' LF and indeed no brain-language" (581), one might nevertheless admit the possibility that LF exists and that it might have at least some memetic component. That is, the underlying (proto)syntax of (musi)language might have a culturally evolved element in addition to its – in Chomsky's formulation – biologically evolved dimension. As the theory of memetic drive (§3.7.1) hypothesises, meme-driven selection pressures are a potentially powerful factor in directing genetic evolution and so any nascent capacity for syntax – a partly soft/memetic, partly hard/genetic proto-LF (§3.8.3, §3.8.6) – might have been seized upon by other memes and used to favour their replication. If this proto-LF had conferred aptive benefits to its possessors, then its genetic underpinning would likely have been favoured for replication into the next generation, ready to receive a potentially more evolved – and potentially more memetic-drive-potent – meme component.

Returning to their explanatory power to elucidate consciousness, both cognitivism and communicativism arguably rely on appeals to what are still poorly understood processes, where often, in an infinite regress, the explanation for consciousness recedes, mirage-like, ever further into the distance. Cognitivism appeals to the swarms of memes that, seemingly by brute force, boot-up consciousness like the loading of a computer's operating system and the associated colourful illumination of the machine's monitor; whereas communicativism appeals to the ToM module that, somehow, makes lexeme-tokened LF conscious – as Carruthers asserts in the passage quoted on page 264, "perceptual and imagistic states *get to be* phenomenally conscious by virtue of their availability to the higher-order thoughts generated by the theory of mind system" (my emphasis added here). In both cases, and for all the light they shed upon the neurobiological encoding and cultural evolution of music and language, the nature of consciousness as felt experience – as a series of qualia – remains elusive in both perspectives. What is at least defensible in both is the claim that evolutionary processes are a strong candidate for sustaining brain-states/drafts – in a Darwin machine made up of competing hexagonal plaques and powered by the VRS algorithm – because entities that can make copies of themselves – and that includes patterns of neuronal minicolumn interconnection just as much as patterns of base-pair combination – will tend to prevail according to how successfully they are able to survive selection and to achieve replication. Yet, in summary, it seems clear that any exclusive alignment of memetics with cognitivism or communicativism is over-simplistic. In reality, there appear to be three dynamically intersecting continua at play: (i) that connecting cognitivism with communicativism; (ii) that connecting neurobiological and psychological backgrounds with foregrounds; and (iii) that connecting un-consciousness with consciousness. As continua, these are likely gradualistic, in terms of ontogeny and phylogeny and also in terms of the "user-illusion" of consciousness itself.

7.5 Tonal-System Evolution as (Musical) Consciousness

If, after §7.3.2, one accepts that consciousness is a form of rapid evolution, and that evolution is a form of slow consciousness, then where might one look for evidence of this phenomenon in relation to music? One clear candidate is the process of tonal-system evolution in western music, the widely observed fact that, over time, the hierarchic relationships between pitches, chords and keys has not remained static but has changed, and that these changes have been in the direction, arguably, of greater chromaticism, dissonance and richness. At the risk of oversimplifying a complex process, the localised post-modal tonalities of early-Baroque music (such as the transient key areas in Monteverdi's *Orfeo* of 1607), gave way to the stable "unified tonality" (LaRue, 2011, p. 53) of the eighteenth and early-nineteenth centuries, with its increasing reliance on the tension-generating power of the tonic-dominant polarity. After Beethoven, the chromatic freedom he had wedded to an overarching tonic increased, leading to an almost Gaussian return to tonal fragmentation. By the end of the nineteenth century, localised areas of relative tonal stability, some articulating non-diatonic organisation, gave way, in Schoenberg and others, to total chromaticism and non-hierarchic pitch relationships. Except when viewed from the perspective of an infinitesimally thin slice through time, western tonality – and, by extension, all systems of tonal organisation in music – was in constant dynamic flux, this fluidity providing a diachronic counterpoint to the concept of replication hierarchies (§1.6.2 see also §4.3 and §4.4), with its implications of synchronic immutability.

7.5.1 Style Hierarchies and Music-Systemic Evolution

Table 1.4 aligns, at level two, systems of rules in culture (which encompass tonal systems in music) (Meyer, 1996, p. 17) with biochemical systems in biology. While both are subject to physical laws (level one) – the laws of chemistry (and thus of physics) in the case of biology; the (physically controlled) laws of acoustics and the (genetically controlled) constraints of psychology in the case of music – phenomena at level two are mutable, albeit perhaps more evidently so in culture than in nature. Given sufficient bottom-up musemic pressure, transformations manifesting themselves in several dialects are able to reorientate a particular configuration of cultural rules. The same principles hold in biology, although top-down forces are perhaps stronger than bottom-up ones here, owing to the relatively static nature of physical laws (§1.5.2), whereas the converse appears to be the case in culture. Thus, species evolution might reconfigure certain aspects of biochemistry in order to open up the capacity to occupy certain ecological niches, such as aptations to deep-sea environments (Somero, 1992; Saito, 2007). As argued, and like a species, a dialect is difficult to define, in that it represents a "smeary continuum" (§1.7.3, §4.3.2, §4.3.3), not a discrete entity. This gradualism means that not only is a species or a dialect different at its end from its beginning, but also that its transformations (and the location and nature of its end-state) are intrinsically ambiguous: at what point do species or dialects $x^{1 \cdots n}$ cease to be instances of category x (i.e., variants of x) and become instead instances of category y (i.e., something different from x)? Because dialects token a system of rules, these observations apply to tonal systems: the rule-systems are fluid because the dialects that generate them are themselves constantly changing as a result of museme-transforming cultural evolution.

As the foregoing implies, a tonal system is a diachronic reality, not a synchronic abstraction, existing concretely through the musemes that underpin

it. It follows that the various characteristics, qualities, tendencies and relationships of these musemes give rise, as bottom-up forces, to the attributes
and dynamics that constitute and define the system. Cumulatively, such
lower-order, intraopus-, idiom- and dialect-level processes fed into and determined the complexion of higher-order, rule-level systems. Thus, it is
axiomatic to memetics – by virtue of the recursive ontology of which it is an
element (§1.5.5) – that large-scale cultural phenomena, including tonal systems, are manifestations of the attributes of "real" m(us)emes at lower levels
of a cultural hierarchy feeding upwards to engender larger scale "virtual"
networks and relationships at higher, systemic levels. In this view there is no
central authority governing a tonal system – how could there be, when there
are so many independent agents engaged in musemic replication? – and
thus no omniscient arbiter of the realm. In this sense, such systems might
be regarded as macrocosmic analogues of human consciousness, being the
"serial" outcomes of myriad "parallel" musemic processes. Adapting Dennett's "Thumbnail Sketch" of the MDM cited on page 573 to tonal-system
evolution, one might argue that

> [t]here is no single, definitive 'stream of [tonality]', because there is no
> central Headquarters, no Cartesian [Concert Hall] where 'it all comes
> together' for the perusal of a Central Meaner. Instead of such a single
> stream (however wide), there are multiple channels in which specialist
> [tonalities] try, in parallel pandemoniums, to do their various things
> [i.e., engender the replication of their generating musemes and muse-
> meplexes], creating Multiple Drafts as they go. Most of these fragment-
> ary drafts of '[tonality]' play short-lived roles in the modulation of
> current activity but some get promoted [by practice and theorisation] to
> further functional roles, in swift succession, by the activity of a virtual
> machine in the [culture]. The [apparent] seriality of this machine ... is
> not a 'hard-wired' design feature, but rather the upshot of a succession
> of coalitions of these [practitioners and theorists]. (after Dennett, 1993a,
> pp. 253–254)

A central issue in this tonal-system consciousness/evolution is the tendency
for theory to lag significantly behind practice in many artistic realms. As
argued in §4.6, the metalanguage of music theory and analysis is also an
evolutionary system, but one that often takes a significant period of time
to adapt to the language (music) that it evolves to describe/prescribe. This

lag is manifested specifically in the tendency for new tonal-harmonic phenomena often to take many years to be recognised as normative by music theorists. On initial appearance in the work of a single composer – as a result of localised musemic mutation – certain phenomena may be framed as transgressive or aberrant by theory. They eventually become legitimised by the practice of increasing numbers of composers – as the museme or musememeplex is more widely replicated – which creates the selective environment that impels theory to accept what had previously been rejected. In terms of the paraphrase of Dennett's summary of the MDM given above, the function of the "virtual machine" is accomplished – at a higher hierarchic level than that of the individual brain – by culture, specifically the "analytical discourse" in Figure 4.9, which brings together theorists in "coalitions" of agreement upon which verbal-conceptual memeplexes are most optimally coadapted with the musemes and musemeplexes in question.

Anthony Pople coined the term "tonalities" to convey a sense of the multiplicity of practice in harmonic language and tonal organisation in the European music of the late-nineteenth and early-twentieth centuries (Pople, 2004; Russ, 2004). The term characterised a problem that was the impetus for his development of the "prolongation-analysis" software *Tonalities* (Pople, 2002) (discussed more fully in §7.5.3). This tool was designed to map the differences between the output of a Debussy and a Schoenberg and, in so doing, to help formulate a "*tonal* set theory" (Pople, 2004, p. 155; emphasis in the original) – i.e., an expansion of the concerns of pitch-class set theory (Forte, 1973) to encompass (late-)tonal music, and not just the atonal music for which it was initially developed. Pople's pluralisation is useful because, at the turn of the twentieth century, starkly divergent approaches to tonal organisation – specifically in relation to the "localised areas of relative tonal stability" referred to at the start of this section – arose in the work of contemporaneous composers in a way that was not evident a century earlier. The software is useful for illuminating present concerns, because it allows one to determine the tonal-harmonic complexion of a particular passage and – although not explicitly theorised by Pople – to relate this to the musemes that engender it. Tonal-systemic evolution can be captured, qualitatively or quantitatively, by comparing analyses against each other in order to relate observed changes in tonal-harmonic configuration to chronology and to potential composer-to-composer intertextual influences.

Tonalities also allows one to explore the tensions between language (music) and metalanguage (theory) referred to above via various manipulations of the program's "language settings" – its numerous configuration parameters, determining which among a large range of chord- and scale-types the software is able to detect. Essentially, one can make the program more or less "aware" of (sensitive to) various tonal-harmonic phenomena. Activating only a few settings (such as selecting a restricted palette of chord- and/or scale-types) makes the program behave like a conservative music theorist, one inclined to see phenomena cautiously, in older, more diatonically inclined ways. Activating many settings (such as selecting a wide range of chord- and/or scale-types) gives *Tonalities* the mindset of a radical composer, inclined to entertain more adventurous chromaticisms. Aspects of this approach are covered in §7.5.3.

7.5.2 Mechanisms of Tonal-System Evolution

How does lower-level museme-mutation feed into higher-level tonal-systemic evolution? As argued in §1.5.1, evolution is a process of aptive change – the "S" of the VRS algorithm referring to selection according to some set of environmental conditions – and not necessarily one where that change leads to an increase in "the logarithm of the total information content of the biosystem (genes plus memes)" (Ball, 1984, p. 154) (§3.6.6). Nevertheless, the cultural environment of post-Renaissance western music has generally favoured novelty over stability – the former often driven by pursuit of the value that forms the other aspect of creativity (§5.5.1) – on account of the arguably greater replicative advantages possessed by musemes that are, on account of their novelty, more perceptually-cognitively salient than their rivals; and this tendency has been a significant factor driving the increasing combinatorial and chromatic richness of western music of the past four hundred years.

This richness is manifested in the ongoing assaults on diatonic organisation (hereafter "DIA") by forces that lead to increasing hexatonic (hereafter "HEX"), octatonic (hereafter "OCT"), whole-tone organisation (hereafter

"WT") and chromatic (hereafter "CHR").[296] In a nutshell, juxtaposition and mutation change musemes and musemeplexes that articulate DIA organisation (horizontally and/or vertically) into variant non-DIA forms – i.e., into HEX-, OCT-, WT- or CHR-articulating patterns. Sometimes, this mutation consists of perturbations of triads by parsimonious voice-leading, according to neo-Riemannian principles (Cohn, 1996; Gollin & Rehding, 2011). By sheer weight of numbers, these non-DIA musemes and musemeplexes cumulatively change the profile of the parent dialect and, ultimately, reorientate the level of rules in their image.

There are at least two mechanisms, the first itself subdivided, by which this process appears to operate. These are summarised below and represented in Figure 7.1 (after Jan, 2015b, pp. 151–152, Fig. 1):

- *Juxtapositional*: Non-DIA pitch-collections initially appear at the foreground and shallow-middleground levels as the inter-museme consequence of the juxtaposition of DIA musemes in linear sequences and in musemeplexes (§3.5.2). In this sense, non-DIA organisation is the outcome of *first*:

  – DIA musemes being horizontally juxtaposed (·|·) in museme adjacencies and in musemeplexes in ways that create localised foreground- and shallow-middleground-level HEX, OCT, WT and CHR collections "across the cracks" (inter-museme horizontal juxtaposition, hereafter "IMHJ"); *and then …*

  – DIA musemes being vertically juxtaposed (÷) in museme simultaneities and in musemeplexes in ways that create localised foreground- and shallow-middleground-level HEX, OCT, WT and CHR collections "between the layers" (inter-museme vertical juxtaposition, hereafter "IMVJ"); *and then …*

- *Mutational*:

---

[296] In summary, DIA organisation uses seven-note scales generated by cycles of interval-class 7, such as C♮–D♮–E♮–F♮–G♮–A♮–B♮; HEX organisation uses six-note scales generated by cycles of interval-class 4, such as C♮–E♭–E♮–G♮–G♯–B♮; OCT organisation uses eight-note scales generated by cycles of interval-class 3, such as C♮–D♮–E♭–F♮–F♯–G♯–A♮–B♮; WT organisation uses six-note scales generated by cycles of interval-class 2, such as C♮–D♮–E♮–F♯–G♯–A♯; and CHR organisation uses twelve-note scales generated by cycles of interval-class 1, i.e., C♮–C♯–D♮–E♭–E♮–F♮–F♯–G♮–G♯–A♮–B♭–B♮ (Straus, 2016, Ch. 5).

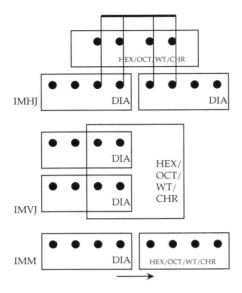

Figure 7.1: Generation of HEX, OCT, WT and CHR Collections.

– DIA musemes being mutated, giving rise directly to HEX, OCT, WT
and CHR collections (intra-museme mutation, hereafter "IMM"). As
IMHJ- and IMVJ-generated HEX, OCT, WT and CHR organisation became widely propagated, these collections may then have been directly
generated – mimicked? – by IMM.

These mechanisms align with the theory of consciousness discussed in §7.3.1,
in that both juxtapositional categories (IMHJ and IMVJ) and the mutational
category (IMM) are implemented, as are all aspects of museme-encoding, by
the structures and processes described by the HCT. Apropos the discussion
on page 267, and in the case of IMHJ and IMVJ, there is (literal) abutting/
overlapping of two or more museme-encoding cortical hexagons (or rather
colonies of hexagons), such that their triangular arrays interdigitate in ways
that engender a hybrid hexagon, one in which the pitch relationships have
been recalibrated. Thus, the "undecided [hybrid, juxtaposed] region may
receive equal doses of both melodies [i.e., musemes]" (Calvin, 1998, p. 59;
see also Jan, 2011a, sec. 4.1.2, paras. 64–68). In the case of IMM, a given
hexagon's arrays are reconfigured in ways that "retune" certain pitches. This
arises partly because a "barrier" (i.e., an area in cortex that, for various
reasons, will not support triangular-array extension) prevents the normal

"error-correction" of a variant pattern, which is therefore not forced back into conformity with its normative neighbours (1998, pp. 87–88). Thereafter, for both mechanisms, "[i]f two copies of the same variant get started, this novel spatiotemporal pattern may be able to clone. If it is closer to a basin of attraction, it may successfully compete for territory with the parent pattern[s]" (1998, p. 88), and may thus be replicated.

The relationship of these mechanisms with consciousness inheres in the fact that the various musemes and musemeplexes involved (and indeed not those involved) in IMHJ, IMVJ and IMM – whether separate, interdigitating, "normal" or variant, in terms of their cortical encoding – are just as much "drafts", the outcomes of "parallel pandemoniums", as are those other types of mental content encompassed by the MDM. All are museme alleles engaged with their rivals in competition for the precious resource of cortical territory, with some motivating, via phemotypic expression, their replication. Beyond a certain threshold point, this replication engenders the expression of these brain-as-Darwin-machine processes at the higher structural-hierarchic level – that of culture-as-Darwin-machine – articulated in the tonality-specific para-phrase of the MDM (page 588). Driven by aptive imperatives, these drafts occupy regions of cortex over microscopic time-scales, and they inscribe their traces on the artefacts of culture over macroscopic time-scales, thereby integrating consciousness as a form of evolution with evolution as a form of consciousness (§7.3.2).

7.5.3 Two Strategies to Evidence Tonal-System Evolution

To evidence the claim that tonal-system evolution is the result of myriad lower-level musemic changes that feed up to affect the profile of the higher-level system is intrinsically difficult, on account of the enormous body of music that must be investigated. One way to achieve this would be to develop a computer program — one might call it *Aristoxenus*, after the first known western music theorist-taxonomist — that could scrutinise every piece of music in a given corpus, segment it into perceptually-cognitively meaningful units at various structural-hierarchic levels, and then cross-map these units synchronically and diachronically. In terms of the distinction drawn in §6.1, this would constitute a form of high-level style analysis, but it might be implemented using some of the strategies for music synthesis discussed in Chapter 6, including machine learning. This approach would allow one to build up a near-complete picture — possibly in the form of a multidimensional musemic hypervolume (§3.6.5, §5.5.2, §6.5), in which each musical parameter is represented by a dimension — of all the musemes in that corpus and of the hypothesised nexus of transmission that connects them. It would also allow "snapshots" to be taken of the system at specific time-points, allowing one to determine its state of evolution at any given point. While there are programs that can accomplish some of this analytical work (Lartillot, 2009; Hawkett, 2013), albeit not always with a specifically memetic focus; and others that can simulate the synthetic processes that might be taking place within musical culture (§6.5), none to my knowledge can accomplish the complete task, namely to offer a comprehensive description of a given museme-pool and to chart its population memetics in detail.

In the absence of such a program, there are two alternative (but complement-ary) strategies to garner the necessary evidence for the claim of a bottom-up musemic basis for tonal-system evolution. The first strategy is to sample very selectively a given museme from various stages in its hypothesised evolutionary history and then attempt to determine its tonal-systemic implic-ations at these various stages, in order to extrapolate from this information wider conclusions about the status of the system as a whole. The second strategy is to examine an extract of music, tracing the antecedent coindexes of its constituent musemes and identifying the nature of any shifts from DIA to non-DIA organisation resulting from IMHJ, IMVJ and IMM. Figure 7.2 illustrates the first strategy and Figure 7.4 illustrates the second.

Figure 7.2 is naturally very selective, taking only five "snapshots" over a long time-span and therefore ignoring numerous intermediate stages.[297] It shows that there are various intersecting museme allele-classes replicated in the five passages, depending upon segmentation and coindexation, the

---

[297] Thus, it is not intended to suggest that the museme from Handel (Figure 7.2a), a work Mozart probably would not have known, was directly transmitted to the latter's Clarinet Quintet (Figure 7.2b) (the other connections are, however, more strongly motivated if not necessarily direct). Rather, these two musemes, in particular, were connected by a complex web of interme-diates, in Mozart's case perhaps filtered via J. S. Bach and facilitated by his access to Baron van Swieten's library in Vienna (which held various manuscripts by J. S. Bach and Handel). In fact, and while not material to the present discussion, Handel's authorship of the sonata in Figure 7.2a, claimed to be among the composer's earliest music, is in doubt.

(a) Museme x^1: Handel, Trio Sonata in E♭ major, HWV 382 (?*c*. 1696), III, bb. 1–2.

(b) Museme x^2: Mozart, Clarinet Quintet in A major K. 581 (1789), I, bb. 42–44.

(c) Museme x^3: Beethoven, Thirty-Three Variations on a Waltz by Diabelli op. 120 (1823), Var. III, bb. 0–4.

(d) Museme x^4: Liszt, *Années de Pèlerinage, deuxième année, Italie* S. 161 (1838–1861), no. 6, *Sonnetto del Petrarca no. 123* (*Io vidi in terra angelici costumi*), bb. 15–17.

(e) Museme x^5: Strauss, *Der Rosenkavalier* TrV 227 (1910), Introduction to Act I, bb. 2–4.

Figure 7.2: Evolution of Museme x.

instantiating musemes coalescing to form a musemeplex allele-class centred around the $\hat{3}$–$\hat{7}$–$\hat{1}$–$\hat{5}$ scale-degree sequence – Museme x itself – that forms the class's structural core. Instantiating the musemeplex allele-class, two partly intersecting sub-classes might be identified. The first sub-class is represented by Figure 7.2a, where the scale-degree sequence is $\hat{1}$–$\hat{2}$–$\hat{3}$–$\hat{7}$–$\hat{1}$–$\hat{5}$–$\hat{3}$ .... Discounting mode, Figure 7.2c shares the $\hat{3}$–$\hat{7}$–$\hat{1}$–$\hat{5}$–$\hat{3}$ ... segment and, on this basis, also instantiates the first sub-class; but it nevertheless has a different continuation to Figure 7.2a and it has no opening (pre-core) museme. The second sub-class is represented by Figure 7.2b, where the scale-degree sequence is ... $\hat{1}$–$\hat{2}$–$\hat{3}$–$\hat{7}$–$\hat{1}$–$\hat{5}$–$\hat{6}$ ....[298] Despite their different continuation from the two members of the first sub-class – that between the post-core $\hat{3}$ ... or $\hat{6}$ ... taken to be the distinguishing feature – Figure 7.2b and Figure 7.2d (the latter also an instance of the second sub-class) share the pre-core museme, $\hat{1}$–$\hat{2}$–$\hat{3}$, of the first sub-class's Figure 7.2a, attenuating the differences between the sub-classes. Its chromatic complications – discussed more fully below – make assigning Figure 7.2e to one of these two sub-classes difficult; but reading it from its starting tonality of A♭ major and ignoring the shift to E major in b. 3, it aligns most closely with the second sub-class, even though it has no $\hat{1}$–$\hat{2}$–$\hat{3}$ prefix-museme and has a different continuation to that of Figure 7.2b and Figure 7.2d.

These musemeplex allele-class sub-classes can be represented as in Figure 7.3 (Feuersänger, 2014, after), which shows a notional three-dimensional hypervolume in which musemes, museme allele-classes, and the latter's sub-classes are depicted as curved surfaces, and in which elements common to two unitary or -plex replicators – in this case, the $\hat{3}$–$\hat{7}$–$\hat{1}$–$\hat{5}$ core scale-degree sequence of Museme x – are represented by the area of intersection between surfaces.

Despite the implication of the first of the two strategies outlined on page 594, all but the last of the five musemes in Figure 7.2 integrate smoothly with their horizontally and vertically adjacent musemes and articulate a stable DIA context. In terms of the mechanisms discussed in §7.5.2, there is no perturbation of the prevailing DIA by means of IMHJ, IMVJ or IMM evident

---

[298] See also Mozart's String Quartet in D major K. 575 (1789), I, bb. 5–6 and his *Die Zauberflöte* K. 620 (1791), no. 19, bb. 18–19 for two other instances of this sub-class.

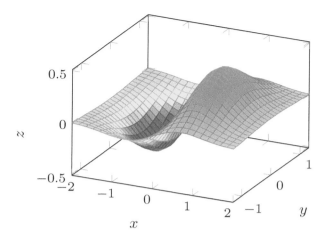

Figure 7.3: Two Intersecting Musemeplex Allele Sub-Classes in a Multidimensional Musemic Hypervolume.

from the deployment of musemes x^1–x^4. This is not the case, however, with
museme x^5, which is best considered in terms of the second strategy.

The passage from which Figure 7.2e is taken is shown in Figure 7.4. This
adopts the approach of Jan (2015a, 2015b) – which discuss music by Mahler
and Debussy, respectively – in using the *Tonalities* software to analyse a segment of music in terms of its tonal-harmonic structure. Taking the opening of
Strauss's *Der Rosenkavalier*,[299] Figure 7.4 shows: (a) a harmonic/voice-leading
reduction; (b) *Tonalities'* own harmonic analysis; (c) *Tonalities'* analysis of
prolonging and connective gamuts, the former shown in (c i), the latter
in (c ii);[300] (d) a reduction of the score; and (e) posited antecedent coin-

---

[299] It might be argued that *Der Rosenkavalier* is not typical of the music of this period, given its
ironic use of jewel-like figures reminiscent of eighteenth-century music (the setting is Vienna
in the early years of Maria Theresa's reign (1740–1780)) set in the gold of a modern harmonic
language. Aside from the fact that there was little stylistic consistency in European music at this
time, one key feature of the opera – the engendering of tonal-harmonic richness by juxtaposition
and mutation of musemes from earlier musics – is also observable in much other music of this
period.

[300] A gamut is Pople's term for a pitch collection, one that transcends the more limited concept
of a scale. A prolonging gamut is a superset pitch collection within which a subset harmony
is active; whereas a connective gamut is an intersection set between two prolonging gamuts.
Tonalities calculates connective gamuts by determining a candidate superset of which two
trichords (three-note chords) extracted from two adjacent prolonging gamuts are subsets (Jan,
2015b, p. 151). A museme may be encompassed by either type of gamut.

dexes of certain of Strauss's musemes.[301] Table 7.2 shows *Tonalities'* output analysis of this passage, detailing the tonal-harmonic configuration of each segment (Table 7.2a, Table 7.2b) before aggregating these in a summary (Table 7.2c).[302]

---

[301] Strauss's musemes are labelled M1, M2, etc., to distinguish them from those in Figure 7.2. As can be seen, museme M2 in Figure 7.4 = museme x^5 in Figure 7.2e. The antecedent coindexes are as follows: Figure 7.4 (e i; for M1): Chopin, Waltz in E♭ major op. 18 (1832), bb. 5–7; (e ii; for M3): Schumann, Piano Concerto in A minor op. 54 (1845), III, bb. 283–287; (e iii; for M4): Wagner, *Lohengrin* WWV 75 (1850), Prelude to Act III, bb. 16–18; (e iv; for M5) Tchaikovsky, *Les saisons* op. 37b (1876), no. 11 (Novembre; Troika), bb. 1–2; and (e v; for M6): Haydn, String Quartet in D major op. 76 no. 5 (1797), II, bb. 3–4 (here the antecedent coindex represents the whole allele-class of major and minor $\hat{7}$–$\hat{1}$–$\hat{4}$–$\hat{3}$ musemes, this allele-class integrating aspects of the *Meyer* and *Fenaroli* schemata (Gjerdingen, 2007a, pp. 111–112; 225)). For clarity, musemes in Figure 7.4 are not given the analytical overlay-symbology used in other music examples (§2); instead, their antecedent coindexes are shown boxed.

[302] *Tonalities'* language settings for this particular analysis were largely the program's defaults, save that: (i) all the "Standard chords" were activated (in addition to the default "Common-practice chords"); and (ii) HEX, OCT and WT were activated, as both prolonging gamuts and as connective gamuts, all "spellable" (see below). Note that there are as many potential analyses of a passage as there are configurations of language settings, and so constraints of space prevent the exploration of the potentially very wide range of configurations. Nevertheless, an alternative configuration is explored at one point in the analysis below. The segmentation of the music, symbolised in Figure 7.4 (c) and (d), and in the *Excel*®spreadsheets that form *Tonalities'* input data encoding, by the dollar ($) symbol, is that employed in the file prepared by Pople himself for this passage and it aligns with the principal harmonic changes of the passage. Not all elements of Figure 7.4 (d) are encoded in Pople's data file, but his omissions (and my additions) do not affect the analysis. Output from *Tonalities* cited in the main text is shown in `typewriter` font.

[303] The forward-slash symbol in *Tonalities'* output indicates that those pitches listed before the slash constitute members of the set representing the identified chord or gamut, whereas those pitches listed after the slash are present in the segment but do not form part of the identified chord- or gamut-set.

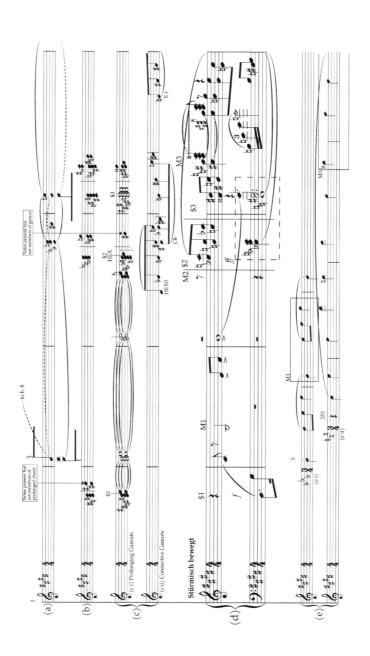

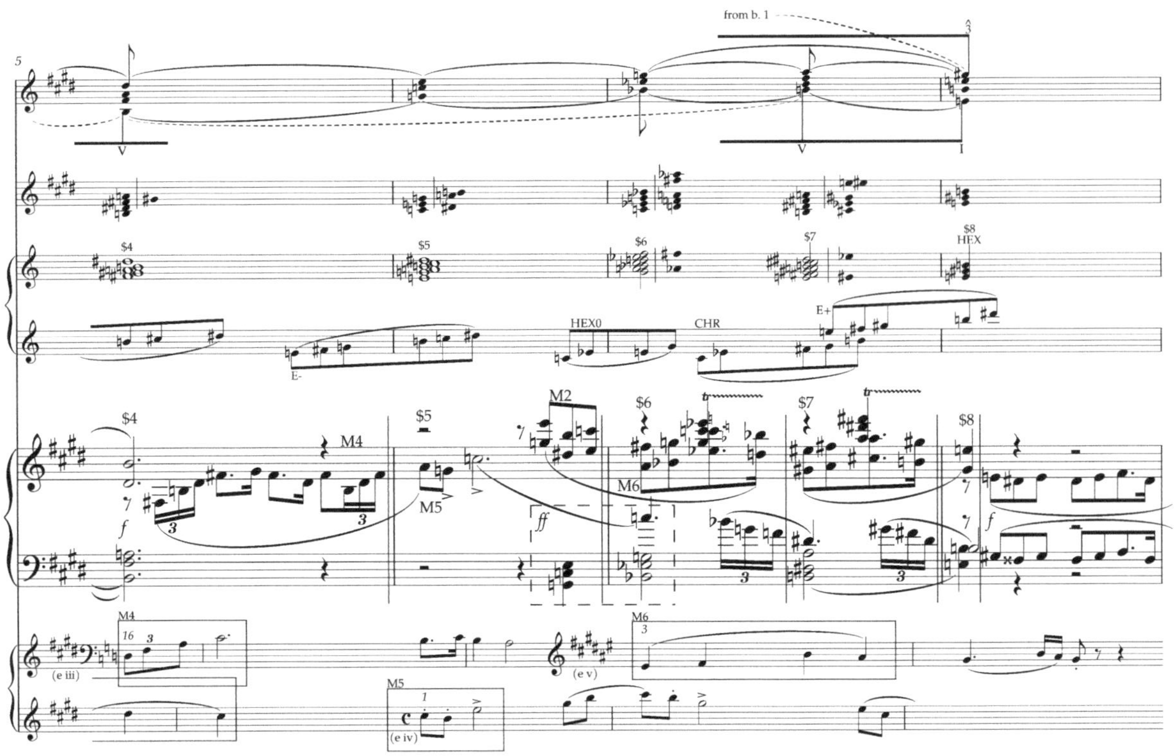

Figure 7.4: Evidence of Tonal-System Evolution in Strauss: *Der Rosenkavalier* TrV 227 (1910), Introduction to Act I, bb. 1–8. *Key:* (a) Harmonic/Voice-Leading Reduction; (b) *Tonalities'* Harmonic Analysis; (c) *Tonalities'* Analysis of Prolonging Gamuts (c i) and Connective Gamuts (c ii); (d) Score Reduction; (e) Antecedent Coindexes of Musemes.

Segment	Analysis
1	*Prolonged chord*: major triad on E [E G♯ B /³⁰³ F♯ C♯] *Prolonging gamut*: E major scale [E F♯ G♯ B C♯] *Chord function within segment*: I *Pitch-class content*: 5–35 (t=4) [1 4 6 8 11]
2	*Prolonged chord*: major triad on A♭ [A♭ C E♭ / G♯ B G] *Prolonging gamut*: hexatonic scale on C [C E♭ G A♭ B / G♯] *Connective gamut*: hexatonic collection 0 [C E♭ E G♯ B] *Trichord distance*: 2 *Root movement*: I–III in terms of previous prolonging gamut (E major) *Pitch-class content*: 5–21A (t=7) [0 3 7 8 11]
3	*Prolonged chord*: minor seventh on C♯ [C♯ E G♯ B / D♯ F♯ G F× A A♯ B♯] *Prolonging gamut*: E major scale [E F♯ G♯ A B C♯ D♯ / G F× A♯ B♯] *Chord function within segment*: VI *Connective gamut*: C♯ melodic minor collection [C♯ E♭ E G♯ C] *Chord progression*: V–I within connective gamut (C♯ melodic minor) *Pitch-class content*: 10–3 (t=6) [0 1 3 4 6 7 8 9 10 11]
4	*Prolonged chord*: dominant seventh on B [B D♯ F♯ A / G♯] *Prolonging gamut*: E major scale [F♯ G♯ A B D♯] *Chord function within segment*: V *Connective gamut*: E major collection [E F♯ G♯ B C♯ D♯] *Chord progression*: VI–V *Pitch-class content*: 5–25B (t=3) [3 6 8 9 11]

(a) Analysis of Segments 1–4.

Segment	Analysis
5	*Prolonged chord*: major triad on C [C E G / D♯ A B] *Prolonging gamut*: E harmonic minor scale [E G A B C D♯] *Chord function within segment*: vi *Connective gamut*: E harmonic minor collection [E F♯ G B C D♯] *Chord progression*: V–vi *Pitch-class content*: 6–31B (t=7) [0 3 4 7 9 11]
6	*Prolonged chord*: minor seventh on C [C E♭ G B♭ / D F F♯ A♭ A] *Prolonging gamut*: G diatonic minor scale [G A B♭ C D E♭ F / A♭ F♯] *Chord function within segment*: IV *Connective gamut*: hexatonic collection 0 [C E♭ E G] *Trichord distance*: 1 *Root movement*: none *Pitch-class content*: 9–7B (t=2) [0 2 3 5 6 7 8 9 10]
7	*Prolonged chord*: dominant seventh on B [B D♯ F♯ A / C♯ E♭ E E♯ G♯] *Prolonging gamut*: E major scale [E F♯ G♯ A B C♯ D♯ / E♯ E♭] *Chord function within segment*: V *Connective gamut*: chromatic [C E♭ F♯ G B] *Common tones*: 1 *Root movement*: ♭VI–V in terms of prolonging gamut (E major) *Pitch-class content*: 8–22A (t=3) [1 3 4 5 6 8 9 11]
8	*Prolonged chord*: major triad on E [E G♯ B] *Prolonging gamut*: hexatonic scale on E [E G♯ B] *Connective gamut*: E major collection [E F♯ G♯ B D♯] *Chord progression*: V–I within connective gamut (E major) *Pitch-class content*: 3–11B (t=4) [4 8 11]

(b) Analysis of Segments 5–8.

Criterion	Summary
Chord types prolonged	major triad: 50.0% (4) minor seventh: 25.0% (2) dominant seventh: 25.0% (2) [15 other common-practice chord types active but unused] [18 standard chord types active but unused]
Prolonging gamuts	E major: 50.0% (4) E minor: harmonic 12.5% (1) G minor: diatonic 12.5% (1) hexatonic 0: 25.0% (2) [3 other gamut types active but unused]
Connective gamuts	E major: 28.6% (2) C♯ minor: melodic 14.3% (1) E minor: harmonic 14.3% (1) hexatonic 0: 28.6% (2) chromatic: 14.3% (1) [3 other selectable connective gamut types active but unused]

(c) Summary of Analysis.

Table 7.2: *Tonalities'* Analysis of Richard Strauss: *Der Rosenkavalier* TrV 227 (1910), Introduction to Act I, bb. 1–8.

There is a lot of information in Figure 7.4 and Table 7.2, and exploring all its implications in detail is beyond the scope of this chapter; but some suggestive conclusions can nevertheless be drawn in support of the hypotheses advanced in §7.5.2. As might be expected from the frequent harmonic shifts between chords a third apart – such as the E major–A♭ major progression of bb. 2–3, the converse progression in bb. 3–4, and the C major–E♭ major progression of bb. 6–7 (see note 305 on page 606) – HEX is invoked by *Tonalities* for certain connective gamuts. Indeed HEX is the dominant non-DIA mode of organisation here: no OCT or WT prolonging or connective gamuts are read in this passage.

Specifically, hexatonic collection 0 [C E♭ E G♯ B] is invoked as the $1–$2 connective gamut and hexatonic collection 0 [C E♭ E G] is also invoked as the $5–$6 connective gamut.[304] This collection would also be viable as the $2–$3 connective, given that $2–$3 reverses the harmonic shift, E major–A♭ major, of $1–$2; but *Tonalities* instead prefers a C♯ melodic minor collection [C♯ E♭ E G♯ C] here, reading E♭ as enharmonically equivalent to D♯ and C♮ as enharmonically equivalent to B♯. This highlights the theoretical tension between the more conservative C♯ minor reading and the more progressive HEX_0 interpretation. The C♯ melodic minor collection is preferred here because this gamut is, by default, "spellable". In Pople's definition, "[s]pelled matches of chords or gamuts adhere to the [DIA-correct] note-class definitions — so that, for example, C F♭ G won't be recognised as a C major triad, but C E G will. In an unspelled match [available when a gamut is set as spellable], the pitches in the segment are interpreted as pitch-classes, so that C F♭ G would be recognised as an unspelled [i.e., incorrectly spelled] C major triad" (2002, p. 10). On account of this capacity, *Tonalities'* looks both for DIA-correct note-class names, and therefore their normative tonal-harmonic implications and functions, *and* for their more abstract, ostensibly non-DIA pitch-class representations. The latter ability to read E♭ and C♮ as $\hat{2}$ and ♯$\hat{7}$, respectively, in C♯ minor pushes *Tonalities* – as far as is possible to discern, given the current lack of detailed "under-the-bonnet" knowledge of

---

[304] There are four HEX (sub-)collections – four distinct forms of set-class 6–20 – represented by Cohn (1996, p. 24, Fig. 5) in terms of a "hyper-hexatonic system" consisting of collections normally labelled HEX_0, HEX_1, HEX_2 and HEX_3. Only the first of these – the pitch-classes 0 (C♮), 3 (E♭), 4 (E♮), 7 (G♮), 8 (G♯) and 11 (B♮) – is found in the passage analysed in Figure 7.4.

the program's algorithms – towards favouring the more conservative reading over the more radical one.

Perhaps more significantly, HEX_0 is also invoked as the prolonging gamut in $2 and $8, although the reasons for *Tonalities'* alighting upon this reading in the latter segment are unclear, given that the data file encoding this extract only contains the first beat of b. 8 and thus omits the f× (b. 8^2) that, understood enharmonically as g♮, would help support a HEX_0 reading. The former segment, $2, however, is pure HEX_0, with its arresting combination of a sounding A♭ major and residual elements of the E major of $1, sustained in $2 by the A♭ ($= G♯$) and the reiterated B♮, these prolonging the memory of E major from $1. In an inversion of the situation discussed above apropos the C♯ melodic minor collection [C♯ E♭ E G♯ C] spanning $2–$3, if the analysis were rerun and the language settings adjusted (as mentioned in note 302 on page 598) so that HEX was not spellable – which essentially serves to make HEX a less credible interpretation – then *Tonalities* would not find a HEX prolonging gamut in $2 and $8. Rather, and unsurprisingly, it would read an A♭ major scale [A♭ C E♭ G / G♯ B] and an E major scale [E G♯ B], respectively. As with the C♯ melodic minor collection, this indicates, again, that the flexibility afforded by spellability has a significant liberalising effect on which gamuts are able to be recognised.

In terms of the generation of these HEX connective and prolonging gamuts, it is clear that commonplace figures that arose in the largely DIA music of earlier styles are often used to engender them by means of the by IMHJ, IMVJ and IMM discussed in §7.5.2. In the case of the connective gamuts, the $1–$2 hexatonic collection 0 [C E♭ E G♯ B] arises from the IMHJ of M1 and M2. The terminal G♯ of M1 becomes its enharmonic equivalent, A♭, in b. 2, over which M2 unfolds. M2 terminates with the three-note sequence d♯^{2}–e♮^{2}–a♮^{2} (owing to the closural force of the ♪. a♮^{2} of b. 3^{2-3}), to align with the return to E major harmony in b. 3. The three-note sequence is an artefact of IMM, one perhaps impelled by the A♭ major–E major harmonic shift, because the antecedent coindexes of M2 (musemesx^1–x^4) in Figure 7.2 are – in terms of their $\hat{3}$–$\hat{7}$–$\hat{1}$–$\hat{5}$ core – four-note patterns, while Strauss's form (x^5/M2) arguably has six notes, as symbolised by the dotted line in Figure 7.2e. Yet its first four notes preserve the interval structure of musemesx^2–x^4

(i.e., $\downarrow5\uparrow1\downarrow5\uparrow1$), despite the internal harmonic shift. The broadly analogous $5–$6 `hexatonic collection 0` [C E♭ E G♯ B] is generated by a repeat of M2 that overlaps with M6: in b. 3, M2 is terminated by the ♪. a^2, that, via museme overlapping (Jan, 2007, pp. 74–77), also forms the initial node of M3. In b. 7, a different continuation, reinforced by repetition (b. $7^{1-2} \rightarrow {}^{3-4}$), engenders two iterations of a separate museme, M6 (whose parent allele-class, understood broadly, is that of the various changing-note patterns of schema theory (Gjerdingen, 2007a)), the first three pitches of which overlap with the final three of M2. Thus, the $5–$6 HEX connective arises from IMHJ or, more precisely, from what might be termed IMHO – Inter-Museme Horizontal Overlapping.[305]

In the case of the prolonging gamuts, the `hexatonic scale on C` [C E♭ G A♭ B / G♯] of $2 arises in part because the normal distinction drawn in tonal harmony between chord notes and non-chord notes is subverted by the prevailing context – the E major–A♭ major–E major of $1–$3 – that, as suggested in the previous paragraph, perhaps drives the IMM of M2. Here, the $g\natural^2$ of b. 2^4 and its inner-voice shadow $b\natural^1$ would normally be heard as unstable appoggiaturas to the more stable following $a\flat^2$ and c^2, respectively; but the previous $1–$2 HEX connective, with its persisting $g\sharp^1$ and remembered b, appears to motivate *Tonalities* – as it might also a human listener – to reconceive the relationship between these four notes such that the inner-voice $b\natural^1$ becomes essential while the upper-voice g^2 retains its in-essential status as an appoggiatura (reheard as f×) to an also reheard (as $g\sharp^2$) $a\flat^2$. As noted above, it is not clear why a `hexatonic scale on E` [E G♯ B] prolonging gamut is read in $8: as *Tonalities'* bare listing of the components of an E-major triad tacitly admits, there appear to be no strong musemic motivation for this analogous to the contextually driven rehearing evident in $2. Rather, it may be a resonant artefact of the CHR connective read across $6–$7. As an element of the aforementioned black-box nature of *Tonalities'*

---

[305] There are also discrete harmonic musemes here – i.e., two-element chord progressions – coadapted with the melodic musemes discussed, two of these being shown in dashed-line boxes in Figure 7.4. As reported by *Tonalities*, the $5–$6 progression articulates a `Root movement`: `none`, a reading at variance with the evident $C4–E\flat4$ (I–♭III in C major) harmony. The analogous $2–$3 progression, while not associated with a HEX connective gamut (as noted, the $2–$3 connective is a `C♯ melodic minor collection` [C♯ E♭ E G♯ C]), articulates a `Chord progression`: `V-I within connective gamut` (`C♯ melodic minor`), a reading similarly at variance with the evident $A\flat4–E4$ (III–I in A♭ major) harmony.

algorithms, it is not entirely clear how much the program can "remember" of past events; but such memory is clearly a factor in human music cognition and would presumably be a factor in the processes that drove the replication and intermeshing of these musemes.

What seems clear from the necessarily selective discussion of *Tonalities'* analysis of these bars is the power of musemes to drive perturbations of an increasingly unstable DIA equilibrium. Strauss's musemes, individually and locally DIA, seem to grate against each other, wresting the tonality from one region to another and engendering, in places here, a distinct HEX sound-world that invites a progressive hearing, and a progressive theory (one arguably not arrived at until the 1990s), to recognise it. Of course, for this reading to be valid one has to endorse the model of individual selfish replicators competing in Strauss's mind for phemotypic expression. Some might argue that the genesis of *Der Rosenkavalier* involved more than the kind of creative somnambulism that an unsympathetic reading of this account might suggest. But – to reiterate the thesis of §7.3 and §7.5 – a thoroughgoing memetic interpretation of consciousness and culture would suggest that, just as the former is driven (in part) by the relentless competition between selfish replicators for (intra-agent) survival in cortex, so the latter (including music-systemic culture) is driven, at a higher structural-hierarchic level, by the same (albeit additionally inter-agent) processes. While the former gives the illusion of an intentional self (Blackmore, 1996) whereas the latter appears more random, both are manifestations of the Universal-Darwinian operation of the VRS algorithm. In this reading, both fleeting mental states and the ever-changing configurations of culture are, to recall Dennett's phrase, the products of replicators operating in "multiple channels in which specialist circuits try, in parallel pandemoniums, to do their various things, creating Multiple Drafts as they go" (1993a, pp. 253–254).

7.6 Cultural Evolution and Internet Consciousness

By design, the internet – a network of interconnected computers – is a medium for information transmission. Since the inception in the 1990s of the World Wide Web – a network of interconnected documents – this hardware and software infrastructure has increasingly been understood as a fertile medium for the propagation of memes (Marshall, 1998). As discussed in §3.1, while the term "meme" has become to some extent debased by its recent restricted usage, this does not alter the fact that the internet is a conduit for the replication of an almost unimaginably large body of information, be it programming-language code and associated executables, text, images, videos and, of course, music-related data such as score-image files and sound files. To quantity one must add speed: the rate of cultural evolution on the internet appears constantly to accelerate, outstripping the pace of pre-electronic cultural evolution, just as cultural evolution out-paces biological evolution. In this section, the nature and implications of music-cultural evolution on the internet are considered, and a connection is hypothesised between the kind of music-systemic consciousness discussed in §7.5 and the yet higher-level consciousness that appears nascent on the internet.

7.6.1 Replicators and Vehicles in Internet Evolution

The transmission of information on the internet – and in digital/electronic environments more generally – subverts the distinction between replicators and vehicles. As outlined in §1.6.1, in biological evolution, genes are the replicators – together they constitute the organism's genome – and the physical body is the vehicle – the phenotypic product that facilitates replication. Similarly, in (non-electronic) cultural evolution, brain-encoded memes are the replicators – together they constitute the organism's memome – and the artefacts and behaviours they motivate are the vehicles – the phemotypic products that facilitate replication. These alignments prompt two questions: (i) is information transmitted on the internet a subtype of cultural evolution, understandable using the same categories of memomic replicators and phemotypic vehicles; or (ii) does it represent, as suggested in §1.5, a new phase of evolution on earth – termed there a seventh phase of Darwinism – requiring a separate category, and a new conceptual framework, to those employed that section?

If the first question is answered in the affirmative, the units of internet-replicated information are primarily the human-phemotypic ("*h*-phemotypic") products of brain-stored memes ("*h*-memes"), on the grounds that much information transmission on the internet is directly mediated by human activity. On this reading, elements of such first-order phemotypes ("1*h*-phemotypes") of first-order memes ("1*h*-memes") – such as text-information entered into a web browser (§7.6.2) – have a double function, themselves acting as memes ("*i*-memes" ≡ "2*h*-memes"). The latter may subsequently give rise to their own phemotypes ("*i*-phemotypes") – such as the actions that such text might motivate, including text generated by others in response to the initial information – that, from the perspective of the *i*-meme, are first-order phemotypes ("1*i*-phemotypes") but that, from the perspective of the originating 1*h*-memes, are second-order phemotypes ("2*h*-phemotypes").

If the second question is answered in the affirmative, however, and in situations where information propagation on the internet proceeds without direct human intervention, then the electronic impulses underpinning this information, while analogous to the Calvinian structures of human-centred memetics (implementing 1*h*-memes and "1*h*-memomes"; §3.8.3), are nevertheless independent of them and thus constitute autonomous first-order replicators. Individually, they are *i*-memes; collectively, when associated in some functional or systemic grouping, they constitute "*i*-memomes", although they transcend the organic structures that bind 1*h*-memes into 1*h*-memomes. Their *i*-phemotypic products are similarly independent of human control. Blackmore (2015) terms *i*-memes "tremes" (§6.5.3.2) – she previously named them "temes" (2008; see also Dennett, 2017, p. 392) – or third-order replicators: in the complete ontology (i.e., that encompassing replicators in Velardo's biological, psychological and socio-cultural ontological categories; §1.5.5), tremes (iii), the products of which are their "tremotype", build upon meme-products (ii), which themselves build upon gene-products (i).[306] I generally reserve the term treme to refer to independent replicators in this second category, thus distinguishing them from the dependent *i*-memes of the first category with which they align, structurally if not ontologically.

Extending Table 1.3, the relationships between the three evolutionary systems – biological, human-cultural and digital-cultural – are summarised in Table 7.3 (after Jan, 2007, p. 30, Tab. 2.1), where, as indicated above, "*b*-" denotes "biological", "*h*-" indicates "human(/cultural)" and "*i*-" represents

---

[306] It should be noted that *i*-memes/tremes function as replicators whether or not they exist as elements of programs implementing genetic/evolutionary algorithms (§6.5.3.2).

"internet(/cultural)". While the second (strong) model, outlined in the previous paragraph, seems more viable than the first (weak) model, in part due to the growth of Artificial Intelligence, including the music-generative systems discussed in §6.5, both are outlined, as (i) and (ii), in the relevant part of Table 7.3.

Gene/Genome	Phenotype
The genetic material of an organism, coded, in humans, in DNA.	The genome-motivated morphology and non-learned (instinctive) behaviours of – Skinnerian and Popperian (Table 3.1) – organisms ("1*b*-phenotype"); the extended-phenotypic consequences of these morphologies and behaviours in the world, including structural modifications to the organism's environment and to other phenotypes (§1.5.3).

Meme/Memome	Phemotype
[A] replicator existing as a sound/image/concept-encoding SFP embedded as a series of basins of attraction in the underlying minicolumnar connectivity of the cortex by recurrent excitation resulting from sensory or motor input and capable of colonising large areas of cortex (and of other brains' cortices) according to Universal-Darwinian principles of variation, replication and selection. It aligns partially with other SFPs in the "Library of Aristoxenus",[307] such that similarity relationships connect the discrete and particulate into a wider continuum of structure and meaning relationships across cortical, idiostructural and cultural space (after Jan, 2016c, p. 462).	The meme-motivated behaviours, and the artefacts resulting from these behaviours, of culture-manifesting – Gregorian – organisms ($\equiv$ "2*b*-phenotype").

---

[307] After Borges' Library of Babel. This library, a memetic hypervolume, "is total and ... its shelves register all the possible combinations of the twenty-odd orthographical symbols (a number which, though extremely vast, is not infinite): in other words, all that it is given to express, in all languages" (Borges, 1970, p. 81; see also Jan, 2007, pp. 199–201). In a telling alignment with the HCT, the library is constructed of a series of interconnected hexagonal galleries (Borges, 1970, p. 78).

Treme/Tremome	Tremotype
Either (i) a dependent replicator arising from the $1h$-phemotype of a $1h$-meme, and giving rise, as a $2h$-meme $\equiv$ *i*-meme, to $1h$-phemotypic effects of the *i*-meme and thus to $2h$-phemotypic effects of the $1h$-meme; *or* (ii) an independent replicator, *i*-meme $\equiv$ treme, existing as a series of electromagnetic impulses transmitted via the hardware of the internet and capable of colonising large areas of storage space according to Universal-Darwinian principles of variation, replication and selection. It aligns partially with other coordinated impulses in the "Library of Berners-Lee", such that similarity relationships connect the discrete and particulate into a wider continuum of structure and meaning relationships across informational space (after Jan, 2016c, p. 462).	*Either* (i) the "traces" (Nattiez, 1990, p. 12) of a $1h$-phemotype $\equiv$ *i*-meme, these being the former's (extended) $2h$-phemotype; *or* (ii) the traces of a treme, these being its tremotype. Such traces take the form of the audiovisual outputs of computer systems together with the "extended-tremotypic" (Dawkins, 1983a) effects of these outputs on individuals and the wider world ($\equiv$ "$3b$-phenotype").

Table 7.3: Genes/Genomes, Memes/Memomes, and Tremes/Tremomes; and Phenotypes, Phemotypes and Tremotypes in Biological, Human-Cultural and Digital-Cultural Replication.

Favouring the second model of tremes over the first has certain ontological implications. If we define a replicator not only as something capable of causing copies to be made of itself but also as a means of storing information, then it is the *relationships* encoded, rather than the *substrate* in which they are encoded, that is significant. In the case of genes, DNA information is fundamentally stored as base-pair sequences of nucleotides, but there is no reason why this information (which codes for protein-synthesis) could not be stored in other forms. Indeed, genome-mapping has effectively converted it into letter-sequences (A[denine], C[ytosine], G[uanine], T[hymine], U[racil]), which can be stored as text in physical and electronic formats (National Human Genome Research Institute, 2020). The issue then arises as to whether such "translated" letter-sequences are: (i) different incarnations of the same genes; (ii) the extended-phenotypic products of the "untranslated" genes; or (iii) the phemotypic products of independent, text-encoding memes. In the case of the latter replicator, memes' information content is fundamentally stored in the form of interconnections between (gene-built) neurons but, again, this information can be translated into other formats. Paralleling the translation of gene-information into meme-information – (iii) above – meme-information can itself be rendered as impulses in (meme-built) computer systems – as treme-information. As Table 7.3 indicates, however, preservation of the replicator-vehicle distinction becomes more difficult when memes leave the human brain and enter the digital realm. Invoking third-order replicators helps to transcend memes' constraints of physicality and materiality because the information content of tremes is encoded fundamentally by electrical impulses, coalitions of electrons that emit patterns of electromagnetic radiation; and their tremotypic products are themselves forms of electromagnetic radiation, such as the visible-wavelength light emitted by monitors, together with the sound waves that this radiation impels speakers to produce.

7.6.2 Evidence for Memetic Evolution on the Internet

A number of studies, sometimes framed in memetic terms, have been conducted in order to demonstrate the evolution of information on the internet (Spiliopoulou, 2011). While many of these studies are concerned with text-based information, others have explored the evolution of the behaviours motivated by memes – understood, apropos the distinction in §7.6.1, primarily as dependent *i*-memes rather than as independent tremes – propagated in internet videos (Schlaile et al., 2018). This field of research is to some extent related to that conducted under the rubrics of corpus linguistics (Cortes & Csomay, 2015) and stylistics (Jeffries & McIntyre, 2010), in that it seeks to explore pattern-distributions in large corpora. In a pioneering early study, one that advocated the need to identify a unit of cultural selection in order to develop an evolutionary model of culture, Pocklington and Best (1997) tracked the occurrence of patterns, framed as memes, in posts on discussion lists and, among other things, concluded that the frequency of occurrence of certain word-combinations was positively correlated with the degree to which they might be regarded as inflammatory (Jan, 2007, pp. 137–138). More recently, Adamic et al. (2014) investigated the transmission of certain types of text, also understood as memes, on *Facebook* – "a large petri dish in which memes can mutate and replicate over the substrate of the network of friendship ties" (2014, p. 1) – attempting to understand the extent to which such information propagation could be compared with mechanisms governing genetic replication. They conclude that

> information evolves as it is passed from individual to individual in a social network, sometimes exactly, and sometimes with a modification which produces a new variant. This process is well-described by the Yule model,[308] with the mutation rate predicting the distribution of popularity among variants. Although many variants appear to emerge from neutral drift, there is evidence of some selection, as successful subsequences were found across memes, and individual meme variants were found to match [political] preferences of individuals transmitting them. (Adamic et al., 2014, pp. 11–12)

Their results confirm the Yule-model principle that replicators, here memes, "with a low mutation rate will have variants distributed according to a power-law distribution with an exponent close to 2, which is what we observed ....[309] The Yule model also predicts that memes with a high mutation rate will deviate from a power law because frequent mutation prevents any single variant from achieving an extremely high number of identical copies" (Adamic et al., 2014, p. 4), a result confirmed in this study. Such mutations – quantified by Adamic et al. (2014) using an edit-distance metric (§3.6.5) – are often the consequence of the fact that, at the time of the study, *Facebook* had not yet implemented a "share" functionality, so users had to copy and paste text from other users into their own status updates, which afforded the opportunity for accidental or intentional mutation (Adamic et al., 2014,

---

[308] The Yule model (Yule, 1925) describes the statistics of replication and mutation in evolutionary systems in order to model replicator populations (Adamic et al., 2014, p. 3).

[309] In a power-law distribution, one quantity varies in proportion with another according to a power relation, so an increase of x in one quantity is correlated with an increase of x^n in another. The Yule-model exponent, as noted, is x^{-2}.

p. 1). Some of these mutations involve text accidentally or intentionally pre- and/or postpended to a message, or changes to its central portion (Adamic et al., 2014, p. 3). Often, the intentional mutations can be correlated with the political affiliations of those making the changes.

There are certain significant differences between the model advanced by Adamic et al. (2014) and that outlined in §7.6.1. For one thing, they maintain that, "[f]or textual memes, the string is the information that is being passed, or the 'genotype'. The 'phenotype' is what is expressed by the meme, which can include the meme's message and replication instructions" (2014, p. 10). The argument developed here, by contrast, regards the "string" (the text copied on *Facebook*) as the 1h-phemotype arising from a 1h-meme in the brains of the website's users. Moreover, what Adamic et al. (2014) term a meme would appear to be a memeplex in my formulation, because the "successful subsequences ... found across memes" referred to above are the optimon (§1.6.2) in these VRS-algorithm cycles – they are the "indivisibly particulate" units, in Dawkins' phrase (1989, p. 33). Beyond these issues, what Adamic et al. (2014) do not explore, for understandable methodological reasons, are the underlying meme dynamics driving the evident mutations (Lynch, 1996; Lynch, 1998). These are presumably a function of the verbal-conceptual memeplexes underpinning the political, social and religious views that motivate the replication, with or without mutation, of the *Facebook* memes. As the replication of a gene in biological evolution is governed, to a greater or lesser extent, by that of other genes, so in cultural evolution the connection of memes in memeplexes, and the connection of memeplexes to form vast interconnected networks, means that a single meme does not simply stand or fall on its own intrinsic fecundity (§1.6.3.2). Rather, that fecundity, or perceptual-cognitive salience, is partly a function of the attributes of the wider networks of which the meme forms a part, and this is a powerful factor, albeit one difficult to model, in the dynamics of the replication of memes on (and off) the internet.

The majority of information transmission on the internet appears to occur in the medium of text, given that it is the most readily user-malleable substrate. This, and not just methodological constraints, might explain the focus on verbal-conceptual memes, as opposed to those in still images or videos, in the studies surveyed by (Adamic et al., 2014, p. 2). Music-cultural evolution occurs on the internet by means of processes acting upon the sound files that constitute the main container – a kind of *i*-chromosome – for *i*-musemes (§7.6.1). These processes are of two types: (i) the mutational operations performed upon sound files by specialist software, which are the digital equivalent of the edit-distance type modifications performed by composers and improvisers working with pen and paper or from memory, or of the memory-related changes and depredations attendant upon the transmission of non-notated musics; and (ii) the selection pressure, mediated by the other elements of musical culture, of public taste on specific genres, forms and styles of music – specifically on their constituent musemes – manifested in differential downloads, likes and other forms of community-visible endorsement. The evolution of *i*-musemes has been demonstrated in such cases as the *DarwinTunes* project (§6.5.3.2), where user-selection of *i*-Tremotypes drives the evolution – some might argue in the direction of a generalised levelling-down – of *i*-musemes (equivalent to process (ii) above). While *DarwinTunes* formalises this process in a quasi-experimental framework, there is no reason to think that it is not occurring "naturally" across the internet.

If it is accepted that information evolves on the internet, then it is not a significantly further step to hypothesise the operation of a form of memetic drive (§3.7.1, §5.2) in this medium, which might be termed "tremic drive", after Blackmore's (2008, 2015) term. As previously discussed, memetic drive is the process whereby the survival advantages of being able to imitate – and then to imitate imitators, and then to mate with imitators – impels genes to build ever bigger brains. This mechanism, once under way, can be hijacked and accelerated by memes, whose thus-expedited evolution can sometimes give rise to phemotypes that are meme-advantageous but gene-deleterious. It is possible to extend this process to the realm of tremes if we accept that an analogue to the imitative and memory capacity of brains is the processing power and data-storage capacity, respectively, of individual and networked ("cloud") computers.

By way of context, humans who use computer technology – most of our species in the developed world, and a significant part in the developing world – are led by those companies that produce it to believe that it will make their lives better by reducing the time and effort spent on complex or laborious tasks. Yet phenomena such as email overload – which is perhaps marked by "hypervigilance" to (generally work-related) email alert sounds, even when such musemes are less salient than (generally non-work-related) text-message alert sounds (Uther et al., 2018, p. 2) – suggest that the technology is having the opposite effect to the happiness-through-efficiency agenda promoted by its advocates. Beyond "productivity" software, the rise of social media over the last fifteen years promised ever more effortless communication and the fostering of a harmonious community of mutually supportive individuals, yet it seems to be increasingly characterised by bitterness, spleen and vitriol. Writing before social media was invented, Blackmore argues that the selfplex (§7.3.2) is a jumble of competing and often self-contradictory memes overwhelming the physical hardware that they have colonised: "[w]ith constant memetic bombardment our lives and our selves become more and more stressful and complicated. But this is a 'Red Queen' process. No one benefits because everyone has to keep running just to stay in the same place" (1999, p. 233).[310] So not only are our own brains buzzing with the information transmitted to us via traditional broadcast media, but there is a vast network of computers storing and loading us with information that is either of no relevance to us, or that significantly compromises our happiness. Perhaps more significantly, it is detrimental to our genes, because it takes time away from gene-beneficial activities such as child-rearing and what the Victorians called "rational recreation" (Herbert, 2003, p. 153).[311]

To outline briefly how tremic drive might be responsible for this proliferation of information on the internet, and the development of the computational and storage capacity to process it, one needs to invoke a category of "marketing memes". Concerned with winning friends and influencing people (Carnegie, 1936), they regulate the rhetorical highlighting by sellers of the value of a commodity to potential buyers. They constitute an extension of the innate signalling of our primate ancestors, which, as with marketing memes, can

---

[310] The Red Queen hypothesis asserts that, owing to ongoing evolutionary arms-races between rival species, each must run, in an aptive sense, in order to stand still (Liow et al., 2011). Sexual reproduction furnishes the genetic diversity that helps drive this process (Ridley, 1994).

[311] While smartphone "dating" apps ostensibly favour gene-replication, they primarily transmit image-memes (photographs of other app users) and advertising text and images, rather than the genes of (contraceptive-using) humans.

include dishonest as well as honest signals (§2.5.3), and various gradations in between. They are adopted by their hosts (those with commodities to sell) because of the anticipated financial benefits that will accrue to those who have assimilated them, and they are reinforced when they are successfully deployed to sell a product or service. In terms of evolutionary psychology, such memes play on potential buyers' genetically motivated alertness to "anger, fear, hunger, and lust" – attention-stealing imperatives that, in Brodie's term, "push our buttons" (1996, p. 91) – as well as to humans' aversion to social exclusion (often expressed in terms of the "fear of missing out"). Many of these memes relate to the smartphone market, with its high rate of innovation, rapid turnover of model release and consumer renewal, and hierarchically graded social kudos. They stoke users' desires for augmented functionality, greater information storage, better photographic capabilities and slicker responsiveness (often in the context of social media apps). These desires are satisfied by hardware manufacturers and operating system designers – in both the smartphone industry and the wider field of computer and internet technology, with which smartphones are ecosystemically interconnected – creating, inadvertently, an ever more fertile environment for image- and text-based tremes to proliferate, and a concomitant increase in expectations of future performance from users. Similar processes motivate increases in internet speed and capacity, again ostensibly in the service of user satisfaction and convenience; but ultimately they serve, and are driven by, the imperatives of treme replication.

7.6.3 The Internet as (Musical) Consciousness

Given that it is a network made up of multiple interconnected nodes, the internet has been understood as structurally and functionally analogous to the structure and function of the human brain. In Blackmore's formulation,

> [o]ur current digital technology is similarly evolving. Our computers, servers, tablets, and phones evolved piecemeal, new ones being added as and when they were useful and now being rapidly linked together, creating something that looks increasingly like a global brain. Of course in one sense we made these gadgets, even designed them for our own purposes, but the real driving force is the design power of evolution and

selection: the ultimate motivation is the self-propagation of replicating information. (Blackmore, 2015, p. 151)

Perhaps more accurately, the internet – and with it the "internet of things" – more closely resembles the octopus brain than our own. Whereas our species has the majority of neurons in the brain and spinal cord, in the octopus

> there is a division of labor between the CNS [Central Nervous System] and the PNS [Peripheral Nervous System]: a relatively small central brain (~50 million neurons out of a total of ~500 million neurons) controls the large, complex, and highly autonomous PNS of the arms (~300 million neurons), as well as integrating processed information from the huge visual system (~120 million neurons). The intermingled and distributed neural networks ... might point to a unique organization wherein single cells or groups of cells are dynamically recruited into several different higher control networks. (Zullo et al., 2009, p. 1635)

This configuration appears to be evolutionarily correlated with the octopus's highly flexible range of motion and its "nonsomatotopic" neurobiology. In humans, every part of the body is correlated with a corresponding brain region, this termed a "somatotopic" organisation. By contrast, the octopus has a neurobiology whereby "movements are represented in the higher motor centers by a number of overlapping circuits that are not somatotopically organized" (Zullo et al., 2009, p. 1634). This collection of attributes appears to facilitate the kind of quasi-autonomous movement and behaviour regulation that has culturally evolved in certain robotic systems using an "embodied intelligence" design. This relies upon "the dynamic interplay of information and physical processes between ... the controller, the mechanical system, the sensory system and the task environment" (Hochner, 2012, p. 887). In cybernetics, this architecture "has proved efficient for solving complex robotic problems. It does not seem unreasonable that biological evolution has followed similar principles" (2012, p. 887). Stressing the evolutionary significance of the octopus brain, Godfrey-Smith argues that

> [c]ephalopods are an island of mental complexity in the sea of invertebrate animals. Because our most recent common ancestor was so simple and lies so far back, cephalopods are an *independent experiment* in the evolution of large brains and complex behavior. If we can make *contact*

with cephalopods as sentient beings, it is not because of a shared history, not because of kinship, but because evolution built minds twice over. This is probably the closest we will come to meeting an intelligent alien. (Godfrey-Smith, 2016, p. 9; emphases in the original)

The point of this octopic excursus is not only to marvel at the complexity and sophistication of these creatures. Rather, it is primarily to stress that our own discrete brain – albeit one augmented by a degree of embodied cognition (as in Damasio's model of consciousness outlined in §7.2.2) – is not the only design that evolution has built on earth capable of sustaining intelligence and possibly, in the case of the octopus, (proto-)consciousness.[312] For all its boundedness – in a large CNS and small PNS – the human brain is, in its "parallel pandemoniums", nevertheless functionally decentralised (§7.3.1); yet the octopus nervous system – with its small CNS and large PNS – trumps ours for decentralised organisation, being both functionally and structurally distributed: its whole organism is evolved to create Multiple Drafts.

The cephalopod nervous system therefore offers not only a structural analogy with the parallel-processing functionality of the human brain, but also a conceptual analogy with the distributed information-processing structure and function of the internet. Indeed, the internet is even more highly distributed and parallel than the cephalopod nervous system, because octopi have, as the ultimate arbiter, a CNS – albeit, after Zullo et al. (2009), comprising only *c.* 10% of its total neural complement – that oversees and responds to the various delegated processing carried out by the PNS, whereas the internet bows to no such authority. For this reason, might the internet not only be capable of storing and processing large quantities of information, but also potentially able to sustain a kind of meta-intelligence even, in the future, a meta-consciousness (Koch, 2004; Koch, 2012)? The internet-as-distributed-brain analogy thus draws together points made in §7.3.1 and §7.5, suggesting far-reaching structural and functional parallels between phenomena in seemingly very different substrates. In summary, consciousness, even localised in individual human brains, is a massively parallel and distributed VRS-algorithm-driven phenomenon. This architecture is re-implemented at a

---

[312] There is, however, no evidence in the octopus of the kind of vocal learning (§2.7.5) that, in humans, certain birds and certain cetaceans (§5.4), is associated with high intelligence, imitative culture, and potentially – apropos the Carrutherian extension (§5.6) – (proto-)consciousness.

higher level when multiple individual consciousnesses interact in cultural communities, giving rise to a collective consciousness. The powers of this collective are significantly augmented when the speed and interconnectedness of digital technologies are used to facilitate communication, but they also afford the possibility of tremes slipping the bonds of human-cultural control and sustaining a separate evolutionarily conscious system. In this sense, Figure 1.2 is incomplete, requiring an additional ontological category above the socio-cultural, namely the "digital-cultural". I return to this issue of the internet as consciousness in §7.8.

7.7 Summary of Chapter 7

Chapter 7 has argued that:

1. A comprehensive explanation of consciousness, particularly the hard problem, remains elusive. The strongly rationalistic agenda adopted in this book nevertheless motivates the rejection of any candidate explanation for it other than some form of materialism.

2. Dennett's Multiple Drafts Model offers a Darwinian hypothesis for consciousness. When the VRS algorithm operates upon genes, it is normally understood in terms of evolution, but its action might also be regarded as a form of slow, systemic consciousness; conversely, consciousness might be regarded as a form of fast, internalised operation of the VRS algorithm acting upon the drafts – encoded as hexagonally organised neuronal configurations – of the MDM.

3. Integrating the MDM (as theory) and HCT (as mechanism) with memetics (as metatheory) not only affords a hypothesis for consciousness but also suggests a means of reconciling the cognitivist and communicativist conceptions of thought and language.

4. Large-scale systems of musical organisation, such as forms of tonality, are the high-level, virtual artefacts of low-level, real processes driven by the operation of the VRS algorithm on musemes. As such, they represent a form of systemic consciousness that arrives at "decisions", that changes its "mind", and that thus has a degree of aptive flexibility.

5. The internet represents an environment in which the memome/phemotype distinction of classical memetics becomes blurred. It sustains a new replicator,

the treme, new forms of (digital-cultural) evolution, and, potentially, a new mode of consciousness.

7.8 Epilogue: How Music Thinks

I borrow the title of this final section, deliberately singularised, from Liza Lim's composition *How Forests Think* (Lim, 2016a). In a natural equivalent to Blackmore's internet-as-global-brain model (§7.6.3) – sometimes referred to as a "wood-wide web" (Beiler et al., 2010) – Lim explains that

> *How Forests Think* reflects on the work of anthropologist Eduardo Kohn who writes about forest ecologies as the 'living thought' of human and non-human selves.[313] Each of these selves may have its own subjectivity, creating the world with its own registers of knowledge, sensation and meaning. These selves organize into communities: in ancient forests, a stump may be kept alive for centuries by the surrounding trees through underground fungal networks that nourish the old connections and keep a song going. One might think of a forest as a choir or certainly as an ensemble. Stories, dreams and thoughts inhabit multiple forms in a living matrix; they ask us to look beyond our limited human gaze and limited human time-span. (Lim, 2016b)

Thus, the boundaries of the vehicle (§1.6.1), fragile at best, are transcended by interconnections between organisms that, to serve the selfish interests of their generative replicators, form channels of intercommunication and so build a super-organism from a multiplicity of ostensibly separate life-forms. In a less rose-tinted view than Lim's, such "communities" are built by replicators to serve their selfish interests, and the appeals to immortality in her last sentence are in reality in the gift of the replicator, not the vehicle. The notion of the super-organism aligns quite closely with certain ideas from idealist philosophy (§4.4.1), which held there was "a strong interrelationship between all things: in [the British philosopher Bernard] Bosanquet's words, 'every finite existence necessarily transcends itself and points toward other existences and finally to the whole'" (Solie, 1980, p. 149). Leibniz attempted to understand such transcendence in terms of the binarism between concrete

---

[313] Kohn's work (2013) itself draws upon the "Gaia" hypothesis of James Lovelock (2000).

objects (including living organisms) and the "real"/ideal essences connecting them (1980, p. 149). According to Russell,

> [a]ssuming that the human being, consisting of mind and body, is a true unity he [Leibniz] extended the notion of organism to cover all beings endowed with substantial forms. A substantial form, for Leibniz, was something analogous to a mind and capable of 'perception' (the lowest degree of mental activity, not involving either self-consciousness or thought). It is through its perception that any individual 'expresses' what goes on in the universe. (in Solie, 1980, p. 149)

To recast the language of idealism in the terms repeatedly emphasised in this book, one might equate "concrete" objects with the vehicle and the "ideal" with the replicator. The former represent "merely the time-space relationships between the 'real' (ideal) substances" (Solie, 1980, p. 149), whereas the latter are the permanent "essences" of things – the information content, as a network of relationships (§7.6.1), of the replicator – forming "matrices" (in Lim's term) of self-interest in order to serve their fundamental quest for immortality.

If, as §7.3.2 asserts, one can regard consciousness as a form of rapid (cognitive) evolution and, vice versa, evolution as a form of slow (systemic) consciousness; and if, as §7.6.2 indicates, information evolves on the internet; then music, as a cultural-evolutionary system operating over decades and centuries, represents a kind of thought, perhaps even instantiating a distributed selfplex. This is not thought in the traditional sense of music's encompassing and embodying the ideas and feelings of its human composers and performers and the socio-cultural traditions they represent (which is a form of association between musemeplexes and verbal-conceptual memeplexes). Rather, it is thought in the sense of a complex dynamic system unfolding over time and, in its memetic evolution, representing a form of consciousness that "thinks" and "feels" at the systemic level – a form of thought just as much "living", in the Kohnian sense, as that taking place in our own individual consciousness. Were we to accelerate this process, compressing centuries into milliseconds, then we would perhaps apprehend music-cultural evolution as exemplifying the reactivity and (self-) awareness evident in human consciousness. Indeed, as §7.6 has suggested, the internet provides an environment in which this acceleration is already taking place. A tractable example of this evolutionary-systemic parallel between intra- and extra-brain processes – between the psychological and socio-cultural ontological categories – is to be found in information transmission between communities of birds. This process has been studied, in groups of zebra finches (*Taeniopygia guttata*), by Stowell et al. (2016). Using a form of network modelling called the Generalised Linear Model, point-process (GLMpp) developed in Paninski (2004) and Pillow et al. (2008), they were able to track imitative call-and-response patterns between conspecifics (some all-female and some in mated pairs) and develop a social-network analysis of the birds' interactions (Stowell et al., 2016, p. 10, Fig. 9). They note that this model "was originally developed in computational neurology for analysis of spiking neural networks" (Stowell et al., 2016, p. 1). That an approach developed to model the "social networks" of a community of neurons – encoding and transmitting memes – can also model social networks in bird species – encoding and transmitting sonemes – affords further evidence for the deep structural commonalities between systems at seemingly disparate levels of organisation arising from their implementation of the VRS algorithm.

But there is a deeper, if radically ultra-reductionist, way of understanding music in this domain, one even more abstract than the notion of the *i*-museme coursing across the internet in a sound file. This is to see music as not just *on* the internet but also *in* the internet. That is, the electrical signals that constitute the information content of the internet, *musical and otherwise*, might be regarded as a kind of music. This is because the audible patterns of music are a series of (phemotypic) waveforms in the sound spectrum arising from (memomic) electrochemical activity in the brain; and the electrical signals driving the internet are similarly waveforms in the electromagnetic spectrum: both are forms of cyclic vibration or oscillation. Thinking in this way takes us back to the notion of the harmony of the spheres (§4.1), wherein the sounding ratios inherent in the waveforms of vibrating strings and columns of air were seen as being writ large in the positions and motions of cosmic bodies, this harmony being "audible to but unnoticed by mortals who hear it from birth" (Haar, 2001). While this is not necessarily the most illuminating level of description for the purposes of this book – which is concerned with those coalitions of waveforms that constitute replicators – in a quantum-mechanical view everything devolves (or dissolves) to music, be it understood as particle or wave.[314] – and vice versa. More fundamentally, quantum mechanics itself bows to the Vanchurin machine implemented in the "microscopic neural network that undergoes learning evolution" (Vanchurin, 2020, p. 2) (§1.5.2).

Despite its ostensible focus upon the seemingly self-contained domain of human music and the musicality that sustains it, this book has sought to blur the distinction between this domain and a number of others to which it is closely related. In particular, it has used the perspective of evolution to argue that the similarities between music and language, the similarities between music/language and learned animal vocalisations, the similarities between music/language and the creative products of music-generative systems, and the similarities between neuron-borne musemes and electron-borne tremes are all substantially greater than their differences. In this sense it has argued for a Universal-Darwinian view in which music is not *sui generis*, but is rather one realm of a vast nexus – Velardo's "being", a "universal brain" made up of interconnected Darwinian systems in a number of domains – whose structural and functional commonalities, and its evolution, are driven by the limitless power of the VRS algorithm. In doing so, it has argued that music and musicality are a powerful driving force in the evolution of human anatomy, physiology, consciousness and culture. Arising from our primal instinct to produce structured, expressive vocalised sound, music – far from being merely auditory cheesecake – has nourished, sustained and shaped us in ways that are fundamental to our very humanity.

---

[314] In quantum mechanics, certain phenomena, such as light, have a dual existence as both particles and waves (Greiner, 2001, p. 29).

References

Abeles, H. (2009). Are musical instrument gender associations changing? *Journal of Research in Music Education*, *57*(2), 127–139. https://doi.org/10.1177/0022429409335878

Abler, W. L. (1989). On the particulate principle of self-diversifying systems. *Journal of Social and Biological Structures*, *12*(1), 1–13. https://doi.org/10.1016/0140-1750(89)90015-8

Abler, W. L. (1997). Gene, language, number: the particulate principle in nature. *Evolutionary Theory*, *11*(4), 237–248.

Ablinger, P. (2013). Black square and bottle rack: noise and noises. In A. Cassidy & A. Einbond (Eds.), *Noise in and as music* (pp. 5–8). University of Huddersfield Press. https://doi.org/10.5920/noise.01

Adam, O., Cazau, D., Gandilhon, N., Fabre, B., Laitman, J. T., & Reidenberg, J. S. (2013). New acoustic model for Humpback whale sound production. *Applied Acoustics*, *74*(10), 1182–1190. https://doi.org/10.1016/j.apacoust.2013.04.007

Adamic, L. A., Lento, T. M., Adar, E., & Ng, P. C. (2014). *Information evolution in social networks*. arXiv: 1402.6792. https://doi.org/10.1145/2835776.2835827

Adkins, M. (2009). The application of memetic analysis to electroacoustic music. *Sonic Ideas*, *1*(2), 34–41. http://www.ems-network.org/ems08/papers/adkins.pdf

Adler, G. (1885). Umfang, Methode und Ziel der Musikwissenschaft. *Vierteljahresschrift für Musikwissenschaft*, *1*, 5–20.

Adorno, T. W. (2002). Late style in Beethoven (S. H. Gillespie, Trans.). In R. Leppert (Ed.), *Essays on music* (pp. 564–568). University of California Press.

Agawu, V. K. (1991). *Playing with signs: a semiotic interpretation of classic music*. Princeton University Press. https://doi.org/10.1515/9781400861835

Ahmad, S. F., Singchat, W., Jehangir, M., Suntronpong, A., Panthum, T., Malaivijitnond, S., & Srikulnath, K. (2020). Dark matter of primate genomes: satellite DNA repeats and their evolutionary dynamics. *Cells*, *9*(2714), 1–34. https://doi.org/10.3390/cells9122714

Aiello, L. C., & Dunbar, R. I. M. (1993). Neocortex size, group size, and the evolution of language. *Current Anthropology*, *34*, 184–193. https://doi.org/10.1086/204160

AIMC. (2021). *AI music creativity*. Retrieved August 4, 2021, from https://aimusiccreativity.org/

Albright, D. (Ed.). (2004). *Modernism and music: an anthology of sources*. University of Chicago Press.

Allanbrook, W. J. (1992). Two threads through the labyrinth: topic and process in the first movements of K. 332 and K. 333. In W. J. Allanbrook, J. M. Levy & W. P. Mahrt (Eds.), *Convention in eighteenth- and nineteenth-century music: essays in honor of leonard g. ratner* (pp. 125–171). Pendragon Press.

Allen, G. (2011). *Intertextuality*. Routledge. https://doi.org/10.1093/acrefore/9780190201098.013.1072

Amabile, T. M. (1982). Social psychology of creativity: a consensual assessment technique. *Journal of Personality and Social Psychology*, *43*(5), 997–1013. https://doi.org/10.1037/0022-3514.43.5.997

Angliss, S. (2011). *The Bird fancyer's delight*. Retrieved May 14, 2020, from https://www.sarahangliss.com/birdfancyersdelightnotes/

Angliss, S. (2019). *On birdsong and music*. Retrieved May 14, 2020, from http://www.sarahangliss.com/birdsongandmusic

Antonicek, T., Beales, D., Botstein, L., Klein, R., & Goertz, H. (2001). *Vienna* (D. L. Root, Ed.). https://doi.org/10.1093/gmo/9781561592630.article.29326

Apicella, C. L., Feinberg, D. R., & Marlowe, F. W. (2007). Voice pitch predicts reproductive success in male hunter-gatherers. *Biology Letters*, *3*(6), 682–684. https://doi.org/10.1098/rsbl.2007.0410

Ariza, C. (2009). The interrogator as critic: the Turing test and the evaluation of generative music systems. *Computer Music Journal*, *33*(2), 48–70. https://doi.org/10.1162/comj.2009.33.2.48

Ariza, C. (2011). Two pioneering projects from the early history of computer-aided algorithmic composition. *Computer Music Journal, 35*(3), 40–56. https://doi.org/10.1162/COMJ_a_00068

Arndt, M. (2011). Schenker and Schoenberg on the will of the tone. *Journal of Music Theory, 55*(1), 89–146. https://doi.org/10.1215/00222909-1219205

Arnx, A. (2019). First neural network for beginners explained. Retrieved December 19, 2019, from https://towardsdatascience.com/first-neural-network-for-beginners-explained-with-code-4cfd37e06eaf

Aubert, M., Lebe, R., Oktaviana, A. A., Tang, M., Burhan, B., Hamrullah, Jusdi, A., Abdullah, Hakim, B., Zhao, J.-x., Geria, I. M., Sulistyarto, P. H., Sardi, R., & Brumm, A. (2019). Earliest hunting scene in prehistoric art. *Nature, 576*, 442–445. https://doi.org/10.1038/s41586-019-1806-y

Aunger, R. (2000). *Darwinizing culture: the status of memetics as a science*. Oxford University Press. https://doi.org/10.1093/acprof:oso/9780192632449.001.0001

Aunger, R. (2002). *The electric meme: a new theory of how we think*. Free Press.

Avis, J., & Harris, P. L. (1991). Belief-desire reasoning among Baka children: evidence for a universal conception of mind. *Child Development, 62*(3), 460–467. https://doi.org/10.2307/1131123

Azumagakito, T., Suzuki, R., & Arita, T. (2018). An integrated model of gene-culture coevolution of language mediated by phenotypic plasticity. *Scientific Reports, 8*(1), 1–11. https://doi.org/10.1038/s41598-018-26233-7

Babbitt, M. (1961). Set structure as compositional determinant. *Journal of Music Theory, 5*(1), 72–94. https://doi.org/10.2307/842871

Backlund, A. (2000). The definition of system. *Kybernetes, 29*(4), 444–451. https://doi.org/10.1108/03684920010322055

Baker, M. C. (1996). Depauperate meme pool of vocal signals in an island population of Singing Honeyeaters. *Animal Behaviour, 51*, 853–858. https://doi.org/10.1006/anbe.1996.0089

Ball, J. A. (1984). Memes as replicators. *Ethology and Sociobiology, 5*(3), 145–161. https://doi.org/10.1016/0162-3095(84)90020-7

Bandura, A. (1997). *Self-efficacy: the exercise of control*. W.H. Freeman. https://doi.org/10.1891/0889-8391.13.2.158

Bannan, N. (1999). Out of Africa: the evolution of the human capacity for music. *International Journal of Music Education*, 33(1), 3–9. https://doi.org/10.1177/025576149903300102

Bannan, N. (2012). *Music, language, and human evolution* (N. Bannan, Ed.). Oxford University Press.

Bannan, N. (2019). *Every child a composer: music education in an evolutionary perspective*. Peter Lang.

Bannan, N., Bamford, J. S., & Dunbar, R. I. M. (2023). The evolution of gender dimorphism in the human voice: the role of octave equivalence [Forthcoming]. *Current Anthropology*. https://doi.org/10.31234/osf.io/f4j6b

Bannan, N., & Montgomery-Smith, C. (2008). "singing for the brain": reflections on the human capacity for music arising from a pilot study of group singing with Alzheimer's patients. *The Journal of the Royal Society for the Promotion of Health*, 128(2), 73–78. https://doi.org/10.1177/1466424007087807

Baptista, L. F., & Petrinovich, L. (1984). Social interaction, sensitive phases and the song template hypothesis in the White-crowned sparrow. *Animal Behaviour*, 32(1), 172–181. https://doi.org/10.1016/S0003-3472(84)80335-8

Barber, B. L., Eccles, J. S., & Stone, M. R. (2001). Whatever happened to the Jock, the Brain, and the Princess? young adult pathways linked to adolescent activity involvement and social identity. *Journal of Adolescent Research*, 16(5), 429–455. https://doi.org/10.1177/0743558401165002

Barkow, J. H., Cosmides, L., & Tooby, J. (1992). *The adapted mind: evolutionary psychology and the generation of culture*. Oxford University Press. http://cogweb.ucla.edu/Abstracts/AdaptedMind_92.html

Bates, H. J., & Busenbarn, R. L. (1958). Train your bird in stereo (lp recording). http://blog.wfmu.org/freeform/2006/09/train_your_bird.html

Baudrillard, J. (1988). *The ecstasy of communication* (S. Lotringer, Ed.; B. Schutze & C. Schutze, Trans.). Autonomedia. https://doi.org/10.4135/9781446269534.n7

Bauman, T. (2001). *Oberon, König der Elfen* (D. L. Root, Ed.). https://doi.org/10.1093/gmo/9781561592630.001.0001/omo-9781561592630-e-5000903623

Bedau, M. A. (2013). Minimal memetics and the evolution of patented technology. *Foundations of Science, 18*(4), 791–807. https://doi.org/10. 1007/s10699-012-9306-7

Beiler, K. J., Durall, D. M., Simard, S. W., Maxwell, S. A., & Kretzer, A. M. (2010). Architecture of the wood-wide web: rhizopogon spp. genets link multiple Douglas-fir cohorts. *New Phytologist, 185*(2), 543–553. https://doi.org/10.1111/j.1469-8137.2009.03069.x

Bent, I. D., & Pople, A. (2001). *Analysis* (D. L. Root, Ed.). https://doi.org/10. 1093/gmo/9781561592630.article.41862

Bentley, P. J., & Corne, D. W. (2002). An introduction to creative evolutionary systems. In P. J. Bentley & D. W. Corne (Eds.), *Creative evolutionary systems* (pp. 1–75). Academic Press. https://doi.org/10.1016/b978-155860673-9/50035-5

Benton, M. J. (2015). *Vertebrate palaeontology* (4th ed.). Wiley Blackwell. https://doi.org/10.1007/978-1-4899-2865-8

Benzer, S. (1957). The elementary units of heredity. In W. D. McElroy & B. Glass (Eds.), *The chemical basis of heredity* (pp. 70–93). Johns Hopkins University Press.

Berg, J. M., Tymoczko, J. L., Gatto, Gregory J., J., & Stryer, L. (2019). *Biochemistry* (9th ed.). W.H. Freeman.

Bergeron, K., & Bohlman, P. V. (1992). *Disciplining music: musicology and its canons* (K. Bergeron & P. V. Bohlman, Eds.). University of Chicago Press. https://doi.org/10.2307/843948

Bergevin, C., Narayan, C., Williams, J., Mhatre, N., Steeves, J. K. E., Bernstein, J. G. W., & Story, B. (2020). Overtone focusing in biphonic Tuvan throat singing. *eLife, 9*, 1–42. https://doi.org/10.7554/eLife.50476

Bermúdez-de-Castro, J. M., Martinón-Torres, M., Martín-Francés, L., Modesto-Mata, M., Martínez-de-Pinillos, M., García, C., & Carbonell, E. (2017). Homo antecessor: the state of the art eighteen years later. *Quaternary International, 433*, 22–31. https://doi.org/10.1016/j.quaint.2015.03. 049

Bernard, H. R., & Gravlee, C. C. (Eds.). (2014). *Handbook of methods in cultural anthropology* (2nd ed.). Rowman; Littlefield. https://doi.org/10. 5860/choice.36-4846

Besson, M., Barbaroux, M., & Dittinger, E. (2017). Music in the brain: music and language processing. In R. Ashley & R. Timmers (Eds.), *The Routledge companion to music cognition* (pp. 37–48). Routledge.

Bickerton, D. (2000). Can biomusicology learn from language evolution studies? In N. L. Wallin, B. Merker & S. Brown (Eds.), *The origins of music* (pp. 153–163). MIT Press.

Bickerton, D. (2003). Symbol and structure: a comprehensive framework for language evolution. In M. H. Christiansen & S. Kirby (Eds.), *Language evolution* (pp. 77–93). Oxford University Press. https://doi.org/10.1093/acprof:oso/9780199244843.003.0005

Biles, J. A. (2007). Improvising with genetic algorithms: *genjam*. In E. R. Miranda & J. A. Biles (Eds.), *Evolutionary computer music* (pp. 137–169). Springer.

Biles, J. A. (2013). Straight-ahead jazz with *genjam*: a quick demonstration. In P. Pasquier, A. Eigenfeldt, O. Bown & G. McCaig (Eds.), *Proceedings of the second international workshop on musical metacreation* (*MuMe 2013*), *in conjunction with the ninth annual AAAI conference on artificial intelligence and interactive digital entertainment* (*AIIDE 13*) (pp. 20–23). AAAI Press. https://www.aaai.org/ocs/index.php/AIIDE/AIIDE13/paper/view/7414

Biles, J. A. (2019). *"you go to my head": al Biles and genjam*. Retrieved August 10, 2021, from https://www.youtube.com/watch?time_continue=127%5C&v=RDgJw2kiuWU%5C&feature=emb_logo

Biles, J. A. (2020). Al Biles and *genjam*. Retrieved January 2, 2020, from https://genjam.org/al-biles/genjam/

Blackmore, S. J. (1996). Memes, minds and selves. *Seminar in the series About Biology*. http://www.memes.org.uk/lectures/mms.html

Blackmore, S. J. (1999). *The meme machine*. Oxford University Press.

Blackmore, S. J. (2000a). The memes' eye view. In R. Aunger (Ed.), *Darwinizing culture: the status of memetics as a science* (pp. 25–42). Oxford University Press. https://doi.org/10.1093/acprof:oso/9780192632449.003.0002

Blackmore, S. J. (2000b). The power of memes. *Scientific American*, *283*(4), 64–73. https://doi.org/10.1038/scientificamerican1000-64

Blackmore, S. J. (2001). Evolution and memes: the human brain as a selective imitation device. *Cybernetics and Systems, 32*(1–2), 225–255. https://doi.org/10.1080/019697201300001867

Blackmore, S. J. (2005a). *Consciousness: a very short introduction.* Oxford University Press. https://doi.org/10.1093/actrade/9780198794738.001.0001

Blackmore, S. J. (2005b). Evidence for memetic drive?: commentary on Iacoboni. In S. Hurley & N. Chater (Eds.), *Perspectives on imitation: from neuroscience to social science. volume 1: mechanisms of imitation and imitation in animals* (pp. 203–205). MIT Press.

Blackmore, S. J. (2007). Memes, minds, and imagination. In I. Roth (Ed.), *Imaginative minds: concepts, controversies and themes* (pp. 61–78). Oxford University Press. https://doi.org/10.5871/bacad/9780197264195.003.0003

Blackmore, S. J. (2008). *Memes and temes.* https://www.ted.com/talks/susan_blackmore_on_memes_and_temes

Blackmore, S. J. (2009). *Ten Zen questions.* Oneworld.

Blackmore, S. J. (2015). The next replicator. In J. Brockman (Ed.), *What to think about machines that think: today's leading thinkers on the age of machine intelligence* (pp. 150–152). Harper.

Blackmore, S. J., & Troscianko, E. T. (2018). *Consciousness: an introduction* (3rd ed.). Routledge. https://doi.org/10.4324/9781315755021

Blute, M. (2002). The evolutionary ecology of science. *Journal of Memetics: Evolutionary Models of Information Transmission, 7*(1).

Blute, M. (2006). Gene-culture coevolutionary games. *Social Forces, 85*(1), 151–166. https://doi.org/10.1353/sof.2006.0115

Boas, H. C., & Sag, I. A. (Eds.). (2012). *Sign-based construction grammar.* Center for the Study of Language; Information. https://doi.org/10.1093/oxfordhb/9780195396683.013.0008

Boden, M. A. (2004). *The creative mind: myths and mechanisms* (2nd ed.). Routledge.

Boghossian, P., & Lindsay, J. A. (2020). *The conceptual penis as a social construct: a Sokal-style hoax on gender studies.* Retrieved April 16, 2020, from https://www.skeptic.com/reading_room/conceptual-penis-social-contruct-sokal-style-hoax-on-gender-studies/

Bohlman, P. V. (2002). *World music: a very short introduction.* Oxford University Press. https://doi.org/10.1093/actrade/9780198829140.001.0001

Bolhuis, J. J., & Everaert, M. (Eds.). (2013). *Birdsong, speech, and language: exploring the evolution of mind and brain.* MIT Press. https://doi.org/10.7551/mitpress/9322.003.0006

Bonabeau, E. (2002). Agent-based modeling: methods and techniques for simulating human systems. *Proceedings of the National Academy of Sciences of the United States of America, 99,* 7280–7287. https://doi.org/10.1073/pnas.082080899

Bonds, M. E. (1991). *Wordless rhetoric: musical form and the metaphor of the oration.* Harvard University Press. https://doi.org/10.4159/harvard.9780674733411

Bonnici, H. M., & Maguire, E. A. (2018). Two years later – revisiting autobiographical memory representations in vmPFC and hippocampus. *Neuropsychologia, 110,* 159–169. https://doi.org/10.1016/j.neuropsychologia.2017.05.014

Borges, J. L. (1970). *Labyrinths: selected stories and other writings* (D. A. Yates & J. E. Irby, Eds.). Penguin.

Borges, J. L. (1998). *Collected fictions* (A. Hurley, Trans.). Viking Penguin.

Bosse, T., Jonker, C. M., & Treur, J. (2008). Formalisation of Damasio's theory of emotion, feeling and core consciousness. *Consciousness and Cognition, 17*(1), 94–113. https://doi.org/10.1016/j.concog.2007.06.006

Bourdieu, P. (1984). *Distinction: a social critique of the judgement of taste* (R. Nice, Trans.). Harvard University Press. https://doi.org/10.4324/9781315680347-10

Bowden, D. M., Dubach, M. F., McArthur, E., Song, E., Kocheleva, I., & Moore, E. (Eds.). (2020). *Braininfo.* https://doi.org/10.1007/978-1-4614-7320-6_485-1

Bown, O. (2021). *Beyond the creative species making machines that make art and music.* MIT Press. https://doi.org/10.7551/mitpress/10913.001.0001

Boyd, R., & Richerson, P. J. (1985). *Culture and the evolutionary process.* University of Chicago Press. https://doi.org/10.2307/2803086

Braitenberg, V., & Braitenberg, C. (1979). Geometry of orientation columns in the visual cortex. *Biological Cybernetics, 33,* 179–186. https://doi.org/10.1007/bf00337296

Bringsjord, S., Bello, P., & Ferrucci, D. (2001). Creativity, the Turing Test, and the (better) Lovelace Test. *Minds and Machines, 11,* 3–27. https://doi.org/10.1007/978-94-010-0105-2_12

Briot, J. P. (2021). From artificial neural networks to deep learning for music generation: history, concepts and trends. *Neural Computing and Applications*, *33*(1), 39–65. https://doi.org/10.1007/s00521-020-05399-0

British Library. (2010). Secret songs of birds: the hidden beauty of birdsong revealed.

Brodie, R. (1996). *Viruses of the mind: the new science of the meme.* Integral Press.

Brodmann, K. (1909). *Vergleichende Lokalisationslehre der Grosshirnrinde*. Barth.

Bronson, B. H. (1959). *The traditional tunes of the Child Ballads: with their texts, according to the extant records of Great Britain and North America.* Princeton University Press.

Brown, S. (2000). The "musilanguage" model of musical evolution. In N. L. Wallin, B. Merker & S. Brown (Eds.), *The origins of music* (pp. 271–300). MIT Press.

Brown, S., Martinez, M. J., & Parsons, L. M. (2006). Music and language side by side in the brain: a PET study of the generation of melodies and sentences. *European Journal of Neuroscience*, *23*(10), 2791–2803. https://doi.org/10.1111/j.1460-9568.2006.04785.x

Brown, S., Merker, B., & Wallin, N. L. (2000). An introduction to evolutionary musicology. In N. L. Wallin, B. Merker & S. Brown (Eds.), *The origins of music* (pp. 3–24). MIT Press.

Browning, T., & Freund, K. (1931). Dracula.

Budka, M., & Osiejuk, T. S. (2017). Microgeographic call variation in a non-learning species, the Corncrake (Crex crex). *Journal of Ornithology*, *158*(3), 651–658. https://doi.org/10.1007/s10336-017-1438-7

Bulhak, A. C. (1996). *Postmodernism generator*. Retrieved April 16, 2020, from http://www.elsewhere.org/journal/pomo/

Bull, L., Holland, O., & Blackmore, S. J. (2000). On meme-gene coevolution. *Artificial Life*, *6*(3), 227–235. https://doi.org/10.1162/106454600568852

Burak, Y., & Fiete, I. R. (2009). Accurate path integration in continuous attractor network models of grid cells. *PLoS Computational Biology*, *5*(2), e1000291. https://doi.org/10.1371/journal.pcbi.1000291

Burton, G. O. (Ed.). (2007). *Silva rhetoricae: the forest of rhetoric*. Retrieved September 6, 2020, from http://rhetoric.byu.edu/

Busoni, F. (Ed.). (1894). *Bach-Busoni: the first twenty-four preludes and fugues of The well-tempered clavichord*. Schirmer.

Butler, J. (1990). *Gender trouble: feminism and the subversion of identity*. Routledge. https://doi.org/10.4324/9780203824979

Byros, V. (2009). *Foundations of tonality as situated cognition, 1730–1830: an enquiry into the culture and cognition of eighteenth-century tonality, with Beethoven's Eroica Symphony as a case study* [Doctoral dissertation, Yale University]. http://vasilibyros.com/byros_dissertation.pdf

Cain, A. J. (2020). *Taxonomy*. https://doi.org/10.21273/hortsci.25.6.603a

Callender, C., Quinn, I., & Tymoczko, D. (2008). Generalized voice-leading spaces. *Science*, *320*(5874), 346–348. https://doi.org/10.1126/science.1153021

Calvin, W. H. (1987a). Bootstrapping thought: is consciousness a Darwinian sidestep? *Whole Earth Review*, *55*, 22–28.

Calvin, W. H. (1987b). The brain as a Darwin machine. *Nature*, *330*, 33–34. https://doi.org/10.1038/330033a0

Calvin, W. H. (1996). *How brains think: evolving intelligence, then and now*. Basic Books.

Calvin, W. H. (1998). *The cerebral code: thinking a thought in the mosaics of the mind*. MIT Press. https://doi.org/10.7551/mitpress/1775.001.0001

Cambouropoulos, E. (2001). Melodic cue abstraction, similarity, and category formation: a formal model. *Music Perception*, *18*(3), 347–370. https://doi.org/10.1525/mp.2001.18.3.347

Campbell, D. T. (1960). Blind variation and selective retention in creative thought as in other knowledge processes. *Psychological Review*, *67*, 380–400. https://doi.org/10.1037/h0040373

Campbell, D. T. (1965). Variation and selective retention in socio-cultural evolution. In H. R. Barringer, G. I. Blanksten & R. W. Mack (Eds.), *Social change in developing areas: a reinterpretation of evolutionary theory* (pp. 19–49). Schenkman.

Campbell, D. T. (1974). Evolutionary epistemology. In P. A. Schilpp (Ed.), *The philosophy of karl popper* (pp. 413–463). Open Court.

Campbell, D. T. (1990). Epistemological roles for selection theory. In N. Rescher (Ed.), *Evolution, cognition, and realism: studies in evolutionary epistemology* (pp. 1–19). University Press of America.

Caplin, W. E. (1998). *Classical form: a theory of formal functions for the instrumental music of Haydn, Mozart, and Beethoven*. Oxford University Press.

Caplin, W. E. (2005). On the relation of musical *topoi* to formal function. *Eighteenth-Century Music*, 2(1), 113–124. https://doi.org/10.1017/S1478570605000278

Caplin, W. E., Hepokoski, J. A., & Webster, J. (2009). *Musical form, forms and Formenlehre: three methodological reflections* (P. Bergé, Ed.). Leuven University Press.

Carbone, L., Harris, R. A., Gnerre, S., Veeramah, K. R., Lorente-Galdos, B., Huddleston, J., Meyer, T. J., Herrero, J., Roos, C., Aken, B., Anaclerio, F., Archidiacono, N., Baker, C., Barrell, D., Batzer, M. A., Beal, K., Blancher, A., Bohrson, C. L., Brameier, M., ... Gibbs, R. A. (2014). Gibbon genome and the fast karyotype evolution of small apes. *Nature*, 513(7517), 195–201. https://doi.org/10.1038/nature13679

Carnegie, D. (1936). *How to win friends and influence people*. Simon; Schuster. https://doi.org/10.2307/20629470

Carr, B. (2007). *Universe or multiverse?* Cambridge University Press. https://doi.org/10.1111/j.1468-4004.2008.49229.x

Carroll, L. (1993). *Alice's adventures in wonderland and Through the looking-glass*. Wordsworth Editions.

Carroll, S. B. (2003). Genetics and the making of Homo sapiens. *Nature*, 422(6934), 849–857. https://doi.org/10.1038/nature01495

Carroll, S. B. (2005). *Endless forms most beautiful: the new science of Evo Devo and the making of the animal kingdom*. Norton.

Carruthers, P. (2002). The cognitive functions of language. *Behavioral and Brain Sciences*, 25, 657–726. https://doi.org/10.1017/S0140525X02000122

Carruthers, P. (2005). *Consciousness: essays from a higher-order perspective*. Oxford University Press.

Carter, T. (1987). *W. a. Mozart Le nozze di Figaro*. Cambridge University Press. https://doi.org/10.2307/941909

Cassidy, A., & Einbond, A. (Eds.). (2013). *Noise in and as music*. University of Huddersfield Press. https://doi.org/10.5920/noise.2013

Cavalli-Sforza, L. L., & Feldman, M. W. (1981). *Cultural transmission and evolution: a quantitative approach*. Princeton University Press.

Cavett-Dunsby, E. (1988). Mozart's codas. *Music Analysis*, 7(1), 31–51. https://doi.org/10.2307/939245

Chalmers, D. J. (2010). *The character of consciousness*. Oxford University Press. https://doi.org/10.1093/acprof:oso/9780195311105.001.0001

Chamorro-Premuzic, T., & Furnham, A. (2007). Personality and music: can traits explain how people use music in everyday life? *British Journal of Psychology*, *98*(2), 175–185. https://doi.org/10.1348/000712606X111177

Changizi, M. (2011). *Harnessed: how language and music mimicked nature and transformed ape to man*. BenBella Books.

Chantler, A. (2006). *E.T.A. Hoffmann's musical aesthetics*. Ashgate. https://doi.org/10.4324/9781315094779

Charlton, B. D. (2014). Menstrual cycle phase alters women's sexual preferences for composers of more complex music. *Proceedings of the Royal Society B: Biological Sciences*, *281*(1784), 1–6. https://doi.org/10.1098/rspb.2014.0403

CHARM. (2017). *The AHRC research centre for the history and analysis of recorded music*. Retrieved August 8, 2017, from http://www.charm.rhul.ac.uk/index.html

CHARM. (2019a). *Comparing two performances of Mazurka in F minor op. 7 no. 3*. http://www.mazurka.org.uk/info/tempocurve/mazurka07-3/

CHARM. (2019b). *The mazurka project*. http://www.mazurka.org.uk/

Charnley, J., Pease, A., & Colton, S. (2012). On the notion of framing in computational creativity. In M. L. Maher, K. Hammond, A. Pease, R. P. y. Pérez, D. Ventura & G. Wiggins (Eds.), *Proceedings of the third international conference on computational creativity* (pp. 77–81). University College Dublin. https://www.computationalcreativity.net/proceedings/ICCC-2012-Proceedings.pdf

Chen, C. (2006). CiteSpace ii: detecting and visualizing emerging trends and transient patterns in scientific literature. *Journal of the American Society for Information Science and Technology*, *57*(3), 359–377. https://doi.org/10.1002/asi.20317

Chen, C. (2014). *CiteSpace manual*. http://cluster.ischool.drexel.edu/~cchen/citespace/CiteSpaceManual.pdf

Chen, C. (2019a). *CiteSpace: creating visualizations with Scopus (RIS) data*. Retrieved April 3, 2020, from https://www.youtube.com/watch?v=Pr5CeiIq8A0

Chen, C. (2019b). *How to use CiteSpace*. Leanpub. https://leanpub.com/howtousecitespace

Chen, C. (2020). *CiteSpace 101*. Retrieved April 3, 2020, from https://sites.google.com/site/citespace101

Chen, C., & Song, M. (2019). Visualizing a field of research: a methodology of systematic scientometric reviews. *PLoS ONE, 14*(10), 1–25. https://doi.org/10.1371/journal.pone.0223994

Cheney, D. L., & Seyfarth, R. M. (1991). Truth and deception in animal communication. In C. A. Ristau (Ed.), *Cognitive ethology: the minds of other animals: essays in honor of donald r. griffin.* (pp. 127–151). Lawrence Erlbaum Associates, Inc.

Child, F. J. (Ed.). (1904). *The English and Scottish popular ballads*. Houghton Mifflin. https://doi.org/10.1017/cbo9781107711143.047

Chomsky, N. (1959). A review of B. F. Skinner's Verbal behavior. *Language, 35*(1), 26–58. https://doi.org/10.4159/harvard.9780674594623.c6

Chomsky, N. (1965). *Aspects of the theory of syntax*. MIT Press. https://doi.org/10.21236/ad0616323

Chomsky, N. (1986). *Knowledge of language: its nature, origin, and use*. Praeger. https://doi.org/10.2307/2185417

Chomsky, N. (2006). *Language and mind* (3rd ed.). Cambridge University Press. https://doi.org/10.1017/cbo9780511791222

Chomsky, N. (2009). *Cartesian linguistics: a chapter in the history of rationalist thought* (J. McGilvray, Ed.; 3rd ed.). Cambridge University Press. https://doi.org/10.1017/cbo9780511803116

Christensen, T. (2002). *The Cambridge history of western music theory*. Cambridge University Press. https://doi.org/10.2307/4127121

Chua, D. K. L. (1999). *Absolute music and the construction of meaning*. Cambridge University Press. https://doi.org/10.1017/cbo9780511481697

Cireşan, D. C., Meier, U., Masci, J., Gambardella, L. M., & Schmidhuber, J. (2011). Flexible, high performance convolutional neural networks for image classification. In T. Walsh (Ed.), *Proceedings of the twenty-second international joint conference on artificial intelligence* (*IJCAI-11*) (pp. 1237–1242, Vol. 2). AAAI Press/International Joint Conferences on Artificial Intelligence. https://doi.org/10.5591/978-1-57735-516-8/IJCAI11-210

Clark, S., & Rehding, A. (2001). *Music theory and natural order from the Renaissance to the early twentieth century.* Cambridge University Press.

Clarke, D. (2017). North indian classical music and Lerdahl and Jackendoff's generative theory: a mutual regard. *Music Theory Online, 23*(3). https://doi.org/10.30535/mto.23.3.3

Clarke, J. A., Chatterjee, S., Li, Z., Riede, T., Agnolin, F., Goller, F., Isasi, M. P., Martinioni, D. R., Mussel, F. J., & Novas, F. E. (2016). Fossil evidence of the avian vocal organ from the mesozoic. *Nature, 538*(7626), 502–505. https://doi.org/10.1038/nature19852

Clegg, M. (2012). The evolution of the human vocal tract: specialized for speech. In N. Bannan (Ed.), *Music, language, and human evolution* (pp. 58–80). Oxford University Press.

Cloak, F. T. (1975). Is a cultural ethology possible? *Human Ecology, 3,* 161–182. https://doi.org/10.1007/bf01531639

Clynes, M. (1978). *Sentics: the touch of the emotions.* Anchor Press/Doubleday.

Cohen, D., & Kitayama, S. (Eds.). (2019). *Handbook of cultural psychology* (2nd ed.). Guilford Press.

Cohn, R. L. (1996). Maximally smooth cycles, hexatonic systems, and the analysis of late-romantic triadic progressions. *Music Analysis, 15*(1), 9–40. https://doi.org/10.2307/854168

Cohn, R. L. (1997). Neo-Riemannian operations, parsimonious trichords, and their *tonnetz* representations. *Journal of Music Theory, 41*(1), 1–66.

Coleridge, S. T. (2014). *Biographia literaria* (A. Roberts, Ed.). Edinburgh University Press. https://doi.org/10.2307/3713748

Collins, A. G., & Valentine, J. W. (2001). Defining phyla: evolutionary pathways to metazoan body plans. *Evolution and Development, 3*(6), 432–442. https://doi.org/10.1046/j.1525-142X.2001.01048.x

Collins, N. (2018). "… there is no reason why it should ever stop": large-scale algorithmic composition. *Journal of Creative Music Systems, 3*(1). https://doi.org/10.5920/jcms.525

Collins, N., & Brown, A. R. (2009). Generative music editorial. *Contemporary Music Review, 28*(1), 1–4. https://doi.org/10.1080/07494460802663967

Collins, N., & D'Escrivàn, J. (Eds.). (2017). *The Cambridge companion to electronic music* (2nd ed.). Cambridge University Press. https://doi.org/10.1017/9781316459874

Collins, T., Tillmann, B., Barrett, F. S., Delbé, C., & Janata, P. (2014). A combined model of sensory and cognitive representations underlying tonal expectations in music: from audio signals to behavior. *Psychological Review, 121*(1), 33–65. https://doi.org/10.1037/a0034695

Colombelli-Négrel, D., Hauber, M. E., Evans, C., Katsis, A. C., Brouwer, L., Adreani, N. M., Kleindorfer, S., & Kleindorfer, S. (2021). Prenatal auditory learning in avian vocal learners and non-learners. *Philosophical Transactions of the Royal Society B, 376,* 1–6. https://doi.org/10.1098/rstb.2020.0247

Colton, S. (2008). Creativity versus the perception of creativity in computational systems. In D. Ventura, M. L. Maher & S. Colton (Eds.), *Proceedings of the AAAI symposium on creative systems* (pp. 14–20). AAAI Press. https://www.aaai.org/Library/Symposia/Spring/ss08-03.php

Colton, S., Charnley, J., & Pease, A. (2011). Computational creativity theory: the FACE and IDEA descriptive models. In D. Ventura, P. Gervás, D. F. Harrell, M. L. Maher, A. Pease & G. Wiggins (Eds.), *Proceedings of the second international conference on computational creativity* (pp. 90–95). Universidad Autónoma Metropolitana – Unidad Cuajimalpa. https://computationalcreativity.net/iccc2011/proceedings/index.html

Conard, N. J., Malina, M., & Münzel, S. C. (2009). New flutes document the earliest musical tradition in southwestern Germany. *Nature, 460*(7256), 737–740. https://doi.org/10.1038/nature08169

Conklin, D. (2013). Multiple viewpoint systems for music classification. *Journal of New Music Research, 42*(1), 19–26. https://doi.org/10.1080/09298215.2013.776611

Conklin, D., & Anagnostopoulou, C. (2006). Segmental pattern discovery in music. *INFORMS Journal on Computing, 18*(3), 285–293. https://doi.org/10.1287/ijoc.1040.0122

Conklin, D., & Witten, I. H. (1995). Multiple viewpoint systems for music prediction. *Journal of New Music Research, 24*(1), 51–73. https://doi.org/10.1080/09298219508570672

Conner, S. (2014). The score of Babylon: outline of a framework for reconstructing ancient songs. In L. C. Eneix (Ed.), *Archaeoacoustics: the archaeology of sound. publication of the 2014 conference in malta* (pp. 195–210). OTS Foundation.

Cook, K. M. (2015). Text mining and early music: using lexomics in research. *Early Music, 43*(4), 661–665. https://doi.org/10.1093/em/cav085

Cook, N. (1990). *Music, imagination, and culture.* Clarendon Press. https://doi.org/10.2307/854006

Cook, N. (1994). *A guide to musical analysis.* Oxford University Press. https://doi.org/10.2307/843388

Cook, N. (1996). *Analysis through composition: principles of the classical style.* Oxford University Press.

Cook, N. (1998). *Music: a very short introduction.* Oxford University Press. https://doi.org/10.1093/actrade/9780198726043.001.0001

Cook, N. (2007a). Performance analysis and Chopin's mazurkas. *Musicae Scientiae, 11*(2), 183–207. https://doi.org/10.4324/9781003075059-25

Cook, N. (2007b). *The Schenker project: culture, race, and music theory in fin-de-siècle Vienna.* Oxford University Press. https://doi.org/10.1093/acprof:oso/9780195170566.001.0001

Cook, P., Rouse, A., Wilson, M., & Reichmuth, C. (2013). A California Sea Lion (*zalophus californianus*) can keep the beat: motor entrainment to rhythmic auditory stimuli in a non vocal mimic. *Journal of Comparative Psychology, 127*(4), 412–427. https://doi.org/10.1037/a0032345

Cooke, D. (1968). *The language of music.* Oxford University Press. https://doi.org/10.2307/843055

Cope, D. (1996). *Experiments in musical intelligence.* A-R Editions.

Cope, D. (1998). Signatures and earmarks: computer recognition of patterns in music. In W. B. Hewlett & E. Selfridge-Field (Eds.), *Melodic similarity: concepts, procedures, and applications* (pp. 129–138). MIT Press.

Cope, D. (2001). *Virtual music: computer synthesis of musical style.* MIT Press. https://doi.org/10.7551/mitpress/7106.001.0001

Cope, D. (2003). Computer analysis of musical allusions. *Computer Music Journal, 27*(1), 11–28. https://doi.org/10.1162/01489260360613317

Cope, D. (2015). *Experiments in musical intelligence.* http://artsites.ucsc.edu/faculty/cope/experiments.htm

Corballis, M. C. (2014). Left brain, right brain: facts and fantasies. *PLoS Biology, 12*(1), 1–6. https://doi.org/10.1371/journal.pbio.1001767

Cortes, V., & Csomay, E. (2015). *Corpus-based research in applied linguistics: studies in honor of Doug Biber* (V. Cortes & E. Csomay, Eds.). John Benjamins.

Costall, A. (1991). The "meme" meme. *Cultural Dynamics*, *4*, 321–335. https://doi.org/10.1177/092137409100400305

Cox, A. (2011). Embodying music: principles of the mimetic hypothesis. *Music Theory Online*, *17*(2), 1–24. https://doi.org/10.30535/mto.17.2.1

Cox, A. (2016). *Music and embodied cognition: listening, moving, feeling, and thinking*. Indiana University Press. https://doi.org/10.2307/j.ctt200610s

Crewdson, J. (2010). *Music: an etiological perspective* [Doctoral dissertation, Royal Holloway, University of London]. London.

CRM Records. (2008). Songs of the Humpback whale.

Cross, I. (1999). Is music the most important thing we ever did? music, development and evolution. In S. W. Yi (Ed.), *Music, mind and science* (pp. 10–39). Seul National University Press.

Cross, I. (2012). Music as an emergent exaptation. In N. Bannan (Ed.), *Music, language, and human evolution* (pp. 263–276). Oxford University Press. https://doi.org/10.1093/acprof:osobl/9780199227341.003.0010

Cross, I., & Woodruff, G. E. (2009). Music as a communicative medium. In *The prehistory of language* (pp. 77–98). https://doi.org/10.1093/acprof:oso/9780199545872.003.0005

Crystal, D. (Ed.). (2019). *The Cambridge encyclopedia of the English language* (3rd ed.). Cambridge University Press.

Csikszentmihalyi, M. (1996). *Creativity: flow and the psychology of discovery and invention*. Harper Collins.

Dadabots. (2021). *Dadabots*. Retrieved August 6, 2021, from https://dadabots.com/

Dahlhaus, C. (1982). *Esthetics of music* (W. W. Austin, Trans.). Cambridge University Press. https://doi.org/10.2307/940647

Dahlhaus, C. (1983). *Foundations of music history* (J. B. Robinson, Trans.). Cambridge University Press. https://doi.org/10.1017/cbo9780511627309

Damasio, A. R. (1989). Time-locked multiregional retroactivation: a systems-level proposal for the neural substrates of recall and recognition.

Cognition, *33*(1–2), 25–62. https://doi.org/10.1016/0010-0277(89) 90005-x

Damasio, A. R. (2000). *The feeling of what happens: body, emotion and the making of consciousness*. Vintage.

Damasio, A. R., & Meyer, K. (2009). Consciousness: an overview of the phenomenon and of its possible neural basis. In S. Laureys & G. Tononi (Eds.), *The neurology of consciousness: cognitive neuroscience and neuropathology* (First, pp. 3–14). Academic Press.

Danforth, C. M. (2013). *Chaos in an atmosphere hanging on a wall*. Retrieved September 25, 2019, from http://mpe.dimacs.rutgers.edu/2013/03/ 17/chaos-in-an-atmosphere-hanging-on-a-wall/

Darwin, C. (2004). *The descent of man, and selection in relation to sex*. Penguin. https://doi.org/10.1093/owc/9780199580149.003.0008

Darwin, C. (2006). *The Origin of species: a variorum text* (M. Peckham, Ed.). University of Pennsylvania Press. https://doi.org/10.9783/ 9780812200515

Darwin, C. (2008). *On the origin of species by means of natural selection, or the preservation of favoured races in the struggle for life* (G. Beer, Ed.). Oxford University Press. https://doi.org/10.1093/owc/9780199580149.003. 0005

Darwin, C. (2012). *Online variorum of Darwin's Origin of species* (B. Bordalejo, Ed.). http://darwin-online.org.uk/Variorum/index.html

David, H. T., Mendel, A., & Wolff, C. (Eds.). (1998). *The new Bach reader: a life of Johann Sebastian Bach in letters and documents*. Norton. https: //doi.org/10.5860/choice.36-1499

Dawkins, R. (1983a). *The extended phenotype: the long reach of the gene*. Oxford University Press.

Dawkins, R. (1983b). Universal Darwinism. In D. S. Bendall (Ed.), *Evolution from molecules to men* (pp. 403–425). Cambridge University Press. https://doi.org/10.1017/cbo9780511730191.035

Dawkins, R. (1988). The evolution of evolvability. In C. G. Langton (Ed.), *Artificial life: proceedings of the interdisciplinary workshop on the synthesis and simulation of living systems* (pp. 201–220). Addison-Wesley. https: //doi.org/10.1016/b978-012428765-5/50046-3

Dawkins, R. (1989). *The selfish gene* (2nd ed.). Oxford University Press. https: //doi.org/10.1515/9781400848393-029

Dawkins, R. (2006). *The blind watchmaker: why the evidence of evolution reveals a universe without design* (Thirtieth anniversary). Penguin.

Dawkins, R. (2007). *The god delusion*. Transworld Publishers.

Dawkins, R. (2020). *Watchmaker suite by Richard Dawkins*. Retrieved May 2, 2020, from http://watchmakersuite.sourceforge.net/

De Angeli, S., Both, A. A., Hagel, S., Holmes, P., Jiménez Pasalodos, R., & Lund, C. S. (Eds.). (2018). *Music and sounds in ancient Europe: contributions from the European music archaeology project*. European Music Archaology Project. https://doi.org/10.1017/CBO9781107415324.004

De Clercq, T., & Temperley, D. (2011). A corpus analysis of rock harmony. *Popular Music, 30*(1), 47–70. https://doi.org/10.1017/S026114301000067X

Dean, R. T., & McLean, A. (Eds.). (2018). *The Oxford handbook of algorithmic music*. Oxford University Press. https://doi.org/10.1093/oxfordhb/9780190226992.001.0001

Dearmer, P., Vaughan Willams, R., & Shaw, M. (Eds.). (1928). *The Oxford book of carols*. Oxford University Press. https://doi.org/10.2307/898363

Deliège, I. (2000). Listening to a piece of music: a schematization process based on abstracted surface cues. In D. Greer (Ed.), *Musicology and sister disciplines: past, present, future. proceedings of the sixteenth international congress of the International Musicological Society, London, 1997* (pp. 71–87). Oxford University Press.

Delius, J. D. (1989). Of mind memes and brain bugs: a natural history of culture. In W. A. Koch (Ed.), *The nature of culture: proceedings of the international and interdisciplinary symposium, October 7–11, 1986 in Bochum* (pp. 26–79). Brockmeyer.

Delius, J. D. (1991). The nature of culture. In M. S. Dawkins, T. R. Halliday & R. Dawkins (Eds.), *The Tinbergen legacy* (pp. 75–99). Chapman; Hall. https://doi.org/10.1007/978-0-585-35156-8_6

Dennett, D. C. (1988). Précis of *the intentional stance*. *Behavioral and Brain Sciences, 11*(3), 495–546. https://doi.org/10.1017/S0140525X00058611

Dennett, D. C. (1989). *The intentional stance*. MIT Press. https://doi.org/10.2307/2026682

Dennett, D. C. (1993a). *Consciousness explained*. Penguin. https://doi.org/10.2307/2940970

Dennett, D. C. (1993b). Précis of *consciousness explained*. *Philosophy and Phenomenological Research, 53*(4), 889–892.

Dennett, D. C. (1995). *Darwin's dangerous idea: evolution and the meanings of life*. Penguin.

Dennett, D. C. (2017). *From bacteria to Bach and back: the evolution of minds*. Allen Lane.

Deutsch, D. (1999). Grouping mechanisms in music. In D. Deutsch (Ed.), *The psychology of music* (2nd ed., pp. 299–348). Academic Press. https://doi.org/10.1016/b978-0-12-213562-0.50008-5

Díaz Jerez, G. (2012). *Iamus computer: Colossus, for piano solo*. Retrieved August 11, 2021, from https://www.youtube.com/watch?v=yGrzzZupYVI

Diaz-Jerez, G. (2011). Composing with melomics: delving into the computational world for musical inspiration. *Leonardo Music Journal, 21*, 13–14. https://doi.org/10.1162/LMJ_a_00053

Diaz-Jerez, G., & Vico, F. J. (2017). *Iamus* (*computer*). Retrieved December 7, 2017, from http://melomics.com/iamus

Díaz-Muñoz, S. L., & Bales, K. L. (2016). "monogamy" in primates: variability, trends, and synthesis: introduction to special issue on primate monogamy. *American Journal of Primatology, 78*(3), 283–287. https://doi.org/10.1002/ajp.22463

Dick, P. K. (1968). *Do androids dream of electric sheep?* Doubleday.

Diogo, R., Siomava, N., & Gitton, Y. (2019). Development of human limb muscles based on whole-mount immunostaining and the links between ontogeny and evolution. *Development, 146*(20), 1–17. https://doi.org/10.1242/dev.180349

Dissanayake, E. (2000). Antecedents of the temporal arts in early mother-infant interaction. In N. L. Wallin, B. Merker & S. Brown (Eds.), *The origins of music* (pp. 389–410). MIT Press.

Dissanayake, E. (2008). If music is the food of love, what about survival and reproductive success? *Musicae Scientiae, 12*(Special Issue: Narrative in Music and Interaction), 169–195. https://doi.org/10.1177/1029864908012001081

Dissanayake, E. (2012). *Art and intimacy: how the arts began*. University of Washington Press.

Distin, K. (2005). *The selfish meme: a critical reassessment*. Cambridge University Press. https://doi.org/10.1017/cbo9780511614286

Dobson, E. (2018). Digital audio ecofeminism (DA'EF): the glocal impact of all-female communities on learning and sound creativities. In L. R. de Bruin, P. Burnard & S. Davis (Eds.), *Creativities in arts education, research and practice: international perspectives for the future of learning and teaching* (pp. 201–220, Vol. 15). Brill.

Dobzhansky, T. (1973). Nothing in biology makes sense except in the light of evolution. *American Biology Teacher, 35*, 125–129. https://doi.org/10.2307/4444260

Doeller, C. F., Barry, C., & Burgess, N. (2010). Evidence for grid cells in a human memory network. *Nature, 463*, 657–661. https://doi.org/10.1038/nature08704

Domínguez, M. (2015). Evolution of metaphors: phylogeny of oil slick cartoons in Spanish press. *Discourse and Society, 26*(2), 184–204. https://doi.org/10.1177/0957926514556208

Dumbrill, R. J. (2005). *The archaeomusicology of the ancient Near East.* Trafford Publishing.

Dunbar, R. I. M. (2017). Group size, vocal grooming and the origins of language. *Psychonomic Bulletin and Review, 24*, 209–212. https://doi.org/10.3758/s13423-016-1122-6

Dunsby, J., & Whittall, A. (1988). *Music analysis in theory and practice.* Faber. https://doi.org/10.2307/j.ctt1xp3t38

Durham, W. H. (1991). *Coevolution: genes, culture, and human diversity.* Stanford University Press. https://doi.org/10.1515/9781503621534

Düring, D. N., Ziegler, A., Thompson, C. K., Ziegler, A., Faber, C., Müller, J., Scharff, C., & Elemans, C. P. H. (2013). The songbird syrinx morphome: a three-dimensional, high-resolution, interactive morphological map of the zebra finch vocal organ. *BMC Biology, 11*(1), 1–27. https://doi.org/10.1186/1741-7007-11-1

Durrell, M., Kohl, K., Kaiser, C., & Loftus, G. (2015). *Essential German grammar* (2nd ed.). Routledge. https://doi.org/10.4324/9781315728070

Ebcioğlu, K. (1988). An expert system for harmonizing four-part chorales. *Computer Music Journal, 12*(3), 43–51. https://doi.org/10.2307/3680335

Eck, R. V., & Dayhoff, M. O. (1966). *Atlas of protein sequence and structure 1966.* National Biomedical Research Foundation. https://doi.org/10.2307/2412074

Edelman, G. M. (1987). *Neural Darwinism: the theory of neuronal group selection.* Basic Books.

Eigenfeldt, A. (2014a). Generative music for live performance: experiences with real-time notation. *Organised Sound, 19*(3), 276–285. https://doi.org/10.1017/S1355771814000260

Eigenfeldt, A. (2014b). *An unnatural selection (2014).* Retrieved January 30, 2020, from https://aeigenfeldt.wordpress.com/an-unnatural-selection/

Eigenfeldt, A., Bown, O., Pasquier, P., & Martin, A. (2013). Towards a taxonomy of musical metacreation: reflections on the first musical metacreation weekend. *Proceedings of the second international workshop on musical metacreation (MuMe 2013), in conjunction with the ninth annual AAAI conference on artificial intelligence and interactive digital entertainment (AIIDE 13).* http://philippepasquier.com/

Ekroll, V., Faul, F., & Golz, J. (2008). Classification of apparent motion percepts based on temporal factors. *Journal of Vision, 8*(4), 1–22. https://doi.org/10.1167/8.4.31

Eldredge, N., & Gould, S. J. (1972). Punctuated equilibria: an alternative to phyletic gradualism. In T. J. M. Schopf (Ed.), *Models in paleobiology* (pp. 82–115). Freeman, Cooper & Co.

Enard, W., Przeworsky, M., Fisher, S. E., Lai, C. S. L., Wiebe, V., Kitano, T., Monaco, A. P., & Pääbo, S. (2002). Molecular evolution of FOXP2, a gene involved in speech and language. *Nature, 418*, 869–872. https://doi.org/10.1038/nature01025

Epstein, D. (1979). *Beyond Orpheus: studies in musical structure.* MIT Press. https://doi.org/10.2307/940192

Eriksen, N., Miller, L. A., Tougaard, J., & Helweg, D. A. (2005). Cultural change in the songs of Humpback whales (*Megaptera novaeangliae*) from Tonga. *Behaviour, 142*(3), 305–328. https://doi.org/10.1163/1568539053778283

Fagan, B. M., & Durrani, N. (2020). *World prehistory: a brief introduction* (10th ed.). Routledge. https://doi.org/10.4324/9780429430381

Falk, D. (2000). Hominid brain evolution and the origins of music. In N. L. Wallin, B. Merker & S. Brown (Eds.), *The origins of music* (pp. 197–216). MIT Press.

Falk, D. (2004). Prelinguistic evolution in early hominins: whence motherese? *Behavioral and Brain Sciences, 27*(4), 491–503. https://doi.org/10.1017/s0140525x04000111

Fang, X. (2019). *Sound from antiquity: a music-archaeological study of chime stones in ancient China (c. 2,400 BCE–8 CE)* [Doctoral dissertation, University of Huddersfield]. http://eprints.hud.ac.uk/id/eprint/35175/

Farzaneh, M., & Toroghi, R. M. (2020). Music generation using an interactive evolutionary algorithm. In C. Djeddi, A. Jamil & I. Siddiqi (Eds.), *Pattern recognition and artificial intelligence: proceedings of the third Mediterranean conference* (pp. 207–217). Springer. https://doi.org/10.1007/978-3-030-37548-5

Fasold, R. W., & Connor-Linton, J. (Eds.). (2014). *An introduction to language and linguistics* (2nd ed.). Cambridge University Press.

Fazenda, B., Scarre, C., Till, R., Pasalodos, R. J., Guerra, M. R., Tejedor, C., Peredo, R. O., Watson, A., Wyatt, S., Benito, C. G., Drinkall, H., & Foulds, F. (2017). Cave acoustics in prehistory: exploring the association of palaeolithic visual motifs and acoustic response. *The Journal of the Acoustical Society of America, 142*(3), 1332–1349. https://doi.org/10.1121/1.4998721

Febres, G., & Jaffe, K. (2017). Music viewed by its entropy content: a novel window for comparative analysis. *PLoS ONE, 12*(10), 1–30. https://doi.org/10.1371/journal.pone.0185757

Fedurek, P., Machanda, Z. P., Schel, A. M., & Slocombe, K. E. (2013). Pant hoot chorusing and social bonds in male chimpanzees. *Animal Behaviour, 86*(1), 189–196. https://doi.org/10.1016/j.anbehav.2013.05.010

Felsenstein, J. (2018). *Phylip v. 3.695.* University of Washington. http://evolution.genetics.washington.edu/phylip.html

Fernández, J. D., & Vico, F. J. (2013). AI methods in algorithmic composition: a comprehensive survey. *Journal of Artificial Intelligence Research, 48*, 513–582. https://doi.org/10.1613/jair.3908

Fernández-Armesto, F. (2001). *Food: a history.* Macmillan.

Fernando, C. T., Szathmáry, E., & Husbands, P. (2012). Selectionist and evolutionary approaches to brain function: a critical appraisal. *Frontiers in Computational Neuroscience, 6*(24), 1–28. https://doi.org/10.3389/fncom.2012.00024

Ferrari, L., & Addessi, A. R. (2014). A new way to play music together: the *continuator* in the classroom. *International Journal of Music Education*, *32*(2), 171–184. https://doi.org/10.1177/0255761413504706

Feuersänger, C. (2014). *Surface plot of a math function*. Retrieved September 9, 2019, from http://pgfplots.net/tikz/examples/surface-plot-math/

Fisher, R. A. (1915). The evolution of sexual preference. *Eugenics Review*, *7*(3), 184–192. https://doi.org/10.1109/61.25587

Fisher, R. A. (1930). *The genetical theory of natural selection*. Clarendon Press. https://doi.org/10.5962/bhl.title.27468

Fitch, W. T. (2006). The biology and evolution of music: a comparative perspective. *Cognition*, *100*(1), 173–215. https://doi.org/10.1016/j.cognition.2005.11.009

Fitch, W. T. (2010). *The evolution of language*. Cambridge University Press. https://doi.org/10.1017/cbo9780511817779

Flores-Ferrer, A., Nguyen, A., Glémin, S., Deragon, J.-M., Panaud, O., & Gourbière, S. (2021). The ecology of the genome and the dynamics of the biological dark matter. *Journal of Theoretical Biology*, *518*(110641), 1–11. https://doi.org/10.1016/j.jtbi.2021.110641

Fober, D., Kilian, J. F., & Pachet, F. (2019). *Real-time score notation from raw MIDI inputs* (tech. rep. No. hal-02158966). Grame Computer Music Research Lab.

Fodor, J. A. (1983). *The modularity of mind: an essay on faculty psychology*. MIT Press. https://doi.org/10.1017/cbo9780511814273.046

Fodor, J. A., & Piattelli-Palmarini, M. (2011). *What Darwin got wrong*. Profile Books.

Foley, R. A. (2012). Music and mosaics: the evolution of human abilities. In N. Bannan (Ed.), *Music, language, and human evolution* (pp. 31–57). Oxford University Press.

Forkel, J. N. (1920). *Johann Sebastian Bach: his life, art and work (über Johann Sebastian Bachs Leben, Kunst und Kunstwerke)* (C. S. Terry, Trans.). Harcourt, Brace; Howe. http://www.gutenberg.org/files/35041/35041-pdf.pdf?session_id=f071b5feb00aa69e0e4c612dea2cf918cdf0e0b8

Forte, A. (1973). *The structure of atonal music*. Yale University Press. https://doi.org/10.2307/843643

Foubert, K., Collins, T., & De Backer, J. (2017). Impaired maintenance of interpersonal synchronization in musical improvisations of patients with borderline personality disorder. *Frontiers in Psychology, 8*, 1–17. https://doi.org/10.3389/fpsyg.2017.00537

Franklin, T. B., Russig, H., Weiss, I. C., Grff, J., Linder, N., Michalon, A., Vizi, S., & Mansuy, I. M. (2010). Epigenetic transmission of the impact of early stress across generations. *Biological Psychiatry, 68*(5), 408–415. https://doi.org/10.1016/j.biopsych.2010.05.036

Freer, P. K. (2010). Two decades of research on possible selves and the "missing males" problem in choral music. *International Journal of Music Education, 28*(1), 17–30. https://doi.org/10.1177/0255761409351341

Freud, S. (1981). *The standard edition of the complete psychological works of Sigmund Freud* (J. Strachey, A. Freud, A. Strachey & A. Tyson, Eds.; Vol. XIX (1923-). The Hogarth Press; The Institute of Psycho-Analysis.

Friedman, J. C. (Ed.). (2013). *The Routledge history of social protest in popular music*. Routledge. https://doi.org/10.4324/9780203124888

Frith, S. (1981). *Sound effects: youth, leisure, and the politics of rock 'n' roll*. Pantheon Books. https://doi.org/10.2307/2068513

Fuhs, M. C., & Touretzky, D. S. (2006). A spin glass model of path integration in rat medial entorhinal cortex. *The Journal of Neuroscience, 26*(16), 4266–4276. https://doi.org/10.1523/jneurosci.4353-05.2006

Fux, J. J. (1965). *The study of counterpoint. from Johann Joseph Fux's Gradus ad Parnassum* (A. Mann, Ed. & Trans.). Norton.

Gabrielsson, A., & Juslin, P. N. (1996). Emotional expression in music performance: between the performer's intention and the listener's experience. *Psychology of Music, 24*(1), 68–91. https://doi.org/10.1177/0305735696241007

Gamble, C. (2012). When the words dry up: music and material metaphors half a million years ago. In N. Bannan (Ed.), *Music, language, and human evolution* (pp. 81–106). Oxford University Press.

Geberzahn, N., & Aubin, T. (2014). Assessing vocal performance in complex birdsong: a novel approach. *BMC Biology, 12*(1), 1–9. https://doi.org/10.1186/s12915-014-0058-4

Geetha Ramani, R., & Priya, K. (2019). Improvised emotion and genre detection for songs through signal processing and genetic algorithm. *Concurrency and Computation: Practice and Experience, 31*(14), 1–8. https://doi.org/10.1002/cpe.5065

Geissmann, T. (2000). Gibbon songs and human music from an evolutionary perspective. In N. L. Wallin, B. Merker & S. Brown (Eds.), *The origins of music* (pp. 103–123). MIT Press.

Gilliam, B., & Youmans, C. (2001). *Strauss, Richard (Georg)* (D. L. Root, Ed.). Retrieved July 20, 2020, from http://www.oxfordmusiconline.com/subscriber/article/grove/music/40117

Gilmurray, J. (2013). *Beyond phonography: an ecomusicological analysis of contemporary approaches to composing with the sounds of the natural world.* https://www.academia.edu/6208853/BEYOND_PHONOGRAPHY_An_Ecomusicological_Analysis_of_Contemporary_Approaches_to_Composing_with_the_Sounds_of_the_Natural_World

Gimenes, M. (2015). Artificial worlds and the simulation of music evolution. *Study day on computer simulation of musical creativity, University of Huddersfield, 27 June 2015.* https://simulationofmusicalcreativity.wordpress.com/programme/%5C#marcelo

Gimenes, M., Miranda, E. R., & Johnson, C. (2007). Musicianship for robots with style. In L. Crawford (Ed.), *Proceedings of the seventh international conference on new interfaces for musical expression* (pp. 197–202). Association for Computing Machinery. https://doi.org/10.1145/1279740.1279778

Gjerdingen, R. O. (1988). *A classic turn of phrase: music and the psychology of convention.* University of Pennsylvania Press. https://doi.org/10.2307/854046

Gjerdingen, R. O. (1989a). Meter as a mode of attending: a network simulation of attentional rhythmicity in music. *Integral, 3,* 67–92.

Gjerdingen, R. O. (1989b). Using connectionist models to explore complex musical patterns. *Computer Music Journal, 13*(3), 67–75. https://doi.org/10.2307/3680013

Gjerdingen, R. O. (1990). Categorization of musical patterns by self-organizing neuronlike networks. *Music Perception, 7*(4), 339–370. https://doi.org/10.2307/40285472

Gjerdingen, R. O. (1992). Learning syntactically significant temporal patterns of chords: a masking field embedded in an ART 3 architecture. *Neural Networks, 5,* 551–564. https://doi.org/10.1016/s0893-6080(05)80034-6

Gjerdingen, R. O. (1999). An experimental music theory? In N. Cook & M. Everist (Eds.), *Rethinking music* (pp. 161–170). Oxford University Press.

Gjerdingen, R. O. (2007a). *Music in the galant style*. Oxford University Press.

Gjerdingen, R. O. (2007b). Partimento, que me veux-tu? *Journal of Music Theory, 51*(1), 85–135. https://doi.org/10.1215/00222909-2008-024

Gjerdingen, R. O. (2010). Mozart's obviously corrupt minuet. *Music Analysis, 29*(1–3), 61–82. https://doi.org/10.1111/j.1468-2249.2011.00326.x

Gjerdingen, R. O., & Bourne, J. (2015). Schema theory as a construction grammar. *Music Theory Online, 21*(2). https://doi.org/10.30535/mto.21.2.3

Gleick, J. (1998). *Chaos: making a new science*. Vintage. https://doi.org/10.2307/1059589

Godfrey-Smith, P. (2016). *Other minds: the octopus, the sea, and the deep origins of consciousness*. Farrar, Straus; Giroux.

Godwin, J. (Ed.). (1993). *The harmony of the spheres: a sourcebook of the Pythagorean tradition in music*. https://doi.org/10.2307/898329

Goehr, L. (1992). *The imaginary museum of musical works: an essay in the philosophy of music*. Clarendon Press. https://doi.org/10.1093/0198235410.001.0001

Goldberg, A. E. (2003). Constructions: a new theoretical approach to language. *Trends in Cognitive Sciences, 7*(5), 219–224. https://doi.org/10.1016/S1364-6613(03)00080-9

Goldberg, A. E. (2013). Constructionist approaches to language. In T. Hoffmann & G. Trousdale (Eds.), *Handbook of construction grammar* (pp. 15–31). Oxford University Press.

Gollin, E., & Rehding, A. (2011). *The Oxford handbook of neo-Riemannian music theories* (E. Gollin & A. Rehding, Eds.). Oxford University Press.

Gonzaga, M. V. (Ed.). (2020). *Homeostasis*. https://doi.org/10.1007/978-94-007-7335-6_1

Gonzales, W. G., Zhang, H., Harutyunyan, A., & Lois, C. (2019). Persistence of neuronal representations through time and damage in the hippocampus. *Science, 365*(6455), 821–825. https://doi.org/10.1126/science.aav9199

Goodfellow, I., Bengio, Y., & Courville, A. (2016). *Deep learning*. MIT Press. https://doi.org/10.1038/nature14539

Goodfellow, I. J., Pouget-Abadie, J., Mirza, M., Xu, B., Warde-Farley, D., Ozair, S., Courville, A., & Bengio, Y. (2014). Generative adversarial nets. In Z. Ghahramani, M. Welling, C. Cortes, N. D. Lawrence & K. Q. Weinberger (Eds.), *Proceedings of the twenty-seventh international conference on neural information processing systems* (pp. 2672–2680, Vol. 2). MIT Press. https://doi.org/10.1145/3422622

Google. (2021). *Magenta: music and art generation with machine intelligence*. Retrieved August 12, 2021, from https://opensource.google/projects/magenta

Gould, S. J. (1977). *Ontogeny and phylogeny*. Harvard University Press. https://doi.org/10.2307/2412825

Gould, S. J. (1997). Darwinian fundamentalism. *New York Review of Books, 44*, 34–37.

Gould, S. J. (2002). *The structure of evolutionary theory*. Harvard University Press. https://doi.org/10.4159/9780674417922

Gould, S. J., & Lewontin, R. C. (1979). The spandrels of San Marco and the Panglossian paradigm: a critique of the adaptationist programme. *Proceedings of the Royal Society of London B, 205*, 581–598.

Gould, S. J., & Vrba, E. S. (1982). Exaptation: a missing term in the science of form. *Paleobiology, 8*(1), 4–15. https://doi.org/10.1017/s0094837300004310

Green, L. (1997). *Music, gender, education*. Cambridge University Press. https://doi.org/10.1017/cbo9780511585456

Greiner, W. (2001). *Quantum mechanics: an introduction* (4th ed.). Springer.

Grier, J. (1996). *The critical editing of music: history, method, and practice*. Cambridge University Press.

Griesinger, G. A. (1810). *Biographische Notizen über Joseph Haydn*. Breitkopf und Härtel.

Griffiths, A. J. F., Wessler, S. R., Carroll, S. B., & Doebley, J. (2015). *Introduction to genetic analysis* (11th ed.). W.H. Freeman.

Grimaldi, D., & Engel, M. S. (2005). *Evolution of the insects*. Cambridge University Press. https://doi.org/10.1080/10635150600755461

Gritten, A., & King, E. (Eds.). (2006). *Music and gesture*. Ashgate. https://doi.org/10.1093/oso/9780190653637.003.0004

Gritten, A., & King, E. (Eds.). (2011). *New perspectives on music and gesture*. Ashgate. https://doi.org/10.4324/9781315598048

Grossberg, S. (1987). Competitive learning: from interactive activation to adaptive resonance. *Cognitive Science, 11*(1), 23–63. https://doi.org/10.1111/j.1551-6708.1987.tb00862.x

Große Ruse, M., Hasselquist, D., Hansson, B., Tarka, M., & Sandsten, M. (2016). Automated analysis of song structure in complex birdsongs. *Animal Behaviour, 112,* 39–51. https://doi.org/10.1016/j.anbehav.2015.11.013

Groves, C. (2017). Primates (taxonomy). In A. Fuentes (Ed.), *The international encyclopaedia of primatology.* John Wiley; Sons. https://doi.org/10.1002/9781119179313.wbprim0045

Guberman, S. (2017). Gestalt theory rearranged: back to Wertheimer. *Frontiers in Psychology, 8*(1782), 1–8. https://doi.org/10.3389/fpsyg.2017.01782

Guéguen, N., Meineri, S., & Fischer-Lokou, J. (2014). Men's music ability and attractiveness to women in a real-life courtship context. *Psychology of Music, 42*(4), 545–549. https://doi.org/10.1177/0305735613482025

Guinee, L. N., & Payne, K. B. (1988). Rhyme-like repetition of songs in Humpback whales. *Ethology, 79*(4), 295–306.

Guo, R., Simpson, I., Magnusson, T., Kiefer, C., & Herremans, D. (2020). A variational autoencoder for music generation controlled by tonal tension. In B. L. T. Sturm (Ed.), *Proceedings of the first joint conference on AI music creativity.* Royal Institute of Technology (KTH), Stockholm. https://doi.org/10.5281/zenodo.4285344

Gutiérrez, S., & García, S. (2016). Landmark-based music recognition system optimisation using genetic algorithms. *Multimedia Tools and Applications, 75*(24), 16905–16922. https://doi.org/10.1007/s11042-015-2963-0

Haar, J. (2001). *Music of the spheres* (D. L. Root, Ed.). https://doi.org/10.1093/gmo/9781561592630.article.19447

Habib, M. B. (2019). New perspectives on the origins of the unique vocal tract of birds. *PLoS Biology, 17*(3), 4–7. https://doi.org/10.1371/journal.pbio.3000184

Hadjeres, G., Pachet, F., & Nielsen, F. (2016). *DeepBach: harmonization in the style of Bach generated using deep learning.* Retrieved January 18, 2020, from https://www.youtube.com/watch?v=QiBM7-5hA6o

Hadjeres, G., Pachet, F., & Nielsen, F. (2017). DeepBach: a steerable model for Bach chorales generation. In D. Precup & Y. W. Teh (Eds.), *Proceedings of the thirty-fourth international conference on machine learning* (pp. 1362–1371, Vol. 70).

Hagel, S. (2009). *Ancient Greek music: a new technical history*. Cambridge University Press. https://doi.org/10.1017/cbo9780511691591

Hameroff, S. (2021). "orch OR" is the most complete, and most easily falsifiable theory of consciousness. *Cognitive Neuroscience, 12*(2), 74–76. https://doi.org/10.1080/17588928.2020.1839037

Harari, Y. N. (2014). *Sapiens: a brief history of humankind*. Harvill Secker.

Harne, G. A. (2012). Unstable embodiments of musical theory and practice in the *speculum musicae*. *Plainsong and Medieval Music, 21*(2), 113–136. https://doi.org/10.1017/S0961137112000034

Harvey, A. R. (2017). *Music, evolution and the harmony of souls*. Oxford University Press. https://doi.org/10.1093/acprof:oso/9780198786856.001.0001

Harvey, A. R. (2018). Music and the meeting of human minds. *Frontiers in Psychology, 9*(762), 1–6. https://doi.org/10.3389/fpsyg.2018.00762

Harvey, A. R. (2020). Links between the neurobiology of oxytocin and human musicality. *Frontiers in Human Neuroscience, 14*(350), 1–19. https://doi.org/10.3389/fnhum.2020.00350

Hasty, C. (1981). Segmentation and process in post-tonal music. *Music Theory Spectrum, 3*, 54–73. https://doi.org/10.2307/746134

Hattori, Y., & Tomonaga, M. (2020). Rhythmic swaying induced by sound in chimpanzees *(Pan troglodytes)*. *Proceedings of the National Academy of Sciences, 117*(2), 936–942. https://doi.org/10.1073/pnas.1910318116

Hauser, M. D. (2000). The sound and the fury: primate vocalizations as reflections of emotion and thought. In N. L. Wallin, B. Merker & S. Brown (Eds.), *The origins of music* (pp. 77–102). MIT Press.

Hawkett, A. (2013). *An empirical investigation into the concept of musical memes in western classical music using data mining techniques on MusicXML documents* [Doctoral dissertation, University of Huddersfield]. http://eprints.hud.ac.uk/id/eprint/19290/

Head, M. (1997). Birdsong and the origins of music. *Journal of the Royal Musical Association, 122*(1), 1–23. https://doi.org/10.1093/jrma/122.1.1

Heartz, D. (2003). *Music in European capitals: the galant style 1720–1780.* Norton.

Hebb, D. O. (1949). *The organization of behavior: a neuropsychological theory.* Wiley. https://doi.org/10.2307/1418888

Hebdige, D. (1979). *Subculture: the meaning of style.* Routledge. https://doi.org/10.1111/j.1467-8705.1995.tb01063.x

Heimerdinger Clench, M., Austin, O. L., & Gill, F. (2020). *Passeriform.* Retrieved August 25, 2020, from https://www.britannica.com/animal/passeriform

Hennessey, B. A., Amabile, T. M., & Mueller, J. S. (2011). Consensual assessment. In M. A. Runco & S. R. Pritzker (Eds.), *Encyclopedia of creativity* (2nd ed., pp. 253–260, Vol. 1). Academic Press. https://doi.org/10.1016/b978-0-12-375038-9.00046-7

Hennig, W. (1999). *Phylogentic systematics* (3rd ed.). University of Illinois Press. https://doi.org/10.1146/annurev.en.10.010165.000525

Hepokoski, J. A., & Darcy, W. (2006). *Elements of sonata theory: norms, types, and deformations in the late-eighteenth-century sonata.* Oxford University Press.

Herbert, T. (2003). Social history and music history. In M. Clayton, T. Herbert & R. Middleton (Eds.), *The cultural study of music: a critical introduction* (pp. 146–156). Routledge.

Herman, L. M., Pack, A. A., Spitz, S. S., Herman, E. Y. K., Rose, K., Hakala, S., & Deakos, M. H. (2013). Humpback whale song: who sings? *Behavioral Ecology and Sociobiology, 67,* 1653–1663. https://doi.org/10.1007/s00265-013-1576-8

Herremans, D. (2022). *The computer-generated music repository.* Retrieved February 12, 2022, from http://dorienherremans.com/cogemur/

Herremans, D., Chuan, C.-H., & Chew, E. (2017). A functional taxonomy of music generation systems. *ACM Computing Surveys, 50*(5), 1–33. https://doi.org/10.1145/3108242

Herremans, D., & Sörensen, K. (2013). Composing fifth species counterpoint music with a variable neighborhood search algorithm. *Expert Systems with Applications, 40*(16), 6427–6437. https://doi.org/10.1016/j.eswa.2013.05.071

Herremans, D., Sörensen, K., & Martens, D. (2015). Classification and generation of composer-specific music using global feature models and variable neighborhood search. *Computer Music Journal, 39*(3), 71–91. https://doi.org/10.1162/COMJ

Herrnstein, R. J., & Murray, C. (1994). *The bell curve: intelligence and class structure in American life*. Free Press. https://doi.org/10.2307/3121812

Herwig, U. (2010). *Me, myself and i: how the brain maintains a sense of self*. https://www.scientificamerican.com/article/me-myself-and-i/

Heylighen, F. (2006). *The Newtonian world view*. Retrieved October 8, 2020, from http://pespmc1.vub.ac.be/NEWTONWV.html

Hickmann, E. (1984). Terminology, problems and goals of archaeomusicology. *Progress reports in ethnomusicology, 1*(3), 1–9.

Hiller, L., & Isaacson, L. M. (1957). *Illiac Suite for string quartet*. New Music Edition.

Hindley, D. G. (1990). The music of birdsong. *Wildlife Sound, 6*(4), 25–33.

Hindley, D. G. (1995). *The musical transcription and simulation of bird song*. The Author.

Hladký, V., & Havlíček, J. (2013). Was Tinbergen an Aristotelian? comparison of Tinbergen's four whys and Aristotle's four causes. *Human Ethology Bulletin, 28*(4), 3–11.

Hochner, B. (2012). An embodied view of octopus neurobiology. *Current Biology, 22*(20), 887–892. https://doi.org/10.1016/j.cub.2012.09.001

Hockett, C. F. (1960). Logical considerations in the study of animal communication. In W. E. Lanyon & W. N. Tavolga (Eds.), *Animal sounds and communication* (pp. 392–430). American Institute of Biological Sciences.

Hoeschele, M., & Fitch, W. T. (2022). Cultural evolution: conserved patterns of melodic evolution across musical cultures. *Current Biology, 32*(6), R265–R267. https://doi.org/10.1016/j.cub.2022.01.080

Hoffmann, E. T. A. (1998). Beethoven's instrumental music. In W. O. Strunk, L. Treitler & R. A. Solie (Eds.), *Source readings in music history: the nineteenth century* (Revised, pp. 151–156, Vol. 6). Norton.

Hofstadter, D. (1985). *Metamagical themas: questing for the essence of mind and pattern*. Basic Books. https://doi.org/10.2307/4611504

Honing, H. (2018a). Musicality as an upbeat to music: introduction and research agenda. In H. Honing (Ed.), *The origins of musicality* (pp. 3–20). MIT Press.

Honing, H. (Ed.). (2018b). *The origins of musicality.* MIT Press. https://doi.org/10.7551/mitpress/10636.001.0001

Howe, B., Jensen-Moulton, S., Lerner, N., & Straus, J. N. (Eds.). (2015). *The Oxford handbook of music and disability studies.* Oxford University Press. https://doi.org/10.1093/oxfordhb/9780199331444.001.0001

Howe, C. J., & Windram, H. F. (2011). Phylomemetics: evolutionary analysis beyond the gene. *PLoS Biology, 9*(5), 1–5. https://doi.org/10.1371/journal.pbio.1001069

Huang, P., Wilson, M., Mayfield-Jones, D., Coneva, V., Frank, M., & Chitwood, D. H. (2017). *The evolution of western tonality: a corpus analysis of 24,000 songs from 190 composers over six centuries.* https://doi.org/10.31235/osf.io/btshk

Hughes, D. P. (2014). On the origins of parasite-extended phenotypes. *Integrative and Comparative Biology, 54*(2), 210–217. https://doi.org/10.1093/icb/icu079

Hull, D. L. (1976). Are species really individuals? *Systematic Zoology, 25*(2), 174–191. https://doi.org/10.2307/2412744

Hull, D. L. (1988a). Interactors versus vehicles. In H. C. Plotkin (Ed.), *The role of behaviour in evolution* (pp. 19–50). MIT Press/Bradford Books.

Hull, D. L. (1988b). *Science as a process: an evolutionary account of the social and conceptual development of science.* University of Chicago Press. https://doi.org/10.7208/chicago/9780226360492.001.0001

Hunt, K. D. (1994). The evolution of human bipedality: ecology and functional morphology. *Journal of Human Evolution, 26*(3), 183–202. https://doi.org/10.1006/jhev.1994.1011

Huron, D. (1997). Humdrum and Kern: selective feature encoding. In E. Selfridge-Field (Ed.), *Beyond MIDI: the handbook of musical codes* (pp. 375–401). MIT Press.

Huron, D. (2002). Music information processing using the Humdrum Toolkit: concepts, examples, and lessons. *Computer Music Journal, 26*(2), 11–26. https://doi.org/10.1162/014892602760137158

Huron, D. (2006). *Sweet anticipation: music and the psychology of expectation.* MIT Press. https://doi.org/10.7551/mitpress/6575.001.0001

Huron, D. (2022). *Humdrum.* Retrieved January 7, 2021, from https://www.humdrum.org/

Huron, D., Kornstädt, A., Sapp, C. S., & Aarden, B. (2021). *Themefinder*. Retrieved August 3, 2021, from http://www.themefinder.org/

Iacoboni, M. (2005). Understanding others: imitation, language and empathy. In S. Hurley & N. Chater (Eds.), *Perspectives on imitation: from neuroscience to social science. volume 1: mechanisms of imitation and imitation in animals* (pp. 77–99). MIT Press.

Iamus. (2012). *Iamus (album)*. http://www.melomicsrecords.com/index.php?page=iamus-2

IMDb. (2019). *Shafted*. Retrieved October 14, 2019, from https://www.imdb.com/title/tt0302191/

Inglis, D., & Almila, A.-M. (Eds.). (2016). *The SAGE handbook of cultural sociology*. SAGE Publications.

Jablonka, E., & Lamb, M. J. (2014). *Evolution in four dimensions: genetic, epigenetic, behavioral, and symbolic variation in the history of life* (Revised). MIT Press. https://doi.org/10.7551/mitpress/9689.001.0001

James, W. (1950). *The principles of psychology* (Vol. 1). Dover. https://doi.org/10.1037/11059-000

Jan, S. B. (2004). Meme hunting with the Humdrum Toolkit: principles, problems, and prospects. *Computer Music Journal*, *28*(4), 68–84. https://doi.org/10.1162/0148926042728403

Jan, S. B. (2007). *The memetics of music: a neo-Darwinian view of musical structure and culture*. Ashgate. https://doi.org/10.4324/9781315085951

Jan, S. B. (2010). Memesatz contra Ursatz: memetic perspectives on the aetiology and evolution of musical structure. *Musicae Scientiae*, *14*(1), 3–50. https://doi.org/10.1177/102986491001400101

Jan, S. B. (2011a). Music, memory, and memes in the light of Calvinian neuroscience. *Music Theory Online*, *17*(2). https://doi.org/10.30535/mto.17.2.4

Jan, S. B. (2011b). Replication, parataxis, and evolution: meme journeys through the first movement of a Mozart sonata. In E. R. Miranda (Ed.), *A-life for music: music and computer models of living systems* (pp. 217–260). A-R Editions.

Jan, S. B. (2012). "the heavens are telling": a memetic-Calvinian reading of a Haydn chord progression. *Interdisciplinary Science Reviews*, *37*(2), 113–130. https://doi.org/10.1179/0308018812Z.0000000009

Jan, S. B. (2013). Using galant schemata as evidence for universal Darwinism. *Interdisciplinary Science Reviews*, *38*(2), 149–168. https://doi.org/10.1179/0308018813Z.00000000042

Jan, S. B. (2014). Similarity continua and criteria in memetic theory and analysis. *Journal of Music Research Online*, *5*. http://www.jmro.org.au/index.php/mca2/article/view/125

Jan, S. B. (2015a). Evolutionary thought in music theory and analysis: a corrective to "babelization"? In X. Hascher, M. Ayari & J.-M. Bardez (Eds.), *L'analyse musicale aujourd'hui/music analysis today* (pp. 55–75). Delatour France.

Jan, S. B. (2015b). Memetic perspectives on the evolution of tonal systems. *Interdisciplinary Science Reviews*, *40*(2), 145–167. https://doi.org/10.1179/0308018815Z.000000000110

Jan, S. B. (2016a). "understood at last"?: a memetic analysis of Beethoven's "bloody fist". In R. Kronland-Martinet, M. Aramaki & S. Ystad (Eds.), *Music, mind, and embodiment: 11th international symposium, cmmr 2015, plymouth, uk, june 16-19, 2015, revised selected papers* (pp. 420–437). Springer. https://doi.org/10.1007/978-3-319-46282-0_27

Jan, S. B. (2016b). From holism to compositionality: memes and the evolution of segmentation, syntax and signification in music and language. *Language and Cognition*, *8*(4), 463–500. https://doi.org/10.1017/langcog.2015.1

Jan, S. B. (2016c). A memetic analysis of a phrase by Beethoven: calvinian perspectives on similarity and lexicon-abstraction. *Psychology of Music*, *44*(3), 443–465. https://doi.org/10.1177/0305735615576065

Jan, S. B. (2018a). "the two brothers": reconciling perceptual-cognitive and statistical models of musical evolution. *Frontiers in Psychology*, *9*(344), 1–15. https://doi.org/10.3389/fpsyg.2018.00344

Jan, S. B. (2018b). The theory and analysis of computer-generated music: a case-study of *colossus*. In R. Loughran (Ed.), *Proceedings of the third conference on the computer simulation of musical creativity, University College Dublin, 20–22 August 2018*. University College Dublin. https://csmc2017.wordpress.com/

Jander, O. (1993). The prophetic conversation in Beethoven's "Scene by the brook". *The Musical Quarterly*, *77*(3), 508–559. https://doi.org/10.1093/mq/77.3.508

Janik, V. M. (2009). Whale song. *Current Biology, 19*(3), 109–111. https://doi.org/10.1016/j.cub.2008.11.026

Janssen, B., van Kranenburg, P., & Volk, A. (2017). Finding occurrences of melodic segments in folk songs employing symbolic similarity measures. *Journal of New Music Research, 46*(2), 118–134. https://doi.org/10.1080/09298215.2017.1316292

Jeffries, L. (2019). *Hansard at Huddersfield*. https://hansard.hud.ac.uk/site/index.php

Jeffries, L., & McIntyre, D. (2010). *Stylistics*. Cambridge University Press. https://doi.org/10.1017/cbo9780511762949

Jeppesen, K. (1992). *Counterpoint: the polyphonic vocal style of the sixteenth century*. Dover.

Jerison, H. (2000). Paleoneurology and the biology of music. In N. L. Wallin, B. Merker & S. Brown (Eds.), *The origins of music* (pp. 177–196). MIT Press.

Johns, P. (2014). *Clinical neuroscience: an illustrated colour text*. Churchill Livingstone. https://doi.org/10.1016/B978-0-443-10321-6.00003-5

Johnson, D. P., Tyson, A., & Winter, R. S. (1985). *The Beethoven sketchbooks: history, reconstruction, inventory*. Clarendon Press. https://doi.org/10.2307/897833

Jõks, M., & Pärtel, M. (2019). Plant diversity in oceanic archipelagos: realistic patterns emulated by an agent-based computer simulation. *Ecography, 42*(4), 740–754. https://doi.org/10.1111/ecog.03985

Jones, R. (2014). Beethoven and the sound of revolution in Vienna, 1792–1814. *Historical Journal, 57*(4), 947–971. https://doi.org/10.1017/S0018246X14000405

Jones, S. (1999). *Almost like a whale: the Origin of species updated*. Doubleday.

Jordanous, A. K. (2012). *Evaluating computational creativity: a standardised procedure for evaluating creative systems and its application* [DPhil]. University of Sussex. http://sro.sussex.ac.uk/44741/1/Jordanous,_Anna_Katerina.pdf

Juslin, P. N., & Laukka, P. (2003). Communication of emotions in vocal expression and music performance: different channels, same code? *Psychological Bulletin, 129*(5), 770–814. https://doi.org/10.1037/0033-2909.129.5.770

Kalonaris, S. (2018). Satisficing goals and methods in human-machine music improvisations: experiments with *dory*. *Journal of Creative Music Systems*, 2(2), 1–21. https://doi.org/10.5920/jcms.2018.03

Kaminska, Z., & Woolf, J. (2000). Melodic line and emotion: cooke's theory revisited. *Psychology of Music*, 28(2), 133–153. https://doi.org/10.1177/0305735600282003

Karmiloff-Smith, A. (1992). *Beyond modularity: a developmental perspective on cognitive science*. MIT Press. https://doi.org/10.7551/mitpress/1579.001.0001

Kassler, J. C. (1983). Heinrich Schenker's epistemology and philosophy of music: an essay on the relations between evolutionary theory and music theory. In D. Oldroyd & I. Langham (Eds.), *The wider domain of evolutionary thought* (pp. 221–260). D. Reidel. https://doi.org/10.1007/978-94-009-6986-5_8

Kauffman, S. A. (1993). *The origins of order: self-organization and selection in evolution*. Oxford University Press. https://doi.org/10.1142/9789814415743_0003

Keller, H. (1955). Strict serial technique in classical music. *Tempo*, 37, 12–24. https://doi.org/10.1017/s0040298200055212

Keller, H. (1956). Key characteristics. *Tempo*, 40, 5–10, 13–16. https://doi.org/10.1017/s0040298200052827

Keller, H. (1957). Functional analysis: its pure application. *The Music Review*, 18, 202–206.

Keller, H. (1958). Functional analysis of Mozart's D minor quartet. *The Score*, 22, 56–64.

Keller, H. (1985). Functional analysis of Mozart's G minor quintet. *Music Analysis*, 4(1–2), 73–94. https://doi.org/10.2307/854236

Keller, H. (1994). *Hans Keller: essays on music* (C. Wintle, B. Northcott & I. Samuel, Eds.). Cambridge University Press.

Keller, H. (2001). *Functional analysis: the unity of contrasting themes. complete edition of the analytical scores* (G. W. Gruber, S. Bradshaw & M. Meixner, Eds.). Peter Lang.

Keller, M. S. (2012). Zoomusicology and ethnomusicology: a marriage to celebrate in heaven. *Yearbook for Traditional Music*, 44, 166–183. https://doi.org/10.5921/yeartradmusi.44.0166

Kellermann, N. P. F. (2013). Epigenetic transmission of Holocaust trauma: can nightmares be inherited? *Israel Journal of Psychiatry and Related Sciences*, *50*(1), 33–39.

Kendal, J. R., & Laland, K. N. (2000). Mathematical models for memetics. *Journal of Memetics: Evolutionary Models of Information Transmission*, *4*. http://cfpm.org/jom-emit/2000/vol4/kendal_jr%5C&laland_kn.html

Kerman, J. (1985). *Musicology*. Fontana. https://doi.org/10.2307/854343

Kerman, J. (1994a). A profile for American musicology. In *Write all these down: essays on music* (pp. 3–11). University of California Press. https://doi.org/10.2307/830725

Kerman, J. (1994b). *Write all these down: essays on music*. University of California Press. https://doi.org/10.2307/899075

Keysers, C. (2009). Mirror neurons. *Current Biology*, *19*(21), 971–973. https://doi.org/10.1016/j.cub.2009.08.026

Killian, N. J., Jutras, M. J., & Buffalo, E. A. (2012). A map of visual space in the primate entorhinal cortex. *Nature*, *491*, 761–764. https://doi.org/10.1038/nature11587

Kinderman, W., & Krebs, H. (1996). *The second practice of nineteenth-century tonality*. University of Nebraska Press. https://doi.org/10.2307/899959

Kirby, S. (2001). Spontaneous evolution of linguistic structure: an iterated learning model of the emergence of regularity and irregularity. *IEEE Transactions on Evolutionary Computation*, *5*(2), 102–110. https://doi.org/10.1109/4235.918430

Kirby, S. (2007). The evolution of language. In R. I. M. Dunbar & L. Barrett (Eds.), *Oxford handbook of evolutionary psychology* (pp. 669–681). Oxford University Press. https://doi.org/10.1093/oxfordhb/9780198568308.013.0046

Kirby, S. (2013). Transitions: the evolution of linguistic replicators. In P. M. Binder & K. Smith (Eds.), *The language phenomenon: human communication from milliseconds to millennia* (pp. 121–138). Springer. https://doi.org/10.1007/978-3-642-36086-2_6

Kirby, S., Tamariz, M., Cornish, H., & Smith, K. (2015). Compression and communication in the cultural evolution of linguistic structure. *Cognition*, *141*, 87–102. https://doi.org/10.1016/j.cognition.2015.03.016

Kirke, A. J., Freeman, S., Miranda, E. R., & Ingram, S. (2011). Application of multi-agent whale modelling to an interactive saxophone and whales duet. *Proceedings of the international computer music conference 2011*, 350–353. http://hdl.handle.net/2027/spo.bbp2372.2011.072

Klein, R. G. (2009). *The human career: human biological and cultural origins* (3rd ed.). University of Chicago Press. https://doi.org/10.2307/2409685

Knopoff, L., & Hutchinson, W. (1981). Information theory for musical continua. *Journal of Music Theory*, *25*(1), 17–44. https://doi.org/10.2307/843465

Koch, C. (2004). *The quest for consciousness: a neurobiological approach*. Roberts.

Koch, C. (2012). *Consciousness: confessions of a romantic reductionist*. MIT Press. https://doi.org/10.7551/mitpress/9367.001.0001

Kochiyama, T., Ogihara, N., Tanabe, H. C., Kondo, O., Amano, H., Hasegawa, K., Suzuki, H., Ponce de León, M. S., Zollikofer, C. P. E., Bastir, M., Stringer, C., Sadato, N., & Akazawa, T. (2018). Reconstructing the Neanderthal brain using computational anatomy. *Scientific Reports*, *8*(6296), 1–9. https://doi.org/10.1038/s41598-018-24331-0

Koda, H., Lemasson, A., Oyakawa, C., Rizaldi, Pamungkas, J., & Masataka, N. (2013). Possible role of mother-daughter vocal interactions on the development of species-specific song in gibbons. *PLoS ONE*, *8*(8), 1–10. https://doi.org/10.1371/journal.pone.0071432

Koelsch, S. (2013). *Brain and music*. Wiley-Blackwell.

Kohn, E. (2013). *How forests think: toward an anthropology beyond the human*. University of California Press. https://doi.org/10.1525/california/9780520276109.001.0001

Kornstädt, A. (1998). Themefinder: a web-based melodic search tool. In W. B. Hewlett & E. Selfridge-Field (Eds.), *Melodic similarity: concepts, procedures, and applications* (pp. 231–236). MIT Press.

Korshunova, I. (2016). *folk-rnn training data*. Retrieved December 23, 2019, from https://github.com/IraKorshunova/folk-rnn/blob/master/data/allabcwrepeats_parsed

Korsyn, K. (1991). Towards a new poetics of musical influence. *Music Analysis*, *10*(1–2), 3–72. https://doi.org/10.2307/853998

Koza, J. R. (1992). *Genetic programming: on the programming of computers by means of natural selection*. MIT Press.

Kraft, D. (2000). *Birdsong in the music of Olivier Messiaen* [PhD]. Middlesex University. http://eprints.mdx.ac.uk/6445/

Kramer, J. D. (2016). *Postmodern music, postmodern listening* (R. Carl, Ed.). Bloomsbury. https://doi.org/10.5040/9781501306051.ch-015

Kramer, L. (2002). *Musical meaning: toward a critical history*. University of California Press. https://doi.org/10.1525/9780520928329

Kramer, L. (2010). *Music as cultural practice: 1800–1900*. University of California Press. https://doi.org/10.2307/854306

Kronfeldner, M. (2014). *Darwinian creativity and memetics*. Routledge. https://doi.org/10.4324/9781315729107

Kroodsma, D. E. (2004). The diversity and plasticity of birdsong. In P. Marler & H. Slabbekoorn (Eds.), *Nature's music: the science of birdsong* (pp. 108–131). Elsevier Academic Press. https://doi.org/10.1016/b978-012473070-0/50007-4

Krumhansl, C. L. (1990). *Cognitive foundations of musical pitch*. Oxford University Press. https://doi.org/10.1093/acprof:oso/9780195148367.001.0001

Krumhansl, C. L., & Kessler, E. J. (1982). Tracing the dynamic changes in perceived tonal organization in a spatial representation of musical keys. *Psychological Review, 89*(4), 334–368. https://doi.org/10.1037/0033-295x.89.4.334

Kuhn, T. S. (2012). *The structure of scientific revolutions* (4th ed.). University of Chicago Press. https://doi.org/10.7208/chicago/9780226458106.001.0001

Kuijper, B., Pen, I., & Weissing, F. J. (2012). A guide to sexual selection theory. *Annual Review of Ecology, Evolution, and Systematics, 43*, 287–311. https://doi.org/10.1146/annurev-ecolsys-110411-160245

Kunej, D., & Turk, I. (2000). New perspectives on the beginnings of music: archeological and musicological analysis of a middle paleolithic bone "flute". In N. L. Wallin, B. Merker & S. Brown (Eds.), *The origins of music* (pp. 235–268). MIT Press.

Kuper, A. (2000). If memes are the answer, what is the question? In R. Aunger (Ed.), *Darwinizing culture: the status of memetics as a science* (pp. 175–188). Oxford University Press. https://doi.org/10.1093/acprof:oso/9780192632449.003.0009

Lack, D. L. (1983). *Darwin's finches* (L. M. Ratcliffe & P. T. Boag, Eds.). Cambridge University Press. https : / / doi . org / 10 . 1038 / scientificamerican0453-66

Laland, K. N., & Galef, B. G. (2009). *The question of animal culture*. Harvard University Press. https://doi.org/10.1007/bf02692251

Lalitte, P., Bigand, E., Kantor-Martynuska, J., & Delbé, C. (2009). On listening to atonal variants of two piano sonatas by Beethoven. *Music Perception, 26*(3), 223–234. https://doi.org/10.1525/mp.2009.26.3.223

Lamarck, J.-B. P. A. (2011). *Philosophie zoologique: ou exposition des considérations relative à l'histoire naturelle des animaux*. Cambridge University Press. (Original work published 1809). https://doi.org/10.1017/cbo9781139103800

Lansley, C. M. (2018). *Charles Darwin's debt to the romantics: how Alexander von Humboldt, Goethe and Wordsworth helped shape Darwin's view of nature.* Peter Lang.

Lartillot, O. (2009). Taxonomic categorisation of motivic patterns. *Musicae Scientiae, Discussion Forum 4B: Musical Similarity*, 25–46. https://doi.org/10.1177/102986490901300103

Lartillot, O. (2019). Miningsuite: a comprehensive Matlab framework for signal, audio and music analysis, articulating audio and symbolic approaches. In I. Barbancho, L. J. Tardón, A. Peinado & A. M. Barbancho (Eds.), *Proceedings of the sixteeenth sound and music computing conference* (p. 489). Sound; Music Computing Network.

LaRue, J. (2011). *Guidelines for style analysis* (M. G. LaRue, Ed.; 2nd ed.). Harmonie Park Press. https://doi.org/10.2307/896363

Laurent, J. (1999). A note on the origin of "memes"/"mnemes". *Journal of Memetics: Evolutionary Models of Information Transmission, 3*(1). http://cfpm.org/jom-emit/1999/vol3/laurent_j.html

Ledbetter, D. (2013). Fugal improvisation in the time of J. S. Bach and Handel. *The Organ Yearbook, 42*, 53–75.

Leech-Wilkinson, D. (2009a). *The changing sound of music: approaches to studying recorded musical performances*. CHARM. http://www.charm.kcl.ac.uk/studies/chapters/intro.html

Leech-Wilkinson, D. (2009b). Review of Steven Jan, the memetics of music: a neo-Darwinian view of musical structure and culture. *Music and Letters, 90*(1), 148–150. https://doi.org/10.1093/ml/gcn079

Leff, G. (1992). The trivium and the three philosophies. In H. de Ridder-Symoens (Ed.), *A history of the university in Europe. vol. I: universities in the middle ages* (pp. 307–336). Cambridge University Press.

Lehmann, C. (2018). Wilhelm von Humboldts Theorie der Sprachevolution. *Zeitschrift für Literaturwissenschaft und Linguistik, 48*(4), 689–715. https://doi.org/10.1007/s41244-018-0110-x

Leman, M. (1995). *Music and schema theory: cognitive foundations of systematic musicology.* Springer. https://doi.org/10.2307/3687199

Leman, M. (2008). *Embodied music cognition and mediation technology.* MIT Press. https://doi.org/10.7551/mitpress/7476.001.0001

Leng, X., & Shaw, G. L. (1991). Toward a neural theory of higher brain function using music as a window. *Concepts in Neuroscience, 2,* 229–258.

Leng, X., Wright, E. L., & Shaw, G. L. (1990). Coding of musical structure and the trion model of cortex. *Music Perception, 8,* 49–62. https://doi.org/10.2307/40285485

Lerdahl, F. (1992). Cognitive constraints on compositional systems. *Contemporary Music Review, 6*(2), 97–121. https://doi.org/10.1080/07494469200640161

Lerdahl, F. (2001). *Tonal pitch space.* Oxford University Press. https://doi.org/10.1093/acprof:oso/9780195178296.001.0001

Lerdahl, F., & Jackendoff, R. (1983). *A generative theory of tonal music.* MIT Press. https://doi.org/10.7551/mitpress/12513.001.0001

Levenshtein, V. I. (1966). Binary codes capable of correcting deletions, insertions, and reversals. *Soviet Physics Doklady, 10,* 707–710.

Levitin, D. (2008). *This is your brain on music: understanding a human obsession.* Atlantic Books.

Levitin, D. (2009). *The world in six songs: how the musical brain created human nature.* Dutton.

Levitz, T. (2004). The chosen one's choice. In A. Dell'Antonio (Ed.), *Beyond structural listening? postmodern modes of hearing* (pp. 70–108). University of California Press.

Lewens, T. (2015). *Cultural evolution: conceptual challenges.* Oxford University Press. https://doi.org/10.1093/acprof:oso/9780199674183.001.0001

Lewin, D. (2011). *Generalized musical intervals and transformations*. Oxford University Press. https://doi.org/10.1093/acprof:oso/9780195317138.001.0001

Lewontin, R. C. (1970). The units of selection. *Annual Review of Ecology and Systematics, 1,* 1–18. https://doi.org/10.1146/annurev.es.01.110170.000245

Ligrone, R. (2019). *Biological innovations that built the world: a four-billion-year journey through life earth history*. Springer.

Lim, L. (2016a). *How forests think (composition)*. https : / / issuu . com / casaricordi/docs/lim_how_forests_think_wm

Lim, L. (2016b). *How forests think (programme note)*. Retrieved September 10, 2021, from https://limprogrammenotes.wordpress.com/2016/02/06/howforeststhink/

Lindsay, J., & Boyle, P. (2017). The conceptual penis as a social construct. *Cogent Social Sciences, 3*(1330439), 1–7. https://doi.org/10.1080/23311886.2017.1330439

Liow, L. H., Van Valen, L., & Stenseth, N. C. (2011). Red queen: from populations to taxa and communities. *Trends in Ecology and Evolution, 26*(7), 349–358. https://doi.org/10.1016/j.tree.2011.03.016

Lockwood, L., & Gosman, A. (Eds.). (2013). *Beethoven's "Eroica" sketchbook: a critical edition*. University of Illinois Press.

Lomax, A. (1976). *Cantometrics: an approach to the anthropology of music*. University of California Extension Media Center. https://doi.org/10.2307/851562

Lord, A. B. (1964). *The singer of tales*. Harvard University Press. https://doi.org/10.2307/4344494

Lord, A. B. (1965). Yugoslav epic folk poetry. In A. Dundes (Ed.), *The study of folklore* (pp. 265–268). Prentice-Hall. https://doi.org/10.2307/835775

Loughran, R., & O'Neill, M. (2017). Limitations from assumptions in generative music evaluation. *Journal of Creative Music Systems, 2*(1). https://doi.org/10.5920/jcms.2017.12

Lovejoy, A. O. (1976). *The great chain of being: a study of the history of an idea*. Harvard University Press. https://doi.org/10.2307/j.ctvjsf71g

Lovelock, J. (2000). *Gaia: a new look at life on earth*. Oxford University Press. https://doi.org/10.1016/0004-6981(80)90149-3

Low, T. (2016). *Where song began: australia's birds and how they changed the world*. Yale University Press. https://doi.org/10.12987/9780300226805

Lucretius, T. C. (2007). *The nature of things* (A. E. Stallings, Trans.). Penguin.

Lumaca, M., & Baggio, G. (2017). Cultural transmission and evolution of melodic structures in multi-generational signaling games. *Artificial Life, 23*(3), 406–423. https://doi.org/10.1162/ARTL_a_00238

Lumsden, C. J., & Wilson, E. O. (1981). *Genes, mind and culture: the coevolutionary process*. Harvard University Press. https://doi.org/10.1142/5786

Lynch, A. (1996). *Thought contagion: how belief spreads through society – the new science of memes*. Basic Books.

Lynch, A. (1998). Units, events and dynamics in memetic evolution. *Journal of Memetics: Evolutionary Models of Information Transmission, 2*. http://jom-emit.cfpm.org/1998/vol2/lynch_a.html

Mabley, C. (2015). *Bach's authentic chorale harmony: a progressive guide to his principles and practices*. The Choir Press.

MacCallum, R. M., Leroi, A. M., Mauch, M., Welburn, S., & Bussey, C. (2012). *DarwinTunes: survival of the funkiest*. http://darwintunes.org/

MacCallum, R. M., Mauch, M., Burt, A., & Leroi, A. M. (2012). Evolution of music by public choice. *Proceedings of the National Academy of Sciences, 109*(30), 12081–12086. https://doi.org/10.1073/pnas.1203182109

Madison, G., Holmquist, J., & Vestin, M. (2018). Musical improvisation skill in a prospective partner is associated with mate value and preferences, consistent with sexual selection and parental investment theory: implications for the origin of music. *Evolution and Human Behavior, 39*(1), 120–129. https://doi.org/10.1016/j.evolhumbehav.2017.10.005

Maeterlinck, M. (1927). *The life of the white ant*. George Allen; Unwin.

Manser, M. B. (2013). Semantic communication in vervet monkeys and other animals. *Animal Behaviour, 86*(3), 491–496. https://doi.org/10.1016/j.anbehav.2013.07.006

Manzano, Ö. d., & Ullén, F. (2018). Same genes, different brains: neuroanatomical differences between monozygotic twins discordant for musical training. *Cerebral Cortex, 28*(1), 387–394. https://doi.org/10.1093/cercor/bhx299

Marais, E. N. (2017). *The soul of the white ant*. A Distant Mirror.

Marcaggi, G., & Guénolé, F. (2018). Freudarwin: evolutionary thinking as a root of psychoanalysis. *Frontiers in Psychology*, *9*(892), 1–9. https://doi.org/10.3389/fpsyg.2018.00892

Margulis, E. H., & Beatty, A. P. (2008). Musical style, psychoaesthetics, and prospects for entropy as an analytic tool. *Computer Music Journal*, *32*(4), 64–78. https://doi.org/10.1162/comj.2008.32.4.64

Marin, O. S. M., & Perry, D. W. (1999). Neurological aspects of music perception and performance. In D. Deutsch (Ed.), *The psychology of music* (2nd ed., pp. 653–724). Academic Press. https://doi.org/10.1016/b978-012213564-4/50018-4

Marler, P. (1970). A comparative approach to vocal learning: song development in white-crowned sparrows. *Journal of Comparative and Physiological Psychology*, *71*, 1–25. https://doi.org/10.1037/h0029144

Marler, P. (2000). Origins of music and speech: insights from animals. In N. L. Wallin, B. Merker & S. Brown (Eds.), *The origins of music* (pp. 31–48). MIT Press.

Marler, P., & Slabbekoorn, H. (Eds.). (2004). *Nature's music: the science of birdsong*. Elsevier Academic Press. https://doi.org/10.5860/choice.42-5277

Marshall, G. (1998). *The internet and memetics*. Retrieved October 8, 2020, from http://pespmc1.vub.ac.be/Conf/MemePap/Marshall.html

Martinelli, D. (2017). *Give peace a chant: popular music, politics and social protest*. Springer.

Marx, A. B. (1997). *Musical form in the age of Beethoven: selected writings on theory and method* (S. Burnham, Ed. & Trans.). Cambridge University Press. https://doi.org/10.1017/cbo9780511582721

Masel, J. (2011). Genetic drift. *Current Biology*, *21*(20), R837–R838. https://doi.org/10.1016/j.cub.2011.08.007

Matsubara, M., Ishiwa, Y., Uehara, Y., & Tojo, S. (2018). Computational detection of local cadence on revised TPS. In R. Loughran (Ed.), *Proceedings of the third conference on the computer simulation of musical creativity, University College Dublin, 20–22 August 2018*. University College Dublin. https://csmc2018.wordpress.com/

Mattheson, J., & Harriss, E. C. (1981). *Johann Mattheson's Der vollkommene Capellmeister: a revised translation with critical commentary*. UMI Research Press.

Maul, M. (2013). Bach versus Scheibe: hitherto unknown battlegrounds in a famous conflict. In A. Talle (Ed.), *J.s. bach and his german contemporaries* (pp. 120–143). University of Illinois Press.

Maynard Smith, J. (1982). *Evolution and the theory of games*. Cambridge University Press. https://doi.org/10.1017/cbo9780511806292

Mayr, E. (1982). *The growth of biological thought: diversity, evolution, and inheritance*. Harvard University Press.

Mayr, G. (2016). *Avian evolution: the fossil record of birds and its paleobiological significance*. John Wiley; Sons. https://doi.org/10.1002/9781119020677

McClary, S. (1986). A musical dialectic from the Enlightenment: mozart's Piano Concerto in G major, K. 453, movement 2. *Cultural Critique, 4,* 129–169. https://doi.org/10.2307/1354338

McClary, S. (1987). Getting down off the beanstalk: the presence of a woman's voice in Janika Vandervelde's *Genesis II. Minnesota Composers' Forum Newsletter.*

McClary, S. (1991). *Feminine endings: music, gender, and sexuality* (First). University of Minnesota Press.

McClary, S. (1993). Narrative agendas in "absolute" music: identity and difference in Brahms's Third Symphony. In R. A. Solie (Ed.), *Musicology and difference: gender and sexuality in music scholarship* (pp. 326–344). University of California Press. https://doi.org/10.1525/9780520916500-017

McClary, S. (1994). Narratives of bourgeois subjectivity in Mozart's *Prague* Symphony. In J. Phelan & P. J. Rabinowitz (Eds.), *Understanding narrative* (pp. 65–98). Ohio State University Press.

McClary, S. (2002). *Feminine endings: music, gender, and sexuality* (2nd ed.). University of Minnesota Press.

McClary, S. (2004). Rap, minimalism, and structures of time in late twentieth-century culture. In C. Cox & D. Warner (Eds.), *Audio culture: readings in modern music* (pp. 289–298). Continuum. https://doi.org/10.5040/9781501318399.ch-055

McClary, S. (2007). *Reading music: selected essays*. Ashgate. https://doi.org/10.4324/9781315089140

McCormack, J., & D'Inverno, M. (Eds.). (2012). *Computers and creativity*. Springer. https://doi.org/10.1016/b978-0-12-375038-9.00041-8

McKay, J. Z. (2015). The problem of improbability in music analysis. In M. Ayari, J.-M. Bardez & X. Hascher (Eds.), *L'analyse musicale aujourd'hui/music analysis today* (pp. 77–90). Delatour France.

Mcloughlin, M., Lamoni, L., Garland, E. C., Ingram, S., Kirke, A. J., Noad, M. J., Rendell, L., & Miranda, E. R. (2018). Using agent-based models to understand the role of individuals in the song evolution of Humpback whales (*megaptera novaeangeliae*). *Music & Science, 1,* 1–17. https://doi.org/10.1177/2059204318757021

McLuhan, M. (1969). *Counterblast.* McClelland; Stewart.

McNamara, A. (2011). Can we measure memes? *Frontiers in Evolutionary Neuroscience, 3,* 1–7. https://doi.org/10.3389/fnevo.2011.00001

Mehr, S. A., Krasnow, M. M., Bryant, G. A., & Hagen, E. H. (2021). Origins of music in credible signaling. *Behavioural and Brain Sciences, 44*(e60), 23–39. https://doi.org/10.1017/S0140525X20000345

Melott, A. L., & Thomas, B. C. (2019). From cosmic explosions to terrestrial fires? *Journal of Geology, 127*(4), 475–481. https://doi.org/10.1086/703418

Mendel, G. (1901). Experiments in plant hybridization (tr. druery, c. t. and bateson, w.) *Journal of the Royal Horticultural Society, 26,* 1–32. http://www.esp.org/foundations/genetics/classical/gm-65.pdf

Meraviglia, M. (2020). *Computer generated music: a new empirical approach* [PhD]. London Metropolitan University.

Merchant, H., Grahn, J., Trainor, L. J., Rohrmeier, M., & Fitch, W. T. (2018). Finding the beat: a neural perspective across humans and nonhuman primates. In H. Honing (Ed.), *The origins of musicality* (pp. 171–203). MIT Press. https://doi.org/10.1098/rstb.2014.0093

Merchant, H., & Honing, H. (2014). Are non-human primates capable of rhythmic entrainment? evidence for the gradual audiomotor evolution hypothesis. *Frontiers in Neuroscience, 7*(274), 1–8. https://doi.org/10.3389/fnins.2013.00274

Meredith, D. (Ed.). (2016). *Computational music analysis.* Springer. https://doi.org/10.1007/978-3-319-25931-4

Merker, B. (2000a). Synchronous chorusing and human origins. In N. L. Wallin, B. Merker & S. Brown (Eds.), *The origins of music* (pp. 315–327). MIT Press.

Merker, B. (2000b). Synchronous chorusing and the origins of music. *Musicae Scientiae, 3*(1), 59–73. https://doi.org/10.1177/10298649000030S105

Merker, B. (2002). Music: the missing Humboldt system. *Musicae Scientiae, 6*(1), 3–21. https://doi.org/10.1177/102986490200600101

Merker, B. (2012). The vocal learning constellation: imitation, ritual culture, encephalization. In N. Bannan (Ed.), *Music, language, and human evolution* (pp. 215–260). Oxford University Press.

Merker, B., & Cox, C. (1999). Development of the female great call in *hylobates gabriellae*: a case study. *Folia Primatologica, 70*(2), 97–106. https://doi.org/10.1159/000021680

Meyer, L. B. (1956). *Emotion and meaning in music*. University of Chicago Press. https://doi.org/10.7208/chicago/9780226521374.001.0001

Meyer, L. B. (1973). *Explaining music: essays and explorations*. University of Chicago Press. https://doi.org/10.2307/843142

Meyer, L. B. (1996). *Style and music: theory, history, and ideology*. University of Chicago Press. https://doi.org/10.2307/941770

Mhatre, H., Gorchetchnikov, A., & Grossberg, S. (2012). Grid cell hexagonal patterns formed by fast self-organized learning within entorhinal cortex. *Hippocampus, 22*(2), 320–334. https://doi.org/10.1002/hipo.20901

Miller, G. (2000). Evolution of human music through sexual selection. In N. L. Wallin, B. Merker & S. Brown (Eds.), *The origins of music* (pp. 329–360). MIT Press. https://doi.org/10.1177/004057368303900411

Miller, G. (2001). *The mating mind: how sexual choice shaped the evolution of human nature*. Vintage.

Miller, G., Tybur, J. M., & Jordan, B. D. (2007). Ovulatory cycle effects on tip earnings by lap dancers: economic evidence for human estrus? *Evolution and Human Behavior, 28*(6), 375–381. https://doi.org/10.1016/j.evolhumbehav.2007.06.002

Miller, G. A. (1956). The magical number seven, plus or minus two: some limits on our capacity for processing information. *Psychological Review, 63*(2), 81–97. https://doi.org/10.1037/h0043158

Miller, J., & Van Loon, B. (2010). *Introducing Darwin: a graphic guide*. Icon Books.

Milne, A. A., & Shepard, E. H. (2016). *The house at Pooh corner*. Egmont.

Miranda, E. R. (2001). *Composing music with computers.* Taylor; Francis. https://doi.org/10.4324/9780080502403

Miranda, E. R. (2003). On the evolution of music in a society of self-taught digital creatures. *Digital Creativity, 14*(1), 29–42. https://doi.org/10.1076/digc.14.1.29.8812

Miranda, E. R. (2004). At the crossroads of evolutionary computation in music: self-programming synthesizers, swarm orchestras and the origins of melody. *Evolutionary Computation, 12*(2), 137–158. https://doi.org/10.1162/106365604773955120

Miranda, E. R. (2008). Emergent songs by social robots. *Journal of Experimental and Theoretical Artificial Intelligence, 20*(4), 319–334. https://doi.org/10.1080/09528130701664640

Miranda, E. R. (Ed.). (2021). *Handbook of artificial intelligence for music: foundations, advanced approaches, and developments for creativity.* Springer International Publishing. https://doi.org/10.1007/978-3-030-72116-9

Miranda, E. R., & Biles, J. A. (2007). *Evolutionary computer music.* Springer. https://doi.org/10.1007/978-1-84628-600-1

Miranda, E. R., & Drouet, E. (2006). Evolution of musical lexicons by singing robots. In M. Witkowski, U. Nehmzow, C. Melhuish, E. Moxey & A. Ellery (Eds.), *Towards autonomous robotic systems 2006 (TAROS-06): incorporating the Autumn Biro-net symposium, 4-6 September 2006, Surrey, UK.* Imperial College London.

Miranda, E. R., Kirby, S., & Todd, P. M. (2003). On computational models of the evolution of music: from the origins of musical taste to the emergence of grammars. *Contemporary Music Review, 22*(2), 91–110. https://doi.org/10.1080/0749446032000150915

MIREX. (2020). *MIREX.* Retrieved August 3, 2021, from https://www.music-ir.org/mirex/wiki/MIREX_HOME

Mirka, D. (Ed.). (2014). *The Oxford handbook of topic theory.* Oxford University Press. https://doi.org/10.1093/oxfordhb/9780199841578.001.0001

Mithen, S. (2006). *The singing Neanderthals: the origins of music, language, mind and body.* Phoenix.

Mitrano, P., Lockman, A., Honicker, J., & Barton, S. (2017). Using recurrent neural networks to judge fitness in musical genetic algorithms. In P. Pasquier, O. Bown & A. Eigenfeldt (Eds.), *Proceedings of the fifth inter-*

national workshop on musical metacreation (*MuMe 2017*), *in conjunction with the eighth international conference on computational creativity* (*ICCC 2017*). http://musicalmetacreation.org/mume2017/proceedings/Mitrano.pdf

Monelle, R. (2006). *The musical topic: hunt, military and pastoral*. Indiana University Press.

Mordvintsev, A., Olah, C., & Tyka, M. (2015). *DeepDream: a code example for visualizing neural networks*. Retrieved December 20, 2019, from https://ai.googleblog.com/2015/07/deepdream-code-example-for-visualizing.html

Morgan, R. P. (2003). The concept of unity and musical analysis. *Music Analysis, 22*(1–2), 7–50. https://doi.org/10.1111/j.0262-5245.2003.00175.x

Morgan, R. P. (2014). *Becoming Heinrich Schenker: music theory and ideology*. Cambridge University Press. https://doi.org/10.1017/cbo9781107705579

Morley, I. (2012). Hominin physiological evolution and the emergence of musical capacities. In N. Bannan (Ed.), *Music, language, and human evolution* (pp. 109–141). Oxford University Press. https://doi.org/10.1093/acprof:osobl/9780199227341.003.0005

Morris, D. (1967). *The naked ape: a zoologist's study of the human animal*. Jonathan Cape. https://doi.org/10.2307/2799430

Moseley, R. (2016). *Keys to play: music as a ludic medium from Apollo to Nintendo*. University of California Press. https://doi.org/10.1515/9780520965096

Mosing, M. A., Verweij, K. J. H., Madison, G., Pedersen, N. L., Zietsch, B. P., & Ullén, F. (2014). Did sexual selection shape human music? testing predictions from the sexual selection hypothesis of music evolution using a large genetically informative sample of over 10,000 twins. *Evolution and Human Behavior, 36*(5), 359–366. https://doi.org/10.1016/j.evolhumbehav.2015.02.004

Mountcastle, V. B. (1978). An organizing principle for cerebral function: the unit module and the distributed system. In G. M. Edelman & V. B. Mountcastle (Eds.), *The mindful brain: cortical organization and the group-selective theory of higher brain function* (pp. 7–50). MIT Press.

Müllensiefen, D., & Frieler, K. (2004). Cognitive adequacy in the measurement of melodic similarity: algorithmic vs. human judgments. In W. B. Hewlett & E. Selfridge-Field (Eds.), *Music query: methods, models, and user studies* (pp. 147–177). MIT Press.

Müllensiefen, D., & Frieler, K. (2006). Evaluating different approaches to measuring the similarity of melodies. In V. Batagelj, H.-H. Bock, A. Ferligoj & A. Žiberna (Eds.), *Data science and classification* (pp. 299–306). Springer. https://doi.org/10.1007/3-540-34416-0_32

Murray, C. (2020). *Human diversity: the biology of gender, race, and class*. Twelve.

Mussorgsky, M. (1987). *Boris Godunov* (N. Rimsky-Korsakov, G. Kirkor & I. Iordan, Eds.). Dover. https://doi.org/10.2307/897697

Narmour, E. (1977). *Beyond Schenkerism: the need for alternatives in music analysis*. University of Chicago Press. https://doi.org/10.2307/843728

Narmour, E. (1989). The "genetic code" of melody: cognitive structures generated by the implication-realization model. *Contemporary Music Review*, 4(1), 45–63. https://doi.org/10.1080/07494468900640201

Narmour, E. (1990). *The analysis and cognition of basic melodic structures: the implication-realization model*. University of Chicago Press. https://doi.org/10.2307/897927

Narmour, E. (1992). *The analysis and cognition of melodic complexity: the implication-realization model*. University of Chicago Press. https://doi.org/10.2307/898334

Narmour, E. (1999). Hierarchical expectation and musical style. In D. Deutsch (Ed.), *The psychology of music* (2nd ed., pp. 441–472). Academic Press. https://doi.org/10.1016/b978-012213564-4/50013-5

National Human Genome Research Institute. (2020). *The human genome project*. https://doi.org/10.32388/842425

Nattiez, J.-J. (1985). The concepts of plot and seriation process in music analysis. *Music Analysis*, 4(1–2), 107–118. https://doi.org/10.2307/854238

Nattiez, J.-J. (1990). *Music and discourse: toward a semiology of music* (C. Abbate, Trans.). Princeton University Press. https://doi.org/10.2307/942137

Negrete-Yankelevich, S., & Morales-Zaragoza, N. (2014). The apprentice framework: planning, assessing creativity. In S. Colton, D. Ventura, N. Lavrač & M. Cook (Eds.), *Proceedings of the fifth international conference on computational creativity* (pp. 280–283). Jožef Stefan Institute. http: //kt.ijs.si/publ/iccc_2014_proceedings.pdf

Nielsen, J. A., Zielinski, B. A., Ferguson, M. A., Lainhart, J. E., & Anderson, J. S. (2013). An evaluation of the left-brain vs. right-brain hypothesis with resting state functional connectivity magnetic resonance imaging. *PLoS ONE, 8*(8), 1–11. https://doi.org/10.1371/journal.pone.0071275

Nielsen, S. G. (2004). Strategies and self-efficacy beliefs in instrumental and vocal individual practice: a study of students in higher music education. *Psychology of Music, 32*(4), 418–431.

Nierhaus, G. (2009). *Algorithmic composition: paradigms of automated music generation.* Springer.

Nikolsky, A. (2015). Evolution of tonal organization in music mirrors symbolic representation of perceptual reality. part 1: prehistoric. *Frontiers in Psychology, 6*, 1–36. https://doi.org/10.3389/fpsyg.2015.01405

Nikolsky, A. (2016). Evolution of tonal organization in music optimizes neural mechanisms in symbolic encoding of perceptual reality. part 2: ancient to seventeenth century. *Frontiers in Psychology, 7*, 1–32. https://doi.org/10.3389/fpsyg.2016.00211

Noad, M. J., Cato, D. H., Bryden, M. M., Jenner, M.-N., & Jenner, K. C. S. (2000). Cultural revolution in whale songs. *Nature, 408*(6812), 537. https://doi.org/10.1038/35046199

Nolte, D. D. (2014). *Introduction to modern dynamics: chaos, networks, space and time.* Oxford University Press. https://doi.org/10.1093/oso/9780198844624.001.0001

Norman-Haignere, S., Kanwisher, N. G., & McDermott, J. H. (2015). Distinct cortical pathways for music and speech revealed by hypothesis-free voxel decomposition. *Neuron, 88*(6), 1281–1296. https://doi.org/10.1016/j.neuron.2015.11.035

North, A. C., Hargreaves, D. J., & O'Neill, S. A. (2000). The importance of music to adolescents. *British Journal of Educational Psychology, 70*(2), 255–272. https://doi.org/10.1348/000709900158083

North, J. (1992). The quadrivium. In H. de Ridder-Symoens (Ed.), *A history of the university in Europe. vol. I: universities in the middle ages* (pp. 337–359). Cambridge University Press.

Notman, H., & Rendall, D. (2005). Contextual variation in chimpanzee pant hoots and its implications for referential communication. *Animal*

Behaviour, 70(1), 177–190. https://doi.org/10.1016/j.anbehav.2004.08.024

Nottebohm, G. (1979). *Two Beethoven sketchbooks: a description with musical extracts* (J. Katz, Trans.). Gollancz.

Nowacki, E. (2020). *Greek and Latin music theory: principles and challenges.* University of Rochester Press. https://doi.org/10.1017/9781787449169

O'Hara, W. (2020). Music theory on the radio: theme and temporality in Hans Keller's first functional analysis. *Music Analysis, 39*(1), 3–49. https://doi.org/10.1111/musa.12129

Orpen, K., & Huron, D. (1992). Measurement of similarity in music: a quantitative approach for non-parametric representations. *Computers in Music Research, 4*, 1–44.

Oudeyer, P.-Y., & Hurford, J. R. (2006). *Self-organization in the evolution of speech.* Oxford University Press. https://doi.org/10.1093/acprof:oso/9780199289158.001.0001

Pachet, F. (2003). The *continuator*: musical interaction with style. *Journal of New Music Research, 32*(3), 333–341.

Pachet, F., & Roy, P. (2011). Markov constraints: steerable generation of Markov sequences. *Constraints, 16*(2), 148–172. https://doi.org/10.1007/s10601-010-9101-4

Paninski, L. (2004). Maximum likelihood estimation of cascade point-process neural encoding models. *Network: Computation in Neural Systems, 15*(4), 243–262. https://doi.org/10.1088/0954-898X_15_4_002

Parri, S., Alatalo, R. V., Kotiaho, J. S., Mappes, J., & Rivero, A. (2002). Sexual selection in the wolf spider *hygrolycosa rubrofasciata*: female preference for drum duration and pulse rate. *Behavioral Ecology, 13*(5), 615–621. https://doi.org/10.1093/beheco/13.5.615

Parry, M. (1930). Studies in the epic technique of oral versemaking: i. homer and Homeric style. *Harvard Studies in Classical Philology, 41*, 73–147. https://doi.org/10.2307/310626

Parry, M. (1932). Studies in the epic technique of oral versemaking: ii. the Homeric language as the language of poetry. *Harvard Studies in Classical Philology, 43*, 1–50.

Pasquier, P. (2019). *Metacreation lab for creative AI.* Retrieved December 13, 2019, from http://metacreation.net/

Pastille, W. A. (1984). Heinrich Schenker, anti-organicist. *19th-Century Music,*
    8(1), 29–36. https://doi.org/10.1525/ncm.1984.8.1.02a00020

Patel, A. D. (2008). *Music, language, and the brain.* Oxford University Press.
    https://doi.org/10.1093/acprof:oso/9780195123753.001.0001

Patel, A. D. (2018). Music as a transformative technology of the mind: an
    update. In H. Honing (Ed.), *The origins of musicality* (pp. 113–126).
    MIT Press.

Payne, K. B. (2000). The progressively changing songs of Humpback whales:
    a window on the creative process in a wild animal. In N. L. Wallin,
    B. Merker & S. Brown (Eds.), *The origins of music* (pp. 135–150). MIT
    Press.

Payne, K. B., & Payne, R. S. (1985). Large-scale changes over 19 years in songs
    of Humpback whales in Bermuda. *Zeitschrift für Tierpsychologie, 68*(2),
    89–114. https://doi.org/10.1111/j.1439-0310.1985.tb00118.x

Payne, K. B., Tyack, P. L., & Payne, R. S. (1983). Progressive changes in the
    songs of Humpback whales (*megaptera novaeangliae*): a detailed ana-
    lysis of two seasons in Hawaii. In R. S. Payne (Ed.), *Communication*
    and behavior of whales (pp. 9–57). Westview Press.

Pearce, M., & Müllensiefen, D. (2017). Compression-based modelling of
    musical similarity perception. *Journal of New Music Research, 46*(2),
    135–155. https://doi.org/10.1080/09298215.2017.1305419

Pearce, M. T., & Wiggins, G. A. (2012). Auditory expectation: the information
    dynamics of music perception and cognition. *Topics in Cognitive*
    Science, 4(4), 625–652. https://doi.org/10.1111/j.1756-8765.2012.
    01214.x

Penrose, R. (1989). *The emperor's new mind: concerning computers, minds and*
    the laws of physics. Oxford University Press. https://doi.org/10.1093/
    oso/9780198519737.001.0001

Penrose, R. (1994). *Shadows of the mind: a search for the missing science of con-*
    sciousness. Oxford University Press.

Penrose, R. (1997). *The large, the small, and the human mind.* Cambridge Uni-
    versity Press.

Pepper, S. C. (1945). *The basis of criticism in the arts.* Harvard University Press.
    https://doi.org/10.4159/harvard.9780674424005

Pepperberg, I. M. (1998). Talking with Alex: logic and speech in parrots.
    Scientific American, 9(4), 60–65.

Pepperberg, I. M. (2017). Animal language studies: what happened? *Psychonomic Bulletin and Review*, *24*(1), 181–185. https://doi.org/10.3758/s13423-016-1101-y

Pereira, A. S., Kavanagh, E., Hobaiter, C., Slocombe, K. E., & Lameira, A. R. (2020). Chimpanzee lip-smacks confirm primate continuity for speech-rhythm evolution. *Biology Letters*, *16*(5), 1–6. https://doi.org/10.1098/rsbl.2020.0232

Pigliucci, M. (2008). Is evolvability evolvable? *Nature Reviews Genetics*, *9*, 75–82. https://doi.org/10.1038/nrg2278

Pillow, J. W., Shlens, J., Paninski, L., Sher, A., Litke, A. M., Chichilnisky, E. J., & Simoncelli, E. P. (2008). Spatio-temporal correlations and visual signalling in a complete neuronal population. *Nature*, *454*(7207), 995–999. https://doi.org/10.1038/nature07140

Pinker, S. (1997). *How the mind works*. Norton. https://doi.org/10.2307/j.ctv1jk0jrs.35

Pinker, S. (2007). *The language instinct: how the mind creates language*. Harper Perennial Modern Classics. https://doi.org/10.2307/416234

Pippin, R. B. (2005). *The persistence of subjectivity: on the Kantian aftermath*. Cambridge University Press. https://doi.org/10.1017/CBO9780511614637

Pirger, Z., Crossley, M., László, Z., Naskar, S., Kemenes, G., O'Shea, M., Benjamin, P. R., & Kemenes, I. (2014). Interneuronal mechanism for Tinbergen's hierarchical model of behavioral choice. *Current Biology*, *24*(17), 2018–2024. https://doi.org/10.1016/j.cub.2014.07.044

Piston, W. (1962). *Harmony* (3rd ed.). Norton. https://doi.org/10.2307/934287

Plotkin, H. C. (1995). *Darwin machines and the nature of knowledge: concerning adaptations, instinct and the evolution of intelligence*. Penguin.

Plotkin, H. C., & Odling-Smee, F. J. (1981). A multiple-level model of evolution and its implications for sociobiology. *Behavioral and Brain Sciences*, *4*(2), 225–235. https://doi.org/10.1017/S0140525X00008566

Pluckrose, H., Lindsay, J. A., & Boghossian, P. (2018). Academic grievance studies and the corruption of scholarship. Retrieved April 16, 2020, from https://areomagazine.com/2018/10/02/academic-grievance-studies-and-the-corruption-of-scholarship/

Plut, C., & Pasquier, P. (2020). Generative music in video games: state of the art, challenges, and prospects. *Entertainment Computing, 33*, 100337. https://doi.org/10.1016/j.entcom.2019.100337

Pocklington, R., & Best, M. L. (1997). Cultural evolution and units of selection in replicating text. *Journal of Theoretical Biology, 188*, 79–87. https://doi.org/10.1006/jtbi.1997.0460

Podlipniak, P. (2016). The evolutionary origin of pitch centre recognition. *Psychology of Music, 44*(3), 527–543. https://doi.org/10.1177/0305735615577249

Podlipniak, P. (2017a). The role of the Baldwin Effect in the evolution of human musicality. *Frontiers in Neuroscience, 11*(542), 1–12. https://doi.org/10.3389/fnins.2017.00542

Podlipniak, P. (2017b). Tonal qualia and the evolution of music. *Avant, 8*(1), 33–44. https://doi.org/10.26913/80102017.0101.0002

Podlipniak, P. (2020). Pitch syntax as an evolutionary prelingual innovation. *Musicae Scientiae, 26*(2), 280–302. https://doi.org/10.1177/1029864920941551

Pople, A. (2002). *Getting started with the tonalities music analysis software.* Retrieved November 25, 2021, from https://research.hud.ac.uk/media/universityofhuddersfield/content/image/research/mhm/tonalities/Getting_Started_with_Tonalities.pdf

Pople, A. (2004). Using complex set theory for tonal analysis: an introduction to the *tonalities* project. *Music Analysis, 23*(2–3), 153–194.

Popper, K. (1959). *The logic of scientific discovery.* Hutchinson. https://doi.org/10.4324/9780203994627

Potengowski, A. F., & Wagner, G. W. (2017). The edge of time: palaeolithic bone flutes of France and Germany (CD recording).

Powys, V., Taylor, H., & Probets, C. (2013). A little flute music: mimicry, memory, and narrativity. *Environmental Humanities, 3*(1), 43–70. https://doi.org/10.1215/22011919-3611230

Pressing, J. (1988). Improvisation: methods and models. In J. A. Sloboda (Ed.), *Generative processes in music: the psychology of performance, improvisation, and composition* (pp. 129–178). Clarendon Press. https://doi.org/10.1093/acprof:oso/9780198508465.003.0007

Preston, S. (2004). *Bird song as a basis for new techniques and improvisational practice with the baroque flute* [Doctoral dissertation, University of

Plymouth]. https://pearl.plymouth.ac.uk/bitstream/handle/10026.1/854/403476.pdf?sequence=4%5C&isAllowed=y

Prothero, D. R. (2007). *Evolution: what the fossils say and why it matters.* Columbia University Press. https://doi.org/10.7312/prot18064

Provine, R. R. (2001). *Laughter: a scientific investigation.* Penguin.

Puy, N. G.-C. (2017). On the ontological category of computer-generated music scores. *Journal of Creative Music Systems, 1*(2). https://doi.org/10.5920/jcms.2017.06

Quick, D., & Hudak, P. (2013). Grammar-based automated music composition in Haskell. In P. Hudak & C. Elliott (Eds.), *Proceedings of the first ACM SIGPLAN workshop on functional art, music, modeling, and design (FARM 2013)* (pp. 59–70). Association for Computing Machinery. https://doi.org/10.1145/2505341.2505345

Rafael, B., Oertl, S., Affenzeller, M., & Wagner, S. (2009). Music segmentation with genetic algorithms. In A. M. Tjoa & R. R. Wagner (Eds.), *Proceedings of the twentieth international workshop on database and expert systems applications (DEXA 2009)* (pp. 256–260). IEEE Computer Society/Conference Publishing Services. https://doi.org/10.1109/DEXA.2009.16

Rahn, J. (1980). *Basic atonal theory.* Longman. https://doi.org/10.2307/843362

Randel, D. M. (1992). The canons in the musicological toolbox. In K. Bergeron & P. V. Bohlman (Eds.), *Disciplining music: musicology and its canons* (pp. 10–22). Chicago University Press.

Ratner, L. G. (1970). *Ars combinatoria*: chance and choice in eighteenth-century music. In H. C. R. Landon & R. E. Chapman (Eds.), *Studies in eighteenth-century music: a tribute to Karl Geiringer on his seventieth birthday* (pp. 343–363). George Allen; Unwin.

Ratner, L. G. (1980). *Classic music: expression, form, and style.* Schirmer. https://doi.org/10.2307/843564

Ratner, L. G. (1991). Topical content in Mozart's keyboard sonatas. *Early Music, 19*(4), 615–619. https://doi.org/10.1093/earlyj/xix.4.615

Ravignani, A. (2018). Darwin, sexual selection, and the origins of music. *Trends in Ecology and Evolution, 33*(10), 716–719. https://doi.org/10.1016/j.tree.2018.07.006

Rawbone, T., & Jan, S. B. (2020). The butterfly schema in the classical instrumental style: a product of the tendency for congruence. *Music Analysis, 39*(1), 85–127. https://doi.org/10.1111/musa.12133

Reichl, L., Heide, D., Löwel, S., Crowley, J. C., Kaschube, M., & Wolf, F. (2012a). Coordinated optimization of visual cortical maps (I): symmetry-based analysis. *PLoS Computational Biology, 8*(11), 1–24. https://doi.org/10.1371/journal.pcbi.1002466

Reichl, L., Heide, D., Löwel, S., Crowley, J. C., Kaschube, M., & Wolf, F. (2012b). Coordinated optimization of visual cortical maps (II): numerical studies. *PLoS Computational Biology, 8*(11), 1–26. https://doi.org/10.1371/journal.pcbi.1002756

Ren, Y., Guo, S., Labeau, M., Cohen, S. B., & Kirby, S. (2020). Compositional languages emerge in a neural iterated learning model. *Proceedings of the eighth international conference on learning representations (ICLR 2020)*, 1–18.

Ren, Z. (2020). Style composition with an evolutionary algorithm. In B. L. T. Sturm (Ed.), *Proceedings of the first joint conference on AI music creativity*. Royal Institute of Technology (KTH), Stockholm. https://doi.org/10.5281/zenodo.4285346

Reti, R. (1951). *The thematic process in music*. Macmillan. https://doi.org/10.2307/891225

Reti, R. (1967). *Thematic patterns in sonatas of Beethoven*. Faber. https://doi.org/10.2307/893992

Reybrouck, M. (1997). Gestalt concepts and music: limitations and possibilities. In M. Leman (Ed.), *Music, Gestalt, and computing: studies in cognitive and systematic musicology* (pp. 57–69). Springer. https://doi.org/10.1007/bfb0034107

Reznikoff, I. (2002). Prehistoric paintings, sound and rocks. In E. Hickmann, A. D. Kilmer & R. Eichmann (Eds.), *The achaeology of sound: origin and organisation* (pp. 39–56). Verlag Marie Leidorf.

Rice, T. J. (1997). *Joyce, chaos, and complexity*. University of Illinois Press. https://doi.org/10.2307/3201446

Richerson, P. J., & Boyd, R. (2005). *Not by genes alone: how culture transformed human evolution*. University of Chicago Press. https://doi.org/10.7208/chicago/9780226712130.001.0001

Richman, B. (2000). How music fixed "nonsense" into significant formulas: on rhythm, repetition, and meaning. In N. L. Wallin, B. Merker & S. Brown (Eds.), *The origins of music* (pp. 301–314). MIT Press.

Ridley, M. (2004). *Evolution* (3rd ed.). Blackwell. https://doi.org/10.1007/978-3-0348-6133-5

Ridley, M. (1994). *The red queen: sex and the evolution of human nature*. Penguin.

Riede, T., Eliason, C. M., Miller, E. H., Goller, F., & Clarke, J. A. (2016). Coos, booms, and hoots: the evolution of closed-mouth vocal behavior in birds. *Evolution, 70*(8), 1734–1746. https://doi.org/10.1111/evo.12988

Rieger, E. (1992). "i recycle sounds": do women compose differently? *Journal of the International League of Women Composers,* 22–25.

Riepel, J. (1755). *Anfangsgründe zur musikalischen Setzkunst* (Vol. 2). Lotter.

Ringer, A. L. (1961). Clementi and the *eroica. The Musical Quarterly, 47*(4), 454–468.

Ríos-Chelén, A. A., Salaberria, C., Barbosa, I., Macías Garcia, C., & Gil, D. (2012). The learning advantage: bird species that learn their song show a tighter adjustment of song to noisy environments than those that do not learn. *Journal of Evolutionary Biology, 25*(11), 2171–2180. https://doi.org/10.1111/j.1420-9101.2012.02597.x

RISM. (2021). *Incipit search.* Retrieved August 3, 2021, from https://opac.rism.info/metaopac/start.do?View=rism%5C&SearchType=2%5C&Language=en

Ritchie, G. (2007). Some empirical criteria for attributing creativity to a computer program. *Minds and Machines, 17,* 67–99. https://doi.org/10.1007/s11023-007-9066-2

Robertson, L. C. (2005). Attention and binding. In L. Itti, G. Rees & J. K. Tsotsos (Eds.), *Neurobiology of attention* (pp. 135–139). Academic Press. https://doi.org/10.1016/B978-012375731-9/50028-8

Robertson, S. (2020). *BC, Before Computers: on information technology from writing to the age of digital data*. Open Book Publishers. https://doi.org/10.11647/obp.0225

Robinson, M. A. (2001). *New Testament textual criticism: the case for Byzantine priority.* http://www.reltech.org/TC/v06/Robinson2001.html

Rodgers, T. (2010). *Pink noises: women on electronic music and sound.* Duke University Press. https://doi.org/10.1515/9780822394150

Rogalsky, C., Rong, F., Saberi, K., & Hickok, G. (2011). Functional anatomy of language and music perception: temporal and structural factors investigated using functional magnetic resonance imaging. *Journal of Neuroscience, 31*(10), 3843–3852. https://doi.org/10.1523/JNEUROSCI.4515-10.2011

Rosa, J. P. S., Guerra, D. J. D., Horta, N. C. G., Martins, R. M. F., & Lourenço, N. C. C. (2020). Overview of artificial neural networks. In *Using artificial neural networks for analog integrated circuit design automation* (pp. 21–44). Springer Nature. https://doi.org/10.1007/978-3-030-35743-6_3

Rosati, D. P., Woolhouse, M. H., Bolker, B. M., & Earn, D. J. D. (2021). Modelling song popularity as a contagious process. *Proceedings of the Royal Society A, 477*(2253), 1–16. https://doi.org/10.1098/rspa.2021.0457

Rose, S., Tuppen, S., & Drosopoulou, L. (2015). Writing a big data history of music. *Early Music, 43*(4), 649–660. https://doi.org/10.1093/em/cav071

Rosen, C. (1988). *Sonata forms* (2nd ed.). Norton. https://doi.org/10.2307/940317

Rosen, C. (1995). *The romantic generation.* Harvard University Press. https://doi.org/10.2307/898378

Rosen, C. (1997). *The classical style: Haydn, Mozart, Beethoven* (3rd ed.). Norton. https://doi.org/10.2307/1851210

Rosen, C. (2001). *Critical entertainments: music old and new.* Harvard University Press.

Rouget, G., & Buckner, M. (2011). Musical efficacy: musicking to survive; the case of the pygmies. *Yearbook for Traditional Music, 43*, 89–121. https://doi.org/10.5921/yeartradmusi.43.0089

Rubner, Y., Tomasi, C., & Guibas, L. J. (2000). The Earth Mover's Distance as a metric for image retrieval. *International Journal of Computer Vision, 40*(2), 99–121.

Rumph, S. (2004). *Beethoven after Napoleon: political romanticism in the late works.* University of California Press. https://doi.org/10.1525/9780520930124

Runco, M. A. (2014). *Creativity: theories and themes: research, development, and practice* (2nd ed.). Academic Press.

Russ, M. (2004). "fishing in the right place": analytical examples from the *tonalities* project. *Music Analysis, 23*(2–3), 195–244.

Sachs, C. (1962). *The wellsprings of music* (J. Kunst, Ed.). Martinus Nijhoff. https://doi.org/10.1007/978-94-015-1059-2

Sacks, O. (2011). *Musicophilia: tales of music and the brain*. Picador.

Said, E. W. (2006). *On late style: music and literature against the grain*. Bloomsbury.

Saito, H. (2007). Identification of novel *n*-4 series polyunsaturated fatty acids in a deep-sea clam, *calyptogena phaseoliformis*. *Journal of Chromatography A, 1163*(1–2), 247–259. https://doi.org/10.1016/j.chroma.2007.06.016

Salzer, F., & Schachter, C. (1989). *Counterpoint in composition: the study of voice leading*. Columbia University Press.

Sánchez-Quintana, C., Moreno-Arcas, F., Albarracín-Molina, D., Fernández Rodríguez, J. D., & Vico, F. J. (2013). Melomics: a case-study of AI in Spain. *AI Magazine, 34*(3), 99–103. https://doi.org/10.1609/aimag.v34i3.2464

Savage, P. E. (2017). *Measuring the cultural evolution of music: with case studies of British-American and Japanese folk, art, and popular music* [PhD]. Tokyo University of the Arts. https://www.researchgate.net/publication/303333952_Measuring_the_cultural_evolution_of_music_With_case_studies_of_British-American_and_Japanese_folk_art_and_popular_music

Savage, P. E. (2018). Alan Lomax's Cantometrics project: a comprehensive review. *Music and Science, 1*, 1–19. https://doi.org/10.1177/2059204318786084

Savage, P. E. (2019). Cultural evolution of music. *Palgrave Communications, 5*(16), 1–12. https://doi.org/10.1057/s41599-019-0221-1

Savage, P. E., Brown, S., Sakai, E., & Currie, T. E. (2015). Statistical universals reveal the structures and functions of human music. *Proceedings of the National Academy of Sciences, 112*(29), 8987–8992. https://doi.org/10.1073/pnas.1414495112

Savage, P. E., Loui, P., Tarr, B., Schachner, A., Glowacki, L., Mithen, S., & Fitch, W. T. (2021). Music as a coevolved system for social bonding. *Behavioral and Brain Sciences, 44*(e59), 1–22. https://doi.org/10.1017/S0140525X20000333

Savage, P. E., Passmore, S., Chiba, G., Currie, T. E., Suzuki, H., & Atkinson, Q. D. A. (2022). Sequence alignment of folk song melodies reveals cross-cultural regularities of musical evolution. *Current Biology*, *32*(6), 1395–1402. https://doi.org/10.1016/j.cub.2022.01.039

Sawyer, G. J., Deak, V., Sarmiento, E., & Milner, R. (2007). *The last human: a guide to twenty-two species of extinct human ancestors*. Yale University Press.

Scarre, C., & Lawson, G. (Eds.). (2006). *Archaeoacoustics*. McDonald Institute for Archaeological Research.

Schaefer, N. K., Shapiro, B., & Green, R. E. (2021). An ancestral recombination graph of human, Neanderthal, and Denisovan genomes. *Science Advances*, *7*(29), 1–16. https://doi.org/10.1126/sciadv.abc0776

Schenker, H. (1979). *Free composition (Der freie Satz)* (E. Oster, Ed. & Trans.). Longman.

Schenker, H. (1980). *Harmony* (O. Jonas, Ed.; E. Mann Borgese, Trans.). University of Chicago Press. https://doi.org/10.2307/25293112

Schenker, H. (2004). *Der Tonwille: pamphlets in witness of the immutable laws of music* (I. D. Bent & W. Drabkin, Eds. & Trans.; Vol. 1). Oxford University Press.

Schenker, H. (2005). *Der Tonwille: pamphlets in witness of the immutable laws of music* (I. D. Bent & W. Drabkin, Eds. & Trans.; Vol. 2). Oxford University Press.

Schlaile, M. P., Knausberg, T., Mueller, M., & Zeman, J. (2018). Viral ice buckets: a memetic perspective on the ALS ice bucket challenge's diffusion. *Cognitive Systems Research*, *52*, 947–969. https://doi.org/10.1016/j.cogsys.2018.09.012

Schleidt, W. (1962). Die historische Entwicklung der Begriffe "Angeborenes auslösendes Schema" und "Angeborener Auslösemechanismus" in der Ethologie. *Zeitschrift für Tierpsychologie*, *19*(6), 697–722. https://doi.org/10.1111/j.1439-0310.1962.tb00800.x

Schmidhuber, J. (2015). Deep learning in neural networks: an overview. *Neural Networks*, *61*, 85–117. https://doi.org/10.1016/j.neunet.2014.09.003

Schoenberg, A. (1983). *Structural functions of harmony* (L. Stein, Ed.). Faber. https://doi.org/10.2307/893016

Schoenberg, A. (1995). *The musical idea and the logic, technique and art of its presentation* (P. Carpenter & S. Neff, Eds.). Columbia University Press.

Schoenberg, A. (2010). *Style and idea: selected writings of Arnold Schoenberg* (L. Stein, Ed.; L. Black, Trans.; Sixtieth anniversary). University of California Press. https://doi.org/10.2307/832549

Schubert, E., & Pearce, M. (2016). A new look at musical expectancy: the veridical versus the general in the mental organization of music. In R. Kronland-Martinet, M. Aramaki & S. Ystad (Eds.), *Music, mind, and embodiment: 11th international symposium, CMMR 2015, Plymouth, UK, June 16–19, 2015, revised selected papers* (pp. 358–370). Springer. https://doi.org/10.1007/978-3-319-46282-0

Schulkin, J. (2013). *Reflections on the musical mind: an evolutionary perspective.* Princeton University Press. https://doi.org/10.23943/princeton/9780691157443.001.0001

Schultz, R. (2008). Melodic contour and nonretrogradable structure in the birdsong of Olivier Messiaen. *Music Theory Spectrum, 30*(1), 89–137. https://doi.org/10.1525/mts.2008.30.1.89

Scopus. (2020). *Scopus.* https://www.scopus.com

Scott-Phillips, T. C., & Kirby, S. (2010). Language evolution in the laboratory. *Trends in Cognitive Sciences, 14,* 411–417. https://doi.org/10.1016/j.tics.2010.06.006

Scruton, R. (1997). *The aesthetics of music.* Oxford University Press. https://doi.org/10.1093/019816727x.001.0001

Selfridge-Field, E. (1997). *Beyond MIDI: the handbook of musical codes.* MIT Press. https://doi.org/10.2307/900186

Semon, R. W. (1909). *Die mnemischen Empfindungen in ihren Beziehungen zu den Originalempfindungen: erste Fortsetzung der Mneme.* Wilhelm Engelmann.

Semon, R. W. (1911). *Die Mneme als erhaltendes Prinzip im Wechsel des organischen Geschehens* (3rd ed.). Wilhelm Engelmann. https://doi.org/10.5962/bhl.title.10234

Semon, R. W. (1921). *The Mneme* (L. Simon, Trans.). George Allen; Unwin. https://doi.org/10.1097/00005053-192509000-00076

Semon, R. W., Duffy, B., & Lee, V. (1923). *Mnemic psychology.* George Allen; Unwin.

Sereno, M. I. (1991). Four analogies between biological and cultural/linguistic evolution. *Journal of Theoretical Biology*, *151*, 467–507. https://doi.org/10.1016/s0022-5193(05)80366-2

Serrat, O. (2010). Taxonomies for development. *Knowledge Solutions*, *91*, 1–7. https://doi.org/10.1007/978-981-10-0983-9_124

Sewell, A. (2012). *London Symphony Orchestra to perform music made by computer Iamus*. Retrieved January 20, 2020, from http://www.digitaljournal.com/article/327916

Shamshad, A., Bawadi, M. A., Wanhussin, W., Majid, T. A., & Ahmad, M. S. S. (2005). First and second order Markov chain models for synthetic generation of wind speed time series. *Energy*, *30*(5), 693–708. https://doi.org/10.1016/j.energy.2004.05.026

Shannon, C. E. (1948). A mathematical theory of communication. *Bell System Technical Journal*, *27*, 379–423, 623–656. https://doi.org/10.2307/410457

Shapiro, L. A. (2011). *Embodied cognition*. Routledge. https://doi.org/10.4324/9781315180380

Sharma, S., Tim, U. S., Wong, J., Gadia, S., & Sharma, S. (2014). A brief review on leading big data models. *Data Science Journal*, *13*, 138–157. https://doi.org/10.2481/dsj.14-041

Shazam. (2019). *Shazam*. Retrieved December 13, 2019, from https://www.shazam.com/

Shennan, S. (2002). *Genes, memes, and human history: darwinian archaeology and cultural evolution*. Thames; Hudson.

Shifman, L. (2013). Memes in a digital world: reconciling with a conceptual troublemaker. *Journal of Computer-Mediated Communication*, *18*(3), 362–377. https://doi.org/10.1111/jcc4.12013

Shrager, Y., Kirwan, C. B., & Squire, L. R. (2008). Neural basis of the cognitive map: path integration does not require hippocampus or entorhinal cortex. *Proceedings of the National Academy of Sciences*, *105*(33), 12034–12038. https://doi.org/10.1073/pnas.0805414105

Simon, H. A. (1975). How big is a chunk? *Science*, *183*(4124), 482–488. https://doi.org/10.1126/science.183.4124.482

Simpson, J. A., & Weiner, E. S. C. (2018). *Evolution, n.* http://www.oed.com/view/Entry/65447?redirectedFrom=evolution

Sisman, E. (1982). Small and expanded forms: koch's model and Haydn's music. *Musical Quarterly, 68,* 444–475. https://doi.org/10.1093/mq/lxviii.4.444

Skinner, B. F. (1953). *Science and human behaviour.* Macmillan.

Skinner, B. F. (2014). *Verbal behavior.* B.F. Skinner Foundation. https://doi.org/10.1037/11256-000

Slater, P. J. B. (2000). Birdsong repertoires: their origins and use. In N. L. Wallin, B. Merker & S. Brown (Eds.), *The origins of music* (pp. 49–63). MIT Press.

Slatkin, M. (2008). Linkage disequilibrium: understanding the genetic past and mapping the medical future. *Nature Reviews Genetics, 9*(6), 477–485. https://doi.org/10.1038/nrg2361.Linkage

Sluming, V., Brooks, J., Howard, M., Downes, J. J., & Roberts, N. (2007). Broca's area supports enhanced visuospatial cognition in orchestral musicians. *Journal of Neuroscience, 27*(14), 3799–3806. https://doi.org/10.1523/jneurosci.0147-07.2007

Smithsonian Institution. (2019). *Human evolution timeline.* Retrieved November 11, 2019, from http://humanorigins.si.edu/evidence/human-evolution-timeline-interactive

Smoliar, S. W. (1994). *The language of music* by Deryck Cooke: review by Stephen W. Smoliar. *Computer Music Journal, 18*(2), 101–105.

Snarrenberg, R. (1997). *Schenker's interpretive practice.* Cambridge University Press. https://doi.org/10.1017/cbo9780511583056

Sneath, P. H. A., & Sokal, R. R. (1973). *Numerical taxonomy* (2nd ed.). W.H. Freeman. https://doi.org/10.2307/2406364

Sniegowski, P. D., & Murphy, H. A. (2006). Evolvability. *Current Biology, 16*(19), 831–834. https://doi.org/10.1016/j.cub.2006.08.080

Snow, C. P. (1964). *The two cultures.* Cambridge University Press. https://doi.org/10.2307/1578601

Snyder, B. (2000). *Music and memory: an introduction.* MIT Press.

Snyder, B. (2009). Memory for music. In S. Hallam, I. Cross & M. Thaut (Eds.), *The Oxford handbook of music psychology* (pp. 107–117). Oxford University Press. https://doi.org/10.1093/oxfordhb/9780199298457.013.0010

Soha, J. (2017). The auditory template hypothesis: a review and comparative perspective. *Animal Behaviour, 124*, 247–254. https://doi.org/10.1016/j.anbehav.2016.09.016

Sokal, A. D. (1996). *Transgressing the boundaries: towards a transformative hermeneutics of quantum gravity.* https://doi.org/10.2307/466856

Solie, R. A. (1980). The living work: organicism and musical analysis. *19th-Century Music, 4*(2), 147–156. https://doi.org/10.2307/746712

Solomon, M. (1995). *Mozart: a life.* Hutchinson. https://doi.org/10.2307/899717

Solomon, M. (1998). *Beethoven* (2nd ed.). Schirmer. https://doi.org/10.2307/898050

Solomon, M. (2003). *Late Beethoven: music, thought, imagination.* University of California Press.

Somero, G. N. (1992). Biochemical ecology of deep-sea animals. *Experientia, 48*(6), 537–543. https://doi.org/10.1007/BF01920236

Sonic Visualiser. (2021). *Sonic visualiser.* Retrieved November 25, 2021, from https://www.sonicvisualiser.org/

Sony CSL. (2012). *György Kurtág and the continuator.* Retrieved August 7, 2021, from https://www.youtube.com/watch?v=AXBBhpATlP0%5C&list=PLvoqwxjRRNfmLD2kNGnp9LlSeb5CzI3Kh

Spicer, M. (2004). (ac)cumulative form in pop-rock music. *Twentieth-Century Music, 1*(1), 29–64. https://doi.org/10.1017/S1478572204000052

Spiliopoulou, M. (2011). Evolution in social networks: a survey. In C. C. Aggarwal (Ed.), *Social network data analytics* (pp. 149–175). Springer. https://doi.org/10.1007/978-1-4419-8462-3_6

Spitzer, M. (2004). *Metaphor and musical thought.* University of Chicago Press. https://doi.org/10.7208/chicago/9780226279435.001.0001

Spitzer, M. (2006). *Music as philosophy: adorno and Beethoven's late style.* Indiana University Press. https://doi.org/10.2307/j.ctv20pxxv8

Spitzer, M. (2021). *The musical human: a history of life on earth.* Bloomsbury.

Steblin, R. (1996). *A history of key characteristics in the eighteenth and early nineteenth centuries.* University of Rochester Press. https://doi.org/10.2307/941305

Steiner, F. G. (2016). *Heinrich Christoph Kochs Versuch einer Anleitung zur Composition im Spiegel der zeitgenössischen Kompositionslehren.* Schott.

Stensola, H., Stensola, T., Solstad, T., Frøland, K., Moser, M.-B., & Moser, E. I. (2012). The entorhinal grid map is discretized. *Nature, 492*, 72–78. https://doi.org/10.1038/nature11649

Stoker, B. (2003). *Dracula*. Penguin. https://doi.org/10.1093/owc/9780199564095.001.0001

Storer, R. W., Rand, A. L., & Gill, F. (2020). *Bird*. Retrieved August 25, 2020, from https://www.britannica.com/animal/bird-animal

Stowell, D., Gill, L., & Clayton, D. (2016). Detailed temporal structure of communication networks in groups of songbirds. *Journal of the Royal Society Interface, 13*(119), 1–13. https://doi.org/10.1098/rsif.2016.0296

Straus, J. N. (2005). *Introduction to post-tonal theory* (3rd ed.). Prentice-Hall.

Straus, J. N. (2008). Disability and late style in music. *The Journal of Musicology, 25*(1), 3–45. https://doi.org/10.1525/jm.2008.25.1.3

Straus, J. N. (2016). *Introduction to post-tonal theory* (4th ed.). Norton.

Stravinsky, I. F. (2006). *The Firebird*. Dover Publications.

Street, A. (1989). Superior myths, dogmatic allegories: the resistance to musical unity. *Music Analysis, 8*(1–2), 77–123. https://doi.org/10.2307/854327

Stringer, C. (2003). Out of Ethiopia. *Nature, 423*, 692–694. https://doi.org/10.1038/423692a

Strunk, W. O., Treitler, L., & Solie, R. A. (Eds.). (1998). *Source readings in music history: the nineteenth century* (Vol. 6). Norton.

Sturm, B. L. T. (2017a). *folk-rnn (v2) tune #2857*. Retrieved August 6, 2021, from https://highnoongmt.wordpress.com/2017/12/02/folk-rnn-v2-tune-2857/

Sturm, B. L. T. (2017b). *folk-rnn session books, volumes 1–10, and v3 volumes 1–4*. Retrieved August 6, 2021, from https://highnoongmt.wordpress.com/2017/08/10/folk-rnn-session-books-volumes-1-10-and-v3-volumes-1-4/

Sturm, B. L. T., & Ben-Tal, O. (2017). Taking the models back to music practice: evaluating generative transcription models built using deep learning. *Journal of Creative Music Systems, 2*(1). https://doi.org/10.5920/jcms.2017.09

Sturm, B. L. T., Santos, J. F., Ben-Tal, O., & Korshunova, I. (2016). Music transcription modelling and composition using deep learning. In V.

Velardo (Ed.), *Proceedings of the first conference on computer simulation of musical creativity, University of Huddersfield, 17–19 June 2016* (pp. 1–16). University of Huddersfield. https://csmc2016.wordpress.com/proceedings/

Sturm, B. L. T., Santos, J. F., & Korshunova, I. (2015). Folk music style modelling by recurrent neural networks with long short term memory units. In M. Müller & F. Wiering (Eds.), *Proceedings of the sixteenth international society for music information retrieval conference.* International Society for Music Information Retrieval. https://dblp.org/db/conf/ismir/ismir2015.html

Suthers, R. A. (2004). How birds sing and why it matters. In P. Marler & H. Slabbekoorn (Eds.), *Nature's music: the science of birdsong* (pp. 272–295). Elsevier Academic Press. https://doi.org/10.1016/b978-012473070-0/50012-8

Sznajder, B., Sabelis, M. W., & Egas, M. (2012). How adaptive learning affects evolution: reviewing theory on the Baldwin Effect. *Evolutionary Biology, 39*, 301–310. https://doi.org/10.1007/s11692-011-9155-2

Tagg, P. (1999). *Introductory notes to the semiotics of music.* Retrieved November 25, 2021, from http://www.tagg.org/xpdfs/semiotug.pdf

Tarr, B., Launay, J., & Dunbar, R. I. M. (2014). Music and social bonding: "self-other" merging and neurohormonal mechanisms. *Frontiers in Psychology, 5*(1096), 1–10. https://doi.org/10.3389/fpsyg.2014.01096

Taruskin, R. (1995). *Text and act: essays on music and performance.* Oxford University Press. https://doi.org/10.2307/900110

Taruskin, R. (2005). *The Oxford history of western music.* Oxford: Oxford University Press.

Tatar, K., & Pasquier, P. (2019). Musical agents: a typology and state of the art towards musical metacreation. *Journal of New Music Research, 48*(1), 56–105. https://doi.org/10.1080/09298215.2018.1511736

Taylor, H. (2017). *Is birdsong music? outback encounters with an Australian songbird.* Indiana University Press. https://doi.org/10.2307/j.ctt2005zrr

Taylor, M. (2007). *The philosophy of Herbert Spencer.* Bloomsbury.

Tchaikovsky, P. I. (1900). *The sleeping beauty (suite), op. 66a* (A. Siloti, Ed.). D. Rahter.

Teilhard de Chardin, P. (2008). *The phenomenon of man*. Harper Perennial. https://doi.org/10.2307/2422954

Temperley, D. (2001). *The cognition of basic musical structures*. MIT Press.

Tennyson, A. (2007). *Alfred Lord Tennyson: selected poems* (C. Ricks, Ed.). Penguin.

Terleph, T. A., Malaivijitnond, S., & Reichard, U. H. (2018). An analysis of white-handed gibbon male song reveals speech-like phrases. *American Journal of Physical Anthropology, 166*(3), 649–660. https://doi.org/10.1002/ajpa.23451

Tesar, J. C. (2000). Mozart, dice, and glass selection. *Proceedings of the international symposium on optical science and technology*, 1–6. https://doi.org/10.1117/12.402410

Thinh, V. N., Hallam, C., Roos, C., & Hammerschmidt, K. (2011). Concordance between vocal and genetic diversity in crested gibbons. *BMC Evolutionary Biology, 11*(36), 1–9. https://doi.org/10.1186/1471-2148-11-36

Thompson, W. F., Marin, M. M., & Stewart, L. (2012). Reduced sensitivity to emotional prosody in congenital amusia rekindles the musical proto-language hypothesis. *Proceedings of the National Academy of Sciences, 109*(46), 19027–19032. https://doi.org/10.1073/pnas.1210344109

Thorpe, W. H. (1958a). Further studies on the process of song learning in the Chaffinch (*fringilla coelebs gengleri*). *Nature, 152*, 554–557.

Thorpe, W. H. (1958b). The learning of song patterns by birds, with especial reference to the song of the Chaffinch, *fringilla coelebs*. *Ibis, 100*(4), 535–570. https://doi.org/10.1111/j.1474-919X.1958.tb07960.x

Thrasher, A. R., Lam, J. S. C., Stock, J. P. J., Mackerras, C., Rebollo-Sborgi, F., Kouwenhoven, F., Schimmelpenninck, A., Jones, S., Mei, H., Ben, W., Rees, H., Trebinjac, S., & Lee, J. C. (2001). *China, People's Republic of* (D. L. Root, Ed.). https://doi.org/10.1093/gmo/9781561592630.001.0001/omo-9781561592630-e-0000043141

Till, R. (2010). *Pop cult: religion and popular music*. Continuum.

Till, R. (2014). Sound archaeology: terminology, palaeolithic cave art and the soundscape. *World Archaeology, 46*(3), 292–304. https://doi.org/10.1080/00438243.2014.909106

Till, R. (2017). An archaeoacoustic study of the Hal Saflieni Hypogeum on Malta. *Antiquity, 91*(355), 74–89. https://doi.org/10.15184/aqy.2016.258

Till, R. (2019). Sound archaeology: a study of the acoustics of three world heritage sites, Spanish prehistoric painted caves, Stonehenge, and Paphos Theatre. *Acoustics, 1*(3), 661–692. https://doi.org/10.3390/acoustics1030039

Till, R., Scarre, C., Fazenda, B., Pettitt, P., Kang, J., Watson, A., Wyatt, S., Rojo Guerra, M., Arias Mendoza, P., Jiménes Pasalodos, R., Garcia Benito, C., & Tejedor, C. (2014a). *Songs of the caves: interactive maps*. Retrieved September 17, 2019, from https://songsofthecaves.wordpress.com/sound-maps-of-the-caves/

Till, R., Scarre, C., Fazenda, B., Pettitt, P., Kang, J., Watson, A., Wyatt, S., Rojo Guerra, M., Arias Mendoza, P., Jiménes Pasalodos, R., Garcia Benito, C., & Tejedor, C. (2014b). *Songs of the caves: soundgate app*. Retrieved September 17, 2019, from https://songsofthecaves.wordpress.com/multimedia/soundgate-app/

Tinbergen, N. (1951). *The study of instinct*. Oxford University Press. https://doi.org/10.2307/4510368

Tinbergen, N. (1963). On aims and methods of ethology. *Zeitschrift für Tierpsychologie, 20*, 410–433. https://doi.org/10.1111/j.1439-0310.1963.tb01161.x

Tischbirek, C. H., Noda, T., Tohmi, M., Birkner, A., Nelken, I., & Konnerth, A. (2019). In-vivo functional mapping of a cortical column at single-neuron resolution. *Cell Reports, 27*(5), 1319–1326. https://doi.org/10.1016/j.celrep.2019.04.007

Todd, P. (2000). Simulating the evolution of musical behavior. In N. L. Wallin, B. Merker & S. Brown (Eds.), *The origins of music* (pp. 361–388). MIT Press.

Todd, P. M., & Loy, D. G. (1991). *Music and connectionism*. MIT Press. https://doi.org/10.2307/899412

Tolbert, E. (2001). Music and meaning: an evolutionary story. *Psychology of Music, 29*(1), 84–94. https://doi.org/10.1177/0305735601291006

Tooby, J., & Cosmides, L. (2005). Conceptual foundations of evolutionary psychology. In D. M. Buss (Ed.), *The handbook of evolutionary psychology* (pp. 1–63). Wiley. https://doi.org/10.1002/9780470939376.ch1

Tovey, D. F. (2015). *Symphonies and other orchestral works: selections from Essays in musical analysis*. Dover.

Truss, L. (2003). *Eats, shoots and leaves: the zero tolerance approach to punctuation*. Profile.

Turing, A. (1950). Computing machinery and intelligence. *Mind, 59*(236), 433–460. https://doi.org/10.1007/978-1-4020-6710-5_3

Tymoczko, D. (2006). The geometry of musical chords. *Science, 313*(5783), 72–74. https://doi.org/10.1126/science.1126287

Tymoczko, D. (2011). *A geometry of music: harmony and counterpoint in the extended common practice*. Oxford University Press.

Typke, R. (2007). *Music retrieval based on melodic similarity* [Doctoral dissertation, University of Utrecht].

Typke, R., Giannopoulos, P., Veltkamp, R. C., Wiering, F., & van Oostrum, R. (2003). Using transportation distances for measuring melodic similarity. In H. H. Hoos & D. Bainbridge (Eds.), *Proceedings of the fourth international conference on music information retrieval (ISMIR 2003)* (pp. 107–114). Johns Hopkins University Press.

Typke, R., Wiering, F., & Veltkamp, R. C. (2007). Transportation distances and human perception of melodic similarity. *Musicae Scientiae, 11*(Discussion Forum 4A: Similarity Perception in Listening to Music), 153–181. https://doi.org/10.1177/102986490701100107

Uther, M., Cleveland, M., & Jones, R. (2018). Email overload? brain and behavioral responses to common messaging alerts are heightened for email alerts and are associated with job involvement. *Frontiers in Psychology, 9*(1206), 1–13. https://doi.org/10.3389/fpsyg.2018.01206

Valiant, L. G. (2009). Evolvability. *Journal of the ACM, 56*(1), 1–21. https://doi.org/10.1145/1462153.1462156

Vanchurin, V. (2020). The world as a neural network. *Entropy, 22*(11), 1–20. https://doi.org/10.3390/e22111210

Various. (2012). Special issue: mathematical and computational approaches to music: three methodological reflections. *Journal of Mathematics and Music, 6*(2). https://doi.org/10.1080/17459737.2012.712354

Various. (2015). *European music archaology project*. http://www.emaproject.eu/

Various. (2021). *The session*. Retrieved August 6, 2021, from https://thesession.org/

Vazza, F., & Feletti, A. (2020). The quantitative comparison between the neuronal network and the cosmic web. *Frontiers in Physics, 8,* 1–8. https://doi.org/10.3389/fphy.2020.525731

Velardo, V. (2014). The sound/music dilemma: why is it that all music is sound but only some sounds are music? *Proceedings of the sound ambiguity conference.* http://ambiguity.amuz.wroc.pl

Velardo, V. (2016). Recursive ontology: a systemic theory of reality. *Axiomathes, 26*(1), 89–114. https://doi.org/10.1007/s10516-015-9272-0

Velardo, V. (2019). *Making kantor: human-machine collaboration to build artistic VR.* Retrieved August 12, 2021, from https://medium.com/the-sound-of-ai/making-kantor-human-machine-collaboration-to-build-artistic-vr-387ceabe59db

Velardo, V., & Vallati, M. (2016). *A general framework for describing creative agents.* arXiv: 1604.04096.

Velardo, V., Vallati, M., & Jan, S. B. (2016). Symbolic melodic similarity: state of the art and future challenges. *Computer Music Journal, 40*(2), 70–83. https://doi.org/10.1162/COMJ_a_00359

Victorri, B. (2007). Analogy between language and biology: a functional approach. *Cognitive Processing, 8*(1), 11–19. https://doi.org/10.1007/s10339-006-0156-5

Voltaire. (1918). *Candide, ou l'optimisme.* Boni; Liveright. https://doi.org/10.2307/321984

Wade, R. W. (1977). Beethoven's Eroica sketchbook. *Fons Artis Musicae, 24*(4), 254–289.

Wallin, N. L. (1991). *Biomusicology: neurophysiological, neuropsychological and evolutionary perspectives on the origins and purposes of music.* Pendragon Press. https://doi.org/10.2307/898296

Wallin, N. L., Merker, B., & Brown, S. (2000). *The origins of music* (N. L. Wallin, B. Merker & S. Brown, Eds.). MIT Press.

Walser, R. (1993). *Running with the devil: power, gender and madness in heavy metal music.* Wesleyan University Press of New England. https://doi.org/10.2307/3052258

Walsh, J. (1717). *The bird fancyer's delight.* John Walsh.

Walshaw, C. (2019). *ABC notation.* Retrieved December 20, 2019, from http://abcnotation.com/

Wangerman, E. (1973). *The Austrian achievement, 1700–1800*. Harcourt Brace Jovanovich.

Waugh, E. (1962). *Brideshead revisited: the sacred and profane memories of Captain Charles Ryder*. Penguin.

Wei, Y., Schatten, H., & Sun, Q.-Y. (2014). Environmental epigenetic inheritance through gametes and implications for human reproduction. *Human Reproduction Update, 21*(2), 194–208. https://doi.org/10.1093/humupd/dmu061

Werneburg, I., Laurin, M., Koyabu, D., & Sánchez-Villagra, M. R. (2016). Evolution of organogenesis and the origin of altriciality in mammals. *Evolution & Development, 18*(4), 229–244. https://doi.org/10.1111/ede.12194

Werner, G. M., & Todd, P. M. (1997). Too many love songs: sexual selection and the evolution of communication. In P. Husbands & I. Harvey (Eds.), *Proceedings of the fourth European conference on artificial life* (pp. 434–443). MIT Press.

Wey, Y. (2020). Transformations of tonality: a longitudinal study of yodeling in the Muotatal Valley, central Switzerland. *Analytical Approaches to World Music, 8*(1), 144–163.

Wheatland, P. S. K. (2009). *MelodicMatch music analysis software*. http://www.melodicmatch.com/

White, B. (1998). The life of birds.

White, C. W. (2017). A metrically based generative system of harmony. In R. Laney (Ed.), *Proceedings of the second conference on computer simulation of musical creativity, The Open University, 11–13 September 2017* (pp. 1–11). The Open University. https://csmc2017.wordpress.com/

Whitehead, H., & Rendell, L. (2014). *The cultural lives of whales and dolphins*. University of Chicago Press. https://doi.org/10.7208/chicago/9780226187426.001.0001

Whorf, B. L. (1956). *Language, thought, and reality: selected writings*. MIT Press.

Wiering, F., Typke, R., & Veltkamp, R. C. (2004). Transportation distances and their application in music-notation retrieval. In W. B. Hewlett & E. Selfridge-Field (Eds.), *Music query: methods, models, and user studies* (pp. 113–128). MIT Press.

Wiggins, G. A. (2012). The future of (mathematical) music theory. *Journal of Mathematics and Music, 6*(2), 135–144. https://doi.org/10.1080/17459737.2012.698151

Wiggins, G. A., Müllensiefen, D., & Pearce, M. T. (2010). On the non-existence of music: why music theory is a figment of the imagination. *Musicae Scientiae, 14*(1), 231–255. https : / / doi . org / 10 . 1177 / 10298649100140s110

Wiggins, G. A., Tyack, P., Scharff, C., & Rohrmeier, M. (2018). The evolutionary roots of creativity: mechanisms and motivations. In H. Honing (Ed.), *The origins of musicality* (pp. 287–308). MIT Press. https://doi.org/10.1098/rstb.2014.0099

Wikipedia. (2020). *Prehistory*. Retrieved August 27, 2020, from https://en.wikipedia.org/wiki/Prehistory

Wilson, E. O. (1978). *On human nature*. Harvard University Press. https://doi.org/10.4159/9780674076549

Wilson, E. O. (2000). *Sociobiology: the new synthesis*. Harvard University Press. https://doi.org/10.2307/2063068

Wilson, M., O'Bryan, L. R., Plummer, A. R., Beckman, M. E., & Munson, B. (2018). Tracking chimpanzee pant-hoot changes across time and space. *The Journal of the Acoustical Society of America, 143*(3), 1786. https://doi.org/10.1121/1.5035846

Wilsson, L. (1968). *My beaver colony* (J. Bulman, Trans.). Doubleday. https://doi.org/10.2307/1378381

Wolkewitz, M., Allignol, A., Graves, N., & Barnett, A. G. (2011). Is 27 really a dangerous age for famous musicians? retrospective cohort study. *British Medical Journal, 343*(7837), 1–6. https://doi.org/10.1136/bmj.d7799

Woodman, J. P., & Moore, N. R. (2012). Evidence for the effectiveness of Alexander Technique lessons in medical and health-related conditions: a systematic review. *International Journal of Clinical Practice, 66*(1), 98–112. https://doi.org/10.1111/j.1742-1241.2011.02817.x

Wrangham, R. (2009). *Catching fire: how cooking made us human*. Basic Books.

Wray, A. (1998). Protolanguage as a holistic system for social interaction. *Language and Communication, 18*(1), 47–67. https://doi.org/10.1016/s0271-5309(97)00033-5

Wright, E., Grawunder, S., Ndayishimiye, E., Galbany, J., McFarlin, S. C., Stoinski, T. S., & Robbins, M. M. (2021). Chest beats as an honest signal of body size in male mountain gorillas (*gorilla beringei beringei*). *Scientific Reports, 11*(1), 1–8. https://doi.org/10.1038/s41598-021-86261-8

Xenakis, I. (2001). *Formalized music: thought and mathematics in composition* (2nd ed.). Pendragon Press. https://doi.org/10.2307/896037

Xu, X., Zhou, Z., Dudley, R., Mackem, S., Chuong, C. M., Erickson, G. M., & Varricchio, D. J. (2014). An integrative approach to understanding bird origins. *Science, 346*(6215). https://doi.org/10.1126/science.1253293

Yehuda, R., Daskalakis, N. P., Bierer, L. M., Bader, H. N., Klengel, T., Holsboer, F., & Binder, E. B. (2016). Holocaust exposure induced intergenerational effects on FKBP5 methylation. *Biological Psychiatry, 80*(5), 372–80. https://doi.org/10.1016/j.biopsych.2015.08.005

Yeston, M. (1976). *The stratification of musical rhythm*. Yale University Press. https://doi.org/10.2307/897288

Young, H. (2017a). A categorial grammar for music and its use in automatic melody generation. In M. Sperber & J. Bresson (Eds.), *Proceedings of the fifth ACM SIGPLAN international workshop on functional art, music, modeling, and design (FARM 2017)* (pp. 1–9). Association for Computing Machinery. https://doi.org/10.1145/3122938.3122939

Young, H. (2017b). *Categorial music*. Retrieved January 11, 2020, from https://github.com/HalleyYoung/CategorialMusic

Yule, G. U. (1925). A mathematical theory of evolution, based on the conclusions of Dr J. C. Willis FRS. *Transactions of the Royal Society of London. Series B, 213*(402–410), 21–87. https://doi.org/10.1098/rstb.1925.0002

Zahavi, A., & Zahavi, A. (1997). *The handicap principle: a missing piece of Darwin's puzzle*. Oxford University Press.

Zatorre, R. J. (2003). Neural specializations for tonal processing. In I. Peretz & R. J. Zatorre (Eds.), *The cognitive neuroscience of music* (pp. 231–246). Oxford University Press. https://doi.org/10.1093/acprof:oso/9780198525202.003.0016

Zbikowski, L. M. (2011). Music, language, and kinds of consciousness. In D. Clarke & E. Clarke (Eds.), *Music and consciousness: philosophical, psychological, and cultural perspectives* (pp. 179–192). Oxford Univer-

sity Press. https://doi.org/10.1093/acprof:oso/9780199553792.001.
0001/acprof-9780199553792-chapter-010

Zon, B. (2016). *Music and metaphor in nineteenth-century British musicology.*
Routledge. https://doi.org/10.4324/9781315090955

Zou, J., Han, Y., & So, S.-S. (2009). Overview of artificial neural networks. In
D. J. Livingstone (Ed.), *Artificial neural networks: methods and applications* (pp. 15–23). Humana Press. https://doi.org/10.1007/978-1-
60327-101-1_2

Zuidema, W., Hupkes, D., Wiggins, G. A., Scharff, C., & Rohrmeier, M. (2018).
Formal models of structure building in music, language, and animal
song. In H. Honing (Ed.), *The origins of musicality* (pp. 253–286). MIT
Press.

Zullo, L., Sumbre, G., Agnisola, C., Flash, T., & Hochner, B. (2009). Nonsomatotopic organization of the higher motor centers in octopus. *Current
Biology, 19*(19), 1632–1636. https://doi.org/10.1016/j.cub.2009.07.067

Glossary

A

allele An alternative form of a replicator such that members of the same allele-class are functionally and/or structurally analogous. As such they might be regarded as rivals of each other. *See*: **choreoeme**; **gesteme**; **lexeme**; **meme**; **museme**; **replicator**; **soneme**; **treme**.

allometry The study of the body size and shape ratios of an organism in relation to other characteristics, including physiology and behaviour. *See*: **encephalisation**.

altriciality Referring to species whose young are hatched/born in an undeveloped/immobile state, and thus require substantial parental care. *See*: **precociality**.

archaeomusicology The study of evidence for human music-making in the material record.

B

b-, h-, i- Relating to replicators and vehicles, designates biological, human-cultural, and internet-cultural forms, respectively. *See*: **genome**; **memome**; **phemotype**; **phenotype**; **replicator**; **vehicle**.

bipedalism Using the legs for locomotion. *See*: **brachiation**.

brachiation Using the arms for locomotion, including swinging from branch to branch. *See*: **bipedalism**.

C

choreoeme A meme in the domain of physical movement related to dance, existing as a pattern of bodily (re)configurations. *See*: **gene; gesteme; lexeme; meme; museme; soneme; treme**.

chromatin The material constituting chromosomes, consisting of DNA plus various other molecules. *See*: **chromosome; epigenetic; DNA (deoxyribonucleic acid); epigenome; epimemetic; epimemome; methylation**.

chromosome A long strand of DNA, segments of which code for a specific phenotypic feature. *See*: **chromatin; DNA (deoxyribonucleic acid); gene; nucleotide; phenotype**.

clade A set of species *s* descended from an ancestral species *a* common to them all. *See*: **cladistics; monophyletic**.

cladistics A branch of phylogenetic taxonomy in which relationships between organisms are hypothesised on the basis of evolutionary descent. *See*: **clade; cladogram; phenetics; phylogenetics; taxonomy**.

cladogram A taxonomic diagram, organised in the form of a tree, showing hypothesised evolutionary relationships between organisms. *See*: **cladistics; clade**.

cognitivism A theory of consciousness that holds that language is the medium in which human thought is (primarily or exclusively) conducted. *See*: **communicativism**.

communicativism A theory of consciousness that holds that language is a vehicle for the articulation of thought conducted in a more fundamental "brain-language" or "mentalese". *See*: **cognitivism**.

copying-fidelity An attribute of a replicator referring to the accuracy with which copies of it are made. *See*: **fecundity; longevity; replicator**.

D

dimorphism (sexual) The presence of differences in average body-sizes between males and females. *See*: **monomorphism, sexual**.

DNA (deoxyribonucleic acid) A complex polymer made up of sequences of nucleotide molecules, by means of which biological information is encoded and transmitted. *See*: **chromatin; chromosome; gene; nucleotide**.

E

E-language/E-music Language and music externalised within a cultural community. *See*: **I-language/I-music**.

encephalisation An increase in the absolute or relative (to body) brain size in a species. *See*: **allometry**.

entelechy A motivation or drive that realises an inherent potential in life, development or growth. *See*: **ontogeny**.

epigenesis The origin of structures from undifferentiated material during ontogeny. *See*: **ontogeny**.

epigenetic Inheritance that does not involve the transmission of DNA; inheritance "over"/"on top of" DNA-based inheritance. *See*: **chromatin; chromosome; DNA (deoxyribonucleic acid); gene; genome; epigenome; epimemetic; epimemome; methylation**.

epigenome That which is transmitted alongside, but which is not part of, the genome. *See*: **epigenetic; epimemetic; epimemome; gene; genome**.

epimemetic Inheritance that does not involve the direct transmission of memes. *See*: **epigenetic; epigenome; epimemome; meme; memome**.

epimemome That which is transmitted alongside, but which is not part of, the memome. *See*: **epigenetic; epigenome; epimemetic; meme; memome**.

eukaryota A classification encompassing organisms (such as plants and animals) whose cells contain a nucleus, and other organelles, enclosed by a membrane. *See*: **prokaryota; organelle**.

evolution, convergent Homoplasies arising from the operation of the same selection pressure on two or more species. *See*: **evolution, Darwinian**; **homoplasy**.

evolution, Darwinian The theory that patterning in the universe has diversified from antecedent forms as a result of the operation of variation, replication and selection. *See*: **evolution, Lamarckian; evolution, convergent; replicator; VRS (variation, replication, selection) algorithm**.

evolution, Lamarckian The theory that evolution is the result of organisms striving to adapt to their environments, and the inheritance of such acquired characteristics. *See*: **evolution, Darwinian**.

F

fecundity An attribute of a replicator referring to its propensity to make copies of itself. *See*: **copying-fidelity; longevity; replicator**.

G

gene The unit of biological heredity, a segment of a chromosome coding for a specific phenotypic feature. *See*: **allele; choreoeme; chromatin; chromosome; gesteme; lexeme; meme; museme; nucleotide; operon; phenotype; soneme; treme**.

genome An organism's genetic material, encoded in DNA. *See*: **DNA (deoxyribonucleic acid); memome; phemotype; phenotype**.

gesteme A meme in the domain of physical movement related to musical performance, existing as a pattern of bodily (re)configurations. *See*: **choreoeme; gene; lexeme; meme; museme; soneme; treme**.

glossogeny/musogeny Cultural-historical linguistic/musical change. *See*: **E-language/E-music; I-language/I-music**.

gradualism The theory that evolution proceeds at a steady pace over time, by means of small, incremental modifications. *See*: **evolution, Darwinian; punctuated equilibrium; saltationism**.

g-t-r (generate, test, regenerate) heuristic An equivalent to the VRS algorithm, where g = variation, t = selection and r = replication. *See*: **evolution, Darwinian; replicator; VRS (variation, replication, selection) algorithm**.

H

Hexagonal Cloning Theory A theory of neuronal information encoding of William Calvin's proposing the existence of triangular arrays of neuronal minicolumns coordinated into hexagonally organised spatiotemporal firing patterns. *See*: **meme; mnemon; museme**.

hominid Modern great apes and their immediate ancestors: humans, gorillas, chimpanzees and orangutans. *See*: **hominin**.

hominin Modern humans and our immediate ancestors: the genera *Homo*, *Australopithecus*, *Paranthropus* and *Ardipithecus*. *See*: **hominid**.

homology A characteristic shared between two or more species $a^1, a^2, \ldots, a^n$ that *was present* in their common ancestor a. *See*: **homology, ancestral; homology, derived; homoplasy**.

homology, ancestral Characteristics present in the common ancestor a of a set of species $s = a^1, a^2, \ldots, a^n$. *See*: **homology; homology, derived; homoplasy**.

homology, derived Homologies evolving after the common ancestor a in the set of species s. *See*: **homology; homology, ancestral; homoplasy**.

homoplasy A characteristic shared between two or more species $a^1, a^2, \ldots, a^n$ that *was not present* in their common ancestor a. *See*: **homology; homology, ancestral; homology, derived**.

I

I-language/I-music Language and music internalised within the human brain. *See*: **E-language/E-music**.

L

lexeme A meme in the domain of language, existing as a pattern of sound information. *See*: **choreoeme; gene; gesteme; meme; museme; soneme; treme.**

longevity An attribute of a replicator referring to the length of time a single copy survives. *See*: **copying-fidelity; fecundity; replicator.**

M

Markov chain An event-sequence where the probability (often abstracted from statistical regularities) of an event occurring is dependent upon the previous event(s). *See*: **neural network.**

meme The unit of cultural transmission, consisting of a network of interconnected neurons coding for a discrete item of cultural information. *See*: **allele; choreoeme; gene; Hexagonal Cloning Theory; lexeme; memetics; mnemon; museme; musemeplex; replicator; soneme; treme.**

memeplex A complex of memes that, while independently replicated, are also replicated as part of the complex. *See*: **meme; memeplex, verbal-conceptual; museme; musemeplex.**

memeplex, verbal-conceptual A complex of memes in the domain of language and propositional thought. *See*: **meme; memeplex; museme; musemeplex.**

memetics The study of cultural evolution in terms of the variation, replication and selection of memes. *See*: **meme; museme; VRS (variation, replication, selection) algorithm.**

memome A human's memetic information, encoded in the brain. *See*: **genome; phemotype; phenotype.**

methylation The process whereby a methyl group (CH_3) in the non-DNA chromatin is attached to elements of DNA. *See*: **chromatin; chromosome; epigenetic; DNA (deoxyribonucleic acid); epigenome; epimemetic; epimemome.**

mnemon An item of unreplicated memory that, when replicated, becomes a meme. *See*: **choreoeme**; **gesteme**; **Hexagonal Cloning Theory**; **lexeme**; **meme**; **memeplex**; **memeplex, verbal-conceptual**; **mnemonplex**; **museme**; **musemeplex**; **soneme**; **treme**.

mnemonplex A complex of mnemons that, when replicated, becomes a memeplex. *See*: **choreoeme**; **gesteme**; **Hexagonal Cloning Theory**; **lexeme**; **meme**; **memeplex**; **memeplex, verbal-conceptual**; **mnemon**; **museme**; **musemeplex**; **soneme**; **treme**.

monomorphism (sexual) The absence of differences in average body-sizes between males and females. *See*: **dimorphism, sexual**.

monophyletic A set of species s containing an ancestral species a and all its descendant species $a^1, a^2, \ldots, a^n$. *See*: **clade**; **paraphyletic**; **polyphyletic**.

museme A meme in the domain of music, existing as a pattern of pitch and rhythm information, in the vertical (harmonic) and horizontal (melodic/contrapuntal) dimensions. *See*: **choreoeme**; **gene**; **Hexagonal Cloning Theory**; **gesteme**; **lexeme**; **meme**; **memetics**; **mnemon**; **musemeplex**; **soneme**; **treme**.

musemeplex A complex of musemes that, while independently replicated, are also replicated as part of the complex. *See*: **meme**; **memeplex**; **mnemonplex**; **museme**.

musemesatz A higher-order structure, loosely analogous to a juxtaposition of the Schenkerian *erster Schicht* and *Ursatz*, resulting from the assemblage of musemes in a musemeplex. *See*: **allele**; **meme**; **memeplex**; **museme**; **musemeplex**.

N

neoteny The retention into adulthood of features found in infants or juveniles.

neural network A virtual representation, in software, of the real connections between neurons in the brain, capable of learning by abstracting regularities in input information. *See*: **Hexagonal Cloning Theory**; **Markov chain**.

nucleotide A class of molecules assembled upon five bases (adenine, cytosine, guanine, thymine and uracil) the first four of which form the building blocks of DNA. *See*: **chromatin**; **chromosome**; **DNA (deoxyribonucleic acid)**; **gene**.

O

ontogeny The development of an organism, from fertilisation to maturity, but sometimes extended to incorporate its whole life-span. *See*: **epigenesis**; **ontomemy**; **phylogeny**; **phylomemy**.

ontomemy The accumulation and development of an individual's meme complement/profile via education and enculturation over the course of their lifetime. *See*: **meme**; **ontogeny**; **phylogeny**; **phylomemy**.

operon A group of genes that function together, resulting in their joint (non-)expression (i.e., (non-)production of a protein). *See*: **chromatin**; **chromosome**; **DNA (deoxyribonucleic acid)**; **gene**; **meme**; **memeplex**; **memeplex, verbal-conceptual**; **museme**; **musemeplex**; **nucleotide**.

organelle A structure within a cell, sometimes enclosed by a membrane. *See*: **eukaryota**; **prokaryota**.

P

paraphyletic A set of species *s* containing an ancestral species *a* and some of its descendants. Included species resemble *a*; excluded species, while deriving from *a*, do not resemble *a*. *See*: **monophyletic**; **polyphyletic**.

phemotype The extrasomatic products and behavioural manifestations of a memome. *See*: **genome**; **memome**; **phenotype**.

phenetics A taxonomic methodology based upon the measurement of morphological similarities. *See*: **cladistics**; **phylogenetics**; **taxonomy**.

phenotype The somatic and behavioural manifestations of a genome. *See*: **genome**; **memome**; **phemotype**.

phylogenetics A taxonomic methodology based upon the reconstruction of evolutionary relationships. *See*: **cladistics**; **phenetics**; **taxonomy**.

phylogeny The development of a species, understood in terms of descent from and branching into other species. *See*: **ontogeny**; **ontomemy**; **phylomemy**.

phylomemy The development of a cultural category, phenomenon or type, understood in terms of descent from and branching into other categories, phenomena or types. *See*: **ontogeny**; **ontomemy**; **phylogeny**.

polyphyletic A set of species s descended from two or more common ancestral species, $a, b, \ldots$. The original common ancestor of $a, b, \ldots, o$, is not a member of s. *See*: **monophyletic**; **paraphyletic**.

precociality Referring to species whose young are hatched/born in a developed/mobile state, and thus require little parental care. *See*: **altriciality**.

prokaryota A classification encompassing organisms (such as bacteria) whose cells contain no membrane-enclosed organelles. *See*: **eukaryota**; **organelle**.

punctuated equilibrium The theory that evolution is relatively static for long periods of time, these being interrupted by short periods of rapid change. *See*: **evolution, Darwinian**; **gradualism**; **saltationism**.

R

rank (taxonomy) The relative position of a taxon in a taxonomic hierarchy. *See*: **taxon**; **taxonomy**.

recursive ontology The theory that being is divided into four hierarchical categories (physical, biological, psychological and (socio-)cultural), each subdivided into levels, with all categories governed by common laws of organisation.

replicator Any entity that causes, directly or indirectly, copies to be made of itself. *See*: **allele; choreoeme; gesteme; lexeme; meme; museme; soneme; treme; vehicle; VRS (variation, replication, selection) algorithm.**

S

saltationism The theory that evolution proceeds, at times, by rapid changes. *See*: **evolution, Darwinian; gradualism; punctuated equilibrium.**

soneme A meme in the domain of sound, existing as a pattern of pitch and rhythm information, in the vertical (harmonic) and horizontal (contrapuntal) dimensions, but one that (particularly in the case of animal vocalisations) might not be perceived as musical by human listeners. *See*: **choreoeme; gene; gesteme; lexeme; meme; museme; treme.**

speciation, allopatric The formation of a new species when members of a population become separated from its main body and are subsequently unable to interbreed with members of the antecedent species. *See*: **speciation, sympatric.**

speciation, sympatric The formation of a new species that occupies the same territory as, and coexists with, the antecedent species. *See*: **speciation, allopatric.**

T

taxon A group of organisms of sufficient coherence to be assigned a taxonomic rank. *See*: **rank (taxonomy); taxonomy.**

taxonomy The science of classification, conducted according to a number of methods that vary in the significance assigned to evolutionary relationships. *See*: **cladistics; phenetics; phylogenetics.**

treme A meme propagated in electronic systems. *See*: **choreoeme; gesteme; lexeme; meme; museme; soneme.**

V

vehicle The means by which a replicator secures its replication. *See*: **allele; choreoeme; gesteme; lexeme; meme; museme; replicator; soneme; treme; VRS (variation, replication, selection) algorithm.**

VRS (variation, replication, selection) algorithm The underlying process driving Darwinian evolution, involving modification, copying and selection of replicators. *See*: **evolution, Darwinian; g-t-r (generate, test, regenerate) heuristic; replicator.**

Z

zoomusicology The comparative study of animal behaviour in terms of music-like characteristics.

Index

About the Team

Alessandra Tosi was the managing editor for this book.

Lucy Barnes performed the copy-editing and proofreading.

Anna Gatti designed the cover. The cover was produced in *InDesign* using the Fontin font.

The author typeset the book using LaTeX. The text font is Tex Gyre Pagella.

Luca Baffa produced the paperback and hardback editions. Luca also produced the AZW3, HTML and XML editions. Michal Hoftich produced the EPUB edition using his open-source *tex4ebook* software (https://github.com/michal-h21/tex4ebook).

This book need not end here ...

Share

All our books – including the one you have just read – are free to access online so that students, researchers and members of the public who can't afford a printed edition will have access to the same ideas. This title will be accessed online by hundreds of readers each month across the globe: why not share the link so that someone you know is one of them?

This book and additional content is available at:

https://doi.org/10.11647/OBP.0301

Donate

Open Book Publishers is an award-winning, scholar-led, not-for-profit press making knowledge freely available one book at a time. We don't charge authors to publish with us: instead, our work is supported by our library members and by donations from people who believe that research shouldn't be locked behind paywalls.

Why not join them in freeing knowledge by supporting us:

https://www.openbookpublishers.com/section/104/1

Like Open Book Publishers:
https://www.facebook.com/OpenBookPublish

Follow @OpenBookPubl:
https://twitter.com/OpenBookPublish

Read more at the Open Book Publishers blog:
https://blogs.openbookpublishers.com/

You may also be interested in:

The Power of Music
An Exploration of the Evidence
Susan Hallam and
Evangelos Himonides
https://doi.org/10.11647/OBP.0292

Behaviour, Development and
Evolution
Patrick Bateson
https://doi.org/10.11647/OBP.0097

Human Cultures through the
Scientific Lens
Essays in Evolutionary Cognitive
Anthropology
Pascal Boyer
https://doi.org/10.11647/OBP.0257

CPSIA information can be obtained
at www.ICGtesting.com
Printed in the USA
BVHW012048200223
658864BV00012B/210